The MANIFESTO in Literature

VOLUME **3**

The MANIFESTO *in Literature*

ACTIVISM, UNREST, AND THE NEO-AVANT-GARDE

THOMAS RIGGS, *editor*

ST. JAMES PRESS
A part of Gale, Cengage Learning

GALE
CENGAGE Learning·

Detroit • New York • San Francisco • New Haven, Conn • Waterville, Maine • London

GALE
CENGAGE Learning·

The Manifesto in Literature

Thomas Riggs, Editor

Lisa Kumar, Project Editor

Artwork and photographs for *The Manifesto in Literature* covers were reproduced with the following kind permission.

Volume 1
For foreground painting "Writing the Declaration of Independence in 1776" by Jean Leon Gerome Ferris. © Virginia Historical Society, Richmond, VA/The Bridgeman Art Library.
For background image of the Declaration of Independence of the thirteen United States of America, 1776. © Private Collection/The Bridgeman Art Library.

Volume 2
For foreground portrait of Adolf Hitler. © INTERFOTO/awkz/Mary Evans.
For background image of the title page from the original publication of Mein Kampf, 1925-1926. © INTERFOTO/Alamy.

Volume 3
For foreground portrait of Albert Einstein. © Mary Evans/AISA Media.
For background image of the first page of the Russell-Einstein Manifesto. Courtesy Ava Helen and Linus Pauling Papers, Oregon State University Libraries.

LIBRARY OF CONGRESS CATALOGING-IN-PUBLICATION DATA

The Manifesto in Literature / Edited by Thomas Riggs.
   v. cm. — ()
   Includes bibliographical references and index.
   ISBN - 13: 978-1-55862-866-3 (set) -- ISBN - 13: 978-1-55862-867-0 (vol. 1) -- ISBN - 13: 978 1-55862-868-7 (vol. 2) -- ISBN - 13: 978-1-55862-869-4 (vol. 3)
   1. Revolutionary literature—History and criticism. 2. Literary manifestos.
3. Political manifestoes. 4. Politics and literature. 5. Authors—Political and social views.
I. Riggs, Thomas, 1963—editor of compilation.
   PN51.M26785 2013
   809.935—dc23

Gale
27500 Drake Rd.
Farmington Hills, MI, 48331-3535

978-1-55862-866-3 (set)	1-55862-866-5 (set)
978-1-55862-867-0 (vol. 1)	1-55862-867-3 (vol. 1)
978-1-55862-868-7 (vol. 2)	1-55862-868-1 (vol. 2)
978-1-55862-869-4 (vol. 3)	1-55862 869-X (vol. 3)

This title will also be available as an e-book.
ISBN-13: 978-1-55862-880-9 ISBN-10: 1-55862-880-0
Contact your Gale, a part of Cengage Learning, sales representative for ordering information.

Printed in the United States of America
1 2 3 4 5 6 7 17 16 15 14 13

ADVISORY BOARD

CHAIR

Martin Puchner
Byron and Anita Wien Professor of Drama and of English and Comparative Literature, Harvard University, Cambridge, Massachusetts. Author of *The Drama of Ideas: Platonic Provocations in Theater and Philosophy* (2010); *Poetry of the Revolution: Marx, Manifestos, and the Avant-Gardes* (2006); and *Stage Fright: Modernism, Anti-Theatricality, and Drama* (2002). Editor of *The Norton Anthology of World Literature,* 3rd edition (2012); and *The Communist Manifesto and Other Writings* (2005). Coeditor, with Alan Ackerman, of *Against Theatre: Creative Destructions on the Modernist Stage* (2006). Founding Director, Mellon Summer School of Theater and Performance Research.

ADVISORS

Rita Felski
William R. Kenan, Jr. Professor of English, University of Virginia, Charlottesville. Author of *Uses of Literature* (2008); *Literature after Feminism* (2003); *Doing Time: Feminist Theory and Postmodern Culture* (2000); *The Gender of Modernity* (1995); and *Beyond Feminist Aesthetics: Feminist Literature and Social Change* (1989). Editor of *Rethinking Tragedy* (2008). Coeditor of *Comparison: Theories, Approaches, Methods* (2013). Editor of *New Literary History.*

Janet Lyon
Associate Professor of English; Science, Technology and Society; and Women's Studies, Pennsylvania State University, University Park. Author of *Manifestoes: Provocations of the Modern* (1999). Contributor to *Gender in Modernism: New Geographies, Complex Intersections,* edited by Bonnie Kime Scott (2007); *The Cambridge Companion to American Modernism,* edited by Walter Kalaidjian (2005); and *Geomodernisms: Race, Modernism, Modernity,* edited by Laura Doyle and Laura Winkiel (2005).

Peter Nicholls
Professor of English, New York University, New York City. Author of *George Oppen and the Fate of Modernism* (2009); *Modernisms: A Literary Guide,* 2nd

edition (2009); and *Ezra Pound: Politics, Economics and Writing* (1984). Coeditor, with Sara Crangle, of *On Bathos: Literature, Art, Music* (2010); and, with Laura Marcus, of *The Cambridge History of Twentieth-Century English Literature* (2004). Contributor to *The Oxford Handbook of Modern and Contemporary American Poetry*, edited by Cary Nelson (2012); and *The Cambridge Companion to Modernist Poetry*, edited by Alex Davis and Lee M. Jenkins (2007).

Laura Winkiel

Associate Professor of English, University of Colorado Boulder. Author of *Modernism, Race and Manifestos* (2008). Coeditor, with Laura Doyle, of *Geomodernisms: Race, Modernism, Modernity* (2005). Contributor to *The Routledge Companion to Experimental Literature*, edited by Joe Bray, Alison Gibbons, and Brian McHale (2012); *The Invention of Politics in the European Avant-Garde* (1906-1940), edited by Sascha Bru and Gunther Martens (2006); and *Decentering the Avant-Garde: Towards a New Topography of the International Avant-Garde*, edited by Per Backstrom and Hubert van den Berg (forthcoming). Book project provisionally titled "Epic Proportions: Genre, Debt and Anticolonial Modernism." Senior editor of *English Language Notes*.

Sarah G. Wenzel

Librarian, English and Romance Literatures, University of Chicago, Illinois.

Editorial and Production Staff

ASSOCIATE PUBLISHER
Marc Cormier

PRODUCT MANAGER
Philip J. Virta

PROJECT EDITOR
Lisa Kumar

EDITORIAL ASSISTANCE
Andrea Henderson, Michelle Lee, and Rebecca Parks

ART DIRECTOR
Kristine Julien

COMPOSITION AND IMAGING
Evi Seoud, John Watkins

MANUFACTURING
Wendy Blurton

RIGHTS ACQUISITION AND MANAGEMENT
Kimberly Potvin, Robyn V. Young

TECHNICAL SUPPORT
Luann Brennan, Mike Weaver

TABLE OF CONTENTS

INTRODUCTION

Among the hundreds of manifestos that are represented in these three volumes, one stands out: *The Manifesto of the Communist Party* (1848). In a collaborative process that spanned several countries and included much trial and error, the two authors, Karl Marx and Friedrich Engels, did nothing less than invent the manifesto as we know it. To be sure, there were earlier texts that called themselves manifestos, but they existed side by side with declarations, proclamations, open letters, admonitions, refutations, theses, defenses, vindications, catechisms, and much more. "Manifesto" was just one more convenient name to give to a document intent on stating publicly—on making manifest—a set of rules or beliefs.

When they were charged with drawing up the beliefs of the newly established Communist League, Marx and Engels experimented with all of these rival forms. For example, they initially thought that the best way of expressing the principles of the new party would be in the form of a catechism, the question-and-answer testing of knowledge introduced by theologians of the Catholic Church. The finished text of the *Communist Manifesto* still bears traces of this early experiment. Gradually, however, the two authors realized that they were facing an unprecedented challenge—a challenge they needed to meet with an entirely new kind of text.

The problem they set themselves in 1847 was how to write a revolution. All across Europe monarchies and empires were entrenched, fortifying their positions of power. They watched jealously for any sign of new revolutionary groups threatening the status quo. The French revolution had long ago receded into history, but it had not been forgotten. Word was going around of a radical new movement sowing discontent abroad, but no one knew anything specific about it. Apparently, it was called communism.

There was something to the rumor. Carefully, Marx and Engels had begun to establish a network of the revolutionaries scattered across the continent. "There is a specter haunting Europe," the *Communist Manifesto* begins. With discontent in the air, the time had come for the secret society to become visible, public—manifest. To accomplish this purpose, the two authors recreated the manifesto as a new genre.

This manifesto did much more than make manifest the principles of communism. Marx, a trained philosopher, had developed a philosophy of history based on the struggle among different classes. This history culminated in the present moment, in the manifesto itself, which declared a kind of point zero: all subsequent history would be shaped by this crucial document. At the center of this turning point stood the proletariat, a newly defined class of workers utterly dependent on the owners of factories and capital. Everyone knew about disenfranchised workers, of course, but the *Communist Manifesto* took the unusual step of describing them as the future sovereigns of Europe and the world.

In addition to articles of belief, Marx and Engels's treatise includes this history of mankind, told at breathtaking speed, leading up to the present and into the future. In order to bring about this revolutionary future, the document introduced a new historical agent—the proletariat—and now had to call this agent into being. The burden of the *Communist Manifesto* was to forge out of the disenfranchised workers a coherent class. This class must be roused to action. If there was going to be a revolution, the manifesto itself must incite it. Ingeniously, Marx and Engels combined the crucial elements—declaration of principle; long view of history; creation of a turning point; introduction of a new agent—and couched them in a style singularly intent on transforming their ideas into action. Out of disparate ingredients the authors created a formula that was exemplified, for the first time, in the *Communist Manifesto*. Without this document, the three volumes presented here would not exist.

The *Communist Manifesto* is a lens through which we can look backward and forward, backward at the prehistory of the genre and forward to the many successors and imitators. A look back reveals a striking fact: many early manifestos were not revolutionary documents. They tended to be declarations by heads of states, emperors, or the Church, utterances by those with the power and authority to make laws and impose a vision of the world. Marx and Engels would cunningly change the genre, turning the manifesto into a tool not for those in power but for those seeking to usurp it.

Alongside these authoritative declarations, other, more subversive texts existed, although they didn't always designate themselves as manifestos. Martin Luther's *Ninety-Five Theses* (1517), nailed to the church door in Wittenberg, had the long-term, if perhaps unintended, consequence of revolutionizing the Church. Other, more explicitly insurrectional documents—for example those (such as the 1649 "Digger's Song") emanating from the so-called Diggers and Levellers in seventeenth-century England, who hoped to claim common property from landlords—explicitly sought to change the status quo. Like Luther, they made ample use of Christian texts to articulate their demands, quoting liberally from the Bible.

Religion was not the only language available to revolutionaries. In the eighteenth century, philosophers began to formulate, more and more cogently, a worldview premised on the human exercise of reason; their beliefs freed humanity from the humble subservience to God that had characterized many earlier revolutionary texts. The new philosophical attitude created a new age, the Enlightenment, and its principal philosopher, Immanuel Kant, authored the seminal text (which might have been called, retrospectively, the Enlightenment Manifesto) "What Is Enlightenment?" This undertaking was not just a matter of philosophy. It aided those hoping to reorganize the social order without recourse to older authorities—to place society on a new foundation.

The most famous experiment along these lines happened not in Europe but in the English colonies of North America, where revolutionaries declared their independence from England and from the monarchy. The Americans expressed the principles of their freedom in a text that soon became world famous and found many imitators of its own: the *Declaration of Independence* (1776). Like the *Communist Manifesto,* the *Declaration of Independence* did not just state new principles; together with the *Constitution* (1787), it called into being a new entity, the United States of America. More particularly, it created a new agent, the people of the United States of America, who would henceforth govern their own fate.

Although these documents and other, lesser-known manifestos tended to be phrased in the radical idiom of universality—as in the opening of the *Declaration of Independence,* which proclaimed, "All men are created equal"—their practice was often a good deal more restrictive, excluding slaves and women, among others. In response these discounted groups began to articulate their demands with recourse to the *Declaration,* holding the document, and those who endorsed it, to its original, radical vision. In 1848 a women's rights convention in Seneca Falls, New York, modeled its *Declaration of Sentiments* explicitly on the *Declaration of Independence,* demanding freedom and independence for the half of the nation that had been excluded in the original *Declaration.* Eighty years earlier, on the French colonial island of Saint-Dominique, a slave revolt inspired by the *Declaration of the Rights of Man and of the Citizen* (1789) had found expression in Jean-Jacques

Dessalines's "Liberty or Death" (1804), which charged Europeans with not living up to their own revolutionary ideas. Despite these forceful new manifestos, it would take centuries for their mandates to receive wider acceptance.

Protest literature, Enlightenment philosophy, a new type of Republican constitution—these were some of the strands that Marx and Engels knit into a new kind of text, the manifesto proper. Despite the later success of this document, which truly changed the world, its immediate effects were disappointing. The timing was right, or almost right—revolutions were erupting across Europe (although the *Communist Manifesto* was published in London, which was relatively isolated from those revolutions, and it was written in German). When the revolutionary energy of 1848 ebbed, however, enthusiasm for the document and its ilk ebbed as well, and it took decades and a concerted program of translation to catapult the *Communist Manifesto* to the forefront again. At the end of the nineteenth century, the treatise finally began its triumphant rise. Marx and Engels's new formula had taken a long time to become popular.

Two developments resulted from the increasingly visible success of the *Communist Manifesto.* The first was that the genre became the preferred form of political expression for the Left: Marx and Engels had inaugurated a long tradition of manifestos seeking to found communist or socialist parties or to update and revitalize the international communist movement. Several of these are collected in the second volume of this set, "The Modernist Movement." They include Emma Goldman's "Anarchism" (1910), in which the author explains the tenets of that movement; the "Zimmerwald Manifesto" (1915), a World War I socialist document condemning the fierce nationalism that held Europe's Left in its grip; and the *Spartacus Manifesto* (1918), a Marxist revolutionary treatise written by Rosa Luxemburg in postwar Germany. From time to time right-leaning groups tried to answer this leftist tradition with manifestos of their own but never with lasting success.

The second development, also represented in volume two, was more surprising. As the *Communist Manifesto* was gaining prominence, artists started to write texts specifically styled as manifestos. Most did not hope to create social revolutions; instead, they wanted to revolutionize the arts. Their treatises adopted many elements from political manifestos: the telling of a grand history (of art) that culminated in a complete rupture; the creation of a new entity or movement; an aggressive denunciation of predecessors or rivals; and lists of demands or actions to be taken. The trend began in the late nineteenth century, when a new group called the symbolists sought to articulate their break with the dominant artistic mode of the time, realism. The art manifesto movement really took off when the obscure Italian symbolist poet F. T. Marinetti recognized the form's potential in the artistic sphere and authored *Futurist Manifesto* (1909). The document created quite a stir, which encouraged Marinetti to write more manifestos until he was flooding the art market with his missives. No futurist artwork had been created yet; the new movement existed simply by virtue of having been founded, defended, and explained through manifestos. With the proclamation of futurism, the new artistic offshoot of the political manifesto had come into its own.

The artistic manifesto, too, had predecessors. Artists had always wanted to articulate their principles and views, sometimes quite succinctly or polemically; examples of these texts appear in the first volume of this series, "Origins of the Form." Percy Bysshe Shelley's *Defence of Poetry* for instance, written in 1821 and published in 1840, exalts Romantic poetry and poets in the face of detractors. Shelley's contemporary William Wordsworth had contented himself with writing the pointed "Preface" to the 1800 edition of *Lyrical Ballads* (poems by Wordsworth and Samuel Taylor Coleridge), which accomplished a similar purpose. Over the course of the nineteenth century, these declarations of aesthetic principles edged closer to the manifesto; Émile Zola's *Naturalism in the Theater* (1880) is a prominent example of this trend. Only after the turn of the century, with futurism, did the genre fully arrive in the world of art.

Once the manifesto gained entry into the artistic sphere, art was never the same again. Groups, splinter groups, and subformations sprang up everywhere, fiercely fighting over minor points of aesthetic doctrine, and most of the fighting was done through manifestos. The immediate effect was a new artistic landscape dominated by a proliferation of "isms." Many artists were no longer content simply to exercise their craft; they now felt the need to be part of a movement—futurism, Dadaism, surrealism, suprematism, and numerous others—until finally the war of the manifestos became more important than the artwork created under the auspices of any particular movement.

The competition even extended to the form of the manifesto itself. Marinetti had perfected a particularly aggressive style, intent on driving home its often extreme points with utmost force. The Dadaists responded with playful, whimsical manifestos that seemed not only to disagree with the content of futurist treatises but also with their bellicose tone. The surrealists differentiated themselves from both of these movements, not only by emphasizing the importance of dreams and of free association but also by writing meandering, essay-like manifestos that mirrored this new emphasis.

A term began to circulate throughout the new landscape: "avant-garde." Originally a military term designating the advanced guard of an army, it now described the ambition of artists to found the latest and most advanced ism through the latest and most advanced manifesto.

The two strands of the manifesto, the political and the artistic, existed side by side, sometimes merging, sometimes diverging. During World War II and its aftermath, however, the fortunes of the manifesto waned as fascism and fascist-leaning regimes took hold in Europe, quelling both leftist revolutionary energy and artistic revolutions. Even movements that had sided with fascism, such as Italian futurism, quieted, and once the war was over, these groups found themselves discredited. The time of the manifesto seemed to have ended.

Not for long. A second wave of both political and artistic manifestos swelled in the 1950s and gained momentum as the 1960s wore on. This next wave, represented in the third volume of this series, "Activism, Unrest, and the Neo-Avant-Garde," was different. The political manifestos, although still primarily leftist, were no longer used predominantly by communist parties but rather by disenfranchised groups seeking recognition and justice, including African Americans, feminists, immigrants, and gays.

Many of these groups could claim a substantial history of manifesto writing. Harlem Renaissance writers of the 1920s and 1930s, including Alain Locke and Richard Wright, outlined the aesthetic and political principles of their art in manifestos or manifesto-like statements, including Locke's "Legacy of Ancestral Arts" (1925) and Wright's "Blueprint for Negro Writing" (1937) (both represented in the second volume of the series). In 1966 the Black Panthers demanded rights for African Americans in a more political and forceful manifesto, the Black Panther Party Platform. They strategically ended their document with the first paragraph of the *Declaration of Independence,* recalling one of the most important documents in the prehistory of the manifesto. In her 1967 *SCUM* (Society for Cutting Up Men) *Manifesto,* Valerie Solanas notably used the standard "we" even though her movement consisted only of herself. She, too, could look back on a long history of feminist manifestos, including Mary Wollstonecraft's *A Vindication of the Rights of Woman* (1792), one of the most important early examples of the form.

Artistic and political manifestos had emerged outside Europe and the United States during the first part of the twentieth century, driven by the global rise of communism, an increasingly international modernism, and the avant-garde movements in the arts. In 1914 the Chilean poet Vicente Huidobro delivered the lecture "Non Serviam" (Latin for "I will not serve"), a manifesto declaring independence from authority in various forms; and in 1917 the future cofounder of the Chinese Communist Party Chen Duxiu wrote "On Literary Revolution," importing the form and its revolutionary zeal to China. By the 1960s the manifesto's international reach was no longer an exception but a commonplace occurrence. Frantz Fanon's *The Wretched of the Earth* (1961) became a manifesto for the independence movements of former colonies all over the world, and Nelson Mandela's 1961 "Manifesto of Umkhonto we Sizwe" played a role in the struggle against Apartheid in South Africa.

By the middle of the twentieth century, writing political manifestos was no longer an original act. On the contrary, it now meant joining a long tradition; it meant pledging allegiance to the institution of leftist thought even as the origin of the tradition, the *Communist Manifesto,* receded into history.

The artistic manifesto was going through a similar experience. Originally conceived as a means of declaring a new point of departure, a complete rupture with all preceding art, avant-garde manifestos now had to admit that they were part of a tradition—a tradition of manifesto writing. What to do? Some artists tried to surpass their early-twentieth-century predecessors by being even more radical and revolutionary; one group, the Situationists (whose founder Guy Debord produced "Situationist Theses on Traffic" in 1959), even declared that they were against the production of anything resembling art. Others found novelty in new technologies, from which they hoped a complete revolution would arise. Donna Haraway's "Manifesto for Cyborgs" (1985) envisioned a new form of existence in the symbiosis of humans and machines, while McKenzie Wark's *Hacker Manifesto* (2004) elevated hacking to the status of a new creative and radical activity.

The end of the twentieth century saw the demise of communism in politics and the emergence of the postmodernist movement in the arts—both seemed to spell, once again, the end of the manifesto. Without communism as a credible alternative to capitalism, how could political activists write in a genre inaugurated by the *Communist Manifesto*? And with the art world declaring that "anything goes," how could activist artists claim to do away with all preceding and rival art forms? If the late twentieth century did not experience the "end of history," as the political scientist Francis Fukuyama predicted in 1992 that it would, it certainly seemed to experience the end of the manifesto.

The manifesto has not disappeared entirely, however. An increasingly global capitalism still breeds resistance and resentment in those left behind; and 9/11 demonstrated that we still live in a world dominated by rival political systems and their sometimes violent clashes. At the same time, the ever-changing social media allow for new forms of revolutionary organizing, and new technological revolutions are changing the face of art even more rapidly now than during the early twentieth century.

The evidence of several hundred years of manifesto writing assembled in these volumes captures a breathtaking history of innovation, a history of men and women trying to make the world anew. The enduring impulse to declare a point zero and to envision a new departure, the audacity to break with tradition and to found new traditions, is nothing less than a history of modernity itself. Manifestos, the most characteristic form in which these ambitions have been expressed, can thus be regarded as the most representative and important documents of the modern world, a literature unto themselves.

Manifestos have routinely predicted the future even as they have tried to bring that future about. They may well continue to shape our world for the foreseeable future.

Martin Puchner,
Advisory Board Chair

Editor's Note

*T*he Manifesto in Literature, a three-volume reference guide, provides critical introductions to 300 manifestos throughout the world. As manifestos, all the works share a common trait. They challenge a traditional order, whether in politics, religion, social issues, art, literature, or technology, and propose a new vision of the future.

Among the earliest manifestos discussed in the guide are the *Ninety-Five Theses* (1517), a critique of the Roman Catholic Church by German priest and professor Martin Luther, and the *Politics of Obedience* (1552-53), in which French writer Étienne de la Boétie argues that people allow themselves to be ruled by tyrants out of habit and hope for personal gain. Of the twentieth-century art manifestos covered in the book, "Art, Revolution, and Decadence" (1926), by Peruvian marxist José Carlos Mariátegui, discusses the relationship between revolutionary art and politics, and "Gutai Manifesto" (1956), by Japanese artist Jiro Yoshihara, contends that representational art perpetuates a "fraud" by creating illusions. More recently, *Why Facebook Exists* (2012), by Mark Zuckerberg, the American founder of the social network, offers an idealistic vision for his company, arguing that its mission is not profit but increased interpersonal connectivity throughout the world and thus more democratic social, political, and economic institutions.

The structure and content of *The Manifesto in Literature* was planned with the help of the project's advisory board, chaired by Martin Puchner, Byron and Anita Wien Professor of Drama and of English and Comparative Literature at Harvard University. In his introduction to this guide, he discusses how *The Manifesto of the Communist Party,* written in 1848 by the German theorists Karl Marx and Frederick Engels, helped define the very idea of the manifesto.

ORGANIZATION

All entries share a common structure, providing consistent coverage of the works and a simple way of comparing basic elements of one text with another. Each entry has six parts: overview, historical and literary context, themes and style, critical discussion, sources, and further reading. Entries also have either an excerpt from the manifesto and/or a sidebar discussing a related topic, such as the life of the author.

The Manifesto in Literature is divided into three volumes, each with 100 entries. Volume 1, "Origins of the Form: Pre-1900," has six sections focusing on early concerns of manifesto writers—church and state, citizens and revolutionaries, proletarians, emancipation and independence, women, and artists and writers. "Church and State," for example, contains nineteen entries, such as the *People's Charter* by English activist William Lovett, who advocated electoral reforms aimed at helping British working classes. Volume 2, "The Modernist Movement: 1900-WWII," includes three sections—social and political upheavals, Harlem Renaissance, and avant gardes—the latter two including entries on art and literature manifestos. Volume 3, "Activism, Unrest, and the Neo-Avant-Garde," has eleven sections: art and architecture; film; feminisms; radical politics; queer politics; America left and right; global militants; philosophies; poetry and performance; students, activists, and situations; and technologies.

Among the criteria for selecting entry topics were the importance of the work in university curricula, the region and country of the author and text, and the time period. Entries can be looked up in the author and title indexes, as well as in the general subject index.

ACKNOWLEDGMENTS

Many people contributed time, effort, and ideas to *The Manifesto in Literature*. At Gale, Philip J. Virta, manager of new products, developed the original plan for the book, and Lisa Kumar, senior content project editor, served as the in-house manager for the project. *The Manifesto in Literature* owes its existence to their ideas and involvement.

We would like to express our appreciation to the advisors, who, in addition to creating the organization of *The Manifesto in Literature* and choosing the entry topics, identified other scholars to work on the project and answered many questions, both big and small. We would also like to thank the contributors for their accessible essays, often on difficult topics, as well as the scholars who reviewed the text for accuracy and coverage.

I am grateful to Erin Brown, senior project editor, especially for her work with the advisors and on the entry list; Greta Gard, project editor, who managed the writers; Mary Beth Curran, associate editor, who oversaw the editing process; David Hayes, associate editor, whose many contributions included organizing the workflow; and Hannah Soukup, assistant editor, who identified and corresponded with the academic reviewers. Other important assistance came from Mariko Fujinaka, managing editor; Anne Healey, senior editor; and Janet Moredock and Lee Esbenshade, associate editors. The line editors were Heather Campbell, Cheryl Collins, Tony Craine, Holli Fort, Laura Gabler, Harrabeth Haidusek, Ellen Henderson, Joan Hibler, Dehlia McCobb, Kathy Peacock, Donna Polydoros, Natalie Ruppert, Mary Russell, Lisa Trow, Will Wagner, and Whitney Ward.

Thomas Riggs

 CONTRIBUTORS

DAVID AITCHISON

Aitchison is a PhD candidate in literary studies and a university instructor.

GREG BACH

Bach holds an MA in classics and is a freelance writer.

KIM BANION

Banion is a PhD student in English literature and a high school English instructor.

LISA BARCA

Barca holds a PhD in romance languages and literatures and is a university professor.

KATHERINE BARKER

Barker holds an MA in English literature.

CRAIG BARNES

Barnes holds an MFA in creative writing and has been a university instructor and a freelance writer.

MARIE BECKER

Becker holds an MA in humanities.

KAREN BENDER

Bender holds an MFA in creative writing and an MPhil in Anglo-Irish literature. She has taught high school English.

KATHERINE BISHOP

Bishop is a PhD student in English literature and has been a university instructor.

ALLISON BLECKER

Blecker is a PhD candidate in Near Eastern languages.

ELIZABETH BOEHEIM

Boeheim holds an MA in English literature and has been a university instructor.

MELANIE BREZNIAK

Brezniak is a PhD candidate in English literature and has been a university instructor.

WESLEY BORUCKI

Borucki holds a PhD in American history and is a university professor.

JOSEPH CAMPANA

Campana holds an MA in English literature and has been a university professor.

GERALD CARPENTER

Carpenter holds an MA in U.S. intellectual history and a PhD in early modern French history. He is a freelance writer.

CHRISTINA BROWN CELONA

Celona holds a PhD in English literature and creative writing and has been a university instructor and a freelance writer.

CURT CLONINGER

Cloninger holds an MFA in studio arts and is a university professor.

KEVIN COONEY

Cooney holds a PhD in English literature and is a university professor.

ALEX COVALCIUC

Covalciuc is a PhD candidate in English literature. He has been a university instructor and a freelance writer.

GIANO CROMLEY

Cromley holds an MFA in creative writing and is a university instructor.

MARIE DAVOL

Davol holds an MA in writing.

VICTORIA DeCUIR

DeCuir holds an MA in art history and is a university instructor.

ANNA DEEM

Deem holds an MA in education and is a freelance writer.

CAMERON DODWORTH

Dodworth holds a PhD in English literature and is a university instructor.

RICHARD ESBENSHADE

Esbenshade holds a PhD in history and has been a university professor and a freelance writer.

TAYLOR EVANS

Evans is a PhD student in English literature and has been a university instructor.

DENNIS FEHR

Fehr holds a PhD in art education and is a university professor.

ELEANOR FOGOLIN

Fogolin is pursuing an MA in English literature.

CAROL FRANCIS

Francis holds an MA in English literature and has been a university instructor.

DANIEL FRIED

Fried holds a PhD in East Asian studies and is a university professor.

DAISY GARD

Gard is a freelance writer with a background in English literature.

GRETA GARD

Gard is a PhD candidate in English literature and has been a university instructor and a freelance writer.

CLINT GARNER

Garner holds an MFA in creative writing and is a freelance writer.

KRISTEN GLEASON

Gleason holds an MFA in creative writing and has been a university instructor.

RODNEY HARRIS

Harris is pursuing a PhD in history and has been a university instructor.

JOSH HARTEIS

Harteis holds an MA in English literature and is a freelance writer.

MICHAEL HARTWELL

Hartwell holds an MFA in creative writing and has been a university instructor and a freelance writer.

RON HORTON

Horton holds an MFA in creative writing and has been a high school English instructor and a freelance writer.

ANNA IOANES

Ioanes is a PhD student in English language and literature and has been a university instructor.

MIRANDA JOHNSON

Johnson is a freelance writer with a background in art history.

EMILY JONES

Jones holds an MFA in creative writing and has been a university instructor.

REBECCA KASTLEMAN

Kastleman is a PhD candidate in English literature and a freelance writer.

KRISTIN KING-RIES

King-Ries holds an MFA in creative writing and has been a university instructor.

LISA KROGER

Kroger holds a PhD in English literature and has been a university instructor.

DAVID LOVE

Love is pursuing an MFA in creative writing and has been a freelance writer.

JENNY LUDWIG

Ludwig holds an MA in English literature and has been a university instructor and a freelance writer.

GREGORY LUTHER

Luther holds an MFA in creative writing and has been a university instructor and freelance writer.

KATIE MACNAMARA

Macnamara holds a PhD in English literature and has been a university instructor.

MAGGIE MAGNO

Magno has an MA in education. She has been a high school English teacher and a freelance writer.

ABIGAIL MANN

Mann holds a PhD in English literature and is a university professor.

THEODORE MCDERMOTT

McDermott holds an MFA in creative writing and has been a university instructor and a freelance writer.

LISA MERTEL

Mertel holds an MA in library science and an MA in history.

STEPHEN MEYER

Meyer holds an MFA in creative writing and has been a university instructor and a freelance writer.

RACHEL MINDELL

Mindell holds an MFA in creative writing and has been a freelance writer.

JIM MLADENOVIC

Mladenovic holds an MS in clinical psychology and is pursuing an MA in library science.

CAITIE MOORE

Moore holds an MFA in creative writing and has been a university instructor.

ROBIN MORRIS

Morris holds a PhD in English literature and has been a university instructor.

JANET MULLANE

Mullane is a freelance writer and has been a high school English teacher.

ELLIOTT NIBLOCK

Niblock holds an MTS in the philosophy of religion.

ELIZABETH ORVIS

Orvis is a freelance writer with a background in English literature.

JAMES OVERHOLTZER

Overholtzer holds an MA in English literature and has been a university instructor.

JONATHAN REEVE

Reeve holds an MA in humanities and an MA in English literature and has been a university instructor.

EVELYN REYNOLDS

Reynolds is pursuing an MA in English literature and an MFA in creative writing and has been a freelance writer.

RICHARD ROTHROCK

Rothrock hold an MA in mass communication and has been a university instructor and a freelance writer.

REBECCA RUSTIN

Rustin holds an MA in English literature and is a freelance writer.

CARINA SAXON

Saxon is a PhD candidate in English literature and has been a university instructor and a freelance editor.

CATHERINE E. SAUNDERS

Saunders holds a PhD in English literature and is a university professor.

JACOB SCHMITT

Schmitt holds an MA in English literature and has been a freelance writer.

NANCY SIMPSON-YOUNGER

Simpson-Younger is a PhD candidate in literary studies and a university instructor.

NICHOLAS SNEAD

Snead is a PhD candidate in French language and literature and has been a university instructor.

HANNAH SOUKUP

Soukup holds an MFA in creative writing.

STEPHEN SQUIBB

Squibb is a PhD candidate in English literature and a freelance writer.

SARAH STOECKL

Stoeckl holds a PhD in English literature and is a university instructor and a freelance writer.

MARTHA SUTRO

Sutro holds an MFA in creative writing and is a university instructor and a freelance writer.

ELIZABETH VITANZA

Vitanza holds a PhD in French and Francophone studies and has been a university and a high school instructor.

GRACE WAITMAN

Waitman is pursuing a PhD in educational psychology. She holds an MA in English literature and has been a university instructor.

JOHN WALTERS

Walters is pursuing a PhD in English literature and has been a university instructor.

JOSHUA WARE

Ware holds a PhD in creative writing and has been a university instructor.

KATRINA WHITE

White is a PhD candidate in Spanish language and literature and a university instructor.

ACADEMIC REVIEWERS

JOSEPH ACQUISTO

Associate Professor of French, University of Vermont, Burlington.

ANN MARIE ADAMS

Professor of English, Morehead State University, Kentucky.

RAPHAEL ALLISON

Assistant Professor of English, MAT Program, Bard College, Annandale-on-Hudson, New York.

JOHN ALVIS

Professor of English and Director, American Studies Program, University of Dallas, Irving, Texas.

NAOMI ANDREWS

Assistant Professor of History, Santa Clara University, California.

PETER ARNADE

Dean, College of Arts and Humanities, University of Hawaiapos;i at Manoa, Honolulu.

BERNARDO ALEXANDER ATTIAS

Professor and Chair, Department of Communication Studies, California State University, Northridge.

SYLVIA BAKOS

Associate Professor of Fine Arts, SUNY Buffalo State, New York.

J. T. BARBARESE

Associate Professor of English and Creative Writing, Rutgers-Camden, New Jersey.

ROANN BARRIS

Associate Professor of Art History, Radford University, Virginia.

ADAM BARROWS

Associate Professor of English, Carleton University, Ottawa, Ontario, Canada.

WILLIAM BAUER

Associate Professor of History, University of Nevada-Las Vegas.

ROSALYN BAXANDALL

Retired Distinguished Teaching Professor, SUNY Old Westbury, New York, and Professor, Bard Prison Project and CUNY Labor School, New York.

JEREMY BEAUDRY

Assistant Professor and Director, Master of Industrial Design Program, University of the Arts, Philadelphia, Pennsylvania.

THOMAS OLIVER BEEBEE

Edwin Erle Sparks Professor of Comparative Literature and German, Pennsylvania State University, University Park.

STEPHEN BEHRENDT

University Professor and George Holmes Distinguished Professor of English, University of Nebraska, Lincoln.

JUSTYNA BEINEK

Assistant Professor of Slavic Languages and Literatures and Director, Polish Language, Literature, and Culture Program, Indiana University-Bloomington.

WILLIAM BELDING

Professorial Lecturer, School of International Service, American University, Washington, D.C.

EVGENII BERSHTEIN

Associate Professor of Russian, Reed College, Portland, Oregon.

ALEX BLAZER

Assistant Professor of English and Coordinator, Teaching Fellows,

Georgia College & State University, Milledgeville.

DAVID BLITZ

Professor of Philosophy and Director, Honors Program, Central Connecticut State University, New Britain.

JULIA BLOCH

Assistant Professor of Literature, MAT Program, Bard College, Annandale-on-Hudson, New York.

SAM BOOTLE

Teaching Fellow in French, University of St. Andrews, Fife, Scotland, United Kingdom.

MARK CAMERON BOYD

Professor of Fine Arts and Academics, Corcoran College of Art and Design, Washington, D.C.

MICHAEL P. BREEN

Associate Professor of History and Humanities, Reed College, Portland, Oregon.

DANIEL H. BROWN

Assistant Professor of Spanish, Western Illinois University, Macomb.

JAMES BROWN

Assistant Professor of English, University of Wisconsin-Madison.

ERNESTO CAPELLO

Associate Professor of History and Latin American Studies, Macalester College, St. Paul, Minnesota.

MICHAEL CARIGNAN

Associate Professor of History, Elon University, North Carolina.

TERRELL CARVER

Professor of Political Theory, University of Bristol, United Kingdom.

MALCOLM CHASE

Professor of Social History, University of Leeds, United Kingdom.

EWA CHRUSCIEL

Associate Professor of Humanities, Colby-Sawyer College, New London, New Hampshire.

ANN CIASULLO

Assistant Professor of English and Women's and Gender Studies, Gonzaga University, Spokane, Washington.

CURT CLONINGER

Assistant Professor of New Media, University of North Carolina, Asheville.

RUSSELL COOK

Professor of Communications, Loyola University Maryland, Baltimore.

RAYMOND CRAIB

Associate Professor of History, Cornell University, Ithaca, New York.

JANE CRAWFORD

Faculty, History and Political Science Department, Mount St. Mary's College, Los Angeles, California.

LESLEY CURTIS

Visiting Lecturer in French, Humanities, and Women's Studies, University of New Hampshire, Durham.

VICTORIA ESTRADA BERG DeCUIR

Assistant Director and Registrar, UNT Art Gallery and Art in Public Places, and Adjunct Faculty, Department of Art History, College of Visual Arts and Design, University of North Texas, Denton.

GABRIELE DILLMANN

Associate Professor of German, Denison University, Granville, Ohio.

EDUARDO DE JESÚS DOUGLAS

Associate Professor of Art History, University of North Carolina at Chapel Hill.

ELLEN DuBOIS

Professor of History, University of California, Los Angeles.

HUGH DUBRULL

Associate Professor of History, St. Anselm College, Manchester, New Hampshire.

ELIZABETH DUQUETTE

Associate Professor of English, Gettysburg College, Pennsylvania.

MICHAEL J. DUVALL

Associate Professor of English, College of Charleston, South Carolina.

TAYLOR EASUM

Assistant Professor of Global Histories; Faculty Fellow of Draper Program, New York University.

LORI EMERSON

Assistant Professor of English, University of Colorado-Boulder.

ALEŠ ERJAVEC

Professor of Philosophy, Aesthetics, and Contemporary Art History, Institute of Philosophy, Slovenian Academy of Sciences and Arts, Ljubljana, Slovenia.

SEBASTIAAN FABER

Professor of Hispanic Studies, Director, Oberlin Center for Languages and Cultures, and Chair, Latin American Studies, Oberlin College, Ohio.

BREANNE FAHS

Associate Professor of Women and Gender Studies, Arizona State University, Glendale.

DANINE FARQUHARSON

Associate Professor of English, Memorial University of Newfoundland, St. John's, Canada.

JIMMY FAZZINO

Lecturer in the Literature Department and Writing Program, University of California, Santa Cruz.

ODILE FERLY

Associate Professor of Francophone Studies, Clark University, Worcester, Massachusetts.

JOSHUA FIRST

Croft Assistant Professor of History and International Studies, University of Mississippi, University.

LEONARDO FLORES

Associate Professor of English and Fulbright Scholar in Digital Culture, Universidad de Puerto Rico, Mayagüez.

LISA FLORMAN

Associate Professor, History of Art, Ohio State University, Columbus.

WILLIAM FRANKE

Professor of Comparative Literature and Religious Studies, Vanderbilt University, Nashville, Tennessee, and Professor of Philosophy and Religions, University of Macao, China.

SUSAN GALLAGHER

Associate Professor of Political Science, University of Massachusetts Lowell.

JAMES GIGANTINO

Assistant Professor of History, University of Arkansas, Fayetteville.

DAWN GILPIN

Assistant Professor of Journalism, Walter Cronkite School of Journalism and Mass Communication, Arizona State University, Phoenix.

DALE GRADEN

Professor of History, University of Idaho, Moscow.

PATRICK RYAN GRZANKA

Honors Faculty Fellow at Barrett, the Honors College, Arizona State University, Tempe.

ANDREW P. HALEY

Associate Professor of American Cultural History, University of Southern Mississippi, Hattiesburg.

M. SÜKRÜ HANIOGLU

Garrett Professor in Foreign Affairs, Chair, Near Eastern Studies Department, and Director, Near Eastern Studies Program, Princeton University, New Jersey.

MARK HARRISON

Professor of Theatre and Performance Studies, Evergreen State College, Olympia, Washington.

CHENE HEADY

Associate Professor of English, Longwood University, Farmville, Virginia.

MICHAEL C. HICKEY

Professor of History, Bloomsburg University, Pennsylvania.

STEPHEN HICKS
Professor of Philosophy, Rockford College, Illinois.

BENEDIKT HJARTARSON
Adjunct Professor of Comparative Literature, University of Iceland, Reykjavik.

TAMARA HO
Assistant Professor of Women's Studies, University of California, Riverside.

WALTER HÖLBLING
Professor of American Studies, Karl-Franzens-Universität, Graz, Austria.

PIPPA HOLLOWAY
Professor of History and Program Director, Graduate Studies, Middle Tennessee State University, Murfreesboro.

MARYANNE HOROWITZ
Professor of History, Occidental College, Los Angeles, California. Editor-in-Chief, New Dictionary of the History of Ideas.

BOZENA KARWOWSKA
Associate Professor of Polish Language and Literature, University of British Columbia, Vancouver, Canada.

ANTHONY KEMP
Associate Professor of English, University of Southern California, Los Angeles.

ALICIA A. KENT
Associate Professor of English, University of Michigan-Flint.

MATTHEW KINEEN
Professor of Comparative Literature, St. Louis University-Madrid, Spain.

JASMINE KITSES
PhD candidate in English, University of California, Davis.

SCOTT KLEINMAN
Professor of English, California State University, Northridge.

CHRISTOPHER KNIGHT
Professor of English, University of Montana, Missoula.

ANDREAS KRATKY
Assistant Professor of Media Arts and Interim Director, Media Arts and Practice

PhD Program, University of Southern California, Los Angeles.

CHARLES KURZMAN
Professor of Sociology, University of North Carolina at Chapel Hill.

JOSÉ LANTERS
Professor of English, University of Wisconsin-Milwaukee.

SHARON LARSON
Visiting Instructor of Modern Languages, University of Central Florida, Orlando.

KEITH LAYBOURN
Diamond Jubilee Professor, University of Huddersfield, West Yorkshire, United Kingdom.

BRENT LAYTHAM
Professor of Theology and Dean, Ecumenical Institute of Theology, St. Mary's Seminary and University, Baltimore, Maryland.

KAREN J. LEADER
Assistant Professor of Art History, Florida Atlantic University, Boca Raton.

ESTHER LESLIE
Professor of Political Aesthetics, University of London-Birkbeck, United Kingdom.

ESTHER LEVINGER
Professor of Art History, University of Haifa, Israel.

MARK LEVY
Professor of Art, California State University-East Bay, Hayward.

MARTIN LOCKSHIN
Professor of Humanities and Chair, Humanities Department, York University, Toronto, Ontario, Canada.

XIAOFEI LU
Gil Watz Early Career Professor in Language and Linguistics, as well as Associate Professor of Applied Linguistics, Pennsylvania State University, University Park.

CARY MAZER
Associate Professor of Theatre Arts and English, University of Pennsylvania, Philadelphia.

WILLIAM MCBRIDE
Associate Professor of English, Illinois State University, Normal.

KEVIN MCCOY
Associate Professor of Art and Art Education, New York University-Steinhardt.

PETER MCPHEE
Professorial Fellow of History, University of Melbourne, Australia.

GREGORY METCALF
Adjunct Professor of Art History and Theory & Criticism, University of Maryland; Maryland Institute College of Art, Baltimore.

DARREN MIDDLETON
Professor of Religion, Texas Christian University, Fort Worth.

GRÜNFELD MIHAI
Associate Professor of Hispanic Studies, Vassar College, Poughkeepsie, New York.

GAVIN MURRAY-MILLER
Adjunct Professor of History, Virginia Commonwealth University, Richmond.

DAVID N. MYERS
Professor of History and Chair, Department of History, University of California, Los Angeles.

WENDY NIELSEN
Assistant Professor of English, Montclair State University, New Jersey.

DRAGANA OBRADOVIC
Assistant Professor of Slavic Languages and Literatures, University of Toronto, Ontario, Canada.

ELAINE O'BRIEN
Professor of Modern and Contemporary Art History and Criticism, California State University, Sacramento.

JENNIFER PAP
Associate Professor of French, University of Denver, Colorado. Sanja Perovic Lecturer in French, King's College, London, United Kingdom.

EMMANUEL PETIT
Associate Professor of Architecture, Yale University, New Haven, Connecticut.

MICHEL PHARAND
Director, Disraeli Project, Queen's University, Kingston, Ontario, Canada.

JANET POWERS

Professor Emerita of Interdisciplinary Studies and Women, Gender, and Sexuality Studies, Gettysburg College, Pennsylvania.

EPHRAIM RADNER

Professor of Historical Theology, Wycliffe College, University of Toronto, Ontario, Canada.

MICHAEL RAPPORT

Professor of History and Politics, University of Stirling, Scotland, United Kingdom.

HOLLY RAYNARD

Lecturer in Czech Studies, University of Florida, Gainesville.

JONATHAN REES

Professor of History, Colorado State University-Pueblo.

JOHN RIEDER

Professor of English, University of Hawaii at Manoa, Honolulu.

PATRICIO RIZZO-VAST

Instructor in Spanish and Portuguese, Northeastern Illinois University, Chicago.

HUGH ROBERTS

Associate Professor of English, University of California, Irvine, California.

MOSS ROBERTS

Professor of Chinese, New York University.

LETHA CLAIR ROBERTSON

Assistant Professor of Art and Art History, University of Texas at Tyler.

AARON ROSEN

Lecturer in Sacred Traditions and the Arts, King's College-London, United Kingdom.

ELI RUBIN

Associate Professor of History, Western Michigan University, Kalamazoo.

GREGORY SHAYA

Associate Professor of History and Chair, History Department, College of Wooster, Ohio.

NOAH SHUSTERMAN

Assistant Professor of Intellectual Heritage, Temple University, Philadelphia, Pennsylvania.

JOEL SIPRESS

Professor of History, University of Wisconsin-Superior.

ADAM SITZE

Assistant Professor of Law, Jurisprudence, and Social Thought, Amherst College, Massachusetts.

CRAIG SMITH

Associate Professor of Art, University of Florida, Gainesville.

ROGER SOUTHALL

Honorary Professor in SWOP (Southwest Organizing Project) and Head, Sociology Department, University of the Witwatersrand, Johannesburg, South Africa.

ROBERT SPAHR

Assistant Professor of Media and Media Production, Southern Illinois University, Carbondale.

ANIA SPYRA

Assistant Professor of English, Butler University, Indianapolis, Indiana.

MARY ZEISS STANGE

Professor of Women's Studies and Religion, Skidmore College, Saratoga Springs, New York.

ELIZABETH STARK

Visiting Fellow, Yale Information Society Project, and Lecturer in Computer Science, Yale University, New Haven, Connecticut.

JANET WRIGHT STARNER

Associate Professor of English, Wilkes University, Wilkes-Barre, Pennsylvania.

R. VLADMIR STEFFEL

Professor Emeritus of History and Director, Honors Programs, Ohio State University-Marion.

SARAH STOECKL

PhD, Department of English, University of Oregon, Eugene.

MASON STOKES

Associate Professor of English and Chair, English Department, Skidmore College, Saratoga Springs, New York.

MATTHEW STRATTON

Assistant Professor of English, University of California, Davis.

WOODMAN TAYLOR

Associate Professor of Art History, American University of Dubai.

CHARISSA TERRANOVA

Assistant Professor of Aesthetic Studies, University of Texas at Dallas, Richardson.

DOUGLASS THOMSON

Professor of English, Georgia Southern University, Statesboro.

LARRY THORNTON

Professor of History, Hanover College, Indiana.

JOHN G. TURNER

Assistant Professor of Religious Studies, George Mason University, Fairfax, Virginia.

THOMAS UNDERWOOD

Senior Lecturer (Master Level), College of Arts and Sciences Writing Program, Boston University, Massachusetts.

ELIZABETH VITANZA

French Instructor, Marlborough School, Los Angeles, California.

ALICIA VOLK

Associate Professor of Art History and Director, Graduate Studies, University of Maryland, College Park.

DONALD WELLMAN

Professor of Literature and Writing, Daniel Webster College, Nashua, New Hampshire.

E. J. WESTLAKE

Associate Professor of Theatre, University of Michigan, Ann Arbor.

RACHEL WILLIAMS

Associate Professor of Studio Art and Gender, Women's, and Sexuality Studies, University of Iowa, Iowa City.

SIMONA WRIGHT

Professor of Italian, College of New Jersey, Ewing Township.

RALPH YOUNG

Professor of History, Temple University, Philadelphia, Pennsylvania.

PIERANTONIO ZANOTTI

Adjunct Professor of Japanese Language, Università Ca' Foscari Venezia, Italy.

America Left and Right

CONTRACT WITH AMERICA

Richard Armey, John Boehner, Tom DeLay, Newt Gingrich, Larry Hunter

OVERVIEW

Written in 1994 by economist Larry Hunter with Republican legislators Newt Gingrich, Richard Armey, Tom DeLay, and John Boehner, *Contract with America* argues for conservative principles to be enacted in government on a variety of levels. The document calls for specific bills, such as those related to increased personal responsibility, the reinforcement of families, and the strengthening of national defense, to be proposed in the first one hundred days of the 104th Congress. *Contract with America* was published six weeks before the 1994 U.S. midterm elections, when the administration of Democratic President Bill Clinton was in its second year and Democrats held the majority in both the Senate and the House of Representatives. The conservative legal agenda declared government reforms and policy that would be enacted if the Republican Party gained control of Congress. Addressed to American voters, the ten-point legislative program was signed by all but two House Republicans and by all nonincumbent Republican candidates, for a total of 367 signatories. As a unifying document for Republican candidates across the nation, the policy statement reaffirmed general conservative principles but avoided any explicit statements on social issues deemed too controversial, such as abortion and school prayer.

The document resonated with voters, and in the 1994 elections the Republican Party gained control of the House and Senate for the first time since 1954. Many saw *Contract with America* as a symbol of triumph for Republican Party leaders, particularly Gingrich, and for the American conservative movement. However, when House Republicans put each item from the contract to a vote, most of the bills failed to pass the Senate or faced vetoes from Clinton, who referred to it as the "Contract *on* America." The acrimonious debate over the principles outlined in the document presaged the contentious climate that persisted in Washington throughout the late 1990s. Ultimately considered a failure by many, including Gingrich, the contract articulates themes that have remained prevalent in conservative political campaigns.

HISTORICAL AND LITERARY CONTEXT

Contract with America was intended to restate and repopularize conservative ideals while taking advantage of public discontent with the country's large deficit and with the Clinton administration's failure to pass either an economic stimulus package or health care reform. Before the 1994 midterm elections, the Democratic Party had controlled the House of Representatives for forty years, and Clinton's election in 1992 had been viewed by conservatives and Republican Party strategists as a major setback following three Republican presidential administrations. The Republican Party's success in the election was dubbed by many as the "Republican revolution" or the "Gingrich revolution," referring to Gingrich, who was the figure most associated with the contract—and ultimately became Speaker of the House because of it. In addition to gaining fifty-four seats in the House of Representatives and eight seats in the Senate, the Republican Party gained twelve gubernatorial seats and 472 legislative seats at the state level.

Gingrich, a Republican representative from Georgia, had been urging Republican Party leaders for years to be more aggressive and more unified in their campaign language. He founded the Conservative Opportunity Society in 1983, and the group's ideas, particularly Gingrich's analysis of public opinion polls, were increasingly adopted in President Ronald Reagan's second term. The opening of *Contract with America* reiterated these basic ideas in a three-part form: the federal government is too big and unresponsive (lacking accountability), government programs sap individual willpower (diminishing responsibility), and ultimately an overtaxed and over-regulated citizenry cannot pursue the American Dream (stunted opportunity). The first part of the contract, relating to congressional procedure, was presented as the means to restore governmental accountability, while the national policy proposals primarily reinforced this concept of responsibility (welfare reform, anti-crime measures) and opportunity (small business incentives, limits on liability and punitive damages).

✣ Key Facts

Time Period:
Late 20th Century

Movement/Issue:
Political conservatism

Place of Publication:
United States

Language of Publication:
English

GOVERNMENT IN CRISIS: BUDGET SHUTDOWN OF 1995 AND 1996

The U.S. federal government shutdown of 1995 resulted from conflicts between Democratic President Bill Clinton and the Republican-controlled Congress over funding for Medicare, education, and the environment. When Clinton refused to accept the proposed budget, U.S. Representative Newt Gingrich, as House speaker, threatened to refuse to raise the debt limit, putting the government in danger of default. The government suspended all nonessential services for a total of twenty-eight days, the longest shutdown in U.S. history. A 2010 congressional report detailed the effects, including curtailment of veteran services, losses to the tourism and airline industries, and billions lost in federal contracts.

Clinton's approval ratings fell during the shutdown but rose significantly after it had ended. Many commentators attribute this to an increasingly negative perception of Gingrich, whose comments regarding a perceived snub by Clinton on *Air Force One* led many to question his motives for the standoff. Additionally, the budget crisis caused tensions within the Republican Party, as Gingrich and Senator Bob Dole, then potential rivals for the 1996 Republican presidential ticket, took different stances on the negotiations, with Dole wanting to resolve the crisis sooner and Gingrich wanting to continue the shutdown until the Republicans' budget was accepted. Although Gingrich came to regret his comments, he maintains that the Republicans' hardline stance influenced the balanced-budget deal in 1997 and contributed to the Republicans' retaining their majority in the 1996 elections, despite Clinton's reelection.

Contract with America draws on the tradition of American revolutionary documents as well as traditional conservative and federalist themes. The opening language of the contract, as well as the public signing ceremony on the steps of the Capitol, were intended to evoke the Declaration of Independence. The contract also drew on Republican Party history by invoking Abraham Lincoln as being symbolic of a reformer: "Like Lincoln, our first Republican president, we intend to act 'with firmness in the right, as God gives us to see the right.'" Reagan biographer Lou Cannon has suggested that large parts of the contract, both in content and in rhetorical style, were drawn from Reagan's 1985 State of the Union address. At the same time, the authors positioned the contract as revolutionary: Gingrich said, "There is no comparable congressional document in our two-hundred-year history."

The impact of *Contract with America* has continued into the new millennium. In September 2011 Gingrich released an expanded *21st Century Contract with America* as part of his campaign for the Republican presidential nomination. Conservative Tea Party activists also evoked *Contract with America* when they published a ten-point *Contract from America* in April 2010, based on points developed from online balloting. Both Armey and Gingrich offered support of *Contract from America,* while Democratic National Committee communications director Brad Woodhouse criticized the proposals as "bumper sticker solutions."

THEMES AND STYLE

The central theme of *Contract with America* adopts ideas from the Declaration of Independence to argue that the U.S. government has become too big, too wasteful, and too intrusive in individuals' lives. The contract opens with the pledge that "as Republican Members of the House of Representatives and as citizens seeking to join that body we propose not just to change its policies, but even more important, to restore the bonds of trust between the people and their elected representatives." Therefore, the 1994 congressional elections were presented as an opportunity not only for specific policy changes but for systemic changes if a Republican majority were elected. The idea of trust suggested in the contract is emphasized in the prominence of organizational reforms meant to indicate a commitment to changing the government status quo.

Contract with America is phrased in simple language that is meant to suggest a contrast with the "era of official evasion and posturing" the Republicans propose to end. The document's eight organizational reforms are to be passed on the first day after taking office. The other ten points (laws), to be enacted within the first one hundred days, are presented to Congress as a series of bullet points, and the proposed national policy laws are briefly summarized with titles using emotionally evocative language. These include the American Dream Restoration Act (relating to a $500 child tax credit and changes to tax policy for married couples and retirement accounts), the Personal Responsibility Act (relating to cuts to programs assisting unwed mothers on welfare), and the Common Sense Legal Reform Act (relating to limits on punitive damages and changes to product liability laws). The contract was written to emphasize what GOP polling strategist Frank Luntz referred to as "60 percent" issues, meaning policies that had already proven popular with focus groups and avoiding more divisive topics of social policy.

Stylistically, the contract positions itself as direct and unambiguous, "a written commitment with no fine print," in contrast with a government that is perceived as unnecessarily bloated and obscure. This is reiterated through repetitions of expressions relating to trust, faith, common sense, and personal responsibility—all of which are core Republican principles. The contract also emphasizes immediate action and rapid results through pledging to immediately pass the operational reforms and to bring the policy measures to the floor within the first hundred days of the congressional session, providing a sharp contrast to the "four decades of one-party control." Although the contract proffers specific bills by name and economic measures, critics pointed out that it does not specify how the promised budget reductions would be accomplished.

CRITICAL DISCUSSION

Some observers believe *Contract with America* helped secure a decisive victory for the Republicans in the 1994 elections. Jeffrey Gaynor of the Heritage Foundation argued in 1995 that future historians would look at the contract as "one of the most significant developments in the political history of the United States," emphasizing its degree of detail as campaign material and the amount of legislation it inspired in the House of Representatives. However, others disputed the contract's importance to the election, noting its late introduction into the campaign. Polls at the time suggested relatively little awareness of the contract among voters. Critics condemned the contract as a "gimmick" more concerned with electability than policy, and they criticized the explicit use of polling data in formulating the contents of the contract. Others suggested that the focus on relatively popular and broadly termed issues was purposefully misleading about the Republican agenda, while some social conservatives felt betrayed by the lack of attention given to social issues, especially in contrast with the full Republican platform.

The polarized political atmosphere engendered by the contract ultimately contributed to the government shutdown of 1995 and the impeachment of Clinton in 1998. The shutdown left many people disenchanted with Republican hardline tactics on enforcing the contract in the face of opposition from Senate Republicans as well as congressional Democrats and Clinton. Only three of the bills became law: the Congressional Accountability Act of 1995, requiring Congress to follow eleven workplace laws; the Unfunded Mandates Reform Act of 1995, which restricts Congress from imposing state mandates without adequate funding; and the Paperwork Reduction Act of 1995. However, some of the elements of the contract were influential in the ultimate passage of the Welfare Reform Act of 1996 and Balanced Budget Act of 1997.

Ultimately, *Contract with America* is considered by many to have failed, at least in bringing its specific promises to fruition. Edward Crane, president of the libertarian Cato Institute, claimed in 2000 that "the combined budgets of the 95 major programs that the *Contract with America* promised to eliminate have increased by 13%." However, others have suggested that the contract continues to have influence in more discrete ways. Conservative commentator Major Garrett has argued that *Contract with America* paved the way for the election of George W. Bush and that the economic policies it suggested became incorporated

Former House Speaker Newt Gingrich giving a lecture in 2004. © ZUMA WIRE SERVICE/ALAMY

in Democratic as well as Republican campaign platforms. Law professor David E. Bernstein has argued that *Contract with America* represented a demonstrated commitment by the Republican Party to principles of federalism and limited national government that continues to impact policy in all branches of government, such as United States v. Lopez (1995), the first Supreme Court decision since the New Deal to limit congressional power under the Commerce Clause of the Constitution.

BIBLIOGRAPHY

Sources

Bernstein, David E. "Constitutional Doctrine and the Constitutionality of Health Care Reform." The Volokh Conspiracy. N.p., 15 Dec. 2010. Web. 10 June 2012.

Crane, Edward H. "On My Mind: GOP Pussycats." Forbes. 13 Nov. 2000. *Cato Institute*. Web. 9 June 2012.

Davis, Teddy. "Tea Party Activists Unveil 'Contract from America.'" *ABC News.com*. ABC News Internet Ventures, 15 April 2010. Web. 8 June 2012.

Garrett, Major. "Beyond the Contract." *Mother Jones*. Mother Jones, March/April 1995. Web. 8 June 2012.

———. *The Enduring Revolution: How the Contract with America Continues to Shape the Nation*. New York: Crown Forum, 2005. Print.

Gaynor, Jeffrey. "The *Contract with America*: Implementing New Ideas in the U.S." *The Heritage Foundation*. Heritage Foundation, 12 Oct. 1995. Web. 8 June 2012.

Further Reading

Bader, John B. *Taking the Initiative: Leadership Agendas in Congress and the Contract with America*. Washington, DC: Georgetown UP, 1996. Print.

Balz, Daniel, and Ronald Brownstein. *Storming the Gates: Protest Politics and the Republican Revival*. New York: Little, Brown, 1996. Print.

Gross, Neil, Thomas Medvetz, and Rupert Russell. "The Contemporary American Conservative Movement." *Annual Review of Sociology* 37 (2011): 325-54.

Hershey, Marjorie Randon. "Do Constructed Explanations Persist? Reframing of the 1994 Republican Takeover of Congress." *Congress & the Presidency* 38.2 (2011): 131-51.

Rae, Nicol C. *Conservative Reformers: The Republican Freshmen and the Lessons of the 104th Congress.* Armonk, NY: ME Sharpe, 1998. Print.

Woolridge, Adrian, and John Micklethwait. *The Right Nation: Conservative Power in America.* London: Penguin Press, 2004. Print.

Marie Becker

A COUNTRY FOR ALL
An Immigrant Manifesto
Jorge Ramos

OVERVIEW

Journalist and news anchor Jorge Ramos's book *A Country for All: An Immigrant Manifesto* (2010), first published in Spanish as *Tierra de todos: Nuestro momento para crear una nación de iguales* (2009), describes the dysfunctional state of U.S. immigration policy in the first decade of the twenty-first century and delineates a pragmatic strategy to overcome policy challenges and to make effective reforms. At the time of the book's publication, Ramos was the second-most watched news anchor in the United States, appearing on the leading Spanish-language news program *Noticiero Univision*. From a position of power within the rapidly growing Spanish-speaking U.S. population, Ramos used *A Country for All* to criticize president Barack Obama and other elected officials for failing to implement immigration reform and to call on Americans to change the way they think about immigration in the United States. Addressed to all Americans, Ramos's book targets federal inaction in the face of anti-immigrant sentiment and legislation, and it offers policy solutions to problems faced by millions of undocumented workers.

When first published, *A Country for All* made waves for its staunch, unabashed proimmigration stance. Responses to the book were polarized. Discussion surrounding Ramos's manifesto tended to address the issue of immigration in general rather than the text specifically. Ramos, a Mexican immigrant, took up immigration reform as a personal cause. Appearing on television and in other (English-language and Spanish-language) media outlets, the author and other pundits broadly debated the issue of immigration. Ramos's high profile and the soundness of his argument helped spur dialogue about reform and put additional pressure on President Obama to work with Congress to address immigration.

HISTORICAL AND LITERARY CONTEXT

A Country for All responds to the immigration crisis facing the United States in the early twenty-first century, when political battles over undocumented residents escalated in response to controversial anti-immigration laws and a growing Hispanic population. Many like Ramos decried the lack of basic rights and protections for the millions of undocumented workers on whom many American businesses depend. However, the economic downturn and high unemployment in 2008 prompted many Americans to blame undocumented immigrants for having a negative impact on the economy.

By the time Ramos published his book, the need for immigration reform had reached a critical point. The number of undocumented immigrants in the United States had exceeded 10 million, and sentiment toward immigrants was increasingly hostile. The passage of Arizona Senate Bill 1070, strict anti-immigration legislation that empowered police officers to investigate alleged criminals' residency, made it a misdemeanor to be in the state without legal documentation. Seen by many as a way to legitimize racial profiling, the bill sparked renewed interest in immigration reform. However, many were disappointed that, despite campaign promises to reform immigration, President Obama had not fulfilled his pledge after two years in office.

A Country for All is part of a wide body of American immigration literature ranging from novels such as T.C. Boyle's *Tortilla Curtain* (1995), which describes the experience of crossing the U.S.-Mexico border, to historical studies such as *Guarding the Golden Door* (2004), in which Roger Daniels provides an overview of American immigration policy since the late-nineteenth century. The call to action in *A Country for All* builds on that of other manifestos, such as the *Chicano Manifesto* (1971), by Armando B. Redón, which demands rights for Americans of Mexican descent. Ramos's manifesto also develops ideas put forth in his other works, including *Lo que vi* (1999; What I've Seen), an account of his migration from Mexico; *No Borders: A Journalist's Search for Home* (2003); *The Latino Wave: How Hispanics Are Transforming Politics in America* (2005); *Dying to Cross: The Worst Immigrant Tragedy in American History* (2006); and *The Other Face of America: Chronicles of the Immigrants Shaping Our Future* (2006).

Following the publication of *A Country for All*, Ramos continued ardently to support immigration reform and to pursue sweeping political change. A variety of media outlets called on him to comment

✣ *Key Facts*

Time Period:
Early 21st Century

Movement/Issue:
American immigration reform; Growth of Hispanic population; Election of President Barack Obama

Place of Publication:
United States

Language of Publication:
Spanish; English

THE "NO ONE IS ILLEGAL MANIFESTO"

While much contemporary attention has focused on the immigration reform debate in the United States, many European nations are embroiled in similar discussions. In the United Kingdom attention has been drawn to hundreds of thousands of "illegal" immigrants who have entered the country without proper documents or have overstayed their tourist or student visas. On September 6, 2003, the UK-based No One Is Illegal group reacted to pervasive anti-immigration sentiment with the "No One Is Illegal Manifesto." The text embraces a world without borders or immigration regulations and opposes the idea that it is possible to be an "illegal" immigrant.

Among the arguments outlined in the manifesto are that immigration laws represent a systematic means of restricting human rights and perpetuating misery; that arguments for immigration control (most notably, that "people coming here are a 'burden' on welfare or are 'flooding' the country") are false; and that such positions originate in racism and misplaced fear. The manifesto calls upon its readers to join the fight against immigration controls, deportations, and detention centers. It also exhorts state welfare workers to ignore anti-immigrant regulations and urges trade unions to actively recruit undocumented workers.

on immigration policy in light of his proimmigration stance in his work as host of *Noticiero Univision*. His strongly held views have helped underscore the urgency of and demand for immigration reform in the United States, which remains a relevant, if not dominant, topic in American politics.

THEMES AND STYLE

The central theme of *A Country for All* is that the most pressing need for the United States in the twenty-first century is legislation that facilitates the immigration process and ends the forceful deportation and detention of undocumented workers. Ramos asks, "what is gained by annually deporting some six thousand of those arrested during raids at a cost of millions of dollars when thousands more will enter the country every year?" With

a wealth of statistics and anecdotes, he demonstrates why the current immigration system is ineffectual and conveys a deep conviction that giving undocumented immigrants official residency would benefit the nation in myriad ways. To this end, he outlines three steps to strategically address the issue of reform: legalization, integration, and long-term investment.

The manifesto achieves its rhetorical effect through appeals to foundational American values that transcend ethnic and cultural differences. Ramos asserts, "The unity that defines this nation is the result of shared values and the marvelous concept, established in the Declaration of Independence, that all men and women are created equal. We speak many languages, come in all colors and believe very strongly that our future lies in this great land." After describing injustices that undocumented workers have suffered, he writes, "This is not who we are in the United States of America." By invoking moral values that transcend racial boundaries, he demonstrates that reform is important not only to undocumented workers but to all Americans as well.

Stylistically, *A Country for All* is distinguished by the tension between its pragmatism and its emotional exigency. The text opens with a succinct statement: "Now is the time." Ramos repeats these words throughout the text, reinforcing the urgency of immigration reform. Although in the first half of the book he uses anecdotes and data to illustrate the current state of affairs and to rectify misconceptions about immigration, he maintains an urgent, even fervent, tone. In the latter half of the book, he offers recommendations and strategies for the next steps in immigration reform. Despite an obvious emotional commitment to the cause, he maintains a rational tone in discussing policy solutions: "It would be disingenuous to take the position that reform will prevent undocumented immigration. Whether it's in greater or lesser numbers, people will continue to come into the United States illegally. We have to be very realistic and look at the situation objectively in order to make an effective plan." The manifesto's closing lines call for a "*United* States. Nothing more. Nothing less," encapsulating Ramos's sense of urgency and the need for measured, practical steps forward.

CRITICAL DISCUSSION

When *A Country for All* was first published in English in 2010, it received generally positive reviews, although the author's fervent proimmigration stance garnered some criticism. The book made headlines and gained the attention of such well-known media outlets as *Time* magazine and the *New York Times*. Popular concern about Arizona's S. 1070 also furthered interest in *A Country for All*, which roundly condemned the bill. In a 2010 review for *Newsweek*, Tasnim Shamma attests, "It's not called a 'manifesto' for nothing…. Above all, it's an inspiring book that, if passionate to a fault, is soundly reasoned." However, some criticized Ramos for overstating the importance

Newscaster and author Jorge Ramos wrote *A Country for All: An Immigrant Manifesto*, which calls for reform of and offers a solution to the broken immigration system in place in the United States. AP PHOTO/LYNNE SLADKY

of undocumented workers and for using his position as a journalist to advocate for a political cause. In a 2010 article for *Culture and Media Institute,* Alana Goodman writes, "Ramos's brand of journalism represents an unsettling style among Spanish-language TV news reporters, whose musings on U.S. policy often go beyond mere political bias and into the realm of political advocacy."

In the years since *A Country for All* first appeared, immigration reform has continued to be part of the national political conversation. S. 1070 came under review for its constitutionality, and President Obama instituted a policy to allow young undocumented immigrants to attend school and remain in the United States. The manifesto had its greatest impact on Ramos himself, indelibly linking his persona to his views on immigration. In a 2012 entry for his Center for Immigration Studies blog, Jerry Kammer writes, "Ramos's unconstrained advocacy has made him a hero among illegal immigrants. It has also made him one of the most polarizing figures in the discussion of national immigration policy." In spite of criticism of his lack of objectivity, Ramos is frequently called on by news sources to comment on immigration and is perceived to be an authority on policy reform.

Few scholars have written about *A Country for All* as a text that deals with a hotly contested political issue. Most relevant scholarship broadly addresses the issue of immigration and the impact of media figures like Ramos on the policy debate. Nevertheless, Ramos's arguments and the data he includes in *A Country for All* have been cited in immigration reform debates, and his book has been adopted in university courses on public policy and immigration. The continuing attention attests to the importance of his perspective to the immigration debate.

BIBLIOGRAPHY

Sources

Cohen, Steve, Harriet Grimsditch, Teresa Hayter, Bob Hughes, and Dave Landau. "'No One Is Illegal Manifesto." *No One Is Illegal: The UK Campaign for Freedom of Movement and Settlement, and an End to Immigration Controls.* No One Is Illegal UK, 6 Sept. 2003. Web. 28 Nov. 2012.

Goodman, Alana. "Media Darling Univision Anchor Brings Pro-Illegal Immigration Bias to Latino Households." *Culture and Media Institute.* Media Research Center, 7 July 2010. Web. 13 Aug. 2010.

Hunt, Albert R. "Deflating the Myths about Immigration in the U.S." *New York Times.* New York Times, 11 July 2010. Web. 12 Aug 2012.

Kammer, Jerry. "Senator Marco Rubio Takes on Jorge Ramos, and Wins." *Jerry Kammer's Blog.* Center for Immigration Studies, 25 June 2012. Web. 12 Aug. 2012.

Pisani, Michael J. Rev. of *A Country for All: An Immigrant Manifesto,* by Jorge Ramos. *American Journal of Business* 27.1 (2012): 91-93. Print.

Ramos, Jorge. *A Country for All: An Immigrant Manifesto.* New York: Vintage, 2010. Print.

Shamma, Tasnim. Rev. of *A Country for All: An Immigrant Manifesto,* by Jorge Ramos. *Newsweek* 1 July 2010. Web. 17 Aug. 2012.

Further Reading

Bancroft, Colette. "'No Human Being Is Illegal.'" *Saint Petersburg Times* 25 July 2010: 7. Print.

Colarusso, Laura M. "The Anchor." *Washington Monthly* 44.5-6 (2012): 13-19. Print.

"Jorge Ramos: Prioritize Immigration Reform." *American Morning CNN.* CNN, 5 July 2010. Web. 12 Aug. 2012.

Kammer, Jerry. "Jorge Ramos's Problem with President Obama." *Jerry Kammer's Blog.* Center for Immigration Studies, 25 Aug. 2009. Web. 12 Aug. 2012.

Montané, Diana. "A Nation for All." *Hispanic* June 2009: 52-53. Print.

Nieblas, Nelly G., and Celina Moreno. "Twenty Years of Journalistic Justice." *Harvard Journal of Hispanic Policy* 19 (2006): 17-23. Print.

"Ten Questions for Jorge Ramos." *Time* 9 Aug. 2010: 6. Print.

Elizabeth Boeheim

DECLARATION OF THE OCCUPATION OF NEW YORK CITY

Occupy Wall Street

❖ *Key Facts*

Time Period:
Early 21st Century

Movement/Issue:
Great Recession;
Increasing corporate
power

Place of Publication:
United States

**Language of
Publication:**
English

OVERVIEW

Composed by members of the Occupy Wall Street protest movement, the *Declaration of the Occupation of New York City* (2011) enumerates a litany of grievances against the "corporate forces of the world" and urges people to organize for solutions to these injustices. The manifesto was drawn up through the collective effort of the New York City General Assembly, a decision-making body open to all members of the Occupy Wall Street protest, which was ongoing as of July 2012. Inspired in part by protests in Tunisia and Egypt during the so-called Arab Spring in 2011, Occupy Wall Street began on September 17, 2011, when hundreds of activists filled Zuccotti Park in Manhattan's Financial District to protest economic inequality and corruption, among other issues. Protesters established an encampment in the park and refused to leave, until they were forced out on November 15, 2011. Addressed to "the people of the world," the *Declaration of the Occupation of New York City* expresses "a feeling of mass injustice" and an urgent need to "generate solutions accessible to everyone."

Upon its issuance on September 27, the *Declaration* catalyzed a protest movement known as the Occupy movement that quickly spread across the United States and around the world. The movement was distinguished by its decentralized structure, diverse membership, and the breadth of its aims. Although the ongoing Occupy movement had not achieved by its first anniversary the kind of fundamental economic and political change it advocated, the movement drew significant popular and media attention to economic inequality in the United States and elsewhere in the western capitalist world. Both observers and participants consider the *Declaration of the Occupation of New York City* an important foundational document in the most vital ongoing protest movements against contemporary capitalism, corporatism, and globalization.

HISTORICAL AND LITERARY CONTEXT

The *Declaration of the Occupation of New York City* responds to the political and economic crisis facing the United States in the early 2010s, when recession, corporate bailouts, and growing economic disparity created a pervasive sense of disaffection among people in the lower and middle classes. Between 1979 and 2007, according to economists Paul Krugman and Robin Wells, the wealthiest one percent of the population of the United States saw its real income nearly quadruple. The remaining ninety-nine percent of the population saw much smaller gains. The result was cavernous economic disparity. In 2008 the United States experienced its greatest economic downturn since the Great Depression. In response, the U.S. government initiated a series of bailouts of banks and corporations. Meanwhile, home foreclosures, bankruptcies, and layoffs of average Americans dramatically rose. This resulted in a mounting sense of economic and political injustice.

KALLE LASN: CULTURE JAMMER

If the amorphous, collectivist, consensus-driven Occupy movement has a founder, it would be Kalle Lasn, a Canadian who was born in Estonia in 1942, spent time in German refugee camps, and grew up in Australia. He studied mathematics, then designed computer software and moved to Japan, where he started a market-research company. After that, he moved to Vancouver to make experimental films and advocate for environmental causes. In 1989 he founded *Adbusters,* a bimonthly magazine devoted to what Lasn deemed "culture jamming," or subverting mainstream cultural conventions.

The idea for Occupy Wall Street emerged in mid-2011 as part of an ongoing conversation between Lasn and Micah White, a senior editor of *Adbusters,* about the need for a grassroots response to what they saw as pervasive economic, political, and social injustice in the United States. That June, they sent an e-mail to *Adbusters* subscribers calling for a mass protest along the lines of the one in Cairo's Tahrir Square. Soon thereafter, on July 13, they sent out a second e-mail that provided a detailed plan for a protest encampment in New York City's Financial District that was set to begin on September 17. As that message spread across the web, the Occupy movement began the process of leaving Lasn's grasp and becoming the province of a broad, decentralized group of amateur organizers—just as Lasn had planned.

By the time the *Declaration of the Occupation of New York City* was written in 2011, political and social unrest was growing in the United States and around the world. An organized conservative response to Americans' disaffection had begun to take shape in 2009 in the form of the Tea Party movement. However, many Americans, particularly those on the left, were alienated by the Tea Party's campaign for free-market, rather than government, solutions to the nation's economic downturn. Then, in early 2011, the success of popular revolutions in Tunisia and Egypt launched a wave of regional insurrection known as the Arab Spring. During this same time period, protesters in numerous European countries campaigned against austerity measures that were meant to end ongoing recession. These various strands of protest and resistance inspired Kalle Lasn and Micah White of the Canadian magazine *Adbusters* to initiate a new protest targeting Wall Street.

The *Declaration of the Occupation of New York City* draws from an array of declarations on democracy and in particular from the *Port Huron Statement.* Largely written by Tom Hayden and issued by the Students for a Democratic Society in 1962 in response to the burgeoning civil rights movement, nuclear arms race, and the apathy of the liberal establishment, the *Port Huron Statement* advocates citizens' direct involvement not only in government but also in all institutional bodies that affected their lives. This form of "participatory democracy," as the *Port Huron Statement* labeled it, was not merely a political imperative

but a moral one. The authors of the *Declaration of the Occupation of New York City* made a similar case, arguing "that the future of the human race requires the cooperation of its members."

In the months following its publication, the *Declaration* inspired a wide range of polemical writing in response to the Occupy movement. On April 8, 2012, for example, the *Declaration from Occupy San Francisco General Assembly* was issued. One month later, on May 11, 2012, the International Occupy General Assembly issued the *GlobalMay Manifesto.* It, too, draws from the *Declaration of the Occupation of New York City*'s indictment of corporate power and demand for social and economic justice. It declares, "We want another world, and such a world is possible." Today the *Declaration of the Occupation of New York City* continues to serve as a source of inspiration for the ongoing and evolving Occupy movement.

THEMES AND STYLE

The central theme of the *Declaration of the Occupation of New York City* is that the contemporary political, economic, and social system is fundamentally corrupt and unjust and thus must be reformed. Written collectively in the midst of a large and amorphous protest, the manifesto opens with a call for focus: "As we gather together in solidarity to express a feeling of mass injustice, we must not lose sight of what brought us together." To this end, the manifesto enumerates a wide-ranging list of twenty-three injustices perpetrated by the "corporate forces of the world" against

PRIMARY SOURCE

DECLARATION OF THE OCCUPATION OF NEW YORK CITY

As we gather together in solidarity to express a feeling of mass injustice, we must not lose sight of what brought us together. We write so that all people who feel wronged by the corporate forces of the world can know that we are your allies.

As one people, united, we acknowledge the reality: that the future of the human race requires the cooperation of its members; that our system must protect our rights, and upon corruption of that system, it is up to the individuals to protect their own rights, and those of their neighbors; that a democratic government derives its just power from the people, but corporations do not seek consent to extract wealth from the people and the Earth; and that no true democracy is attainable when the process is determined by economic power. We come to you at a time when corporations, which place profit over people, self-interest over justice, and oppression over equality, run our governments. We have peaceably assembled here, as is our right, to let these facts be known.

- They have taken our houses through an illegal foreclosure process, despite not having the original mortgage.

- They have taken bailouts from taxpayers with impunity, and continue to give Executives exorbitant bonuses.

- They have perpetuated inequality and discrimination in the workplace based on age, the color of one's skin, sex, gender identity and sexual orientation.

- They have poisoned the food supply through negligence, and undermined the farming system through monopolization.

- They have profited off of the torture, confinement, and cruel treatment of countless animals, and actively hide these practices.

- They have continuously sought to strip employees of the right to negotiate for better pay and safer working conditions.

- They have held students hostage with tens of thousands of dollars of debt on education, which is itself a human right.

- They have consistently outsourced labor and used that outsourcing as leverage to cut workers' healthcare and pay.

- They have influenced the courts to achieve the same rights as people, with none of the culpability or responsibility.

- They have spent millions of dollars on legal teams that look for ways to get them out of contracts in regards to health insurance.

the protesters and their allies. The manifesto's authors call on their allies to "exercise your right to peaceably assemble; occupy public space; create a process to address the problems we face, and generate solutions accessible to everyone."

The manifesto achieves its rhetorical effect through an appeal to a sense of inclusiveness that transcends class, identity, or ideology. This sense of inclusiveness is achieved through the use of sweeping language that speaks to the broadest possible audience. "As one people, united," the manifesto reads, "we acknowledge the reality: that the future of the human race requires the cooperation of its members." Elsewhere, the manifesto directly addresses "the people of the world" and "all communities that take action and form groups in the spirit of direct democracy." The manifesto's inclusiveness is emphasized by its use of the first-person plural ("we"), which reflects its status as a collectively authored document. Rather than a list of specific demands, the *Declaration of the*

Occupation of New York City evokes a pervasive sense of disaffection. This, too, is a rhetorical means of appealing to the broadest possible audience.

Stylistically, the *Declaration of the Occupation of New York City* is distinguished by its use of repetition. For example, every item in the manifesto's extensive list of grievances employs the same sentence structure. All of them begin "they," and all but a few of the twenty-three begin "they have." This repetitiousness imbues the document with a sense of insistence and conviction. The first item on the list reads, "They have taken our houses through an illegal foreclosure process, despite not having the original mortgage." The other items accuse this same "they" of everything from "poison[ing] the food supply" to "keep[ing] people misinformed and fearful through their control of the media." In this way, the document's syntactic repetition provides a mechanism for joining together a diverse set of issues into a single, overarching concern about the unfairness of contemporary society.

- They have sold our privacy as a commodity.

- They have used the military and police force to prevent freedom of the press.

- They have deliberately declined to recall faulty products endangering lives in pursuit of profit.

- They determine economic policy, despite the catastrophic failures their policies have produced and continue to produce.

- They have donated large sums of money to politicians, who are responsible for regulating them.

- They continue to block alternate forms of energy to keep us dependent on oil.

- They continue to block generic forms of medicine that could save people's lives or provide relief in order to protect investments that have already turned a substantial profit.

- They have purposely covered up oil spills, accidents, faulty bookkeeping, and inactive ingredients in pursuit of profit.

- They purposefully keep people misinformed and fearful through their control of the media.

- They have accepted private contracts to murder prisoners even when presented with serious doubts about their guilt.

- They have perpetuated colonialism at home and abroad.

- They have participated in the torture and murder of innocent civilians overseas.

- They continue to create weapons of mass destruction in order to receive government contracts.*

To the people of the world,

We, the New York City General Assembly occupying Wall Street in Liberty Square, urge you to assert your power.

Exercise your right to peaceably assemble; occupy public space; create a process to address the problems we face, and generate solutions accessible to everyone.

To all communities that take action and form groups in the spirit of direct democracy, we offer support, documentation, and all of the resources at our disposal.

Join us and make your voices heard!

*These grievances are not all-inclusive.

SOURCE: *Declaration of the Occupation of Wall Street,* September 29, 2011.

CRITICAL DISCUSSION

When the *Declaration of the Occupation of New York City* was issued in September 2011, it provided a template for the nascent Occupy movement and received a mixed response from the popular American media. While many in the media initially ignored the protest and its declaration, those who did respond in the protest's first days primarily critiqued Occupy Wall Street for its lack of clear purpose or message. On *Mother Jones*'s Political Mojo blog, Lauren Ellis wrote of the movement's demands, "There's something there for everyone, but no one clear message that can carry a movement forward." Two weeks later, on October 11, Katrina vanden Heuvel, editor and publisher of the liberal *Nation* magazine, wrote approvingly of the protest and its manifesto despite its lack of a unified agenda: "The movement doesn't need a policy or legislative agenda to send its message. The thrust of what it seeks—fueled both by anger and deep principles—has moral clarity."

Occupy protests spread beyond Zuccotti Park to reach across the country and around the world, but the *Declaration of the Occupation of New York City* has remained an important statement of the movement's founding principles. The document's expression of moral outrage about social injustice, economic disparity, political corruption, and undue corporate power motivated protesters to form Occupy encampments that lasted for weeks and months. The manifesto attracted significant scholarly consideration for its role in expressing growing American disaffection and catalyzing newfound left-wing resistance to economic inequality.

Much of the scholarship on the *Declaration of the Occupation of New York City* has viewed the document in historical terms. In their essay "The Widening Gyre: Inequality, Polarization, and the Crisis," which is included in *The Occupy Handbook*, economists Krugman and Wells argue that the origins of the Occupy movement can be seen in interrelated economic, political, and social terms: "Inequality bred a polarized political system, in which the right went all out to block any and all efforts by a modestly liberal president to do something about job creation." Commentators have also considered the manifesto in relation to prior protest movements. James Miller, a professor of politics, is cited in *The Occupy Handbook* as describing Occupy's mission as the result of "an unstable political idealism, an amalgam of direct action and direct democracy, with many of the virtues of a utopian and romantic revolt … but also some of the vices."

BIBLIOGRAPHY

Sources

Byrne, Janet, ed. *The Occupy Handbook.* New York: Back Bay, 2012. Print.

"Declaration from Occupy San Francisco General Assembly." Occupy San Francisco, 8 April 2012. Web. 2 August 2012.

Declaration of the Occupation of New York City. New York City General Assembly, 29 Sept. 2011. Web. 2 August 2012.

Ellis, Lauren. "Is #OccupyWallStreet Working?" *Mother Jones.* Political Mojo, 27 Sept. 2011. Web. 3 August 2012.

"The 'GlobalMay Manifesto' of the International Occupy Assembly." *Guardian,* 11 May 2012. Web. 2 August 2012.

Hayden Tom. "Participatory Democracy: From the Port Huron Statement to Occupy Wall Street." *Nation* 27 March 2012. Web. 3 August 2012.

"#OCCUPYWALLSTREET: A Shift in Revolutionary Tactics." *Adbusters.* Adbusters Blog, 13 July 2011. Web. 2 August 2012.

Schwartz, Mattathais. "Pre-Occupied: The Origins and Future of Occupy Wall Street." *New Yorker* 28 Nov. 2011. Web. 3 August 2012.

vanden Heuvel, Katrina. "Will Occupy Wall Street's Spark Reshape our Politics?" *Washington Post* 11 October 2011. Web. 3 August 2012.

Further Reading

Botz, Dana La. "The Emergence of a Mass Movement." *New Politics* 13.4 (2012): 11-16. Web. 2 August 2012.

Engler, Mark. "Let's End Corruption—Starting with Wall Street." *New Internationalist* 30 Sept. 2011. Web. 2 August 2012.

Fleming, Andrew. "Adbusters Sparks Wall Street Protests." *Vancouver Courier* 27 Sept. 2011. Web. 2 August 2012.

Graeber, David. "Occupy's Liberation from Liberalism: The Real Meaning of May Day." *Guardian* 7 May 2012. Web. 2 August 2012.

Grusin, Richard. "Premediation and the Virtual Occupation of Wall Street." *Theory & Event* 14.4 (2011). Web. 2 August 2012.

Schneider, Nathan. "Some Assembly Required: Witnessing the Birth of Occupy Wall Street." *Harper's Magazine* February 2012: 45-54. Web. 2 August 2012.

Theodore McDermott

FOR A NEW LIBERTY
The Libertarian Manifesto
Murray N. Rothbard

OVERVIEW

Published in 1973 by American economist and historian Murray N. Rothbard, *For a New Liberty: The Libertarian Manifesto* is considered the blueprint for the modern Libertarian movement. The book advances a form of anarchy known as anarcho-capitalism, in which all forms of government are considered ineffective and immoral and must be overthrown. Additionally, the manifesto promotes individual sovereignty in a free market. In this society, the judicial system, law enforcement, and other types of security are provided and regulated through privately funded organizations rather than through taxation and traditional politics. Money is circulated in a private and competitive open market. Rothbard traces his ideology to the classical liberal philosopher John Locke and the writings of John Trenchard and Thomas Gordon. The core of Rothbard's philosophy is the nonaggression axiom, which states that "no man or group of men may aggress against the person or property of anyone else."

Initially, *For a New Liberty* caused little noticeable stir. After a brief time, however, it began to quickly gain momentum. In 1974 Rothbard, along with Libertarian Party leader Ed Crane and Charles Koch, chairman and CEO of Koch Industries, founded a Libertarian think tank called the Charles Koch Foundation. In 1977 the name would be changed to the Cato Institute, named after *Cato's Letters,* a series of essays published in eighteenth-century England on civil and religious liberty from government oppression. The institute's stated mission is "to increase the understanding of public policies based on the principles of limited government, free markets, individual liberty, and peace." Likewise, Libertarianism in general has grown in a multitude of ways. The Tea Party movement, which formed in 2009, is a major outlet for Libertarian ideas; Ron Paul, a longtime leader in the movement, made an unsuccessful bid for the 2012 presidency, and Koch Industries was the second largest privately held company in the United States, with annual revenue of $98 billion.

HISTORICAL AND LITERARY CONTEXT

For a New Liberty was a response to a U.S. economic system that was both out of touch and out of date. Economic models were slow to adapt to the changing economy, contributing to private interests' moves to evade what they considered troublesome tax structures. As private industry began to improve its production, the U.S. government stifled the economy with reforms that controlled private enterprise even further, adding to the argument supporting a stateless society as envisioned by Rothbard. Worldwide, the 1970s were perhaps the worst years of economic development since the Great Depression of the 1930s. In October 1973 the members of the multinational organization OPEC (Organization of the Petroleum Exporting Countries) decided to initiate an oil embargo in response to U.S. support for Israel during the Yom Kippur War. The result was dramatic worldwide inflation and recession. In the United States, both unemployment and inflation skyrocketed with interest rates passing twenty percent by the end of the decade. This phenomenon became known as stagflation.

When *For a New Liberty* was published in 1973, the country's confidence in its government was at an all-time low. Citizens were demanding a solution to the profusion of problems the country faced beyond what the two traditional political parties—the Democrats and the Republicans—had to offer. Libertarians did not let this opportunity pass. On December 11, 1971, the Libertarian Party was officially organized in Westminster, Colorado. Within six months they would hold their first national convention. In 1978 Dick Randolph of Alaska became the first Libertarian elected to state office. By 1980 Ed Clark appeared on the ballot in all fifty states and the District of Columbia, garnering almost one million votes. This growth continued unabated; in 2010 there were more than 800 Libertarians running for office. Those running for the U.S. House of Representatives alone received 1,073,000 votes. By the end of the year, there were 154 Libertarians in elected office.

The seed of the Libertarian movement was planted 2,000 years ago by a Roman statesman and politician named Cato the Younger. A noted orator, he was known for his moral integrity. During the Enlightenment in eighteenth-century Europe, he became a symbol of republican principles. It was during this time that a series of essays, collectively called *Cato's Letters,* were published by two

❖ *Key Facts*

Time Period:
Late 20th Century

Movement/Issue:
Libertarianism

Place of Publication:
United States

Language of Publication:
English

MURRAY N. ROTHBARD: A BIOGRAPHY

Murray N. Rothbard was an American political economist and historian whose ideas and theories have formed the basis of today's Libertarian movement. Much of Rothbard's philosophy of anarcho-capitalism stems from the Austrian School's concept of spontaneous order, which states that, if left unrestricted, a free market economy will naturally organize itself in the most fair, efficient, and productive system of commerce. Rothbard considered any form of government to be the greatest threat to freedom and individual well-being. He was also an isolationist, believing that military, political, and/or economic intervention in the affairs of other nations was not only immoral but also criminal.

During the early 1950s, while working on his doctorate in economics at Columbia University in New York City, Rothbard attended seminars at New York University by the Austrian economist Ludwig von Mises and was greatly influenced by his theories. About this same time, Rothbard also became enamored with the fiction and philosophy of Russian-born American writer Ayn Rand, describing her novel *Atlas Shrugged* (1957) as "not merely the greatest novel ever written, it is one of the very greatest books ever written, fiction or nonfiction." On a more personal level, Rothbard's leisure interests included chess, church architecture, and early jazz. He also enjoyed action films of the 1930s and 1940s and was a great fan of the work of director Woody Allen.

British writers, Trenchard and Gordon. These essays focused on the political philosophy of seventeenth-century Englishman John Locke and freeing society of excessive governmental intervention. Locke, who eventually became known as the Father of Classical Liberalism, advocated, among other things, that everyone had a natural right to defend their "life, health, liberty, or possessions" and that revolution is not only a right but an obligation under certain circumstances. His ideas would influence Rothbard's doctrines in the mid-twentieth century, just as Rothbard would fine-tune the tenets of traditional anarchism for his purposes, rejecting the notion of private capital as an enemy and focusing on the government as the force to defeat.

Since the publication of *For a New Liberty,* two major and intertwined schools of Libertarianism have developed. On the one hand is the philosophy of Austrian-born British economist Friedrich Hayek, a supporter of classical Liberalism and winner of the 1974 Nobel Prize in Economics. Along with his mentor, American economist Ludwig von Mises, he was an important contributor to the Austrian School of economic thought. His more moderate version of Liberalism, which would be supported by the Cato Institute (partially founded by Rothbard), advocated for the state and market as codependent entities. On the other hand is the Rothbardian school of thought

promoted by presidential hopeful Ron Paul and the Ludwig von Mises Institute. This latter movement, which wants no government interference in economic matters, is by far the most popular because of its exposure and promotion by Paul as well as the Tea Party.

THEMES AND STYLE

The central theme of *For a New Liberty* is that any form of government is oppressive or even criminal and must be minimized or eradicated completely so that individuals can truly be free. Rothbard quotes *Cato's Letters* often to support his ideas:

> Human history is a record of irrepressible conflict between Power and Liberty, with Power (government) always standing ready to increase its scope by invading people's rights and encroaching upon their liberties.... Power must be kept small and faced with eternal vigilance and hostility on the part of the public to make sure that it always stays within its narrow bounds.

From this concept, Rothbard formulated his nonaggression axiom. The axiom forms a narrative thread elaborating upon a wide variety of services controlled by government that could be better handled by private groups or individuals. Each chapter defines a particular issue—such as taxation, education, business, or foreign policy—elaborates on the variety of problems caused by government intervention in that area, and then explains in detail how and why a private solution would be better and more effective. Each solution reinforces the idea that "the Libertarian favors the right to unrestricted private property and free exchange; hence, a system of laissez-faire capitalism."

The manifesto achieves its rhetorical effect by constantly and consistently reiterating the ideas that government is evil and that government and freedom cannot coexist. "While opposing any and all private or group aggression against the rights of person and property, the libertarian sees that throughout history and into the present day, there has been one central, dominant, and overriding aggressor upon all of these rights: the State." Rothbard extends his basic definition of freedom to include property rights. Property is claimed through the gathering and/or processing of natural resources. "As much land as a man tills, plants, improves, cultivates, and can use the product of, so much is his property. He by his labour does, as it were, enclose it from the common." In other words, a man may claim as much as he can leave his mark upon. "Everywhere a powerful hand is divined which has molded matter and an intelligent will which has adapted it ... to the satisfaction of the wants of one same being." It may be argued that this type of thinking might cause problems at the societal level, but Rothbard rejects even the concept of society.

Libertarians believe "that only individuals exist, think, feel, choose, and act; and that 'society' is not a living entity but simply a label for a set of interacting individuals."

Stylistically, *For a New Liberty* is an aggressive, uncompromising, unrepentant work. Whereas many intellectuals over the years have attempted to explain or promote Libertarianism in a more moderate version to make it more palatable to the masses, Rothbard's attitude is black and white: either accept it or do not. In the introduction to the manifesto's 2006 edition, Lew Rockwell of the Mises Institute asks:

> Why … make a case for statelessness or anarchism when a case for limited government might bring more people into the movement.… Why go into such depth about privatizing courts and roads and water when doing so might risk alienating people … trimming and compromising for the sake of the times or the audience was just not his way.

Throughout his manifesto, Rothbard is clear and consistent in his ideas, and he leaves no room for compromise. He describes government in the most vitriolic terms; he sees freedom as an all or nothing concept, and his solutions are meant to fit all situations.

CRITICAL DISCUSSION

The publication of Rothbard's *For a New Liberty* did not garner a huge reaction when it was first published, but it did something even more important: the book gained the attention of many of the right people and organizations. The Ludwig von Mises Institute called it "relentless, scientific, analytical, and morally energetic" and referred to Rothbard as "the State's greatest living enemy." In the book *Radicals for Capitalism* (2007), Brian Doherty suggests that one of the main reasons for its eventual popularity was that "Rothbard hits the harder anarcho-capitalism stuff, but slips it in so smoothly than many readers might not notice that this 'libertarian manifesto' promotes anarchism." In other words, it was true that most people were dissatisfied with their government, but did that necessarily mean that they wanted no government at all?

As economic, social, and political issues worsened during the 1970s, the solutions offered by *For a New Liberty* became even more appealing. Initially, the radical concepts of the book were acceptable only by hard-core Libertarians; most preferred a more moderate process. As economist Robert Wenzel wrote in 2010, "the Uptights tend to promote the work of Nobel Prize winning economist Friedrich Hayek, over the work of the Austrian economists Ludwig von Mises and Murray Rothbard." This one-sidedness, however, would soon change. Though people in general were upset with both primary parties, Libertarians at the time were particularly angry

A Libertarian protester in costume as Uncle Sam. Murray N. Rothbard's anarcho-capitalist manifesto helped launch the Libertarian political movement in the United States. © VISIONS OF AMERICA, LLC/ALAMY

with the (conservative) Right. Rockwell explains, "It was to defend a pure liberty against the compromises and corruptions of conservatism—beginning with Nixon but continuing with Reagan and the Bush presidencies—that inspired the birth of Rothbardian political economy."

Since the financial collapse of 2008, much attention has been focused on the economic ideals promoted in *For a New Liberty*. Although Rothbard demanded less government regulation and more freedom for businesses to operate as they wished, it would appear that these specific conditions were significantly responsible for the greatest financial meltdown since the Great Depression. As underscored by critic Stephen Metcalf in "The Liberty Scam," according to Libertarians, "economic rights are the only rights, and that insofar as there are political rights, they are nothing more than a framework in support of private property and freedom of contract."

BIBLIOGRAPHY

Sources

Buchanan, James M. "Utopia, the Minimal State, and Entitlement." *Public Choice* 23.3 (1975): 121-26. Web. 29 June 2012.

Cato Institute. *CATO 25: 25 Years at the Cato Institute– The 2001 Annual Report*. Washington DC: Cato Institute, 2001. Web. 29 June 2012.

Doherty, Brian. *Radicals for Capitalism*. New York: Public Affairs, 2007. Print.

Frech III, H. E. "The Public Choice Theory of Murray N. Rothbard, a Modern Anarchist." *Public Choice* 14.1 (1973): 143-54. Web. 29 June 2012.

Horn, Walter. "Libertarianism and Private Property in Land: The Positions of Rothbard and Nozick, Critically Examined, Are Disputed." *American Journal of Economics and Sociology* 43.3 (1984): 341-55. Web. 29 June 2012.

McMaken, Ryan. "The Rothbardian School." *LewRockwell. com.* LewRockwell.com. August 31, 2010. Web. 29 June 2012.

Metcalf, Stephen. "The Liberty Scam." *Slate.com.* The Washington Post Company, 20 June 2011. Web. 29 June 2012.

Wenzel, Robert. "Kelly Evans, Again." *EconomicPolicyJournal. com.* EconomicPolicyJournal, 30 Aug. 2010. Web. 29 June 2012.

Further Reading

Attas, Daniel. *Liberty, Property and Markets: A Critique of Libertarianism.* Burlington, VT: Ashgate, 2005. Print.

Boaz, David. *Libertarianism: A Primer.* New York: Free Press, 1998. Print.

Casey, Gerard. *Murray Rothbard.* New York: Continuum, 2010. Print.

Duncan, Craig, and Tibor Machan. *Libertarianism: For and Against.* Lanham, MD: Rowman and Littlefield, 2005. Print.

Hamowy, Robert, ed. *The Encyclopedia of Libertarianism.* Los Angeles: SAGE, 2008. Print.

Huebert, Jacob H. *Libertarianism Today.* Santa Barbara, CA: Praeger, 2010. Print.

Machan, Tibor R. *Libertarianism Defended.* Burlington, VT: Ashgate, 2006. Print.

Narveson, Jan. *The Libertarian Idea.* Orchard Park, NY: Broadview, 2001. Print.

Palmer, Tom G. *Realizing Freedom: Libertarian Theory, History and Practice.* Washington DC: Cato Institute, 2009. Print.

Vallentyne, Peter, and Hillel Steiner, eds. *The Origins of Left-Libertarianism: An Anthology of Historical Writings.* New York: Palgrave, 2000. Print.

Jim Mladenovic

MANIFESTO OF A TENURED RADICAL

Cary Nelson

OVERVIEW

Written by professor Cary Nelson, *Manifesto of a Tenured Radical* (1997) explores the political nature of all things academic through the lens of his own discipline, English literature. A main thrust of the work is the crisis in academic labor in the United States during the 1990s. Amid external pressures to operate under a profit-making model, institutions of higher learning stepped up reliance on part-time, adjunct, and graduate student teaching assistants (TAs) and reduced tenure-track positions, the result being a growing underclass of academics. Unabashedly leftist in its slant, the manifesto is designed to goad full-time faculty into engaging in collective action. Groups of TAs began lobbying for collective bargaining rights as early as the 1960s, but it remained a fringe issue until *Manifesto of a Tenured Radical* was published. Nelson's work was instrumental in keeping campus labor issues on the agendas of U.S. colleges, universities, and professional organizations. A key element in the text is the author's twelve-step program on how to reform institutions of higher learning and fulfill what he calls their "commitment to democratic values." In this collection of previously published essays, Nelson rails at "careerists" who fail to understand that corporatization of education threatens not only the livelihood of TAs but also every aspect of academic life that educators hold sacred.

Criticized in scholarly journals for lacking a unifying thread, for substituting anecdotes for methodological rigor, and for its condescending and score-settling tone, *Manifesto of a Tenured Radical* was nonetheless welcomed by mainstream scholars as providing a much-needed examination of the ills within the profession. Many hoped that the manifesto would have political significance, and some saw it as a reawakening of leftist scholars of the 1960s who had been active critics of the institution before shifting focus in the 1970s and 1980s in exchange for tenure. Nelson's manifesto received its sharpest criticism from Marxist scholars who found it to be far from the radical prescriptive it claimed to be. In the twenty-first century, *Manifesto of a Tenured Radical* is occasionally cited for its arguments advocating diversity in the canon, and its twelve-step program for reform still provides intellectual underpinnings and inspiration for campus activists involved in the ongoing labor crisis.

HISTORICAL AND LITERARY CONTEXT

Manifesto of a Tenured Radical reacts against growing unemployment and underemployment among graduate student TAs and other part-time teachers in the 1990s. In the United States, a movement to unionize TAs achieved its first success in 1968, when faculty at City University in New York voted to allow TAs to join their collective bargaining unit. The following year a TA union at the University of Wisconsin was the first to enter a contract with the administration. Most actions, however, met with strong resistance from administrations and legislatures, and three decades later there were still fewer than a dozen TA unions with collective bargaining agreements. At the 1995 annual meeting of the Modern Language Association (MLA), the main disciplinary organization in English, the efforts of TAs to unionize at Yale University met with sharp disapproval from a group of tenured faculty. In his manifesto, an outraged Nelson describes how these professors failed to make the connection between their own progressive scholarship (one of them taught the history of the labor movement) and the plight of their underpaid colleagues.

When *Manifesto of a Tenured Radical* was published in 1997, the numbers of poorly paid, part-time faculty teachers at U.S. colleges and universities had increased, but the movement to fix academic labor had gained little ground. Nelson's arguments in the manifesto forced tenured professors and their professional organizations to examine the gap between their progressive scholarship and the political realities of campus labor. Media coverage of the struggle between Yale's Graduate Student Union and the administration in the mid-1990s, as well as the manifesto, were instrumental in bringing the issue to the attention of a national audience. Prior to the manifesto's publication, scholarly articles on the subject of collective bargaining in the university setting dealt primarily with faculty unions. Few had tackled the issue of TAs and other part-time faculty, with Gary Rhoades's *Managed Professionals: Unionized Faculty and Restructuring Academic Labor* (1998) being one notable exception. Although Nelson's proposals to create a university employee bill of rights, organize graduate teaching assistant unions, and raise wages were not new, his work provided intellectual grounding and inspiration for campus activists of the day.

✛ *Key Facts*

Time Period:
Late 20th Century

Movement/Issue:
Collective bargaining rights for academic labor

Place of Publication:
United States

Language of Publication:
English

THE COLLECTIVE BARGAINING RIGHTS OF GRADUATE STUDENT TEACHING ASSISTANTS

Labor laws governing student employees hinge on the question of whether a teaching assistant's (TA's) primary function is as a student or as an employee. If the TA is foremost a student, then laws governing labor practices view the right to collective bargaining as interfering with the educational system. If the TA is an employee, then the relationship between student and school, at least in the context of the teaching assistantship, is an economic one. The National Labor Relations Board (NLRB), which governs federal labor laws, defines TAs as students, whereas the Internal Revenue Service taxes TAs as if they were employees of the university.

Labor laws in the United States differ depending on whether an institution is public or private. Public colleges and universities are not covered by federal bargaining rights because their employees fall under an exclusion in the Taft-Hartley Act, which dictates labor-management relations. TAs at private universities, however, can engage in collective bargaining under state law where permitted. At present, students at private colleges and universities have no collective bargaining rights under federal or state law. Employee rights at private institutions are governed by the National Labor Relations Act (NLRA) as interpreted by the NLRB.

Manifesto of a Tenured Radical draws on a history of radical manifestos that take their inspiration from Karl Marx's *Communist Manifesto*. Written in 1848, the *Communist Manifesto* called on workers of the world to unite against the forces of capitalism. Nelson's text makes reference to capitalism and collective struggle in an attempt to place itself within that earlier tradition. He explains his use of the word "manifesto" as both "serious and ironic," the serious part being his proposals for "a series of progressive cultural commitments within academia" and the ironic part being a jab at a term coined by the political Right, "tenured radical." Nelson also acknowledges that his secure position as a tenured professor makes him less than radical relative to the university radicals during Senator Joseph McCarthy's communist witch hunt of the 1950s as well as to political radicals outside of academia.

Following publication, *Manifesto of a Tenured Radical* was reviewed in several academic journals, including the *Chronicle of Higher Education, Academe,* and *Contemporary Literature*. It also has received occasional mention in newspaper articles and scholarly essays in connection with the ongoing battle to reform campus labor practices and on issues of diversity in the literary canon. The twelve proposals for reforming

universities still provide inspiration and intellectual support for graduate teaching assistants and part-time university teachers amid the ongoing fight for higher wages and better working conditions.

THEMES AND STYLE

Manifesto of a Tenured Radical contains multiple unrelated themes that are divided into three parts. The first part is called "The Politics of English" and covers the literary canon, multiculturalism, and the "new" discipline of cultural studies. The second part, "The Academy and the Culture Debates," covers the politics of teaching, the New Right, and hate speech on campus. The third part, "Lessons from the Job Wars," deals with the academic labor crisis. Nelson extrapolates lessons for the entire academic world from anecdotes about his own discipline, English literature: "Literary studies has reformed and opened its intellectual life in such a way as to fulfill a commitment to democratic values. Yet because English departments often hire large numbers of graduate students or part-time faculty to teach lower-division courses, [it] also harbors some of the most exploitive labor practices in the academy." The theme the manifesto is best known for is that of the academic labor crisis, particularly its proposals for equitable treatment of academic workers.

Nelson's text is perhaps most effective when he speaks against his own interests, such as when he recommends that academics "challenge the priority given to faculty salaries." In these instances, the manifesto invites the reader to be in league with the author. "I believe it would be better to get this usually hidden conflict out in the open rather than deny its existence." Here Nelson explains that he has done just that, even though it might mean taking a cut in salary. The author's repeated use of irony is less effective. "David Bromwich, on stage with me when I made my comments in support of unionization, reacted in such a way as to look for all the world like a vampire bat suddenly exposed to a shaft of sunlight." The tone invites the reader to laugh with the author at the absurdity of anyone or anything with which he disagrees. "Some faculty cared deeply; others were indifferent to the nature of the community they worked in or the values of the institution to which they were devoting their labor. After all, their lives proceeded on a higher plane." Notably absent from the manifesto, in spite of its sweeping statements about the problems plaguing academia as a whole, are evidence or examples from the sciences, the arts, or the professional schools.

Distinguished by its mix of scholarly terms of art with conversational language, *Manifesto of a Tenured Radical* reads more like a memoir or exposé than an academic tome. The author proudly "names names" and tells tales about closed-door meetings, cocktail parties, and conferences. Its emphasis on firsthand experience makes the work more engaging than most academic writing, and at the same time the absence of methodology caused scholars to question whether or not it can be considered scholarship. Where Nelson succeeds in persuading, he achieves his result through sheer force of personality. The manifesto irritates, amuses, and attempts to shame readers into taking action.

CRITICAL DISCUSSION

Manifesto of a Tenured Radical received mixed reviews upon its publication. According to Joan Bean's review in the *Journal of Higher Education* in 2000, the work, far from fulfilling the title's promise of radicalism, was "a benchmark defense of old-fashioned liberal education." British scholar Kevin White wrote in his 1999 review of the text that while it was flawed, it must be viewed as "a major contribution to the higher education debate in the U.S." deserving of "wide attention." The manifesto continues to influence labor movements on campuses nationwide. Others dismissed the book as fuzzy radical thinking. Roger Shattuck wrote in the journal *Salmagundi* that *Manifesto of a Tenured Radical* was "self-absorbed and self-aggrandizing." In her review, Marxist academic Barbara Foley found that the work's recommendations fell far short of its radical claims. She felt it showed "blindness to the class function that higher education has always served, and continues to serve, in the U.S." Nelson's harsh criticisms of his peers, his proud tactics of naming names and telling tales, and his self-important asides antagonized his audience, but his calls for collective action and his proposals to change academia also managed to inspire some people to action. In the article "Not off the Hook Yet" (1998), academic John Irwin Fischer notes that Nelson needlessly antagonizes the people he hopes to engage in collective action. Even so, Fischer found the twelve steps invigorating. In an article published in *Science & Society* in 1999, Corey Dolgon hoped that the manifesto, along with Nelson's *Will Work for Food* (1997), would serve as "a clarion call for academics to move from political critique to social action."

Nelson continued to advocate for collective bargaining for teaching assistants and other part-time university teachers in his role as an activist and as a member of the American Association of University Professors, where he served as president from 2006 to 2012. In 2006 he was arrested along with fifty others during a protest at New York University over the school's refusal to recognize the graduate student union.

Since its publication, *Manifesto of a Tenured Radical* and its ideas have been the subject of work by notable scholars such as Gerald Graff, Michael Berube, and Andrew Ross. Scholarship in the humanities continues to examine questions of tenure, academic freedom, and the academic labor crisis, as well as the state of the canon in English literature departments, and Nelson's manifesto receives

Professor Cary Nelson is the author of the *Manifesto of a Tenured Radical*. The activist was elected the president of the American Association of University Professors in 2006. AP PHOTO/ DARRELL HOEMANN, THE NEWS-GAZETTE/FILE

occasional mention. However, the large-scale changes proposed in *Manifesto of a Tenured Radical* have yet to be realized, and parity in the academic labor force remains an elusive goal.

BIBLIOGRAPHY

Sources

Bean, John P. Rev. of *Manifesto of a Tenured Radical*, by Cary Nelson. *Journal of Higher Education* 71.4 (2000): 496-503. *JSTOR*. Web. 26 Sept. 2012.

Dolgon, Corey. Rev. of *Will Work for Food*, by Cary Nelson. *Science & Society* 63.2 (1999): 259-62. *JSTOR*. Web. 29 Sept. 2012.

Fischer, John Irwin. "Not off the Hook Yet: Cary Nelson and the Crisis in MLA Disciplines." *South Central Review* 15.2 (1998): 46-55. *JSTOR*. Web. 26 Sept. 2012.

Foley, Barbara. "'Lepers in the Acropolis': Liberalism, Capitalism and the Crisis in Academic Labor." Rev. of *Manifesto of a Tenured Radical*, by Cary Nelson. *Contemporary Literature* 39.2 (1998): 317-35. *JSTOR*. Web. 27 Sept. 2012.

Rowe, John Carlos. Review of *Manifesto of a Tenured Radical*, by Cary Nelson. *Academe* 84.3 (1998): 76-77. *JSTOR*. Web. 27 Sept. 2012.

Shattuck, Roger. "Education: Higher and Lower." Rev. of *Manifesto of a Tenured Radical*, by Cary Nelson. *Salmagundi* 116/117 (1997): 41-54. *JSTOR*. Web. 27 Sept. 2012.

White, Kevin. Rev. of *Manifesto of a Tenured Radical*, by Cary Nelson. *Journal of American Studies* 33.3 (1999): 547-49. *JSTOR*. Web. 26 Sept. 2012.

Further Reading

Ellis, John M. *Literature Lost: Socialist Agendas and the Corruption of the Humanities.* New Haven, CT: Yale UP, 1997. Print.

Nelson, Cary. "Affiliation and Change: A Year of Campus Labor Activism." *symploke* 7.1 (1999): 85-96. *JSTOR.* Web. 28 Sept. 2012.

Rhoades, Gary. *Managed Professionals: Unionized Faculty and Restructuring Academic Labor.* Albany: State U of New York P, 1998. Print.

Ross, Andrew. "Beyond the Siege Mentality." *Academe* 94.5 (2008): 8-10. *JSTOR.* Web. 28 Sept. 2012.

Kristin King-Ries

Manifesto: Mad Farmer Liberation Front

Wendell Berry

OVERVIEW

Written by Wendell Berry, the poem "Manifesto: Mad Farmer Liberation Front" (1973) cautions its audience on the potential social, moral, and environmental ills that are caused by mass consumption. Although the initial stanza critiques the industrialized landscape, Berry celebrates the often-neglected aspects of culture rather than lamenting their loss. The poem quietly weaves in aspects of public and private life, highlighting the seemingly mundane aspects of daily life to remind the reader that spontaneity is a fundamental aspect of existence that has been subsumed under the desire to possess objects. Targeting the growing affluent middle class of the 1970s, the manifesto presents an antiurban and antimodern romanticism that fears the potential loss of the connection between human beings and nature.

The manifesto was equally applauded and condemned when it was initially published. Its meditative focus on nature led people to label Berry as an anachronism, a Luddite, and an out-of-touch romantic. Environmentalists and regionalists applauded his ideas, focusing on his simple prose and moralizing concepts concerning the relationship between society and nature. The manifesto articulates a set of communitarian values that chastise society for its failure to address the looming environmental and existential crises caused by mass consumption and mass production. Today the poem is seen as a foreshadowing voice in the evolving environmental, conservation, agrarian, and sustainability movements. Berry suggests that the imagination can once again be set free to contemplate life through a direct relationship with the land.

HISTORICAL AND LITERARY CONTEXT

"Manifesto: Mad Farmer Liberation Front" responds to what Berry sees as the profit motive behind U.S. Congressional farm policy leading into the 1970s. The ecological agrarianism that underlies the poem seeks to defend the integrity of the land against the effects of modernization. The manifesto rests on the idea that nature can be used as a ground from which we seek to discover a standpoint of critique of consumerism. What's more, the manifesto critiques any notion of a pragmatic relationship with the land by offering a reflective mysticism. Profit motives separate the farmer from the household as well as from the

land, disrupting both personal and public relationships to the community.

Written during the transition between conservation-based first-wave and activist-driven second-wave environmentalism, the manifesto represents one of a host of similar voices that called for deep ecological action and a return to a spiritual relationship with the land. In the early 1970s, despite the federal government's implementation of a series of environmental regulations, Berry's politics called for an extreme revision to how people relate to the land. "Mad Farmer Liberation Front" models its name after radical organizations such as the Animal Liberation Front; however, Berry articulates a pacifist vision rather than the militant visions announced by the other groups. Berry also operates from a rural and agrarian perspective that looks toward stewardship as a means by which people can heal the land.

"Manifesto: Mad Farmer Liberation Front" carries on a rich tradition of American romanticism. Following the lines of Ralph Waldo Emerson, Henry David Thoreau, and Walt Whitman, Berry places great importance on an individual's relationship with the landscape and how such a relationship or lack of one affects the larger social relationships he or she is able to maintain. Berry originated the voice of the Mad Farmer in "The Man Born to Farming" (1970), and he developed the character in thirteen poems featuring the Mad Farmer. Through the voice of the recurring character, Berry articulates what he envisions as the most sane response to a world that has lost its way. In the initial manifesto, the Mad Farmer calls for a retreat from technology-based solutions and, instead, hearkens back to a more intimate relationship with the local land. In "The Mad Farmer Manifesto: The First Amendment" (1973), the Mad Farmer suggests that he is one sane voice in the world ruled by consumption.

The philosophical meditation of the manifesto influenced writers such as David Abram, who developed an anthropomorphic system of environmental ethics. Other writers, such as Philip Fisher and Dana Phillips, have used Berry's agrarian ethics to develop a system of environmental aesthetics, focusing on a distinct sense of place as a means by which people can ground themselves in the world. Some environmental philosophers, such as Timothy Morton, Bruno

✤ *Key Facts*

Time Period:
Mid-20th Century

Movement/Issue:
Consumerism;
Industrialization;
Environmentalism

Place of Publication:
United States

Language of Publication:
English

WENDELL BERRY: ACTIVIST FARMER

No stranger to controversy, Wendell Berry exemplifies a man who practices what he preaches. Since 1968 he and his wife have operated a small farm in Kentucky. In addition to his essays and poems, Berry has written eight novels and about forty short stories. Like his philosophy, his fiction is deeply rooted in an individual place, providing a narrative history for the fictional town of Port William, Kentucky. Much of Berry's prose stems from the imaginative impulses created from working the land. Berry advocates for an intimate knowledge of nature that can only be achieved through the daily joy and toil of farming. His soft voice and contemplative prose call for people to lead a good life by engaging in sustainable practices, connecting with their bioregion, participating in their communities, and taking pleasure in the simple goods of food, work, and company.

Berry began as an activist for traditional farming, but through the years he has participated in nonviolent protests against nuclear power plants, war, and racism. Following the U.S. invasion of Iraq, Berry wrote a scathing essay, "A Citizen's Response to the National Security Strategy of the United States," that condemned President George W. Bush's policies. He has spoken out against abortion and the death penalty and has continued to participate in nonviolent protests against coal mining, soil erosion, and industrial farming practices.

Latour, and Georges Teyssot, have taken some of Berry's work to task while still acknowledging that his thought has profoundly influenced generations of environmental activists campaigning for small agrarian-based communities. Contemporary feminist scholars such as Jane Smiley and Sonya Salamon have looked to Berry's exaltation of the small farm as a means by which they can sketch out an agrarian-based ethics that both elevates domesticity and empowers rural women through their work.

THEMES AND STYLE

The guiding theme of the manifesto is to depict the relationship between people and the land, which provides for a richer understanding of the world and, in turn, establishes an ethical framework. The poem opens with a critique of capitalism: "Love the quick profit, the annual raise, / vacation with pay. Want more / of everything ready-made. Be afraid / to know your neighbors and to die." It is a world that leaves nothing to chance, where "not even your future will be a mystery / any more." The poem then shifts to the demonstration of a possible solution to current social and environmental ills. In a quasi-Eden framework, Berry subtly portrays a natural connection between the people and the land. As the landscape ages, it slowly decays and revitalizes itself through the "two inches of humus / that will build under the trees / every thousand years." Berry suggests that we do something every day that cannot be quantitatively measured. He asks the reader to "Love the Lord. / Love the world. Work for nothing." Akin to Thomas Jefferson, Berry seeks to embrace a deep-rooted Christianity with the simplicity of agrarian principles. He instructs the reader to invest time and energy in planting trees, farming the land, communing with neighbors, and taking delight in existence in spite of the existential malaise that may arise in the face of life's problems. In order to salvage one's autonomy, Berry writes that "as soon as the generals and the politicos / can predict the motions of your mind, / lose it."

The poem relies upon simple and direct language. Meaning is not something that the reader must excavate from a series of metaphors and symbols. In one sense, the manifesto is almost accepting of the conditions it rails against. At the close of the first stanza, Berry paints a bleak picture where there is no means of escape from the system. He warns that "when they want you to buy something / they will call you. When they want you / to die for profit they will let you know." By addressing the readers as friends, the poem establishes a sense of community in which people can "love someone who does not deserve it" and find hope to realize the American promise of life, liberty, and happiness. His poetic enterprise clings to hope and the promise of the future. He asks the reader to listen to the carrion "and hear the faint chattering / of the songs that are to come." The poem concludes with the promise of new birth and the imperative to "practice resurrection."

"Manifesto: Mad Farmer Liberation Front" maintains a sermonlike force as it weaves together its solution. The majority of its lines begin with directives to "love," "ask," "say," and "go." The calmness of the voice helps ease the tensions that Berry sees in the world. Although he asks us to "denounce the government," he wishes for us to "embrace the flag." In line with the resounding imperatives to love, the manifesto compels the reader to find faith and to pledge allegiance to the emotional concepts that create a community. As a poem, the manifesto is able to unshackle itself from political discourse and offer a moment of contemplation. However, the contrast between the style and the subject matter creates an uneasiness in its language. Although the direct prose provides for a clear demonstration of the problems, immeasurable notions of "love" and "laughter" allow for individual interpretations. The initial stanza blankets the manifesto in despair, but the possibilities articulated by Berry draw in the reader through its repetition and imperative structure.

CRITICAL DISCUSSION

When "Manifesto: Mad Farmer Liberation Front" was first published, it was seen as a radical new voice in environmental politics. In his introduction to *Wendell Berry: Life and Work*, Jason Peters comments that "Berry's indefatigable judgment of an economy predicated on competition—that it not only facilitates

Wendell Berry in the White House with First Lady Michelle Obama after accepting the 2010 National Humanities Medal. President Barack Obama stands in the background. © WHITE HOUSE PHOTO/ALAMY

but also encourages the accumulation of wealth and power into fewer and fewer hands—accords with the sentiment in Thoreau that unites his naturalism and his political grumpiness." Berry's agrarianism sought for a way in which people could locate moments of resistance without entirely retreating from society. Although radical environmental groups such as Environmental Life Force initially found agrarianism to be too passive, other conservationist groups celebrated Berry's call for "an integrated life, a life of integrity … characterized by membership in a community in which one lives, works, worships, and conducts the vast majority of other human activities."

In the decades that followed the poem's publication, environmental and communitarian activists continually returned to the thoughts outlined in Berry's manifesto. In the face of industrial farming, clear-cutting of forests, and the pollution of streams, rivers, and oceans, many activists and scholars returned to Berry's imperatives to live more simply. Summarizing Berry's influence, Norman Wirzbau claims that "Berry has clearly tapped into a widespread sentiment that our culture is deeply flawed because of its denial and destruction of the many good sources of life." During this period, organic farming, permaculture, and farmers' markets became part of popular culture.

Much of the scholarship on Berry's "Manifesto" concerns itself with the philosophical imperatives that it attempts to articulate. Eric Freyfogle notes that "society has come to view [environmental issues] in broader terms, as a more fundamental crisis involving all of the ways that people interact with the nonhuman parts of the natural world." Many critics follow Freyfogle's line of thought and attempt to reconcile Berry's thought with contemporary issues. For example, Barbara Kingsolver suggests that Berry's model of working the land asks us to weigh continually our choices between want and need. She comments that "the siren song of needless want inflicts internal damage on people of every class. Buying new things accosts our stability, our satisfaction with ourselves and one another as we already are." Berry has not been without his detractors. Feminist critics in particular have taken issue with his depiction of women's roles on the farm. In an attempt to reconcile agrarian philosophy with feminism, Kimberly Smith argues that the "concern about gender roles is to some extent an artifact of industrial capitalism; agrarian life is famous for maintaining less rigid divisions between work and home than industrialism requires." The attempt to bridge seemingly two contradictory worldviews points to Berry's lasting influence on sociopolitical and environmental politics and philosophy.

BIBLIOGRAPHY

Sources

Freyfogle, Eric T. "The Dilemma of Wendell Berry." *U of Illinois Law Review* 1994.2 (1994): 363-85. Print.

Kingsolver, Barbara. "The Art of Buying Nothing." *Wendell Berry: Life and Work.* Lexington: UP of Kentucky, 2007. 287-95. Print.

Peters, Jason. Introduction. *Wendell Berry: Life and Work.* Lexington: UP of Kentucky, 2007. 1-11. Print.

Smith, Kimberly K. "Wendell Berry's Feminist Agrarianism." *Women's Studies: An Inter-Disciplinary Journal* 30:5 (2001): 623-46. Print.

Wirzbau, Norman. "An Economy of Gratitude." *Wendell Berry: Life and Work.* Lexington: UP of Kentucky, 2007. 145-55. Print.

Further Reading

Angyal, Andrew J. *Wendell Berry.* New York: Twayne, 1995. Print.

Berry, Wendell. *Mad Farmer Poems.* New York: Counterpoint, 2008. Print.

Grubbs, Morris Allen, ed. *Conversations with Wendell Berry.* Jackson: UP of Mississippi, 2007. Print.

Leonard, Sarah. "Nature as an Ally: An Interview with Wendell Berry." *Dissent Magazine.* Dissent Magazine, Spring 2012. Web. 19 July 2012.

Oehlschlaeger, Fritz. *The Achievement of Wendell Berry: The Hard History of Love.* Lexington: UP of Kentucky, 2011. Print.

Peters, James, ed. *Wendell Berry: Life and Work.* Lexington: UP of Kentucky, 2007. Print.

Scigaj, Leonard M. *Sustainable Poetry: Four American Eco-Poets.* Lexington: UP of Kentucky, 1999. Print.

Josh Harteis

POWELL MEMO

Lewis F. Powell, Jr.

OVERVIEW

Written by corporate attorney Lewis F. Powell, Jr. on August 23, 1971, the Powell Memo proposes a U.S. government-led movement to help corporations counter extremists on the Left, who Powell perceives as a serious threat to the survival of capitalism. Activists and other liberal voices of dissent, sometimes referred to as the New Left, gained a mainstream audience during the 1960s for their antiestablishment views and criticism of the Vietnam War. Powell, believing that the free enterprise system had become apathetic and inept, saw the need for conservatives and corporate leaders to launch a counterattack against the broad-based anticapitalist assault by "Communists, New Leftists and other revolutionaries who would destroy the entire system, both political and economic." Addressed to his friend Eugene B. Sydnor Jr., director of the U.S. Chamber of Commerce, the memo, titled "Attack on American Free Enterprise System," outlines an organized program of speakers, educators, publications, paid advertisements, and political and judicial action focused on building support for corporations.

Initially, only Sydnor and a select number of associates read the memo. However, after Powell was appointed to the U.S. Supreme Court and the document was leaked to syndicated newspaper columnist Jack Anderson, the chamber published the memo in full. Public response was mixed. Some doubted Powell's fitness to serve on the bench; others agreed with the grave predictions that socialism would overtake American capitalism. Among liberals the memo called into question Powell's objectivity in several court opinions, such as a decision that corporations have a First Amendment right to make campaign contributions. Today the Powell Memo is known as an influential blueprint for empowering corporate interests and enhancing their presence in Washington.

HISTORICAL AND LITERARY CONTEXT

The Powell Memo calls for the unification of a disorganized and indifferent corporate community against what was perceived as a focused and aggressive effort on the Left to discredit big business and to diminish its power and influence to the point of collapse. Powell believed that leftist extremists permeated nearly every facet of American life and were working toward the downfall of capitalism. He saw the university system, which was rapidly expanding and increasingly admitting women and minorities, as indoctrinating bright young minds into "the politics of despair." Because graduates went on to become professors, journalists, speakers, and business leaders who further spread the subversive, anticorporate message, Powell emphasized the importance of giving conservatives a louder voice on college campuses.

Powell's memo was the culmination of several months of communication with Sydnor about the systematic takeover of the media, academia, and religious and political establishments by extremists who claimed that corporations hurt the poor and benefited only the rich. Powell also communicated with other conservative executives about the same topic. For example, on August 20, three days before he wrote the memo, he received a letter from William Gill, president of News Perspective International, which detailed an elaborate plan to infiltrate network television and the wire services to send a more business-friendly message over the airwaves. Powell, a respected educator and attorney, had been repeatedly offered a nomination to the high court by President Richard M. Nixon, but Powell did not accept until two months after he wrote the memo.

One of the primary inspirations for Powell's memo was a May 21, 1971, article by Jeffrey St. John in *The Wall Street Journal* titled, "Memo to GM: Why Not Fight Back?" Many of Powell's major points can be traced to the article, which Powell even quotes: "General Motors, like American business in general, is 'plainly in trouble' because intellectual bromides have been substituted for a sound intellectual exposition of its point of view." Like Powell, St. John refers to pervasive negative criticism of big business and the need for a more consistent and intelligent message that communicates the meaning and value of a free capitalist system. Powell's ominous predictions echo St. John's warning that "[t]ough decisions must be made by all of us, and soon."

Since the Powell Memo was released to the public in 1972, its ideas have gained supporters, resources, and momentum. The Chamber of Commerce has incorporated many of the document's recommendations, including creating a grassroots advocacy network and increasing lobbying expenditures, which

⁘ *Key Facts*

Time Period:
Late 20th Century

Movement/Issue:
Free enterprise economics; Political conservatism

Place of Publication:
United States

Language of Publication:
English

CORPORATE PERSONHOOD AND THE U.S. SUPREME COURT

After the Powell Memo was made public, the debate about whether corporations are entitled to the same legal rights as people has significantly expanded. Many have argued that corporations deserve elevated status because of their social benefit: they make executives wealthy and powerful and give citizens good-paying jobs and a sense of purpose. The U.S. Supreme Court has clarified the legal rationale for this elevated status, dubbed corporate personhood, in several high-profile decisions, many of which regard corporations' First Amendment right to make political campaign contributions.

For example, the 1976 decision in *Buckley v. Valeo* sets limits on corporate contributions to political campaigns but affirms under the First Amendment the right of businesses to spend money to influence elections. In *First National Bank of Boston v. Bellotti* (1978), the court supports the right of corporations to spend money in noncandidate elections. Congress, in response to expanding corporate influence following these decisions, passed the Bipartisan Campaign Reform Act of 2002, which bans corporate funding of issue advocacy ads that mention candidates thirty to sixty days before an election. However, in 2010 the Supreme Court overturned a portion of that act in *Citizens United v. Federal Election Commission,* which affirms that, under the First Amendment, corporations have the right to fund independent political broadcasts in candidate elections.

in 2011 totaled $66.3 million. In particular, business advocates have emphasized the right of corporations to influence American politics through campaign contributions. Echoes of Powell's ideas can be heard in the landmark Supreme Court decision in *Citizens United v. Federal Election Commission* (2010), which affirms that the First Amendment prohibits the government from restricting independent political expenditures by corporations and unions. Critics of the ideas expressed in the Powell Memo also have been vocal. Greenpeace, an environmental activist group, has devoted a large section of its website to articles, books, blogs, and other resources that respond to Powell and the activities of the Chamber of Commerce.

THEMES AND STYLE

The central theme of the Powell Memo is that in the face of growing pressure from hostile left-wing forces, American capitalists must study their opponents' methods and plan a long-term, broad-based approach to reversing the damage to corporate America. Powell envisions the most likely course of success in recruiting the support of the Chamber of Commerce: "independent and uncoordinated activity by individual corporations ... will not be sufficient. Strength lies in organization, in careful long-range planning and implementation, in consistency of action over an

indefinite period of years, in the scale of financing available only through joint effort, and in the political power available only through united action and national organizations." He elaborates a series of objectives for retaliating against antibusiness sentiment, including increasing the number of probusiness scholars at colleges and universities; evaluating and replacing social science textbooks that are "biased and unfair"; monitoring national television networks and aggressively complaining to the Federal Communications Commission; publishing books, pamphlets, scholarly journals, and paid advertisements that advocate capitalism; and encouraging swift and decisive political and judicial action.

Powell's memo achieves its rhetorical effect through frank, stark contrasts between the Left's efforts to attack the business community and corporations' weak attempts to defend themselves. Powell creates a sense of urgency by focusing on the Left's successes and corporations' failures: "The painfully sad truth is that business[es] ... at all levels, often have responded—if at all—by appeasement, ineptitude and ignoring the problem." He implicates capitalists in contributing to their own demise: "one of the bewildering paradoxes of our time is the extent to which the enterprise system tolerates, if not participates in, its own destruction." After startling his audience with his bleak and urgent message, he lays out his vision for a counterassault on each front where the Left has gained traction.

Stylistically, the Powell Memo is notable for its unwavering, paternalistic tone and militaristic depiction of the threat to corporate America. Powell scolds the business community for not fighting back: "It's time to grow up. You are better than this." He compares the Left's program of anticapitalism to "rifle shots," "a frontal assault," and a "broad, shotgun attack," urging capitalists to arm themselves and prepare for war. He appeals to nationalist pride by comparing the conflict to the Vietnam War, arguing that like U.S. soldiers who must learn to fight the Viet Cong on its terms, "businessmen have not been trained or equipped to conduct guerrilla warfare with those who propagandize against the system." By comparing corporate executives to American patriots—and by extension, liberal activists to foreign insurgents—Powell calls his troops to rally: "The time has come—indeed, it is long overdue— for the wisdom, ingenuity and resources of American business to be marshaled against those who would destroy it."

CRITICAL DISCUSSION

Although the Powell Memo was sent in August 1971, only two months before President Nixon nominated Powell as an associate justice of the Supreme Court, the memo was not published until the following year. In late September 1972 it was leaked to nationally syndicated liberal columnist Jack Anderson, who published articles about the "confidential memo" and questioned Powell's legal objectivity. Anderson laments, "Senators … never got a chance to ask Powell whether he might use his position on the Supreme Court to put his ideas into practice and to influence the court in behalf of business interests." Although the columnist succeeded in stirring up enough debate to prompt the Chamber of Commerce to publish the memo in its newsletter, *Washington Report,* few other high-profile journalists took up the story, and the controversy soon died out.

Decades later, the ideas expressed in the Powell Memo have proved to be far reaching. The chamber implemented several of Powell's recommendations and mobilized corporate resources across the country to shift public opinion about the U.S. capitalist system. The memo helped inspire the creation of many powerful right-wing think tanks, including the Manhattan Institute, the Cato Institute, Citizens for a Sound Economy, and Accuracy in Academe. Probusiness lobbyists have been highly successful in their campaign to relax or repeal many important business regulations, which according to some scholars led in 2008 to the largest economic collapse since the Great Depression. Despite backlash, however, capitalist supporters have continued unabated. In 2010 they gained an important victory in *Citizens United v. Federal Election Commission,* which secures corporations' First Amendment rights to influence politics through unlimited campaign contributions.

Although the effects of the Powell Memo have been widespread, little outside of political blogs has been written about its influence. Liberal bloggers have focused on the memo in relation to such issues as the *Citizens United* decision and the First Amendment, lobbying, conservative media bias, the Supreme Court's lack of objectivity, and aggressive political advertising. The Occupy movement also has drawn attention to Powell's ideas and the efforts of powerful corporations to influence public opinion, suggesting that corporate America's battle against left-wing extremists is today a war on the majority of Americans, dubbed the "ninety-nine percenters."

BIBLIOGRAPHY

Sources

Anderson, Jack. "Powell's Advice to Business." *Fredericksburg Free-Lance Star* 28 Sept. 1972: 4, 12. Web. 3 July 2012.

Giroux, Henry A. "Academic Freedom under Fire: The Case for Critical Pedagogy." *College Literature* 33.4 (2006): 1-42. Web. 16 June 2012.

Kerr, Robert L. "Transforming Corporate Political Media Spending into Freedom of Speech: A Story of Alchemy and Finesse, 1977-78." *American Journalism* 28:1 (2011): 34-74. Web. 16 June 2012.

"Lewis F. Powell, Jr. Archives." *Washington and Lee University School of Law.* Washington and Lee U School of Law. Web. 16 June 2012.

Olbrys, Stephen G. "Dissoi Logoi, Civic Friendship, and the Politics of Education." *Communication Education* 55:4 (2006): 353-69. Web. 16 June 2012.

St. John, Jeffrey. "Memo to GM: Why Not Fight Back?" *Wall Street Journal* 21 May 1971: 8. Web. 16 June 2012.

Further Reading

Clements, Jeffrey. *Corporations Are Not People.* San Francisco: Berrett-Koehler, 2012. Print.

Giroux, Henry A. *Zombie Politics and Culture in the Age of Casino Capitalism.* New York: Peter Lang, 2011. Print.

Hartmann, Thom. *Unequal Protection: How Corporations Became People—and How You Can Fight Back.* San Francisco: Berrett-Koehler, 2010. Print.

Jacob, John N. *The Lewis F. Powell, Jr. Papers: A Guide.* Lexington: Washington and Lee U School of Law, 1997. Print.

Jeffries, John. *Justice Lewis F. Powell: A Biography.* New York: Scribner's, 2001. Print.

Shulman, Bruce. *The Seventies: The Great Shift in American Culture, Society, and Politics.* Cambridge: Da Capo P, 2002. Print.

Jim Mladenovic

U.S. Supreme Court justice Lewis F. Powell, Jr. in 1983. He wrote his 1971 memorandum prior to his appointment to the court in 1972. © NATIONAL GEOGRAPHIC IMAGE COLLECTION/ALAMY

SOUTHERN MANIFESTO

Strom Thurmond

‡ *Key Facts*

Time Period:
Mid-20th Century

Movement/Issue:
Racial segregation

Place of Publication:
United States

**Language of
Publication:**
English

OVERVIEW

The *Southern Manifesto,* formally known as the *Declaration of Constitutional Principles,* was created by South Carolina senator Strom Thurmond and presented to Congress on March 12, 1956, as a rejection of racial integration in general and *Brown v. Board of Education* in particular. The document accused the Supreme Court of a "clear abuse of judicial power" and pledged to do everything that was legally possible to reverse the landmark 1954 decision, which ruled that "separate educational facilities are inherently unequal." By reading the entire *Southern Manifesto* into the Congressional Record, the 101 senators and representatives who had signed their names to the document aimed to send a message that the country was not ready for desegregation and would not be bullied into accepting it by an overreaching Supreme Court. These elected officials from the "Old South" were making it clear that their white constituents wanted to maintain the status quo.

The manifesto had a polarizing effect. Senator Albert Gore of Tennessee, one of a handful of southern politicians who had refused to sign the manifesto, described it as "a dangerous, deceptive propaganda move which encouraged Southerners to defy the government and to disobey its laws, particularly orders of the federal courts." Much of the national press agreed with Gore's assessment, calling the manifesto an exercise in obstruction and an attempt to make defiance of the Supreme Court and the Constitution acceptable in the South. Evidence of this assertion materialized a month after the document was presented, when Alabama, Georgia, Mississippi, South Carolina, Tennessee, and Virginia all passed acts intended to invalidate *Brown v. Board of Education* within their jurisdictions. In Virginia, Senator Harry F. Byrd, Sr., had already introduced the policy of Massive Resistance, a campaign to enact laws preventing desegregation of public schools that attracted support throughout the South. Arkansas, Florida, Louisiana, and Texas also passed laws aimed at blocking school desegregation.

HISTORICAL AND LITERARY CONTEXT

The primary purpose of the *Southern Manifesto* was to rally support for the argument that the Supreme Court had erred in its decision in *Brown v. Board of Education.* In an attempt to do this, the manifesto portrays the decision in *Brown v. Board of Education* as an overreach of power by the judiciary. It states that the decision was a "derogation of the authority of Congress" and an encroachment "upon the reserved rights of the States and the people," adding that "parents should not be deprived by Government of the right to direct the lives and education of their own children." The manifesto even blames the Supreme Court for "destroying the amicable relations between the white and negro races that have been created through 90 years of patient effort by the good people of both races."

The *Southern Manifesto* was presented within weeks of the two-year anniversary of the *Brown v. Board of Education* decision. The idea came from Thurmond, who envisioned the document as a rallying cry for all opposed to desegregation. In February 1956, Thurmond received backing from Byrd, who helped him generate three drafts of the manifesto. Initially, they had difficulty garnering support for the document because of its endorsement of interposition [*see sidebar*], in which a state overrides a federal decision. Given that the courts had not upheld interposition, lawmakers were fearful of including it in the manifesto. After three more revisions, during which the language regarding interposition was removed and the general tone was made more moderate, the manifesto was signed by 101 of the South's 128 senators and representatives. On March 12, 1956, Georgia senator Walter George read the full document into the Congressional Record.

In order to bolster its argument, the *Southern Manifesto* points to established case law to demonstrate that segregation was legal and should therefore continue. The manifesto argues that because the matter of education is not dealt with in either the Constitution or the Fourteenth Amendment (a Reconstruction amendment ratified after the Civil War), the *Brown v. Board of Education* decision was "a clear abuse of judicial power." When the Fourteenth Amendment was ratified in 1868, there were thirty-seven states; twenty-six of these approved the segregation of schools. Furthermore, the *Southern Manifesto* contends that the doctrine of "separate but equal schools" could be traced to *Roberts v. City of Boston* (1849), implying that segregation originated in the northern states, not in the South. It goes on to say that the decisions in *Plessy v. Ferguson* (1896) and *Lum v. Rice* (1927) reinforced the doctrine of "separate but equal" and did not conflict with the Fourteenth Amendment.

The congressmen who refused to sign the *Southern Manifesto* eventually exerted more influence on U.S. social policy than those who did. Three in particular—Lyndon Johnson of Texas and Gore and Estes Kefauver of Tennessee—became key players in the civil rights movement. As for Thurmond, he would continue to fight for segregation. In 1957, he conducted the longest filibuster ever sustained by an individual, speaking for twenty-four hours eighteen minutes in an unsuccessful attempt to prevent the Civil Rights Act of 1957 from becoming law. As the civil rights movement continued to gain momentum, most proponents of a separatist agenda faded into the dark recesses of history.

THEMES AND STYLE

The key theme of the *Southern Manifesto* is spelled out in the very first sentence: "The unwarranted decision of the Supreme Court in the public school cases is now bearing the fruit always produced when men substitute naked power for established law." Every detail of the 934-word document was crafted not only to renounce the legitimacy of the Supreme Court's decision but also to portray desegregation as a horrific solution to an imagined problem. The manifesto paints a picture of the Jim Crow South as a harmonious world where whites and blacks worked together to create mutually beneficial segregation. Desegregation, the *Southern Manifesto* argues, would ruin this carefully constructed relationship: "It has planted hatred and suspicion where there has been heretofore friendship and understanding."

Thurmond's mastery of Aristotelian oratory is evident in the manifesto. He utilizes all three means of persuasion identified by Aristotle—grounded in ethos (credibility), pathos (emotion), and logos (reason), respectively—in mounting his argument. To establish credibility, he speaks of the basic principles of American government, situating them historically ("the Founding Fathers gave us a Constitution of checks and balances") and morally (in "elemental humanity and commonsense") and then connecting them to the way of life in the South. Next, he attempts to stir the emotions of his audience with phrases such as "unwarranted exercise of power," "planted hatred and suspicion," and "judicial usurpation" in describing the Supreme Court's ruling. Finally, in tying everything together logically (logos), he deconstructs desegregation through his interpretations of the Constitution, the Fourteenth Amendment, and a series of Supreme Court rulings involving "separate but equal."

The *Southern Manifesto* is precise in the language it invokes to cast the Supreme Court as activist body that has no regard either for the Constitution or the

INTERPOSITION AND THE STRUGGLE FOR THE RIGHTS OF STATES

Interposition is based on an "asserted" right of U.S. states to declare federal actions to be unconstitutional. This concept has not been upheld by the courts. Interposition is similar to nullification, though there are differences. Whereas interposition merely dictates that a federal law is unconstitutional, nullification is the declaration of unconstitutionality followed by a second declaration that the law is void and, therefore, will not be enforced within a particular state. Moreover, nullification is enacted by an individual state; interposition involves several states working together. Interposition is characterized by several follow-up options, including petitioning Congress to repeal the law, submitting constitutional amendments, or holding a constitutional convention.

Interposition was first introduced by James Madison in the Virginia Resolution of 1798, which stated that the Alien and Sedition Acts were unconstitutional. The resolution argued that a state had the right to declare acts of Congress unconstitutional that were not authorized by the Constitution. During the 1950s, there were several attempts other than the *Southern Manifesto* to promote interposition. At least ten southern states passed interposition or nullification laws in order to prevent integration of their school systems. In the ongoing battle over states' rights, the Supreme Court ruled in *Cooper v. Aaron* (1958) that states cannot nullify federal laws. Most recently, interposition featured in the debate about the Patient Protection and Affordable Care Act of 2010, more commonly known as "Obamacare."

Senator Strom Thurmond in 1997. AP PHOTO/JOE MARQUETTE

rights of states. The author refers to abuses of "power" five separate times, using emotionally charged language such as "substitute naked power for established law," "clear abuse of judicial power," and "unwarranted exercise of power." The manifesto contends that this abuse has resulted in an "explosive and dangerous condition" rife with "chaos and confusion" and "threatening immediate and revolutionary changes." The author wants to leave no doubt that the integration policies upheld by the Supreme Court are both wrong and perilous.

CRITICAL DISCUSSION

Not surprisingly, the *Southern Manifesto* created an atmosphere of divisiveness. The *Wall Street Journal* recognized the source of the document's angst, saying, "This is not the voice of any calloused demagogue. The hundred men spoke for millions of people, some frustrated, some bewildered, some disheartened, and some fearful." Michigan senator Pat McNamara, on the other hand, called the manifesto "a matter so shameful that it will forever be a dark page in American history." In his book *Black, White, and Southern*, David Goldfield argues that the document is not even significant historically because it did not initiate the movement against the *Brown v. Board of Education* decision but merely introduced a more rancorous tone. Goldfield writes that "respectable resistance was already well established in the South by the time of the Manifesto."

Although the manifesto encapsulated the ideas of the widespread Massive Resistance movement, its adherents could not overcome the momentum that the movement toward desegregation gained as a result of *Brown v. Board of Education.* By 1957, groups such as the Southern Christian Leadership Conference, the "Little Rock Nine," the Student Nonviolent Coordinating Committee, and the Freedom Riders were making their presence felt in the Jim Crow South. Meanwhile, the segregationist movement gradually lost support and ultimately collapsed.

Contemporary scholarly works have concluded that the coalition behind the *Southern Manifesto* was not as unified as initially believed. Many of the politicians who signed their names to the document did so for reasons other than a firm belief in the cause of segregation. Some congressmen, such as Thurmond and Byrd, genuinely wanted to raise a groundswell of southern opposition to desegregation. Many others, however, signed the document simply because they felt intimidated or feared not being reelected. Arkansas Representative Wilbur Mills, for example, claimed, "I had to sign it, I felt like … if I hadn't signed it, I'd have been beaten on that. They would

have beat me about the least, any little thing that you might have done or not done that indicated that you weren't on their side in maintaining segregation." On the other hand, many politicians believed that siding with the manifesto would be a career-ending move. Evidence also suggests that infighting at local levels thwarted attempts to present unified regional fronts on race. In the end, there was not enough political muscle to carry out the aims of the *Southern Manifesto.*

BIBLIOGRAPHY

Sources

Aucoin, Brent. "The Southern Manifesto and Southern Opposition to Desegregation." *Arkansas Historical Quarterly* 55.3 (1996): 173-93. Web. 24 June 2012.

Badger, Tony. "'The Forerunner of Our Opposition': Arkansas and the Southern Manifesto of 1956." *Arkansas Historical Quarterly* 56.3 (1997): 353-60. Web. 24 June 2012.

Badger, Tony. "Southerners Who Refused to Sign the Southern Manifesto." *Historical Journal* 42.2 (1999): 517-34. Web. 24 June 2012.

———. "The South Confronts the Court: The Southern Manifesto of 1956." *Journal of Policy History* 20.1 (2008): 126-42. Web. 24 June 2012.

Goldfield, David R. *Black, White, and Southern: Race Relations and Southern Culture, 1940 to the Present.* Baton Rouge: Louisiana State UP, 1990. Print.

Lalka, Robert T. "I'll Live and Die for Dixie: The Rhetoric of the Southern Manifesto." *Southern Historian* 28 (2007): 32-54. Web. 24 June 2012.

Lewis, George. *Massive Resistance: The White Response to the Civil Rights Movement.* New York: Hodder Arnold, 2006. Print.

"Statement from the South." *Wall Street Journal.* 14 March, 1956: 12.

Further Reading

Badger, Anthony J. *New Deal / New South: An Anthony J. Badger Reader.* Fayetteville: U of Arkansas P, 2007. Print.

Bass, Jack, and Marilyn Thompson. *Strom: The Complicated Personal and Political Life of Strom Thurmond.* New York: PublicAffairs, 2005. Print.

Cohadas, Nadine. *Strom Thurmond and the Politics of Southern Change.* New York: Simon, 1993. Print.

Humphrey, Hubert. *School Desegregation: Documents and Commentaries.* New York: Crowell, 1964. Print.

Telgen, Diane. *Brown v. Board of Education.* Detroit: Omnigraphics, 2005. Print.

Thurmond, Strom. *The Faith We Have Not Kept.* San Diego: Viewpoint, 1968. Print.

Jim Mladenovic

ART AND ARCHITECTURE

AUTO-DESTRUCTIVE ART MANIFESTO

Gustav Metzger

OVERVIEW

Written by Gustav Metzger, a German national living in exile in London, the series of auto-destructive art manifestos—*Auto-Destructive Art* (1959), *Auto-Destructive Art Manifesto* (1960), and *Auto-Destructive Art Machine Art Auto-Creative Art* (1961)—outlines a politically and ethically driven public art that rejects the commodification of art objects in favor of a presentation of their disintegration and destruction. The first of the manifestos was written on pieces of cardboard at Metzger's first auto-destructive exhibition, *Cardboards,* held in London in 1959. The subsequent texts were produced to coincide with publicity for two other exhibitions: *Model for an Auto-Destructive Monument* (1960), which was to consist of three towers that would disintegrate over a period of ten years (the full-scale exhibition never materialized; thus the publication coincided with the event's publicity only), and Metzger's most famous performance, in which he painted, hurled, and sprayed hydrochloric acid onto nylon canvases in front of an audience of construction workers and passersby in an installation in front of the International Union of Architects Congress in 1961.

Although these manifestos received some publicity in London's *Daily Express,* they received little attention outside the world of avant-garde art, and even within that world, reception was limited. According to art historian Kristine Stiles in her essay "Survival Ethos and Destruction Art," auto-destructive art never culminated in a "movement" because it was never "systematically organized or methodically publicized." Today Metzger's manifestos are considered important documents that underpinned the political and ethical motivations of auto-destructive art and influenced various avant-garde movements, such as the Argentinian Arte Destructivo and the Viennese Aktionismus group.

HISTORICAL AND LITERARY CONTEXT

The auto-destructive art manifestos respond to certain social concerns of the 1950s and 1960s, such as nuclear proliferation, as well as the aesthetic desire, expressed by many avant-garde artists of the day, to integrate art with the structures of society and daily life. Fourteen years prior to the issuance of the first manifesto, the United States had dropped the "Little Boy" atomic bomb on Hiroshima, thereby catalyzing

the nuclear arms race that would give rise to the Cold War. British antinuclear groups such as the Committee for Nuclear Disarmament and the Direct Action Committee against Nuclear War, in which Metzger was involved, opposed the arms race and supported the occupation of U.S. missile bases. Along with these political concerns, Metzger's manifestos were influenced by the avant-garde's use of the daily or "found" objects in their art, such as Kurt Schwitters's incorporation of refuse, a development that art critic Alan Bowness describes as "a protest against the false and shiny standards of modern society."

By the time Metzger published his third manifesto, *Auto-Destructive Art Machine Art Auto-Creative Art,* in 1961, antinuclear sentiment was growing and avant-garde art movements with aesthetic similarities to auto-destructive art, such as new realism, were in ascendancy. In 1960 the Committee of 100 (an antinuclear proliferation group) was established with the signature of one hundred public figures, including Metzger, Bertrand Russell, and Michael Shoenman. The committee conducted massive acts of civil disobedience, such as sit-down demonstrations at the Ministry of Defense and protests at Holy Loch and Trafalgar Square in September 1961 that led to the arrest of Metzger, Russell, and others. In the art world, only several days after the publication of Metzger's 1960 manifesto, the new realist Jean Tinguely exhibited *Homage to New York,* a self-destroying structure that shared the aesthetic preoccupation with demolition found in much of Metzger's work from the period.

The auto-destructive art manifestos respond to a long history of avant-garde art manifestos, most specifically the "Futurist Manifesto" (1909), composed by Filippo Tommaso Marinetti. The "Futurist Manifesto" served to define the aesthetic of the futurists and outline their relationship to the contemporary world. According to Andrew Wilson in his essay "Gustav Metzger's Auto-Destructive/Auto-Creative Art," the futurist manifestos (of which Marinetti's "Futurist Manifesto" was but one of more than fifty) "provided the critical space whereby Futurism could be seen to extend both aesthetically and politically beyond painting and sculpture," a project that resonated well with the political and ethical underpinnings of Metzger's art.

In the sixty some years since their publication, the auto-destructive art manifestos have inspired a

+ *Key Facts*

Time Period:
Mid-20th Century

Movement/Issue:
Aesthetics; Avant-gardism; Nuclear proliferation

Place of Publication:
England

Language of Publication:
English

GUSTAV METZGER: CHILD REFUGEE

Remembered as the creator of auto-destructive art, Gustav Metzger was born in 1926 to Polish Jewish parents in Nuremburg, Germany. As a child he watched on numerous occasions as Adolf Hitler addressed the amassed ranks before they marched through the medieval city of Nuremburg. Metzger was also exposed to Nazi cinema as a child. He watched and adored writer-director Leni Riefenstahl's propaganda films such as *The Triumph of the Will,* which portrayed the Nuremburg marches, and *Olympia,* a Nazi hymn to the athletic body.

By 1939, however, with Nazi Germany on the verge of the Holocaust, Metzger and his brother were forced to flee the country. He was only thirteen years old. They escaped Germany with the help of the Refugee Children's Movement, also known as Kinder transport, the rescue mission that evacuated more than 10,000 predominantly Jewish children from Germany, Austria, Czechoslovakia, and Poland prior to the outbreak of World War II. The rest of the Metzger family remained in Germany. His sisters eventually escaped into Sweden, but by 1943 his parents were deported to Poland, where they were killed as part of the Nazi extermination of the Jews. Metzger continued to reside in Great Britain until 1980, but he never found it to be much of a home. Since 1948 he has referred to himself as "stateless."

small body of scholarly literature. Most notably, in "Liquid Arts", the Polish sociologist Zygmunt Bauman uses Metzger's writings as a lens through which one can view postmodern consumption. Bauman argues that by creating an art and literature in which

"the disposal of the component is considered from the earlier design stage," Metzger made a prescient observation about "liquid modernity," about a new consumerism that is obsessed with disposability and thus "not accumulation, not acquisition, but change."

THEMES AND STYLE

The central theme of the auto-destructive art manifestos is that auto-destructive art—or, in other words, art that incorporates and embraces the means of its own disintegration—reenacts and criticizes modern society's obsession with destruction. While the first manifesto seeks, primarily, to define the auto-destructive aesthetic by stating that auto-destructive art objects "have a lifetime varying from a few moments to twenty years," the later manifestos provide more explicit articulations of the movement's political and ethical underpinnings. In the manifesto of 1960, Metzger claims that auto-destructive art "mirrors the compulsive perfectionism of arms manufacture—polishing to destruction point." While the screed from 1961 incorporates new elements, such as the idea that auto-destructive art aims "at the integration of art with the advances of science and technology," it continues to argue that auto-destructive art, in which disposal is already contained in the design, is "an attack on capitalist values and the drive to nuclear annihilation."

The auto-destructive art manifestos achieve their rhetorical aim by capitalizing on a presumed dislike of nuclear proliferation and capitalist ideologies among the British avant-garde. By calmly opposing our "drive to nuclear annihilation," Metzger engenders trust in the reader and appeals to a broad humanistic and pacifistic audience. The manifestos also incur greater

In this 1961 photograph, artist Gustav Metzger demonstrates his auto-destructive art for a crowd in London. KEYSTONE/ HULTON ARCHIVE/GETTY IMAGES

authority through a cumulative publication style. The first manifesto was published alone, but the second work, *Auto-Destructive Art Manifesto* (1960), included the text from 1959. The third publication included both previous manifestos, which helped establish a sense of historical continuity to the movement, thereby granting Metzger's work a greater authority.

Stylistically, the auto-destructive art manifestos vary widely, from the six simple sentences of the 1959 manifesto to the declamatory and performative utterances of the subsequent works. The repetition of "Auto-Destructive art is" at the beginning of most paragraphs in the 1960 manifesto imbues the text with an immediacy and urgency that is lacking from the previous manifesto. The short, single-sentence paragraphs are marked by non sequiturs, and the manifesto's claims are often forwarded by implication as opposed to argument, such as when Metzger writes, "Not interested in ruins (the picturesque)," which suggests that it is not the art object (or ruin) that is of importance but rather the process of its disintegration. Although the manifestos vary in the types of language they deploy, the message that auto-destructive art is a public art engaged with contemporary political and ethical issues is maintained throughout.

CRITICAL DISCUSSION

When the first manifesto, *Auto-Destructive Art,* was published in 1959, it received little notice, but the publication of the subsequent manifestos, along with exhibitions and lecture-demonstrations, provoked a growing interest among the British avant-garde, despite continued skepticism from the general public. After initially granting permission for an auto-destructive exhibit, the International Union of Architects (IUA) Congress refused to allow it to proceed, and Metzger was forced to perform his exhibit near the IUA pavilion. In the *Daily Express,* journalist John Rydon conveyed his deprecatory view of the movement by writing, "Then the ex-joiner [Metzger] who has studied at art schools in Britain and the Continent asked whether I was interested in hearing his theory of 'auto-destructive art.' I said I had heard enough." Not all reception, however, was so negative. Metzger's work attracted the attention of mathematician Ian Sommerville, William Burroughs's partner and collaborator, who invited him to lecture at the Heretics Society of Corpus Christi in Cambridge, and art critic Jasia Reichardt expressed her approval by drawing comparisons between Metzger's work and that of contemporary artist Jean Tinguely.

After the appearance of the initial text and the publication of the subsequent manifestos, *Auto-Destructive Art* remained an important statement about Metzger's political aims. In "Gustav Metzger's Auto-Destructive/ Auto-Creative Art," Andrew Wilson writes that Metzger was the "founder for the local Committee Against Nuclear War" and that it was "impossible to isolate his practice as an artist and his engagement in different kinds of political activism." The series of auto-destructive art manifestos has served, throughout Metzger's career,

as a statement about the ability of art to "be critical of the society in which it is situated." In the decades since its publication, *Auto-Destructive Art* has attracted a limited body of scholarly inquiry that has considered its legacy in aesthetic, political, and ethical terms.

Many scholars have focused on the social criticisms inherent in auto-destructive art and its manifestos. In her article "The Art of Suicide," Jasia Reichardt notes the political and ethical dimensions of Metzger's work, stating, "Art can only be the mirror of society, and a civilisation half-hypnotised by the prospect of atomic suicide, geared to consumer 'durables' which seldom last five years … may well be fairly reflected in works of art containing the seeds of their own decay." While also addressing the ethical aspects of Metzger's work, Wilson places Metzger in a long line of avant-garde artists and acknowledges Metzger's indebtedness to Duchampian ready-mades and Russian constructivism.

BIBLIOGRAPHY

Sources

Bauman, Zygmunt. "Liquid Arts." *Theory, Culture & Society* 24.1 (2007): 117-26. *Sage Journals.* Web. 7 Aug. 2012.

Fisher, John. "Destruction as a Mode of Creation." *Journal of Aesthetic Education.* 8.2 (1974): 57-64. *JSTOR.* Web. 7 Aug. 2012.

Jones, Jonathon. "Liquid Crystal Revolutionary." *Guardian* 29 Sept. 2009: 19. *Lexis Nexis Academic.* Web. 7 Aug. 2012.

Metzger, Gustav. *Auto-Destructive Art. Radical Art.* Amsterdam: Institute of Artificial Art, 1959. Web. 19 Sept. 2012.

Reichardt, Jasia. "The Art of Suicide." *Time and Tide* 25 June 1960. Print.

Schwitters, Kurt, and Alan Bowness. *Kurt Schwitters 1887-1948.* London: Lord's Gallery, 1958.

Stiles, Kristine. "Survival Ethos and Destruction Art." *Discourse* 14.2 (1992): 74-102. *JSTOR.* Web. 26 Sept. 2012.

Wilson, Andrew. "Gustav Metzger's Auto-Destructive/ Auto-Creative Art—An Art of Manifesto." *Third Text* 22.2 (2008): 177-94. *Taylor & Francis Online.* Web. 7 Aug. 2012.

Further Reading

Berridge, David. "The Conversation Series 16: Gustav Metzger by Hans Ulrich Obrist." *The Art Book* 17.1 (2010): 34. *Sage Journals.* Web. 7 Aug. 2012.

Landy, Michael. "Homage to Destruction." *Tate etc.* no. 17 (2009): 114. *OmniFile Full Text Mega.* Web. 7 Aug. 2012.

Metzger, Gustav. "The Third Culture." *Theory, Culture & Society* 24.1 (2007): 137-45. *Sage Journals.* Web. 7 Aug. 2012.

Metzger, Gustav, and Breitwieser, Sabine. *Gustav Metzger—History History.* Ostfildern: Generali Foundation, 2005. Print.

Scharrer, Eva. "Gustav Metzger." *Artforum Intl.* 44.9 (2009): 301. *Cengage Learning.* Web. 7 Aug. 2012.

Gregory Luther

DELIRIOUS NEW YORK
A Retroactive Manifesto for Manhattan
Rem Koolhaas

❖ *Key Facts*

Time Period:
Late 20th Century

Movement/Issue:
"Manhattanism";
Urbanism; Architecture

Place of Publication:
United States

**Language of
Publication:**
English

OVERVIEW

Delirious New York: A Retroactive Manifesto for Manhattan (1978) is the first major publication of Dutch architect Rem Koolhaas, one in which he attempts to identify and describe the ideological forces underlying Manhattan's distinctive architecture. These forces in aggregate he calls "Manhattanism," a set of largely utopian ideals that encourage the cultivation of man-made fantasy and the suppression of the natural. Beginning with the urban grid set down in 1807, Koolhaas surveys a variety of the physical and legal structures that comprise Manhattan, including amusement parks, skyscrapers, and public transit systems. He concludes that from the foundation of European settlement on the island through the 1930s, Manhattan's planners and architects produced the physical evidence—much of it still standing—of an underlying "intellectual program" that "in its indifference to topography, to what exists, ... claims the superiority of mental construction over reality."

Well received by its initial reviewers, *Delirious New York* soon became, for better or worse, a tremendously influential text both among architectural thinkers and in broader circles of cultural criticism. Indeed, the question of "better or worse?" has pervaded much of the discussion of the book for the past thirty years; some consider the "book-as-practice" trend exemplified by Koolhaas to be a boon for architects, while others see the work and the postmodern architectural texts that followed it as little more than vehicles for cynical self-promotion. In addition, Koolhaas's formulation of "Manhattanism" has sometimes been critiqued for giving inadequate attention to the problems of capitalism and the growing power of multinational corporations. Nonetheless, the ideas of *Delirious New York* have been applied not only to the projects of the author and his architectural colleagues but also to a wide range of cultural phenomena that share the "Manhattanistic" preoccupation with spectacle, grandeur, and human triumph over the natural world.

HISTORICAL AND LITERARY CONTEXT

Koolhaas's work is unusual among manifestos in that it addresses a set of historical circumstances that have already run their course. The author sees the emergence of "Manhattanism" as early as 1626, when the fictitious purchase of Manhattan from a group of Native Americans provided the first of the island's many controlling fantasies. Two other events in the legal history of the borough are of special importance for Koolhaas's argument: the 1807 charting of the Manhattan Grid, which "defines a new balance between control and de-control in which the city can be at the same time ordered and fluid, a metropolis of rigid chaos," and the establishment of its 1916 zoning laws, which extrapolated this balance of order and chaos into the vertical dimension.

The most exciting and representative episodes in the life of Manhattanism are, for Koolhaas, those of the early twentieth century, when a massive wave of skyscraper construction took place and many of New York City's most iconic buildings were conceived. The projects of these decades gave physical form to a succession of "Manhattanistic" ideals: the Coney Island annex known as Dreamland (1904) dramatized the importance of technological fantasy; the Woolworth Building (1913), as a "Cathedral of Commerce," united pragmatic usage with religious architectural tradition; and the Downtown Athletic Club (1931) exemplified the skyscraper's "Vertical Schism" of different floors for different functions. For Koolhaas, Rockefeller Center (1939) represents a final expression of these and other seemingly discordant objectives, a "fulfillment of the promise of Manhattan" in which "all paradoxes have been resolved."

The architectural manifesto as a genre predates Koolhaas's work by at least five decades. The most famous early example is Le Corbusier's *Toward an Architecture* (1923), which calls upon architects to set aside nostalgia and base their practice on principles then more closely associated with engineers: streamlining, standardization, and utility. Responding a generation later to this emphatic functionalism, Robert Charles Venturi Jr. would produce his own "gentle manifesto" in *Complexity and Contradiction in Architecture* (1966); that same year Aldo Rossi published *The Architecture of the City,* which extends the concerns of the architectural manifesto to metropolitan scale. In his brief critique of Koolhaas's work in a 2009 essay for *AA Files,* Adam Caruso suggests that

Venturi and Rossi each "provide obvious models" for *Delirious New York*.

Critics consider *Delirious New York* to be opposed to the modern tradition in manifesto writing in architecture, not in continuity with it. According to Caruso and Martino Stierli, also writing for *AA Files*, like its predecessors, Koolhaas's book represents a "decisive shift" in architectural publishing, broadening the modern architect's role as a cultural critic. Numerous late-twentieth-century discussions of architecture followed *Delirious New York* in working to make sense of past architectural fashions. Koolhaas and his firm OMA would make their own further contribution in the form of the much longer *S,M,L,XL* (1995); subsequent works, including the *Harvard Design School Guide to Shopping* (2002) and the 2002 documentary *Lagos/Koolhaas*, also reflect Koolhaas's interest in the ideologies underlying urban planning. Some architectural writers, including Gabrielle Esperdy in her 1999 article in *Perspecta*, have adopted Koolhaas's concept of the "retroactive manifesto" wholesale, providing alternate histories of urban development. Esperdy's "counter-manifesto" focuses "not [on] high-rise offices, but [on] low-rise dwellings" to propose "the recuperation of the Grid not as a laboratory of congestion, as Koolhaas would have it, but as a laboratory of decongestion."

THEMES AND STYLE

Delirious New York aims to articulate the ideology behind Manhattan after centuries of architectural history. Koolhaas suggests that this is a valuable exercise because Manhattan, in its present shape, is "a mountain range of evidence without manifesto … the 20th century's Rosetta Stone." The author/architect often distances himself from the political and economic results of Manhattanism, preferring to discuss them in terms of the ideals they represent and sometimes realize. This is also the case with the Grid itself, which he hails as "the most courageous act of prediction in Western civilization: the land it divides, unoccupied; the population it describes, conjectural; the buildings it locates, phantoms; the activities it frames, nonexistent." Koolhaas admires—and encourages the reader to admire—the ambition of Manhattanism, which he considers to be heightened by the "drastic disconnection between actual and stated intentions" in almost every official document establishing the borough's shape.

After describing the role of the Grid, Koolhaas proceeds to examine a group of notable Manhattan architectural projects, including the Daily News, Chrysler, and Empire State buildings. These serve to reinforce Koolhaas's view of the island as a collection of parallel, self-contained worlds in which human control over the environment is the height of achievement. In this regard, the movie-set atmosphere of the Waldorf-Astoria and the canny artificiality of Radio

FROM THEORY TO PRACTICE

The grandson of an architect and the son of a writer, Rem Koolhaas was born in Rotterdam, Holland, in 1944. Just four years earlier, at the beginning of the Second World War, the invading German army had destroyed much of the city. Soon after the war was over, Koolhaas's family moved to Amsterdam and then to Jakarta, the capital of the newly independent nation of Indonesia. After returning to Holland and working briefly as a journalist, Koolhaas embarked on a career in architecture, relocating to London in the late 1960s. As he continued his exploration of urban spaces in writings such as *Delirious New York* (1978), he also entered numerous architectural competitions and designed buildings that were rarely constructed.

In the 1990s Koolhaas was finally able to put his radical urbanistic theories into practice on the outskirts of the French city of Lille. There, he began work on a project known as Euralille. A sprawling development linked to a new high-speed rail line, it consists of a wide range of structures, including a mall, office towers, a parking garage, a conference center, and a train station. The Euralille project gave substance to Koolhaas's long-simmering ideas about architecture. Since then, he and his international Office for Metropolitan Architecture have built a series of widely admired and highly controversial buildings, including the Seattle Central Library and the Central China Television headquarters building.

City Music Hall are also specimens. Koolhaas charts the progress of Manhattanism through several early twentieth-century examples before announcing its consummation in Rockefeller Center and its almost immediate demise at the 1939 World's Fair: "Among the multiple anxieties of the late thirties, Manhattanism runs out of time; [the New York pavilion at the fair] suggests that Manhattan itself is doomed to remain an imperfect approximation of its theoretical model."

The text of *Delirious New York* is structured into a series of "blocks," relatively homogeneous in layout but varying in content, that provide a "simulacrum of Manhattan's Grid"; their "proximity and juxtaposition reinforce their separate meanings." In more literal terms, the book is divided into brief paragraphs and passages with evocative headings such as "Astronauts" and "Infrastructure," each giving part of the history of Koolhaas's Manhattan and appearing with hundreds of photographs and illustrations. These pictures often take the form of small multiples, showing, for example, the gradual whittling of the Daily News building plan from the envelope provided by zoning law to the final design. The mimetic block structure persists through the chapter titled "Postmortem," which discusses the borough's life after Manhattanism. But it disappears almost entirely in the appendix,

which takes a somewhat more freeform and essayistic approach, presenting Koolhaas's own visions for a future New York.

CRITICAL DISCUSSION

Contemporary reviews of *Delirious New York* were generally favorable. Andrew MacNair, writing in 1979 for the *Journal of Architectural Education,* considered the work "highly useful" and praised it for "releas[ing] architectural theory from its dreary, private, quasi-intellectual language." The *Wilson Quarterly* reviewer that year was even more enthusiastic, acclaiming Koolhaas's description of New York as "a zany, surrealistic Coney Island that spawned other Coney Islands as diverse as Rockefeller Center and the Downtown Athletic Club."

Subsequent discussions of *Delirious New York* were more critical, often focusing on perceived omissions and biases within the text. In a 1997 interview with Koolhaas, literary critic Masao Miyoshi noted the virtual absence of an economic perspective from the book and expressed concern that Koolhaas was presenting a portrait of New York idealized beyond recognition. Miyoshi also critiqued Koolhaas's work for "construct[ing] a whole New York out of ... signature buildings and projects" while neglecting the perspective of the brownstone-dwelling masses.

The events of September 11, 2001, prompted further reexamination of Koolhaas's text; most assessments were inclined to endorse rather than critique the author's nostalgia. Such was the case with Hal Foster's 2002 essay "The ABCs of Contemporary Design," which acknowledges *Delirious New York* as a mainstay of design thinking. Foster suggests that Manhattanism represented a set of ideals well worth preserving: "the 'urbanistic ego' and cultural diversity that Koolhaas celebrates ... are under enormous pressure.... New York Beauty will be delirious or will not be."

Foster is not alone in assigning such iconic status to Koolhaas's book. Other scholars have worked to establish the place of *Delirious New York* in the intellectual history of architecture, though its contribution has been a contentious one. Stierli maintains that Koolhaas (along with other authors) "shifted the role of architect to that of reader and interpreter of an extant urban reality." For Stierli, this is evidently a worthwhile transformation, but Caruso takes a less optimistic view: "Koolhaas has initiated the unfortunate trend of 'the book as practice,' now perpetuated by lonely academics and vast commercial practices alike. These authors are motivated by the desire to practice 'critically,' or by vanity, self-promotion, or often by all of the above."

Despite (perhaps, in part, because of) this ongoing and sometimes strident debate, *Delirious New York* has established itself as one of the modern classics of architectural thought.

BIBLIOGRAPHY

Sources

Caruso, Adam. "Whatever Happened to Analogue Architecture." *AA Files* 59 (2009): 74-75. *JSTOR.* Web. 28 Aug. 2012.

Esperdy, Gabrielle. "Defying the Grid: A Retroactive Manifesto for the Culture of Decongestion." *Perspecta* 30 (1999): 10-33. *JSTOR.* Web. 28 Aug. 2012.

Foster, Hal. "The ABCs of Contemporary Design." *October* 100 (2002): 191-99. *JSTOR.* Web. 28 Aug. 2012.

MacNair, Andrew. Rev. of *Delirious New York,* by Rem Koolhaas. *JAE* 32.4 (1979): 32. *JSTOR.* Web. 28 Aug. 2012.

Miyoshi, Masao, and Rem Koolhaas. "XL in Asia: A Dialogue between Rem Koolhaas and Masao Miyoshi." *boundary 2* 24.2 (1997): 1-19. Stanford University Libraries' HighWire Press. Web. 28 Aug. 2012.

Rev. of *Delirious New York,* by Rem Koolhaas. *Wilson Quarterly* 3.3 (1979): 161-62. The Woodrow Wilson International Center for Scholars. Web. 28 Aug. 2012.

Stierli, Martino. "The Power of Imagination." *AA Files* 58 (2009): 42-44. *JSTOR.* Web. 28 Aug. 2012.

Further Reading

Kanna, Ahmed, and Arang Keshavarzian. "The UAE's Space Race: Sheikhs and Starchitects Envision the Future." *Middle East Report* 248 (2008): 34-39. Middle East Research and Information Project. Web. 28 Aug. 2012.

Koolhaas, Rem. "The Future's Past." *Wilson Quarterly* 3.1 (1979): 135-40. The Woodrow Wilson International Center for Scholars. Web. 28 Aug. 2012.

Koolhaas, Rem, et al. *Mutations.* New York: ACTAR, 2001. Print.

Koolhaas, Rem, and Bruce Mau. *S,M,L,XL.* New York: Monacelli, 1995. Print.

Petit, Emmanuel J. "Botox-ing Architecture's Hermeneutical Wrinkles: From Differential to Integrative Thinking in Architecture, 1965-2005." *Perspecta* 38 (2006): 28-38. *JSTOR.* Web. 28 Aug. 2012.

Porphyrios, Demetri. "Pandora's Box: An Essay on Metropolitan Portraits." *Perspecta* 32 (2001): 18-27. *JSTOR.* Web. 28 Aug. 2012.

Puchner, Martin. "Manifesto = Theatre." *Theatre Journal* 54.3 (2002): 449-65. *Project MUSE.* Web. 28 Aug. 2012.

Michael Hartwell

First Diasporist Manifesto

R. B. Kitaj

❖ **Key Facts**

Time Period:
Late 20th Century and
Early 21st Century

Movement/Issue:
London School;
Aesthetics;
Postmodernism

Place of Publication:
England and United
States

**Language of
Publication:**
English

OVERVIEW

R.B. Kitaj's *First Diasporist Manifesto* (1989) places the author's work as a painter within an artistic movement that embraces geographic dispersion and aesthetic alienation. This "Diasporist tendency," as Kitaj deems it, is described as an at once fundamental and open trait of those artists who lack traditional "rootedness" and instead straddle cultural, religious, and physical boundaries. Though born in the United States, Kitaj had been living, teaching, and painting in London for some forty years at the time of the work's composition. As a result of this self-imposed exile, as well as his steadfast Jewishness, Kitaj identified as an outsider and pariah. His text explores the ways in which this positioning in opposition to dominant culture is formative in the work of artists who share his diasporist position.

After the *First Diasporist Manifesto* appeared it proved controversial within the art world. Many critics, particularly in Britain, had long viewed Kitaj's colorful figurative paintings with suspicion and even derision. For them his manifesto was viewed as a distracting and pretentious addendum to a body of work that should have been left to stand on its own merits. Kitaj was criticized, in particular, for dealing with politicized content at a time when the main critical debate was between "content-less" abstract expressionism and "object-less" conceptualism. Over time, however, Kitaj's engagement with themes of political and cultural marginalization proved farsighted, as postmodernist artists embraced his blending of image and text and his explorations of social and political alienation. Today the *First Diasporist Manifesto* is widely read, taught, and discussed for its role in anticipating the newly global art world.

HISTORICAL AND LITERARY CONTEXT

The *First Diasporist Manifesto* responds to the British art world of the late 1980s, when Kitaj was navigating a rapidly changing scene in London. Four years after moving to England in 1959, Kitaj held his first solo exhibition. These early paintings showed the influence of Pop Art, which had resuscitated figurative imagery after a period of increasing abstraction. Kitaj also looked back to the early modernism of expressionists such as Max Beckman and Edvard Munch. He often added esoteric textual commentary with his paintings that engaged his audience with his furious social conscience and aesthetic opinion. In the late 1970s Kitaj became associated with other innovative figurative painters such as Leon Kossoff, Frank Auerbach, Lucian Freud, Francis Bacon, and David Hockney. He named himself and his notable group of artist friends the London School.

By the time the *First Diasporist Manifesto* appeared in 1989, Kitaj's work had become deeply engaged with Jewish thought and with the artist's own Jewishness. As he read widely in literature, philosophy, and theology, he became interested in the notion that the Jewish peoples' history of exile was intrinsically connected to their iconoclastic creativity. Through his readings of the Zionist activist Ahad Ha-am, the critic Walter Benjamin, and the novelist Franz Kafka, he understood his art within the larger context of the dispersion of the Jewish Diaspora. In his work he confronted not only his Jewish identity but also the history of anti-Semitism. This manifested itself in striking ways. For example, he began to incorporate chimneys in his paintings in order to allude to the horrors of the Holocaust. These ideas weren't merely present within his paintings' imagery; they were also explicated in texts that accompanied his works. His *First Diasporist Manifesto* offered a more thorough exploration of his theory about the Diaspora and aesthetics.

The *First Diasporist Manifesto* draws from a range of writing on art, exile, and Jewish thought and identity. As with his art, Kitaj's text responds to the rebellious tumult of modernism, which is typified in Tristan Tzara's *Dada Manifesto of 1918*. Tzara wrote, "Dada: the abolition of logic.... Dada: abolition of all the social hierarchies and equations set up by our valets to preserve values." This spirit of upending artistic and social convention is echoed in Kitaj's text: "I can only posit a new aesthetic for myself (to recreate myself) because I don't want to become a mouthpiece for the traditions of general art." Kitaj's primary interest, however, was in Jewish thinkers such as Benjamin and Ha'am. From them he derived his idea that, as he wrote, "Jewishness, this complex of qualities, would be a presence in art as it is in life."

After an eighteen-year gap, Kitaj followed his *First Diasporist Manifesto* with his *Second Diasporist Manifesto*. Published in 2007, this second manifesto was composed of 615 verse-like observations. In it he returned to the question of the relationship between the Jewish exilic tradition and his own output as an artist. He also explored his relationship with his dead wife, Sandra, as well as his interest in the mysticism of the Kabbalah. It ended with a direct statement to the reader about the work's purpose and technique: "You've been reading a long unfinished poem called HOW TO DO JEWISH ART." Today Kitaj's manifestos are considered important keys to the influential and innovative art he produced over the course of his lengthy career.

THEMES AND STYLE

The central theme of the *First Diasporist Manifesto* is that the author's work belongs within the larger context of works that emerge from the experience of exiles, émigrés, refugees, and other outcasts. As Kitaj writes, "I want to suggest and manifest a commonality (for painting) in dispersion which has mainly been seen before only in fixed places." The fact of being dispersed and unrooted creates in people a "pariah condition" that declares itself in "aesthetic matters." Though this does not result in an easily identifiable style, it elicits a certain common attitude of opposition to tradition and convention. Ultimately it is a fickle and unstable label: "*In the end, the Diasporist knows he is one,* even though he may one day settle down and sort of cease to be one." For Kitaj, the usefulness of the term is personal: "It is the way I do my pictures."

The text achieves its rhetorical effect by making a personal appeal that is cautious, limited, and inviting. Rather than make strict declarations about what diasporism is or should be, Kitaj offers observations from his own point of view. This is signaled in the opening sentence: "Since this is a manifesto, albeit not a very aggressive one … I want it to be somewhat declarative because I think art and life are fairly married and I think I owe it to my pictures to put their stressful birth with some idiosyncratic precision." As he develops his "somewhat declarative" argument, he retains this tone of humility. In so doing, Kitaj invites his audience into the essay, even as he makes a primarily personal case for diasporism.

Stylistically, the *First Diasporist Manifesto* is distinguished by its mix of erudition and informality. Instead of a carefully structured argument, Kitaj digresses from one subject to the next, following the pattern of thought. Along the way he cites numerous artists and thinkers and draws from a large body of historical and art-historical examples. The result is a text that is grounded in the authority of sources without being overwhelmed by the weight of the information it contains. Kitaj writes, "Although my Diasporist painting grows out of art, as, for instance, Cubism or Surrealism did, it owes its greatest debt to the terms and passions of my own life and growing sense of myself as a Diasporist Jew." This is one

R. B. KITAJ: THE GREAT DIASPORIST

R.B. Kitaj was born Ronald Brooks in Cleveland, Ohio, in 1932. In 1941 he assumed the surname of Walter Kitaj, who had become his stepfather. He joined the merchant marines at age seventeen and served for four years. At that point Kitaj began his art education, starting at the Cooper Institute of New York (1950), continuing at the Academie der Bildenden Künsten in Vienna (1951-54), then (following a stint in the U.S. Army) at Oxford University's Ruskin School (1957), and ending at the Royal College of Art (1959-62). An exceptional draftsman, Kitaj traced himself to Edgar Degas with some justification—his instructor at the Ruskin School was Percy Horton, who studied with Degas's pupil, Walter Sickert.

Kitaj left England when the 1994 opening of his retrospective at the Tate Gallery generated a storm of vindictive criticism. His penchant for writing textual accompaniments to his work elicited particular venom, with his critics insisting that text prevented artworks from standing on their own merits. Kitaj read the charges as veiled anti-Semitism, and when, two weeks after the close of the show, his beloved wife, Sandra Fisher, died of a brain aneurysm, Kitaj felt that the stress of the critical onslaught had caused it. He took his own life in Los Angeles in 2007.

example of the ways in which Kitaj deftly weaves fact into the inviting texture of his essay.

CRITICAL DISCUSSION

After the *First Diasporist Manifesto* was published in 1989, it generated a mixed response within artistic and critical circles. For many, Kitaj's various writings, for which the manifesto served as the centerpiece, roused deep skepticism. The mid-twentieth-century presumption set forth by aesthetic theorists such as Clement Greenberg was that an artwork must stand on its own in a presumably pristine state that text could only sully; Kitaj's rebellion against that idea roused controversy. The negative response peaked in 1994, in response to his one-artist show at London's Tate Gallery. However, the vitriol of critics also brought attention—and large crowds—to the show. As Richard Morphet wrote in the *Independent* in 2007, "The controversial texts roused considerable interest in those visitors not sufficiently daunted by the criticism to attend, and the exhibition was enormously successful later at the Metropolitan Museum, New York."

Though Kitaj did find acceptance for his work and for his essay's argument about diasporism, the venomous criticism from the British press compelled him to move back to the United States after his 1994 show. Thus his peregrinations continued, as did his obsessions with the exilic condition of Jews and with

The Wedding (1989-1993), a painting by artist and author R.B. Kitaj. TATE, LONDON/ART RESOURCE, NY

painting. Over the next thirteen years he continued to paint on the theme of diasporism and his Jewish identity. Through all his work Kitaj sought active rather than passive responses from viewers by attempting to give them intellectual as well as aesthetic experiences. His polyglot references—literary, artistic, historical, philosophical, scientific, and theological—contributed significantly to the hybridizing of the definition of art. Kitaj published his *Second Diasporist Manifesto* just weeks before his death in 2007. It represented the culmination of his long rumination on the diasporist tendency in art. Since the *First Diasporist Manifesto* appeared in 1989, scholars have viewed Kitaj's writing in aesthetic, political, and art-historical terms.

Much scholarship has been focused on Kitaj's definition of diasporism. In her essay "R.B. Kitaj: The Tate Fiasco and Some Key History Paintings," scholar Carol Salus argues that the term extends beyond a purely Jewish context: "Diasporism, Kitaj believes, is a common plight not only of the Jews. He also applies this thesis to all classes outside the mainstream of power in their society, including women, foreigners, homosexuals, and those of non-Caucasian racial origins." Commentators have also drawn attention to the relationship between Kitaj's two manifestos. In his review, scholar John Sears writes that the *Second Diasporist Manifesto* "condenses, extends and reworks the projects announced in the first into a text that displays its own readerly erudition alongside a volatile, endlessly stimulating aesthetic sensibility."

BIBLIOGRAPHY

Sources

Bell, Clive. "Art and Significant Form." *Art*. 1913. *denis-dutton.com*. Web. 3 Sept. 2012.

Danchev, Alex. "Kitaj: Portraits and Reflections." *Times Higher Education*. TSL Education, 21 July 2011. Web. 29 Aug. 2012.

Greenberg, Clement. "The Pasted-Paper Revolution." *ArtNews*. 57.5 (1958): 34-37. Print.

Kamhi, Michelle. "Understanding Contemporary Art." *Aristos.* 1 Sept. 2012. Web. 1 Sept. 2012.

Morphet, Richard. "R.B. Kitaj Obituary." *Independent.* The Independent, 25 Oct. 2007. Web. 4 Oct. 2012.

Salus, Carol. "R.B. Kitaj: The Tate Fiasco and Some Key History Paintings." *Shofar: An Interdisciplinary Journal of Jewish Studies* 25.2 (2007) 63-81. *Project MUSE.* Web. 4 Oct. 2012.

Sears, John. Rev. of *Second Diasporist Manifesto,* by R.B. Kitaj. *Art Book* 15.2 (2008): 44-45. *Wiley Online Library.* Web. 4 Oct. 2012.

Further Reading

Aulick, James, and John Lunch, eds. *Critical Kitaj.* New Brunswick: Rutgers UP, 2001. Print.

Choi, Bo-Kyung. "R.B. Kitaj's Paintings in Terms of Walter Benjamin's Allegory Theory." May 2009. *Stony Brook University.* Web. 2 Sept. 2012.

Derrida, Jacques. "Of the Humanities and the Philosophical Discipline: The Right to Philosophy from the Cosmopolitical Point of View." Trans. Thomas Dutoit. *PUM.* Université de Montréal, 28 May 2002. Web. 12 Sept. 2012.

Motherwell, Robert, ed. *The Dada Painters and Poets: An Anthology.* Boston: George Wittenborn, 1989. Print.

Myers, David. "R.B. Kitaj and the State of "Jew-on-the-Brain." 2005. *UCLA Division of Social Sciences.* Web. 2 Sept. 2012.

Paul, Christiane. *Digital Art.* 2nd ed. London: Thames & Hudson, 2008. Print.

Scholem, Gershom. *The Messianic Idea in Judaism and Other Essays on Jewish Spirituality.* New York: Schocken, 1971. Print.

Dennis Fehr

FLUXUS MANIFESTO

George Maciunas

❖ **Key Facts**

Time Period:
Mid-20th Century

Movement/Issue:
Aesthetics; Avant-gardism; Conceptualism;
Fluxus

Place of Publication:
United States

**Language of
Publication:**
English

OVERVIEW

Composed by Lithuanian American artist George Maciunas, the *Fluxus Manifesto* (1963) calls for a radical form of "anti-art" that will offer an accessible antidote to the elitism of the contemporary art culture. In 1961, two years before issuing his statement, Maciunas started the Fluxus art movement in New York. Inspired by Dadaism, the improvisatory works of John Cage, and the found art of Marcel Duchamp, Fluxists attempted to reinvigorate the avant-garde tradition by moving art beyond the confines of museums and galleries. The art of the Fluxists was, to varying degrees, playful, performative, and conceptual. In that spirit, Maciunas's piece is a collage of various photocopied dictionary definitions of "flux" along with handwritten text. The result is a metaphorical call for a "purging" of the "sickness" of culture to make way for a revolutionary new art accessible to "all peoples."

When it was first issued, Maciunas's *Fluxus Manifesto* was viewed warily by many within the Fluxus movement. The document, which called for "a united front & action" for revolution, was viewed by those within the movement as confirmation of Maciunas's turn away from the fluidity of Fluxus and toward an increasingly rigid stance on art and culture. Despite this rigidity, *Fluxus Manifesto* makes an enduringly influential case for an end to "professional and commercialized culture" and for a new brand of "anti-art." While it reached its height of activity in the 1960s, the Fluxus movement continues today. Maciunas's document is viewed by contemporary scholars and artists as one of the movement's most important artistic statements and as a vital work of the twentieth-century avant-garde.

HISTORICAL AND LITERARY CONTEXT

The *Fluxus Manifesto* reflects the cultural and artistic climate in the early 1960s, when mass media began to exert considerable influence on fine art production. Up to this time, modernism had dominated the art world and upheld the distinction between aesthetic refinement and crass popular entertainment. Duchamp and the Dadaists of the early 1920s initiated one of the first attempts to move art outside the confines of aesthetics and to infuse it with characteristics of popular culture, including mass production, reproducibility, and commodification. In the late 1950s

and early 1960s, Pop Art emerged as a movement that adopted the conventions of popular culture.

When the *Fluxus Manifesto* was issued in 1963, the Fluxus movement was beginning to unravel. Many of the movement's original members met in a music class taught by avant-garde composer Cage at the New School for Social Research in New York. They were inspired by Cage's aesthetic openness and willingness to take chances in artistic production. The influence of Cage, combined with the precedent of Dadaism, loomed large when Maciunas met concept artist Henry Flynt, composer La Monte Young, poet Jackson Mac Low, artist Yoko Ono, and others in mid-1961. Their collaborations—in experimental music, conceptual art, poetry, and "anti-films" such as Nam June Paik's soundless, imageless *Zen for Film* (1962)—led to performances in New York and in Germany, where Maciunas had moved to work as a designer for the U.S. Army. While abroad, Maciunas distributed a series of Fluxus newsletters that aimed to give the movement direction—and to keep Maciunas at its helm.

The *Fluxus Manifesto* draws on a tradition of avant-garde manifestos and responds to those of the early 1960s, such as the *Situationist Manifesto*. Issued in 1960, the *Situationist Manifesto* was composed by members of the Situationist International, a French revolutionary group that called for an end to society's "existing framework." The document foresees a new kind of art that exists in opposition to "preserved," "particularized," and "unilateral" art. "At a higher stage," situationists argue, "everyone will become an artist, i.e., inseparably a producer-consumer of total culture creation, which will help the rapid dissolution of the linear criteria of novelty." The *Fluxus Manifesto* echoes the situationists; Maciunas calls for an end to "dead art" and for the emergence of art accessible to "all peoples." Other important sources for the *Fluxus Manifesto* are Hugo Ball's *Dada Manifesto* (1916) and Cage's writings on artistic composition.

The *Fluxus Manifesto* inspired a number of other texts on the Fluxus project. In 1965 Maciunas himself wrote a second manifesto, *FLUXMANIFESTO ON FLUXAMUSEMENT—VAUDEVILLE—ART?* In it, he declares that "anything can substitute art and anyone can do it." Dick Higgins, another Fluxus member, published his own Fluxus manifesto on a rubber stamp in 1966. It read, "Fluxus is not: / —a moment in history, or / —an art movement." In 1970, artist Joseph Beuys slightly altered Maciunas's statement, changing "EUROPANISM" to "AMERICANISM" and signing his name. This new work was simply called *Manifesto*.

THEMES AND STYLE

The central theme of the *Fluxus Manifesto* is that a revolutionary new form of art is necessary to counteract the dominant mode of culture. After offering collaged photocopies of dictionary definitions of "flux," Maciunas gives the first of his three instructions: "Purge the world of bourgeois sickness, 'intellectual,' professional & commercialized culture, PURGE the world of dead art, imitation, artificial art, abstract art, illusionistic art, mathematical art,—PURGE THE WORLD OF 'EUROPANISM!'" His next imperative is the promotion of "NON ART REALITY to be fully grasped by all peoples"—meaning an artistic mode that explodes the conventions and confines of traditional art creation and consumption. He ends with a call to "FUSE the cadres of cultural, social & political revolutionaries into united front and action."

The *Fluxus Manifesto* achieves its rhetorical effect through its use of the metaphor of flux. Maciunas places reproduced fragments of various dictionary entries defining the term above each passage of his handwritten text, thereby positioning his argument as a radical elaboration of the term's conventional meanings. One of the included definitions is a "flowing or fluid discharge from the bowels or other part; esp. an excessive and morbid discharge." By placing this authoritative text above his own writing, Maciunas prepares the reader to accept his metaphorical call for purging cultural "sickness." This strategy is repeated throughout the document. For example, he precedes his call for "A REVOLUTIONARY FLOOD AND TIDE IN ART" with the definition of "flux" as "the setting in of the tide toward the shore."

Stylistically, the *Fluxus Manifesto* is distinguished by its combination of objectivity and exhortation. This sense is evoked immediately and visually by the manifesto's juxtaposition of cut-up dictionary entries, which are black, and scrawled handwriting, which is written on beige paper. By contrasting visual and graphic elements—the various styles of typography themselves serve to make the point that anything can be art—the *Fluxus Manifesto* appropriates and subverts the authority of the dominant culture. Maciunas's collage technique demonstrates that even the fundamental conventions of language must be purged in favor of new forms. The manifesto's handwritten passages, meanwhile, are illustrative of the new "flood and tide" that has come to replace those staid conventions. As a result, these sections are written with an urgency that exceeds the bounds of correct syntax.

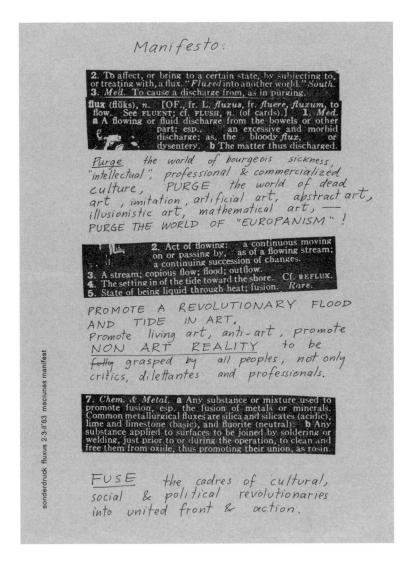

George Maciunas's *Fluxus Manifesto*. © THE MUSEUM OF MODERN ART/LICENSED BY SCALA/ART RESOURCE, NY

Words are underlined, crossed out, and unconventionally capitalized; sentences are run-ons; the handwriting leans forward. The manifesto's style helps make its polemical case for an end to the "dead" forms of middle-class culture.

CRITICAL DISCUSSION

After its initial distribution to attendees of the Düsseldorf Fluxfestival on February 2, 1963, the *Fluxus Manifesto* was received with skepticism. According to scholar Michael Oren in his 1993 article in *Performing Arts Journal*, other Fluxists perceived that Maciunas was attempting to "consolidate his grip, all in the name of the common good, on his little [Fluxus] empire of contacts and itinerant performers, through a series of high-energy letters and circular newsletters." He had also begun to propose terroristic art actions and advocate for civil disruption through such actions as clogging New York traffic, exploding balloons filled with fake money, and mailing unwanted objects to cultural institutions. Oren writes that Maciunas's increasing emphasis on "rigidity and purity" and sabotage were "in direct contradiction to its [Fluxus's] suggestions of flowing and intermingling." As a result, the manifesto's call for a "united front and action" was viewed as extreme and alienating. Even so, the manifesto's call for a new brand of "anti-art" resonated with artists within and outside the Fluxus movement.

Even as the Fluxus movement began to break apart, Maciunas's document remained an important source of artistic inspiration. As David Hopkins writes in *After Modern Art: 1945-2000* (2000), the "oppositional tendencies" found in the Fluxus movement and manifesto "introduced a powerful note of anti-(art) institutional negativity into the 1960s." These "oppositional tendencies" can be seen in the performances and conceptual works of artists such as Ono and Ray Johnson, both of whom were involved in the movement. The influence of Maciunas's message can be observed as well in the body art and performance art of the 1970s, and it continues to resonate with artists around the world.

Scholars have viewed the *Fluxus Manifesto* in terms of the relationship between the aesthetic and the concrete. Writing for *Inside/Out,* Gillian Young calls the manifesto "a scatological critique of the commercial art market and bourgeois culture." According to Young, "Maciunas positions bodily release as its [the manifesto's] primary meaning." Other commentators place the manifesto within the context of other modern art movements. In a 1993 piece for the *Chicago Reader,* critic Fred Camper writes that "the main tradition in Fluxus is neither negation nor social critique but rather affirmation." The manifesto's promotion of a "NON ART REALITY," according to Camper, "is a key to the thinking of Maciunas and other Fluxus artists: they not only wished, like many other artists of this century, to blur or dissolve the distinctions between art and life—they wished to use art to help 'all peoples,' as Maciunas wrote, to redirect their attention to life."

BIBLIOGRAPHY

Sources

Camper, Fred. "The Fluxus Manifesto." *Chicago Reader.* Sun-Times Media, 2 Dec. 1993. Web. 28 Aug. 2012.

Hopkins, David. *After Modern Art: 1945-2000.* New York: Oxford UP, 2000. Print.

Oren, Michael. "Anti-Art as the End of Cultural History." *Performing Arts Journal* 15.2 (1993): 1-30. Print.

Situationist International. *Situationist Manifesto.* Situationist International Online. Web. 28 Aug. 2012.

Tofts, Darren. "Fluxus Thirty-Eight Degrees South: An Interview with Ken Friedman." *Postmodern Culture* 21.3 (2011). Print.

Young, Gillian. "Unpacking Fluxus: An Artist's Release." *Inside/Out* 30 June 2010. Museum of Modern Art. Web. 27 Aug. 2012.

Further Reading

Dezeuze, Anna, ed. *The 'Do-It-Yourself' Artwork: Participation from Fluxus to New Media.* New York: Manchester UP, 2010. Print.

Friedman, Ken. "The Literature of Fluxus." *Visible Language* 40.1 (2006): 90-112. Print.

Higgins, Hannah. *Fluxus Experience.* Berkeley: U of California P, 2002. Print.

Jenkins, Janet, ed. *In the Spirit of Fluxus.* Minneapolis: Walker Art Center, 1993. Print.

Kellein, Thomas. *Fluxus.* London: Thames and Hudson, 1995. Print.

———. *George Maciunas: The Dream of Fluxus.* London: Thames and Hudson, 2007. Print.

Robinson, Julia. "Maciunas as Producer: Performative Design in the Art of the 1960s." *Grey Room* 33 (2008): 56-83. Print.

Williams, Emmet. *A Flexible History of Fluxus Facts and Fictions.* London: Edition Hansjorg Mayer, 2006. Print.

Williams, Emmet, and Ann Noel, eds. *Mr. Fluxus: A Collective Portrait of George Maciunas, 1931-1978.* London: Thames and Hudson, 1998. Print.

Theodore McDermott

Gutai Manifesto

Jiro Yoshihara

OVERVIEW

Written by Japanese artist Jiro Yoshihara and addressed to the Western and Japanese avant-garde, the "Gutai Manifesto" aggressively states a view that was radical when the work appeared in 1956: "Under the cloak of an intellectual aim, the [artists'] materials have been completely murdered and can no longer speak to us." Representational art, Yoshihara proclaims in the document, perpetuates a "fraud" by creating illusions. He and another artist, Shozo Shimamoto, assembled a group of artists who embraced the idea that art materials should be allowed to speak for themselves. Shimamoto named the group the Gutai, and other members of note included Akira Kanyama, Sadamasa Motonaga, Kazuo Shiraga, and Atsuko Tanaka. The group's theories gained visibility that peaked in Japan during the late 1950s and early 1960s. In adherence to the Gutai's principles, Yoshihara eventually gave up painting everything except circles, never creating two identically.

Although Gutai members exchanged ideas with American artist Jackson Pollock and influenced several major modernist movements, widespread recognition in the West eluded them. Upon Yoshihara's death in 1972, the group's visibility faded in Japan too. Today they are rarely mentioned in Western art history survey books or university courses. However, their ideas continue to be felt on a global scale, and their growing presence in scholarship suggests that the Gutai might yet receive recognition for the contributions they made half a century ago.

HISTORICAL AND LITERARY CONTEXT

Following World War II, the Japanese struggled with deeply held reverence for tradition amid pressure to modernize under U.S. President Harry Truman's Marshall Plan. The Gutai artists embraced this modernization, rejecting history in order to create innovative means of expression that they felt would create a new and better world.

The appearance of the "Gutai Manifesto" in the art journal *Geijutsu Shincho* in 1956 might have been just another mid-twentieth-century refutation of artistic tradition if not for two key points: (1) It was one of the precious few artistic statements to emerge in Asia and not Europe or the United States,

and (2) it was ahead of its time. Philosophically, the Gutai fall between minimalism and conceptualism, neither of which existed when the "Gutai Manifesto" was written. In *Assemblage, Environments, and Happenings* (1965), Allan Kaprow describes the Gutai as the "forerunner of happenings" such as environmental art, which is an alteration of the natural environment to create sculpture, at times on a monumental scale. The minimal attention accorded the group at the time of the essay's publication is more a comment on the West's practice of ignoring works from other cultures than on the Gutai's theoretical importance.

Yoshihara argues in his text that raw materials and the "human spirit" are the artist's greatest concerns; the more the materials are manipulated, the less able they are to create a spiritual connection. He writes:

> Gutai Art gives life to the material. Gutai Art does not distort the material. In Gutai Art, the human spirit and the material shake hands but keep being in conflict with each other. The material never assimilates itself into the spirit. The spirit never subordinates the material. When the material exposes its characteristics remaining intact, it starts telling a story and even screaming out.

This evokes Pollock's statement in the Winter 1947-48 issue of *Possibilities* about the need for a new art: "It seems to me that the modern painter cannot express this age, the airplane, the atom bomb, the radio, in the old forms of the Renaissance or of any other past culture." Indeed, Yoshihara repeatedly mentions Pollock in his text, though the Gutai felt that even the styles of manipulation employed by abstract expressionists such as Pollock intruded on the form's honesty.

A metaphor for the Gutai's influence on Western modernism is found in the ongoing confusion about how to translate the group's name, which, in full, is *Gutai Bijutsu Kyokai* (Gutai Art Association). *Gutai* is at times translated as "concrete," but the first syllable, "gu," means "tool," or "accomplishing something," and "tai" means "body"; hence, the more commonly accepted translation, "embodiment." "Concrete" in Gutai terms means "not abstract," which is to say that

❖ *Key Facts*

Time Period:
Mid-20th Century

Movement/Issue:
Aesthetics; Avant-gardism; Abstraction

Place of Publication:
Japan

Language of Publication:
Japanese

JIRO YOSHIHARA'S CIRCLES

Jiro Yoshihara's circles are perhaps his most singular act of creativity. Reminiscent of *satori,* or Zen Buddhist enlightenment, the circle was his only subject during the latter part of his career, despite his statement at one point that he was unsatisfied with every circle he ever created. The lines of the circles are generally a few inches thick with open centers. Some of the circles are solid brown, dark gray, or black on light gray, beige, or white backgrounds; other circles are the reverse.

The years Yoshihara spent pursuing the perfect circle indicate his seriousness of purpose and represent the essence of Gutai: freeing the material from representing other things to let it simply be itself. Through this act, the material reaches mystical heights that enliven the human spirit. Yoshihara admired the approaches of Jackson Pollock and Georges Mathieu toward materials and encouraged the members of his group, the Gutai, to explore them. The Gutai artists published their results in an eponymous journal, *Gutai,* which ran from 1955 to 1965 and counted Pollock among its subscribers.

the group's work is not like that of New York's action painters (who counted Pollock among their ranks). In other words, Gutai members felt that even the dripping and flinging of the action painters stifled the power of the paint to reveal itself. Several years before the publication of the "Gutai Manifesto," Shimamoto demonstrated the extreme nature of his convictions about materials. Unable to afford canvases, he began gluing sheets of newspaper together to create surfaces for his work. Inevitably, he accidentally poked holes in the newspaper. Instead of throwing the damaged paper away, he showed it to Yoshihara, who encouraged him to explore the process. Shimamoto eventually began piercing the surfaces of canvases. The feisty Gutai had room for both definitions—concrete and embodiment—and the two can be traced in Western art to the present day.

THEMES AND STYLE

The "Gutai Manifesto" trumpets the following theme: no burden shall be assigned to art materials other than to simply exist, thus enabling the artist to achieve spiritual oneness with them. Yoshihara writes, "Gutai art does not transform matter. Gutai art brings matter to life." The Gutai members were able to align themselves with superstars of Western movements such as art informel's Georges Mathieu ("Mathieu's works … emit the loud outcry of the material") and abstract expressionism's Pollock ("Pollock's splendor will never be extinguished"). This gives the text's extremist message—the rejection of nearly all art of the past—credibility with the Gutai's two target audiences: the

American and European avant-garde as well as its smaller but equally robust Japanese counterpart.

The "Gutai Manifesto" achieves its rhetorical effect by, in part, tapping into the changing face of Japan. The postwar Japanese experienced profound pressure to Westernize—to replace the power of the Chrysanthemum Throne with that of the ballot box and loyalty to the group with the supremacy of the individual. The Gutai, while embracing this Western definition of a better world, reacted against the pressure by imbuing their work with deliberate freedom and spontaneity. One senses this spirit in the tenor of the essay's language:

> The spray pictures created by smashing a bottle full of paint, or the large surface made in a single moment by firing a small, hand-made cannon filled with paint by means of an acetylene gas explosion, etc., display a breathtaking freshness. Other works which deserve mention are those of Yasuo Sumi produced with a vibrator or Toshio Yoshida, who uses only one single lump of paint. All their actions are full of a new intellectual energy which demands our respect and recognition…. Gutai art put the greatest importance on all daring steps which lead to an undiscovered world.

The "Gutai Manifesto" generously employs the florid prose that burdens many art manifestos. It personifies art materials, for example, by stating that they are "loaded with false significance" and "completely murdered." These materials are "corpses" locked into "their tombs." Gutai art, however, can restore them "to life" by providing them with "the human spirit" to "reach out their hands to each other." At that point, they will be able to speak "with a mighty voice." The sometimes hyperbolic tone distracts the reader from the text's intellectual argument. For example, Yoshihara writes that Kazuo Shiraga can "confront and unite the material" with his "spiritual dynamics" to achieve "an extremely convincing result." Such linguistic choices can be taken as a revolt against academe, which was at least as staid in Japan as it was in the West.

CRITICAL DISCUSSION

The response to the "Gutai Manifesto" was similar to that of the Gutai artwork itself: befuddlement bordering on scorn. In a 1956 essay in *Biiku Bunka,* Sanami Hajime states that Tokyo's art critics described the Gutai as "immature" and "unable to measure up to accepted categories of painting and sculpture." However, such assessments did not prove to be accurate measures of the Gutai. By the mid-1950s modernism had evolved to the point of abstract expressionism, but minimalism and Fluxus had not begun, nor had conceptualism, environmental art, or happenings. The Gutai anticipated all of these movements.

The Gutai inspired Western artists such as Conrad Bo, Allan Kaprow, Yoko Ono, Nam June Paik, and Wolf Vostell, yet they are rarely credited by Western scholars with having done so. They seldom are mentioned in university art history courses or in books on twentieth-century art. This oversight can be explained in simple, if uncomfortable, terms: the West has not yet fully embraced non-Western contributions to the modernist canon. A case in point is the difference in the West's reaction to the oeuvres of the canvas slasher Shimamoto and Argentine arte povera member Lucio Fontana, who is known for his "Cut Series"—slashed canvases that "expose" what is behind the Western oil-on-canvas tradition. He began his series at about the same time Shimamoto was piercing his canvases, although the artists were not aware of each other's work. Fontana even had a similar motivation, writing in *White Manifesto* (1946), "Matter, colour and sound in motion are the phenomena whose simultaneous development makes up the new art." Today Fontana, unlike Shimamoto, receives mention in Western texts, and his work is included in a number of major collections.

Nevertheless, the Gutai are starting to be recognized for challenging prevailing notions of art in Japan and beyond and staking out territory as central players in the avant-garde. Recent confirmation of this can be found in the fiftieth-anniversary issue of *Art Forum,* issued in August 2012. It contains a full-page advertisement for a Gutai exhibition at Hauser & Wirth, a respected Manhattan gallery. Fittingly, the piece featured in the advertisement is *Work,* one of Yoshihara's circle paintings, dated 1967.

BIBLIOGRAPHY

Sources

Fontana, Lucio. *White Manifesto.* Milan: Apollinaire Gallery, 1946. Print.

Hajime, Sanami. "Gutai Artists and Their Works." *Biiku Bunka (Art Education and Culture)* 6.11 (1956). Print.

"Jackson Pollock and Gutai Artists of Japan." *YouTube.* YouTube, 8 Aug. 2009. Web. 19 Sept. 2012.

Johnson, Ellen, ed. *American Artists on Art from 1940 to 1980.* New York: Harper & Row, 1982. Print.

Kaprow, Allan. *Assemblages, Environments, Happenings.* New York: Abrams, 1965.

Mansanari, Murai. "The Attack of the Kansai Artists." *Geijutsu Shinchu* 6.12 (1955). Print.

Pollock, Jackson. "My Painting." *Possibilities* 1.1 (1947-48). Print.

Shimamato, Shozo. "Profile." *Shozo Shimamoto.* Web. 5 Sept. 2012.

Further Reading

Blackwood, Michael. "Japan: The New Art." *YouTube.* Web. 29 Aug. 2012.

"Gutai: Multimedia." *Nippon.* Web. 16 Oct. 2012.

Munroe, Alexandra. *Scream against the Sky: Japanese Art after 1945.* New York: Abrams, 1994. Print.

Tapié, Michel. *Un Art Autre.* Paris: Gabriel-Giraud. 1952. Print.

"Yasuo Sumi—Gutai tra passato epresente." *YouTube.* YouTube, 2009. Web. 6 Sept. 2012.

Dennis Fehr

In Jiro Yoshihara's "Gutai Manifesto", he praises painter Jackson Pollock, pictured here, and his relationship with his material as an artist.
© PHOTO RESEARCHERS/ALAMY

HOW TO WRITE AN AVANT-GARDE MANIFESTO

Lee Scrivner

❖ *Key Facts*

Time Period:
Early 21st Century

Movement/Issue:
Avant-gardism

Place of Publication:
England

Language of Publication:
English

OVERVIEW

Lee Scrivner's "How to Write an Avant-Garde Manifesto" (2008) is ostensibly a manual on how to craft one's own avant-garde manifesto, but the text also provides a parodic overview of the history of the manifesto and its techniques and aims in avant-garde art. The London Consortium, where Scrivner received his PhD, lists the date of publication as 2006, but it was not until 2008 that the manifesto was featured as part of a roundtable discussion titled "A Slap in the Face of Public Taste: The Art of Manifestos," held at the British Library during the exhibition "Breaking the Rules: The Printed Face of the European Avant Garde 1900-1937." The manifesto claims that there are five rules for composition but actually gives six (one rule is numbered as two-and-a-half), and it summarizes them as: "drink coffee, don't use explosives, never use French expressions (*bien sur!*), never involve yourself in dialectics with precedents, never publish nor write nor think your manifesto," and repeat these rules.

Although "How to Write an Avant-Garde Manifesto" was aired during the British Library roundtable discussion, the response to the manifesto was limited almost exclusively to those who attended the discussion. Nevertheless, Scrivner maintained an interest in the form, and he published four other manifestos: "'With Usura' with Bells and Manifesto" (2008), "The Sound Moneyfesto" (2008), "The Memory of Futurism and the Rise of the Insomnauts" (2009), and "Manifest-o-Meter" (2009). However, it is "How to Write an Avant-Garde Manifesto," Scrivner's first manifesto, that is considered a unique parody and overview of the manifesto form.

HISTORICAL AND LITERARY CONTEXT

"How to Write an Avant-Garde Manifesto" responds to the state of the manifesto in avant-garde art at the beginning of the twenty-first century, when many scholars and artists had come to believe that the genre was outdated. Perry Anderson articulates this crisis in his 1998 piece, *The Origins of Postmodernity*, writing that "since the seventies, the very idea of an avant-garde, or an individual genius, has fallen under suspicion." He asserts that "the universe of the postmodern is not one of delimitation, but intermixture.... In this climate, the manifesto becomes outdated, a relic of assertive purism at variance with the spirit of the

age." The manifestos published in the late twentieth century, such as *Dogme 95* (1995), composed by a collective of Danish filmmakers that included Lars von Trier and Thomas Vinterberg, and *Delirious New York: A Retroactive Manifesto for Manhattan* (1978) by Rem Koolhaas, often harken toward older movements and ideas as opposed to futurist aesthetics.

By the time "How to Write an Avant-Garde Manifesto" was featured at "A Slap in the Face of Public Taste" in 2008, the manifesto itself was an increasingly compromised and ineffective genre. In 2002 the market further co-opted the genre when an advertisement for Isabella Rossellini cosmetics adopted the manifesto form. The advertisement featured two women in red lipstick who read "Isabella Rossellini's Manifesto," followed by instructions on how to "write your own manifesto," assumably with their lipstick. Scrivner's "How to Write an Avant-Garde Manifesto," which appeared only a few years later, is thus in a position to take a historiographical viewpoint of the developments and efficacy of the manifesto within avant-garde art.

"How to Write an Avant-Garde Manifesto" draws on and analyzes a long history of avant-garde manifestos, but the parodic elements of the text, such as the "Founding" section, focus primarily on the *Futurist Manifesto*. Composed primarily by Filippo Marinetti in 1909, the *Futurist Manifesto* served to define the aesthetic of the Italian futurists, who valorized aggressive activity, motion, speed, and violence. By framing his manifesto as a parody of the *Futurist Manifesto*, Scrivner imitates Tristan Tzara's *Dada Manifesto* of 1918, which satirizes Marinetti's rationally defined aesthetic territories: "To launch a manifesto you have to want A. B. & C., and fulminate against 1, 2, 3." Using this approach, Scrivner, like Tzara, provides an analysis of the genre and instructions on manifesto writing.

In the years since its publication, "How to Write an Avant-Garde Manifesto" inspired Scrivner to write other screeds, most notably the "Sound Moneyfesto" and "Manifest-o-Meter," which were featured, respectively, in the 2008 and 2009 Serpentine Gallery Manifesto Marathon, in London. These performances, which featured numerous contemporary manifesto writers, were accompanied by the publication of a contemporary manifesto anthology (the *Serpentine*

Gallery Manifesto Marathon) that, according to art historian Martin Puchner in his essay "It's Not Over ('Til It's Over)," amounted "to a defense of the avant-garde of the present."

THEMES AND STYLE

The central theme of "How to Write an Avant-Garde Manifesto" is that the avant-garde, which has historically used the manifesto as a means to critique and overthrow established artistic movements, has succeeded in creating its own status quo—one of revolution—that is now in itself passé. For most of the manifesto, Scrivner forwards his argument by implication, presenting the reader with the historical narrative of artistic revolution; that is, how futurism was toppled by vorticism, which was in turn toppled by Dadaism, which was in turn toppled by something newer, more *avant*. Along with painting this broad narrative of the avant-garde, the text concerns itself with the history and development of the manifesto genre. For example, he argues that Marinetti's verbal pyrotechnics evince a need to be heard, a development taken to the extreme when Ted Kaczynski, the man known as the Unabomber, used the threat of continued violence to force the *New York Times* and *Washington Post* to publish his manifesto. "How to Write an Avant-Garde Manifesto" also traces other lines of development, noting how the *Dada Manifesto*'s use of parody presages the postmodern self-reflexivity seen in manifestos from the situationists and neoists. In the concluding section of the text, Scrivner is more explicit about the future of the genre. He addresses the would-be manifesto writer, for whom "it will be clear that it is the rupture itself that has become vainglorious and status-quo, rather than the status-quo, with which you are rupturing your ties."

"How to Write an Avant-Garde Manifesto" achieves its rhetorical effects through parody of the language of many early avant-garde art manifestos. "I've been up all night," the manifesto begins, parodying Marinetti's *Futurist Manifesto,* which commences with a similar phrase: "We have been up all night, my friends and I, beneath mosque lamps whose cupolas are as bright as our souls." Such bombastic language, while bold and daring at the turn of the century, is now somewhat humorous to the contemporary reader. Scrivner uses this language to make his complex historical analysis of the avant-garde more palatable to the reader, who might otherwise avoid such a tract. A sense of unity is also engendered through this language, as Scrivner addresses readers directly and occasionally refers to them as "comrades," a term that nods to the manifesto genre's history as a revolutionary political form.

Stylistically, "How to Write an Avant-Garde Manifesto" is distinguished by its faux instructional nature. Written ostensibly as a writing manual, replete with suggestions and tips that necessitate historical examples, the manifesto uses its structure to launch

LEE SCRIVNER: SCHOLAR OF SLEEP

Along with being recognized for his parodic contributions to the history of manifestos in avant-garde art, Lee Scrivner has written numerous scholarly and creative works on insomnia. After graduating with a master's degree in British and American literature from the University of Utah, Scrivner pursued a PhD at the University of London, where he drafted his doctoral dissertation, "Modern Insomnia: Vicious Circles and Paradoxes of Attention and Will." According to the author's website, the dissertation "traces insomnia as a subject of increasing medical and cultural interest in the late nineteenth century" and "how this 'rise' of insomnia influenced literary modernism."

Scrivner's interest in insomnia is not restricted to scholarly inquiry; the theme is also present in much of his creative work. In 2009, at Birbeck College, possibly on the occasion of the centenary of Marinetti's publication of the *Futurist Manifesto,* Scrivner presented a manifesto titled *The Memory of Futurism and the Rise of the Insomnauts.* The Insomnauts, however, are not just a theoretical group named in a parodic manifesto but a loosely knit avant-garde collective (of which Scrivner is the founding member) known for its "anachronistic, lyrical theatrical productions."

an analysis and critique of the manifesto genre and its functions in the history of avant-garde art. Thus the section titled "Rule One: Do Drink Coffee" is on one level a practical writing tip, one that the founding futurist Marinetti took seriously; it is also an analysis of the frenetic and agitated energy of the futurist aesthetic. Although this art history critique proves to be a rather dense and well-cited academic argument, the text's playful nature as a how-to guide clothes the text in a humorous garb that seduces the reader to continue reading.

In "How to Write an Avant-Garde Manifesto," Lee Scrivener's number-one rule is "DO drink coffee."
© DUNCAN SNOW/ALAMY

CRITICAL DISCUSSION

When "How to Write an Avant-Garde Manifesto" was first issued, it received little notice except as part of the discussion held at the British Library's 2008 exhibition "Breaking the Rules: The Printed Face of the European Avant Garde 1900-1937," which was lauded for its broad view of the historical avant-garde. The exhibit included manifestos, pamphlets, artist's books, and magazines from cities typically associated with modernism, such as Paris, Moscow, Vienna, and Berlin, as well as underappreciated locations such as Bucharest, Belgrade, Krakow, and Copenhagen. The panel discussion "A Slap in the Face of Public Taste," which debated the motives behind avant-garde screeds, included not only Scrivner but also Gustav Metzger, the author of the *Auto-Destructive* art manifestos.

Although "How to Write an Avant-Garde Manifesto" has not engendered any broad aesthetic legacy of its own, its appearance did coincide with a rejuvenated cultural interest in the manifesto genre. In 2007 *Rett Kopi,* the Norwegian cultural magazine, dedicated a special issue to the genre of the manifesto, "Rett Kopi Documents the Future," which included Norwegian translations of a broad range of texts, from the *Futurist Manifesto* to more contemporary tracts such as McKenzie Wark's *Hacker Manifesto.* The issue also included articles on the genre by scholars such as Janet Lyon, Marjorie Perloff, and Puchner. This resurgence of interest can also be seen in the Serpentine Gallery's Manifesto Marathon (2008), which consisted of a published anthology of contemporary manifestos as well as a "marathon" performance of manifesto works, including Scrivner's "Sound Moneyfesto."

Scrivner's "How to Write an Avant-Garde Manifesto" has not commanded significant scholarly attention, perhaps because of its somewhat recent publication, but the general resurgence of interest in the form has generated a small body of scholarly inquiry. Puchner's essay "It's Not Over ('Til It's Over)" views this resurgence as a defense of the contemporary avant-garde. According to Puchner, neo-Marxist historical narratives, forwarded by thinkers such as Anderson, consign the avant-garde to history; its achievements cannot be replicated or equaled because modernism and the avant-garde thrived on "tensions between capitalism and older forms of production," tensions that have disappeared in a world "entirely saturated by capitalism." In this view, such a historical narrative condemns contemporary art to a dim future. Puchner argues that *Rett Kopi* and the Manifesto Marathon avoid this narrative of progress and decline and "draw on the history of the avant-garde … as a springboard for their own practices."

BIBLIOGRAPHY

Sources

Anderson, Perry. *The Origins of Postmodernity.* London: Verso, 1998. Print.

Blinkhorn, Annie. "The Last Laugh." *Apollo,* Apollo Magazine. 22 May 2008. Web. 24 Sept. 2012.

Puchner, Martin. "It's Not Over ('Til It's Over)." *New Literary History* 41.4 (2010): 914-28. *Project Muse.* Web. 26 Sept. 2012.

Scrivner, Lee. "How to Write an Avant-Garde Art Manifesto: A Manifesto." *The London Consortium.* London Consortium, 2008. Web. 24 Sept. 2012.

Further Reading

Baudrillard, Jean. *Simulacra and Simulation.* Ann Arbor: U of Michigan P, 1994. Print.

Duman, Alberto. "Public Art U Need, Public Art for All, Public Art as Boycott: Directions in Artists' Responses to the Present State of Public Art in the UK." *Alberto Duman.* Alberto Duman, 2008. Web. 24 Sept. 2012.

Lyon, Janet. *Provocations of the Modern.* Ithaca: Cornell UP, 1999. Print.

Puchner, Martin. *Poetry of the Revolution: Marx, Manifestos and the Avant-Gardes.* Princeton: Princeton UP, 2006. Print.

Sykes, Lewis. "A Visual Music Manifesto." *The Augmented Tonoscope.* Lewis Sykes, 10 Nov. 2011. Web. 24 Sept. 2012.

Gregory Luther

I Am for an Art

Claes Oldenburg

OVERVIEW

Written by Claes Oldenburg and first published in 1961, "I Am for an Art" is a short essay in which Oldenburg, an American artist, declares himself in favor of, and therefore demands the reconsideration of, the "art" of a sweeping variety of everyday objects, occurrences, and activities. Originally published as a catalog statement alongside an exhibit of Oldenburg's work, the essay seeks to present "an art that grows up not knowing it is art at all, an art given the chance of having a starting point of zero." Formally, "I Am for an Art" is a list of nearly 150 types of art Oldenburg claims to be "for," which range from the utilitarian ("art that tells you the time of day") to the grotesque ("the art of flies walking on a slick pear in the electric light"). In contrast, the artist is "against" little, demanding only that art "[do] something other than sit on its ass in a museum." This last statement, along with Oldenburg's advocacy of representative art (i.e., "the art of" recognizable physical objects), is typically construed as a break from the abstract expressionist movement of the 1940s and 1950s.

"I Am for an Art" was quickly regarded as a manifesto for the pop art movement in general; art historians well into the twenty-first century cite it as a starting point in discussing the principles and practices that Oldenburg shared with such artists as Andy Warhol and Roy Lichtenstein. Oldenburg continued, over a subsequent half century of work, to engage with ideas he first presented in "I Am for an Art." As if to make good on his claim, he produced gigantic sculptural versions of dozens of the objects listed therein. In the early twenty-first century, "I Am for an Art" was also analyzed as a statement on the broader relationship between art and consumerism and as a critique of the iconic status of many consumer goods.

HISTORICAL AND LITERARY CONTEXT

In the years following World War II, the New York–based abstract expressionist movement rose from relative obscurity to become an internationally influential phenomenon. Assisted in part by the promotional efforts of critics such as Clement Greenberg and Harold Rosenberg, the paintings of Jackson Pollock, the color field works of Barnett Newman, and various works of their contemporaries came to be viewed as the quintessence of American high art. Abstract expressionist works were also widely regarded as inaccessible to the public, although for critics this often constituted a badge of honor rather than a defect. Rosenberg, for example, notes in an article in a 1961 issue of *London Magazine* with apparent approbation that "the vanguard artist has an audience of nobody.... The public ... accepts the choices made for it as phenomena of The Age of Queer Things."

Oldenburg is one of a generation of pop artists to offer a rebellious alternative to abstract expressionism, frankly embracing commercial and lowbrow subjects in a manner that scandalized the champions of high artistic concept. His early work, presented under the collective title *The Store,* takes the form of a set of enamel-painted plaster sculptures of such objects as hamburgers, bottle caps, and lingerie. Some of these were presented in the 1961 exhibition to which "I Am for an Art" provided commentary; others were exhibited and sold in an actual storefront on Manhattan's Lower East Side, a space which constituted a major artistic statement in itself.

It is often suggested that Oldenburg's reappraisal of everyday objects takes its cue from Dada, an originally European avant-garde art movement that emphasized absurdity and upheld ready-made manufactured goods as art. Certainly, Marcel Duchamp's 1917 *Fountain* (an autographed porcelain urinal) prefigures Oldenburg's own sculptural renditions of such household fixtures as bathtubs and kitchen sinks. Yet "I Am for an Art" also departs from Dada in its focus on an affirmative "I am for" that consciously risks sentimentality rather than the nihilistic and avowedly unsentimental "We are against" that prevails in the manifestos of Dada cofounder Tristan Tzara. According to Tzara in his "Dada Manifesto" in the book *Manifesto: A Century of Isms,* where the earlier movement "strip[ped] its chapel of every useless awkward accessory," Oldenburg seeks new uses for the awkward accessories of both art and life.

The central ideas of "I Am for an Art" were current among several of Oldenburg's pop art contemporaries, including Roy Lichtenstein, whose works draw on the visual language of comic books. Oldenburg's upholding of commercial subjects as art worthy anticipates such works as Warhol's *Campbell's Soup*

❖ *Key Facts*

Time Period:
Mid-20th Century

Movement/Issue:
Aesthetics; Pop art; Avant-gardism

Place of Publication:
United States

Language of Publication:
English

EVERYDAY OBJECTS

The work for which Claes Oldenburg is best known in the twenty-first century bears little overt resemblance to *The Store,* although it shares with those early sculptures a commitment to finding the art in everyday objects. Since the late 1960s Oldenburg has become internationally famous for his series of monumental renditions of common household and industrial wares, executed in collaboration with his wife, Coosje van Bruggen. These pieces include *Knife Slicing through Wall* (1989) and the towering *Lipstick (Ascending) on Caterpillar Tracks* (1974). Perhaps the pair's best-known work is *Dropped Cone* (2001), a thirty-two-foot ice-cream cone dropped on the rooftop of a Köln shopping mall. One of Oldenburg and Van Bruggen's collaborative projects, a series of giant thumbtacks dubbed *Tumbling Tacks,* was installed in 2009 on the grounds of the Kistefos Museum in Norway.

An exhibition of works by Claes Oldenburg at the Hamburger Kunsthalle in Hamburg, Germany. HAMBURGER KUNSTHALLE, HAMBURG, GERMANY/THE BRIDGEMAN ART LIBRARY

Cans, a set of screen-printed canvases that in 1962 prompted a referendum on the merits and motives of pop art in general. Fluxus, a movement roughly contemporary with pop art, also shared with Oldenburg an interest in the artistic potential of such everyday objects as matchsticks and playing cards. "I Am for an Art," however, is generally seen as a critical touchstone for historical discussions of pop art rather than as an influential document for specific artists.

THEMES AND STYLE

"I Am for an Art" describes the ordinary components of modern experience as a seemingly inexhaustible resource for artists. The five statements with which the essay opens furnish a theoretical overview of Oldenburg's position before he delves, for the remainder of the text, into specific imagery. In addition to arguing for an art that is unselfconscious yet "politicalerotical-mystical," Oldenburg favors art "that embroils itself with the everyday crap & still comes out on top." To this end he often draws upon the language of the supermarket ("US Government Inspected art, Grade A art, Regular Price art") and the workplace ("art that you can hammer with, stitch with, sew with, paste with, file with"). His opposition to preconceived notions of art also includes abstract materials: he calls for "an art that imitates the human, that is comic, if necessary, or violent, or whatever is necessary."

As a free-form lyrical catalog of objects, "I Am for an Art" is often described as Whitmanesque. In many places, the essay indeed seems concerned to demonstrate the sheer variety of things and experiences that form a basis for art. Thus Oldenburg often juxtaposes items that are disparate, even jarringly so, in their connotations. For example, the artist is "for an art of teddy bears and guns and decapitated rabbits"; for "sweetheart hearts, full of nougat"; and for "worn meathooks and singing barrels of … meat." This show of capaciousness extends to traditional tools of visual art ("crayons and weak grey pencil-lead, and grainy wash and sticky oil paint"), which are accorded equal status with "the art of the finger on a cold window … or in the bubbles on the sides of a bathtub." It seems central to Oldenburg's point that, rhetorically, no particular class of item is given pride of place in these long lists.

Oldenburg often uses alliteration and repetition in an almost lyrical fashion, encouraging the reader to form connections between "bones and boxes," "phonographs," and "pharaohs." In the last paragraphs, the essay enters a kind of accelerando as the types of art enumerated become more succinct: the artist is for "Extra Fancy art, Ready-to-eat art, Best-for-less art … apple art, turkey art, cake art, cookie art." However, Oldenburg then deflates this briefly triumphant conclusion by appending a final paragraph in which he declares himself, in a more relaxed cadence, "for" the art of jewelry, makeup, socks, and a few other items. The essay closes with the enigmatic phrase "square which becomes blobby" printed on a separate line.

CRITICAL DISCUSSION

Oldenburg's essay quickly acquired the status of a pop-art manifesto. Art critic Jill Johnston took particular notice of "I Am for an Art" in her *Village Voice* review of the 1961 exhibition at which it first appeared, deeming the text "a mud-luscious Whitmanesque catalogue of the materials of art." Johnston also notes that while Oldenburg is seemingly "for an art that

PRIMARY SOURCE

"I AM FOR AN ART"

I am for an art that is political-erotical-mystical, that does something other than sit on its ass in a museum.

I am for an art that grows up not knowing it is art at all, an art given the chance of having a starting point of zero.

I am for an art that embroils itself with the everyday crap & still comes out on top.

I am for an art that imitates the human, that is comic, if necessary; or violent, or whatever is necessary.

I am for all art that takes its form from the lines of life itself, that twists and extends and accumulates and spits and drips, and is heavy and coarse and blunt and sweet and stupid as life itself.

…

I am for the art of bread wet by rain. I am for the rat's dance between floors.

I am for the art of flies walking on a slick pear in the electric light. I am for the art of soggy onions and firm green shoots.

I am for the art of clicking among the nuts when the roaches come and go. I am for the brown sad art of rotting apples.

I am for the art of meowls and clatter of cats and for the art of their dumb electric eyes.

I am for the white art of refrigerators and their muscular openings and closings.

I am for the art of rust and mold. I am for the art of hearts, funeral hearts or sweetheart hearts, full of nougat. I am for the art of worn meathooks and singing barrels of red, white, blue and yellow meat.

I am for the art of things lost or thrown away; coming home from school. I am for the art of cock-and-ball trees and flying cows and the noise of rectangles and squares. I am for the art of crayons and weak grey pencil-lead, and grainy wash and sticky oil paint, and the art of windshield wipers and the art of the finger on a cold window, on dusty steel or in the bubbles on the sides of a bathtub.

I am for the art of teddy-bears and guns and decapitated rabbits, exploded umbrellas, raped beds, chairs with their brown bones broken, burning trees, firecracker ends, chicken bones, pigeon bones and boxes with men sleeping in them.

I am for the art of slightly rotten funeral flowers, hung bloody rabbits and wrinkly yellow chickens, bass drums & tambourines, and plastic phonographs.

I am for the art of abandoned boxes, tied like pharaohs. I am for an art of watertanks and speeding clouds and flapping shades.

I am for US Government Inspected Art, Grade A art, Regular Price art, Yellow Ripe art, Extra Fancy art, Ready-to-eat art, Best-for-less art, Ready-to-cook art, Fully cleaned art, Spend Less art, Eat Better art, Ham art, pork art, chicken art, tomato art, banana art, apple art, turkey art, cake art, cookie art.

add:

I am for an art that is combed down, that is hung from each ear, that is laid on the lips and under the eyes, that is shaved from the legs, that is brushed on the teeth, that is fixed on the thighs, that is slipped on the foot.

square which becomes blobby

does everything," he expresses a clear preference for "everything that is *not* self-consciously refined, in other words that is raw, quick, smelly, holy." Within three years, "I Am for an Art" was widely reprinted and anthologized.

Many later critics treated Oldenburg and his essay as successors to the absurdist tradition of Dada. In this regard, "I Am for an Art" is a sort of rhetorical battle standard for critics wishing to see pop art accorded the same serious consideration as its precursor movement. In an article in a 2012 issue of *Art Education,*

Robert Arnold asserts that Oldenburg's essay displays a "Duchampian view of art and life" and maintains that the labeling of pop art as "a somewhat flippant put-on of American popular culture" was a naive denial of the movement's "more radical implications."

In the late twentieth and early twenty-first centuries, "I Am for an Art" found new life in cultural studies of various commercial goods that, like Oldenburg's hamburgers or Warhol's soup cans, have attained iconic significance. For example, the essay forms part of the theoretical backdrop to Jennifer

Price's "The Plastic Pink Flamingo: A Natural History," a cultural history of the pink plastic lawn flamingo, published in a 1999 issue of *American Scholar*. It is also seen, in the branch of literary and cultural criticism known as "thing theory," as a valuable commentary on the emotions attending consumers' relationships to utilitarian objects. In his inaugural article, "Thing Theory," in a 2001 issue of *Critical Inquiry*, Bill Brown notes that Oldenburg was critiqued, especially in his early career, for his supposedly sentimental approach to his sculptural subjects. Brown then refers to "I Am for an Art," however, to show that Oldenburg displays an "aggressive consciousness of his sentimentality" in his allusion to "sweetheart hearts, full of nougat" alongside "worn meathooks" and "rust and mold."

BIBLIOGRAPHY

Sources

Arnold, Robert. "The Development of a Pluralistic Avant-Garde." *Art Education* 29.8 (1976): 18-21. *JSTOR*. Web. 5 Oct. 2012.

Brown, Bill. "Thing Theory." *Critical Inquiry* 28.1 (2001): 1-22. *JSTOR*. Web. 5 Oct. 2012.

Johnston, Jill. "'Environments' at Martha Jackson's." *Village Voice* 6 July 1961: 13. *Art Agenda*. Web. 14 Oct. 2012.

Price, Jennifer. "The Plastic Pink Flamingo: A Natural History." *American Scholar* 68.2 (1999): 73-88. *JSTOR*. Web. 5 Oct. 2012.

Rosenberg, Harold. "The American Action Painters." *London Magazine* 1.4 (1961): 45-56. *Saison Poetry Library*. Web. 14 Oct. 2012.

Tzara, Tristan. "Dada Manifesto." *Manifesto: A Century of Isms*. Ed. Mary Ann Caws. Lincoln: U of Nebraska P, 2001. 297-304. Print.

Further Reading

Grunenberg, Christoph. "The Modern Art Museum." *Contemporary Cultures of Display*. Ed. Emma Barker. New Haven: Yale UP, 1999. 26-49. Print.

Hopkins, David. *Neo-Avant-Garde*. New York: Rodopi, 2006. Print.

Kelly, Edward T. "Neo-Dada: A Critique of Pop Art." *Art Journal* 23.3 (1964): 192-201. *JSTOR*. Web. 5 Oct. 2012.

Oldenburg, Claes, and Coosje van Bruggen. "Dropped Cone." *Claes Oldenburg/Coosje van Bruggen*. Web. 14 Oct. 2012.

Osterwold, Tilman. "Claes Oldenburg." *Pop Art*. Köln: Taschen, 2003. 192-201. Print.

Rottner, Nadja, ed. *Claes Oldenburg*. Cambridge: MIT P, 2012. Print.

Sommer, Richard M. "Four Stops along an Architecture of Postwar America." *Perspecta* 32 (2001): 76-89. *JSTOR*. Web. 5 Oct. 2012.

Wood, Paul. "The 'Neo-Avant-Garde.'" *Varieties of Modernism*. Ed. Paul Wood. New Haven: Yale UP, 2004. 271-314. Print.

Michael Hartwell

INFLAMMATORY ESSAYS

Jenny Holzer

OVERVIEW

Between 1979 and 1982, installation artist Jenny Holzer illegally posted her *Inflammatory Essays* around the streets of New York City. The collection of twenty-four essays, each one hundred words and twenty lines long, was inspired by the works of "Emma Goldman, [Adolf] Hitler, [Vladimir Ilich] Lenin, Mao [Zedong] and [Leon] Trotsky as well as by some crackpot writings," according to biographer Diane Waldman in her 1989 book on the artist. The essays incorporate violent language in order to call for change; one begins, "SENTIMENTALITY DELAYS THE REMOVAL / OF THE DANGEROUSLY BACKWARD AND THE / UNFIT." Holzer writes each essay from a different perspective, evacuating the series of a singular authorial voice. Nevertheless, the essays share totalizing language, grandiose claims, and incitements to violence.

People who came across the essays on telephone poles, buildings, and street signs sometimes revised or commented directly on them. In 1979 Holzer self-published a selection of the essays in *The Black Book,* which first appeared anonymously. Eventually, her essays moved to galleries, as Holzer began to show her work in Europe. In 1990 she was the first woman chosen to represent the United States at the Venice Biennale, where she won the Golden Lion award for her installation. Excerpts from the *Inflammatory Essays* have been displayed at the Solomon R. Guggenheim Museum in New York, joining selections from Holzer's other language-based public art pieces.

HISTORICAL AND LITERARY CONTEXT

Holzer's site-specific work is informed by earlier "guerrilla art" movements, such as Dadaism, surrealism, and situationism. Situationists protested the encroachment of corporations and mass media on daily life in the 1960s. Intervening in the everyday experience of moving through the city, situationists valued surprise and playfulness as feelings that could disrupt the monotony and disempowerment of modern life. The *Inflammatory Essays* extended these ideas, appearing in the midst of the technological innovation and rapid proliferation of media that are hallmarks of postmodernity.

The *Inflammatory Essays* demonstrate the effect of postmodern culture on the ability of language to represent the world. Although terms used in the essays—such as "domination," "security," "overthrow," "enemy," and "apocalypse"—seem as if they should carry descriptive weight, they proliferate so widely in modern society that they float free of their meanings. The broad cultural changes affected by postmodern media and culture also laid bare the role language plays in shaping our experiences of the world and sense of self. In the 1960s and 1970s, these ideas were explored by poststructuralist philosophers such as Roland Barthes and Jacques Derrida, who argued that language creates meaning through its function as a system. Words, Barthes and Derrida contended, only carry meaning because they are different than other words, not because they have any natural relationship to what they represent. Holzer's work explores these ideas by juxtaposing the powerful language of the manifesto form with the voicelessness and lack of perspective produced in the absence of a specific "I" or "you."

Like other conceptual artists, Holzer produces works that are significant because of the ideas they introduce to the viewer. As Paula Geyh writes in her essay on the artist in *Postmodernism: The Key Figures* (2002), Holzer creates "art of the mind rather than of the eye." Conceptual art often examines the society around it, pointing out racism, sexism, and classism or critiquing the art world's own complicity with capitalism and consumer culture. Holzer's essays share the critical mode of other language-based conceptual artists, such as Barbara Kruger, who famously juxtaposed mass-mediated images of women with ironic statements such as "I shop, therefore I am" in order to emphasize the extent to which consumer culture shapes individual identity and values.

As a prominent female artist, Holzer has helped pave the way for a newer generation of female installation artists. For example, the young street artist Swoon installs portraits on walls and street corners that resemble the *Inflammatory Essays* in that they are, according to writer Winfried Fluck, "unexpected and unsettling in their new context." Holzer was included in the PBS documentary series *Art21* and the feminist documentary *!Women Art Revolution* [*sic.*], which brings together archival footage of and interviews with twentieth-century female artists.

✥ *Key Facts*

Time Period:
Late 20th Century

Movement/Issue:
Guerrilla art;
Postmodernism;
Post-structuralist

Place of Publication:
United States

Language of Publication:
English

PROJECTIONS OF PROTECTION

After making, distributing, and displaying her *Inflammatory Essays* (1979-82), Jenny Holzer further pursued the possibilities of textual, rather than imagistic, art. In 1982, soon after posting the last of her paper essays around New York City, Holzer turned to LED signs as a means of disseminating her textual messages. During the 1990s and early 2000s, she experimented with creating curved LED installations. In 1996, in Florence, Italy, she began to project text in public spaces. Since then her textual projections have appeared around the globe, from Rio de Janeiro to Portland, Oregon. In the 2000s she started incorporating not only her own writing into her art but also excerpts from declassified government documents largely related to the ongoing "War on Terror."

In 2009 a retrospective of Holzer's work was displayed at the Whitney Museum of American Art in New York City. Called "Jenny Holzer: PROTECT PROTECT," the exhibition included selections from throughout the artist's three-decade career, focusing on her work since the late 1990s. The show was widely lauded. In the journal *Art in America,* critic Nick Obourn called it "a forceful illustration of her ability to marry her text to the electronics associated with commercial signage without sacrificing her anti-establishment ambitions."

THEMES AND STYLE

Instead of developing a single unifying theme or line of argument, the *Inflammatory Essays,* observes Geyh, "prompt a consideration, beyond their immediate discursive content, of the form and function of the manifesto itself." Although ideas of violent overthrow, the nature of pain, and the relationship between power and desire recur throughout the series, the essays move easily from statements such as "A CRUEL BUT ANCIENT LAW / DEMANDS AN EYE FOR AN EYE" to "FREEDOM IS IT! YOU'RE SO SCARED, YOU WANT TO LOCK UP EVERYBODY." One essay describes the "real torture" that could be produced by building a "sparkling cage" in which young girls would dance, presumably tantalizing "everyone who watches." Indeed, Holzer explores the nature of suffering and torture, a theme that she later developed in work based on declassified government documents from the U.S. prison at Guantanamo Bay and the wars in Iraq and Afghanistan. The *Inflammatory Essays,* however, cannot be linked to specific incidents or people; instead, the pronouncements are generalized.

In Waldman's book, Holzer explains her rhetorical strategies thusly: "I wanted to move between, or include both sides of manifesto-making, one being the scary side where it's an inflamed rant to no good end, and then the positive side, when it's the most deeply felt description of how the world should be." The political character of each essay varies, ranging from far left to far right to no position at all. In one essay, Holzer gestures toward a critique of violent torture but keeps it universal and decontextualized: "SHRIEK WHEN THE PAIN HITS / DURING INTERROGATION … FORM A NOISE SO / TRUE THAT YOUR TORMENTOR / RECOGNIZES IT AS A VOICE THAT / LIVES IN HIS OWN THROAT." While readers may glean the notion that empathy can override any justification for torture, they must supply their own context for the language Holzer uses in order to do so.

Holzer describes violence and evokes the body in order to emphasize the disjuncture between the essays and the context in which the viewer finds them. For example, she writes, "WHAT SCARES PEASANTS IS / THINKING THEIR BODIES WILL / BE THROWN OUT IN PUBLIC AND / LEFT TO ROT." Such statements are meant to provoke feelings of shock, discomfort, and disorientation in the viewer. Although one essay states that "THREATENING BODILY HARM IS CRUDE," another threatens, "I'LL CUT THE SMILE OFF YOUR FACE." When Holzer vacillates between rational detachment and direct threats, she confuses the distinction between the perpetrator and victim, demanding that viewers identify with both the instigator and the target of the harm. The end result is a sense of fragmentation.

CRITICAL DISCUSSION

Less critical attention has been paid to the *Inflammatory Essays* than to Holzer's later installations, which, after 1982 began to use projected LED lights and inscribed plaques to bring her text-based work into public spaces on a broader scale. Nevertheless, initial responses to the *Inflammatory Essays* were largely glowing, and she has since become a fixture in the art world. In 1980 art critic Lucy Lippard called the *Inflammatory Essays* "dangerously conventional collages of propaganda with lethal reminders built in for anyone who swallows them whole," highlighting the potential negative effects of Holzer's ambiguity but ultimately celebrating the essays for their confrontational nature. In 1988 the Solomon R. Guggenheim museum held a solo exhibition of her work, and her later series have appeared around the world.

Stylistically, the clean graphics and direct address of the *Inflammatory Essays* have influenced the aesthetics of political activism. In the 1980s and 1990s the environmentalist group Greenpeace used the power of ironic juxtaposition in its critique of the environmental effects of capitalism, and the AIDS activism group ACT UP has juxtaposed images and language to critique the Ronald Reagan administration's policies on AIDS and homophobia more generally. Holzer's influence can also be seen in the rising prominence of street art, which, in the past two decades has been bought in increasing numbers by museums and private collectors.

DON'T TALK DOWN TO ME. DON'T
BE POLITE TO ME. DON'T
TRY TO MAKE ME FEEL NICE.
DON'T RELAX. I'LL CUT THE
SMILE OFF YOUR FACE. YOU
THINK I DON'T KNOW WHAT'S
GOING ON. YOU THINK I'M
AFRAID TO REACT. THE JOKE'S
ON YOU. I'M BIDING MY TIME,
LOOKING FOR THE SPOT. YOU
THINK NO ONE CAN REACH YOU,
NO ONE CAN HAVE WHAT YOU
HAVE. I'VE BEEN PLANNING
WHILE YOU'RE PLAYING. I'VE
BEEN SAVING WHILE YOU'RE
SPENDING. THE GAME IS
ALMOST OVER SO IT'S
TIME YOU ACKNOWLEDGE ME.
DO YOU WANT TO FALL NOT
EVER KNOWING WHO TOOK YOU?

One of Jenny Holzer's *Inflammatory Essays* posted on a billboard. JENNY HOLZER/ART RESOURCE, NY

Scholars characterize the *Inflammatory Essays* as a series that explores the relationship between art and politics and between language and meaning. For Fluck, the essays demonstrate the idea that the manifesto declaration can be recognized not by the content of its language but by the rhetorical conventions through which it speaks. Thus, the *Inflammatory Essays* do not call for social change—instead, they reveal how easily calls for change can move from political gestures to aesthetic styles. Likewise, the manifesto's radical language functions in multiple ways simultaneously: it critiques the overabundance and dilution of linguistic signs and acts as just another one of those proliferating signs. Critics such as Robert Hughes believe Holzer's work demonstrates that language has the power to uphold social inequality. Meanwhile, in *Manifestoes: Provocations of the Modern* (1999), Janet Lyon writes that the essays remind us that the manifesto itself is characterized by specific formal conventions, notably historical urgency, and that because those formal features are aesthetically objective, they are also "ideologically reversible." Although their detachment from a particular political commitment may seem frustrating or dangerous, the essays, notes Lyon, serve as an important "reminder that a public genre exists for [social] movements."

BIBLIOGRAPHY

Sources

Fluck, Winfried. "Radical Aesthetics." *Yearbook of Research in English and American Literature: Aesthetics and Contemporary Discourse.* Tübingen: Gunter Narr, 1994. Print.

Geyh, Paula. "Jenny Holzer." *Postmodernism: The Key Figures.* Ed. Hans Bertens and Joseph Natoli. Malden, MA: Blackwell, 2002. 173-79. *Google Books.* Web. 8 Aug. 2012.

Holzer, Jenny. *Writing.* Ed. Noemi Smolik. Ostfildern-Ruit, Germany: Cantz, 1996. Print.

Lippard, Lucy. "Hot Potatoes: Art and Politics in 1980." *The Block Reader in Visual Culture.* Ed. Jon Bird, et. al. London: Routledge, 1996. 7-20. *Google Books.* Web. 14 Aug. 2012.

Lyon, Janet. *Manifestoes: Provocations of the Modern.* Ithaca: Cornell UP, 1999. Print.

Obourn, Nick. "Jenny Holzer: Whitney Museum of American Art." *Art in America* 97.5 (2009): 149. *Academic Search Elite.* Web. 27 Nov. 2012.

Waldman, Diane. *Jenny Holzer.* New York: The Solomon R. Guggenheim Foundation, 1989. Print.

Further Reading

Anastas, Rhea, and Michael Brenson, eds. *Witness to Her Art: Art and Writings by Adrian Piper, Mona Hatoum, Cady Nolan, Jenny Holzer, Kara Walker, Daniela Rossell and Eau de Cologne.* Annandale-on-Hudson: Center for Curatorial Studies, 2006. Print.

Auping, Michael. *Jenny Holzer.* New York: Universe, 1992. Print.

Hershman-Leeson, Lynn, dir. *!Women Art Revolution.* Hotwire Productions, 2010. Film.

Hughes, Gordon. "Power's Script: or, Jenny Holzer's Art after 'Art after Philosophy.'" *Oxford Art Journal* 29:3 (2006): 419-40. Print.

"Jenny Holzer." *Art21,* Season 4, Episode 2: *Protest.* PBS, 2007. Television.

Joselit, David. *Jenny Holzer.* London: Phaidon, 1998. Print.

Kalaidjian, Walter. "Mainlining Postmodernism: Jenny Holzer, Barbara Kruger, and the Art of Intervention." *Postmodern Culture* 2:3 (1992). Print.

Lyon, Janet. "Transforming Manifestoes: A Second-Wave Problematic." *Yale Journal of Criticism* 5:1 (1991): 101-27. *Proquest Information and Learning Company.* Web. 9 Aug. 2012.

Petersen, Anne Ring. "Jenny Holzer and Barbara Kruger at Times Square." *The Urban Lifeworld: Formation, Perception, Representation.* Ed. Peter Madsen and Richard Plunz. London: Routledge, 2002. 366-83. *Google Books.* Web. 13 Aug 2012.

Anna Ioanes

MAINTENANCE ART MANIFESTO

Mierle Laderman Ukeles

OVERVIEW

Written by Mierle Laderman Ukeles, "Maintenance Art Manifesto" (1969) describes a public, feminist performance art that eschews the avant-garde principles of change, progress, and advancement in favor of preservation, renewal, and maintenance. Although Ukeles composed the essay in a single sitting in October 1969, it came as a response to several events, including the development of second-wave feminism, her expulsion from the Pratt Institute on charges of making pornographic art, and the birth of her first child in 1968. The manifesto is divided into two sections. The first part seeks to define maintenance art and contrast its ideals to those of the modernist avant-garde. The second section is a proposal for an exhibition of maintenance art, which includes Ukeles "performing" acts of washing and cleaning at a museum, a set of interviews with workers in different maintenance occupations, and the cleaning and purification of containers filled with trash and pollution in an exhibit called "Earth Maintenance."

Although numerous art institutions rejected the manifesto and the exhibition it proposed, "Maintenance Art Manifesto" was published, in part, in a 1971 issue of *Art Forum* along with several photos of Ukeles performing acts of domestic labor. Through Ukeles's inclusion in Lucy Lippard's 1973 exhibition *7500,* maintenance art and the text that underpins it helped to engender the feminist conceptual art movement of the 1970s. The fourteen public art projects that Ukeles contributed to the exhibition sought to make undervalued domestic labor more visible by performing it. Today "Maintenance Art Manifesto" is considered one of the most important documents in the development of feminist conceptual art.

HISTORICAL AND LITERARY CONTEXT

"Maintenance Art Manifesto" responds to the rise of second-wave feminism and to the state of avant-garde art in the 1960s, when abstract expressionism gave way to a number of competing schools and movements. In 1963 Betty Freidan published *The Feminine Mystique,* a book that articulated, for the first time, American women's growing unease in their role of domestic care providers. This book helped to spark second-wave feminism, which focused on sexuality, gender roles, and employment inequality. In the art world, abstract expressionism, the hitherto dominant trend, was giving way to new forms. The rapid rise of consumerism contributed to pop art's representation of consumer products. Post-painterly abstraction incorporated harder lines, greater clarity, and pure color. Minimalism focused on the simplicity and nonnarrativity of pure geometric forms. The majority of these movements, however, were still male-dominated.

By the time "Maintenance Art Manifesto" was published in 1971, feminist conceptual art was on the rise. One of the key components of the rise was the establishment of Womanhouse. Paul Brach, the dean of the Art School at CalArts, hired conceptual artist Judy Chicago—who was best known for a provocative form she called "cunt art" that sought to reclaim female sexuality—to form a feminist art program. While there she worked with another feminist artist, Miriam Schapiro, who, along with Chicago, was instrumental in establishing Womanhouse, "a collaborative art-environment addressing the gendered experiences of women in the context of a real house located in an urban neighborhood of Los Angeles." Lippard, the art critic, curator, and activist, was also active in the scene at the time, and in an article in a 1971 issue of *Art Forum* she invited the relatively unknown Ukeles to participate in *7500,* her CalArts-sponsored exhibit that promoted feminist conceptual art. "Maintenance Art Manifesto" offered a statement of Ukeles's own aims and performances, which endeavored to make domestic work, and maintenance work in general, more visible.

Although "Maintenance Art Manifesto" draws on a long history of avant-garde art manifestos, it owes its political and ethical influences to *The Feminine Mystique,* which argues that "our culture does not permit women to accept or gratify their basic need to grow and fulfill their potentialities as human beings." They are confined to their role as housewives. In "Maintenance Art Manifesto" Ukeles proposes an exhibition in which she will perform this domestic role and thereby "flush" these acts of everyday maintenance "up to consciousness."

Since its publication, "Maintenance Art Manifesto" has propelled Ukeles's career as a conceptual artist. In 1977 she became the artist in residence at the New York City Department of Sanitation (an unsalaried position). With her 1979 performance piece

❖ *Key Facts*

Time Period:
Mid-20th Century

Movement/Issue:
Second-wave feminism; Aesthetics; Conceptualism

Place of Publication:
United States

Language of Publication:
English

THE ART OF TAKING CARE

The daughter of a rabbi, Mierle Laderman Ukeles was born in Denver, Colorado, in 1939 and studied history and international relations at New York City's Barnard College. After graduating in 1961, she studied painting at the Pratt Institute, also in New York, but was kicked out for making allegedly pornographic art. From 1963 to 1967 Ukeles experimented with making inflatable art. As she told an interviewer in *Art in America,* "I just wanted to be able to make these big, inflatable environments stuffed with air that I could fold up and put in my pocket when I was done. I did not want to have to take care of anything. But, there were all sorts of problems, and these things that were supposed to be symbols of freedom, they cracked."

The experience led Ukeles to rethink her artistic process. Recently married and a new mother, she sought a way to reconcile her roles as mother and artist and to incorporate the idea of "taking care" into her creative practice. The result was her "Maintenance Art Manifesto" (1969). As her career progressed, Ukeles further explored the ideas outlined in her manifesto. In various media, including sculpture, installations, performances, ballets, and even parades, she has worked with garbage and sanitation equipment to make an art of and about "taking care."

Touch Sanitation: Handshake and Thanking Ritual, she endeavored to bring greater visibility to unsung sanitation workers by personally shaking the hands of all the sanitation workers in New York City, more than 8,500 people. The theoretical underpinnings of this later work are articulated, most notably, in her 1984 *Sanitation Manifesto!*

THEMES AND STYLE

The central theme of "Maintenance Art Manifesto" is that modernist avant-garde art has neglected to recognize and portray the realm of human activities—cooking, cleaning, shopping, and child rearing—that allow for the arts' continued existence. Avant-garde art, and consequently the public sphere that supports it, is only concerned with the new or the revolutionary, but the essay seeks to draw attention to the labor that supports such developments: "after the revolution, who's going to pick up the garbage on Monday morning?" According to the text, maintenance is a necessity; it is of great importance, but its invisibility contributes to the "lousy status" of housewives and those who hold maintenance jobs. In order to increase visibility, "Maintenance Art Manifesto" proposes an exhibition in which Ukeles will perform acts of domestic labor in public, thereby establishing it as a subject of debate and forcing recognition of the interdependency of the public and domestic/private spheres.

The manifesto achieves its rhetorical effect through appeals to the frustrations of domestic laborers. The author uses colloquial language to express her dissatisfaction with such chores. "Maintenance is a drag; it takes all the fucking time." She appeals to a sense of unity among the general working public by claiming that "everyone does a hell of a lot of noodling maintenance work." Ukeles also includes long lists of responsibilities that emphasize the unending nature of maintenance work and that portray the thoughts of a worker overwhelmed by these responsibilities: "clean your desk, wash the dishes, clean the floor, wash your clothes, wash your shoes, change the baby's diaper, finish the report, correct the typos, mend the fence." The inclusion of such lists allows the author to engage the reader in the important struggle to bring recognition and visibility to undervalued domestic workers.

Stylistically, "Maintenance Art Manifesto" is distinguished by the broad, dualistic comparisons it draws between modernist and maintenance art. By comparing the avant-garde to the death instinct, and maintenance art to the life instinct, Ukeles has couched her argument in philosophical terms that add weight and authority to her text. Her paragraphing emphasizes this dualism: she uses short paragraphs that set these art forms against one another on the page. By establishing this dualistic, systematized approach, Ukeles can make unequivocal but perhaps reductive statements about these art forms, such as the manifesto's comparison between maintenance work and "survival systems and operations," a comparison that highlights the essential nature of such work and the need to make it more visible.

CRITICAL DISCUSSION

When "Maintenance Art Manifesto" was written, it received little attention within and outside of artistic circles. The essay's proposal for an exhibition was not accepted for several years. It was not until a portion of the text was published in *Art Forum* in 1971 that Ukeles began to receive critical attention. Lippard invited Ukeles to perform her piece *Washing/Track/Maintenance: Outside* at the Wadsworth Athenaeum in Hartford, Connecticut. Despite the exposure at this and subsequent exhibitions, there were few contemporary critical responses to the manifesto and the incipient movement. According to Beth Anne Lauritis in her dissertation "Lucy Lippard and the Provisional Exhibition," much of Ukeles's work goes "unremarked in important texts on the subject" of conceptual art.

After the initial run of performances for the *7500* exhibit ended in 1974, "Maintenance Art Manifesto" remained an important statement of Ukeles's aesthetic aims. Many of her subsequent works continue to embody political ideology set forth in the manifesto. According to Lauritis, "By inserting domestic forms of labor into a conceptual art frame, Ukeles' maintenance process aims for a change that goes beyond aesthetic advances to a politics of recognition." Since its initial publication, "Maintenance Art Manifesto" has attracted limited scholarly interest as an important document in the development of feminist and conceptual art.

Some commentators have considered the essay's significance as a feminist criticism of modern patriarchy. In discussing the visual emphasis Ukeles places on domestic labor, Kelly Rafferty argues in her essay "Regeneration: Tissue Engineering, Maintenance, and the Time of Performance" that the fact that maintenance work is "women's work" when it is done in private is part of why we denigrate and hide the work when it is performed by men." Other commentators have focused on the text as an institutional critique of art museums. According to Helen Molesworth in her piece in *Rewriting Conceptual Art* (1999), "Ukeles took the usually hidden labour of the private sphere and submitted it to public scrutiny in the institutions of art." Molesworth argues that these performances wreaked havoc on the normal museum workday, thereby showing "how absolutely structural it is to patriarchy and capitalism that the labour of maintenance should remain *invisible*."

BIBLIOGRAPHY

Sources

Cart, A.W. *(M)other Work: Feminist Maternal Performance Art.* Thesis. Univ. of Southern California, 2010. *Proquest.* Web. 27 Aug. 2012.

Freeman, Lucy. Rev. of *The Feminine Mystique,* by Betty Friedan. *New York Times.* The New York Times Company, 7 Apr. 1963. Web. 31 Aug. 2012.

Molesworth, Helen. "Cleaning Up the 1970s: The Work of Judy Chicago, Mary Kelly and Mierle Laderman Ukeles." *Rewriting Conceptual Art.* Ed. Michael Newman and Jon Bird. London: Reaktion Books, 1999. 107-22. Print.

Lauritis, Beth Anne. "Lucy Lippard and the Provisional Exhibition: Intersections of Conceptual Art and Feminism, 1970-1980." Diss. Univ. of California, Los Angeles, 2009. *Proquest.* Web. 27 Aug. 2012.

Rafferty, Kelly. "Regeneration: Tissue Engineering, Maintenance, and the Time of Performance." *Drama Review* 56.3 (2012): 83-97. *Project Muse.* Web. 27 Aug. 2012.

Ukeles, Mierle Laderman. "Manifesto for Maintenance: A Conversation with Mierle Laderman Ukeles." Interview by Bartholomew Ryan. *Art in America.* Art in America Magazine, 30 Mar. 2009. Web. 27 Aug. 2012.

———. "Maintenance Art Manifesto: Proposal for an Exhibition, 'Care.'" *Conceptual Art: A Critical Anthology.* Ed. Alexander Alberro and Blake Stimson. Cambridge: MIT P, 1999. 122-25. Print.

Further Reading

Broude, Norma, and Mary D. Garrard. *The Power of Feminist Art: The American Movement of the 1970s, History and Impact.* New York: Harry N. Abrams, 1994. Print.

Carr, C. "Waste. Not!" *Village Voice* 28 May 2002. *Proquest.* Web. 27 Aug. 2012.

Kastner, Jeffrey, and Brian Wallis. *Land and Environmental Art.* London: Phaidon, 1998. Print.

Liss, Andrea. *Feminist Art and the Maternal.* Minneapolis: U of Minnesota P, 2009. Print.

Ryan, Bartholomew. "Manifesto for Maintenance: A Conversation with Mierle Laderman Ukeles." *Art in America.* Art in America Magazine, 30 Mar. 2009. Web. 27 Aug. 2012.

Gregory Luther

Hartford Wash: Washing/ Tracks/Maintenance: Outside (1973), part of a maintenance art performance piece by Mierle Laderman Ukeles in which the artist publicly cleaned the Wadsworth Atheneum Museum in Hartford, Connecticut. WADSWORTH ATHENEUM MUSEUM OF ART/ART RESOURCE, NY

MANIFESTO

Wolf Vostell

✣ Key Facts

Time Period:
Mid-20th Century

Movement/Issue:
Fluxus; Aesthetics; Avant-gardism; Performance art

Place of Publication:
Germany

Language of Publication:
German

OVERVIEW

In "Manifesto" (1963), German painter and sculptor Wolf Vostell defines *décollage* as a theoretical principle underpinning an artistic technique of the same name, one that recognizes and performs the destructive elements of life through its use of torn posters and other altered cultural and mass-media objects. The work appeared in 1963, nine years after Vostell first thought of the concept while reading an account of a plane crash in the French newspaper *Le Figaro*. By the date of the document's publication, Vostell had become a member of the Fluxus movement, a loose-knit avant-garde group that engaged in experimental music, art, and performance events. He was also among the first artists to experiment with the television set as a formal and technological device in his art. Central to "Manifesto" is the idea that "life is not made of up constructive elements" but of a dialectic between construction and destruction.

Much of Vostell's art from the 1960s attracted attention by forcing viewers to confront the violent destruction inherent in modern society, but "Manifesto" drew little notice. The text helped explain in an abstract way the aesthetic foundations of Vostell's new conceptual art, which by 1963 had transformed from the tearing, burning, and altering of posters to full-scale décollage "happenings," in which objects were destroyed in different performances, such as the September 1963 event at which Vostell arranged to have an automobile placed on railroad tracks and struck by a locomotive. His "Manifesto" explicates the project that undergirded many of these productions: to reject the construction of art objects in favor of a performed décollage that acknowledges the "destructive phenomena of our epoch." Today the text is important in helping document the history of European performance art.

HISTORICAL AND LITERARY CONTEXT

"Manifesto," and the concept of décollage that it propounds, responds to both historical and aesthetic concerns: the legacy of the Holocaust and the dematerialization of the art object. In 1940 a young Vostell witnessed bombs falling from the sky "like great flocks of birds," as quoted in Glenn O'Brien's 2001 essay in *Artforum International*. The aftermath of the Holocaust—a period associated with silence, guilt, and repression in Germany—had great effect on a generation that, according to scholar Benjamin Lima's 2009 dissertation *Wolf Vostell's Décollage and Other Forms of Destruction: 1958-1972,* needed "to lay charges of such horrible gravity at the feet of their elders in power." In the art world, the Dada retrospective reached Düsseldorf in October 1958, catalyzing a move away from abstract expressionism. John Cage's performances in Germany that same year emphasized the action or performance, rather than the object, as an artistic medium.

By the time the manifesto was issued in 1963, performance art had supplanted abstract expressionism as the dominant form of art among the European avant-garde. In 1962 George Maciunas, along with Vostell and others, formed Fluxus, an international association of artists who performed events in Fluxus festivals throughout Europe. Along with Fluxus performances, which included work by George Brecht and Maciunas, Vostell was staging his décollage happenings in New York and Germany. Unlike the Fluxus performances, however, Vostell's events were confrontational, often involving the coercive and violent elements that were central to his aesthetic formulation of décollage. His "Manifesto" offers a statement of his aims and processes, which sought to engage with and portray the violent and destructive elements of modern society.

"Manifesto" draws on a long history of avant-garde manifestos. The rekindled interest in Dada at the end of the 1950s, as represented by the 1958 Dada retrospective, suggests that Vostell's text was influenced by the *Dada Manifesto* of 1918. Written by Tristan Tzara, the *Dada Manifesto* underpinned the art movement of the same name, which was in part a reaction to the horrors of World War I, much as Vostell's work bears the scars of World War II. Tzara's claims, such as "the new artist protests: he no longer paints" or "every plastic or pictorial work is unnecessary," presage the ascendance of performance art among the European avant-garde. In composing "Manifesto," Vostell incorporated many of Tzara's ideas for artistic reinvention but reframed them within the new postwar context.

In the decades since its publication, "Manifesto" has provided an abstract, poetic blueprint for Vostell's continued artistic mission. In his 1964 happening *You,* Vostell's work thematized war and violence through mixed media. In 1966 the artist published another manifesto, "dé*coll*/age," which brings greater clarity and definition to the abstractions and metaphors of his previous text. By 1967 he was protesting the U.S. involvement in Vietnam through a piece titled *Miss Vietnam,* which "staged acts of violence on symbolically overcharged objects such as a mannequin and a bombshell." Today Vostell's works command significant scholarly interest for their uncompromising criticism of violence in European and American history.

THEMES AND STYLE

The central theme of "Manifesto" is that life is not made up solely of "constructive elements" but that it also consists of destructive elements, specifically "décollage," which can be translated as "to loosen, to unglue, to take off (as in an airplane) to separate, to go away, or to die." "Manifesto," however, does not offer this definition; in rather repetitive language, it opens with a series of abstract definitions for the word:

> Décollage is your understanding
> Décollage is your accident
> Décollage is your death
> Décollage is your analysis

The text makes no specific mention of art, and it is primarily through performance pieces and later theoretical works that this original manifesto accumulates meaning. It is there that Vostell defines décollage as an artistic technique and relates it to the destructive impulses in modern society. In "Manifesto," however, the disparate definitions of the word suggest that décollage is too broad for definition; it is simply an element of life.

Vostell's text achieves its rhetorical effect not through appeals to a sense of unity or solidarity, as do many manifestos, but through simple, repetitive, declarative sentences that point a finger at the reader. In its use of the second-person possessive pronoun "your" prior to offering a discursive definition of the concept, the text implicates readers in a movement that they did not know existed. This forced confrontation with the concept of décollage—and the claim that "you" too have experienced it—mirrors the confrontation that Vostell seeks through his performance art: to turn the viewer's eye toward the destructive impulses in the history of the twentieth century, alluded to in "Manifesto" as "death," "dirt," "sudden fall," "fever," and "pain."

Stylistically "Manifesto" is distinguished by its line breaks, which, although typical of poetry, make the document read like a list. These line breaks, coupled with short declarative lines, cause the reader to proceed with greater velocity; the text draws the eye downward, thereby imbuing the manifesto with a rapid-fire immediacy. The repetition of twenty-eight sentences that begin with "Décollage is your …,"

THE VIETNAM WAR

Although U.S. involvement in the Vietnam War began with the end of the First Indochina War (1946-54) and the exit of the French in 1955, large-scale combat between U.S. and North Vietnamese communist forces did not begin until President Lyndon B. Johnson took office in the wake of President John F. Kennedy's assassination. In August 1964 brief but deadly naval engagements in the Gulf of Tonkin provoked Johnson to sign the Gulf of Tonkin Resolution, which granted the president power to conduct military operations in Vietnam without declaring war. Through their efforts to combat communism in Southeast Asia, the United States found itself mired in a near decade-long conflict that cost tens of thousands of lives.

Opposition to the war was strong, not only in the United States, where such public figures as Joan Baez and Noam Chomsky and students at campuses across the nation protested the conflict, but also among the European vanguard. Out of protest over the war, Vostell refused to exhibit his work in the United States. He continued to conduct "happenings" in Germany, however, one of which—his 1968 *Miss Vietnam*—was a clear protest against continued U.S. involvement in the region.

followed by a seemingly arbitrary noun—"spot cleaner," for example—euphemistically beats the reader over the head with the idea that décollage is inherent in all aspects of life. Vostell creates a verbal violence that stylistically echoes his claim that "destruction in general and in particular, together with dissolution and change are the strongest elements" in the development of the modern world.

CRITICAL DISCUSSION

When "Manifesto" was first published in 1963, it received almost no attention from the general public or the artistic vanguard, except as an addendum to Vostell's happenings, which generated interest and criticism. In his dissertation, Lima draws on firsthand accounts of participants in the 1964 happening *You* to suggest that the performance, which was staged beside a swimming pool filled with balloons and surrounded by "huge sides of beef and bones and other animal parts," provoked a sense of unease in the audience. Lima notes that according to Al Hansen, one of the show's participants, Vostell's commands—coupled with the mud, the fenced-off area, and the series of exploding smoke bombs—gave *You* a "concentration camp" feeling. Vostell's 1964 *Ulm* happening, which subjected the audience to the sound of a jet engine at full throttle, attracted considerable attention in German-language newspapers.

After the Fluxus events and décollage happenings had wound down in 1970, "Manifesto" remained an

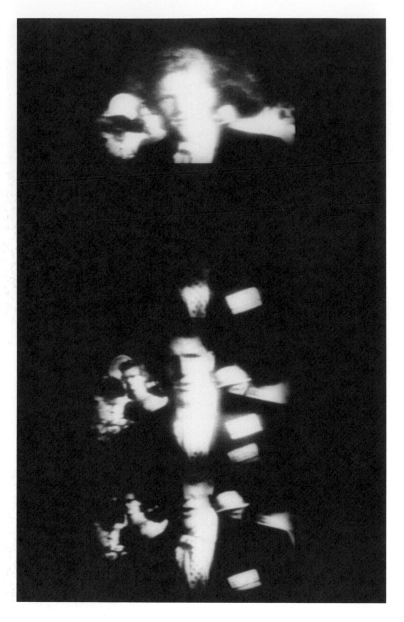

Some scholarship has focused on how décollage and its manifestos can be viewed as a violent reaction to the atrocities of Nazi Germany. Lima points out that Vostell's works display "an aggressive, confrontational and unsettled strain." These "thematizations of violence, of coercion, and of sensory immersion" are perhaps expressions of outrage at "inheriting responsibility" for the legacy of the Holocaust. O'Brien draws similar connections between the Holocaust and décollage, claiming that "Vostell's life was perhaps his greatest work, as he made himself a transformation of the German spirit. Whether or not he was actually a Jew, Vostell took on a rabbinical appearance in his later years, complete with beard, sidelocks, and a Hasidic wardrobe—an act of solidarity and provocation."

BIBLIOGRAPHY

Sources

Lima, Benjamin. *Wolf Vostell's Decollage and Other Forms of Destruction, 1958-1972.* Diss. Yale U, 2009. New Haven, CT: Yale UP, 2009. *Proquest.* Web. 10 Sept. 2012.

O'Brien, Glen. "TV Guide." *Artforum International* 39.8 (2001): 115. *Gale Fine Arts and Music Collection.* Web. 10 Sept. 2012.

Vostell, Wolf. "de-*colll*age." *Theories and Documents of Contemporary Art.* Ed. Kristine Stiles and Peter Selz. Berkeley: U of California P, 1996. 724-25. Print.

———. "Manifesto." *Theories and Documents of Contemporary Art.* Ed. Kristine Stiles and Peter Selz. Berkeley: U of California P, 1996. 723. Print.

Further Reading

Farmer, John Alan. *Art into Television.* New York: Columbia UP, 1998. *Proquest.* Web. 10 Sept. 2012.

Hoffman, Katherine. "Collage in the Twentieth Century: An Overview." *Collage: Critical Views.* Ed. Katherine Ann Hoffman. Ann Arbor: UMI Research, 1989. 1-38. Print.

James, Sara. "Art of Two Germanys/Cold War Cultures." *Art Monthly* Dec. 2009: 21. *Gale Academic OneFile.* Web. 10 Sept. 2012.

Mesch, Claudia. *Modern Art at the Berlin Wall: Demarcating Culture in the Cold War Germanys.* London: I. B. Tauris, 2009. *Elibrary.* Web. 10 Sept. 2012.

Stonard, John-Paul. "Carré d'Art." *Artforum International* 47.1 (2008): 476. *Gale Academic OneFile.* Web. 10 Sept. 2012.

Taylor, Brandon. *Urban Walls: A Generation of Collage in Europe and America.* New York: Hudson Hills, 2008. Print.

Gregory Luther

important statement about Vostell's aesthetic aims. According to Lima, Vostell "continued to organize events and participatory works, but without the topicality and urgency of his production in these earlier years." "Manifesto," however, and its concept of décollage have prevailed as the driving aesthetic principle in Vostell's art. The document has attracted some scholarly interest within the context of the history of the Fluxus Group and the European performance art scene at large.

MANIFESTO

Lebbeus Woods

OVERVIEW

In his 1992 essay "Manifesto," which first appeared in the journal *A+U, Architecture and Urbanism,* Lebbeus Woods makes it clear that he is at war, although his specific targets are less defined. His nebulous cluster of concerns includes "time," "history," "authority," "icons," and "finalities." Of primary interest, however, is architecture. Woods, a cofounder of the Research Institute for Experimental Architecture, regards architecture as a Nietzschean battlefield, saying, "Architecture is war. War is architecture." At the same time, architecture can offer salvation; it is, as Woods writes in his essay, "a constructor of worlds … a silhouette against the darkening sky." He sees himself as an outsider, as someone who does not "fit in" and has "no home, no family, no doctrine." In his text, he does not address a particular audience or even identify himself. Instead, he mysteriously says, "I cannot know your name … [n]or can you know mine."

The text was, and continues to be, met with both admiration and bewilderment among architects and the public. "Manifesto" is in many ways a reflection of Woods's experimental approach to architecture. In his 1993 book *Theory and Experimentation,* Andreas Papadakis compares Woods's designs and drawings to those of Marcel Duchamp, a founder of the Dada movement, and Giovanni Piranesi, creator of fantastic prison etchings that influenced the surrealists. Although the messages in Woods's cryptic essay continue to be debated, his influence as a visionary is such that he has come to be considered, according to Geoff Manaugh in a 2012 article for *BLDGBLOG,* "the avant-garde of the avant-garde."

HISTORICAL AND LITERARY CONTEXT

For Woods, who died in 2012, architecture was a political tool, a means of shaping society. As he states in "Manifesto," "Architecture … has to do with the relations between people and how they decide to change their conditions … Architecture is a prime instrument in making that change." Manaugh places Woods's radicalism in the context of contemporary architecture: "Woods's work is the exclamation point at the end of a sentence proclaiming that the architectural imagination, freed from constraints of finance and buildability, should be uncompromising." Indeed, Woods believed that architecture is nothing short of a way to recreate the way we see and interact with the world. Manaugh writes, "One should imagine entirely new structures, spaces without walls, radically reconstructing the outermost possibilities of the built environment. If need be, we should re-think the very planet we stand on."

At the time "Manifesto" appeared in 1992, the globe was rapidly shrinking. The United States had lifted trade sanctions against China, the Cold War had ended, and the North American Free Trade Agreement was soon to be signed. In architecture, deconstruction, a postmodern style defined by unpredictability, was a dominant trend. Herb Greene's Chicken House in Norman, Oklahoma, perhaps the first postmodern structure, had turned thirty-one years old; JFK International Airport's TWA Flight Center, designed by Woods's mentor Earo Saarinen, was thirty; and the Centre Georges Pompidou in Paris was fifteen. Furthermore, the ideas in the 1977 Charles Jencks classic *The Language of Post-modern Architecture* had taken hold, as evidenced by the postmodernist AT&T Building (later called the Sony Tower) in New York City, which was designed by Philip Johnson. Each of these events rocked the architecture field and startled, if not offended, the public. The world was as ready as it ever would be for the science fiction visions of Woods.

Woods's "Manifesto" shares a number of elements with other manifestos of the twentieth century: it is brief (150 words long), relies on hyperbolic prose, and is impassioned. Tristan Tzara's *Dada Manifesto* (1918) and the Bread and Puppet Theater's *Cheap Art Manifesto* (1984) also fall into this category. With his 150 words, Woods creates the mission statement for a subfield of architecture known as visionary architecture, or architecture that generally cannot be built. The value of his text lies not in its realistic proposals for buildings, of which there are none, but rather in how he expands the ways architects think about what they do.

As a young architect in the 1970s, Woods had a more standard approach and proposed modern designs that were completed. At that same time, architects such as Robert Venturi and Denise Scott Brown were challenging the modernist notion of the square building. Impressed by their new ideas, Woods began to migrate toward spontaneity and unpredictability.

❖ *Key Facts*

Time Period:
Late 20th Century

Movement/Issue:
Visionary architecture;
Postmodernism

Place of Publication:
United States

Language of Publication:
English

LEBBEUS WOODS: HUMANITARIAN

Lebbeus Woods's first public reading of "Manifesto" took place on November 26, 1993, a year after its publication, as he stood on the steps of the ruins of the Olympic Museum in Sarajevo. At that moment, he would have been an easy target for Serbian snipers and artillery gunners, but he delivered the reading without incident. He felt strongly that architecture was part of the cause of the killing of the thousands of innocent men, women, and children in the region. Logically, then, he believed architecture had to be part of the solution.

The Bosnians, not having access to architects, had improvised crude, makeshift repairs of their war-damaged buildings. Woods felt that this demoralizing environment, lived in by people who had been accustomed to a refined culture, played into the hands of the terrorists. For the Bosnians to survive, they needed a sense of order in their lives, which Woods believed architecture could provide. Few architects have demonstrated humanitarianism so inextricably entwined with their professional activities; thus Woods was respected as much for his humanitarianism as for his architectural vision.

Yet instead of becoming just another clever designer of original shapes for human occupancy, he emerged as a visionary who stretched the thinking about a particular discipline. Metaphorically, he both raised the bar (1994's *Havana, radically reconstructed,* which is intended to rise above the ground) and lowered it (1999's *Lower Manhattan,* which is intended to sink below the ground). Woods's influence on his field must be measured in general terms rather than by counting the number of architects who have patterned their work after his, because few today do.

THEMES AND STYLE

In "Manifesto," architecture is more of a concept than a reality. The word "architecture" is mentioned three times in the document's first three sentences. Woods references the term again when he says, "I am an architect." However, little else in his work is specifically about architecture, which is not what one would expect. Much of the text takes the form of surrealistic, stream-of-consciousness blank verse. Woods claims to be guilty of "falseness" and "pitiful fears," a person with "no known beginning or end, no 'sacred and primordial site.'" He is "a constructor of worlds, a sensualist who worships the flesh, the melody, a silhouette against the darkening sky." As with his architectural drawings and proposals, Woods's "Manifesto" is not to be taken literally. In this respect, it is similar to a surrealistic painting.

Starting with the opening line—"Architecture and war are not incompatible"—Woods's aim is to startle the reader. He makes repeated use of war metaphors with phrases such as "I am at war" and "I declare war," giving the document a violent tone. On the one hand, he portrays himself as part of a larger struggle, saying, "I am one of millions" and "Tomorrow, we begin together." On the other hand, he is a lone soldier struggling against the odds, as exemplified by phrases such as "I am at war," and "I declare war." Either way, the concept of fierce upheaval permeates the document.

Woods's text runs the gamut of emotions, opening with despairing, angry cries ("I am at war"), moving toward words of alienation ("I … do not fit in"), and ending on a hopeful note ("Tomorrow, we begin together"). The bleakness of the beginning and the middle gives Woods credibility with the audience because he makes it clear that he will not sugarcoat anything. Thus, the positive ending resonates even more powerfully. In its totality, the text reflects his architectural drawings: compelling imagery, deep passion, singular originality, and ultimate hope for humanity.

CRITICAL DISCUSSION

Woods's "Manifesto," along with his other activities, served to elevate his profile in the 1990s. In 1993 he read his text publicly in war-torn Sarajevo, subjecting himself to the possibility of Serbian sniper attack. During this period, he also created a body of dreary, war-ravaged cityscapes, many of which were designed as shelters for the conflict's victims. He even constructed life-sized models of some of these structures. He was not alone in his social consciousness. Dutch artist Constant Nieuwenhuys, avant-garde architectural group Archigram (based in London), and architectural firm Superstudio (Florence) were conjuring mechanized pedestrian cities and humane megastructures encompassing vast expanses of desert and mountain terrain. The efforts of writer and filmmaker Guy Debord and the neo-Marxist group Situationist International (for which Nieuwenhuys worked) also encouraged oppositionist thinking.

Woods became a hero to architectural students who coveted originality. Projects such as 1980's *Einstein's Tomb* (a space station in which the great physicist's remains would drift endlessly through the universal void) and *Lower Manhattan* (a proposal to dam the north ends of the Hudson and East rivers to create huge trenches for human habitation), combined with written works such as "Manifesto," made Woods a unique voice in the field. Indeed, the notion of the concept in architecture would be forever expanded because of his ideas. Prior to his death, the website for the European Graduate School, where Woods was a professor of visionary architecture (he also taught at the Cooper Union School of Architecture in New York City), stated, "Lebbeus Woods is a revolutionary, experimental, and theoretical architect.

He is regarded as the most original architectural visionary alive today."

Today more than ever, architecture is big business. The field has superstars such as Rem Koolhaas and Daniel Libeskind, who design world-class fine-art warehouses and residential towers for the rich. Woods showed no interest in following this trend. Architecture writer Nicolai Ouroussoff suggests that Woods stood alone among today's major architects, given that social justice is no longer part of the conversation in the field. In a 2008 interview with Ouroussoff in the *New York Times,* Woods states, "With the triumph of liberal democracy and laissez-faire capitalism, the conversation came to an end … What interests me is what the world would be like if we were free of conventional limits. Maybe I can show what could happen if we lived by a different set of rules."

BIBLIOGRAPHY

Sources

"Lebbeus Woods Biography." *European Graduate School.* European Graduate School, n. d. Web. 5 Oct. 2012.

Manaugh, Geoff. "Without Walls: An Interview with Lebbeus Woods." *BLDGBLOG.* Blogspot, 1 Oct. 2012. Web. 4 Oct. 2012.

Ouroussoff, Nicolai. "An Architect Unshackled by the Limits of the Real World." *New York Times.* New York Times, 25 Aug. 2008. Web. 18 Oct. 2012.

Papadakis, Andreas, ed. *Theory and Experimentation.* London: Papadakis, 1993. Print.

Woods, Lebbeus. *Lebbeus Woods: Anarchitecture Architecture Is a Political Act.* Architectural Monographs 22. Hoboken: John Wiley and Sons, 1992. Print.

———. "War and Architecture: The Sarajevo Window." *Lebbeuswoods.* Wordpress, 2 Dec. 2011. Web. 7 Oct. 2012.

Further Reading

Research Institute for Experimental Architecture. "Concept Series." *Research Institute for Experimental Architecture.* RIEA.ch, n.d. Web. 5 Oct. 2012.

Woods, Lebbeus. "Lebbeus Woods." *Lebbeuswoods.* Lebbeus Woods, n.d. Web. 3 Oct. 2012.

———. *The New City.* New York: Touchstone Books, 1992. Print.

———. "The Reality of Theory." *Lebbeuswoods.* Wordpress, 6 Feb. 2008. Web. 5 Oct. 2012.

———. *War and Architecture.* New York: Princeton Architectural Press, 2002. Print.

Dennis Fehr

Ambrogio Lorenzetti' fresco depicting the construction of city walls in Palazzo Pubblico, Siena, Italy, circa 1340.
THE ART ARCHIVE/ PALAZZO PUBBLICO SIENA/ COLLECTION DAGLI ORTI

NOTES ON THE FORMATION OF AN IMAGINIST BAUHAUS

Asger Jorn

✢ *Key Facts*

Time Period:
Mid-20th Century

Movement/Issue:
Aesthetics; Avant-gardism; Bauhaus

Place of Publication:
France

Language of Publication:
French

OVERVIEW

In 1954 Asger Jorn wrote *Notes on the Formation of an Imaginist Bauhaus* as a reaction against the plans of architect Max Bill to re-create the Bauhaus, an art school that emerged in Germany between the world wars and was closed under the Nazis, who opposed the avant-garde. Jorn wrote the document for the eponymous International Movement for an Imaginist Bauhaus (IMIB), a small avant-garde group that emerged from the breakup of CoBrA, a band of Marxist artists whose name derived from the first letters of the cities where they lived: Copenhagen, Brussels, and Amsterdam. A year earlier, Jorn, a former CoBrA member, had sent a note about Bill's plan to Sergio Dangelo and Enrico Baj, the founders of the Italian Arte Nucleare Movement (ANM), a collection of artists who believed the answer to a peaceful world lay in science. The note read in part, "Bill ... wishes to make an academy without painting, without research into the imagination, fantasy, signs, symbols—all he wants is technical instruction. In the name of experimental artists I intend to create an International Movement for an Imaginist Bauhaus."

Dangelo and Baj agreed to join forces with Jorn, whom they saw as a kindred spirit in their fight against pedantry in art education. Indeed, a portion of ANM's manifesto reads: "The Nuclearists desire to demolish all the 'isms' of a painting that ... lapses into academicism.... They desire and have the power to recreate painting." The IMIB then issued a statement claiming that "experimental artists must get hold of industrial means and subject them to their own non-utilitarian ends." Little did the group's members know that in 1968 its agenda would contribute to student rioting in the streets of Paris—or that they would participate in the riots as leaders.

HISTORICAL AND LITERARY CONTEXT

Notes on the Formation of an Imaginist Bauhaus responds to the political and artistic situation in Western Europe after the Second World War. The roots of the IMIB can be traced back to the original Bauhaus movement, which emerged in Germany in the early 1920s and sought to unify art and technology. The aim of that unification was social progress and, eventually, a utopian merger of culture, technology, and society. Jorn's effort to revive the Bauhaus was not his first attempt to recall and renew prior avant-garde movements. In the late 1940s he sought to initiate a new surrealist movement guided explicitly by Marxist ideology. The result was Revolutionary Surrealism, which was short-lived. Upon its collapse, Jorn helped found CoBrA, a new Marxist art movement that repudiated surrealism in favor of a strain of modernism influenced by primitivism. CoBrA lasted from 1948 to 1951. Also in the early 1950s, the ANM emerged in Italy. Influenced by the Concrete Art movement that Bill started in the 1930s, the ANM offered a response to the destructiveness of the new atomic age.

When Jorn wrote *Notes on the Formation of an Imaginist Bauhaus* in 1954, numerous left-wing avant-garde movements were active in Europe. Lettrism, which sought to undermine the bourgeois conceptions of language as a vessel of meaning, had been established in Paris. The London Psychogeographical Association, which concerned itself with "the specific effects of geographical environment on the emotions and behavior of individuals," was active in England. In Italy the ANM was drawing together artists from across the continent to invent new artistic forms. When Bill founded a school of creative design in Ulm, Germany, that was based on the original Bauhaus emphasis on technique and imitation, Jorn issued his manifesto to counter the idea of returning to a conception of art as a craft. In the document he declares that IMIB is "abandoning all efforts at pedagogical action and moving toward experimental activity."

As twentieth-century art became more abstract, and as educational art programs failed to give the public the language to understand it, art movements felt a growing need to explain their work. Like the statements of other avant-garde groups, the IMIB manifesto uses elaborate prose to proclaim that art can heal humanity—if only humanity will sit up and listen. The first such document of note is that of the Dadaists. It emerged in 1918 as World War I raged, and its impassioned rhetoric was in large part a response to the numbing realization that humanity was capable of global conflict. Manifestos proliferated in the decades that followed the war. These documents are priceless in terms of understanding the last century's art, but one could argue that their goal of healing humanity met with little success.

The influence of art manifestos, including that of IMIB, waned as the pop movement returned imagery to art in the 1960s and public opinion toward contemporary art softened. By the postmodern 1980s, no single style or group of styles dominated the art world; therefore, categorizing art via the manifestos of various "-isms" was no longer useful. Art manifestos still occasionally appear, but contemporary artists for the most part have come to rely on the individual "artist's statement," a more tepid version of its predecessor. Some statements are well written and engaging, but as a group such tracts tend to lack the passion, earnestness, and social concern of the twentieth-century art manifesto. Yet because IMIB's manifesto addresses art education more directly than art itself, its influence may be said to continue. The imaginative, rather than technical, approach continues to be debated, at times hotly, in art education programs.

ASGER JORN, NORDIC ARTIST

Understanding Asger Jorn requires awareness of his strong sense of identity as a Nordic artist. He was intensely conscious of how perceptions of art and culture and, in some ways, life itself, differed between southern and northern Europe. Although expressionism emerged from the northern countries, Italy had the Renaissance and France most of the early modernists. In his work *Alpha and Omega* (published posthumously), he wrote, "Nordic art casts a spell on the mind that ranges from laughter to tears and from tears to violent rage. One can see how dangerous it is; a cynical person can tyrannize us with the power of art."

These words are indicative of the impact of another Nordic artist, Edvard Munch, who died in 1944, when Jorn was thirty. Munch influenced Jorn not only artistically but also in terms of his outlook and temperament. The tension between southern European artists and Nordic artists could have been dispiriting to Jorn, but it seemed to be a source of creativity for him. Born in the north, he could have become a prisoner of place, but as Troels Andersen points out in his piece on the artist in *The Situationist International (1957-72)*, Jorn was "one of the few able to escape and survive."

Extase inquiétante, painted by Asger Jorn in 1956, the year before he wrote *Notes on the Formation of an Imaginist Bauhaus.*
© PETER HORREE/ALAMY

THEMES AND STYLE

The primary theme of *Notes on the Formation of an Imaginist Bauhaus* is that academic art instruction dampens creativity and therefore artistic success. A free environment that encourages experimentation, on the other hand, enhances creativity. In 1948 Constant Nieuwenhuys, a member of CoBrA, included in that group's manifesto a fundamental statement that summarizes a substantial portion of Jorn's argument:

> [Destruction] forms the key to the liberation of the human spirit from passivity. It is the basic precondition for the flowering of a people's art…. The satisfaction of this primitive need … is the driving force of life, the cure for every form of vital weakness. It transforms art into a power for spiritual health. As such it is the property of all…. [E]very limitation that reduces art to the reserve of a small group of specialists, connoisseurs, and virtuosi must be removed.

This sentiment is echoed not only in IMIB's manifesto but also in those of the other groups that joined Situationist International. The late 1940s and 1950s witnessed the space race, widespread fear of communism, an army general in the White House, and the growth of the U.S. capitalist economy—matters of concern to the Marxist-leaning members of IMIB and the other Situationists. They very optimistically offered their manifestos to the world as correctives.

Notes on the Formation of an Imaginist Bauhaus is authored by an articulate and careful thinker. With concision, clarity, and lack of jargon, Jorn critiques the "old" Bauhaus: "The leaders of the old Bauhaus were great masters with exceptional talents, but they were bad teachers. The pupils' works were only pious imitations of their masters'. The real influence of the latter was indirect, by force of example: [British art critic John] Ruskin on [Flemish painter and architect Henry] van de Velde, van de Velde on [German architect and Bauhaus founder Walter] Gropius." The mimicry that such linearity implied obviously offended Jorn. His critique of pedagogy, and even the presence of subject matter itself, influenced other fields around the globe, most particularly art education.

CRITICAL DISCUSSION

When *Notes on the Formation of an Imaginist Bauhaus* first appeared in 1954, its message resonated within the European avant-garde community, particularly in Italy. The manifesto garnered enough support that, in 1955, the International Movement for an Imaginist Bauhaus successfully founded a laboratory in Alba, Italy, for "free artistic research." The laboratory was not an instructional institution; rather, it offered "new possibilities for artistic experimentation." Although the laboratory was short-lived, the position Jorn articulated in *Notes on the Formation of an Imaginist Bauhaus* appealed to members and former members of the various left-wing art groups and catalyzed their unification under the rubric of the Situationist International in 1957.

A movement of artists, activists, and theorists, the Situationist International was formed in Alba during the International Congress of Free Artists, a meeting that brought together members of the IMIB, ANM, London Psychogeographical Association, and Lettrist International, among others. The Situationists were devoted to overthrowing the capitalist system, which they viewed as dehumanizing and oppressive. Capitalism, the group's principal thinker Guy Debord famously argued, had created a "society of spectacle," one in which humans were mere passive spectators of a culture designed only for the benefit of capital. As an antidote, the Situationists increasingly called for open revolution and insurrection. This culminated, in May of 1968, with widespread student protests in France. The IMIB's manifesto, which called for an experimental approach to art education that would allow artists to assume a primary role in the capitalist age, is viewed by critics as an important precedent to the later program of the Situationists.

Although no Imaginist Bauhaus school materialized, critiques of curriculum-centered education, including the IMIB manifesto, were popular during the third quarter of the twentieth century. As public frustration grew toward the abstract imagery of the art world's avant-garde, artists and art educators unhelpfully withdrew art history, critical viewing skills, and aesthetic philosophy from art curricula. These developments resulted in generations of artistically unschooled adults. They also ensured art's status as a marginal subject in academia and as a peripheral component of contemporary culture.

Beginning in the 1970s, art education began to move away from the approach advocated in *Notes on the Formation of an Imaginist Bauhaus*. The first change of note was a model called Discipline-Based Art Education (DBAE). Donald Crawford describes this approach in his 1987 article in *Journal of Aesthetic Education*: "[DBAE] involves a knowledge of the theories and contexts of art and abilities to respond to as well as to create art…. Content for instruction is derived primarily from the disciplines of aesthetics, art criticism, art history, and art production."

The second profound change was the inclusion of critical theory, which drew on issues of fairness relating to race, gender, and class. Jorn's manifesto had become something to react against. As significant as IMIB's pedagogical theories were in the third quarter of the last century, they might not be its primary contribution to the art world. The manifesto might rather be remembered for simply invigorating the conversation about art education.

BIBLIOGRAPHY

Sources

Andersen, Troels. "Asger Jorn and the Situationist International: On the Passage of a Few People through a Brief Moment in Time." *The Situationist International (1957-1972)*. Boston: MIT P/ICA, 1989. 62-66. Print.

Crawford, Donald. "Discipline-Based Art Education: Becoming Students of Art." *Journal of Aesthetic Education* 21.2 (1987): 135-41. Print.

Home, Stewart. *The Assault on Culture.* 2nd ed. London: AK, 1991. Print.

Jorn, Asger. *Alpha and Omega.* Copenhagen: Borgen, 1964. Print.

———. *Notes on the Formation of an Imaginist Bauhaus.* 1957. *Situationist International Online.* Web. 19 Oct. 2012.

Further Reading

Adorno, Theodor, and Max Horkheimer. *Dialectic of Enlightenment.* Stanford: Stanford UP, 2002. Print.

Dahms, Harry. *No Social Science without Critical Theory.* Bingley, UK: Emerald, 2008. Print.

Debord, Guy. "Introduction to a Critique of Urban Geography." *Les Lèvres Nues* Sept. 1955: 23-35. Print.

———. *The Society of the Spectacle.* Cambridge, MA: Zone, 1988. Print.

Garoian, Charles R. *Performing Pedagogy: Toward an Art of Politics.* Albany: State U of New York P, 1999. Print.

Gripsrud, Jostein, and Lennart Weibull. *Media, Markets & Public Spheres: European Media at the Crossroads.* Chicago: U of Chicago P, 2010. Print.

Lowenfeld, Viktor. *Creative and Mental Growth.* New York: McMillan, 1947. Print.

Stiles, Kristine, and Peter Selz, eds. *Theories and Documents of Contemporary Art: A Sourcebook of Artists' Writings.* Los Angeles: U of California P, 1994. Print.

Dennis Fehr

SENTENCES ON CONCEPTUAL ART

Sol LeWitt

❖ *Key Facts*

Time Period:
Mid-20th Century

Movement/Issue:
Conceptualism; Avant-gardism; Aesthetics

Place of Publication:
United States

Language of Publication:
English

OVERVIEW

Written by American artist Sol LeWitt, *Sentences on Conceptual Art* (1969) outlines the foundational premises of the conceptual art movement of the late 1960s. Stemming from a reaction against formalism, LeWitt proclaims, through a series of thirty-five declarative sentences, that art does not need to be logical. Unlike the formalist aesthetic, which places all value and meaning within an art object regardless of contextual elements, LeWitt focuses on the process of creating a work, a practice that allows an artist to move away from the object and instead highlight the idea that produced the work of art. Similar to structuralist and post-structuralist philosophy that emerged after World War II, LeWitt posits that there is a concept that underlies an object, and he points to the arbitrariness in assigning meaning to objects.

Upon its publication in the journal *Art-Language,* the manifesto was celebrated and dismissed by the competing aesthetic circles of its time. Some applauded LeWitt's efforts to move art away from the increasingly commercialized art world and articulate a challenge to the ontological category of art. Adherents to modernist and formalist aesthetics, however, derided the artist's efforts, claiming that his principles were prescriptive in nature, violated perception, and inhibited interpretation of a work. Seen as a major expression of minimalist and conceptual concerns, the thirty-five statements in *Sentences on Conceptual Art* detail the role of an artist and the artist's relationship with his or her audience and set out to describe how a concept can remain a work of art even when the concept is devoid of an object. In the years since the manifesto was published, artists and critics have wrestled with its implications, and its influence can still be seen in major artistic trends in pop, digital, and performance art.

HISTORICAL AND LITERARY CONTEXT

Sentences on Conceptual Art responds to the prevailing feeling at the time that conceptual art is a rationalist enterprise firmly grounded in modernist avant-garde aesthetics. LeWitt, however, presents a model in which the actual completion of a work is secondary to the dynamic concept that initiated the piece. He does not suggest that the object itself is completely obsolete, since the process of creating art still necessitates an end result; rather, *Sentences on Conceptual Art* offers a descriptive method whereby an artist can transcend formalist definitions. By focusing on the process involved in producing a work, LeWitt foregrounds an artist over his or her final product. A work of art becomes almost incidental to the actual concept. In a sense, LeWitt liberates the work from prescriptive aesthetics that attempt to designate what is and what is not art.

At the time of its publication, *Sentences on Conceptual Art* was one of many attempts to question the ontological categories of art. Traditional notions held that there was some universal definition of art; however, *Sentences* privileges experience over definition and offers a means by which the individual process is paramount. Similar to Claes Oldenburg's "I Am for an Art" (1961), which rejects abstract expressionism, and George Maciunas's *Fluxus Manifesto* (1963), which uses collage to illustrate the inherent uncertainty in language and expression, LeWitt's manifesto provides a framework by which artists could celebrate the viewer's subjective experience. The manifesto champions conceptual art but also maintains affinities with minimalist art, both of which remain vibrant and influential movements.

The manifesto can be seen as LeWitt's revision to his work *Paragraphs on Conceptual Art* (1967). Drawing upon the earlier manifesto, he pares down his aesthetic by focusing on the most essential components of the process and, unlike in *Paragraphs on Conceptual Art,* permits a more open-ended interpretation of his tenets. In *Sentences,* LeWitt focuses on the difference between a concept and the execution of that concept, but he also allows for more play in the relationship between an artist and his or her audience by providing room for multiple interpretations and experiences to exist simultaneously. Arguing against rationalist motifs such as the principle of non-contradiction, LeWitt advances an aesthetic that allows ideas that are theoretically mutually exclusive to exist without negating each other. In its most radical sense, the manifesto postulates a form of artistic expression in which visual art does not necessarily need to be visual.

The manifesto sparked a rich theoretical debate among artists, critics, scholars, and the general public about both the nature of art and the role it plays in society. Although this was not a new discussion, the seemingly open-ended nature of conceptual art challenged the theoretical core of modernist aesthetics. The focus on process marked a step away from formalism and opened the door for a variety of new modes of expression, including installation, performance, and political feminist art. Much of contemporary art is highly indebted to the ideas that LeWitt articulated.

THEMES AND STYLE

Sentences on Conceptual Art is primarily concerned with rescuing art from the rigidity of formalism by illustrating how the idea or concept of art trumps the physical execution of a work. LeWitt begins by stating that "Conceptual Artists are mystics rather than rationalists. They leap to conclusions that logic cannot reach." Through the thirty-four statements that follow, he demonstrates how rational judgments impede artistic experience and only serve as a means to repeat what has already been accomplished by past artists. The manifesto suggests that artists ought to pursue the idea that generated the work and that "irrational thoughts should be followed absolutely and logically." Only by allowing a concept to develop free of artistic intent, he argues, can an artist truly create a unified experience in which the ideas, concept, and object complement one another. LeWitt further states that art is fundamentally a means to alter perceptions

SOL LeWITT: CONCEPTUAL PIONEER

Sol LeWitt (1928-2007) is primarily remembered for ushering art from the confines of formalism into the more playful realm of conceptual art. Although he focused mainly on wall drawings, LeWitt also participated in a variety of media, including photography and painting. Throughout his career, he championed artistic ideas, sometimes at the expense of the artist and the work. His own art focused on line, color, and simplified shapes that he would organize to stimulate thought. His lines, for instance, would appear to be random; however, the structure of the piece would be governed by a mathematical principle or an appeal to architecture.

As his career progressed, LeWitt attempted to efface the hand of the individual artist even more by employing assistants; he believed that the idea could be infinitely translated and repeated if the instructions were adequately articulated. In this, he further challenged notions of art by calling into question the notion of authorship. He believed that if the emphasis was on the process, the work need not be tied to a specific narrative or intention. New perspectives allowed for ideas to be carried out in similar fashion, creating an artistic object that existed for its own sake and not at the whim of the artist's ego or current artistic trends. LeWitt's legacy continues to be seen in digital and programming art, where the interaction between artists allows for a give and take of ideas and interpretations.

Sol LeWitt's Serial Project, I (ABCD), 1966. DIGITAL IMAGE © THE MUSEUM OF MODERN ART/LICENSED BY SCALA/ART RESOURCE, NY

through innovative and transformative concepts: through the subjective perception of the artists, the audience encounters new concepts that, in turn, lead to new ideas that challenge conventions. Art, for LeWitt, is a process with "many side-effects that the artist cannot imagine."

LeWitt develops his argument by appealing to the idea that experience and perspective are more legitimate grounds for expression than a formally structured work of art. Throughout the manifesto, he plays upon the binary oppositions between rational judgments and spontaneous experience. LeWitt envisions an artistic experience in which an artist can transcend traditional categories and "limitations on the artist who would be reluctant to make art that goes beyond the limitations." The conceptual framework flows from sentence to sentence as each idea is explored, allowing the next sentence to form a new concept. Since *Sentences on Conceptual Art* develops a single concept with ideas that support the document, it could be argued that it is a work of conceptual art; however, LeWitt ends the manifesto with the paradoxical statement that "these sentences comment on art, but are not art."

Sentences on Conceptual Art achieves its goal by presenting seemingly irreconcilable oppositions. LeWitt establishes an initial set of premises in the manifesto by situating rational judgments against illogical ones, illustrating how rational judgments rein in artistic expression and aesthetic experience; however, he counters that "irrational thoughts should be followed absolutely and logically." The apparent contradiction is reconciled by the eleventh sentence, in which LeWitt states that while "ideas do not necessarily proceed in logical order," each idea must reach completion before a new idea is formed and followed. Written in the mode of a logical proof, the manifesto allows the single concept to generate ideas, but it also follows its own internal logic, allowing for new ideas and expressions to emerge. By parodying formalist structures, the manifesto illustrates how ideas and concepts are more important than form or execution. Sentence 32 states that "banal ideas cannot be rescued by beautiful execution," serving as a scathing critique of contemporary art as well as an invitation to take LeWitt's project to task on its own merits.

CRITICAL DISCUSSION

Although *Sentences on Conceptual Art* attempted to articulate a way in which art could transcend its commodity status, many critics and artists differed in their interpretation of its tenets. In *End Moments* (1969), artist Dan Graham praises LeWitt and considers him a major influence on his own artistic projects. Some formalist critics argued that conceptual art's focus on process negated artistic ability, and they lamented the collapse of the division between high and low art. Critics such as Clement Greenberg found that

conceptual art played upon a nonexistent function of taste that betrayed the goals of earlier avant-garde art. In *Homemade Esthetics: Observations on Art and Taste* (2000), Greenberg considers conceptual art "all surprise without satisfaction." He concludes that conceptual art's desire to create an aesthetic sphere that resisted commodification did so at the expense of structures and form and relegated art "as a one-time move that has to be trumped." For Greenberg, the moment celebrated by conceptual art created only a self-serving art world that submerged its audience in boredom and artistic egos.

Over the years, conceptual art has gone in and out of favor, yet its legacy and enduring influence on contemporary art are difficult to ignore. *Sentences on Conceptual Art* placed the focus back on the artist, allowing him or her to articulate an artistic vision that did not need to adhere to aesthetic principles. Performance artists such as Carolee Schneemann contested traditional artistic conventions by revolting against the male-centered art world that ignored the body as a necessary component to human emotions. Conceptual artists in general attempted to upend the museum-dominated world by placing value in the ideas that generated the work, ostensibly resisting the commodity structure surrounding traditional aesthetic categories such as beauty and symmetry. Concepts also allowed for seemingly disparate objects to relate to one another. In a 2010 article in *Art Monthly* discussing LeWitt's serial phase, Stephen Bury suggests that "each object photographed relates to each other simply through a common ownership: they are tied inseparably to one another through the notion of collection." Since its initial publication in 1969, LeWitt's *Sentences* has become a foundational tenet in modern art, despite at times being watered down or taken out of context.

Contemporary scholarship surrounding *Sentences on Conceptual Art* focuses more upon its aesthetic legacy in contemporary art than it does upon the manifesto's individual statements. At the 2010 conference "Artists Publications and the Legacy of Sol LeWitt," Chloe Brown suggested that the creation of artist books allowed for a "democratic means of disseminating ideas to a wider audience. In doing so, the artists' publication challenged the preciousness of the unique work of art." Other scholars have called attention to the difficulty of determining the concept that lies behind a work. In his 2010 essay in *Journal of Aesthetic Education*, Michael Weh suggests that there is no reliable, objective source that can determine the intention of a work of art and there may be "a special problem concerning artists having no particular intention." For Weh, the issue lies in determining when an instance of the object occurs, which, in turn, challenges some of the long-standing paradigms of artistic integrity. Other contemporary scholars find similarities between conceptual art and technologically driven art. In his 2002 article "Art in the Information Age: Technology and Conceptual Art," Edward A. Shanken argues that "advances in electronics, computing and telecommunications—and especially the advent of the Internet—have provided tools that enable artists to interrogate the conventional materiality and semiotic complexity of art objects in ways that were not available 30 years ago."

BIBLIOGRAPHY

Sources

Bury, Stephen. "Sol LeWitt." *Art Monthly* June 2010: 31. Print.

Brown, Chloe. "Artists Publications and the Legacy of Sol LeWitt." *Sheffield Hallam University Research Archive.* Sheffield Hallam University. Web. 11 July 2012.

Graham, Dan. *End Moments.* New York: n.p., 1969. Print.

Greenberg, Clement. *Homemade Esthetics: Observations on Art and Taste.* Oxford: Oxford UP, 2000. Print.

LeWitt, Sol. "Sentences on Conceptual Art." *Art and Its Significance.* 3rd ed. Ed. Stephen David Ross. New York: SUNY, 1994. 691-92. Print.

Shanken, Edward A. "Art in the Information Age: Technology and Conceptual Art." *Leonardo* 35.4 (2002): 433-38. *Project Muse.* Web. 12 July 2012.

Weh, Michael. "Production Determines Category: An Ontology of Art." *Journal of Aesthetic Education* 44.1 (2010): 84-99. *Project Muse.* Web. 09 July 2012.

Further Reading

Alberro, Alexander, and Blake Stimson. *Conceptual Art a Critical Anthology.* Cambridge: MIT UP, 2000. Print.

Buskirk, Martha. *The Contingent Object of Contemporary Art.* Cambridge: MIT UP, 2003. Print.

Meyer, James. *Minimalism: Art and Polemics in the Sixties.* 2nd ed. New Haven: Yale UP, 2004. Print.

Mitchell, W.J.T., ed. "Voices Off: Reflections on Conceptual Art." *Critical Inquiry* 33.1 (2006): 113-35. Print.

Ostrow, Saul, and Sol LeWitt. "Sol LeWitt." *BOMB* 85 (2003): 22-29. Print.

Stimson, Blake. "Conceptual Work and Conceptual Waste." *Discourse* 24.2 (2002): 121-51. Print.

Josh Harteis

THE STUCKISTS

Billy Childish, Charles Thomson

⸙ *Key Facts*

Time Period:
Late 20th Century

Movement/Issue:
Stuckism; Anti-
conceptualism;
Aesthetics

Place of Publication:
England

**Language of
Publication:**
English

OVERVIEW

Composed by Billy Childish and Charles Thomson, *The Stuckists* (1999) rails against postmodern art and advocates a return to figurative, painterly explorations of the self. The manifesto serves as an announcement of the formation of the Stuckists, a group of primarily British artists dedicated to creating figurative art and combating conceptual art. The group and its manifesto were a response to the trend toward conceptualism that had started in the 1970s and was spectacularly revived in Britain in the 1990s, when a group of shocking new conceptualists known as the Young British Artists (YBAs) came to dominate the British art scene and market. Led by Damien Hirst and Tracey Emin—whose admonition that Childish's paintings were "stuck" gave the Stuckists their name—the YBAs were known for making flashy postmodern spectacles. *The Stuckists* rejects the perceived commercialization, cleverness, and irony of the YBAs and other contemporary conceptualists and instead pursues "authenticity" and accessibility through the traditional medium of paint.

When the manifesto first appeared in 1999, it engendered a debate about the state of British art at the end of the twentieth century. The manifesto also led to the formation of the Stuckists, a group of painters who exhibited throughout Britain, spread internationally, and led an assault on the perceived excesses and errors of conceptualism. This assault included protests and demonstrations against the British art establishment and involved the issuance of other manifestos that continued the critique of conceptualism, elaborating the call for a return to painterly expression. Today *The Stuckists* is considered an important contribution to the ongoing debate about the merits and limitations of conceptualism and of figurative painting.

HISTORICAL AND LITERARY CONTEXT

The Stuckists responds to the visual arts scene in Britain at the turn of the twenty-first century, when the YBAs dominated critical and popular attention. The YBAs were led by Hirst, a bold conceptual artist, who beginning in 1988, while he was still an art student, organized a series of shows around London that drew significant interest from dealers and curators. The art displayed by Hirst and his cohort was informed by a conceptual approach that drew from Dada, Fluxus, *arte povera,* and the conceptualism of the 1960s and 1970s. In 1991 Hirst displayed one of his most famous and controversial works: a tiger shark floating in a formaldehyde-filled glass tank. Titled *The Physical Impossibility of Death in the Mind of Someone Living,* the piece became symbolic of the attention-grabbing style of the YBAs.

By the time *The Stuckists* was issued in 1999, a backlash against the commercialism and conceptualism of the YBAs was growing but disorganized. Many critics, scholars, and artists argued that Hirst and his cohort merely "mindlessly recycled the tropes" of prior conceptual movements. The YBAs were also critiqued for their close relationship with the collector Charles Saatchi, who bought their paintings in bulk and relentlessly promoted them. Many commentators viewed Saatchi's dominance of the British art market as engendering gimmickry, hype, and conceptualism at the expense of more subtle, nuanced, and diverse kinds of work. In an attempt to catalyze an organized response to the YBAs, Childish and Thomson, who had been involved in the British art and music scenes since the late 1970s, came together to form Stuckism.

The Stuckists draws on a long history of art manifestos and draws, in particular, from previous manifestos authored by Childish and Thomson. These earlier manifestos laid the groundwork for *The Stuckists'* argument for more accessible and humane forms of art. First issued in 1978, Thomson's *Crude Art Manifesto* announced the founding of the Crude Art Society, which was formed "for the purpose of providing original works of art at an inexpensive price." The manifesto declares, "the exploration and expression of the human spirit, with whatever techniques are necessary, are the over-riding priorities," an argument that returned two decades later in *The Stuckists.* In the *Hangman Manifestos* of 1997 and 1998, Childish also paved the way for Stuckism. "Hangman Communication 0001," for example, begins, "Crimes of the future: The role of the artist against conceptualism and the idiocy of ideas."

After its publication, *The Stuckists* was followed by a series of polemical writings that expanded and clarified its argument about contemporary art. In January 2000 Childish and Thomson issued *Remodernism,* a manifesto that calls for a return to "the original principles of Modernism." With the subtitle "Towards a new spirituality in art," the manifesto advocates "highlighting vision as opposed to formalism" and foresees a "spiritual renaissance in art" led by Stuckism. One month later, in February 2000, the group issued an open letter to Sir Nicolas Serota, the director of Britain's foremost contemporary art museum, the Tate. In it they critiqued the museum's emphasis on postmodern forms and argued for the importance of painting. Throughout 2000 the group continued to issue polemics on contemporary British art.

THEMES AND STYLE

The central theme of *The Stuckists* is that postmodern and conceptual forms of art should be abandoned in favor of a return to expressionistic explorations in paint. The manifesto is preceded by an epigraph from Emin: "Your paintings are stuck, you are stuck! Stuck! Stuck! Stuck!" This is followed by a blunt statement of purpose set in boldface type: "Against conceptualism, hedonism and the cult of the ego-artist." Through the epigraph and statement of purpose, the manifesto's authors immediately set themselves in opposition to the reigning British art movement, that of the YBAs, and announce that their critique will be more than aesthetic. What follows is an assault not only on the style of contemporary conceptual and postmodern art but also on its attitude. In the twenty enumerated points that make up the manifesto, Childish and Thomson pose Stuckism as an antidote to the hedonism of the YBAs and other conceptualists.

The manifesto achieves its rhetorical effect by pitching the Stuckist agenda as an uncomplicated quest to explore shared human experience, while portraying conceptualism as an exclusive and esoteric realm for elitists. To that end, *The Stuckists'* first point is, "Stuckism is the quest for authenticity. By removing the mask of cleverness and admitting where we are, the Stuckist allows him/herself uncensored expression." The idea of art as an open-ended pursuit rather than as a commercial product is emphasized throughout. The manifesto declares, "The Stuckist is not a career artist but rather an amateur (*amare,* Latin, to love) who takes risks on the canvas rather than hiding behind ready-made objects (e.g. a dead sheep)." This self-professed amateurism serves to shrink the distance between the audience and the artist by identifying with the reader's presumed alienation from the conceptualism of modern art and by depicting Stuckism as "alive with all aspects of human experience."

Stylistically, *The Stuckists* is distinguished by an aphoristic quality that allows it to embrace openness and contradiction without abandoning directness of expression. The manifesto is premised on the idea that Stuckism offers a way out of the closed system of conceptual cleverness, which is emphasized by the plain and pithy declarations that begin the text. When, in the fourth point, the authors state, "Artists

BILLY CHILDISH: PROLIFIC PUNK

Billy Childish was born in the English seaside city of Kent. He had a difficult childhood and left school at the age of sixteen to work as an apprentice stonemason in a dockyard. He briefly attended art school before being expelled in 1981. However, his expulsion did not prevent him from continuing to make art. Over the next thirty years, he published more than forty volumes of poetry and several novels, formed numerous bands and recorded more than a hundred albums, wrote manifestos, made films, and produced thousands of paintings. Immensely prolific, he is widely lauded for the consistent quality and inventiveness of his work and for his commitment to the DIY ethos that informed the punk movement during his adolescence in the 1970s.

In the 1980s he met and dated artist Tracey Emin. After they broke up, Emin became increasingly interested in conceptualism and tried to interest Childish, too, though he resisted. When in the early 1990s he refused her invitation to view a performance piece of someone doing cocaine, she admonished him by saying, "Your paintings are stuck, you are stuck! Stuck! Stuck! Stuck!" In 1995 she included his name in her piece "Everyone I Have Ever Slept With 1963-1995." Four years later her upbraiding of Childish became the epigraph for *The Stuckists* and the inspiration for the movement's name. In 2001, however, Childish left the Stuckists, preferring to pursue instead his own idiosyncratic artistic vision.

who don't paint aren't artists," they make clear their unpretentiousness by embracing a traditional vision of artistic practice. In their final point, however, the authors employ a similar aphoristic formulation to make a more cryptic and sophisticated claim: "Stuckism embraces all that it denounces. We only denounce that which stops at the starting point—Stuckism starts at the stopping point!" This paradoxical statement allows Childish and Thomson to end their manifesto with a retreat from the prevailing attack and with a return to the sense of an open-ended quest that begins the text.

CRITICAL DISCUSSION

When *The Stuckists* was first published in 1999, it received a mixed response within the British cultural community. Simon Grant, writing in the *Evening Standard* in 1999, typifies the initial, ambivalent reaction to Stuckism and its first manifesto: "They have a 20-point manifesto that clearly lays out their stance, they have a self-appointed group of artists, led by Childish and Charles Thomson, and they have plenty of shins to kick against…. Again, the problem with Stuck-ism is the narrowness of its target, namely Saatchi's Sensation artists." In a 1999 article for London's *Sunday Times,* critic Rose Aidin writes, "It seems that in a confusing, Stuckist sort of way … the Stuckists are protesting against the cult of celebrity that sees Brit Artists pictured in gossip columns, endorsing

Billy Childish teaching painting in 2006. With Charles Thomson, Childish created the Stuckists, a 1999 manifesto expressing their theories about art. © GEORGE WILSON/ ALAMY

Stuckists proved effective as a mechanism of critique, they were less successful at initiating a new creative movement. However, their manifesto continues to garner critical attention, which has considered *The Stuckists'* legacy in aesthetic, cultural, and historical terms.

Some scholars have viewed *The Stuckists* and the group's other polemics within the context of a larger critique of postmodernism. In his book *Digimodernism: How New Technologies Dismantle the Postmodern and Reconfigure Our Culture* (2009), scholar Alan Kirby writes that the Stuckists' "words and gestures are, like the odd behavior of cattle before a storm, unwitting signals of wider, larger historico-cultural changes, which they don't comprehend." According to Kirby, the Stuckists did not help bring down postmodernism; rather they "chimed with the zeitgeist" by calling for an end to what was already dead. Commentators have also drawn attention to, and critiqued, the manifesto's call for a return to traditional painterly forms. Jonathan Jones in a 2009 article for the *Guardian* writes, "To say 'painting good, ready-made bad' is not a view of art—it's a prejudice…. It's a surrender, a nervous breakdown."

BIBLIOGRAPHY

Sources

Aidin, Rose. "No Tents, No Dead Animals, Please." *Sunday Times* (London) 1 Aug. 1999. *Academic OneFile.* Web. 11 Sept. 2012.

Childish, Billy. "Hangman Manifestos." *Stuckism International.* Stuckism International, 2000. Web. 11 Sept. 2012.

Childish, Billy, and Charles Thomson. *The Stuckists. Stuckism International.* Stuckism International, 1999. Web. 11 Sept. 2012.

Grant, Simon. "Call Me Neurotic but This 'Ism' Isn't Any Good." *Evening Standard* 24 Sept. 1999. *LexisNexis Academic.* Web. 11 Sept. 2012.

Jones, Jonathan. "The Stuckists Are Enemies of Art." *Guardian* (London) 2 Oct. 2009. Web. 11 Sept. 2012.

Kirby, Alan. *Digimodernism: How New Technologies Dismantle the Postmodern and Reconfigure Our Culture.* London: Continuum, 2009. Print.

O'Keefe, Alice. "How Ageing Art Punks Got Stuck into Tate's Serota." *Guardian* (London) 10 Dec. 2005. Web. 10 Sept. 2012.

Thomson, Charles. "Crude Art Manifesto." *Stuckism International.* Stuckism International, 1978. Web. 11 Sept. 2012.

Yanoshevsky, Galia. "Three Decades of Writing on Manifesto: The Making of a Genre." *Poetics Today* 30.2 (2009): 257-86. Web. 10 Sept. 2012.

Further Reading

Alberro, Alexander. *Conceptual Art and the Politics of Publicity.* Cambridge: MIT, 2003. Print.

Archer, Michael. *Art Since 1960.* 2nd ed. London: Thames & Hudson, 2002. Print.

products … and interviewed on every conceivable subject in glossy magazines."

Although Stuckism never gained prominence as an art movement in Britain, *The Stuckists* became an important source of inspiration for ongoing critiques of conceptualism and postmodernism. After issuing a series of manifestos and other polemics in 1999 and 2000, the Stuckists waged protests and demonstrations against the British art establishment, which drew considerable attention. According to Alice O'Keefe in a 2005 article for the *Guardian,* "the group has become rather more than simply an irritating thorn in the side of the Tate's director, Sir Nicholas Serota. They, and in particular their media-savvy spokesman Charles Thomson, are responsible for orchestrating a highly effective media campaign to publicly shame Serota and expose what they claim is the unhealthy favouritism being practised by the gallery." While the

Corris, Michael, ed. *Conceptual Art: Theory, Myth, and Practice.* New York: Cambridge UP, 2004. Print.

Goldie, Peter, and Elisabeth Schellekens. *Who's Afraid of Conceptual Art?* New York: Routledge, 2010. Print.

Harrison, Charles. *Since 1950: Art and Its Criticism.* New Haven: Yale UP, 2009. Print.

Hopkins, David. *After Modern Art: 1945-2000.* New York: Oxford UP, 2000. Print.

Karr, Rick. "Profile: Stuckist Art Movement of Great Britain." *All Things Considered.* National Public Radio. 16 July 2001. *Newspaper Source Plus.* Web. 10 Sept. 2012.

Thomson, Charles. "A Stuckist on Stuckism." *The Stuckists: Punk Victorian.* Ed. Frank Milner. Liverpool: National Museums, 2004. 6-32. Web. 11 Sept. 2012.

Theodore McDermott

THE _____ MANIFESTO

Michael Betancourt

❖ **Key Facts**

Time Period:
Late 20th Century

Movement/Issue:
Postmodernism; Open-source philosophy

Place of Publication:
United States

Language of Publication:
English

OVERVIEW

Written in 1996, Michael Betancourt's "The _____ Manifesto" was first published online and is one of the first examples of a manifesto made with the use of broadly accessible interactive technology. Betancourt, an artist and critical theorist, coded his manifesto with all key words removed. When accessed online, any user is able to fill in the blanks to create his or her own manifesto. The page does not provide a way to save the input but does have a "reset button" that clears any text that has been added to the manifesto. Betancourt's manifesto makes a bold statement about the artistic potential of the then-emerging Internet. His manifesto draws on Dadaist themes of absurdity, nonsense, and formalism without meaning while also participating in the postmodern turn away from strictly defined boundaries and authoritarian proclamations. The manifesto

participates in a broader movement of early light-art and new-media art, such as the work of Roy Ascott and Eduardo Kac. Also, following in the wake of Joseph Beuys's famous declaration that "everyone can be an artist," Betancourt's manifesto is designed to be a user-based project—an interactive artwork that can be accessed by anyone. It effectively foreshadowed the cultural potentials of the distributed networks that have dominated interactive Internet culture in the years since.

Betancourt first published "The _____ Manifesto" on Usenet, a popular text-based Internet discussion network. Betancourt's manifesto was quietly successful within the Usenet community and was soon reposted by several Webzines, foreshadowing the networked feedback loops that have come to characterize user-based interactive art, such as the various "LOLcats" memes. The manifesto was soon printed as a broadsheet in Miami, where Betancourt was pursuing postgraduate studies. More recently, an HTML version of "The _____ Manifesto" has been available on Betancourt's personal website as a part of his artistic archive, where it can be freely accessed, filled in, and printed by anyone with an Internet connection.

HISTORICAL AND LITERARY CONTEXT

"The _____ Manifesto" responds to the aesthetic potential of the rapid growth of the Internet and the theoretical claims of postmodernism. Three years before the manifesto was written, services such as America Online opened up Usenet access to a broad base of new users, democratizing what had been a largely university-centric network. Two years before the manifesto was written, tensions between postmodernists and scientists catalyzed into the so-called science wars, as both sides critiqued the intellectual rigor and social value of the other in very public forums, such as the infamous issue of Duke's postmodern journal *Social Text,* which unknowingly published a prank academic article by physicist Alan Sokal. This animosity between academics at a professional level was balanced somewhat by the informal connections forming between longtime Usenet users, predominantly academics and college students, and the general Internet-going crowd. These connections, combined with a general skepticism of established authority engendered by postmodernism, combined

MICHAEL BETANCOURT: ARTISTIC SCHOLARSHIP

Michael Betancourt published "The _____ Manifesto" when he was studying Communication and Film Studies as a first-year master's student at the University of Miami. In 2002 Betancourt received his PhD in Interdisciplinary Studies from the university, and he joined faculty at the Savannah College of Art and Design. In addition to his impressive academic accolades, Betancourt is a hard-working artist. Describing himself as an "artist-as-theorist/researcher," he has created video installations, academic articles, a book, and a full-length experimental film, all of which function as both theoretical scholarship and artistic production.

Bridging the gap between the academy and the art world, Betancourt offers a model for alternative modes of academic scholarship. Although most artists circulate primarily in the art world, occasionally breaking through into the broader art market, and most scholars associate predominantly with college students and other academics, Betancourt circulates in both groups. His artistic works are sophisticated, scholarly explorations of high-level theoretical issues. At the same time, his rigorous academic work is presented as an aesthetic object. Betancourt proves that the boundary between scholarship and art need not be a strict separation.

to form an open-source milieu and communitarian, antiauthoritarian artistic ethic.

By the time Betancourt posted his manifesto on Usenet in 1996, the Internet was quickly becoming a mainstream destination. Popular services such as America Online repackaged the still highly technical networks of the Internet into user-friendly formats, allowing those without computer science backgrounds a chance to participate in the online experience. This flood of new users was largely met by ambivalence in Usenet communities, as the untrained masses began to disrupt the existing social mores of Usenet. These disruptions came first from the lack of "netiquette" of inexperienced users and then from the flood of spam targeting the increasing number of Usenet users. In addition to his active participation in various Usenet forums, Betancourt began work on an MA in Film history at the University of Miami in 1996, and "The _____ Manifesto" represents one of his earliest attempts at merging artistic production, electronic media, and high-level scholarship.

"The _____ Manifesto" draws on a history of ironic and surrealist artistic manifestos. He composed the manifesto out of various passages from Tristan Tzara's *Dada Manifesto* (1918) from which he removed keywords, replacing them with interactive blanks. Tzara's manifesto mocks the vogue for serious artistic manifestos by mimicking them in form but refusing their seriousness in content. In writing "The _____ Manifesto," Betancourt takes this exercise one step further, referencing the form of the popular Mad Libs word game in which players fill in blanks in premade sentences without knowing the context for their words. In this way, Betancourt, like Tzara, works with an absurdist tone, implicitly contrasting the critical self-assurance usually required of manifesto writers with the potential absurdity of their ideas.

In the years since its publication, "The _____ Manifesto" has served as an important example of the potential uses of new media in experimental artistic productions. The fill-in-the-blank form was prescient, as Betancourt's manifesto forecast, showing up in later online sources as diverse as meme generators and official electronic documents. For Betancourt, "The _____ Manifesto" was the first of a series of online artistic projects. Betancourt has repeatedly made use of both the interactive possibilities of online art and its unique potential for mass distribution and consumption.

THEMES AND STYLE

The central theme of "The _____ Manifesto" is intentionally left ambiguous. Many specific nouns or verbs that give excerpts of Tzara's manifesto particular meaning are removed and left blank: "Today, _____ itself is obsolete. In documenting art on the basis of _____: we are

human and true for the sake of _____, _____, and _____." Visiting users are invited to fill in the blanks with whatever words they feel are appropriate. This is a stark contrast to the manifesto's source, the *Dada Manifesto* (1918). In its original form, the previous passage reads: "But this need itself is obsolete. In documenting art on the basis of the supreme simplicity: novelty, we are human and true for the sake of amusement, impulsive, vibrant to crucify boredom." Users are at once reminded of the original Dada manifesto and invited to reject Tzara's polemic in favor of their own. The manifesto's immediate meaning, then, comes from the user rather than from Betancourt or Tzara.

The manifesto achieves its rhetorical effect through an appeal to interactive participation. The blanks on the manifesto can be selected by a user and filled in with whatever the user decides. By leaving the meaning of the manifesto explicitly ambiguous, Betancourt makes a statement about the artistic potential of interactive, electronic media in a postmodern milieu.

Cover of *Revue Dada*, no. 3, 1918, edited by Tristan Tzara and containing his *Dada Manifesto* (1918). Betancourt used parts of text from Tzara's manifestos, replacing certain words with blanks. BIBLIOTHÈQUE LITTERAIRE JACQUES DOUCET, PARIS, FRANCE/ ARCHIVES CHARMET/THE BRIDGEMAN ART LIBRARY

PRIMARY SOURCE

"THE _____ MANIFESTO"

Today _____ itself is obsolete. In documenting art on the basis of _____: we are human and true for the sake of _____, _____ and _____. At the crossroads of the lights, alert, attentively awaiting _____,

If you find it futile and don't want to waste your time on a _____ that means nothing, consider that here we cast _____ on fertile ground. Here we have a right to do some prospecting, for we have _____. We are ghosts drunk on energy, we dig into _____.

We are a _____ as tropically abundant as _____, which is the art of making _____ established as _____ on a canvas before our eyes, yet today the striving for _____ in a work of art seems _____ to art. Art is a _____ concept, exalted as _____, inexplicable as life, indefinable and _____. The work of art comes into being through the _____ of the elements.

The medium is as _____ as the artist. Essential only is the forming, and because the medium is _____, any _____ whatsoever will _____.

_____ is the name for such art. _____ stands for freedom. _____ changes meaning with the change in the insight of those who view it. Every artist must be allowed to mold a picture out of _____. The _____ of natural elements is _____, to a work of art. Instead, it is the artist who _____ to produce _____, in order to make a better art.

SOURCE: 100 Artists' *Manifestos From the Futurists to the Stuckists,* edited by Alex Danchev, Penguin, 2011. Pp. 417–418. Copyright © Michael Betancourt. All rights reserved. Reproduced by permission.

However, the manifesto is not without any rhetorical agenda. Certain possibilities are constrained by the demands of coherent grammar. For instance, the manifesto ends: "The _____ of natural elements is _____ to a work of art. Instead, it is the artist who _____ to produce _____, in order to make a better art." Although there is no technical constraint of what words can be filled in, for the sentence to make grammatical sense certain conventions must be followed. Also, for all its openness and contingency, "The _____ Manifesto" does have the final word. Regardless of what the user inputs into the blanks, the purpose of the manifesto is fixed: it is a way "to make a better art."

Stylistically, "The _____ Manifesto" is distinguished by its careful structure and many blank spaces. Betancourt breaks the sentences up much the way a modern, open-form poem might, drawing focus to the manifesto's structure as much as to its negative spaces. This heightened sense of structure balances the apparent carelessness of the omitted words. Betancourt also uses carefully selected language to ensure that the manifesto can achieve an appropriately polemical tone even with missing words: "Here we have a right to do some prospecting, for we have _____." The "we" suggests that, regardless of the word or words a user selects, the user is part of a broader movement; the "right" suggests that the manifesto grounds its claim on universal rights as opposed to artistic whims. Although the manifesto reads as a disjointed, incomplete statement, it achieves its rhetorical force through careful manipulation of the conventions of grammar and structure.

CRITICAL DISCUSSION

When "The _____ Manifesto" was first posted in 1996, it received some positive reactions within the small Usenet artistic community, and it was reposted in several art Webzines. Soon after, the manifesto was printed as a broadsheet and distributed around Miami. A decade after its publication, "The _____ Manifesto" was included in Lee Scrivner's ironic "How to Write an Avant-Garde Manifesto (A Manifesto)" where it was described as one of the "exercises in nonexistence" that emerged in postmodern manifesto writing. Scrivner makes particular note of the persistence of the blanks in Betancourt's manifesto: "And even this isn't enough to render all authoritarian agendas blank, since, at the end of the manifesto, there is a *reset* button." Although not as influential as later online manifestos such as the "Stuckist Manifesto" (1999), "The _____ Manifesto" remains relevant as one of the earliest examples of a truly digital manifesto.

Betancourt's manifesto was included in *Incite: Journal of Experimental Media* and referenced in subsequent online manifestos. It also marked a change in Betancourt's own interests, as he shifted to long-term digital projects, such as the experimental Free Art Project, which adapted open-source programs to produce art. In the article "Three Decades of Writing on Manifesto: The Making of a Genre," Galia Yanoshevshy describes a category of "present-day Internet manifestos, which have not yet been studied in current scholarship"—an apt assessment of the current state of scholarship on Betancourt's "The _____ Manifesto." Betancourt, for his part, has moved on to conceptual video art projects, tracking a movement across mediums but maintaining an interest in the various distinctive features of each medium.

Most scholarship focusing on later-twentieth-century manifestos has noted the newfound ease with which manifestos can be written and disseminated. In a 2001 article "Manifesto Destiny" in the *Village Voice,* Simon Reynolds argues that, "One could almost say we are living through a new boom time for the manifesto. The Web allows almost anybody to nail a broadsheet to the virtual wall for all to see." Although, as Yanoshevshy notes, most modern manifestos have not yet been studied academically, the technology and practices that undergirded Benancourt's distribution vector for "The _____ Manifesto" have, with the ever-increasing ubiquity of Internet connections, become the norm. At the same time, the sheer volume of Internet-based electronic manifestos has made rigorous scholarship for any one example exceedingly rare. Crowdsourced online resources have become effective means to survey the state of the manifesto in the Internet age.

BIBLIOGRAPHY

Sources

Betancourt, Micheal. "The _____ Manifesto." *MichaelBetancourt.* 1996. Web. 1 Nov. 2012.

Childish, Billy, and Thomson, Charles. "The Stuckist Manifesto." *Stuckism International.* The Stuckists, 1999. Web. 1 Nov. 2012.

Galia Yanoshevshy. "Three Decades of Writing on Manifesto: The Making of a Genre." *Poetics Today* 30:2 (2009): 257-86. Print.

Reynolds, Simon. "Manifesto Destiny." *Village Voice* 15 May 2001. Web. 1 Nov. 2012.

Scrivner, Lee. "How to Write an Avant-Garde Manifesto (A Manifesto)." *The London Consortium.* London Consortium. Web. 1 Nov. 2012.

Tzara, Tristan. *Dada Manifesto* (1918). *Maria Elena Buszek.* Web. 1 Nov. 2012.

Further Reading

Betancourt, Michael. "Immateralism and Physicality." *CTheory.net.* N.p. 22 June 2010. Web. 1 Nov. 2012.

Breton, André. *Manifestos of Surrealism.* Trans. Richard Seaver and Helen Lane. Ann Arbor: U of Michigan P. 1972. Print.

Buffet-Picabia, Gabrielle. "Arthur Cravan and American Dada." *The Dada Painters and Poets.* 2nd ed. Ed. Robert Motherwell. New York: Hall, 1981. Print.

Lyon, Janet. *Manifestoes: Provocations of the Modern.* Ithaca: Cornell UP, 1999. Print.

Perloff, Marjorie. "Violence and Precision: The Manifesto as Art Form." *Chicago Review* 34.2 (1984): 65-101. Print.

Robbins, Christopher. "Crossing Conventions in Web-Based Art: Deconstruction as a Narrative Device." *Leonardo: International Journal of Contemporary Visual Artists* 40.2 (2007): 161-66. Web. 1 Nov. 2012.

Shanken, Edward A. *Art and Electronic Media.* London: Phaidon, 2009. Print.

Taylor Evans

WHY CHEAP ART? MANIFESTO
Peter Schumann, et al.

❖ Key Facts

Time Period:
Late 20th Century

Movement/Issue:
Marxism; Aesthetics;
Vietnam War protest

Place of Publication:
United States

**Language of
Publication:**
English

OVERVIEW

Written in 1984 by German artist Peter Schumann and other members of the anti-capitalist Bread & Puppet Theater (often referred to as Bread & Puppet), the *WHY CHEAP ART? Manifesto* uses language both aggressive and whimsical to critique the notion of "high" or "fine" art. This notion, according to Bread & Puppet, aligns with the capitalist view of art as an investment commodity. Buying and selling art to make a profit is contrary to the more profound roles art is meant to play—those of personal expression, social commentary, and beauty. The answer, according to the artists and performers of Bread & Puppet, is to sell art for prices low enough to make it available to all social classes. Bread & Puppet's manifesto addresses the entire world, with particular attention to certain entities within the contemporary art community, such as galleries and auction houses, museums, critics, and of course artists themselves.

When *WHY CHEAP ART?* first appeared, it was largely overlooked outside the small world of avant-garde theater in the United States and of the Bread & Puppet community in particular. Within that scene, however, the document's call for a revitalizing, uncommoditized art resonated loudly. When Bread & Puppet first emerged in New York City in the 1960s, the group belonged to a much broader movement toward political avant-gardism. That movement was part of the larger countercultural and student response to the atrocities of the Vietnam War. By the mid-1980s, however, much of the avant-gardism and political radicalism of the 1960s had faded. For many in the American leftist political theater community, *WHY CHEAP ART?* represented a new and clarified commitment to the revitalizing potential of uncommoditized art. Today, the tract is considered among the most important documents in the history of one of the most important and innovative political theater groups in the United States.

HISTORICAL AND LITERARY CONTEXT

Schumann founded the Bread & Puppet Theater in 1963 in New York City in response to the general cultural and political unrest in the United States during the Cold War and, in particular, to the ongoing bloodshed in Vietnam. Schumann was concerned both with the theme of complicity in injustice and with the political potential of popular theater. In the early 1960s, avant-garde theater was undergoing a renaissance in New York. Groups such as the Living Theatre and the Wooster Group sought new dramatic forms in order to respond to a society that was rapidly changing due in part to the civil rights movement, war protests, and the explosion of the hippie counter-culture. Schumann's Bread & Puppet Theater aimed to do the same. Using huge puppets, some reaching twenty feet high, and handing out bread, the group performed at protest events, in theaters, and in informal street shows.

In 1970 Schumann and his group left New York to accept a residency at Goddard College in Plainfield, Vermont. A few years later, in 1974, the group moved from Goddard to a Vermont farm. It was here in 1979 that *WHY CHEAP ART?* was presaged: Schumann and friends drove through small Vermont communities in an old school bus with dozens of small works of art, done on cardboard, Masonite, and newspaper, decorating the bus's exterior. The works' prices—from ten cents to ten dollars—reflected the group's mission to make art accessible and affordable. Between 1976 and 1984, when *WHY CHEAP ART?* was issued, the group focused on public spectacles, including the annual Domestic Resurrection Circus, that relied on amateur performers.

Despite its humane intent, *WHY CHEAP ART?* is characterized by a bellicose tone that places it squarely within the firmament of confrontational twentieth-century art manifestos. It exhorts rather argues. The authors write: "ART SOOTHES PAIN! Art wakes up sleepers! ART FIGHTS AGAINST WAR & STUPIDITY!" In this way, the Bread & Puppet manifesto recalls the vociferousness of Filippo Tommaso Marinetti's *Futurist Manifesto* (1909), among other polemics that emerged from the futurist movement in the early twentieth century. *WHY CHEAP ART?* also draws from a rich tradition of socialist manifestos, particularly those that advocate for peaceful change rather than violent revolution, such as Victor Considerant's *Principes du socialisme, Manifeste de la démocratie au XIXe siècle* (1843; *Principles of Socialism: Manifesto of Nineteenth Century Democracy*).

Modernism was suited to the presence of artists' cliques and the formation of "-isms," each with its own stylistic conceit and conceptions about what art should be. *WHY CHEAP ART?* emerged just as this era was yielding to a postmodern, Internet-driven mash-up of countless art styles. The aggressive trumpeting of manifestos did not fit well in this new historical moment in which no particular artistic style dominated. Individual artists' "statements" have largely replaced the tradition of the manifesto. The legacy of Bread & Puppet's document is largely political, therefore, rather than literary. Its anticapitalist message continues to be discussed in art circles, though the dialog rarely seems to enter the larger public discourse. To a large degree, art still *is* business. Right or wrong, corporations and wealthy collectors control much of it, and few if any signs suggest that matters have or will change.

THEMES AND STYLE

The theme of *WHY CHEAP ART?* is stated clearly in its opening sentence: "PEOPLE have been THINKING too long that ART is a PRIVILEGE of the MUSEUMS & the RICH." The piece continues, declaring that art is "FOOD," that it must be available to "EVERYBODY," "EVERYWHERE," and that it "SOOTHES PAIN!" Art also wakes people up, fights against "WAR" and "STUPIDITY," and sings "HALLELUJA." In addition (despite the above claims to the contrary), art is "CHEAP." The use of present tense suggests that the problem is solved after all, but here again Bread & Puppet seem to write what they wish for rather than what is. The manifesto's title offers a solution, *sell art cheaply,* and the organization's name implies a vague mechanism for achieving it,

WHEN PUPPETS WERE CRIMINALS

At the 2000 Republican Party National Convention in Philadelphia, volunteers from the Bread & Puppet Theater showed up to protest the party's policies. Agents of John Timoney, Philadelphia's chief of police at the time, had infiltrated Bread & Puppet for weeks prior to the event. After the group set up in an old trolley barn and began building their ten- and twenty-foot puppets, the police, lacking a warrant, raided the building. A surreal scene ensued, complete with news helicopters hovering overhead, buzz on the street about terrorist plots and bomb building, and what the Associated Press called "SWAT-style" police tactics on the ground.

By the time the raid ended, more than seventy puppetistas had been arrested. Chief Timoney's conduct later received criticism from the American Civil Liberties Union, Human Rights Watch, the National Lawyers Guild, and Amnesty International.

bread & puppets (i.e., combining humane social action with politically charged entertainment). However, no detailed directive for implementing this agenda is offered, either here or elsewhere in Bread & Puppet's literature.

Although it is not clear from the manifesto itself what Bread & Puppet's plan of action is, the group later issued an introduction to *WHY CHEAP ART?* that clarified the matter, if somewhat obliquely. Bread & Puppet's philosophical position in the introduction

The Bread & Puppet Theater's Cheap Art Store, a broken-down bus where visitors can buy art based on the honor system.
© RANDY DUCHAINE/ ALAMY

is unchanged from that of the manifesto; however, the rhetorical tone has become much more temperate:

> Many of us have felt [that] some popular arts events [are] profit-driven, and priced beyond what the average artist can afford.... There comes a time when pricing at "what the market will bear" holds arts events—and, to some degree, the arts—hostage.... **It's time to stop the nonsense.** Let's earn our money by making & selling art, *not by overcharging students.*

Although this statement refers only to an art market of students, Bread & Puppet is likely suggesting that art be sold at low prices across the board. This inference is supported by the manifesto's mode of production—as a letterpress broadside. In this way, Bread & Puppet demonstrates its fidelity to an art that is tangible, reproducible, and accessible.

The contrast in tone between the introduction and the work itself is marked. The introduction avoids off-putting rhetoric and abuse of capitalization, whereas the body reads as a temper tantrum. Rhetorically Bread & Puppet seems to have become more confident, choosing to rely on the force of its humanitarian argument rather than shouting in uppercase. Consequently, although both the introduction and the work itself address the same matter—long-standing and legitimate concern about the overreaching power of the free market—the manifesto, though perhaps more entertaining, is less effective than the introduction as a mechanism for instigating actual change.

CRITICAL DISCUSSION

When the *WHY CHEAP ART? Manifesto* was first issued in 1984, it was viewed by members of the American avant-garde theater community as an important statement of the ongoing mission of the Bread & Puppet Theater. At the time of its composition, the once prominent avant-garde wing of the U.S. theater scene had been marginalized. Only a few troupes survived, and the Bread & Puppet group had moved from New York to rural Vermont. The document helped refocus the group's mission. In lieu of the concretely defined causes of the 1960s and 1970s, *WHY CHEAP ART?* signaled an embrace of a larger aim: to offer art devoid of the trappings of capitalism and full of a kind of sustaining spiritual nourishment. For those involved in avant-garde theater in the United States in the mid-1980s, this call resonated as a feasible way to continue what had become a largely unprofitable and overlooked endeavor.

In addition to helping guide avant-garde theater through its struggles to remain relevant, *WHY CHEAP ART?* also helped define the mission of the Bread & Puppet Theater. Throughout the 1980s and 1990s and into the twenty-first century, the group has continued to make public and political puppet theater that challenges not only structures of authority, such as the International Monetary Fund, but also common conceptions about the nature of art. Though it has not elicited an extensive body of criticism, *WHY CHEAP ART?* is regarded as a valuable document of late-twentieth-century American avant-gardism.

Commentators have noted the ways in which the Bread & Puppet Theater has modified its tactics, techniques, and mission in order to adjust to an altered social, cultural, and artistic landscape. *WHY CHEAP ART?* is an important part of that process. As John Bell writes in "Beyond the Cold War: Bread and Puppet Theater and the New World Order," the group became increasingly dependent on volunteer performers as funding dried up in the 1980s. He notes, "The volunteer spectacles ... were especially practical techniques in Latin American and other Third World locales visited by Bread and Puppet, where a lack of theater technology and even such resources as electric power was offset by an abundance of spirited volunteer performers." Other commentators have also noted the group's connection to the international theater scene. In *Beyond the Boundaries: American Alternative Theatre,* Theodore Shank describes Bread & Puppet's international influence, arguing that the group "had an important impact upon younger theatre companies" in France, England, and elsewhere.

BIBLIOGRAPHY

Sources

Aucoin, Don. "Bread and Puppet's Imagery Packs Political Punch." *Boston Globe.* NY Times, 1 Feb. 2010. Web. 28 Sept. 2012.

Bell, John. "Beyond the Cold War: Bread and Puppet Theater and the New World Order." *Staging Resistance: Essays on Political Theater.* Ed. Jeanne Colleran and Jenny S. Spencer. Ann Arbor: U of Michigan P, 1998. Print.

Brecht, Stefan. *The Bread and Puppet Theatre, Vol. 2.* New York: Routledge, 1988. Print.

Shank, Theodore. *Beyond the Boundaries: American Alternative Theatre.* Ann Arbor: U of Michigan P, 2002. Print.

Simon, Ronald, and Estrin, Marc. "Rehearsing with Gods; Photographs and Essays on the Bread & Puppet Theater." Chelsea Green Publishing, 29 April 2004. Web. 2 Oct. 2012.

Further Reading

Denniston, George. *An Existing Better World: Notes on the Bread & Puppet Theater.* New York: Farrar, Straus, and Giroux, 2001. Print.

Schumann, Peter. "The Radicality of the Puppet Theatre." *TDR: The Drama Review* 35.4 (1991): 75-83. Print.

———. "Five Reasons Why I Support Air Strikes to Lift the Siege of Sarajevo." *TDR: The Drama Review* 38:2 (1994): 10-11. Print.

Toy, Judith. "Bread and Puppet Theatre Workshop Intensive." *Puppetry Journal* 45:3 (1994): 13-14. Print.

Dennis Fehr

FEMINISMS

THE BITCH MANIFESTO

Joreen (Jo Freeman)

OVERVIEW

The Bitch Manifesto (1968), written by Jo Freeman under her activist name Joreen, calls for the creation of a feminist activist group for women who identify as "bitches" and have been excluded from the budding women's liberation movement because of their bold, unfeminine appearance and personality. It was written during the beginning of what has now been defined as the second wave of feminism, when various women's groups were being formed to discuss and promote ideas of gender equality and the subversion of traditional gender roles. The manifesto was intended for women who did not fit into these emerging groups and who blatantly disregarded the traditional ideas of femininity. *The Bitch Manifesto* calls for bitches to unite, despite their mistrust of other women, in order to discuss and challenge their own problems with social injustice.

The manifesto was met with immediate enthusiasm among certain members of the growing feminist movement, and it was reprinted multiple times because of its ability to reach out to women who had been excluded from developing feminist organizations. The piece's blunt manner and take-action approach were effective in generating excitement, but its somewhat confused ideas about the greater purpose of the feminist movement and who exactly it was fighting against are reflective of early second-wave organizational downfalls. While not solely responsible for the events that unfolded during the rise of women's rights activism, *The Bitch Manifesto*, in combination with Freeman's other theoretical writings, formed an influential collection that set into motion the ideas and opinions that fueled the second-wave feminist movement in 1970s America.

HISTORICAL AND LITERARY CONTEXT

The Bitch Manifesto was written near the beginning of the women's liberation movement in response to the alienation and hostility directed at Freeman by other women involved in feminist activism during the 1960s. Freeman had been a founding member of the Westside Group in Chicago, an early feminist organization designed to protest sexism at home and in the workplace, but was forced to leave because of group dynamics that rejected her bold manner and authoritative leadership role. Feeling unwanted by the very people her activism was trying to liberate, she wrote *The Bitch Manifesto* in order to work out her own feelings of marginalization while searching for other women who experienced similar reactions to their subversion of the prescribed gender roles associated with American women.

The manifesto was written in the infancy of the women's liberation movement as a direct result of Freeman's interactions with the Westside Group. Freeman was still struggling with her sense of rejection and was curious about why she did not fit in with the other feminists. Her theorizing produced *The Bitch Manifesto* and two other articles, "The Tyranny of Structurelessness" (1970) and "Trashing: The Dark

+ *Key Facts*

Time Period:
Mid-20th Century

Movement/Issue:
Second-wave feminism

Place of Publication:
United States

Language of Publication:
English

JO FREEMAN: SCHOLAR, ACTIVIST, AND SOCIAL REFORMER

Jo Freeman, born on August 26, 1945, in Atlanta, was raised in Los Angeles, where her family moved shortly after her birth. Her career as a political activist began at the University of California-Berkeley, where she studied political science and became involved in numerous groups that supported issues of equality. After completing her degree in 1965, Freeman became an activist in the southern states, working for Martin Luther King Jr.'s Southern Christian Leadership Conference and editing activist newspapers and journals.

Freeman's experience with the civil rights movement naturally led her to apply the principles of equality to women's rights, and she became one of the founders of the women's liberation movement in the United States and in Europe, where she traveled to hand out pamphlets and connect with international feminist groups. She returned to America and completed a doctorate in political science at the University of Chicago in 1973, writing and publishing papers that supported her feminist and antisexist beliefs. Her movement name, "Joreen," is an amalgamation of her first and last name, which was common practice among feminists in the late 1960s. She later republished her articles under her real name in order to prevent confusion. She received a law degree in 1982 from New York University, after which she opened a private practice serving as council to prochoice activists and women in politics.

Side of Sisterhood" (1976), which proved to be her most influential pieces of writing. These works are often hailed as two of the founding documents of the women's liberation movement and are considered to be integral pieces for the development and unification of feminist theory through the 1970s.

Although the liberation movement was only just beginning, Freeman had access to theoretical literature that strongly influenced her opinions for *The Bitch Manifesto.* Perhaps the most prominent influence was Simone de Beauvoir's *The Second Sex* (1953), which explores how women's roles have been constructed as separate from and inferior to men's and suggests that women who wish to live as autonomous human beings—with an independent income and an influential place in society—are seen as masculine and dangerous to society and therefore are not taken seriously. In Freeman's interpretation of Beauvoir's ideas, the bitches go one step further: not only are they rejected by society as a whole, but they also are shunned by women claiming to be involved in the very movement that strives for gender equality. Freeman's manifesto thus addresses how women oppress other women, even within the feminist movement.

Despite the passion that characterizes her manifesto, Freeman failed to create the organization that she hoped to: BITCH, for women who identified as bitches. The reconstitution of the term "bitch" as a badge of pride, however, encouraged the rejection of traditional gender roles prescribed for women and inspired women's rights activists to be proud of their gender subversion and demand equality within society, both in the home and in the workplace. Freeman's ideas are still utilized in feminist discussions today: while not directly influenced by *The Bitch Manifesto,* the quarterly feminist magazine *Bitch,* established in 1996, still produces articles about feminist representations in pop culture and plays on the reclamation of the word "bitch" as a badge of pride and honor.

THEMES AND STYLE

The central theme of *The Bitch Manifesto* is the necessity for bitches to unite in order to challenge society's preconceived notions of femininity and the second-class treatment of women. The manifesto begins by defining who qualifies as a bitch, with descriptors pertaining to her personality, her physicality, and her societal orientation: "It is … generally agreed that a Bitch is aggressive, and therefore unfeminine…. She is never a 'true woman.'" According to Freeman, there are different levels of bitches, depending on how many social boundaries they cross, but because of their outsider nature bitches are generally untrusting of other women. Freeman proposes that BITCH, a nonexistent feminist organization, could provide a platform for the unification of bitches as activists for social change.

The text develops its argument through rhetoric aimed at feminists who subvert the gender roles of passivity and domesticity expected of women during 1960s. It suggests that many of these women exist and, if they could overcome their mistrust of each other, they could unite as a powerful force for women's liberation. The sense of identity among these women is created through Freeman's discussion of the term "bitch" and her descriptions of the pressures bitches face in their daily lives, such as being isolated in society because they "do not conform to socially accepted patterns of behavior." Yet the author asserts that despite these pressures, "a woman should be proud to declare she is a Bitch, because Bitch is Beautiful. It should be an act of affirmation by self, and not negation by others." By reclaiming a sense of pride in being a bitch, Freeman presents the idea that these women are not alone in their struggles and that they could unite for social equality in an organization that would celebrate rather than reject them.

Freeman passionately reconstitutes derogatory language in a manner that creates a sense of self-respect in the women she identifies as bitches. By describing bitches with words such as "aggressive," "obnoxious," "ugly," and "domineering," the manifesto transfers the sense of power generated by these words from society at large to the women who feel oppressed by such language. This creates a sense of power that replaces the shame of being an outsider, which, Freeman suggests, should allow bitches to learn to trust each other. Only through trust and pride in themselves can bitches unite to overcome societal ostracism, and only through adopting the rhetorical strategies of their oppressors can bitches reclaim the language used against them and transform it into a vehicle for social change.

CRITICAL DISCUSSION

Initially, *The Bitch Manifesto* was received with excitement, resulting in multiple reprints, because of its reclaiming of the word "bitch" as a positive and proud label for women who did not conform to traditional ideas of feminine behavior or appearance. Jennifer Scanlon notes in her biography of Jo Freeman (1999) that Freeman's early feminist works, including *The Bitch Manifesto*, were minor classics because they "illuminated others' experiences in many movements," including civil rights and feminist movements both in the United States and abroad. Susan Brownmiller writes in her feminist memoir *In Our Time* (1990) that Freeman had a "blunt, peremptory manner" that caused her troubles with the Westside Group but ultimately led to the style and pomp of *The Bitch Manifesto*.

While the manifesto perhaps did not have the desired effect of establishing the BITCH organization, it certainly proved influential for second-wave feminists who began to assert their independence and challenge prescribed gender roles. Winifred Breines in *The Trouble Between Us* (2006) reflects on the empowerment that feminist organizations felt as a result of their newfound theories, stemming from works such as *The Bitch Manifesto*, which proved "that their issues

PRIMARY SOURCE

THE BITCH MANIFESTO

BITCH is an organization which does not yet exist. The name is not an acronym. It stands for exactly what it sounds like.

BITCH is composed of Bitches. There are many definitions of a bitch. The most complimentary definition is a female dog. Those definitions of bitches who are also homo sapiens are rarely as objective. They vary from person to person and depend strongly on how much of a bitch the definer considers herself. However, everyone agrees that a bitch is always a female, dog, or otherwise.

It is also generally agreed that a Bitch is aggressive, and therefore unfeminine (ahem). She may be sexy, in which case she becomes a Bitch Goddess, a special case which will not concern us here. But she is never a "true woman."

Bitches have some or all of the following characteristics.

1. Personality. Bitches are aggressive, assertive, domineering, overbearing, strong-minded, spiteful, hostile, direct, blunt, candid, obnoxious, thick-skinned, hard-headed, vicious, dogmatic, competent, competitive, pushy, loud-mouthed, independent, stubborn, demanding, manipulative, egoistic, driven, achieving, overwhelming, threatening, scary, ambitious, tough, brassy, masculine, boisterous, and turbulent. Among other things. A Bitch occupies a lot of psychological space. You always know she is around. A Bitch takes shit from no one. You may not like her, but you cannot ignore her.

2. Physical. Bitches are big, tall, strong, large, loud, brash, harsh, awkward, clumsy, sprawling, strident, ugly. Bitches move their bodies freely rather than restrain, refine and confine their motions in the proper feminine manner. They clomp up stairs, stride when they walk and don't worry about where they put their legs when they sit. They have loud voices and often use them. Bitches are not pretty.

3. Orientation. Bitches seek their identity strictly thru themselves and what they do. They are subjects, not objects. They may have a relationship with a person or organization, but they never marry anyone or anything; man, mansion, or movement. Thus Bitches prefer to plan their own lives rather than live from day to day, action to action, or person to person. They are independent cusses and believe they are capable of doing anything they damn well want to. If something gets in their way; well, that's why they become Bitches. If they are professionally inclined, they will seek careers and have no fear of competing with anyone. If not professionally inclined, they still seek self-expression and self-actualization. Whatever they do, they want an active role and are frequently perceived as domineering. Often they do dominate other people when roles are not available to them which more creatively sublimate their energies and utilize their capabilities. More often they are accused of domineering when doing what would be considered natural by a man.

were politically legitimate" rather than frivolous complaints. Breines also points out that "an autonomous women's movement was necessary" in order to replace the various emerging women's groups, such as the Westside Group in Chicago, which had different theoretical standpoints and internal conflicts about organization, activism, and ideological positions. Current interest in the manifesto places it as a cornerstone of change at the beginning of an influential social rights movement.

Contemporary scholarship surrounding *The Bitch Manifesto* and the writings of feminists in the 1970s tend to focus on the blind spots of these works vis-à-vis racial, class, and political paradigms. In particular, it is a current trend to divide the second wave of feminism along lines of racial differentiation, with the accusation that Freeman and other prominent writers were concerned only with the issues of middle-class white women during this period. Becky Thompson, in her essay "Multiracial Feminism: Recasting the Chronology of Second Wave Feminism" (2002), describes this type of activism as "hegemonic feminism," which is generally criticized because it "is white led, marginalizes the activism and world views of women of colour, focusses mainly on the United States, and treats sexism as the ultimate oppression." Despite Freeman's earlier activism in the civil rights movement, in which she fought against racism, her work is subject to this criticism because of its reflection of her personal trials as a white woman in the feminist movement.

BIBLIOGRAPHY

Sources

Breines, Winifred. *The Trouble between Us: An Uneasy History of White and Black Women in the Feminist Movement.* Oxford: Oxford UP, 2006. Print.

Brownmiller, Susan. *In Our Time: Memoir of a Revolution.* New York: Dial, 1990. Print.

Scanlon, Jennifer, ed. *Significant Contemporary American Feminists: A Biographical Sourcebook.* Westport: Greenwood, 1999. 104-10. Print.

Thompson, Becky. "Multiracial Feminism: Recasting the Chronology of Second Wave Feminism." *Feminist Studies* 28.2 (2002): 337-452. *Literature Resource Center.* Web. 6 Aug. 2012.

Further Reading

Banaszak, Lee Ann, ed. *The U.S. Women's Movement in Global Perspective.* Lanham: Rowman and Littlefield, 2006.

Beauvoir, Simone de. *The Second Sex.* Ed. and trans. Constance Borde and Sheila Malovany-Chevallier. London: Jonathan Cape, 2009.

Berkeley, Kathleen C. *The Women's Liberation Movement in America.* Westport: Greenwood, 1999.

Echols, Alice. *Daring to Be Bad: Radical Feminism in America 1967-1975.* Minneapolis: U of Minnesota P, 1989. Print.

Freeman, Jo. "On the Origins of the Women's Liberation Movement from a Strictly Personal Perspective." *The Feminist Memoir Project: Voices from Women's Liberation.* Ed. Rachel Blau DuPlessis and Ann Snitow. New York: Three Rivers, 1998.

Katherine Barker

A BLACK FEMINIST STATEMENT

Combahee River Collective

OVERVIEW

Authored by the members of the Combahee River Collective, a nationally recognized black feminist group, *A Black Feminist Statement* (1977), published in 1977, describes the nature of black women's experience of social oppression and insists on political attention to how race, class, gender, and sexuality intersect to shape individuals' lives. Although black women held key roles in the women's liberation and civil rights movements of the 1960s, they were often subject to racism from white feminists and sexism from male activists. Black feminist groups such as the Combahee River Collective formed in response to the failure to recognize the unique needs of black women, who face a double bind of racial and sexual disenfranchisement. Addressed to black women in particular, the statement treats four areas of black feminism: history, beliefs, obstacles to organizing, and areas of focus.

One of the first documents to distinguish the experience of black women from that of black men or white women, the statement was influential in shaping black feminist thought in the 1980s and beyond. As a group, the Combahee River Collective nurtured, educated, and aided in developing major figures in the next generation of the black feminist movement. Over the next several decades, *A Black Feminist Statement* helped usher in a large number of works by women of color exploring new aspects and angles of "intersectionality," or the confluence of gender, race, class, and sexuality (the term itself was not coined until the late 1980s by scholar Kimberlé Crenshaw). Today the statement is recognized as an important work of black feminism and as a key document in the emergence of the third wave of Western feminism.

HISTORICAL AND LITERARY CONTEXT

Although the Combahee River Collective formed as part of the second wave of feminism, its roots reach back to nineteenth-century traditions of black activism. The collective, which takes its name from a South Carolina river where Harriet Tubman helped free slaves, acknowledges the influence of historical black female figures, such as Sojourner Truth, Frances E.W. Harper, Ida B. Wells Barnett, and Mary Church Terrell, as well as thousands of activists who remain unknown. As the black civil rights movement gained national attention in the early 1960s and black men

and women were aligned in their struggle for equality, problems of sexism and misogyny within the black community became apparent. Likewise, when the second wave of feminism began with the 1963 publication of Betty Friedan's *The Feminine Mystique* and the founding of the National Organization for Women (NOW) in 1966, racism in mainstream feminism became apparent. The women's movement was dominated by white middle-class women, though women of color took key roles. Pauli Murray coauthored the original NOW Bill of Rights and Aileen Hernandez became the second president of NOW.

By the late 1970s several black feminist groups had formed, but none had authored a definitive statement about a movement specifically for black women. Black feminist Barbara Smith founded the Combahee River Collective in 1974, perhaps inspired by her work in the National Black Feminist Organization (NBFO), formed in 1973. Members of the Combahee River Collective included Sharon Page Ritchie, Cheryl Clarke, Margo Okazawa Rey, Akasha Gloria Hull, Eleanor Johnson, Demita Frazier, Audre Lorde, Cassie Alfonso, and Chirlane McCray. They met weekly at the Cambridge, Massachusetts, Women's Center and held a number of retreats between 1977 and 1979 to discuss the perils of black feminism. Their 1977 statement, partially the product of one of these retreats, states the major principles of their political project.

A Black Feminist Statement draws on the NBFO's 1973 "Statement of Purpose," which helped pioneer the concept of intersectionality, focusing on "the phenomenon of being black and female, in a country that is *both* racist and sexist." The NBFO document highlights the exclusion of black women from the black and women's liberation movements and posits that black feminism will strengthen both movements by reminding white women and black men of the unique contributions of black women. Although the document was just over five hundred words, it attracted great public interest; ideological differences, however, led to the dissolution of the organization in 1976.

A Black Feminist Statement proved to be a key document in the development of black feminist thought. Several members of the collective went on to become major figures as black feminism gained wider recognition in the 1980s and 1990s. Smith

✛ *Key Facts*

Time Period:
Late 20th Century

Movement/Issue:
African-American Feminism

Place of Publication:
United States

Language of Publication:
English

HARRIET TUBMAN AND THE COMBAHEE RIVER

The Combahee River, which flows through the Port Royal region of South Carolina, was the location of a Civil War military action planned and led by Harriet Tubman, a black abolitionist and antislavery activist. Tubman, an escaped slave, had been serving with the U.S. army to gather intelligence about Confederate positions in order to disrupt supply lines and liberate Confederate slaves. On the first two days of June 1863, she helped lead a raid that resulted in the freeing of around 750 captives.

The raid began on the evening of June 1, when three small U.S. Navy ships departed for the mouth of the Combahee River. The next day Union troops destroyed the pontoon bridge at the Combahee River Ferry and set fire to a number of plantations. Hundreds of slaves working in the fields around the area fled to the riverside, requiring the boats to make multiple trips to evacuate the newly freed men and women to the city of Beaufort. In a written report to U.S. Secretary of War Edwin M. Stanton, Union brigadier general Rufus Saxton noted that the raid was "the only military command in American history wherein a woman, black or white, led the raid and under whose inspiration it was originated and conducted."

formed the Kitchen Table: Women of Color Press in 1980, which published major texts by authors such as Cherríe Moraga and Gloria Anzaldúa. These authors' works were foundational to the third-wave feminism in the 1990s, which paid particular attention to the issues of racial and ethnic intersectionality first raised in the Combahee River Collective's statement.

THEMES AND STYLE

The main theme of *A Black Feminist Statement* is that racial and sexual persecution are inextricably linked and that black women must therefore create their own political and social movement in order to advocate for their unique needs. The statement opens with the declaration "we are actively committed to struggling against racial, sexual, heterosexual, and class oppression … The synthesis of these oppressions creates the conditions of our lives." In each of the following four sections, the authors illustrate how the intersection of multiple oppressions has contributed to the history of black feminism, its principles, the barriers the movement faces, and black feminist issues and projects. The authors state, "our liberation is a necessity not as an adjunct to somebody else's but because of our need as human persons for autonomy."

The statement achieves it rhetorical effect through a highly organized argument for a uniquely black feminist movement built on the experiences of black women. The numbered sections and simple, direct language clarify the complex and often overlooked principle of intersectionality. Although the statement champions the experience of the individual, it does not credit any author in particular, instead attributing itself as the product of "a collective of black feminists … in the process of defining and clarifying our politics." Group authorship eliminates the unfair privileging of a single author and challenges the cultural assumption that ideas may be ethically claimed by individuals. Instead, the statement's use of "we," a tactic notably employed in the Declaration of Independence, grants authority to the group and demonstrates the empowerment, rather than suppression, of individual experiences in the collective.

A Black Feminist Statement makes a direct, emotional appeal to the shared experience of black women, creating new terms to describe black women's unique experience. The authors explore concepts that arose as members of the collective sought to describe their experiences: "We discovered that all of us, because we were 'smart' had also been considered 'ugly,' i.e., 'smart-ugly.' 'Smart-ugly' crystallized the way in which most of us had been forced to develop our intellects at great cost to our 'social' lives." The document is also widely credited with the invention of the term "identity politics," or the idea that "the most profound and potentially radical politics come directly out of our own identity … We reject pedestals, queenhood, and walking ten paces behind. To be recognized as human, levelly human, is enough." These coinages give voice to the experiences of black women that have been left out of the feminist conversation. The authors lament that the result of such exclusion is "[t]he psychological toll of being a Black woman and the difficulties this presents in reaching political consciousness and doing political work."

CRITICAL DISCUSSION

When *A Black Feminist Statement* was published, the ideas expressed in the document were widely discussed in black feminist circles. As a result of these continuing discussions, the statement was reprinted several times, such as in the June 1979 issue of *Off Our Backs,* where it was further refined and transformed. However, because black feminist conversations were taking place outside of the academic mainstream, black feminist publications were all but ignored in scholarship, and academics rarely referred to the document or its significance to expanding the discussion on race and gender in the United States.

A number of publications owe a debt to *A Black Feminist Statement* and its pioneering of the notion of intersectionality. Significant works of black feminist theory that draw on the statement include Moraga and Anzaldúa's *This Bridge Called My Back: Writings by Radical Feminists of Color* (1981), which broadened the collective's focus to include different racial and

ethnic contexts for intersectional analysis. Gloria T. Hull, Patricia Bell Scott, and Barbara Smith's *All the Women Are White, All the Blacks Are Men, But Some of Us Are Brave: Black Women's Studies* (1982) continues an analysis of the gendering of race and the racialization of gender, while Patricia Hill Collins's retrospective *Black Feminist Thought: Knowledge, Consciousness, and the Politics of Empowerment* (1990) insists on the validity of collective and experiential knowledge.

Academic reflections on the value and importance of the collective's statement have become plentiful, as leftist scholars have grown more aware of their intellectual debt to black feminism. A number of texts from the early 2000s chronicle the history of black feminist thought and the importance of *A Black Feminist Statement* to that legacy. In 2001 Duchess Harris credited the "polyvocal political expressions of the Black feminists in the Combahee River Collective [with] defin[ing] the nature of identity politics in the 1980s and 1990s, and challeng[ing] earlier 'essentialist' appeals and doctrines." In the *Encyclopedia of Government and Politics* (2004), M. E. Hawkesworth and Maurice Kogan note that the document "is often seen as the definitive statement regarding the importance of identity politics, particularly for people whose

identity is marked by multiple interlocking oppressions." Recent scholarship, including Brian Norman's 2007 article in *Differences,* has turned to close examination of the rhetorical strategies employed in the text. The statement was included in Estelle B. Freedman's *The Essential Feminist Reader* (2007).

BIBLIOGRAPHY

Sources

Combahee River Collective. "Combahee River Collective: A Black Feminist Statement." *Off Our Backs* 9.6 (1979): 6-8. *JSTOR.* Web. 20 June 2011.

Harris, Duchess. "From the Kennedy Commission to the Combahee Collective: Black Feminist Organizing, 1960-1980." *Sisters in the Struggle: African American Women in the Civil Rights-Black Power Movement.* Ed. Bettye Collier-Thomas and V. P. Franklin. New York: New York UP, 2001. 280-305. Print.

Hawkesworth, M. E., and Maurice Kogan. *Encyclopedia of Government and Politics.* London: Routledge, 1992. Print. Norman, Brian. "'We' in Redux: The Combahee River Collective's Black Feminist Statement." *Differences* 18.2 (2007): 103-132. Print.

Spaine, Daphne. "Women's Rights and Gendered Spaces in 1970s Boston." *Frontiers: A Journal of Women's Studies* 32.1 (2011): 152. Print.

Freedom March participants gather at the Mall in Washington, D.C., on August 28, 1963. *A Black Feminist Statement* addressed social oppression unique to black women and not recognized by the civil rights movement. © BETTMANN/CORBIS

Further Reading

Breines, Wini. *The Trouble between Us: An Uneasy History of White and Black Women in the Feminist Movement.* New York: Oxford UP, 2006. Print.

Collins, Patricia Hill. *Black Feminist Thought: Knowledge, Consciousness, and the Politics of Empowerment.* 2nd ed. New York: Routledge, 2000. Print.

Crenshaw, Kimberlé. "Demarginalizing the Intersection of Race and Sex: A Black Feminist Critique of Antidiscrimination Doctrine, Feminist Theory and Antiracist Politics." *University of Chicago Legal Forum* 139 (1989): 139-67. Print.

James, Stanlie M., Frances Smith Foster, and Beverly Guy-Sheftall. *Still Brave: The Evolution of Black Women's Studies.* New York: Feminist P, 2009. Print.

Sudbury, Julia C. "Toward a Holistic Anti-Violence Agenda: Women of Color as Radical Bridge-Builders." *Social Justice* 30.3 (2003): 134-40. Print.

Ryan, Barbara. *Identity Politics in the Women's Movement.* New York: New York UP, 2001. Print.

Springer, Kimberley. *Living for the Revolution: Black Feminist Organizations, 1968-1980.* Durham: Duke UP, 2005. Print.

Thompson, Becky. "Multiracial Feminism: Recasting the Chronology of Second Wave Feminism." *Feminist Studies* 28.2 (2002): 336-60. Print.

White, Aaronette M. "Talking Feminist, Talking Black: Micromobilization Processes in a Collective Protest against Rape." *Gender and Society* 13.1 (1999): 77-100. Print.

Carina Saxon

A DECLARATION OF WOMEN'S RIGHTS IN ISLAMIC SOCIETIES

Reza Afshari, et al.

OVERVIEW

Originally published in *Free Inquiry,* a bimonthly publication of the Council for Secular Humanism, "A Declaration of Women's Rights in Islamic Societies" (1997) describes the perceived failure of moderate Muslims and Islamic reform movements to address the oppression of women in Islamic societies. A response to increased restrictions on Muslim women's rights during the late twentieth century, the declaration states that all women are entitled to autonomy, equality before the law, and every other basic human right. The document was authored by eighteen original signatories, a mix of scholars, physicians, authors, and political scientists, all born into Muslim families (most came from Iran or South Asia). While conceding that factors other than Islam contribute to the repression of women in Islamic societies, the authors reject contemporary efforts to reinterpret Islam's foundational texts, such as those undertaken by Islamic feminists, and instead demand the complete separation of religion from government and the establishment of fully secular states. This call, addressed to citizens of Islamic states, corresponds to the rise of Islamism, or political Islam, and to the increasing visibility of Muslim political secularists, some of whom envisioned a distinctively Islamic democracy, though others sought simply to ensure that no group, including the Islamists, was excluded from the political process.

The same year it was published, "A Declaration of Women's Rights in Islamic Societies" was reprinted twice more in different journals. However, despite initial interest, the declaration received little critical attention. Although it has not garnered any direct responses, the ideas it puts forth have been advanced by scholars and to remain relevant to contemporary conversations on Islam. Signatories such as Ibn Warraq, Parvin Darabi, and Anwar Shaikh have continued to discuss Muslim women's rights in their subsequent writings.

HISTORICAL AND LITERARY CONTEXT

"A Declaration of Women's Rights in Islamic Societies" responds to the perceived failure of text-based reforms to satisfactorily address the issue of Muslim women's rights. During the twentieth century, women in Muslim societies saw significant advances in provisions for their basic human rights, particularly in terms of suffrage and access to education. Yet, in the last decades of the century, they suffered a number of notable setbacks. Beginning with the success of the 1979 Iranian Revolution, Islamist movements gained momentum throughout the world, and women's rights in many Islamic societies were restricted. For example, after the revolution, Iran reintroduced laws that stripped women of most of their civil rights and forced them to wear a veil, in addition to creating female morality squads to police women's adherence to modesty codes. Similarly, in 1990 a Saudi Arabian custom that prevented women from driving was signed into law, adding to legislation that already denied women the right to work, travel, or even obtain a telephone line without permission from a male guardian.

By the time the declaration was published in 1997, the increasing visibility of a variety of secular and moderate movements, and Islamist groups linked at times to terrorist attacks in the 1980s and 1990s, had sparked a fierce debate among scholars. Some interpreted the teachings of Islam as essentially democratic; others rejected democracy as a Western import but embraced an Islamic understanding of human rights. Still others viewed Islam as an inherent threat to the Western ideals and values they held dear. Many of the signatories of the declaration were already known for their outspoken criticism of Islam. Ibn Warraq, for example, asserted in his 1995 book *Why I Am Not a Muslim,* "Islam is deeply antiwoman. Islam is the fundamental cause of the repression of Muslim women." Bangladeshi author Taslima Nasrin also wrote frequently about the oppression of women in Islam, and her 1993 novel *Lajja* (*Shame*), provoked outrage for its portrayal of the persecution of Bangladeshi Hindus by the Muslim majority in the aftermath of the 1992 Hindu fundamentalist attack on the Babri Mosque in India.

"A Declaration of Women's Rights in Islamic Societies" is a reaction in part to contemporary Islamic feminist works that sought to better understand the problems facing women in Muslim societies through reexamination of foundational texts. Examples of

✜ *Key Facts*

Time Period:
Late 20th Century

Movement/Issue:
Islamic reform; Women's oppression; Rise of political Islam

Place of Publication:
United States

Language of Publication:
English

NAWAL EL SAADAWI'S SECULAR CRITICISM

Feminist, novelist, and writer Nawal El Saadawi was born in Egypt in 1931. Her work is informed by her personal experiences, including her suffering as a victim of female genital mutilation, and by her observations and interactions with other women as a physician. Like the authors of "A Declaration of Women's Rights in Islamic Societies," she criticizes the damaging role of all fundamentalist religions in the struggle for women's equality. However, she ultimately blames socioeconomic and political factors, rather than Islam, for the continued oppression of women in Islamic societies.

El Saadawi argues in an essay published in *The Nawal El Saadawi Reader* (1997), "Islam is not the main obstacle to progress, but rather the oppressive, reactionary, and backward regimes which are often on good terms with certain centres of power in the North." She focuses on poverty and patterns of economic exploitation as the roots of Islamic fundamentalism, admitting the ineffectiveness of wholesale condemnations of Islam, a religion with a multitude of diverse incarnations. Similarly, she decries the forced implementation of "a purely secular approach" in areas where Islam plays a central role in daily life.

such works include the writings of Moroccan sociologist Fatima Mernissi, Egyptian physician and activist Nawal El Saadawi, Pakistani American theologian Riffat Hassan, and Turkish theologian Hidayet Sefkatli Tuksal. In addition, attempts to formulate a declaration of human rights from an Islamic perspective were already underway, as evidenced by the 1981 *Universal Islamic Declaration of Human Rights,* which states, "Islam gave to mankind an ideal code of human rights fourteen centuries ago," and the 1990 *Cairo Declaration of Human Rights*; however "A Declaration of Women's Rights in Islamic Societies" attempted to distance itself from such approaches.

Although the declaration received some attention in the years following its publication, it has mostly faded into obscurity. Nevertheless, several of its signatories have continued to voice many of its key ideas, as in the testimonies of Warraq, Parvin Darabi, and Anwar Shaikh in the edited volume *Leaving Islam: Apostates Speak Out* (2003). Warraq also went on to sign the 2007 "St. Petersburg Declaration," which carefully sidesteps any direct criticism of Islam in its call for secularism. Although the latter declaration addresses forms of oppression of women common in Islamic societies, such as honor killing and forced marriage, it focuses on achieving "the release of Islam from its captivity to the totalitarian ambitions of power-hungry men and the rigid structures of orthodoxy," negating one of the driving principles of "A Declaration of Women's Rights in Islamic Societies."

THEMES AND STYLE

The central theme of the declaration is that women in Islamic societies, including Muslim communities in the West, are barred access to basic human rights and are consistently denied equality with men. The declaration opens with a condemnation of all three of the Abrahamic religions—Judaism, Christianity, and Islam—asserting that their holy books "were devised and enforced by men who claimed divine justification for the subordination of women to men." However, while Christian and Jewish women in the West and in Israel have managed to overcome this history, the declaration states, Muslim women "have been thwarted in their valiant attempts to rise above the inferior position imposed upon them by centuries of Islamic custom and law." Yet, the declaration acknowledges, "Islam may not be the sole factor in the repression of women," citing the importance of social, economic, and cultural factors. Nevertheless, the authors do not acknowledge the many advances made by women in Islamic societies and argue that "Islam and the application of the sharia, Islamic law, remain a major obstacle to the evolution of the position of women." The declaration contains five statements of women's rights, each addressing a different human rights violation associated with Islamic societies: lack of ownership over one's body and unequal inheritance laws, female genital mutilation, forced marriage and imbalanced divorce laws, and lack of educational opportunities and exclusion from public life. The fifth and final declaration is more general, asserting that every woman in an Islamic society "should enjoy the same human rights as those guaranteed under International Human Rights legislation."

"A Declaration of Women's Rights in Islamic Societies" achieves its rhetorical effect by blending the particular situation of women in Islamic societies with a call for universal women's rights. A generalized critique of all three of the major monotheistic religions is followed by a targeted attack on Islamic societies; however, limited attention is paid to the religion of Islam itself. The declaration references the "Islamization programs in Saudi Arabia, Pakistan, Iran, the Sudan, and Afghanistan," as well as "Muslim conservatives" in the Muslim world, "nominally secular India," and the West more broadly, before finally settling on a universalist statement that equates women's rights with human rights and is addressed to "all societies." The conclusion corresponds to the opening paragraph of the declaration, which also speaks to an unparticularized conception of "oppression of women," identifying it as "a grave offense against all of humanity" and "an impediment to social and moral progress throughout the world." In this way, the text seeks to make the issue of women's rights in Islamic societies a global problem with far-reaching repercussions.

Stylistically, "A Declaration of Women's Rights in Islamic Societies" is distinguished by its effort to negotiate the competing languages of confrontation and equivocation. The uncompromising language of censure used to address the historical "oppression of women by orthodox and fundamentalist religions" is tempered by the concession that "local, social, economic, political, and educational forces as well as the prevalence of pre-Islamic customs must also be taken into consideration." Although this inconsistency lessens the impact of the declaration, it reflects the struggle to reconcile attempts to improve the status of women in Islamic societies with universalist rhetoric on women's rights.

CRITICAL DISCUSSION

When "A Declaration of Women's Rights in Islamic Societies" was first published in the fall of 1997, it received little critical attention, although it was reprinted in December of that year in the *Middle East Quarterly,* the journal of the American right-wing Middle East Forum. The short introduction to the text asserts that the "born-Muslim" authors and signatories of the manifesto "stand out as remarkable" in contrast to "most of those concerned with the status of Muslim women" who "reinterpret sacred texts to make Islam compatible with current notions." The same month, the declaration was also reprinted in *International Humanist News,* the magazine of the London-based International Humanist and Ethical Union. The magazine's introduction to the text praises the manifesto in language similar to that found in *Middle East Quarterly* and argues for absolute secularism.

After the reprinting of "A Declaration of Women's Rights in Islamic Societies," the document was largely ignored by scholars. However, several of its signatories remain prominent voices in scholarship on women in Islamic societies. In 1999 writer Parvin Darabi published *Rage against the Veil: The Courageous Life and Death of an Islamic Dissident,* which details the 1994 self-immolation of her sister, doctor and activist Homa Darabi, to raise awareness about the oppression of women in Iran. In *Human Rights in Iran: The Abuse of Cultural Relativism* (2001), author Reza Afshari devotes a chapter to Iran's record on women's rights.

Trends in scholarship on the declaration are diverse. Warren Allen Smith includes it in his encyclopedia-like *Who's Who in Hell: A Handbook and International Directory for Humanists, Freethinkers, Naturalists, Rationalists, and Non-Theists* (2000). In addition, the work of later scholars has addressed many of the declaration's concerns, even if it does not directly engage with the document. In *Feminism and Islamic Fundamentalism: The Limits of Postmodern Analysis* (1999), Haideh Moghissi calls for absolute secularism and outright rejects even the possibility of Islamic feminism. Similarly, Tariq Ali sets out to show through his reading of the Quran in *The Clash*

Three young women study at Yogyakarta University in Java. The authors of the *Declaration of Women's Rights in Islamic Societies* call for Islamic women to have equal access to educational opportunities. © WORLD RELIGIONS PHOTO LIBRARY/ALAMY

of Fundamentalisms: Crusades, Jihads and Modernity (2003) that "the reality of women in Islam is a prefabricated destiny."

BIBLIOGRAPHY

Sources

Ali, Tariq. *The Clash of Fundamentalisms: Crusades, Jihads and Modernity.* New York: Verso, 2003. Print.

Azzam, Salem. "Universal Islamic Declaration of Human Rights." *International Journal of Human Rights* 2.3 (1998): 102-12. Print.

El Saadawi, Nawal. *The Nawal El Saadawi Reader.* New York: Zed, 1997. Print.

"The Rights of Muslim Women." *Middle East Quarterly* 4.4 (1997): 83-84. Print.

"The St. Petersburg Declaration." *Institution for the Secularization of Islamic Society.* Center for Inquiry, 5 Apr. 2007. Web. 28 Sept. 2012.

Warraq, Ibn. *Why I Am Not a Muslim.* Amherst: Prometheus, 1995. Print.

Further Reading

Afshari, Reza. "Egalitarian Islam and Misogynist Islamic Tradition: A Critique of the Feminist Reinterpretation of Islamic History and Heritage." *Critique* 4 (1994): 13-33. Print.

Ahmed, Leila. *Women and Gender in Islam: Historical Roots of a Modern Debate.* New Haven: Yale UP, 1992. Print.

El Saadawi, Nawal. *The Hidden Face of Eve: Women in the Arab World.* Trans. Sherif Hetata. London: Zed, 1980. Print.

Mernissi, Fatima. *The Veil and the Male Elite: A Feminist Interpretation of Women's Rights in Islam.* Trans. Mary Jo Lakeland. Reading: Addison-Wesley, 1991. Print.

Wadud, Amina. *Qur'an and Woman: Rereading the Sacred Text from a Woman's Perspective.* New York: Oxford UP, 1999. Print.

Allison Blecker

MAMA'S BABY, PAPA'S MAYBE
An American Grammar Book
Hortense J. Spillers

OVERVIEW

"Mama's Baby, Papa's Maybe: An American Grammar Book," a 1977 article by scholar Hortense J. Spillers, brings together a historical consciousness of the traumatic effects of slavery on American race relations and a feminist awareness of the possibilities and problems posed by black families' failures to live perfectly within socially defined gender roles. According to Spillers, as a result of the destabilizing effects of slavery, in which female and male bodies were mutilated and isolated and which necessitated the formation of nontraditional kinship systems to replace those lost in the capture and transportation of slaves from Africa to America, traditional divisions between masculinity and femininity do not operate fully in black communities. Often, black women—married or single—are the ones in positions of responsibility and power. Whereas many twentieth-century sociologists interpreted this as a sign of the downfall of black communities, citing the lack of stable or nuclear family structures as a major factor in African American poverty and crime, Spillers's article contends that such a deviation from dominant American gender norms presents an opportunity for social transformation.

Like other black feminist works, "Mama's Baby, Papa's Maybe" helped to establish and develop the concept of intersectionality, which considers various forms of social oppression to be inextricably linked. Spillers's article insists on the necessity of historical awareness in order to analyze contemporary society. "Mama's Baby, Papa's Maybe" represents a watershed moment in academic awareness of American slave history, serving as a manifesto on the effects of that history on African American psyches, families, and extended communities.

HISTORICAL AND LITERARY CONTEXT

In 1965, sociologist and then-Assistant Secretary of Labor Daniel Patrick Moynihan published "The Negro Family: The Case for National Action," commonly known as the "Moynihan Report." This document focuses on a perceived connection between black poverty and the structure of the black family, concluding that the absence of nuclear families adversely affects African American prosperity and social progress. The report was widely criticized by leading figures in the black community, including the Rev. Jesse Jackson and Rev. Al Sharpton, as well as the National Association for the Advancement of Colored People (NAACP). In the view of these critics, the report's portrayal of the black family as a "tangle of pathology" traded in negative stereotypes. The report provided the initial impetus for Spillers's argument, directing her critical and historical investigation into the nature of African American gender roles and kinship structures.

Throughout the 1970s and 1980s, black feminist collectives, groups, and movements—among them the National Black Feminist Association, the Combahee River Collective, and the Third World Women's Alliance—focused on the impact of gender and family roles on African American life. Although many of these organizations were built on communities, strategies, and structures dating from the civil rights movement of the 1960s, black feminists went on to develop the concept of intersectionality, which allowed them to consider the interaction between racial stereotypes and patriarchal gender roles that created the unique frictions surrounding the African American family.

As black feminist thought developed, both mainstream and academic publications on the intersection of race and gender in the American context proliferated. The novels of Alice Walker and the essays of Audre Lorde—particularly her 1984 essay "Man Child," in which she meditates on her position as a black lesbian raising a son—address problems of gender and sexuality within the African American community. Significant academic works responding to these issues include Barbara Smith's *All the Women Are White, All the Blacks Are Men, But Some of Us Are Brave: Black Women's Studies* (1982), *Home Girls: A Black Feminist Anthology* (1983), and the scholarship of bell hooks and Patricia Hill Collins. However, Spillers is relatively unique in her application of psychoanalytic and linguistic methods to the intersection of race and gender. Her emphasis on history, although also seen in germinal works such as *A Black Feminist Statement* by the Combahee River Collective (1977), proved significant in the development of black feminist discourse in academia.

⁘ *Key Facts*

Time Period:
Late 20th Century

Movement/Issue:
Slavery; Black feminism

Place of Publication:
United States

Language of Publication:
English

CONTROVERSY AND TEACHING THE HISTORY OF SLAVERY IN AMERICA

The emotionally intense way in which Hortense J. Spillers's "Mama's Baby, Papa's Maybe: An American Grammar Book" insists on the recognition and confrontation of the pain and horror of American slavery has remained controversial in the twenty-first century, as debates over the teaching of American history question the place of graphic details in public education. In 2010, for example, the Texas School Board voted to redesign public school curricula. The changes included consistently replacing allusions to the Atlantic slave trade with the more euphemistic "Atlantic triangular trade," thereby removing explicit references to slave history. Many educators, academics, and activists protested the change.

However, even when the history of slavery remains present in classrooms, the intensity of the trauma that surrounds it can render lessons fraught with racial tensions. In a history lesson at an Ohio elementary school in 2011, students designated as "masters" sold other students as "slaves" in a mock auction. The incident generated complaints, an investigation, and an apology. Though this is only one example, it indicates that the role-playing of historical trauma for educational purposes continues to be a controversial technique.

Spillers was as an early explicator of the relationship between blackness and gender stereotypes, identifying the limited and limiting names and categories available for black men and women to inhabit. "Neo-slave narratives," retellings of slave history and experience as ways of understanding contemporary black life, have a point of origin in Spillers's work. Although Spillers herself is not well known outside of academia, the conversations she participated in have shaped and generated contemporary forms of black culture and identity.

THEMES AND STYLE

Spillers emphasizes the need to understand the long roots of American race relations, arguing that to examine or critique the twentieth-century black family without reference to slave history is to replicate rather than refute old and damaging stereotypes. The "American grammar" of Spillers's title is one of bodies in historical time:

> The massive demographic shifts, the violent formation of a modern African consciousness, that take place on the subsaharan Continent during the initiative strikes which open the Atlantic Slave Trade in the fifteenth century of our Christ, interrupted hundreds of years of black African culture. We write and think, then, about an outcome of aspects of African-American life in the United States under the pressure of those events.

In the course of her article, Spillers provides an agonized history of the black body in pain, examining sites of communal trauma and scarification that include the violence of the Middle Passage, the sorrow of enslaved reproduction, and the ambivalent place African American women occupy outside of conventional structures of femininity.

Spillers's use of the term "grammar" carries significance at several levels: it indicates the pervasive and systematic nature of the structures of race and gender that she examines but also demonstrates the entangled and mutually constitutive relationship the author sees between language and these structures. As Joan W. Scott notes in "Gender: A Useful Category of Historical Analysis," the use of the term "gender" to describe bodies rather than words was a feminist innovation of the 1970s, one that met with a great deal of controversy. Spillers extends the politicization of grammar to include the intersection of race and gender, examining the dominant effects of language on black bodies, such as in her opening confession: "Let's face it. I am a marked woman, but not everybody knows my name. 'Peaches' and 'Brown Sugar,' 'Sapphire' and 'Earth Mother,' 'Aunty,' 'Granny,' 'God's Holy Fool,' a 'Miss Ebony First,' or 'Black Woman at the Podium'."

The language of "Mama's Baby, Papa's Maybe" oscillates between erudition and mourning, grammatology and suffering. Spillers deliberately draws her readers' attention to the "female body strung from a tree limb, or bleeding from the breast on any given day of field work because the 'overseer,' standing the length of a whip, has popped her flesh open." She refuses to gloss over the negative, even though it may be "'embarrassing,' just as the retrieval of mutilated female bodies will likely be 'backward' for some people. Neither the shameface of the embarrassed, nor the not-looking-back of the self-assured is of much interest to us." Although Spillers cites the elevated discourses of Sigmund Freud and Michel Foucault, she never allows her reader to lose track of the trauma of American slavery.

CRITICAL DISCUSSION

As Farah Jasmine Green says in a 2007 retrospective conversation on Spillers's manifesto, "For so many of us, 'Mama's Baby, Papa's Maybe' was the first we even thought about some of the things [Spillers] cited." In the same conversation, Saidiya Hartman records a more mixed response, noting the disjuncture between Spillers's project and traditional feminism, necessitated by the unique relationship of black men and women as mediated by a history of enslavement. Unlike traditional feminist criticism, Hartman notes, Spillers does not always center women in her cultural critique. In a 1998 overall appraisal of black feminist psychoanalytic scholarship, Sharon Monteith ranks Spillers among the "most successful" critics in the field.

However, the magnitude of the response to "Mama's Baby, Papa's Maybe" may best be observed through the swiftness with which Spillers's ideas were adopted and transformed by other chromatic feminists, activists, authors, and scholars. Kimberlé Crenshaw's important work on race and legality in the late 1980s entered into numerous dialogues with Spillers's writing, helping to develop the academic and social implications of intersectionality. Paul Gilroy's *The Black Atlantic: Modernity and Double Consciousness* (1993) expands on Spillers's historicist methodology, exploring the diasporic cultures created by the Atlantic slave trade, while Deborah R. Grayson's "Mediating Intimacy: Black Surrogate Mothers and the Law" (1998) uses Spillers's work on representations of the black family to study the effects of surrogacy and reproductive laws on African American communities.

While the methodological interventions proposed by Spillers's article have had wide-ranging applications, direct scholarship on her work tends to be retrospective in nature, placing her in the historical context of 1980s black feminism. David M. Jones's "'Women's Lib,' Gender Theory, and the Politics of Home: How I Became a Black Male Feminist" (2001) explores Spillers's thesis from the other side: the impact of the intersection between race and gender on black masculinity. In his influential 2006 article "Feeling Brown, Feeling Down: Latina Affect, the Performativity of Race, and the Depressive Position," José Esteban Muñoz utilizes emergent discourses of affect to further Spillers's investigation of racialized pain. In 2007, Saidiya Hartman, Farah Jasmine Griffin, Shelly Eversley, and Jennifer L. Morgan conversed directly with Spillers about her legacy in forming and interrogating narratives about black feminism and the black family.

Assistant Secretary of Labor Daniel P. Moynihan addresses black urban poverty before the Senate Government Options subcommittee in 1966. Hortense J. Spillers used his 1965 report, "The Negro Family," as a starting point for her essay. © BETTMANN/CORBIS

BIBLIOGRAPHY

Sources

Grayson, Deborah R. "Mediating Intimacy: Black Surrogate Mothers and the Law." *Critical Inquiry* 24.2 (1998): 525-46. Print.

Jones, David M. "'Women's Lib,' Gender Theory, and the Politics of Home: How I Became a Black Male Feminist." *Feminist Teacher* 13.3 (2001): 213-24. Print.

Monteith, Sharon M. Rev. of *Female Subjects in Black and White: Race, Psychoanalysis, Feminism,* by Elizabeth Abel, Barbara Christian, and Helene Moglen. *Journal of American Studies* 32.3 (1998): 557-58. Print.

Scott, Joan W. "Gender: A Useful Category of Historical Analysis." *American Historical Review* 91.5 (1986): 1053-75. Print.

Spillers, Hortense J. "Mama's Baby, Papa's Maybe: An American Grammar Book." *Diacritics* 17.2 (1987): 64-81. Print.

Spillers, Hortense J., Saidiya Hartman, Farah Jasmine Griffin, Shelly Eversley, and Jennifer L. Morgan. "'Whatcha Gonna Do?': Revisiting 'Mama's Baby, Papa's Maybe: An American Grammar Book': A Conversation with Hortense Spillers, Saidiya Hartman, Farah Jasmine Griffin, Shelly Eversley, & Jennifer L. Morgan." *Women's Studies Quarterly* 35.1-2 (2007): 299-309. Print.

Further Reading

Collins, Patricia Hill. *Black Sexual Politics: African Americans, Gender and the New Racism.* New York: Routledge, 2004. Print.

Crenshaw, Kimberlé. "Demarginalizing the Intersection of Race and Sex: A Black Feminist Critique of Antidiscrimination Doctrine, Feminist Theory and Antiracist Politics." *University of Chicago Legal Forum* (1989): 139-67. Print.

Gilroy, Paul. *The Black Atlantic: Modernity and Double Consciousness.* Cambridge: Harvard UP/Verso, 1993. Print.

Lorde, Audre. "Man Child: A Black Lesbian Feminist's Response." *Sister Outsider.* Berkeley: The Crossing, 1984. 72-80. Print.

Lurie, Susan, Ann Cvetkovich, Jane Gallop, Tania Modleski, Hortense Spillers, and Carla Kaplan. "Roundtable: Restoring Feminist Politics to Poststructuralist Critique." *Feminist Studies* 27.3 (2001): 679-707. Print.

Muñoz, José Esteban. "Feeling Brown, Feeling Down: Latina Affect, the Performativity of Race, and the Depressive Position." *Signs* 31.3 (2006): 675-88. Print.

Carina Saxon

MANIFESTO OF THE 343

Simone de Beauvoir

❖ *Key Facts*

Time Period:
Late 20th Century

Movement/Issue:
Women's liberation;
Abortion rights

Place of Publication:
France

**Language of
Publication:**
French

OVERVIEW

Published in *Le Nouvel Observateur* in 1971, *Manifesto of the 343*, also known as *Manifesto of the 343 Bitches* or *Manifesto of the 343 Sluts* (*Manifeste des 343 salopes*), is a French feminist manifesto collectively written by "the women's liberation movement"—although commonly credited to Simone de Beauvoir—that presents 343 signatures of women claiming to have undergone illegal abortions. The manifesto was intended to let other women know that they were not alone in their desire to access free and legal abortions, but it was also intended to open the eyes of political leaders and medical professionals of the time to the injustice of forcing women to resort to criminal measures in order to undergo a relatively simple medical procedure. The manifesto demands that abortions become free for all women and be treated solely as a medical surgery instead of as a political and moral problem. This document appeared during the second-wave feminist movement in France and was signed by some of the leading feminist theorists who influenced both French and American feminism during the 1960s and 1970s, including Beauvoir, Gisèle Halimi, and Monique Wittig.

The manifesto immediately generated discussion in political circles and feminist groups as well as the general public about the issue of abortion and the inadequacy of French laws surrounding the procedure. A week after the manifesto was published, a satirical newspaper, *Charlie Hebdo,* printed an article designed to poke fun at the politicians who were faced with the feminist uprising; the article demanded, "who got the 343 *salopes* pregnant?" Even though all the women who signed the document admitted to breaking the law, none of them were formally prosecuted. The manifesto was highly influential in changing public opinion about the sexist nature of the existing abortion laws in France, which were changed so that the procedure became legal in 1975.

HISTORICAL AND LITERARY CONTEXT

Manifesto of the 343, published during the women's liberation movement in France, deals with one of the fundamental issues concerning the movement: the right of women to control their own bodies. The manifesto seeks to legalize abortions by discussing the procedure as a simple operation that only affects the body of the patient. The signatories of the manifesto claim to have undergone illegal abortions, which were not necessarily sanitary or performed by qualified professionals, thereby exposing themselves as lawbreakers subject to fines and arrest. The manifesto argues that these women should not be seen as criminals just because they have undergone a medical procedure.

When the manifesto was published, it was still a criminal offence for women to have abortions in France, and both the government and the highly influential Catholic Church—which monitored the education system, keeping scholars such as Beauvoir ignorant of some of the philosophical and psychoanalytic theories that would alter her ideas of freedom and citizenship—strongly encouraged women to stay home and raise children in order to repopulate the country after the devastating losses of World War II.

BEAUVOIR AND *THE SECOND SEX*

Although throughout her lifetime Simone de Beauvoir published many influential books about philosophy and feminist theory, her most popular—and perhaps her most influential—theoretical work, which inspired many of her later writings, was *The Second Sex* (*Le deuxième sexe*). Published in 1949, when an organized feminist movement was in its infancy, *The Second Sex* discusses the theory upon which the women's liberation movement would be based. The text separates gender roles from biological sex and includes the famous quote: "One is not born, but rather becomes, a woman." The traits that define women, Beauvoir argues, are subordinate to the traits that define men, and if women want to be considered equal to their male counterparts, they must change the discourse surrounding women and femininity so that the role of women becomes more active and independent, especially in the political and economic spheres.

Despite its influence on many feminist writers and theorists, *The Second Sex* has been criticized for its portrayal of the homemaker and mother as negative feminine roles that women are forced to perform, rather than roles that are freely chosen. The leaders of the Catholic Church were also critical of *The Second Sex,* claiming it contained an "immoral doctrine" that could "damage the family." It was placed on the Vatican Index of Proscribed Books, which only added to the notoriety and popularity of the text.

France was considered a latecomer in its acceptance of women's rights, with women only achieving the status of full citizens—as opposed to legal minors—in 1938 and being granted the right to vote in 1944. Contraceptives were legalized in 1967, but abortion was legalized only under certain circumstances in 1975. Simone de Beauvoir, born in 1908, experienced these changes firsthand but also had a greater perspective on women's rights as a result of her extensive travels across Europe and to Japan and North America, areas where the realization of women's rights was at different stages than in France. These experiences played a significant role in her desire to improve the status of women in France so that they would be on a par with the women in activist movements developing in America and other European countries.

This manifesto was not the first, nor was it the most influential, of the works produced by Beauvoir during the women's liberation movement. Her most famous piece, *The Second Sex* (*Le deuxième sexe*) was published in 1949 and provided the theoretical basis for second-wave feminism in many countries, including France and America. The theories in *The Second Sex* directly influenced the ideas expressed in the *Manifesto of the 343,* including the argument that women were treated as second-class citizens, particularly when it came to making decisions about simple medical procedures that affected their own bodies.

The manifesto initiated discussion about abortion in political and personal spheres and ultimately led to the legalization of some abortions in France in 1975. The final decision to legalize the procedure was made after the Bobigny trial, in which a teenage girl was charged with illegally aborting her pregnancy. Beauvoir testified at this trial, reiterating many of the points outlined in the manifesto about the sexist nature of the laws and culture of France, which forced women to undergo dangerous illegal operations instead of granting them the power to make decisions about their own bodies. Even though abortion is still a morally contested topic today, activism by Beauvoir and other signees of the *Manifesto of the 343* was influential in changing the discourse surrounding abortions and transferring the decision to undergo the operation from the government and medical professionals to the women actually seeking the procedure.

THEMES AND STYLE

The main theme of *Manifesto of the 343* is that women should be allowed access to free abortions without being accused of an illegal offence. Beauvoir outlines three radical changes that each individual woman, and society at large, must come to terms with in order to accept abortion as strictly a medical decision, rather than a political or moral dilemma. The first is that women need to be viewed as the producers of children and, as such, should be able to choose whether or not

Simone de Beauvoir in 1972, appearing as a defense witness at the Bobigny trial, which led to the legalization of abortion in France three years later. AP PHOTO/JEAN-JACQUES LEVY

to have a child. If women went on strike—by refusing to have children altogether—they could put pressure on the system to pay attention to their demands. Second, a woman should only have a child if she feels the society is an accepting place in which to raise it. And third, a woman should only have a child if she feels the political situation is suitable for both her and the child, rather than act as a broodmare producing future soldiers or laborers.

The manifesto is written from the point of view of the generalized "woman"; it speaks for all women, giving the piece the sense of the collective voice of all 343 signees. This perspective works to persuade the audience that the women of France were unified in their opinion that the existing laws did not match societal needs. In order to prove this point, many of the statistics presented in the manifesto were exaggerated, including the claims that "a million women have abortions each year in France" and "5000 of us die" as a result of unsanitary conditions or the inadequate care of unqualified practitioners. While these numbers are difficult to track, it is estimated that 120,000 illegal abortions were performed annually before the procedure was legalized, and deaths from the procedure ranged between forty and fifty a year, according to Sandra Reineke in her book *Beauvoir and Her Sisters* (2011). Beauvoir's intentional exaggeration of the statistics does not detract from the manifesto's overall message but serves to enhance the apparent decision by the women of France to stand together and rebel against the outdated and sexist laws surrounding the control of their bodies.

The manifesto is blunt and unapologetic in tone. It associates women with cattle being bred by society to produce offspring without consideration of the future mother or the potential life of the child. It equates women with slaves, citing the deplorable fact

PRIMARY SOURCE

MANIFESTO OF THE 343

A million women have abortions in France each year. Because they are condemned to secrecy, they are aborted under dangerous conditions. If done under medical control, this operation is one of the simplest. These millions of women have been passed over in silence. I declare that I am one of them, I have had an abortion. Just as we demand free access to birth-control methods, we demand freedom to have abortions.

    Signed:

    Simone de Beauvoir,

    Christiane Rochefort,

    Françoise Sagan,

    Colette Audry,

    Violette Leduc,

    Gisèle Halimi,

    Romy Schneider,

    Delphine Seyrig,

    Jeanne Moreau,

    Catherine Deneuve,

    Micheline Presle,

    among others.

SOURCE: *New French Feminisms: An Anthology,* edited by Elaine Marks and Isabelle de Courtivron. Amherst: University of Massachusetts Press, 1980.

that women do not have control of their own bodies in such a scientifically advanced society. Plural pronouns—such as *we, us,* and *our*—give the sense of a collective speaking with a singular voice, and the repetition of the word *abortion* makes clear the laws that the manifesto is seeking to change. The collective persona was necessary in order to push the politicians to believe their laws no longer suited the public, and the word *abortion* was repeated in order to bring it into the popular discourse of the time and to further press the lawmakers of France to yield to the people in their demands for women's rights.

CRITICAL DISCUSSION

Although the manifesto initially generated the discussion needed to change the political stance on abortions in France, it met with criticism from many women's organizations not directly involved in its writing. Anne Tristan and Annie de Pisan remark in their personal reflections, "Tales from the Women's Movement" (1977), that the organizers of the manifesto were accused of being "reformists" and that the inclusion of Beauvoir in the project generated the

response: "What's that got to do with anything? We don't want any of that kind of feminism here." The reasons for this protest were based on class differences, Tristan and Pisan explain. Thus, some women felt as though *Manifesto of the 343* only dealt with the middle-class issues of a "bunch of bourgeois [who] can all afford abortions." Once the piece was published and the political discussion was focused on the legitimate issue of abortion, feminist discussion proved to be generally supportive.

Following the initial appearance of the manifesto, discussions about abortion led to a change in public opinion. A few months after its publication, a group of six hundred medical professionals published a signed manifesto claiming they had performed illegal abortions and were available to perform more. The discourse surrounding abortion eventually led to a change in the law, but specific conditions had to be met—for example, a pregnancy could only be aborted before the tenth week. Reineke looks at the *Manifesto of the 343* as an important historical document and remarks upon how "Beauvoir and her work became icons for the post war feminist struggle for women's rights and exemplify how feminist high literature can participate in the creation of an empowered 'sisterhood.'" The idea that this manifesto was highly influential in altering French opinion still dominates current scholarship, and the association of this manifesto with Beauvoir only enhances its groundbreaking importance in the development of French feminism.

Most of the scholarship surrounding *Manifesto of the 343* discusses its political impact in changing the abortion laws in France. It is viewed as a cornerstone of feminist literature, having generated social discourse about women's bodies and women's freedom to make decisions regarding their bodies. Deirdre Bair, in her biography of Beauvoir (1990), explains that the manifesto "created an uproar, and naturally much of the attention was focussed on Beauvoir, who had been the favourite target of right-wing writers and publications for years." Similarly, Reineke claims that the manifesto was the first to make the women's liberation movement public in France.

BIBLIOGRAPHY

Sources

Bair, Deirdre. *Simone de Beauvoir, a Biography.* New York: Summit, 1990. Print.

Beauvoir, Simone de. "Manifeste des 343 salopes." *Le Nouvel Observateur.* Le Nouvel Observateur, 5 Apr. 1971. Web. 8 Aug. 2012.

Reineke, Sandra. *Beauvoir and Her Sisters: The Politics of Women's Bodies in France.* Chicago: U of Illinois P, 2011. Print.

Tidd, Ursula. *Simone de Beauvoir.* London: Reaktion, 2009. *Ebrary.* Web. 11 Aug. 2012.

Tristan, Anne, and Annie de Pisan. "Tales from the Women's Movement." Trans. Roisin Mallaghan. *French*

Feminist Thought: A Reader. Ed. Toril Moi. New York: Blackwell, 1987. 33-69. Print.

Further Reading

Beauvoir, Simone de. *Memoirs of a Dutiful Daughter.* 1958. New York: Harper, 2005. Print.

———. *The Second Sex.* New ed. Ed. and Trans. Constance Borde and Sheila Malovany-Chevallier. London: Cape, 2009. Print.

Brison, Susan J. "Beauvoir and Feminism: Interview and Reflections." *The Cambridge Companion to Simone de Beauvoir.* Ed. Claudia Card. Cambridge: Cambridge UP, 2003. 189-207. Print.

Halimi, Gisèle. *The Right to Choose.* Trans. Rosemary Morgan. St. Lucia: U of Queensland P, 1977. Print.

Monteil, Claudine. "Simone de Beauvoir, Witness to a Century." *Simone de Beauvoir Studies* 14 (1997): 5-12. Print.

Schwarzer, Alice. *Simone de Beauvoir Today: Conversations 1972-1982.* Trans. Marianne Howarth. London: Hogarth, 1984. Print.

Siegel, Deborah. *Sisterhood, Interrupted: From Radical Women to Grrls Gone Wild.* New York: Palgrave, 2007. Print.

Katherine Barker

NATIONAL RESOLUTION ON WOMEN

Students for a Democratic Society

✣ *Key Facts*

Time Period:
Mid-20th Century

Movement/Issue:
Socialism; New Left;
Second-wave feminism

Place of Publication:
United States

**Language of
Publication:**
English

OVERVIEW

The "National Resolution on Women" written by members of Students for a Democratic Society (SDS) and passed at their December 1968 National Council meeting, is one of the first acknowledgments of female inequality both within SDS and in U.S. society in general, as well as an outline designed to increase female empowerment within the socialist revolutionary movement. Arising out of the Southern civil rights movement and antiwar demonstrations, SDS was one of the largest organizations of the so-called New Left. But in spite of the organization's progressive politics, many female activists felt dissatisfied with the way their roles in SDS mirrored those in traditional society and with the assertion that other causes were more important than feminist concerns. The "National Resolution on Women" was written as a response to these complaints and in support of the movement's growing feminist consciousness.

For many female SDS activists at the time, this statement was too little, too late. Many women felt that their struggles had not been taken seriously by the organization and that this resolution was merely an insincere attempt to keep them from defecting from SDS to the women's movement. While the resolution admitted that male supremacy was a fact within the organization, it offered no remedies to combat this problem. By 1968 female SDS activists were divided, with liberal feminists hoping to work from within the movement and radical feminists stating that women's liberation could only be achieved via separatism. Drafted only a year before the collapse of SDS, the "National Resolution on Women" was the most progressive statement of feminist values to date by the organization. However, it ultimately represented the way in which the SDS leadership had fallen out of step with the interests of many of its members.

HISTORICAL AND LITERARY CONTEXT

The "National Resolution on Women" responds to increasing complaints by female SDS activists, who were concerned not only that women's issues were not taken seriously within the organization but also that the organization itself echoed the sexism of society at large. Women within SDS were mostly assigned traditionally feminine roles, such as typing minutes and serving food, even as less qualified young men rose within the ranks. Sexual and interpersonal relationships between members were problematic and inherently unequal. Women who wanted feminism to become a more serious part of the SDS platform were ridiculed or told that gender equality was not as important as racial equality or ending the war in Vietnam. College-educated, forward-thinking women saw no more opportunity for themselves inside the movement than they saw outside of it.

By December 1968 these frustrations had been building for quite some time, and several independent women's groups such as Redstockings and WITCH were already in the process of forming. The popularity of the civil rights group Student Nonviolent Coordinating Committee (SNCC), a much more female-driven organization, left SDS seemingly lacking in opportunity. Furthermore, the civil rights movement gave women a framework to talk about their own inequality in society. By 1968 SDS was facing pressure to respond to criticism of its sexual politics. SDS member Noel Ignatin wrote a first draft of the original resolution, which was deemed unsatisfactory by many female activists and was subsequently redrafted.

The "National Resolution on Women" articulated many of the same concerns of earlier writings on gender issues. One of the first writings on women's inequality within the New Left was "Sex and Caste: A Kind of Memo," published anonymously but written by Casey Hayden and Mary King in 1965, which addressed problems within SNCC. A month later, SDS held its first feminist workshop and issued a mild resolution titled "On Roles in SDS." The workshop, however, suffered problems; men became defensive and thought the issue was moot, while women felt as if they were not being heard. For the June 1967 SDS convention, a workshop on women's liberation issued a statement called "Liberation of Women." In spite of the resolution's mild language and attempts to appease men (the statement ends with "we love you!"), the convention dissolved into chaos, hooting, and catcalls when the resolution was presented.

In the months following the publication of the "National Resolution on Women" responses and debates were sparked. Many members, including SDS members Beverly Jones and Judith Brown, believed the statement proved that the SDS was trying to serve too many interests and that an independent female liberation movement was essential. Member Roxanne Dunbar (later Dunbar-Ortiz) criticized the resolution for offering no analysis of male-female relations and the family unit. Although the "National Resolution on Women" went further than any SDS document before it, it largely failed to appease the women it addressed.

THEMES AND STYLE

The primary theme of the "National Resolution on Women" is an acknowledgment of the oppression of women and a delineation of the ways in which women's oppression and eventual liberation can fit into a socialist framework. The document begins by stating that "women form the oldest and largest continually oppressed group in the family of human-kind, their subjugation dating from the downfall of primitive communal society and the rise of private property." The resolution frames women's struggles within a larger class struggle but never directly attributes blame. Instead it attributes "the material basis of women's oppression" to three factors: that women are "a reserve army of labor to bring down wages," that women "perform free services (housekeeping)," and that the structures of society position women to "act as a lightning rod for men's justified frustration, anger, and shame at their inability to control their natural and social environment." The piece concludes with four concrete goals: equal pay for female university workers; improvement of women's educational institutions; awareness of women's oppression in other institutions, such as women's detention centers; and a school curriculum that challenges traditional gender roles instead of reinforcing them.

The work attempts to appeal to female activists through a sense of unified struggle; its point of view is that of the collective. At a time when SDS was trying to rein in splinter groups, it was important to convey a sense that all oppression could be conquered under the umbrella of a socialist revolution. The fight for women's liberation "doesn't stand apart from the fight against capitalism in our society, but rather is an integral part of that fight." The resolution also includes lines that seem intended to quell anger, such as asserting that "male supremacy in the movement mirrors male supremacy in capitalist society," as well as the assertion that "black working-class women are the most oppressed group in society." Although these assertions are significant, they are underdeveloped, and the manifesto offers no concrete framework or goals for eliminating sexism within SDS or understanding of the intersection of gender and racial oppression.

The "National Resolution on Women" differs from other feminist tracts of its time in that its language is broad and somewhat formal, borrowing from Marxist ideology and vocabulary. It assumes an understanding of and sympathy with the ideas

THE DRAMATIC CONCLUSION OF SDS

By 1968 Students for a Democratic Society had nearly one hundred thousand members on almost three hundred college campuses. That year SDS organized the largest student protest in the history of the United States, with nearly one million participants. It seemed unlikely that an organization gaining such traction among young people would fall apart in about a year. Yet the issues underlying the "National Resolution on Women" were only the tip of the iceberg when it came to warring factions within SDS. Most notable among these factions were the pro-Maoist Progressive Labor (PL) group, the Revolutionary Youth Movement (RYM), which would later become the Weather Underground (the Weathermen), and Worker-Student Alliance (WSA). Irreverent anarchist groups like the Youth International Party, or Yippies, and Up Against the Wall Motherfucker encouraged violent action against the state, alienating older members committed to non-violence and grassroots organizing. The growing Black Panther movement and women's movement also had troubled alliances with SDS.

At the 1969 SDS convention in Chicago, events descended into chaos as the warring factions broke out into shouting after a Black Panther speaker advocated "pussy power." Shouts of "End male chauvinism!" were met with "End racism!" The RYM members tried to expel the PL and WSA factions, then staged a walkout led by Bernadine Dohrn. The RYM transformed into the Weather Underground, a smaller, radical organization that advocated and used violence in its mission to overthrow the U.S. government. As a result of the splintering into factions, SDS was effectively destroyed.

behind the "socialist revolution" proposed by SDS. At a time when "the personal is political" was becoming a feminist slogan, the text seems to deliberately deal in generalities and speak as broadly as possible. While the language is strong, it does not convey a sense of urgency to the struggle or place blame with any particular group. Instead, it insists that men's oppression of women is merely part of a "justified frustration" with capitalist society.

CRITICAL DISCUSSION

To many female activists, the "National Resolution on Women" did not go far enough for an organization that had shown such a marked disinterest in feminist causes. In 1968 Jones and Brown published *Toward a Female Liberation Movement*, which argues against the manifesto's claim that women could achieve all of their goals while working within the movement. They accused the women who had worked on the manifesto within SDS of "reject[ing] an identification within their own sex and ... using the language of female power in an attempt to advance themselves personally in the male power structure they are presently concerned with." In *Female Liberation as the*

Members of Students for a Democratic Society march in 1969. The "National Resolution on Women" led to a debate about the role of women in radical political organizations.
© JASON LAURE/THE IMAGE WORKS

Basis for Social Revolution (1974), Dunbar criticizes the SDS resolution for ignoring "marriage or living arrangements" as a political structure. The SDS resolution is also included in Betty and Theodore Roszak's 1969 book *Masculine/Feminine: Readings in Sexual Mythology and the Liberation of Women,* one of the first compendiums of second-wave feminism. The Roszaks call it "an unfortunate example of the pompous jargon employed in SDS literature," in which "defensive feminists" become "trapped by their self-imposed terminology." SDS issued another feminist resolution at its 1969 convention, but the resolution never passed because of philosophical disagreements and the ultimate dissolution of the organization.

In 1969, after the dissolution of SDS, which had been one of the largest and most influential organizations of the New Left, the "National Resolution on Women" illustrated one of the problems that led to its collapse. It showed a movement deeply divided, with ineffective attempts to appease many different groups of people. Still, the document was significant, as David Barber writes in *A Hard Rain Fell: SDS and Why It Failed* (2008), as "the strongest statement SDS had made concerning its own organizational male supremacy." Edith Hoshino Altbach in *From Feminism to Liberation* (2009) calls it "an important document because it set off a debate in the women's movement about the validity of women working in mixed organizations."

Most recent scholarship on the "National Resolution on Women" has centered on its legacy as a failed document and more broadly on SDS as an organization that failed to see how male its perspective was. As Barber writes, "SDS's defense of male supremacy strengthened radical feminism" instead of "build[ing] a movement that really acted in solidarity with the struggles SDS professed to see as important." Similarly, the resolution is of interest for its inclusion of the different issues of women of color, without really taking on what these differences mean. As scholars today still struggle to understand the racial legacy of second-wave feminism, this admission remains relevant.

BIBLIOGRAPHY

Sources

Altbach, Edith Hoshino, ed. *From Feminism to Liberation.* Rev. ed. New Brunswick: Schenkman, 2009. Print.

Barber, David. *A Hard Rain Fell: SDS and Why It Failed.* Jackson: UP of Mississippi, 2008. Print.

Dunbar, Roxanne. *Female Liberation as the Basis for Social Revolution.* Nashville: New England Free Press, 1974. *University of Florida Digital Collections.* Web. 16 Oct. 2012.

Gilbert, Marc Jason, ed. *The Vietnam War on Campus: Other Voices, More Distant Drums.* Westport: Praeger, 2001. Print.

Jones, Beverly, and Judith Brown. *Toward a Female Liberation Movement.* Nashville: New England Free Press, 1968. Web. 18 Oct. 2012.

Roszak, Betty, and Theodore Roszak, eds. "National Resolution on Women." *Masculine/Feminine: Readings in Sexual Mythology and the Liberation of Women.* New York: Harper & Row, 1969. 254-59. Print.

Further Reading

Breines, Wini. "Sixties Stories' Silences: White Feminism, Black Feminism, Black Power." *NWSA Journal* 8.3 (1996): 101. *Academic Search Complete.* Web. 9 Oct. 2012.

"Documents from the Women's Liberation Movement." *Duke University Special Collections.* Duke University, Apr. 1997. Web. 8 October 2012.

Flannery, Kathryn Thomas. "The Passion of Conviction: Reclaiming Polemic for a Reading of Second-Wave Feminism." *Rhetoric Review* 20.1/2 (2001): 113. *Academic Search Complete.* Web. 9 Oct. 2012.

"Links to Resources from SDS." *Students for a Democratic Society Archives and Resources.* Students for a Democratic Society, 10 June 2012. Web. 8 Oct. 2012.

Myers, R. David, ed. *Toward a History of the New Left: Essays from within the Movement.* New York: Carlson, 1989. Print.

Rebels with a Cause: The Women's Movement and Students for a Democratic Society. Dir. Helen Garvy. Shire Films, 2003. Film.

Ryan, Barbara. "Ideological Purity and Feminism: The U.S. Women's Movement from 1966 to 1975." *Gender and Society* June 1989: 239-57. *JSTOR.* Web. 8 Oct. 2012.

Emily Jones

A POSTMODERN FEMINIST LEGAL MANIFESTO

Mary Joe Frug

OVERVIEW

Law professor Mary Joe Frug's "A Postmodern Feminist Legal Manifesto," published in the *Harvard Law Review* (1992), applies postmodern literary criticism to legal language in support of the claim that language affects gender identity and oppresses women. Frug urges American feminists—fractured by issues of politics, race, class, religion, and sexual preference—to unite in a campaign for linguistic change. In the conflict between academic traditionalists and left-leaning reformers over bias in curriculum and lack of diversity among faculty and students, the manifesto stands on the side of change. It sets forth two central principles designed to expose how legal language promotes and even contributes to gender bias, then applies these principles to the text of existing laws in an effort to empower women.

"A Postmodern Feminist Legal Manifesto" generated a great deal of controversy even before its publication. Frug was working on the manifesto when she was murdered on April 4, 1991. The decision to include the draft in the *Harvard Law Review* was contentious. Some called the scholarship mediocre and alleged the journal was considering the article largely because it was submitted by Frug's husband, professor Gerald Frug. Some objected to publishing an article in draft form. Immediately after publication, there was an outpouring of support for Frug, much of which dealt with her death rather than with the substance of the piece. Detractors generally limited their initial critiques of the manifesto to verbal sparring and occasional comments to the media. On the first anniversary of Frug's death, however, the *Harvard Law Review* published a parody titled "He-Manifesto of Post-Mortem Legal Feminism" under the byline "Mary Doe, Rigor Mortis Professor of Law," igniting a storm of controversy and vitriol. As the furor faded, references to the work appeared in substantive law review articles on a range of legal topics.

HISTORICAL AND LITERARY CONTEXT

"A Postmodern Feminist Legal Manifesto" responds to attempts by socially conservative Americans to roll back progressive changes made in the 1960s and 1970s. During the late 1980s and early 1990s, calls to increase diversity in academia were belittled and derisively labeled "politically correct". In 1991 Derrick Bell, Harvard Law School's first—and at the time only—tenured African American professor, took an unpaid leave of absence to protest the paucity of minority and female tenured faculty members. Of fifty-nine tenured professors, only four (including Bell) were men of color and five were women (none of whom were of color); the remaining fifty were white men. According to Robert Gordon, a law professor at Stanford, Harvard saw itself as the pinnacle of academia and "[t]he soul of the country's ruling class." Thus, Gordon writes, Harvard's faculty perceived that whoever won the battle for control of Harvard would by extension win control of American cultural and academic institutions.

Frug's manifesto was published in the context of broad culture wars, particularly struggles for gender equality. Frug, a professor at New England Law School and a pioneer in feminist legal scholarship, had joined with Harvard law professor Clare Dalton to cofound Critical Feminism, a group that offered critiques of gender discrimination. Frug's manifesto is ambitious in scope. It challenges legal rules that discriminate on the basis of gender, demonstrates how mainstream legal discourse contributes to cultural ideas of women as inferior, and attempts to mend a rift among critical feminists over antipornography legislation. Frug takes issue with the divisive nature of the antipornography campaign led by Catharine MacKinnon and Andrea Dworkin, which Frug writes, "assumed its listeners were divisible into only two camps—those who were pro-woman, and, therefore, pro-ordinance, and those who weren't." In closing, she advocates celebrating differences among women in order to undermine oppression by sex.

"A Postmodern Feminist Legal Manifesto" is grounded in a tradition of feminist manifestos, notably MacKinnon's groundbreaking work "Feminism, Marxism, Method and the State: An Agenda for Theory" (1982), the first piece of feminist legal scholarship to adapt Marxist social theories. Frug employs Marxist terms to argue that the history of the U.S. legal system is one of oppression based on gender differences. Unlike MacKinnon's authoritative calls to action, Frug's manifesto offers suggestions, and questions its own authority, encouraging women to engage in "continuous interpretive struggles." Frug's arguments about the power of language

✢ *Key Facts*

Time Period:
Late 20th Century

Movement/Issue:
Postmodernism; Critical feminism

Place of Publication:
United States

Language of Publication:
English

PRIMARY SOURCE

"A POSTMODERN FEMINIST LEGAL MANIFESTO"

The fracturing of feminist criticism has occurred partly because particular sex differences seem so powerfully fixed that feminists are as unable to resist their "naturalization" as liberal jurists. But feminists also cling to particular sex-related differences because of a strategic desire to protect the feminist legal agenda from sabotage. Many feminist critics have argued that the condition of "real" women makes it too early to be post-feminist. The social construction thesis is useful to feminists insofar as it informs and supports our efforts to improve the condition of women in law. If, or when, the social construction thesis seems about to deconstruct the basic category of woman, its usefulness to feminism is problematized. How can we build a political coalition to advance the position of women in law if the subject that drives our efforts is "indeterminate," "incoherent," or "contingent?"

I think this concern is based upon a misperception of where we are in the legal struggle against sexism. I think we are in danger of being politically immobilized by a system for the production of what sex means that makes particular sex differences seem "natural." If my assessment is right, then describing the mechanics of this system is potentially enabling rather than disempowering; it may reveal opportunities for resisting the legal role in producing the radical asymmetry between the sexes.

I also think this concern is based on a misperception about the impact of deconstruction. Skeptics tend to think, I believe, that the legal deconstruction of "woman"—in one paper or in many papers, say, written over the next decade—will entail the immediate destruction of "women" as identifiable subjects who are affected by law reform projects. Despite the healthy, self-serving respect I have for the influence of legal scholarship and for the role of law as a significant cultural factor (among many) that contributes to the production of femininity, I think "women" cannot be eliminated from our lexicon very quickly. The question this paper addresses is not whether sex differences exist—they do—or how to transcend them–we can't–but the character of their treatment in law.

…Now, women get "fucked" in the workplace, too, where we do "women's work" for "women's wages," working for male bosses and working on male schedules. We get assigned to this inferior work track because we are identifiable by our sex. In addition, our past and present economic, social, and physical subordination makes us vulnerable to physical abuse at work, on the way there, and on the way back. We are raped at work or on route to work because of our sex, because we are cunts.

…If women's oppression occurs through sex, then in order to end women's oppression in its many manifestations the way people think and talk and act about sex must be changed.

SOURCE: *Harvard Law Review,* 105.4 (1992): 1051-52, 1072-73.

to construct and deconstruct reality borrow from the work of linguistics scholar Michel Foucault and other postmodernists.

The manifesto uses a nontraditional style popularized by prominent critical feminists, including Robin West and Patricia Williams, to express Frug's disdain for a legal culture controlled by white men and to challenge central tenets such as objectivity, rationality, and the assumption that law is a science. The style of legal writing adopted by Frug has remained relevant in the twenty years since her death, appearing with increasing frequency in law reviews—an ongoing cause of distress for champions of conventional legal writing.

THEMES AND STYLE

The primary theme of "A Postmodern Feminist Legal Manifesto" is the relationship between language, legal rules, and the female body. Frug writes, "legal rules—like other cultural mechanisms—encode the female body with meanings." For example, she argues that laws against rape, ostensibly designed to protect women, effectively grant or deny protection based on a woman's sexual promiscuity. Therefore, the more desirable or "inviting" a woman appears, the less protected she is under the law. Frug also deconstructs rules that reward women for assuming sole responsibility of children and that favor mothers over fathers as parents. To frame her argument, she outlines two main principles—that feminists should recognize legal discourse as a site of political struggle and that even the most seemingly embedded gender differences, such as male aggression and female compassion, are actually rooted in and shaped by language. She then applies these principles to existing laws and legal language to demonstrate how legal rules "encode the female body" in ways that terrorize, maternalize, and sexualize women.

"A Postmodern Feminist Legal Manifesto" eschews traditional law review style, which uses a formal tone, a preponderance of footnotes, and linear logic. The manifesto contains straightforward expressions of self-doubt ("I am worried about the title of this article") to establish the author's feminist credentials and to cement her commitment to women's empowerment. It also appropriates the Harvard Law School's methods in order to expose and deride its members, depicting them as oppressive, privileged white men. By the time "A Postmodern Feminist Legal Manifesto" was published, however, Frug's nontraditional style was neither new nor shocking and had for at least a decade been recognized as valid scholarship. Critics may not have wanted to acknowledge the genre's merit, but there was no denying that Frug's style of rhetoric had gained acceptance in mainstream law reviews.

The manifesto's tone is frank and open. Frug anticipates and answers imagined criticism from different factions of feminist legal scholars as a means of gaining their trust and starting a dialogue; however she does not attempt to anticipate criticism from other quarters. Through first-person narration, the manifesto envisions a unified feminist movement whose diversity is transformed from a perceived weakness into a strength. Frug argues that only by "exploring, pursuing, and accepting differences among women and differences among sexual practices" can feminists "challenge the oppression of women by sex." Unified thusly women will achieve their common goal of legal reform through a variety of channels, including through postmodern linguistic analysis.

CRITICAL DISCUSSION

The initial outpouring of responses to "A Postmodern Feminist Legal Manifesto" in the legal literature focused less on scholarship than on the life—and death—of Frug. Her murder, the controversial decision to publish her manuscript, and the parody "He-Manifesto of Post-Mortem Legal Feminism" all contributed to the sensationalizing of her work. Numerous law reviews published articles dedicated to or in memory of Frug. In one such essay for the *Harvard Law Review* (1991), Martha Minow, law professor and future dean of Harvard Law School, directly addresses Frug: "It is your confidence, I confess, that moves me more than your analysis, your hope even more than your deconstructions."

Over the years, commentators have disagreed vehemently on the merits of the manifesto's scholarship. In *Poisoned Ivy: How Ego, Ideology, and Power Politics Almost Ruined Harvard Law School* (1994), Eleanor Kerlow describes *Harvard Law Review* editor-in-chief David Ellen, who was in favor of publishing Frug's manifesto, as having concerns that the essay was not Frug's best work. Feminist scholar Ruth Colker, in a 1992 response to the manifesto published in the *Harvard Law Review,* wrote that she had "no idea what Mary Joe meant." Even Frug supporter Minow appears to treat the manifesto lightly, characterizing it as "fabulous." The manifesto's greatest critic, professor Arthur Austin, may also be its greatest admirer. A traditionalist, Austin ranked the manifesto as the number one most politically correct law review article ever published, calling it "a verbal kick to the establishment's groin." He credits Frug with successfully subverting the traditional law review article's implied assumption of authority.

Legal scholars have applied Frug's analysis to aspects of the law beyond the usual areas of feminist interest. Her manifesto has served as a touchstone for academic outsiders attempting to root their ideas in established precedent. In a 1994 article for *Columbia Law Review,* Adrienne Hiegel cites the manifesto in support of the Americans with Disabilities Act: "That laws create norms which are not simply legal—medical norms, sexual norms, physical norms—is

Madonna, a figure of both controversy and praise within the feminist movement, performs at Wembley Stadium during her Blond Ambition tour, 1990. AP PHOTO/GIL ALLEN

not a controversial point." Since Frug's manifesto was published, it has been relied upon as a point of departure for the theory of a "different voice" on race, gender, sexual orientation, immigration rights, and other issues. Regardless of the debate over its merit, the manifesto has remained relevant: it has been cited by the U.S. 7th Circuit Court of Appeals and by more than one hundred law review articles as of 2012. Even critics of the manifesto are compelled to recognize its significant impact on the law and on legal literature.

BIBLIOGRAPHY

Sources

Austin, Arthur. "Top Ten Politically Correct Law Review Articles." *Florida State University Law Review* 27 (2001): 233-78. Print.

Colker, Ruth. "The Example of Lesbians: A Posthumous Reply to Professor Mary Joe Frug." *Harvard Law Review* 105.5 (1992): 1084-95. Print.

Frug, Mary Joe. "A Postmodern Feminist Legal Manifesto." *Harvard Law Review* 105.5 (1992): 1045-75. Print.

Hiegel, Adrienne. "Sexual Exclusions: The Americans with Disabilities Act as a Moral Code." *Columbia Law Review* 94 (1994): 1451-94. Print.

Kerlow, Eleanor. *Poisoned Ivy: How Ego, Ideology, and Power Politics Almost Ruined Harvard Law School.* New York: St. Martin's, 1994. Print.

MacKinnon, Catharine A. "Feminism, Marxism, Method and the State: An Agenda for Theory." *Signs: Journal of Women in Culture and Sociology* 7.3 (1982): 515. Print.

Minow, Martha. "Incomplete Correspondence: An Unsent Letter to Mary Joe Frug." *Harvard Law Review* 105.5 (1992): 1096-105. Print.

Further Reading

Austin, Regina, and Elizabeth Schneider. "Speaking Volumes: Musings on Issues of the Day, Inspired by the Memory of Mary Joe Frug." *Columbia Journal of Gender and Law* 12.3 (2003): 660-61. Print.

Bartlett, Katharine T. "Feminist Legal Scholarship: A History through the Lens of the *California Law Review.*" *California Law Review* 100.2 (2012): 381-427. Print.

Bruhl, Elise. "Motherhood and Contracts: Always Crashing the Same Car." *Buffalo Women's Law Journal* 9 (2000-01): 191-224. Print.

Dixon, Rosalind. "Feminist Disagreement (Comparatively) Recast." *Harvard Journal of Law and Gender* 31.2 (2008): 277-321. Print.

Johnson, Barbara. "The Postmodern in Feminism." *Harvard Law Review* 105.5 (1992): 1076-83. Print.

Keller, Susan Etta. "Viewing and Doing: Complicating Pornography's Meaning." *Georgetown Law Journal* 81 (1993): 2195-242. Print.

Rabie, Lisa Limor. "Can You Put on Your Red Light?: Lawrence's Sexual Citizenship Rights in Terms of International Law." *Columbia Journal of Transnational Law* 43.2 (2005): 613-33. Print.

Sachs, Andrea. "Hiring Splits Harvard Law." *ABA Journal* 78.7 (1992): 30. Print.

Subotnik, Dan. "Copulemus in Pace: A Meditation on Rape, Affirmative Consent to Sex, and Sexual Autonomy." *Akron Law Review* 41.4 (2008): 847-48. Print.

West, Robin. "Jurisprudence and Gender." *University of Chicago Law Review* 55.1 (1988): 1-71. Print.

Kristin King-Ries

Redstockings Manifesto

Shulamith Firestone, Ellen Willis

OVERVIEW

Composed by the Redstockings, a radical feminist group, the *Redstockings Manifesto* (1969) is a declaration against male oppression of women, created for distribution at women's liberation events. The Redstockings were considered extremists, especially compared to more mainstream groups such as the National Organization for Women. Their Redstockings' manifesto takes a radical stance in its portrayal of male supremacy as "the oldest, most basic form of domination" and its affirmation that women are not to blame for their centuries-old subjugation to men as breeders, objects of sexual exploitation, and second-class citizens. The manifesto speaks directly to women in an attempt to rally support for the burgeoning women's liberation movement. It contains seven points outlining the perceived offenses against women as a sex and calling for unification among women in order to put an end to discrimination.

At the time of its writing, the *Redstockings Manifesto* was not widely received or recognized beyond New York City, where the Redstockings were based. By the early 1970s, mainstream feminism had become focused on issues of abortion rights and violence against women; however, the core concepts introduced in the manifesto, such as a woman's right to her body and the idea that men and women should be treated equally, remained relevant. Because the manifesto was a foundational document for the Redstockings, the group later included it in the anthology *Feminist Revolution* (1979), a survey of the rebirth of the women's liberation movement. Today, the manifesto is recognized for defining a framework that encourages feminists to question women's roles in society and the historical precedents for gender inequality.

HISTORICAL AND LITERARY CONTEXT

The *Redstockings Manifesto* responds to growing concerns in the United States over the paucity of career choices for women, the lack of a woman's right to her body, and the political system that denied women the ability to gain increased rights. The manifesto was a result of the women's liberation movement, which arose in the wake of the widely televised civil rights movement. As the women's liberation movement gained momentum during the middle to late 1960s, a result in part of the growth of liberalism,

several feminist groups formed to protest and monitor social changes in order to assure that, as men of all backgrounds gained equal rights, so would women. Feminists were particularly outraged by a 1969 New York legislative hearing on abortion, in which the only witnesses were fourteen men and a nun. The Redstockings protested and successfully disrupted the event; later, they staged speak-outs to argue for legalization of abortion.

Less than a year before the *Redstockings Manifesto* was written on July 7, 1969, New York Radical Women, the city's predominant women's group, had broken up due to ideological differences, leading several former members, including feminist activists Ellen Willis (1941-2006) and Shulamith Firestone (1946-), to create the Redstockings. In response to the splintering of the city's women's movement, the manifesto calls for unity and solidarity among women, lending force to what the Redstockings saw as the most critical weapon in the fight for gender equality: consciousness-raising, or "sharing experience and publicly exposing the sexist foundation of all our institutions."

The *Redstockings Manifesto*'s format is most often compared to that of *The Communist Manifesto*. Written in 1848, *The Communist Manifesto* was designed as a declaration of the economic disparity among social classes; its directness of purpose and explanation of class separation have since influenced many political movements. The *Redstockings Manifesto* also describes a social hierarchy, but one that is based on sex, not money. The organization of the *Redstockings Manifesto* most closely resembles that of the *Universal Declaration of Human Rights* (1948), such that the word "woman" could easily be substituted for "human."

In the years following the manifesto's publication, several related essays were published, the most notable being Willis's "Women and the Myth of Consumerism" (1969) and Kathie Sarachild's "Consciousness-Raising: A Radical Weapon" (1973). However, as the feminist agenda shifted toward the topics of abortion rights and violence against women, and as radical feminism faded, the *Redstockings Manifesto* was largely forgotten. Nevertheless, some of the points in the manifesto are still applicable today as women continue to battle for equal rights.

❖ *Key Facts*

Time Period:
Mid-20th Century

Movement/Issue:
Radical feminism

Place of Publication:
United States

Language of Publication:
English

ELLEN WILLIS: RADICALISM, RELIGION, AND ROCK

A founding member of radical feminist groups the Redstockings and No More Nice Girls, Ellen Willis personally embraced the ethos of equality. One of few women working in music criticism in the late 1960s, and the first popular music critic for the *New Yorker*, she published her work in both *Rolling Stone* and the *Village Voice*. Unlike some of her contemporaries, she was strongly opposed to the antipornography movement, considering it puritanical and in defiance of the First Amendment. A contributor to the feminist magazine *Ms.*, Willis helped shaped both mainstream and radical feminist thought.

As the second wave of feminism died out, her writing expanded to cover popular events, such as the O. J. Simpson trial and the Monica Lewinsky scandal. Outspoken in her opposition to the 2003 U.S. invasion of Iraq, she also wrote several essays regarding anti-Semitism and a piece on Judaism. Although self-described as an antiauthoritarian democratic socialist, she was hesitant to align herself with extremists on either side of an issue or political cause. At the time of her death in 2006, she was an adjunct professor of journalism at New York University and the head of the university's Center for Cultural Reporting and Criticism.

THEMES AND STYLE

The central theme of the *Redstockings Manifesto* is that men have oppressed women throughout history and that the creation of equality among the sexes demands political action and unprecedented unity among women. The manifesto opens with the declaration that "[a]fter centuries of individual and preliminary political struggle, women are uniting to achieve their final liberation from male supremacy." The authors develop the theme through seven points: women must unite in order to win their freedom; women are a historically oppressed class; male supremacy underlies all political, economic, and cultural institutions; women should not be blamed for their condition; women must publicly share their experiences as a class; women must unite across economic and racial boundaries; and men should renounce their privilege in order to support the cause.

The manifesto's rhetoric affirms the unity of women as a single political class regardless of educational, racial, or social class differences. The use of the first-person plural reinforces the manifesto's call to unity and resistance of the divisive, masculine rhetoric of "me" and "I." Unequivocal statements such as "all power structures throughout history have been male-dominated" and "all men receive economic, sexual, and psychological benefits from male supremacy" serve less as an appeal to logic and more as a device for evoking an emotional response and for rallying political support for women's liberation. Although the document primarily refers to men as oppressors, it also briefly appeals to men "to give up their male privilege and support women's liberation in the interest of our humanity and their own," implying that at the root of the women's movement is a concern for humankind.

The *Redstockings Manifesto* takes the form of a declaration in order to demonstrate its authority and validity as a statement of class-consciousness. The enumeration of offenses and resolutions derives from a predominantly male historical and literary tradition, suggesting that male oppression is so pervasive that the authors must use the "tools of the oppressor" in order to assert their claim to equality. However, the manifesto denies the absolute authority of male political and social institutions: "We cannot rely on existing ideologies as they are all products of male supremacist culture. We question every generalization and accept none that are not confirmed by our experience." The manifesto's even pacing and poignant, undeviating statements echo the "continual, daily pressure from men" that women must meet with equal force. In establishing the women's movement as a legitimate cause, the document avoids sentimentality, mirroring its call for "honesty, in private and in public, with ourselves and other women."

CRITICAL DISCUSSION

When the *Redstockings Manifesto* was written in 1969, it served as a handout to encourage women to join rallies; however, it was not widely received by the American public. Nevertheless, many women were inspired to attend feminist rallies and to publicly share their experiences as part of the consciousness-raising movement. Men typically responded to the manifesto by asserting that radical feminists wanted to be rid of men altogether and that promoting unity between the sexes was a better way of creating equality for women. As radical feminism declined and abortion rights and violence against women overshadowed issues of historical oppression and revolutionary action, the manifesto's influence waned. In a 2002 interview for *Left Business Observer*, Sarachild acknowledges the dwindling impact of the radical movement: "In the beginning of the movement we would talk about 'women of the world unite,' women have to unite. But we thought of that as kind of an instant revolution. We didn't realize that persisting, the power of persisting, was actually part of the power of unity."

In the decades following the publication of the manifesto, some feminists found that the document's harsh language hindered the pursuit of equality by alienating men. In the anthology *The Vintage Book of Feminism* (1996), Miriam Schneir explains that "the theory that all men are to blame for women's oppression left women isolated from men who did want to fight for genuine liberation." Other commentators

criticized the piece for encouraging women to internalize rather than fight oppression. In a 1996 essay for the *Socialist Workers Party,* Gill Hubbard states that "consciousness raising, which was said to last an average of nine months, led women away from political activity and sent the women's groups into a spiral of inward-looking personalism." Despite the debate over the effectiveness of consciousness-raising and the decline of radical feminism, the Redstockings persisted as an organization and today serve as an activist think tank for the continued struggle for women's liberation.

Modern scholarship has focused on the innovative nature of *The Redstockings Manifesto* as a lesser-known feminist work. Slogans based on the manifesto and the writings it helped inspire remain relevant for contemporary feminists. The phrases "the personal is the political" and "sisterhood is powerful" are still used as calls to unity in the feminist movement. In a 2009 article for *Encyclopaedia Britannica's Guide to Women's History,* Elinor Burkett calls the manifesto "the movement's first analysis of the politics of housework." She points out that the document does not strictly blame men but discusses the possibility of complete equality, even in the home.

BIBLIOGRAPHY

Sources

Burkett, Elinor. "Women's Movement." *Encyclopaedia Britannica's Guide to Women's History.* Encyclopaedia Britannica, 2009. Web. 5 June 2012.

Engels, Friedrich, and Karl Marx. *The Communist Manifesto.* Middlesex: Echo, 2009. Print.

Hubbard, Gill. "Why Has Feminism Failed Women?" *Socialist Workers Party.* June 1996: 2. Web. 6 June 2012.

Redstockings. *Feminist Revolution.* New York: Random, 1979. Print.

Sarachild, Kathie, and Amy Coenen. "Two Redstockings Interviewed." By Doug Henwood. *Left Business Observer.* Left Business Observer, 2002. Web. 7 June 2012.

Schneir, Miriam. *Vintage Book of Feminism.* London: Vintage, 1996. Print.

UN General Assembly. *Declaration of Human Rights.* Paris: United Nations, 1948. Print.

Further Reading

Davidson, Sarah. "An 'Oppressed Majority' Demands Its Rights." *Life* 12 Dec. 1969: 37. Print.

Echols, Alice. *Daring to Be Bad: Radical Feminism in America, 1967-1975.* Minneapolis: U of Minnesota P, 1989. Print.

A women's liberation march in New York City, 1971. the *Redstockings Manifesto* was a controversial work that directly challenged existing gender relations. AP PHOTO/MARTY LEDERHANDLER

Rhodes, Jacqueline. *Radical Feminism, Writing, and Critical Agency: From Manifesto to Modem.* Albany: State U of New York P, 2005. Print.

Smith, Howard. "Scenes." *Village Voice* 13 Mar. 1969. Web. 20 May 2012.

Willis, Ellen. "Radical Feminism and Feminist Radicalism." *No More Nice Girls: Countercultural Essays.* Middletown: Wesleyan UP, 1992. 117-50. Print.

Marie Davol

SCUM Manifesto

Valerie Solanas

OVERVIEW

Self-published by Valerie Solanas in 1967, the *SCUM Manifesto* outlines a case against men and male-centered society and calls on women to rise up and grab power. Made up of an introduction, a list of grievances, and a conclusion, the manifesto calls for the destruction of men, who are blamed for social and political problems ranging from the subjugation of women to the creation of a police state and the denigration of art. The manifesto addresses both women, whom it calls upon to radicalize as "SCUM," and men, from whom it demands an acknowledgment of their unfitness for power and an advocacy of their own destruction. SCUM, according to Solanas, are "dominant, secure, self-confident, nasty, violent, selfish, independent, proud, thrill-seeking, free-wheeling, arrogant females, who consider themselves fit to rule the universe." Such women, she writes, will "sink a shiv into a man's chest or ram an icepick up his asshole as soon as look at him." According to some versions of the text, SCUM also stands for Society for Cutting up Men.

When Solanas first distributed her mimeographed manifesto on the streets of New York City, it elicited a mixed response. Many readers were unsure whether to take the work seriously. Others, however, including Maurice Girodias of Olympia Press, saw in it evidence of Solanas's intelligence, talent, and unique perspective. After Solanas shot and nearly killed artist Andy Warhol in 1968 (see sidebar), interest in the text increased, but commentators were more likely than before to dismiss the text as the work of a deranged mind. The work was subsequently published by Olympia Press in 1968. Today the *SCUM Manifesto* is considered an important early work of militant feminism, and Solanas is viewed more sympathetically as a smart, insightful, and often-funny visionary whose work was underappreciated in its time.

HISTORICAL AND LITERARY CONTEXT

The *SCUM Manifesto,* which Solanas is believed to have begun writing in the late 1950s, reacts against the disempowerment and inequality of women in American society, as well as to social ills and repressive social structures that she attributes to centuries of male domination. The work is generally placed within the context of second-wave feminism, a movement defined by women's attempts to achieve equality in the workplace, eliminate legal and social discrimination, and gain reproductive rights. Second-wave feminism is often dated to 1963, with the report of the Presidential Commission on the Status of Women established by John F. Kennedy and the publication of Betty Friedan's groundbreaking book *The Feminine Mystique,* which forcefully rejects the myth that women necessarily find fulfillment in marriage and motherhood and helped to raise public awareness about the unequal and often unhappy status of females in society.

The *SCUM Manifesto* not only reacts against the historical subjugation of women but also the women's movement of the era. Solanas rejects what she sees as a distinctly middle-class femininity and middle-class feminism, which are antithetical to the SCUM mindset. Asserting that SCUM will never march for their beliefs, for example, she clarifies that such an act is "for the nice, 'privileged, educated,' middle-class ladies." She goes on to note, "If SCUM ever marches, it will be over the President's stupid, sickening face; if SCUM ever strikes, it will be in the dark with a six-inch blade." Ultimately such statements limited the political influence of Solanas's manifesto to the fringes of the women's movement.

As a radical, female-authored, and self-published manifesto addressing the neglected rights of women, the *SCUM Manifesto* is part of a tradition that dates back at least to the French Revolutionary writings of Olympe de Gouges, whose 1791 *Declaration of the Rights of Woman and Citizen* reacted against the disappointing exclusion of women from the reforms proposed by the French National Assembly in *Declaration of the Rights of Man and Citizen* (1789). Recent antecedents of Solanas's mode of production (mimeograph) and distribution (by hand on the street) were the underground political pamphlets that flourished in New York during the period when she produced her work.

As a radical text of second-wave feminism, the *SCUM Manifesto* paved the way for works such as the *Redstockings Manifesto* (1969), which, like Solanas's text, holds men responsible for the creation of a culture of male supremacy and calls upon women to reject the established social and economic structures. Although it is not as well known as some other feminist texts, the *SCUM Manifesto* commands a

✣ *Key Facts*

Time Period:
Mid-20th Century

Movement/Issue:
Radical feminism

Place of Publication:
United States

Language of Publication:
English

VALERIE SOLANAS AND ANDY WARHOL

Valerie Solanas's legacy continues to be shaped by her shooting of Andy Warhol. Solanas, who had played small roles in several of Warhol's films, had given him a copy of her script *Up Your Ass* in the hope that he would purchase and produce it. Over time, she became convinced that Warhol and Olympia Press publisher Maurice Girodias were conspiring to steal her work.

On June 3, 1968, after making unsuccessful attempts to confront Girodias, Solanas waited for Warhol outside his studio and walked in with him. While he took a phone call, she fired three shots at him. Only one hit Warhol, but it did such extensive damage that he was briefly pronounced dead. Solanas also shot Mario Amaya, an art critic, in the hip and attempted to shoot Fred Hughes, Warhol's manager.

Solanas then fled from Warhol's studio, leaving behind a paper bag that contained her address book and a feminine hygiene product. She later turned herself in to a police officer on the street. After spending a year in a psychiatric ward, she was sentenced to three years in prison. Throughout her incarceration, Solanas maintained that the shooting was justified. She continued to believe that Warhol had conspired against her and continued to threaten him following her release from prison in 1971.

significant popular and scholarly following. It has been the subject of such events as the radical feminist SCUM Manifesto Conference in Perth, Australia, in 2011. In addition, the story of Solanas, her manifesto, and her attack on Warhol inspired Mary Harron's controversial but critically acclaimed 1996 independent film *I Shot Andy Warhol*.

THEMES AND STYLE

The central theme of Solanas's manifesto is that men are fatally flawed; that these flaws lead to unjust and tyrannical behavior; and that, accordingly, women ought to destroy men and seize power. Because of their genetic and emotional failings, Solanas explains in her list of grievances, men are responsible for the majority of the world's problems, such as war, emotional isolation, conformity, authoritarian government, boredom, and censorship. In concluding the manifesto, she outlines her plans for the future, which include "destroying, looting, fucking-up and killing until the money-work system no longer exists." The only men exempt from the pillage are those belonging to the SCUM Men's Auxiliary, "who are working diligently to eliminate themselves, men who, regardless of their motives, do good, men who are playing ball with SCUM."

The *SCUM Manifesto* alternates rhetorically between quasi-scientific propositions and satire; like many other feminist texts of the period, it calls for

female solidarity in the face of oppression. Solanas begins by introducing an allegedly scientific argument. She explains that men are genetically flawed due to the Y chromosome, writing that "the male is an incomplete female, a walking abortion, aborted at the gene stage. To be male is to be deficient, emotionally limited; maleness is a deficiency disease and males are emotional cripples." Through her satirical treatment of men, whom she ridicules for harboring the "most hideous fear ... of being discovered to be not a female," she reveals both their threat to women and their ridiculousness. Women, on the other hand, are free of biological defects but have been quashed by male-oriented social, political, and economic structures. Thus, Solanas attempts to unite women by appealing to their common status as outsiders to these structures, asserting that "most women are already dropped out; they were never in." She argues that what will ultimately bring true liberation for women is "the total elimination of the money-work system, not the attainment of economic equality with men within it."

Stylistically, the *SCUM Manifesto* is notable for its ranting tone, vulgar language, and humor. The work's concluding paragraph offers evidence of all three of these qualities: "The sick, irrational men, those who attempt to defend themselves against their disgustingness, when they see SCUM barrelling down on them, will cling in terror to Big Mama with her Big Bouncy Boobies, but Boobies won't protect them against SCUM; Big Mama will be clinging to Big Daddy, who will be in the corner shitting in his forceful, dynamic pants." Her sense of humor is also apparent in her identification of a subclass of men whose membership in the Men's Auxiliary will not save them from extermination, including, most notably, "owners of greasy spoons and restaurants that play Muzak."

CRITICAL DISCUSSION

When Solanas began distributing the *SCUM Manifesto* in 1967, it sold relatively well for a self-published pamphlet, but its reception was mixed. The manifesto won the respect of radical feminists such as Ti-Grace Atkinson, then president of the New York Chapter of the National Organization for Women (NOW), and Florynce Kennedy, a radical lawyer who would defend Solanas after she shot Warhol. The Warhol shooting brought increasingly negative attention to Solanas and her manifesto, particularly after she told reporters to read the text to understand her actions. Because of the shooting and Solanas's subsequent incarceration in a mental health facility and then prison, many dismissed the unusual work as the ravings of a mentally ill woman. Breanne Fahs notes in an article in *Feminist Studies,* for example, that in the popular imagination, the shooting was seen as "evidence of Solanas's instability, insanity, and unreliability."

In the years following Solanas's 1971 release from incarceration, her work continued to command attention in progressive periodicals such as the *Village*

Voice, which published an interview with her in 1977. Many early commentators attempted to ascertain the degree to which the *SCUM Manifesto* is a reflection of its author's biography, often expressing frustration at what they identified as a disjunct between her post-graduate education and the ideas and ranting tone of the manifesto. At the same time, many writers were hesitant to engage with the *SCUM Manifesto* in a serious way out of fear that they too would be tainted by Solanas's alleged mental instability. In her book *Sex Objects,* Jennifer Doyle describes "an unfortunate but not uncommon characterization of feminism—a facile dismissal of feminist intellectual work on women like Solanas as 'merely' an extension of hysterical identification." Over time, however, a broader body of criticism built up around the work, with scholars examining its style and aesthetic influences as well as its politics.

Solanas's manifesto is generally viewed through the myriad lenses of feminist theory. In part because of the author's background in psychology (she earned a bachelor's degree in the subject from the University of Maryland), many commentators have read the manifesto as a reaction against Freudian psychoanalytic theory that rejects the psychotherapist's discussions of penis envy and instead posits that the behavior of men is a response to their own biological shortcomings. Others have noted the marginalization of the text within mainstream feminist theory. Fahs observes that "Solanas redefines the center of feminist scholarship by speaking from an extreme margin." Meanwhile, writers such as Desireé D. Rowe and Karma R. Chávez have applied queer theory to the manifesto, arguing in a 2011 article in *Cultural Studies/Critical Methodologies* that in stirring up the distinctions between sanity and insanity, the manifesto also destabilizes dominant hierarchies of gender and sexuality.

A still from *I Shot Andy Warhol,* a film based on the life of *SCUM Manifesto* author Valerie Solanas, who gained infamy for shooting the famous pop artist. Solanas is played by Lili Taylor, and Warhol is played by Jared Harris. © AF ARCHIVE/ALAMY

BIBLIOGRAPHY

Sources

Doyle, Jennifer. *Sex Objects: Art and the Dialectics of Desire.* Minneapolis: U of Minnesota P, 2006. Print.

Fahs, Breanne. "The Radical Possibilities of Valerie Solanas." *Feminist Studies* 34.3 (2008): 591-617. Print.

Harding, James M. "The Simplest Surrealist Act: Valerie Solanas and the (Re)Assertion of Avantgarde Priorities." *TDR* 45.4 (2001): 142-62. Print.

Rowe, Desireé D., and Karma R. Chávez. "Valerie Solanas and the Queer Performativity of Madness." *Cultural Studies/Critical Methodologies* 11.3 (2011): 274-84. Print.

Solanas, Valerie. *SCUM Manifesto.* London: Verso, 2004. Print.

Further Reading

Echols, Alice. *Daring to Be Bad: Radical Feminism in America, 1967-1975.* Minneapolis: U of Minnesota P, 1989. Print.

Harrison, Katherine. "'Sometimes the Meaning of the Text Is Unclear': Making 'Sense' of the *SCUM Manifesto* in a Contemporary Swedish Context."

Journal of International Women's Studies 10.3 (2009): 33-47. Print.

Heller, Dana. "Shooting Solanas: Radical Feminist History and the Technology of Failure." *Feminist Studies* 27.1 (2001): 167-89. Print.

King, Katie. *Theory in Its Feminist Travels: Conversations in U.S. Women's Movements.* Bloomington: Indiana UP, 1994. Print.

Morgan, Robin, ed. *Sisterhood Is Powerful: An Anthology of Writings from the Women's Liberation Movement.* New York: Random House, 1970. Print.

Rhodes, Jacqueline. *Radical Feminism, Writing, and Critical Agency: From Manifesto to Modem.* Albany: State U of New York P, 2005. Print.

Smith, Hilda, and Bernice A. Carroll. *Women's Political & Social Thought: An Anthology.* Bloomington, Indiana UP, 2000. Print.

Greta Gard

SEXUAL POLITICS
A Manifesto for Revolution
Kate Millett

✦ **Key Facts**

Time Period:
Mid-20th Century

Movement/Issue:
Second-wave feminism

Place of Publication:
United States

Language of Publication:
English

OVERVIEW

Written in 1970, Kate Millett's classic feminist text *Sexual Politics: A Manifesto for Revolution* offers an incisive critique of patriarchal hegemony by analyzing the works of popular male writers. Initially written as a doctoral dissertation in 1969, the expanded text was published as a book at the beginning of the second-wave feminist movement. The manifesto articulates many of the concerns of the movement, including sexual freedom and reproductive issues. It is also one of the first texts of feminist literary criticism: the piece examines the different ways male authors portray women and how this has shaped men's and women's attitudes toward sex and has helped to define gender roles. Addressed to members and supporters of second-wave feminism, *Sexual Politics* argues that women must fight not only the injustice of unequal treatment but also the ideas of injustice prevalent in literature, psychology, and history. Millett argues that only a change in consciousness will alter the fundamental patriarchal values that pervade society.

Despite strong criticism from the mainstream media, *Sexual Politics* and its straightforward critique of male dominance was viewed as a revolutionary document by many second-wave supporters and has remained a popular feminist text. The book galvanized the second-wave movement—which remained active for more than two decades—by revealing yet another kind of female subordination. At a time when other women were focusing on the inequality of governmental policy and traditional values, Millett turned her eye toward attitudes of misogyny and patriarchal entitlement in male-authored texts. *Time* magazine's August 31, 1970, issue featured Millett on the cover with the headline "The Politics of Sex," and her book generated much discussion among journalists and scholars. Today it is seen as one of the defining works of the women's movement of the 1970s and is still considered an important book for feminists and feminist literary critics around the globe.

HISTORICAL AND LITERARY CONTEXT

Sexual Politics responds to the growing dissatisfaction among women in the 1960s who felt that their struggle for personal and political autonomy had gone unnoticed despite the Civil Rights Act of 1964. The act had made discrimination based on sex and race illegal in the workplace, but, as Millett argues, women and people of color still made less money than white men. This economic injustice, coupled with the lack of control women had over their own bodies with respect to marriage, abortion, and sex, fueled the second-wave movement of the 1970s. Many of these feminists had participated in the student protests of the 1960s but felt that those groups had ignored the concerns of women despite arguing for economic, racial, and social equality.

By 1970, when *Sexual Politics* was published, the second-wave movement was becoming well known. Betty Friedan, the author of *The Feminine Mystique* (1963), issued a nationwide plea for women to strike as a way to protest sexual oppression—specifically to draw attention to the lack of job and educational opportunities and to call for the repeal of antiabortion laws. On August 26, 1970, the Women's Strike for Equality began in cities across the country. The demonstration in New York City was so large that it blocked Fifth Avenue. Grassroots feminist groups such as New York Radical Women and the Redstockings marched alongside Millett, Friedan, Gloria Steinem, Alix Kates Shulman, and other leading figures of the feminist movement. Millett published *Sexual Politics* that same month, providing the movement with a discussion of sex and gender in the context of literature, history, and politics.

Although Millett wrote *Sexual Politics,* she describes the book as a collaborative effort because she was heavily influenced by the intense discussions and ideas she had shared with her fellow feminists. During this time, feminist Shulamith Firestone had begun writing *The Dialectic of Sex: The Case for Feminist Revolution* (1970), which analyzes the works of Sigmund Freud, Karl Marx, and Simone de Beauvoir from a feminist perspective. Firestone's text and others were extremely popular within the second-wave movement and informed Millett's writing. Millett also drew heavily on Beauvoir's *Second Sex* (1949), which explores the treatment of women as "other." Millett's book is something of a hybrid because it combines literary theory, politics, psychology, and history in one volume to argue against male authors' depictions of women and sexual intercourse.

Shortly after *Sexual Politics* was published, the second-wave movement gained steam. Many women found Millett's book liberating because it offered a feminist approach to the analysis of literature. The text influenced a number of scholars, including Toril Moi, Sandra Gubar, and Elaine Showalter. Although some second-wave feminists complained that Millett did not offer solutions for combating inequality, others pointed out that her book helped the movement gain national recognition. By the 1980s more books were being published on the subject of feminist literary criticism. Moi's *Sexual/Textual Politics* (1985)—the title is a nod to Millett's book—builds on Millett's theories by discussing why a feminist approach to literature is critical in the political sphere. Although *Sexual Politics* went out of print in the 1980s, it was republished in 1990 and is still considered one of the leading texts of the second-wave movement.

THEMES AND STYLE

The central focus of *Sexual Politics* is the depiction of sex in literature and how it has influenced popular thought about gender roles. Millet achieves this with a line-by-line analysis of the male–female interactions in several male-authored novels, including Henry Miller's *Sexus* (1949) and Norman Mailer's *An American Dream* (1965). Beginning with a close examination of sections of *Sexus,* Millet argues that the images and phrases used by Miller indicate female subjugation. She recounts a passage in which the main characters have sex and then analyzes it, stating, "What the reader is vicariously experiencing at this juncture is a nearly supernatural sense of power—should the reader be male. For the passage is … a male assertion of dominance over a weak, compliant, and rather unintelligent female. It is a case of sexual politics at the fundamental level of copulation." This mention of male assertion of dominance is the key to Millett's argument, insofar as it establishes her definition of politics. In the second part of the book, she states that she does not define politics as Republican or Democratic but rather as "power-structured relationships" where "one group is dominant and the other subordinate." As such, sex is indeed political because it is traditionally depicted in literature as a man exerting his supremacy over a woman.

Throughout the book, Millett's tone is confident and insistent as it confronts its primary target: male writers such as Mailer, Miller, Freud, and John Ruskin. She emphasizes the connection between sex and subordination in the second part when she writes, "In introducing the term 'sexual politics,' one must first answer the inevitable question 'Can the relationship between the sexes be viewed in a political light at all?'" She offers examples from history of the politics of sex and compares the feminist struggle to the plight of

KATE MILLET'S PERSONAL POLITICS

Author, sculptor, and feminist Katherine Murray Millett was born September 14, 1934, in St. Paul, Minnesota. When she was fourteen, her father abandoned her mother, who had to support Millett and Millett's two sisters. After earning a master's degree from Oxford University, Millett moved to Tokyo in 1961 to study sculpting. There she met Japanese sculptor Fumio Yoshimura. The two married in 1965 but established an open marriage so Millett could maintain relationships with other women. She chronicled the complexities of her marriage and her bisexual relationships in her 1974 book *Flying.*

Millett attended Columbia College to obtain her doctorate. She finished her studies with the dissertation that would later become her most famous book, *Sexual Politics: A Manifesto for Revolution.* Within months of its publication, the book had sold 80,000 copies. Millett became instantly famous. She used the money from the book sales to establish an art colony in Poughkeepsie, New York. However, because lesbianism was a polarizing issue for the 1970s women's liberation movement, Millett, despite being supported by feminists such as Gloria Steinem, was ostracized by many of her former colleagues due to her bisexuality. Millett continues to write and sculpt and to support a variety of causes, including the prison reform movement and the antipsychiatric movement.

Kate Millet in 2006, attending the conference "Women's Movements—Today, Yesterday and Tomorrow." © SOPHIE BASSOULS/CORBIS

African Americans during the civil rights movement. She also employs the rhetorical strategy of questioning the reader and then answering the question. For example, at one point she asks why white male power, a power that is so pervasive and obvious, is so rarely discussed. Barely giving the reader a moment to think, she answers, "Partly, I suspect because such discussion is regarded as dangerous in the extreme and because a culture does not discuss its most basic assumptions and most cherished bigotries." *Sexual Politics* does not offer strategies for confronting male hierarchies or dismantling the patriarchal system in favor of a more equitable distribution of power but rather offers its readers an explanation of sexual politics.

Stylistically, *Sexual Politics* is a straightforward discussion of the political attitudes inherent in certain literary texts. Millett chooses popular male authors and persistently combs their work for evidence of misogyny and chauvinism. Moi states in an essay in *The Feminist Reader: Essays in Gender and the Politics of Literary Criticism* (1989) that Millett's style "is that of a hard-nosed street kid out to challenge the author's authority at every turn. Her approach destroys the pervading image of the reader-critic as captive, feminine recipient of authoritarian discourse." Millett displays this fearlessness throughout the text and in the second part of the book asserts her right to offer a critique: "It is opportune, perhaps today even mandatory, that we develop a more relevant psychology and philosophy of power relationships beyond the simple, conceptual framework provided by our traditional formal politics."

CRITICAL DISCUSSION

When *Sexual Politics* was first published, it was heralded by many feminists as one of the most important documents of the second-wave movement. However, outside this circle, Millett was attacked by many journalists, who argued that she had gone too far. Norman Mailer wrote an article for *Harper's Magazine* in which he lambastes *Sexual Politics* while defending his own work and that of his peers. Also writing for *Harper's* in 1970, Irving Howe says of *Sexual Politics,* "There are times when one feels the book was written by a female impersonator." However, Phylis Jacobson, in a 1970 review for *New Politics,* defends the manifesto: "It is the very existence of the Women's Liberation movement that is responsible for the hostile and reactionary response to Miss Millett's book."

The second-wave feminist movement maintained its strength for much of the seventies, and *Sexual Politics* is often credited as a key factor in its success. Although the initial enthusiasm for Millett's work abated during the 1980s and 1990s, the book continued to influence feminist authors and literary critics. In a 1994 article for *The Sociological Quarterly,* Patricia Ticineto Clough writes, "Although in 1970, Kate Millett's *Sexual Politics* would be hailed in the

popular press for providing a theoretical foundation to the newly organized women's liberation movement, what now seems so remarkable about *Sexual Politics* is that it also is a book of literary criticism—the first book of academic feminist literary criticism." In the forty years since the text was first published, it has been reviewed and analyzed numerous times, especially in relation to the second-wave movement.

Much of the scholarship focused on *Sexual Politics* compares it to other 1970s second-wave texts. However, a handful of scholars have studied the manifesto as one of the first feminist critical approaches to literature. As Clough argues, "*Sexual Politics* initiates a revision of the relationship of reality and fantasy, history and fiction, polemic and academic discourse, literary criticism and social science." Her article discusses the different literary arguments Millett employs. Some scholars, however, have criticized Millett's analysis of the literary texts she includes in *Sexual Politics.* Ross Eddington writes in a 2003 article for *Hypatia,* "In labeling Ruskin patriarchal, Millett unjustifiably places Ruskin in the same camp as the widely held contemporary view that did justify women's subordination on the grounds of their supposed inferior rationality and reason." However, others have contended that *Sexual Politics* is a revolutionary text. As Moi states, "Millett destroyed the power of the male author"—something few women authors before her had even attempted.

BIBLIOGRAPHY

Sources

Clough, Patricia Ticineto. "The Hybrid Criticism of Patriarchy: Rereading Kate Millett's *Sexual Politics.*" *Sociological Quarterly* 35.3 (1994): 473-86. *JSTOR.* Web. 26 Sept. 2012.

Eddington, Ross Elliot. "Millett's Rationalist Error." *Hypatia* 18.3 (2003): 193-211. *JSTOR.* Web. 25 Aug. 2012.

Howe, Irving. "The Middle Class Mind of Kate Millett." *Harpers* Dec. 1970: 110-129. Web. 25 Aug. 2012.

Jacobson, Phyllis. "Kate Millett and Her Critics." Rev. of *Sexual Politics,* by Kate Millett. *New Politics* Sept. 1970: 89-94. Web. 26 Sept. 2012.

Millett, Kate. *Sexual Politics.* Champaign: U of Illinois P, 2000. Print.

Moi, Toril. "Feminist, Female, Feminine." *The Feminist Reader: Essays in Gender and the Politics of Literary Criticism.* Ed. Catherine Belsey and Jane Moore. New York: Blackwell, 1989. 117-132. Print.

Further Reading

Albert, Judith Clavir, ed. *The Sixties Papers: Documents of a Rebellious Decade.* New York: Praeger, 1984. Print.

Buchanan, Paul D. *Radical Feminists: A Guide to an American Subculture.* Santa Barbara: Greenwood, 2011. Print.

Evans, Sara M. *Tidal Wave: How Women Changed America at Century's End.* New York: Free Press, 2004. Print.

Gilbert, Sandra M., and Susan Gubar. *No Man's Land: The Place of the Woman Writer in the Twentieth Century.* Vol. 3. New Haven: Yale UP, 1996. Print.

Plain, Gill, and Susan Sellers, eds. *A History of Feminist Literary Criticism.* Cambridge: Cambridge UP, 2007. Print.

Rhodes, Jacqueline. *Radical Feminism, Writing, and Critical Agency: From Manifesto to Modern.* SUNY Series in Feminist Criticism and Theory. New York: State U of New York P, 2004. Print.

Stimpson, Catharine R., Alix Kates Shulman, and Kate Millett. "*Sexual Politics*: Twenty Years Later." *Women's Studies Quarterly* 19.3 (1991): 30-40. *JSTOR.* Web. 25 Aug. 2012.

Wagner, Claire. Rev. of *Sexual Politics,* by Kate Millett. *Australian Quarterly* Dec. 1971: 121-25. *JSTOR.* Web. 25 Aug. 2012.

Hannah Soukup

WITCH Manifesto

Anonymous

✤ *Key Facts*

Time Period:
Mid-20th Century

Movement/Issue:
Women's liberation
movement; New Leftism

Place of Publication:
United States

**Language of
Publication:**
English

OVERVIEW

"WITCH Manifesto" (1968), published anonymously by members of the feminist activist group WITCH (an acronym that originally stood for Women's International Terrorist Conspiracy from Hell), boldly states that witches were the original feminist activists because of the persecution they faced and that all women can become witches simply by proclaiming their status and accepting their inner magic. The essay was written for the feminists involved in the emerging women's liberation movement in the United States who were frustrated with the consciousness-raising style of political engagement and wanted to actively protest. WITCH was distinctive for its theatrical activism, which consisted of "zaps," whereby the group would place a hex on an economic or political institution in a quick and dramatic manner, often by dressing up as witches and chanting curses.

The immediate reaction to "WITCH Manifesto" was mixed, with feminists feeling excited about the bold style of activism but ultimately criticizing the group for its lack of focus and counterproductive objectives. Radical feminist groups felt that the essay addressed fringe concerns that decentralized the feminist movement by targeting economic and capitalist institutions instead of focusing on the misogyny of men and the sexist nature of society. The group was also accused of taking an indirect approach with their theatrics, and consequently their points often were not clearly articulated. The group came into—and went out of—existence rather suddenly, and their activism, including "WITCH Manifesto," is often seen as a disorganized flash of radical excitement that brought attention to feminist activism but was too short-lived and contradictory to be of any lasting significance.

HISTORICAL AND LITERARY CONTEXT

The primary concern of "WITCH Manifesto" is the association of female empowerment with neopagan witchcraft and Wiccan religion and with these movements' applicability to American political feminist activism of the late 1960s. The WITCH organization was formed in response to investigations into communist participation in the August 1968 Democratic Convention demonstrations and the focus on male radicals associated with this involvement. Several politically engaged women felt marginalized and believed they were being overlooked. As a result, they formed WITCH (the meaning of the acronym changed to suit the particular situation being protested), an organization that believed that witches were the first feminist revolutionaries to be harassed and punished because men wanted to suppress the knowledge that these women possessed. The popularity of spirituality, ritual magic, nature worship, and witchcraft during the 1960s helped WITCH members to embrace these influences and to ignite the public's curiosity as they set forth their agenda.

WITCH members took an energetic approach to political activism through a series of guerrilla theater demonstrations. Guerrilla theater, a blending of street theater and protest, became popular in the 1960s, and WITCH was not the first to use theatrical stunts. The Youth International Party (the Yippies) used theatrical feats and pranks—such as presenting a pig as a presidential candidate—to gain public attention and promote their causes. Although aiming for different outcomes, WITCH members employed the same tactics of staged presentations. Two of the group's best-known stagings include the Halloween hex on Wall Street in 1968 and the 1969 crashing of a bridal fair at Madison Square Garden. Some of the women involved in WITCH, including Robin Morgan, Judith Duffett, and Peggy Dobbins, were also active members of New York Radical Women, a feminist group whose ideas and actions often coincided with WITCH's.

"WITCH Manifesto" appeared at a time when producing manifestos was a popular activity among activist groups. The Students for a Democratic Society had penned a 25,000-word piece in 1962 seeking racial equality, disarmament, and a truly democratic process. During the tumultuous decade, feminist writings tended to focus on raising awareness about misogyny and sexism in politics and society. The concentration of "WITCH Manifesto" on capitalism, rather than on men, as the perpetrator of these beliefs, however, went against the developing trends in feminist writings. Thus, the women involved in WITCH who were ultimately responsible for the publication of the manifesto fought to find their own niche, pursuing feminist activism in a bold and creative manner.

WITCH and its primary manifesto created a temporary jolt in the feminist movement of the late 1960s, but its presence as an active feminist group and its influence on further feminist organizations were short-lived. The various WITCH organizations, or covens, that had quickly formed in other influential U.S. cities beyond New York, including Washington, D.C., and Chicago, faced the same criticism as the original branch and died out just as quickly. Accused of reinforcing sexist stereotypes and attacking financial and class institutions instead of focusing on issues of patriarchy and misogyny, the group was ultimately unsuccessful in having any lasting influence on the development of the American women's liberation movement.

THEMES AND STYLE

The main theme of "WITCH Manifesto" is that witches are the original radical feminists because of the persecution they faced for their knowledge and religious practices. The document states that witches were "the first birth-control practitioners and abortionists, the first alchemists" and the "living remnants of the oldest culture of all—one in which men and women were equal sharers in a truly cooperative society." Furthermore, the manifesto claims, "A witch lives and laughs in every woman. She is the free part of each of us…. You are a witch by being female, untamed, angry, joyous and immortal." Therefore, by embracing this identity, women could reclaim their heritage as witches and reform society into the harmonious state of equality that once existed when witches were commonplace. While the group's historical and religious discussion has often been criticized for its inaccuracies, the passionate tone of the text enhances the theme of unity that it strives to generate among feminists.

ROBIN MORGAN: RADICAL FEMINIST, WITCH, AND ACTIVIST

One of the founding members of WITCH was the radical feminist and political activist Robin Morgan, who was born in 1941. From a young age, she was a feature of public media: she had her own nationally broadcast radio show when she was five years old, and in the 1950s she acted in the popular television series *I Remember Mama.* Her activist career began in the 1960s when she joined demonstrations against the Vietnam War (1954-75), becoming a member of numerous protest groups, including Students for a Democratic Society and the Revolutionary Youth Movement. She also helped found the feminist group New York Radical Women.

In addition to her involvement in numerous activist organizations, her contributions to the feminist movement extended into the literary sphere. She was a writer and editor for *Ms.* magazine and wrote poetry, fiction, and nonfiction works that focus on a wide range of topics, including pornography, genital mutilation, welfare and the rights of children, and the abuse and oppression of women. Some of her most influential books are *Sisterhood Is Powerful* (1970) and *Going Too Far: The Personal Chronicle of a Feminist* (1977). She has continued to publish works in the twenty-first century and has been a guest lecturer at numerous universities around the world.

"WITCH Manifesto" achieves its rhetorical effect by directly addressing the reader: "If you are a woman and dare to look within yourself, you are a Witch…. You make your own rules. You are both free and beautiful." By associating freedom and beauty with the

An engraving (circa 1900) by Henriette Goldenberg depicting witches on Walpurgis Night. The 1968 "WITCH Manifesto" uses the term "witch" to describe female proponents of women's rights. CCI/THE ART ARCHIVE AT ART RESOURCE, NY

acknowledgement of an inner witch, the manifesto both appeals to the insecurities of women during the liberation movement of the late 1960s and reinforces the stereotypical construction of women. Despite the use of the word "witch" to describe the supposed inner magic of women, the essay fails to successfully reclaim the word from its negative connotations and only manages to use it according to the stereotypes developed during the neopagan revival—a usage that proved counterproductive for feminists and religious neopagans alike.

Like much of the activism of the women of WITCH, the manifesto is blunt, short, and somewhat lacking in organizational structure. Instead of taking a focused stance against a particular organization or the societal problems facing feminists, WITCH attacks a broad range of institutions and attitudes, stating, "Whatever is repressive, solely male-oriented, greedy, puritanical, authoritarian—those are your targets." The explosive nature of these accusations in "WITCH Manifesto" reflects the group's action-based style of theatrical zaps and dramatic hexes. The discussion of the sisterhood of witches reflects the unifying rhetoric of the text, which attempts to address every woman directly and to tell her to release her inner power.

CRITICAL DISCUSSION

When "WITCH Manifesto" first appeared in 1968, it was met with mixed responses from feminists struggling to find an identity within the emerging women's liberation movement and from the women within the WITCH organization themselves. Despite its limitations, the WITCH movement was able to extend into many parts of the country. Morgan, one of the founding members of WITCH, is quoted in Susan Brownmiller's memoir *In Our Time* (1999) as saying, "WITCH may not have known much about the real history of witches, but WITCH had a joie de vivre." The excitement of the theatrical zaps seemed to be enough to allow small groups of feminists to band together in order to express their views.

The broad social and political legacy of "WITCH Manifesto" was as explosive and brief as the organization itself. Alice Echols, in her survey of radical American feminism *Daring to Be Bad* (1989), notes how the members of WITCH participated in a type of activism where the "sole point seemed to be 'we're liberated and you're not,'" which "only served to distance the movement from its natural consistency." The decentralization of feminist ideas was further enhanced by the group's actions because of its focus on corporate targets rather than on men. Moreover, Echols states that radical feminists of the time felt activism "should be done in a manner that promoted dialogue and developed consciousness," which was not achieved in the theatrical activism of the WITCH women.

Most scholars treat "WITCH Manifesto" as a brief manifestation of the passions of the WITCH activists, who ultimately lacked understanding of the feminist cause and how it affected the women's liberation movement as a whole. The WITCH movement often concentrated on gaining publicity for specific issues that were only relevant to small groups. Margot Adler in *Drawing Down the Moon* (1986) touches on a major trend in criticism that focuses on the ability of the group to tackle different sociopolitical problems, pointing to the name of the organization as the central example: "The original name of the group was Women's International Terrorist Conspiracy from Hell," but "only the letters were fixed; the name kept changing to suit particular needs." Feminist activist Jo Freeman posted further examples of the group's mutability on her website, stating, "The acronym came before the name, which varied with the demonstration" and included such names as "Women Interested in Toppling Consumer Holidays" and "Women Incensed at Telephone Company Harassment."

BIBLIOGRAPHY

Sources

Adler, Margot. *Drawing Down the Moon: Witches, Druids, Goddess-Worshippers, and Other Pagans in America Today.* Rev. ed. Boston: Beacon, 1986. Print.

Brownmiller, Susan. *In Our Time: Memoir of a Revolution.* New York: Dial, 1999. Print.

Echols, Alice. *Daring to Be Bad: Radical Feminism in America 1967-1975.* Minneapolis: U of Minnesota P, 1989. Print.

Freeman, Jo. "W.I.T.C.H.—The Women's International Terrorist Conspiracy from Hell." *Jo Freeman.* Jo Freeman, n.d. Web. 17 Sept. 2012.

"WITCH Manifesto." *Sisterhood Is Powerful: An Anthology of Writings from the Women's Liberation Movement.* Ed. Robin Morgan. New York: Random House, 1970. 539-43. Print.

Further Reading

Berkeley, Kathleen C. *The Women's Liberation Movement in America.* Westport: Greenwood, 1999. Print.

Bradley, Patricia. *Mass Media and the Shaping of American Feminism, 1963-1975.* Jackson: UP of Mississippi, 2004. Print.

Buchanan, Paul D. *Radical Feminists: A Guide to an American Subculture.* Santa Barbara: Greenwood, 2011. Web. 18 Sept. 2012.

Morgan, Robin. *Going Too Far: The Personal Chronicle of a Feminist.* New York: Random House, 1977. Print.

"Robin Morgan." *Feminist Writers.* Ed. Pamela Kester-Shelton. Detroit: St. James, 1996. 340. *Literature Resource Center.* Web. 17 Sept. 2012.

Sempruch, Justyna. *Fantasies of Gender and the Witch in Feminist Theory and Literature.* West Lafayette: Purdue UP, 2008. Print.

Siegel, Deborah. *Sisterhood Interrupted: From Radical Women to Grrls Gone Wild.* New York: Palgrave Macmillan, 2007. Print.

Katherine Barker

FILM

A CERTAIN TENDENCY OF THE FRENCH CINEMA

François Truffaut

OVERVIEW

François Truffaut's "A Certain Tendency of the French Cinema," published in the journal *Cahiers du cinéma* (January 1954), proposes a radical shift in how films should be evaluated by critics and moviegoers alike, establishing the director as the primary creative force behind a movie. During a time when the French film industry was trying to keep up with American, Italian, and other cinema, Truffaut's essay was part of a larger effort by writers at *Cahiers,* such as Jean-Luc Godard, André Bazin, Claude Chabrol, Éric Rohmer, and Jacques Rivette, to redefine the notion of what makes a film great. They argued that the previous "tradition of quality" in French cinema that favored refined literary adaptations no longer spoke to 1950s moviegoers. Instead Truffaut trumpets *"la politique des auteurs,"* which favors individual expression and distinctive directorial styles over bland perfectionism. The essay targets the new generation of French youth who were raised on the movies and who were now starting to take the medium seriously as an art form. It includes a detailed description of what constitutes a bad movie and what makes a good one.

"A Certain Tendency" was particularly well received by cinephiles who had grown up watching American films at the Cinémathèque Française theater in Paris. It laid the groundwork for the type of idiosyncratic, genre-busting films made in the late 1950s by Truffaut and his friends in what became known as the "French New Wave" movement. In the 1960s film critic Andrew Sarris popularized Truffaut's approach in the United States as the "auteur theory." While this theory has since been discredited as too simplistic in its glorification of the director above all other film collaborators, it remains a useful method for examining a director's entire filmography for repeated themes and a sense of the director's worldview.

HISTORICAL AND LITERARY CONTEXT

When Truffaut composed "A Certain Tendency," he claimed to not view it as a revolutionary piece of film criticism but rather to expose a trend in French cinema that he and his colleagues viewed as old-fashioned and detrimental to cinema's development. While still internationally popular, post-World War II French cinema had grown stagnant. Its studio system relied on a staple of big-budget literary adaptations based on

known properties. Truffaut called this the "tradition of quality," in which the primary focus in filmmaking lay with the development of a strong screenplay. Once a screenplay was perfected, directors and actors simply brought that script to life. Their contributions were viewed as inferior to those of the writer. Truffaut felt that this approach to viewing film was outdated and he disagreed with the methods being used to adapt literary works for film.

Truffaut's essay was a natural outgrowth of the work being published in the French cinema journal *Cahiers du cinéma,* the first internationally recognized journal to publish articles about film as art. Cofounded in 1951 by Bazin, Jacques Doniol-Valcroze, and Joseph-Marie Lo Duca, *Cahiers* promoted the view that movies are more than just popular entertainment; they are an art form, and as such they should be held in as high a regard as paintings, theater, or dance. Truffaut and such fellow *Cahiers* writers as Chabrol, Godard, Rivette, Rohmer, and Alain Resnais had grown up watching American movies shown at the Cinémathèque Française, the premier revival house in the world. They rejected the staid interior dramas of French films for the gritty, more urban, more violent films of American filmmakers such as Howard Hawks and Samuel Fuller. Truffaut and his colleagues wanted to establish a critical platform upon which they could communicate their admiration for these filmmakers and explain why they thought their films superior to current French cinema.

While viewed as a watershed publication now, "A Certain Tendency" actually continued a growing trend in French film criticism that sought to identify the primary creative force behind a film. In 1949 the filmmaker and critic Roger Leenhardt had founded the Objectif 49 film club with the aim of establishing a *"cinéma d'auteur."* His pre-World War II film essays heavily influenced Bazin, who argued that a film should reflect a director's personal viewpoint and that the camera should try to capture the world the director envisions.

The success of the essay laid the groundwork for Truffaut and his colleagues to become movie directors themselves. Their debut feature films, including Truffaut's *The 400 Blows* (1959), Godard's *Breathless* (1959), and Renais's *Hiroshima Mon Amour* (1959), launched the French New Wave movement. Rather

+ *Key Facts*

Time Period:
Mid-20th Century

Movement/Issue:
French New Wave

Place of Publication:
France

Language of Publication:
French

FRANÇOIS TRUFFAUT: CRITIC TURNED DIRECTOR

François Truffaut enjoyed a career as one of France's successful and beloved directors in the 1960s and 1970s. He drew particular acclaim for his series of films (from *The 400 Blows* to *Love on the Run*) starring Jean-Pierre Léaud as Truffaut's alter ego, Antoine Doinel. According to the director, these films dramatize his childhood as he wished it had been. In addition to this series, Truffaut directed such classics as *Shoot the Piano Player* (1960), *Jules and Jim* (1962), *Fahrenheit 451* (1966), *The Wild Child* (1970), and *Day for Night* (1973) and starred in Steven Spielberg's science fiction classic *Close Encounters of the Third Kind* (1977). He died of a brain tumor in 1984 at age fifty-two.

Toward the end of his life, Truffaut grew to regret the effects of auteurism on the moviemaking process. He came to feel that contemporary filmmakers placed too much emphasis on the visuals of a movie while neglecting a good screenplay and ignoring basic dramatics. The auteur theory, he admitted, was used primarily as way for the under-thirty generation to wrest control of the movies from older men.

than being slavishly tied to narrative storytelling, these films instead play with the visual conventions of the medium. The critical and financial success of the films made this style of moviemaking acceptable and spurred the eventual creation of the American independent film movement exemplified by such distinctive filmmakers as John Sayles, David Lynch, and Quentin Tarantino.

THEMES AND STYLE

"A Certain Tendency" begins with a discussion of the tradition of quality, which Truffaut claims to have been a hallmark of French film since 1946. The essay focuses on prestige films—of which a handful were released each year and which typically won awards at international film festivals—particularly films made by such directors as Claude Autant-Lara and René Clément. Truffaut declares that these films are locked "in a closed world, barricaded by formulas." Such works are "scenarists' films"—movies in which the primary creative power rests with the screenwriter and not the director. The essay gives particular attention to the work of screenwriters Jean Aurenche and Pierre Bost, who promulgated the idea that film adaptation of books need not be "faithful to the letter" but "faithful to the spirit" of the original. Truffaut argues that Aurenche and Bost advanced this philosophy to "use works of literature to support their own personal biases" by deciding which scenes in a novel are filmable. Unfilmable scenes require the writing of "equivalent scenes" not found in the original work. Truffaut points out specific examples of equivalent scenes from

their movies and then refers to the source material, revealing that many of these invented scenes often run counter to the original intent of the book's author. He attributes this problem to the fact that Aurenche and Bost, along with many of France's top screenwriters, have a literary background. They are "contemptuous of the cinema by underestimating it." A director who merely films these scripts without bringing anything new visually or thematically is labeled a *metteur en scène* (scene setter or stager).

Truffaut suggests that real films can be made only by "a man of the cinema": a filmmaker who thinks in images rather than in words. The tradition of quality, Truffaut argues, should be replaced by an "auteur's cinema." The true filmmakers write their own screenplays as well as direct. In particular, Truffaut praises such directors as Jean Renoir, Jean Cocteau, Max Ophuls, Abel Gance, and Jacques Tati. He closes by saying, "There are no good and bad movies, only good and bad directors."

The writing style throughout "A Certain Tendency" is personal. In the first sentence, Truffaut tries to downplay the importance of the essay by including a disclaimer: "These notes have no other object than to attempt to define a certain tendency of the French cinema." He then proceeds to take on the top French writers and directors of the day. The essay cites specific examples from their work, lacing the excerpts with incredulity and sarcasm. At the end, though, Truffaut backs off and even apologizes by admitting to "a great deal of emotion and taking sides"; he nevertheless deems his commentary necessary because cinema, he feels, is on a dead-end course.

CRITICAL DISCUSSION

Upon publication, "A Certain Tendency" ignited significant controversy. Some critics embraced the auteur theory. The American movie critic Sarris, for example, praises the approach in his essay "Notes on the Auteur Theory in 1962," first published in *Film Culture*. Sarris takes the idea one step further by categorically declaring that "the director is the author of a film, the person who gives it any distinctive quality." Other critics and filmmakers objected to the pedestal on which directors had now been placed. In her 1963 essay "Circles and Squares," the critic Pauline Kael argues that "when a famous director makes a good movie, we look at the movie. We don't think about his personality." Kael suggests that a film with a distinctive style is "a poor film" and that auteur supporters try to elevate trash to the level of art.

In the years following the publication of "A Certain Tendency," Truffaut's ideas gained some popularity in England and in the United States. For a brief time the auteur theory provided a popular way to teach film at colleges, sparking a renewed interest in movie history and the careers of nearly forgotten filmmakers. It also helped spur an American embrace of international filmmakers, such Ingmar Bergman, Akira Kurasawa, and Satyajit Ray.

As the auteur theory gained momentum, people working in the industry questioned the so-called "cult of the director," pointing out that movies are a collaborative medium and that it is difficult to assess the contributions of a particular crew member to a project. Furthermore, they argued that if anyone could have been called an auteur during the heyday of the Hollywood studio system, it would have been a producer, such as David O. Selznick or Darryl Zanuck, because a producer is the only person to oversee a movie through the entire creative process. By the mid-1960s auteurism had been largely replaced in academic circles by other approaches, such as New Criticism, deconstructionist theory, and the study of symbiotics.

BIBLIOGRAPHY

Sources

"François Truffaut." *Conversations at the American Film Institute with the Great Moviemakers: The Next Generation, from the 1950s to Hollywood Today.* Ed. George Stevens Jr. New York: Knopf, 2012. 681-98. Print.

Kael, Pauline, "Circles and Squares." *Film Quarterly* 16.3 (1963): 12-26. Print.

Sarris, Andrew. "Notes on the Auteur Theory in 1962." *Film Culture* 27 (1962-63): 1-8. Print.

Truffaut, François. "A Certain Tendency of the French Cinema." *Movies and Methods.* Ed. Bill Nichols. Berkeley: U of California P, 1976. 224-37. Print.

Further Reading

Balaban, Bob. *Spielberg, Truffaut and Me: An Actor's Diary.* London: Titan Books, 2003. Print.

Bordwell, David. *Film History: An Introduction.* 4th ed. New York: McGraw-Hill, 2009. Print.

Brody, Richard. "Andrew Sarris and the 'A' Word." *New Yorker.* New Yorker, 20 June 2012. Web. 29 June 2012.

Cook, David A. *A History of Narrative Film.* 4th ed. New York: Norton, 2004. Print.

De Baecque, Antoine. *Truffaut: A Biography.* New York: Knopf, 1999. Print.

Giannetti, Louis. *Understanding Movies.* 12th ed. Boston: Allyn & Bacon, 2010. Print.

Godard, Jean-Luc. *Godard on Godard.* London: Da Capo, 1986. Print.

Kael, Pauline. *The Citizen Kane Book.* New York: Bantam Books, 1971. Print.

Sarris, Andrew. *The American Cinema: Directors and Directions 1929-1968.* New York: E. P. Dutton, 1968. Print.

Schatz, Thomas. *The Genius of the System: Hollywood Filmmaking in the Studio Era.* Minneapolis: U of Minnesota P, 2010. Print.

Truffaut, François. *The Films in My Life.* New York: Da Capo, 1994. Print.

———. *Hitchcock.* New York: Simon & Schuster, 1985. Print.

Richard Rothrock

French director François Truffaut behind the camera in 1966. © ANGLO ENTERPRISE/VINEYARD/THE KOBAL COLLECTION/ART RESOURCE

CINEMA AS AN INSTRUMENT OF POETRY

Luis Buñuel

❖ *Key Facts*

Time Period:
Mid-20th Century

Movement/Issue:
Surrealism; Marxism;
Cinematic modernism;
Aesthetics

Place of Publication:
Mexico

**Language of
Publication:**
Spanish

OVERVIEW

Composed by Luis Buñuel, "Cinema as an Instrument of Poetry" (1958) argues for a brand of filmmaking that subverts the superficial conventions of realism as a means of exploring the subconscious and addressing "the fundamental problems of modern man." At the time of the essay's composition, Buñuel was well regarded as a filmmaker, known for his subversive and surrealistic explorations of human psychology and society. Greatly influenced by Freudian theory and the pioneering surrealism of Salvador Dalí and Federico García Lorca, Buñuel began his career as a filmmaker in 1929 with the groundbreaking short *Un Chien Andalou* (An Andalusian Dog), which he made with Dalí. In the decades following, Buñuel moved between Europe and North America, making technically innovative, as well as morally and politically provocative, films. With "Cinema as an Instrument of Poetry" Buñuel offered a defense and explanation of his own filmmaking methodology as well as an assault on the contemporary neorealist movement.

Initially delivered as an address at the University of Mexico in Mexico City and published soon thereafter, "Cinema as an Instrument of Poetry" was met with interest by members of the Mexican film and arts communities, as the essay offered audiences a welcome explanation for Buñuel's often controversial and consistently baffling works. The text also provided Buñuel with an artistic charter that helped guide the rest of his filmmaking career. Soon after delivering and publishing "Cinema as an Instrument of Poetry," Buñuel made a series of films that are widely regarded as the masterpieces of his long and distinguished career. Today the essay is considered among the most important of Buñuel's critical writings and is viewed as an important key to understanding his oeuvre of films.

HISTORICAL AND LITERARY CONTEXT

"Cinema as an Instrument of Poetry" responds to the international filmmaking scene of the mid-twentieth century, when various cinematic styles offered new visions for what the relatively young medium could be. Though born in Spain, Buñuel first emerged as a filmmaker in Paris in the late 1920s as a part of the surrealist movement. Founded by the French writer André Breton in 1924, surrealism was a revolutionary and wide-ranging movement that sought to explore the human subconscious through the use of artistic techniques that dispensed with reason and logic and embraced the productive potential of chance and instinct. Through his interest in surrealism and film, Buñuel became involved with Dalí, a fellow Spaniard. Together they wrote and made the short film *Un Chien Andalou* in 1929. Shocking and technically innovative, it launched Buñuel's career as the foremost surrealist filmmaker.

By the time "Cinema as an Instrument of Poetry" was composed in 1958, Buñuel was a respected filmmaker but had difficulty finding support to make the kinds of movies he was passionate about making. Through his involvement with surrealism, he was exposed to and eventually joined the communist movement. This political stance, combined with the difficulty of his nonnarrative filmmaking vision, made it difficult for Buñuel to find financing for his work. He moved from France to Spain to the United States in pursuit of opportunities. Francisco Franco's victory in the Spanish Civil War (1936-39) made a return to Spain impossible. In 1946 Buñuel moved from the United States to Mexico. There he made many commercial films to finance more personal projects. The result was a number of important films, including *Los Olvidados* (1950), that employed surrealist technique to make powerful social critiques.

"Cinema as an Instrument of Poetry" draws on a tradition of surrealist writing that can be traced back to Breton's *Manifesto of Surrealism*. Written in 1924, it calls for a radical new form of art that upends convention as a means of depicting "the actual functioning of thought." In his urging for filmmaking that "expresses the world of thought, feeling, and instinct," Buñuel echoes Breton's argument of some thirty years before. Buñuel's essay also advances Breton's case against realism on the grounds that it was, as Breton writes, "hostile to any intellectual or moral advancement." In "Cinema as an Instrument of Poetry," Buñuel argues against realism (and neorealism): "I advocate the kind of cinema that will ... give me a whole view of reality, expand my knowledge of things and people, and open up the marvelous world of the unknown, of all that I can't find in the daily press or come across on the street."

Following its publication, "Cinema as an Instrument of Poetry" helped to shape the way critics and writers viewed the films of Buñuel. The essay's argument for the interrelatedness of surrealist methods and left-wing political ambitions influenced later writings in Buñuel's oeuvre. For example, in his essay in *The World of Luis Buñuel* (1978), scholar Randall Conrad uses "Cinema as an Instrument of Poetry" as a lens through which to view Buñuel's later films. Today the work is considered an important key to understanding the artistic vision and ambition of one of the twentieth century's most important filmmakers.

THEMES AND STYLE

The central theme of "Cinema as an Instrument of Poetry" is that film offers an unprecedented means of exploring the subconscious and should be used for this important end. Prepared for a roundtable discussion among Mexican artists and students, the essay takes as its theme "cinema as artistic expression." Buñuel regards its mode of expression as poetic, arguing that poetry and film share "a sense of liberation, subversion of reality, a passage into the marvelous world of the subconscious, and nonconformity to the restrictive society that surrounds us." Unlike the other arts, however, film has not pursued these possibilities. Rather, filmmakers have been more or less content to regurgitate novelistic and theatrical conventions on the screen. In so doing they have missed cinema's true potential: "The cinema seems to have been invented to express the life of the subconscious, the roots of which reach so deeply into poetry, yet it is almost never used toward that end." If it were used toward this end, Buñuel argues, it would "address the fundamental problems of modern man," both psychological and social.

To persuade his audience of the proper, poetic function of film, Buñuel appeals to his reader's (or listener's) intelligence and critical acuity. For example, he declares, "a moderately cultured individual would reject with scorn a book with one of the plots recounted in the biggest films." Writing in the first person, Buñuel allies himself with his audience by offering bold, broad judgments without leaving room for disagreement: "Anyone who hopes to see good films will rarely be satisfied by the big-budget productions or by those that come with the approval of the critics and popular acclaim." Instead of the dissatisfying clichés of convention, "Cinema as an Instrument of Poetry" offers something bright and alluring. "In the hands of a free spirit," Buñuel writes, "the cinema is a magnificent and dangerous weapon."

Stylistically, "Cinema as an Instrument of Poetry" is distinguished by its mix of detached logic and lyrical imagery. The result is a text that is able to make a coherent argument about filmic technique while also offering glimpses of Buñuel's poetic vision. Early in the text he elaborates on a quote from the Mexican poet Octavio Paz when declaring that "the

LUIS BUÑUEL: ITINERANT ARTIST

Luis Buñuel was born in 1900 in the small town of Calanda, Spain, and grew up in the nearby city of Zaragoza. His father was wealthy and sent Buñuel to a strict Catholic school. At seventeen he moved to Madrid to attend university. There he met Salvador Dalí as well as the future poet and playwright Federico García Lorca. Soon after completing his studies in 1924, he went to Paris. Though Buñuel had not yet expressed any particular artistic proclivity, he quickly fell in with artists such as Pablo Picasso and immersed himself in film, often attending three screenings a day.

Over the next several years, he wrote film criticism, studied acting, and worked in the French movie industry. With help from Dalí, Buñuel made his first film, *Un Chien Andalou*, in 1929. After making two other well-received movies in France, he returned to Spain but fled in 1936 due to the outbreak of the Spanish Civil War. He made his way to the United States, bouncing between Los Angeles and New York. Frustrated by his inability to make films in the United States, he left for Mexico, where he found the financing and support he had long been seeking. He made twenty films there over an eighteen-year period. He continued to make films until 1977, when he released the widely acclaimed *Cet obscur object du désir* (*That Obscure Object of Desire*). Six years later he died in Mexico City.

white eyelid of the screen need only reflect the light that is its own to blow up the universe." Though he periodically returns to this lyric tone, Buñuel spends much of the essay quoting from other sources, citing examples, and arguing the specifics of cinematic style, technique, and ambition. Working in concert, these disparate rhetorical modes allow Buñuel to make a cogent argument that relies on the poetic mechanism he champions.

CRITICAL DISCUSSION

When "Cinema as an Instrument of Poetry" was first delivered as a lecture in December 1958, it was met with interest within the Latin American avant-garde cultural community, particularly in Mexico. Immediately after Buñuel's lecture, the text was transcribed from a recording and published in the journal *Universidad de México*. For Buñuel's audience and readership, the essay offered a rare and welcome statement from an important artist who rarely spoke critically or theoretically about his often cryptic and difficult work. Among Latin American artists and writers who were negotiating the lingering influence of surrealism, such as Paz and the Argentinean novelist Julio Cortázar, "Cinema as an Instrument of Poetry" provided a glimpse into Buñuel's take on the ways in which art can explore deeply personal experience without abandoning its larger social engagement.

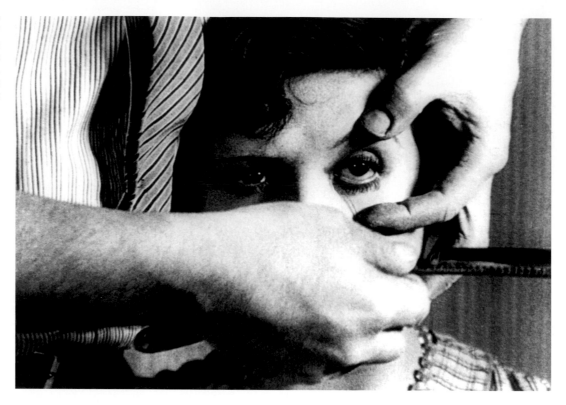

The famous "eye-cutting" scene from Luis Buñuel's early surrealist film *Un Chien Andalou* (1929). © ARENAPAL/TOPFOFO/THE IMAGE WORKS

The essay's argument about the role of film helped guide Buñuel through the final two decades of his career. In 1962, for example, he released *El Ángel exterminador* (The Exterminating Angel). As scholar Gwynne Edwards writes in *A Companion to Luis Buñuel* (2005), the film offered a "ferocious attack on the bourgeoisie ... stripping away its elegant façade in order to reveal its cruelty and hypocrisy, and also, in true surrealist fashion, exposed through dream sequences the anxieties and phobias that lay deep in the subconscious." In this way, Buñuel adhered to the vision laid out in "Cinema as an Instrument of Poetry." Over the course of the rest of his career, he maintained his assault on middle-class convention and continued to employ surrealist technique as his weapon of choice. In the half century since it was written, critics have considered the essay's place not only within Buñuel's cinematic output but also within a larger context of avant-garde art in the twentieth century.

Some commentators have drawn attention to the ways in which Buñuel's essay offers a means of synthesizing the political and the poetic in art. For example, in his 2004 essay in *Discourse,* scholar Victor Fuentes writes, "One could consider this address a 'Buñuelian manifesto.' ... With his concept of an integral vision of reality in which, as surrealism calls for, the real merges with the fantastic and the personal poetic with social commitment, Buñuel arrives at a synthesis of the prevailing antithetical positions in Mexico among the advocates of socially engaged art and the partisans of a poetic art." Commentators have also placed "Cinema as an Instrument of Poetry" within the broader context of Spanish-language literature in the mid-twentieth century. In his 2001 essay in *Bucknell Review,* Antonio Monegal discusses the ways in which these varied artists employed the term "poetic" to discuss their work. Buñuel's essay, Monegal argues, is indicative of Lorca's, Dalí's, and Buñuel's shared approach to poetic works from "the perspective of their enigmatic, or discordant, combination of signs."

BIBLIOGRAPHY

Sources

Buñuel, Luis. *My Last Sigh.* New York: Vintage Books, 1983. Print.

———. *An Unspeakable Betrayal: Selected Writings* of Luis Buñuel. Ed. Garrett White. Berkeley: U of California P, 2000. Print.

Conrad, Randall. "'A Magnificent and Dangerous Weapon': The Politics of Luis Buñuel's Late Films." *The World of Luis Buñuel: Essays in Criticism.* Ed. Joan Mellen. New York: Oxford UP, 1978. Print

Edwards, Gwynne. *A Companion to Luis Buñuel.* Woodbridge: Tamesis, 2005. Print.

Fuentes, Victor. "Buñuel's Cinematic Narrative and the Latin American New Novel." *Discourse* 26.1-2 (2004): 91-110. Web. *Project MUSE.* 25 Sept. 2012.

Monegal, Antonio. "Shall the Circle Be Unbroken? Verbal and Visual Poetry in Lorca, Buñuel, and Dalí." *Bucknell Review* 45.1 (2001): 148-59. Web. *ProQuest.* 25 Sept. 2012.

Further Reading

Aranda, J. Francisco. *Luis Buñuel: A Critical Biography.* Ed. and trans. David Robinson. New York: Da Capo, 1976. Print.

Buache, Freddy. *The Cinema of Luis Buñuel.* New York: A.S. Barnes, 1973. Print.

Buñuel, Luis. *Unspeakable Betrayal: Selected Writings of Luis Buñuel.* Berkeley: U of California P, 2002. Web. 25 Sept. 2012.

Durgnat, Raymond. *Luis Buñuel.* Berkeley: U of California P, 1968. Print.

———. "Theory of Theory: And Buñuel the Joker." *Film Quarterly* 44.1 (1990): 32-44. *JSTOR.* Web. 25 Sept. 2012.

Evans, Peter William. *The Films of Luis Buñuel: Subjectivity and Desire.* New York: Oxford UP, 1995. Print.

Evans, Peter William, and Isabel Santaolalla, eds. *Luis Buñuel: New Readings.* London: British Film Institute, 2004. Print.

Faber, Sebastiaan. "Buñuel's Impure Modernism (1929-1950)." *Modernist Cultures* 7.1 (2012): 56-76. Print.

Hammond, Paul. *The Shadow and Its Shadow: Surrealist Writings on Cinema.* San Francisco: City Lights, 2000. Print.

Paz, Octavio. *On Poets and Others.* New York: Arcade, 1990. Print.

Polizzotti, Mark. *Los Olvidados.* London: British Film Institute, 2006. Print.

Theodore McDermott

DOGME 95 MANIFESTO

Lars von Trier, Thomas Vinterberg

OVERVIEW

Composed by Danish film directors Lars von Trier and Thomas Vinterberg, the *Dogme 95 Manifesto* (1995) briefly critiques contemporary film and aims to remedy the movie industry's failings. Drafted in Copenhagen at von Trier's home on March 13, 1995, and was first distributed by Von Trier on March 20 at the Théâtre de l'Odéon in Paris, where a directors' symposium was being held to commemorate the centennial of filmmaking and to contemplate the film industry's uncertain future. The manifesto was designed to counter contemporary films' overly cosmetic and illusionistic nature and their dependence on expensive technology. Addressed to directors and producers, the manifesto outlines the ten rules of the Vow of Chastity, which require that filmmakers eschew aesthetic and technical gimmicks, and concentrate instead on story, setting, and performance, in order to purify filmmaking.

The manifesto engendered the Dogme 95 movement, which became a film-world phenomenon upon the release of the inaugural Dogme films at the 1998 Cannes Film Festival in France. Although von Trier and Vinterberg personally invited Danish directors Soren Kragh-Jacobsen and Kristian Levring to join the Dogme brotherhood, any filmmaker was welcome to produce a movie in accordance with the Vow of Chastity and to apply for Dogme 95 certification. Thirty-three certified Dogme films were created internationally before the Dogmesecretariat (the administrative department of the group) disbanded in 2002, fearing the movement had inadvertently created a genre, which the Vow of Chastity expressly forbids. Today filmmakers around the world continue to make films that conform to the Vow of Chastity, and many scholars regard the Dogme movement as a significant force in the evolution of cinema.

HISTORICAL AND LITERARY CONTEXT

The *Dogme 95 Manifesto* responds to the overly cosmetic nature, predictability, and superficiality of late-twentieth-century films. The spirit of the manifesto hearkens back to the post-World War II Italian neorealism movement and French new wave cinema of the late 1950s and the 1960s, which rejected traditional cinematic form and sought to depict reality instead of big budget, Hollywood-style fantasy. Both movements attempted to rethink the way characters are depicted and employed avant-garde techniques, such as shooting on location using portable cameras. However, neorealism and new wave cinema were relatively short-lived, and by the 1970s and 1980s, Hollywood blockbusters with outrageous special effects and fantastical plots dominated the box office.

By the time von Trier composed the *Dogme 95 Manifesto* in 1995, he had become frustrated by the onerous process of creating overly cosmetic films. Desiring to strip away artifice from cinema, he asked Vinterberg to join him in creating a new wave of filmmaking. They discussed ways to remedy what they most despised about contemporary film and in less than an hour composed the manifesto and the accompanying Vow of Chastity. Shortly thereafter, when called to speak about the future of film at the Théâtre de l'Odéon, von Trier simply announced that he represented the group Dogme 95, showered the audience with red leaflets bearing the manifesto, and promptly left. Vinterberg directed the first Dogme film in 1998, *The Celebration,* which won the Jury Prize at the 1998 Cannes Film Festival. The film's success helped spur the Dogme movement and the production of a host of Danish and international Dogme films.

The *Dogme 95 Manifesto* draws on a history of cinematic manifestos whose aim is to counter prevailing tendencies in filmmaking. It deliberately mimics François Truffaut's 1954 new wave manifesto "Une certaine tendance du cinéma français" ("A Certain Tendency in French Cinema"), which rejects traditional French cinema in favor of creating films that express the director's vision. Although the *Dogme 95 Manifesto* lauds French new wave ideals, it decries their failure to permanently revolutionize the film industry. Prior to writing the manifesto, von Trier issued three other manifestos lambasting contemporary film; however, unlike the previous works, the *Dogme 95 Manifesto* proposes a solution: the Vow of Chastity.

In the decade following its publication, the *Dogme 95 Manifesto* inspired numerous character-driven films adhering to the Vow of Chastity. Of the Dogme films produced by each of the movement's founding brothers, Vinterberg's *Celebration* and Kragh-Jacobsen's *Mifune's Last Song* (1999) earned the most praise. The success of these films helped gain distribution for other low-budget films. Lone

Scherfig's *Italian for Beginners* (2000), a box office smash in Denmark and the most seen Danish film in the United States to date, became the most financially successful Dogme-certified film. Although the Dogmesecretariat disbanded in 2002 and the founding brothers moved on to new projects, Dogme films continue to be made around the world.

THEMES AND STYLE

The central theme of the *Dogme 95 Manifesto* is that contemporary film has replaced the examination of true feelings and passions with technical and dramatic "trickery." The manifesto opens by claiming to be a "rescue action" with the "express goal of countering 'certain tendencies' in the cinema today." It criticizes the way films have been "cosmeticized to death" by "decadent filmmakers" who conspire to "fool the audience." To counter the overproduced nature of modern cinema and to "force the truth" out of characters and dramatic situations, the manifesto presents the Vow of Chastity. This set of rules challenges filmmakers to shoot on location, to use natural lighting and handheld cameras, and to avoid making postproduction modifications or adding sound or music not recorded on location. The manifesto posits that only when deprived of distracting filmic devices can directors allow a film's narrative and characters to express truth.

The manifesto impudently criticizes the failures of the legendary new wave cineastes and lambasts the decadence of modern cinema in order to provoke filmmakers to reexamine and purify their art. This insolent provocation is primarily achieved through the repeated denunciation of "bourgeois" film, which

LARS VON TRIER: PROVOCATIVE DIRECTOR

Renowned for his role in writing the *Dogme 95 Manifesto* and for cofounding the Dogme movement, director Lars von Trier has dedicated his career to reinventing cinema and to rebelling against filmic convention. Prior to his involvement in the Dogme 95 movement, he wrote three manifestos criticizing the state of contemporary cinema (in 1984, 1987, and 1990). A rebel and opponent of intellectual authority, he describes himself and his work as "a provocation."

While following his experimental, avant-garde cinematic pursuits, he has triumphed in finding a wide audience and commercial success—a rare accomplishment in the art world. He consistently creates films within a predefined set of rules, though he encourages anarchy to reign within that framework. His only Dogme film, *The Idiots* (1998), doggedly adheres to the Vow of Chastity even as it allows its characters, who pretend to be mentally disabled, to unleash chaos in a local community. Critics have decried the film's overt political incorrectness and have generally regarded it as disturbing, though many have reluctantly expressed an appreciation for its boldness. Although *The Idiots* lacks the commercial success and critical acclaim of Vinterberg's *The Celebration* (1998), it is lauded as a nearly perfect example of a Dogme film.

directly references Truffaut's new wave manifesto and its lamentation that antibourgeois films are invariably created by bourgeois filmmakers for consumption by the bourgeoisie. The *Dogme 95 Manifesto*

Thomas Bo Larsen and Therese Glahn in a scene from the Dogme 95 film *The Celebration* (1998), directed by Thomas Vinterberg. In keeping with Dogme 95 principles, it was filmed with handheld cameras and natural lighting. © BUREAU L.A. COLLECTION/SYGMA/CORBIS

PRIMARY SOURCE

DOGME 95 MANIFESTO

THE VOW OF CHASTITY

I swear to submit to the following set of rules drawn up and confirmed by DOGMA 95:

1. Shooting must be done on location. Props and sets must not be brought in (if a particular prop is necessary for the story, a location must be chosen where this prop is to be found).

2. The sound must never be produced apart from the images or vice versa. (Music must not be used unless it occurs where the scene is being shot.)

3. The camera must be hand-held. Any movement or immobility attainable in the hand is permitted.

4. The film must be in color. Special lighting is not acceptable. (If there is too little light for exposure the scene must be cut or a single lamp be attached to the camera.)

5. Optical work and filters are forbidden.

6. The film must not contain superficial action. (Murders, weapons, etc. must not occur.)

7. Temporal and geographical alienation are forbidden. (That is to say that the film takes place here and now.)

8. Genre movies are not acceptable.

9. The film format must be Academy 35 mm.

10. The director must not be credited.

Furthermore I swear as a director to refrain from personal taste! I am no longer an artist. I swear to refrain from creating a "work", as I regard the instant as more important than the whole. My supreme goal is to force the truth out of my characters and settings. I swear to do so by all the means available and at the cost of any good taste and any aesthetic considerations.

Thus I make my VOW OF CHASTITY.

Copenhagen, Monday 13 March 1995

On behalf of DOGMA 95

Lars von Trier

Thomas Vinterberg

---

turns Truffaut's criticism on the French new wave: "The anti-bourgeois cinema itself became bourgeois, because the foundations upon which its theories were based was the bourgeois perception of art." Vinterberg and von Trier openly attack the new wave's failure to resurrect cinema and denigrate Truffaut's auteur concept, which supposes that directors are films' true authors, as "bourgeois romanticism." The manifesto urges directors to rescue the art of filmmaking by stripping it of artifice and strictly disciplining their craft as outlined in the Vow of Chastity.

Stylistically, the *Dogme 95 Manifesto* is distinguished by its dramatic language and punctuation. The style of the manifesto reflects von Trier's radical personality and echoes the dramatic fashion in which he distributed the manifestos. Like the unsuspecting audience at the film conference, the reader is assaulted by the lavish use of exclamation points, which lends a sense of urgency to the manifesto. By declaring "Dogme 95 is a rescue action!" von Trier and Vinterberg hyperbolically cast the film industry as being on the brink of death because of the "technological storm" that is washing "the last grains of truth away in the deadly embrace of sensation." The manifesto's dramatic, stringent diction commands directors to purify their filmmaking, while its decadent language mocks the self-indulgent tendencies of contemporary cinema—a playfulness that is also apparent in its paradoxical homage to and criticism of new wave cinema. Both rebellious and mischievous in tone, the *Dogme 95 Manifesto* achieves its rhetorical force through its insolent yet passionate condemnation of the system it seeks to reform.

CRITICAL DISCUSSION

When the *Dogme 95 Manifesto* was first distributed in 1995, critics generally dismissed it as a publicity stunt or provocative joke. American film critic Jonathan Rosenbaum claims the manifesto's true purpose was "to secure an American release for *The Celebration* and a Hollywood contract for Thomas Vinterberg." Vinterberg seems to confirm Rosenbaum's suspicion that the manifesto's anti-Hollywood rant is a ploy to obtain U.S. distribution for Danish films, when he admits (as quoted in Richard Kelly's 2000 book *The Name of this Book Is Dogme 95*), "When you're a small country, you have to yell to get heard." In a review of *Celebration*, Irish critic Harvey O'Brien states the manifesto has "the sense of a big joke about it" and decries it as "a pale echo of too many greater voices to make any waves." Despite these initial dismissals, the critical success of *Celebration* ensured the spread of the Dogme movement.

After the Dogmesecretariat disbanded in 2002, the manifesto remained an important force in the film world. In the introduction to *Dogme Uncut* (2003), a guide to the origins and influence of Dogme 95, Jack Stevenson argues that Dogme "has changed, broadened, developed," and "survived the departure of the four founding Dogme brothers and has moved out from under the shadow of Lars von Trier." As filmmakers continued to make Dogme films, the movement became part of film school pedagogy around the world. Today scholars continue to debate the movement's importance and historical and aesthetic legacy.

Much scholarship has focused on the success of the *Dogme 95 Manifesto* in effecting an antiestablishment renewal of cinema. Kelly praises the manifesto as "the most audacious and conspicuous attempt to reinvent cinema since, well, Godard." Although others have also likened the movement's influence to that of iconic director Jean-Luc Godard, many have regarded von Trier and Vinterberg's manifesto as childish self-promotion and mere recirculation of old ideas. In a *New York Press* review of von Trier's film *Dogville* (2003), American film critic Armond White (2004) claims the manifesto "brought filmmaking closer to amateur porn," and he refers to the movement as "insignificant." Although critics continue to argue over Dogme's significance, the movement's effects have been felt throughout the film world. As Stevenson writes, "It has survived the failure of individual films and it has survived the *success* of individual films … It has survived innumerable charges of hype and fraud."

BIBLIOGRAPHY

Sources

Beltzer, Thomas. "Lars von Trier: The Little Knight." *Senses of Cinema*. Senses of Cinema, 4 Oct. 2002. Web. 14 Jun. 2012.

Christensen, Ove. "Danish Dogmas." Rev. of *Purity and Provocation: Dogma '95*, ed. Mette Hjort and Scott MacKenzie. *Senses of Cinema*. Senses of Cinema, 28 Oct. 2004. Web. 14 Jun. 2012.

Kelly, Richard. *The Name of this Book Is Dogme 95*. London: Faber and Faber, 2000. Print.

Morgan, Stephen. "Short History of Dogme 95: Lars von Trier and Thomas Vinterberg's Cinematic Challenge." *Foreign Films*. Suite101, 15 March 2009. Web. 3 Jun. 2012.

Nissen, Dan. "Von Trier, Lars." *International Dictionary of Films and Filmmakers*. Vol. 2.2001. Web. 3 Jun. 2012.

O'Brien, Harvey. "Dogme#1—*Festen*." Rev. of *The Celebration*, by Thomas Vinterberg. *Eircom.net*. Eircom Group, 2000. Web. 13 Jun. 2012.

Phillips, William H. *Film: An Introduction*. Boston: Bedford-St. Martin's, 2004. Print.

Rosenbaum, Jonathan. *Movie Wars: How Hollywood and the Media Limit What Movies We Can See*. Chicago: Chicago Review Press, 2002. Print.

Roxborough, Scott. "Blond Ambition: The Next Generation of Scandinavian Filmmakers Is Emerging from the Long Shadow of the Dogme Movement to Make Hollywood-Style Crowd-Pleasers." *Hollywood Reporter* 16 Aug. 2005: 16+. *General OneFile*. Web. 3 Jun. 2012.

Shepard, Jim. "Grand Provocateur: Lars von Trier's War with Himself." *Harper's Magazine* Jan. 2006: 83-88. *Literature Resource Center*. Web. 22 May 2012.

Stevenson, Jack. *Dogme Uncut: Lars von Trier, Thomas Vinterberg, and the Gang That Took on Hollywood*. Santa Monica: Santa Monica Press, 2003. Print.

Van der Vliet, Emma. "Naked Film: Stripping with *The Idiots*." *Post Script* 28.3 (2009): 14-30. *Literature Resource Center*. Web. 22 May 2012.

Walters, Tim. "Reconsidering *The Idiots*: Dogme 95, Lars von Trier, and the Cinema of Subversion?" *Velvet Light Trap* 53 (2004): 40-54. *Literature Resource Center*. Web. 22 May 2012.

White, Armond. "Digital Video Dogpatch." Rev. of *Dogville*, dir. Lars von Trier. *New York Press* 16 Mar. 2004. Web. 13 Jun. 2012.

Further Reading

Bondebjerg, Ib. "Lars von Trier Interview." *The Danish Directors: Dialogues on a Contemporary National Cinema*. Ed. Mette Hjort and Bondebjerg. Bristol: Intellect, 2001. 208-27. Print.

Christensen, Ove. "Authentic Illusions—The Aesthetics of Dogma 95." *P.O.V.* Aarhus University, Dec. 2000. Web. 13 Jun. 2012.

Conrich, Ian, and Estella Tincknell. "Film Purity, the Neo-Bazinian Ideal, and Humanism in Dogma 95." *P.O.V.* Aarhus University, Dec. 2000. Web. 13 Jun. 2012.

Elkington, Trevor G. "Costumes, Adolescence, and Dogma: Nordic Film and American Distribution." *Transnational Cinema in a Global North: Nordic Cinema in Transition*. Ed. Elkington and Andrew Nestingen. Detroit: Wayne State University Press, 2005. 31-52. Print.

Hjort, Mette, and Scott MacKenzie, eds. *Purity and Provocation: Dogma '95*. London: BFI Publishing, 2003. Print.

MacKenzie, Scott. "Direct Dogma: Film Manifestos and the *fin de siècle*." *P.O.V.* Aarhus University, Dec. 2000. Web. 13 Jun. 2012.

Pastorino, Christian C. Vinces. *Alternative Modes: Dialectic of the Hollywood and Dogme 95 Modes of Production and Its Influence in Cuban Cinema*. Saarbrücken: VDM Verlag, 2008. Print.

Roberts, John. "Dogme 95." *New Left Review* Nov. 1999: 141-49. *New Left Review Archive*. Web. 13 Jun. 2012.

Schepelern, Peter. "Film According to Dogma: Ground Rules, Obstacles, and Liberations." *Transnational Cinema in a Global North: Nordic Cinema in Transition*. Ed. Trevor Elkington and Andrew Nestingen. Detroit: Wayne State UP, 2005. 73-107. Print.

Simons, Jan. *Playing the Waves: Lars Von Trier's Game Cinema*. Amsterdam: Amsterdam UP, 2007. Print.

Maggie Magno

METAPHORS ON VISION

James Stanley Brakhage

✥ *Key Facts*

Time Period:
Mid-20th Century

Movement/Issue:
Avant-gardism;
Cinematic theory

Place of Publication:
United States

**Language of
Publication:**
English

OVERVIEW

Composed by James Stanley Brakhage, the 1963 monograph *Metaphors on Vision* calls for an avant-garde form of cinema that portrays, or "sees," the world with an untrained, innocent eye and rejects created rules of perspective and nineteenth-century compositional logic. Brakhage had begun writing *Metaphors on Vision* while working on *Anticipation of the Night* (1957), a film whose evocation of a childlike way of seeing the world embodies many of the monograph's aesthetic concerns. Although the text does not address a specific audience, the manifesto's esoteric content suggests that it is intended for a rather limited group—those concerned with the theoretical underpinnings of avant-garde cinema. Central to the work are two ideas: that sight is conditioned and narrowed by both language and the experience of adulthood and that the task of artists is to increase their ability to see.

Brakhage's films, which number about 400, have provoked considerable critical attention for their experimental, nonnarrative techniques, but *Metaphors on Vision* was hardly noticed when it was first issued. The text was the earliest articulation of the aesthetic theories that underlaid much of Brakhage's art over the next four decades. Indeed, the one defining characteristic of Brakhage's body of work, despite its variety of technique and style, is its attempt at new ways of seeing that were first promulgated in *Metaphors on Vision.* Today the monograph is considered an important document in the aesthetic development of the preeminent avant-garde film director in the United States.

HISTORICAL AND LITERARY CONTEXT

Metaphors on Vision responds to the rise of amateur, avant-garde cinema in the wake of the dominance of Hollywood studio films in the 1940s and 1950s. In 1943, two decades prior to the publication of *Metaphors on Vision,* the Russian-born American filmmaker Maya Deren made *Meshes of the Afternoon,* which film scholar David E. James characterizes in his piece "Amateurs in the Industry Town: Stan Brakhage and Andy Warhol in Los Angeles" as the "foundation film for the next two decades of avant-garde American Cinema." Then in 1947 the House Un-American Activities Committee began to blacklist many actors

and directors, because of their purported association with communism, an act that, according to James, "destroyed all progressive presence in the industry." These experiences led Deren to publish several essays that established a dualism between individual, amateur avant-garde films and industrial, Hollywood projects that were committed to capitalistic modes of production.

By the time *Metaphors on Vision* was published in 1963, American avant-garde cinema was well established but focused on the tradition of the psychodrama. Deren's film, along with Kenneth Anger's *Fireworks* (1947) and Brakhage's own *Reflections on Black* (1955) are all examples of this genre, one that Brakhage would break from with *Anticipation of the Night,* made in 1957, around the time he began writing *Metaphors on Vision.* James claims that it is in this film that Brakhage "committed himself to the intricate splendors of subjective vision and the rejection of Hollywood grammar that marks his mature and signal achievement." These are the aesthetic developments that are outlined in *Metaphors on Vision.*

Metaphors on Vision draws on a long history of avant-garde art manifestos, especially Soviet filmmaker Dziga Vertov's *WE: Variant of a Manifesto* (1919), whose aesthetics included the concept of the "cine-eye" montage method of filmmaking for reflecting the real world rather than the artificial dramatic narrative. Brakhage was also influenced by Deren's essay "Amateur versus Professional," which James described as a prominent work on the American vanguard. Written in 1959, "Amateur versus Professional," defends the artistic freedom of nonindustry directors to produce films that focus less on plot and dialogue and more on visual beauty. The influence of Deren's essay is evidenced not only in *Metaphors on Vision,* where Brakhage advocates for cinema inspired by deep visual perception, but also in his later essay, "In Defense of Amateur," which echoes Deren's appreciation for work done out of love as opposed to financial gain.

For the four decades after its publication, *Metaphors on Vision* served as a template for Brakhage's continued artistic production. The same year he published the monograph, he made *Mothlight,* a gorgeous visual experience created by sandwiching the wings of dead moths between layers of transparent editing tape. Around the same time, he began to hand paint his films. This turn toward an even more abstracted rendition of visual stimuli culminated in his works of the 1990s, when the majority of his films were made using this technique. Today, Brakhage's oeuvre and the monograph that first articulated its vision continue to command significant scholarly interest.

THEMES AND STYLE

The central theme of *Metaphors on Vision* is that artists, having lost the untutored vision of childhood, must develop their sense of visual perception, or their "optical mind," in order to create emotionally moving cinematic experiences. The essay opens with poetic descriptions of this childlike vision: "How many colors are there in a field of grass to the crawling baby unaware of 'Green'? How many rainbows can light create for the untutored eye? How aware of heat waves can that eye be? Imagine a world alive with incomprehensible objects and shimmering with an endless variety of movement and innumerable gradations of color." According to Brakhage, it is not possible to recover this purity of sight, but he claims that pursuing knowledge "founded upon visual communication," as opposed to the normative pursuit of language-based communication, can lead to a deep perception that will approximate this original vision. Brakhage designates this search for vision, and the passage of this visual history from one generation to the next, as a task for the artist.

The manifesto achieves its rhetorical effects by outlining a series of steps that will challenge and provoke the aspiring cinematic artist to view the world differently and more comprehensively. Its direct form of address is emphasized by Brakhage's use of the imperative and the second person pronoun "you." "Become aware," he writes, "of the fact that you are not only influenced by the visual phenomena which you are focused upon and attempt to sound the depths of all influence." This portrayal of deep visual perception as something rare and beautiful is a desirable goal for the artist, because "in these times the development of visual understanding is almost universally forsaken."

Stylistically, *Metaphors on Vision* is characterized by its use of poetic devices. It uses lush imagery to evoke the development of the visual perception it espouses; "shimmering" images and "gradations of color" are present in both the language of the text and in this heightened form of sight. Although these expressions may seemingly contradict Brakhage's claim that the acquisition of language delimits one's vision, his mention of the "new language made possible by the moving picture image" in the final paragraph is suggestive of poiesis, or poetic creation. Brakhage's contemporary, the film historian P. Adams Sitney, sees poiesis as the work's guiding principle and writes in his 2003 article "Celluloid Hero" that "the self-conscious and responsible use of language is poetry."

JAMES STANLEY BRAKHAGE: ORPHAN CHILD

On January 14, 1933, James Stanley Brakhage was born in an orphanage in Kansas City, Missouri. He was soon adopted by a young couple, Ludwig and Clara Brakhage, who led an itinerant life, moving from one Midwestern town to the next. Brakhage was a sickly child, perhaps owing to his sensitivity to his parents' marital troubles: Clara took a lover and Ludwig, some years later, came out as a homosexual. Following the dissolution of the couple's marriage, Brakhage and his mother found themselves in Denver, where the young Stanley, now living in a boy's home, developed a knack for delinquency and petty crime.

Brakhage received a fine arts scholarship to attend Dartmouth, but the difficulty of the academic program and the unwelcoming artistic environment led to a mental breakdown. Stanley was forced to drop out. After a visit with his father in Chicago, Brakhage returned to Denver where he worked menial jobs and reconnected with several friends from high school, two of whom collaborated with Brakhage on his first film. Although that film, *Interim* (1951), a short about a brief erotic encounter, might have seemed an inauspicious beginning, Brakhage eventually became the most influential avant-garde director in the United States in a career that spanned decades and included hundreds of critically acclaimed works.

CRITICAL DISCUSSION

When *Metaphors on Vision* was fist published in 1963, it received almost no reaction in the general press or in the world of avant-garde cinema. As the film scholar Fred Camper explains in his piece, "Glimpses of Greatness: New Films by Stan Brakhage," Brakhage published *Metaphors on Vision* "before he and [Russian director Sergei] Eisenstein

James Stanley Brakhage theorizes that, by using words to define a color such as "green," people might be limiting their ability to perceive the entire range of subtle colors in the spectrum. JULIET WHITE/ PHOTOGRAPHER'S CHOICE/GETTY IMAGES

were paired in a special issue of *Artforum*; before he'd been offered any teaching jobs; before any schools or film museums had bought prints of his films; before the first comprehensive retrospective of his work at New York's Museum of Modern Art. Back then he was almost completely excluded from 'film culture.'" It was only after Brakhage's avant-garde films accumulated some renown that *Metaphors on Vision* was recognized as an important document in film theory.

After Brakhage became recognized as a luminary avant-garde film director, *Metaphors on Vision* was seen as an essential articulation of his avant-garde aims, and those aims were broad. He produced films on a myriad of topics in a myriad of styles, including hand-painted films, antiwar films, silent 8-mm works, and 70-mm IMAX productions. According to Paul Arthur in his essay "Qualities of Light," Brakhage went on to create more films than any other director in the history of cinema. Sitney's article, written after Brakhage's death in 2003, emphasizes the primacy of *Metaphors on Vision* within Brakhage's body of work by claiming that "the center of Brakhage's theoretical discourse was always the poetics of vision." In the five decades since its publication, *Metaphors on Vision* has been the subject of a small body of scholarly inquiry for its significance in the history of American avant-garde cinema.

Some commentators have focused on how Brakhage's conception of language and imagery is present throughout the history of avant-garde cinema. Camper draws comparisons between Brakhage's theoretical work and the films of Dadaist artist Marcel Duchamp and experimentalist and digital filmmaker Hollis Frampton, which all "express the notion that language and imagery exist in a paradoxical and possibly antagonistic relationship to each other." Despite a small amount of criticism about the monograph itself, the vast majority of scholarship focuses on the films that the work underpins. Here, scholarly interpretation abounds, from Bruce Elder's view of Brakhage's films as part of the American poetic tradition of Ezra Pound, Gertrude Stein, and Charles Olson to Rebecca Sheehan's view of Brakhage's films as "establishing an ethos of renewed encounter with the everyday," which "imitates the later writing" of philosopher Ludwig Wittgenstein.

BIBLIOGRAPHY

Sources

Arthur, Paul. "Qualities of Light: Stan Brakhage and the Continuing Pursuit of Vision." *Film Comment* 31.5 (1995): 68-76. *ProQuest.* Web. 20 Sept. 2012.

Brakhage, Stan. *Metaphors on Vision,* in *The Avant-Garde Film: A Reader of Theory and Criticism.* Ed. P. Adams Sitney. New York: Anthology Film Archives, 1978. 120-28. Print.

Camper, Fred. "Brakhage's Contradictions." *Chicago Review* 47/48 (2001): 61-96. *JSTOR.* Web. 20 Sept. 2012.

———. "Glimpses of Greatness: New Films by Stan Brakhage." *Chicago Reader* 10 Sept. 1999. Print.

Elder, R. Bruce. *The Films of Stan Brakhage in the American Tradition.* Waterloo: Wilfred Laurier UP, 1999. Print.

James, David E. "Amateurs in the Industry Town." *Stan Brakhage: Filmmaker.* Ed. David E. James. Philadelphia: Temple UP, 2005. 72-86. *ProQuest.* Web. 20 Sept. 2012.

———. "Introduction: Stan Brakhage: The Activity of His Nature." *Stan Brakhage: Filmmaker.* Ed. David E. James. Philadelphia: Temple UP, 2005. 10-27. *ProQuest.* Web. 20 Sept. 2012.

Macdonald, Scott. "The Filmmaker as Visionary: Excerpts from an Interview with Stan Brakhage." *Film Quarterly* 56.3 (2003): 2-11. *ProQuest.* Web. 20 Sept. 2012.

Sheehan, Rebecca. "Stan Brakhage, Ludwig Wittgenstein and the Renewed Encounter with the Everyday." *Screen* 53.2 (2012): 118-35. *Film and Television Literature Index.* Web. 20 Sept. 2012.

Sitney, P. Adams. "Celluloid Hero: P. Adams Sitney on Stan Brakhage." *Artforum International* 42.1 (2003): 41-42. Print.

Further Reading

Brakhage, Stan, and Johnson, Ronald. "Another Way of Looking at the Universe." *Chicago Review* 47/48 (2002): 31-37. *JSTOR.* Web. 20 Sept. 2012.

James, David E. "The Filmmaker as Romantic Poet." *Film Quarterly* 35.3 (1982): 35-43. *JSTOR.* Web. 20 Sept. 2012.

Nichols, Bill. *Maya Deren and the American Avant-Garde.* Berkeley: U of California P, 2001. Print.

Sitney, P. Adams. *Visionary Film: The American Avant-Garde, 1943-2000.* Oxford: Oxford UP, 1974. Print.

Vertov, Dziga. *Kino-Eye: The Writings of Dziga Vertov.* Berkeley: U of California P, 1984. Print.

Gregory Luther

Minnesota Declaration
Truth and Fact in Documentary Cinema
Werner Herzog

OVERVIEW

Werner Herzog's "Minnesota Declaration: Truth and Fact in Documentary Cinema," delivered during a 1999 appearance in Minneapolis, Minnesota, calls into question the distinction between documentary and feature films. The German filmmaker takes particular aim at the facile notion that documentary films are about real events while feature films are fictional stories. A distinguished director of both types of film, Herzog admits that his documentaries contain fictional moments, just as his feature films contain factual moments. He does not see this manipulation of reality as deceptive. On the contrary, he contends that filmmakers must incorporate both factual and fictional elements in order to achieve what he calls an "ecstatic truth" that will speak to a film's audience.

The "Minnesota Declaration" was embraced by academics and filmmakers alike. It led to the creation and acceptance of more personal and subjective documentaries, such as those by Errol Morris and Chris Marker, which question what is real and whether humans are capable of perceiving "objective reality," given the subjective experience of day-to-day living. The declaration has also been applied to life itself, with wildlife activists and nature photographers using it to support their arguments concerning humans' relationship to and defiling of nature. Herzog himself has striven to live by the tenets of the declaration by making documentaries such as *Grizzly Man* (2005) and *Cave of Forgotten Dreams* (2010).

HISTORICAL AND LITERARY CONTEXT

The intention of Herzog's declaration is to puncture a certain complacency that had, in his estimation, settled into notions of life and documentary film at the end of the twentieth century. In particular, he detests the notion that the movie camera inherently tells the truth. He believes that a camera only captures facts, not truth. Filmmakers who see these facts as absolutes are, according to Herzog, superficial and satisfied with "the truth of accountants." Herzog feels that there is a deeper truth beyond facts and that real filmmakers can find it by using "fabrication and imagination and stylization" to yield a more profound "ecstatic truth" that reaches the soul. Lastly, he emphasizes that nature is indifferent to humanity's presence. Nature does not try to speak to us; it does not care that we are here. By imposing our human thoughts and motivations onto nature, we are missing both its beauty and danger. Life is, after all, inherently unknowable.

Herzog verbalized his declaration in a question-and-answer session with the film critic Roger Ebert during a tribute to his body of work. He claims it was written in a matter of minutes, triggered by his distaste for late-night cable programming and its bland nature documentaries and pornography. Clearly, however, he had been mulling over the ideas expressed in the declaration for most of his career. The director of dozens of films since 1968, Herzog is recognized as one of Germany's premier directors. His movies often deal with the futility of humans' attempts to impose their will on nature and are often made on remote locations that test the endurance of both the characters and the cast and crew trying to capture the stories.

While Herzog downplays its influence, his declaration bears some similarities to the *Oberhausen Manifesto,* written by twenty-two German filmmakers and published in 1962. The manifesto announces these filmmakers' break from the staid post-World War II German cinema and declares their intent to create a new movie style. Herzog's declaration also breaks from the past. It seeks to free filmmakers from outdated definitions and conventions that no longer speak to audiences. Herzog's documentaries reflect this idea. His works do not try to be objective—instead, they flaunt the subjective nature of reality and our inability to truly know a person. Rather than posing as an objective bystander, Herzog often narrates his films and points out the contradictions or falsehoods in what the subjects of his interviews are saying.

Since delivering his declaration, Herzog has spent much of his time making documentaries designed to illuminate its points. For example, *Grizzly Man* profiles late nature activist Tim Treadwell, while *Cave of Forgotten Dreams* explores the origins of humans. He is credited with helping to create a new genre of documentary in which the films are as much about the creator as their subject. His style has influenced filmmakers such as Marker, Morris, and Michael Moore. Herzog's efforts to clarify the points in the

✣ *Key Facts*

Time Period:
Late 20th Century

Movement/Issue:
Film

Place of Publication:
United States

Language of Publication:
English

WERNER HERZOG VS. THE LOCH NESS MONSTER

Werner Herzog is a man with a sense of humor. Though he has dedicated himself to illuminating the points in the "Minnesota Declaration," he also satirizes these efforts in the "mockumentary" *Incident at Loch Ness* (2005).

In the film, Herzog's initially straightforward attempts to make a documentary about the legendary lake creature are routinely undermined by the film's producer (Zak Penn), who wants to make a more "commercial" kind of documentary with mass appeal. His over-the-top attempts include creating matching designer uniforms for team members and hiring a centerfold model (Kitana Baker) for the job of sonar operator. When Penn fears the production crew will get no footage of the actual creature, he has a fake monster built. Herzog attempts to quit the film when the fakery is discovered, but before he can do so, the boat has a memorable encounter with the "real" beast that clouds the audience's beliefs about of what is real and what is not.

Incident at Loch Ness parodies both the shooting style of documentaries and Herzog's own habit of inserting himself into his films. It challenges the viewer not to casually accept that something on film is real just because it appears to be.

"Minnesota Declaration" include a 2010 speech titled "On the Absolute, the Sublime, and Ecstatic Truth."

THEMES AND STYLE

Although Herzog begins by targeting *cinéma vérité* ("truthful cinema") as being anything but truthful, he expands the declaration to challenge notions of life itself. He declares, "Cinéma Vérité is devoid of vérité," adding that filmmakers focused on facts "resemble tourists who take pictures amid ancient ruins." Furthermore, he says, "Tourism is sin" but "travel on foot virtue." This notion comes from Herzog's belief that only by walking to our destinations can humans stay in touch with the physical world and its rhythms. In other interviews, he has asserted that walking can have life-saving benefits. He cites a time in 1974 when noted German author Lotte Eisner was deathly ill in Paris. Urged to see her before she died, Herzog decided to walk from Germany to Paris. When he arrived, he discovered that Eisner had recovered; Herzog credits his choosing to walk with saving her life. He closes his declaration by denouncing humanity's desire to view the world as a romantic and caring place. "The Universe out there knows no smile.... Life in the oceans must be sheer hell. A vast, merciless hell of permanent and immediate danger."

Like any polemic, the "Minnesota Declaration" does not attempt to persuade its audience of the truthfulness of its positions. Instead, it simply announces its beliefs as unassailable facts that cannot be disputed. Its flavor is similar to that of a religious tract, such as the Ten Commandments, complete with the assignment of a number to each statement. The declaration reflects Herzog's longtime interest in nature and humanity's uneasy relationship with it. No matter how hard we try, Herzog believes, most often nature has the last word and levels human dreams through volcanic explosions, floods, droughts, or the simple, remorseless passage of time.

With the aim of stripping all romanticism from life, Herzog adopts a harsh tone in his declaration. Despite this intention, simple declarative sentences such as "7. Tourism is sin, and travel on foot virtue" and "9. The gauntlet is hereby thrown down" are wide open to interpretation. He does not define what he means by "tourism" within the context of the declaration or explain why it is a sin. In his clarifications of the declaration, he has, for example, explained that article 10 ("Mother Nature doesn't call, doesn't speak to you … and don't you listen to the Song of Life") is a rejection of a belief expressed by Katharine Hepburn in a documentary about her life in which her final advice to future generations is to "listen to the song of life." Herzog calls this advice "vanilla ice cream emotions" and asserts that there is no song to hear, although, as he also expresses in article 10, "a glacier eventually farts."

CRITICAL DISCUSSION

Reaction to the "Minnesota Declaration" was almost universally positive. In *The Cinema of Werner Herzog,* Brad Prager praises Herzog's use of fabrication in his documentaries as a way to strive "for an aesthetic height akin to that attainable by poetry…. This capacity to transfigure reality is [what] separates the poets from the accountants." Paul Cronin, writing in *Herzog on Herzog,* concurs: "Cinema, like poetry, is inherently able to present a number of dimensions much deeper than the level of so-called truth." Ebert titled his endorsement of the declaration "In Praise of Rapturous Truth" and lauds the director for acknowledging that "the line between truth and fiction is a mirage." In stating his agreement with the belief that some documentaries contain fiction and some fiction films contain facts, Ebert writes of Herzog, "Your films, frame by frame, contain a kind of rapturous truth that transcends the factually mundane." Herzog's declaration sparked a reevaluation of his earlier work by scholars who used it as their critical prism.

Some critics have complained that Herzog's approach to his films is self-serving, that the story of how he made a film often overshadows the story itself. Kevin Phipps has observed that "Herzog seems to thrive on both the challenges of such projects and the scandal they create." For example, Herzog's collaborations with the actor Klaus Kinski in films such as *Aguirre, the Wrath of God* (1972) and *Cobra Verde* (1987) were fraught with heated on-set arguments that have become legendary. Critic Jim Emerson wonders in "Richard Leacock (1911-2011): 'Screw the Tripod!'" if "the critical winds are blowing in the opposite direction, toward a distrust of craftsmanship … and an embrace of crudity simply because it's undiluted." He cites the "Minnesota Declaration" as a source of this trend and decries the statement for presenting its central tenets as "an either/or choice." "There are all kinds of poetry, and all kinds of cinema," Emerson writes, and surely there is room for both. Other critics have applied the declaration's tenets to life itself. Photographer Harlan Erskine has questioned whether even the use of still cameras to capture nature may be a "sin" as defined by Herzog.

The "Minnesota Declaration" clearly speaks to the current generation of filmmakers, and its influence can be felt both in cinema and in life. Herzog himself remains on the cutting edge of this exploration with his Rogue Film School, where he trains filmmakers. He defines the ideal candidates as "those who have traveled on foot … worked as a bouncer in a sex club or … in a lunatic asylum … in short: for those who have a sense for poetry."

Werner Herzog (left) in Antarctica during the shooting of his 2007 documentary *Encounters at the End of the World.* DISCOVERY FILMS/THE KOBAL COLLECTION/ART RESOURCE

BIBLIOGRAPHY

Sources

Ebert, Roger. "In Praise of Rapturous Truth." *Roger Ebert's Journal.* Sun-Times Media, 17 Nov. 2007. Web. 12 July 2012.

Emerson, Jim. "Richard Leacock (1911-2011): 'Screw the Tripod!'" *Jim Emerson's Scanners.* Sun-Times Media, 31 Mar. 2011. Web. 12 July 2012.

Erskine, Harlan. "Does 'The Minnesota Declaration' Also Apply to Still Images Production?" *Harlan Erskine Photography Blog.* Harlan Erskine, 14 Mar. 2009. Web. 1 July 2012.

Herzog, Werner. *Herzog on Herzog.* Ed. Paul Cronin. New York: Faber, 2002. Print.

———. Interview by Keith Phipps. A.V. *Club.* Onion, 11 June 2003. Web. 1 July 2012.

———. "The Minnesota Declaration: Truth and Fact in Documentary Cinema." *Werner Herzog Film.* Werner Herzog Film, 30 Apr. 1999. Web. 1 July 2012.

———. "Werner Herzog's Rogue Film School." Rogue Film School, 2009. Web. 14 July 2012.

"Oberhausen Manifesto." *Nick Van der Kolk Blog.* Generation PRX, 9 Jan. 2012. Web. 12 July 2012.

Prager, Brad. *The Cinema of Werner Herzog: Aesthetic Ecstasy and Truth.* London: Wallflower, 2007. Print.

Further Reading

Blank, Les, and James Bogan. *Burden of Dreams: Screenplays, Journals, Photographs.* Berkeley: North Atlantic, 1984. Print.

Ebert, Roger. "Herzog and the Forms of Madness." *Roger Ebert's Journal.* Sun-Times Media, 20 July 2008. Web. 12 July 2012.

———. "Werner Herzog: 'Tell Me about the Iceberg, Tell Me about Your Dreams.'" *Roger Ebert's Journal.* Sun-Times Media, 7 July 2007. Web. 12 July 2012.

Herzog, Werner. *Conquest of the Useless: Reflections from the Making of* Fitzcarraldo. New York: Ecco, 2009. Print.

———. "On the Absolute, the Sublime, and Ecstatic Truth." *Arion* 17.3 (2010): n.pag. Web. 8 Aug. 2012.

Lambert, Christopher. "Werner Herzog." *World Film Directors: 1945-1985.* New York: Wilson, 1988. 422-29. Print.

Odorico, Stefano. "Werner Herzog between Documentary and Fiction." *Offscreen* 31 Mar. 2010. Web. 1 July 2012.

Shaughnessy, Adrian. "Werner Herzog and the Deeper Truth." *Design Observer.* Observer Omnimedia, 16 June 2006. Web. 13 July 2012.

Richard Rothrock

GLOBAL MILITANTS

MANIFESTO FOR ARMED ACTION

Ulrike Meinhof

OVERVIEW

Attributed to militant Ulrike Meinhof, *Manifesto for Armed Action,* also known as *Build Up the Red Army!,* first appeared in *Agit 833,* a small underground German newspaper, on June 2, 1970, calling for the West German radical left to organize an armed resistance and to start a communist revolution. The manifesto was the first public statement made by the West German communist group that would later call itself the Red Army Faction and become known popularly as the Baader-Meinhof group. The text appeared just weeks after Meinhof and others successfully sprung the nascent group's leader, Andreas Baader, from prison, where he was incarcerated for committing arson in Frankfurt department stores and then jumping bail. During the escape, shots were fired, and several people were wounded; therefore everyone who helped Baader escape was wanted for attempted murder. Addressed to sympathetic revolutionaries, *Manifesto for Armed Action* seeks to catalyze a violent response to what the Red Army Faction considered the indignity and oppression of the capitalist status quo that existed in West Germany in the 1970s.

When it appeared in June 1970, *Manifesto for Armed Action* fanned the flames of popular outrage in Germany over Baader's violent escape from prison. Within the country's radical left community, however, it helped to turn the participants of the escape into heroes. Members of the Red Army Faction later engaged in more violence, killing and injuring many German citizens, and Meinhof, Baader, and many of the group's other members were eventually arrested and imprisoned. Today *Manifesto for Armed Action* is considered among the most important radical documents to appear in post-World War II Germany.

HISTORICAL AND LITERARY CONTEXT

Manifesto for Armed Action responds to Germany's continuing struggle to move forward, away from the horrors of the country's Nazi past. Members of the Red Army Faction were part of a broader, generational revolt against the older "perpetrator generation" for its participation and complicity in the grave injustices of the Third Reich and the Holocaust. After World War II, many Nazis, including those who had been actively involved in genocide, reintegrated into German society. Meinhof and other members of the

Red Army Faction viewed armed action as a justified response to the violence perpetrated by their enemies during the Third Reich. As West Germany moved forward after the war, it became closely allied with the United States in its opposition to communism. When the Vietnam War escalated in the mid-1960s, West German leftists joined their American counterparts in protesting against the war.

By the time *Manifesto for Armed Action* appeared in 1970, the protest movement against the Vietnam War had evolved into a broader struggle for left-wing ideology known as the New Left. Active in the United States and Europe, New Left activists sought to end the capitalist and imperialist forces that they blamed for widespread social and economic injustice. As they sought alternatives to the capitalist status quo and inspiration for its overthrow, they looked to the ongoing decolonization movements in Asia, Africa, and Latin America for inspiration. While some New Leftists were beholden to the nonviolent origins of the protest movement, others argued that armed struggle was necessary. Two events in the late 1960s proved to be watershed moments in the New Leftists' turn to violence: in 1967 a police officer shot and killed college student Benno Ohnesorg, who was participating in a peaceful protest in West Berlin, and in 1968 Rudi Dutschke, a student leader of the leftist movement, was shot and injured outside his home by a right-wing fanatic. These attacks helped to convince Meinhof and others that violence was necessary. At the time the journal *Konkret* was a major voice of left-wing radicalism in Germany, and through *Konkret,* Meinhof, an editor and journalist, became involved with the radical left and with the effort to free Baader from prison.

The *Manifesto for Armed Action* draws on a history of Marxist polemical writing that can be traced back to *The Communist Manifesto,* written by Karl Marx and Friedrich Engels and originally published in 1848. Marx and Engels' work calls for a "revolutionary movement against the social and political order" and foresees the dawning of a new, egalitarian system led by the disenfranchised proletariat. *Manifesto for Armed Action* echoes Marx and Engels' indictment of the capitalist system and their calls for an armed struggle to overthrow that system.

Following the publication of *Manifesto for Armed Action,* the Red Army Faction issued a series

✣ *Key Facts*

Time Period:
Mid-20th Century

Movement/Issue:
Revolutionary communism

Place of Publication:
Germany

Language of Publication:
German

ULRIKE MEINHOF: A BIOGRAPHY

Ulrike Meinhof was born on October 7, 1934, in the small German city of Oldenburg. Her father was an art historian who moved his family to Jena, where he became a museum curator. When Meinhof was five, her father died, leaving her and her sister, Wienke, and their mother without an income. To make ends meet, her mother took in a female lodger, with whom she fell in love. As a result, the Meinhof girls grew up with two mothers.

Meinhof left home to attend college, where she became involved in antinuclear activism and joined the Socialist German Students' Union in 1958. She became active in the student protest movement and in 1959 joined the staff of the left-wing journal *Konkret* in Hamburg. Two years after joining the journal, she married its publisher, Klaus Rainer Röhl. In 1962 she gave birth to twin girls, and in 1967 she and Röhl divorced. During the next few years, she became an increasingly well-respected journalist, but she also became increasingly radicalized. After helping Baader escape from prison in 1970, Meinhof soon took part in bombings, robberies, and other terrorist acts as part of the Red Army Faction. In 1972 she was arrested, along with Baader and eighteen other members of the group. She died in prison in 1976.

of polemical writings that furthered and altered the work's argument. In 1971 the group produced a communiqué titled *The Urban Guerrilla Concept,* which offered a more thorough defense of the group's violent tactics and a more thorough indictment of the capitalist system. Over the next nearly three decades, the Red Army Faction continued to issue declarations that attempted to clarify and validate their aims and their actions, which ranged from bombings to assassination attempts to hunger strikes. It released its final communiqué, *The Urban Guerilla Is History,* in 1998 and announced the group's official cessation.

THEMES AND STYLE

The central theme of *Manifesto for Armed Action* is that an organized and armed resistance is needed to overthrow an unjust capitalist-imperialist political order. In order to make the case for a comprehensive revolution, the manifesto uses the freeing of Baader as inspiration and explanation. The manifesto begins, "It is pointless to explain the right thing to the wrong people"; therefore it aims "to explain the action to free Baader" only "to the potentially revolutionary section of the people. That is to say, to those who can immediately understand the action, because they are themselves prisoners." The manifesto then describes the diverse membership of this "revolutionary section" and declares that it is for them "that we are building the red army." In order to build this army, the manifesto calls for the formation of an

underground network to facilitate the organization of this force.

The manifesto achieves its rhetorical effect through appeals to a sense of disillusionment that unites the politically, economically, and socially disenfranchised members of German society. This sense of a united yet diverse opposition to the status quo is achieved through the extensive listing of those who are included in the "revolution section of the people." The manifesto addresses "those who are fed up!" and specifies in detail who these people are: "The action to free Bader must be explained to youth from the Märkisch neighbourhood, to the girls from the Eichenhof, Ollenhauer, and Heilignesee, to young people in group homes, in youth centers, in the Grünen Haus and Kieferngrund." The manifesto also includes large families and high school students in its target audience.

Stylistically, the *Manifesto for Armed Action* is distinguished by its mix of informality and vehemence. Filled with fragmented sentences and slang, the manifesto speaks directly to the reader in a hectoring tone that is meant to incite indignation and action. "What do you mean by adventurism?" the manifesto demands to know. "That one only has oneself to blame for informers. Whatever." In this way, the manifesto offers a lecture that superficially resembles a dialogue, thereby creating a sense of exchange while emphatically delivering a pointed message. Elsewhere, the manifesto calls its audience names, such as "you assholes" and "you shitheads." While this method of inciting the reader is potentially alienating, the manifesto is careful to counteract this effect by cultivating a sense of inclusiveness and unity through its extensive definition of the "revolutionary section of the people" and of their enemies, the "babbling intellectuals" and "pigs" of the ruling class.

CRITICAL DISCUSSION

Manifesto for Armed Action elicited a mixed response from readers. The German public, which had been shocked by the brazen, violent escape of Baader three weeks before, condemned it. Within left-wing circles, however, the response was less uniform. Those in the New Left who remained committed to nonviolence viewed the turn to armed struggle derisively, as a kind of betrayal. In his book, *Bringing the War Home* (2004), scholar Jeremy Varon writes that the Red Army Faction and its American counterpart, the Weathermen, "were denounced by leftists in their own countries as everything from self-indulgent fools living out Bonnie-and-Clyde fantasies to 'left-wing adventurists' hopelessly cut off from 'the masses.'" For those in the protest movement who were sympathetic to the idea of using violence, the freeing of Baader and the manifesto's argument helped turn members of the Red Army Faction into heroes of a grander, global movement to end capitalist oppression.

At a press conference after the arrest of RAF terrorist Ulrike Meinhof, police display weapons and ammunition found in her apartment. Meinhof was captured in Hanover, Germany, in 1972. She hanged herself in her cell in 1976. AP PHOTO/ HELMUT LOHMANN

Manifesto for Armed Action helped to turn the freeing of Baader into a catalyst for the formation of an organized revolutionary movement. Although that movement ultimately failed to cohere into anything capable of achieving its aim of overthrowing the German government and the capitalist system, it was able to create enough havoc to destabilize the Federal Republic of Germany during the 1970s. The group carried on even after the arrest of Meinhof, Baader, and the other Red Army Faction members in 1972. Between 1972 and 1976, it carried out a series of bombings that caused numerous casualties. Then, in 1977, its activity heightened. In his 2009 book *Baader-Meinhof,* author Stefan Aust writes, "Above all, the 'German Autumn' of 1977, which saw the abduction and later the murder of Hanns Martin Schleyer, president of the German Employers' Association, and the hijacking of the Lufthansa aircraft Landshut, ending in Mogadishu, was the greatest challenge yet to post-war German society." While the Red Army Faction continued to carry out Meinhof's call for armed action through the 1980s and into the 1990s, her vision of an organized red army was never realized.

In the years since its publication, *Manifesto for Armed Action* has been the subject of a small body of criticism that considers the document in historical terms. Some scholars focus on the rhetorical tactics employed by Meinhof, such as Sarah Colvin, who argues that the manifesto deliberately employs informal and unconventional language as means of enacting the text's radical message. In her 2009 book *Ulrike Meinhof and West German Terrorism,* she writes, "Because formal language is associated with powerful institutions (schools, universities, the government, the law), the deliberate subversion of its rules can be read as rebellious, even as revolutionary." In the 2011 book *Ulrike Meinhof and the Red Army Faction,* author Leith Passmore points to the ways in which the manifesto adheres to the conventions of the capitalist media it aimed in part to undermine. He argues that in so doing, the Red Army Faction "made vast concessions to the way the capitalist media operated," thereby compromising the faction's ability to critique the establishment.

BIBLIOGRAPHY

Sources

Aust, Stefan. *Baader-Meinhof: The Inside Story of the RAF.* Trans. Anthea Bell. New York: Oxford UP, 2009. Print.

"Build Up the Red Army!" *Agit 883* 2 June 1970: n.p. Web. 18 Sept. 2012.

Colvin, Sarah. *Ulrike Meinhof and West German Terrorism: Language, Violence, and Identity.* Rochester: Camden House, 2009. Print.

Marx, Karl, and Friedrich Engels. *The Communist Manifesto.* New York: Penguin, 2006. Print.

Passmore, Leith. *Ulrike Meinhof and the Red Army Faction: Performing Terrorism.* New York: Palgrave-Macmillan, 2011. Print.

Varon, Jeremy. *Bringing the War Home: The Weather Underground, the Red Army Faction, and Revolutionary Violence in the Sixties and Seventies.* Berkeley: U of California P, 2004. Print.

Further Reading

Bauer, Karen, ed. *Everybody Talks About the Weather … We Don't: The Writings of Ulrike Meinhof.* New York: Seven Stories, 2008. Print.

Becker, Jillian. *Hitler's Children: Story of the Baader-Meinhof Terrorist Gang.* New York: Harper, 1979. Print.

Colvin, Sarah. "*Wir Frauen haben kein Vaterland*: Ulrike Marie Meinhof, Emily Wilding Davison, and the 'Homelessness' of Women Revolutionaries." *German Life & Letters* 64.1 (2011): 108-121. *Academic Search Complete.* Web. 11 Sept. 2012.

Fanon, Frantz. *The Wretched of the Earth.* New York: Grove, 1963. Print.

Hockenos, Paul. *Joschka Fischer and the Making of the Berlin Republic: An Alternative History of Postwar Germany.* New York: Oxford UP, 2008. Print.

Kramer, David. "Ulrike Meinhof: An Emancipated Terrorist?" *European Women on the Left.* Ed. Jane Slaughter and Robert Kern. Westport: Greenwood, 1981. 195-219. Print.

Preece, Julian. *Baader-Meinhof and the Novel.* New York: Palgrave-Macmillan, 2012. Print.

Smith, J., and André Moncourt. *Daring to Struggle, Failing to Win: The Red Army Faction's 1977 Campaign of Desperation.* Oakland: PM, 2008. *Ebrary.com.* Web. 18 Sept. 2012.

———. *Red Army Faction: A Documentary History.* Oakland: PM, 2008. *Ebrary.com.* Web. 18 Sept. 2012.

Theodore McDermott

Manifesto of Umkhonto we Sizwe

Nelson Mandela, et al.

OVERVIEW

Written by Nelson Mandela and other members of the newly formed Umkhonto we Sizwe ("Spear of the Nation"), the *Manifesto of Umkhonto we Sizwe* (1961) describes and justifies the group's violent program for fighting South Africa's government, whose policies of apartheid upheld white minority rule. Umkhonto we Sizwe was established by the South African Communist Party (SACP) and the African National Congress (ANC), which operated in alliance, as the armed wing of the liberation movement. These groups had been at the forefront of the nation's nonviolent struggle against the white government's oppression, but they had become disillusioned with the strategy of civil disobedience, which had failed to bring about substantial reform. The *Manifesto of Umkhonto we Sizwe* argues that the violent tactics of the ruling government of South Africa can no longer be tolerated and that the time has come to combat force with force. Addressed to "all the people" of South Africa, the manifesto makes an inclusive call for freedom, equality, and justice at any cost.

Although the *Manifesto of Umkhonto we Sizwe* alienated some members of the resistance, it is credited with catalyzing the armed struggle that helped lead, more than three decades later, to the end of apartheid. The issuance of the manifesto changed the terms of the resistance movement: the mass struggle for reform was replaced by a militant campaign for revolution. Umkhonto we Sizwe led a campaign of sabotage and guerrilla warfare that continued up until 1994, when the pro-apartheid National Party finally granted blacks voting rights and Mandela won the country's presidency. Today, the *Manifesto of Umkhonto we Sizwe* is considered among the most important political documents in South Africa's decades-long movement to end apartheid.

HISTORICAL AND LITERARY CONTEXT

The *Manifesto of Umkhonto we Sizwe* responds to the perceived ineffectiveness of the peaceful movement to end the apartheid policies of South Africa's government. Racial segregation had long existed in South Africa, but it became institutionally entrenched in 1948, when the ruling National Party adopted a comprehensive policy of apartheid (Afrikaans for "apartness"). In place of specific race laws, apartheid introduced a form of institutionalized racism that dominated all aspects of South African society, law, and education. In response, black South Africans began to organize resistance to this oppression. The ANC, which had formed in 1912, adopted its Programme of Action in 1949 to catalyze mass, nonviolent protest. The Communist Party of South Africa, established in 1921, was banned by South Africa's government in 1950, but the group reactivated in 1953 as the SACP.

By the time the *Manifesto of Umkhonto we Sizwe* was adopted in 1961, the resistance movement was well organized but had failed to bring about any practical change. In 1959 certain ANC members broke away and established the Pan-Africanist Congress (PAC), largely because of the alleged overbearing influence of whites and the SACP on the ANC. The PAC organized a protest in the township of Sharpeville in 1960, and authorities responded with violence, killing scores of protestors. That same year, the SACP, influenced by the global communist movement, specifically the Soviet Union, conducted scattered acts of sabotage as a means of signaling its commitment to resisting white oppression. A year later, the ANC, which was being persecuted by the government despite its commitment to peaceful resistance, assisted the SACP in the formation of Umkhonto we Sizwe, an underground organization devoted to sabotage and armed struggle. The *Manifesto of Umkhonto we Sizwe* offers an explanation of and rationalization for the new group's aims and tactics.

The *Manifesto of Umkhonto we Sizwe* draws on a history of polemical writing about apartheid and responds, in particular, to the *Freedom Charter* of 1955. The *Freedom Charter* calls for an end to the racist oppression of apartheid and for the creation of an egalitarian government in its stead. It demands democracy, equality, land redistribution, and nationalization of mines and banks. These demands were culled from lists of grievances compiled by the ANC, the Congress of Democrats, the Indian Congress, and the South African Coloured People's Organization, opposition groups that had united as the Congress Alliance in 1953. The *Manifesto of Umkhonto we Sizwe* seizes upon the *Freedom Charter*'s spirit of inclusiveness and equality while diverging from its calls for "peace and friendship." The *Manifesto of the*

✧ *Key Facts*

Time Period:
Mid-20th Century

Movement/Issue:
Apartheid

Place of Publication:
South Africa

Language of Publication:
English

NELSON MANDELA: PRISONER AND POLITICIAN

As one of the authors of the *Manifesto of Umkhonto we Sizwe*, Nelson Mandela helped to bring about a dramatic change in the tactics of South African opposition to apartheid. In 1962, the year after the manifesto was issued, he was arrested by government authorities and accused of being involved in a conspiracy to overthrow the state. Two years later, he was given a life sentence and was taken to Robben Island, where a prison stood seven miles off the coast of the country's mainland. He remained there for almost twenty-seven years, and the struggle against apartheid continued without his direct participation.

When Mandela was freed by President F.W. de Klerk, he was seventy-one years old and still widely revered by members of the antiapartheid movement. The ruling National Party, under the guidance of de Klerk, was at last ready to negotiate an end to apartheid. Although many groups from both sides of the conflict were unwilling to compromise, Mandela and de Klerk, among others, sought an agreement that would avert civil war. They succeeded, and in 1993 a new national constitution was produced that signaled an end to centuries of institutional racial oppression. A year later, black South Africans voted for the first time within a democratic society and Mandela was elected president. He served one term and then retired, only to continue his fight for justice and equality around the world.

Nelson Mandela on November 19, 1993. Mandela was one of the cofounders of the Umkhonto we Sizwe wing of the African National Congress. © LOUISE GUBB/ CORBIS SABA

ANC Youth League (1944), which was written in part by Mandela and vows to overcome oppression, also strongly influenced the *Manifesto of Umkhonto we Sizwe*.

In the decades following the publication of the *Manifesto of Umkhonto we Sizwe*, a range of polemical writings on the nature of resistance were issued by the ANC and other antiapartheid organizations. Two years after the *Manifesto of Umkhonto we Sizwe* appeared, the ANC produced a leaflet titled *The ANC Spearheads Revolution*, in which the organization describes its mission in more militant terms than it had previously. Beginning with the words, "The South African people are at war," it goes on to advocate "planned, strategic violence." Throughout the 1960s, 1970s, and 1980s, the ANC built on the argument started in the *Manifesto of Umkhonto we Sizwe*. The 1985 tract *Take the Struggle to the White Areas* argues that members of the resistance "must throw in our lot with the fighters for liberation by swelling the ranks of the ANC and Umkhonto We Sizwe underground." Today, the *Manifesto of Umkhonto we Sizwe* commands interest as a source for the tradition of militant antiapartheid writing.

THEMES AND STYLE

The central theme of the *Manifesto of Umkhonto we Sizwe* is that violent resistance is necessary to end the oppressive apartheid government of South Africa's National Party. The manifesto opens declaratively: "Units of Umkhonto we Sizwe today carried out planned attacks against government installations, particularly those connected with the policy of apartheid and race discrimination." Only then, after forthrightly laying claim to violent action, do the text's authors introduce their group and its purpose. The manifesto declares, "The time comes in the life of any nation when there remain only two choices: submit or fight. That time has now come to South Africa. We shall not submit and we have no choice but to hit back by all means within our power in defence of our people, our future and our freedom." As it proceeds, the manifesto describes the contemporary moment in order to rationalize the imperative to fight.

Despite its calls for violence, the *Manifesto of Umkhonto we Sizwe* achieves its rhetorical effect through appeals to a national desire for peace. The authors, who write in the first-person plural, say, "We of Umkhonto we Sizwe have always sought—as the liberation movement has sought—to achieve liberation without bloodshed and civil clash. We do so still. We hope—even at this late hour—that our first actions will awaken every one to a realisation of the disastrous situation to which the Nationalist policy is leading." The manifesto portrays the group's assumption of violent tactics as a means of avoiding the "suffering and bitterness of civil war" and as being "in the best interests of all the people of this country—black, brown and white."

Stylistically, the *Manifesto of Umkhonto we Sizwe* is distinguished by its mix of stridency and resignation. Although the document declares that the group will act as "the fighting arm" and "the striking force of the people," it continually expresses reluctance about doing so. The manifesto even attributes the group's decision to fight back to the actions of its enemies: "The choice is not ours; it has been made by the Nationalist government which has rejected ever peaceable demand by the people for rights and freedom and answered ever such demand with force and yet more force!" The manifesto's authors seek not only to portray their cause and their tactics as just but also to preemptively blame supporters of apartheid for the country's impending violence. With a tone that is simultaneously apologetic and defiant, the manifesto is able to explain the group's turn away from peaceful protest as part of an effort to forge otherwise unattainable and lasting peace.

CRITICAL DISCUSSION

When the *Manifesto of Umkhonto we Sizwe* was issued in 1961, it received a mixed reaction within the resistance movement and was condemned by the apartheid government and its supporters. Some leaders of the ANC opposed the manifesto's advocacy of armed struggle. As scholar Tom Lodge writes in *Black Politics in South Africa Since 1945,* "ANC leaders, still committed to the ideal of a common society, wished to avoid the racial polarisation which might develop with open warfare." Nevertheless, many members of the ANC, SACP, and other opposition groups were inspired by the manifesto's message.

The *Manifesto of Umkhonto we Sizwe* remained an important influence throughout the antiapartheid movement. The manifesto was issued to coincide with a series of bombings of government installations, and it inspired more than one hundred additional bombings and acts of sabotage over the next eighteen months. The group continued in this manner for another two decades before beginning a campaign of urban guerrilla warfare in the 1980s. When Mandela was released from prison in 1990, he argued that the goal of a "democratic and non-racial South Africa" could only be achieved by "a continuation of Umkhonto we Sizwe's armed struggle," according to the scholars Nancy L. Clark and William H. Worger in *South Africa: The Rise and Fall of Apartheid.* In the next four years, negotiations between Mandela and South Africa's president, F.W. de Klerk, helped establish majority rule, and Mandela was elected as the country's new president. In the years since the *Manifesto of Umkhonto we Sizwe* was written, scholars have examined the text and its legacy in political, historical, and linguistic terms.

Much scholarship has been focused on orienting the manifesto and its program of armed struggle within the larger contemporary international political situation. In his article "The Genesis of the ANC's Armed Struggle in South Africa 1948-1961," Stephen Ellis seeks to demonstrate "the degree to which the start of the armed struggle in South Africa was inscribed in the politics of the Cold War." Commentators have also examined the manifesto's role in changing the course of the antiapartheid movement. According to Hein Marais in *South Africa Pushed to the Limit: The Political Economy of Change,* "The turn to armed struggle marked not only a major strategic but also a crucial paradigmatic shift. Henceforth, reforming the system would be considered impossible and practically treasonous."

BIBLIOGRAPHY
Sources
Clark, Nancy L., and William H. Worger. *South Africa: The Rise and Fall of Apartheid.* 2nd ed. Harlow: Pearson, 2011. Print.

Ellis, Stephen. "The Genesis of the ANC's Armed Struggle in South Africa 1948-1961." *Journal of Southern African Studies* 37.4 (2011). Web. 15 July 2012.

Keller, Bill. "Tree Shaker: The Story of Nelson Mandela." *New York Times Upfront* 5 May 2008: 12. Academic OneFile. Web. 15 July 2012.

Lissoni, Arianna. "Transformations in the ANC External Mission and Umkhonto we Sizwe, c. 1960-1969." *Journal of South African Studies* 35.2 (2009). Web. 15 July 2012.

Marais, Hein. *South Africa Pushed to the Limit: The Political Economy of Change.* New York: Zed, 2011. Print.

Further Reading
Curkpatrick, Stephen. "Mandela's 'Force of Law.'" *Sophia* 41.2 (2002): 63-72. Print.

Ellis, Stephen, and Tsepo Sechaba. *Comrades against Apartheid: The ANC and the South African Communist Party in Exile.* Bloomington: Indiana UP, 1991. Print.

Johnson, R.W. *South Africa's Brave New World: The Beloved Country since the End of Apartheid.* New York: Overlook, 2009. Print.

Klein, Naomi. *The Shock Doctrine: The Rise of Disaster Capitalism.* New York: Henry Holt, 2007. Print.

Lodge, Tom. *Black Politics in South African since 1945.* New York: Longman, 1983. Print.

Russell, Alec. *Bring Me My Machine Gun: The Battle for the Soul of South Africa from Mandela to Zuma.* New York: PublicAffairs, 2009. Print.

Thompson, Leonard. *A History of South Africa.* New Haven: Yale UP, 1990. Print.

Worden, Nigel. *The Making of Modern South Africa.* 5th ed. Malden: Wiley-Blackwell, 2012. Print.

Theodore McDermott

SIERRA MAESTRA MANIFESTO

Fidel Castro

❖ *Key Facts*

Time Period:
Mid-20th Century

Movement/Issue:
Cuban Revolution

Place of Publication:
Cuba

Language of Publication:
Spanish

OVERVIEW

Composed primarily by Fidel Castro and signed by Cuban rebel leaders Castro, Raúl Chibás, and Felipe Pazos, the "Sierra Maestra Manifesto" was issued on July 12, 1957, from the guerrilla movement's center of operations in the Sierra Maestra of Cuba and subsequently published in the Cuban magazine *Bohemia* on July 28, 1957. Also known as the "12th of July Manifesto" or the "Manifesto of the Sierra," the document calls for Cubans to unite in the formation of a civic revolutionary movement to bring about the end of Fulgencio Batista's regime. The manifesto was Castro's response to the "Manifesto of the Five," which had been released in June by five anti-Batista groups seeking to reassure the supporters of Castro's July 26th Revolutionary Movement (also known as M-26-7) of their commitment to humanist issues and the group's willingness to work with other organizations, including the *Partido Ortodoxo* (Orthodox Party). Addressed to the rebels' Cuban compatriots, the "Sierra Maestra Manifesto" seeks to unite the different factions in opposition to Batista into one consolidated movement and to sketch out what a post-Batista government would look like.

The "Sierra Maestra Manifesto" initially gained support from the international community, which was witness to Batista's increasingly violent and repressive dictatorial rule. Although the manifesto did bolster the Cuban public's support of Castro's movement, it also highlighted the divisions within the anti-Batista camp as well as certain leaders' attempts to undermine Castro's leadership, including Frank Pais and Carlos Márquez Sterling. The "Sierra Maestra Manifesto" urges all Cuban organizations and political parties to oppose an electoral solution to the country's problems and to refuse any type of negotiation or political compromise with the Batista regime. The manifesto was one of the main documents leading to the victory of the Cuban Revolution, and it appeared to define the political ideology of the new Cuban revolutionary government. It is noteworthy, however, for the numerous ways that Castro and his leadership failed to adhere to the promises they had made within the manifesto and how they quickly distanced themselves from a commitment to humanism.

HISTORICAL AND LITERARY CONTEXT

The "Sierra Maestra Manifesto" responds to the growing divisions among the opponents of the Batista regime and attempts to assuage the fears of the public by calling for unity through a gesture of solidarity to other civic organizations and political parties. While in Mexico earlier in 1957, Castro had broken ties with the *Ortodoxo* leadership because of their insistence on negotiating with Batista. However, upon realizing their error, "the Ortodoxo leadership came to [Castro], implicitly recognizing that Batista's obduracy had proved [Castro] right." The Batista regime's brutal methods of maintaining control and reasserting its power over the Cuban public, including the imprisonment, torture, and execution of early Cuban revolutionary Abel Santamaria, only inspired further discontent and a renewed commitment to revolutionary change among the progressive Cuban population.

By the time the "Sierra Maestra Manifesto" was composed in 1957, growing anti-Batista factions were emerging but had not yet unified in their efforts to overthrow the dictator. Mindful of this divisiveness among Batista opponents, four *Ortodoxo* leaders, including Raul Chibas and Felipe Pazos, traveled to the mountains to meet with Castro in July 1957 in a gesture of support and solidarity. The manifesto was drafted in collaboration with Chibas and Pazos, and it was presented as a clear defiance of Batista's attempts to turn the politicians against the revolutionaries, which was one of the main objectives of the regime's propaganda at the time. When the "Sierra Maestra Manifesto" was published in late July 1957, one of its central messages was the need for unification in order to defeat the threat of Batista's regime.

The "Sierra Maestra Manifesto" participates in a long tradition of Latin American political and revolutionary manifestos dating to the nineteenth-century independence period.

One of the more prominent earlier documents was Jose Martí and Máximo Gómez's 1895 "Manifesto of Montecristi," which declared the goals and philosophy behind the Cuban independence movement. The "Manifesto to the Nation," released in 1953 by Castro's camp, was a direct precursor to his 1957 document. Other influential works leading up to 1957 included *Nuestra Razón: Manifiesto Programa del Movimiento,* issued by the 26th of July Movement in 1956, which set forth the "Doctrine of the Revolution" and addressed national sovereignty, freedom of conscience, and education, among other issues. Marti's influence is clearly present in *Nuestra Razón*'s extensive quoting of the early revolutionary writings. It is widely argued by scholars whether at the time the "Sierra Maestra Manifesto" was issued, Castro's Marxist-Leninist beliefs were not yet fully formed; many academics believe that U.S. acceptance of the manifesto could have altered the Castro's stance on Cuban-U.S. relations.

In the initial years following its publication, Castro's 1957 manifesto influenced a large body of political writing and scholarship from Castro, his fellow revolutionaries, and the new Cuban revolutionary government following their 1959 victory. Not all these documents were approved by or even in direct support of Castro, and as the years progressed the increasingly totalitarian Castro regime faced more intellectual opposition and criticism. The Junta de Liberación Cubana was formed without Castro's direct approval in November 1957 by representatives of several anti-Batista groups, partially in response to the "Sierra Maestra Manifesto"'s demand for a Civic Revolutionary Front. The 1957 manifesto inspired this new Junta's "Document of Unity," which embodied most of the points raised in the manifesto. Castro's own 2007 "Reflection and Manifesto for the People of Cuba" reinforces the "Sierra Maestra Manifesto"'s staunch criticism of the United States and conscious rejection of its influence.

THEMES AND STYLE

According to authors Ramon Bonachea and Marta San Martin, the "Sierra Maestra Manifesto" conveyed an important message "for all movements and parties involved in the opposition to Batista: it called for unity, which at the time was one of the main considerations of the public." The manifesto reads, "Unity is now the only patriotic way. Unity is what all political, revolutionary, and social sectors that combat the dictatorship have in common." Castro identifies the dictatorship as the common enemy of the people, proceeding to list the rights for which their movement was fighting and to lay out the projected foundation of Cuba's future revolutionary government. The manifesto specifically proposes the restoration and protection of the statutes of the 1940 constitution, a strong national economy independent from foreign interests, and a competitive educational system.

The power of the "Sierra Maestra Manifesto" comes from its direct address of the Cuban people and appeals to the common issues uniting them in the face of the oppression of Batista's regime. The manifesto begins, "From the Sierra Maestra, where a sense of duty has united us, we issue this call to our compatriots." The "sense of duty" that unites the

FIDEL CASTRO'S RISE TO POWER

The Cuban Revolution was an armed revolt carried out by the 26th of July Movement led by Fidel Castro against the dictatorship of Fulgencio Batista from 1953 to 1959. The revolution began in July 1953 when Castro's rebels attacked the Moncada Barracks in Santiago, Cuba. Many rebels were killed, but both Fidel and his brother Raul Castro survived and were imprisoned. Fidel proclaimed during his trial, "Condemn me, it does not matter. History will absolve me." Following the Castro brothers' release from prison two years later, they went into exile in Mexico and united with other Cubans in preparation for a revolution to overthrow Batista.

The movement's period of guerrilla warfare began in December 1956 with the landing of the *Granma* yacht, carrying the Castro brothers and 80 other Cuban rebels, on Cuban soil. Two years of guerrilla warfare ensued between the revolutionary forces and the military regime. From the Sierra Maestra, Castro staged numerous successful attacks against Batista troops with the aid of Frank País and Ramos Latour, among others. In December 1938, Castro's forces began their offensive against the military, which prompted Batista to flee to the Dominican Republic. Castro's forces took over the main Cuban cities of Santiago de Cuba and Havana on January 2, 1959, signaling the revolution's victory.

revolutionaries is extended to the Cuban audience addressed by the manifesto, affirming their common identity as Cuban nationals. Another key approach of the manifesto is its privileging of humanist values through its call for an "absolute guarantee of freedom of information, of the spoken and written press, and of all the individual and political rights guaranteed by the Constitution." The manifesto, however, fails to address the issue of race and racial discrimination, which continued to be a central social problem for the country during this period.

Stylistically, the "Sierra Maestra Manifesto" employs a formal, rational tone that nevertheless directly addresses the injustice of the Batista regime. The manifesto notably assumes a "with-me-or-against-me" approach that frames the Cuban situation as taking place between only two factions: Batista and Castro. The manifesto proclaims, "And what do all the opposition political parties, the revolutionary sectors, and the civic institutions have in common? The desire to put an end to a regime based on force, the violation of individual rights ... the desire to seek the peace that we all long for." No matter the differences between the anti-Batista groups, they all face a common enemy, Castro asserts, and unity is the only option if they are going to be victorious. The binary of opposition established by Castro leaves no option for Batista's opponents other than to join his

Men walk past a mural of Fidel Castro in Havana, Cuba, in 1994. The "Sierra Maestra Manifesto" was signed in 1957 by Castro, Raúl Chibás, and Felipe Pazos. © NAJLAH FEANNY/ CORBIS SABA

the Cuban revolutionary cause. Kennedy stated, "I believe that there is no country in the world ... where economic colonization, humiliation and exploitation were worse than in Cuba. I approved the proclamation which Fidel Castro made in the Sierra Maestra, when he justifiably called for justice and especially yearned to rid Cuba of corruption."

After the victory of the Cuban Revolution in 1959, the "Sierra Maestra Manifesto" continued to be viewed as an important document reflecting the early ideology of the Cuban revolutionary movement prior to Castro's turn toward totalitarianism. Famed reporter Robert Taber, the first to interview Castro during the revolution, explains that, "when necessary, as in the Sierra manifesto ... he [Castro] avowed liberal democratic political principles as a temporary political expedient." The widely cited and studied 2003 *Che Guevara Reader,* edited by David Deutschmann, acknowledges the importance of the manifesto in shaping the movement's ideology and Guevara's involvement in the revolution. As critic Leycester Coltman explains, "Guevara did not like the manifesto. He accepted it as a tactical necessity, but thought it made too many concessions to bourgeois ideology." In the five decades since its publication, the "Sierra Maestra Manifesto" has been the subject of much criticism focusing on its political and historical significance.

Much scholarship on the manifesto has focused on the many promises it made that were not fulfilled by Castro's revolutionary government. As Juan Goytisolo states in his 1979 article "20 Years of Castro's Revolution," "In 1960 ... Fidel canceled his repeated promises to call a general election, and contrary to the 'Sierra Maestra Manifesto' signed by Felipe Pazos and Raul Chibas—as well as Castro—he announced that no aid from capitalist North America would be tolerated." Scholars have also emphasized how the manifesto functioned more as a political tactic for Castro to gain the support he needed at the moment rather than a true expression of Castro's political ideology. Other commentators have addressed the notable lack of attention given to the issue of racial tensions and discrimination within the manifesto. In their 1974 book *The Cuban Insurrection, 1952-1959,* Ramon Bonachea and Marta San Martin lament, "What was sadly lacking ... in the 'Sierra Maestra Manifesto' ... was a candid discussion on the subject of social integration. In neither of these declarations was the Negro issue [*sic*] ever spelled out clearly or at all, even though Fidel Castro had in 1949 been a member of the University Committee Against Racial Discrimination."

revolutionary movement, thus reinforcing the manifesto's message.

CRITICAL DISCUSSION

After its publication in July 1957, the "Sierra Maestra Manifesto" received a mixed response, both nationally and internationally. Although the lower- and middle-class Cuban public and progressive international community were quick to identify with the revolutionary movement and its ideals, more conservative politicians and aristocrats interpreted the document more as a political offensive than a true proclamation of the values of the movement. "The U.S Embassy correctly spotted 'bickering' within the movement ... [deducing] that within the anti-Batista opposition 'there is an increasing tendency to question his [Castro's] leadership.'" A large sector of the U.S. population, including President John F. Kennedy, identified with

BIBLIOGRAPHY

Sources

Bonachea, Ramon, and Marta San Martin. *The Cuban Insurrection, 1952-1959.* New Brunswick: Transaction, 1974. Print.

Castro, Fidel. "The Sierra Maestra Manifesto." *Latin American Studies* 15 Dec. 1997. Web. 3 Aug. 2012.

Coltman, Leycester. *The Real Fidel Castro.* New Haven: Yale UP, 2003. Print.

Goytisolo, Juan. "20 Years of Castro's Revolution." Trans. B. Solomon. *New York Review of Books* 22 Mar. 1979. Web. 3 Aug. 2012.

"Jean Daniel Bensaid." *Spartacus Educational.* 3 Aug. 2012. Web.

Kuttruff, Alyson, and Jeffrey Roberg. "Cuba: Ideological Success or Ideological Failure?" *Human Rights Quarterly* 29.3 (2007): 779-95. Print.

Paterson, Thomas G. *Contesting Castro: The United States and the Triumph of the Cuban Revolution.* New York: Oxford UP, 1994. Print.

Stuart, Lyle. Rev. of *M-26. Biography of a Revolution,* by Robert Taber. *The Hispanic American Historical Review* 42.3 (1962): 434-35. Print.

Further Reading

Babun, Teo. *The Cuban Revolution: Years of Promise.* Gainesville: UP of Florida, 2005. Print.

Draper, Theodore. "Castroism." *Marxism in the Modern World.* Ed. M. Drachkovitch. Stanford: Stanford UP, 1965. Print.

Franqui, Carlos. *Diary of the Cuban Revolution.* Trans. Georgette Felix. New York: Viking, 1980. Print.

Guevara, Ernesto. *Che Guevara Reader.* Ed. D. Deustchmann. New York: Ocean P, 2003. Print.

Marquez-Sterling, Manuel. *Cuba 1952-1959: The True Story of Castro's Rise to Power.* Wintergreen: Kleiopatria, 2009. Print.

Nelson, Lowry. *Cuba: The Measure of a Revolution.* Minneapolis: U of Minnesota P, 1972. Print.

Katrina White

World Islamic Front Statement Urging Jihad against Jews and Crusaders

Osama bin Laden

✧ **Key Facts**

Time Period:
Late 20th Century

Movement/Issue:
Jihadism; Zionism

Place of Publication:
England

Language of Publication:
Arabic

OVERVIEW

Released by al-Qaeda leader Osama bin Laden in the pages of the London publication *al-Quds al-Arabi* on February 23, 1998, the "World Islamic Front Statement Urging Jihad against Jews and Crusaders" (1998) authorizes the indiscriminate killing of Americans and their allies "in any country in which it is possible to do it." Eighteen months earlier, bin Laden had published a similar statement, "Declaration of War against the Americans Occupying the Land of the Two Holy Mosques" (1996), helping to pave the way for the al-Qaeda-financed World Islamic Front. Presented as a fatwa, or a legal decree issued by an Islamic religious leader, the 1998 statement condemns U.S. political support of Israel and the presence of American military forces on the holy Arabian Peninsula. Addressed to "all Muslims," the statement is generally viewed as marking the foundation of the World Islamic Front and its collusion with al-Qaeda to root out Western intervention in Middle Eastern politics.

Although alarmingly militant in its rhetoric and aims, the statement elicited few responses until the al-Qaeda bombing of U.S. embassies in Dar es Salaam, Tanzania, and Nairobi, Kenya, in August 1998. The United States responded with an ineffective military action against terrorist bases in Sudan and Afghanistan, and several other al-Qaeda-related strikes ensued, culminating with the attacks of September 11, 2001. Secretary of Defense Donald Rumsfeld frequently cited the 1998 fatwa in building a case against bin Laden following the attacks and referred to the document as a terrorist manifesto. Today the document is seen as one of the first important ideological statements of a consolidated international terrorist movement.

HISTORICAL AND LITERARY CONTEXT

The "World Islamic Front Statement" responds to U.S. efforts to interfere with jihadist activities in the Middle East and Africa. Sometime between August 1988 and October 1989, bin Laden called and moderated the first official meeting of the Islamic fundamentalist terror ring known as al-Qaeda. Throughout the early 1990s, he and his organization funded or participated in most of the jihadist activity in Afghanistan and Sudan, orchestrating a plot to overthrow the Saudi monarchy, attacking American peacekeepers in Somalia in 1993, carrying out an attack on the World Trade Center in 1993, and attempting to assassinate Egyptian president Hosni Mubarak in 1994. After the Persian Gulf War of 1991, the United States become more invested, and increasingly influential, in the Middle East, and bin Laden was stripped of his Saudi citizenship and officially expelled from Sudan.

When his 1998 jihadist statement was published, bin Laden perceived U.S. intervention as proof that American politics had tainted the Islamic homeland and by extension Islam itself. In 1996 he released his first fatwa decrying U.S. military presence in the Arabian Peninsula and calling on Middle Eastern countries to demand the withdrawal of troops. However, there was little to no response from the international Muslim community. As a result, he reached out to radical international Islamic leaders—Ayman al-Zawahiri and Abu-Yasir Rifa-i Ahmad Taha of Egypt, Mir Hamzah of Pakistan, and Fazlul Rahman of Bangladesh—whose fundamentalist groups formed the foundation of the World Islamic Front. However, as Lawrence Wright notes in *The Looming Tower: Al-Qaeda and the Road to 9/11* (2006), many members were outraged to learn that their leaders had secretly joined the new international coalition.

The "World Islamic Front Statement" follows the tradition of Islamic fatwas, which are issued by a legitimate religious authority—usually a state-appointed official called a mufti. A fatwa may take the form of a response to a question asked by an individual or an attempt to situate a specific issue within the Islamic tradition. Because muftis are appointed civil authorities, a fatwa is not binding; however, some officials have used it to attribute moral authority to normally immoral acts. The most notorious of these is the 1989 fatwa in which Iranian Ayatollah Ruhollah Khomeini called for the assassination of author Salman Rushdie for disparaging Islam and the prophet Muhammad in the novel *The Satanic Verses* (1988).

When bin Laden's 1998 statement was issued, it departed from the fatwa tradition by openly inciting Muslims to take militant action against a perceived threat to the integrity and sanctity of Islam. Muslim authorities responded by attacking bin Laden's statement for violating the *fiqh,* or Islamic law, which authorizes lethal force only if Muhammad's name is disparaged aloud and requires that the condemned parties be allowed to defend their positions. However, some radicals in the Islamic community embraced bin Laden's statement, joining his small but unflagging fundamentalist army dedicated to ending Western interference in Middle Eastern politics.

THEMES AND STYLE

The overriding themes of the "World Islamic Front Statement" are opposition to any American presence on the Arabian Peninsula and advocacy of lethal force. In the statement, bin Laden argues, "for over seven years the United States has been occupying the lands of Islam … plundering its riches, dictating to its rulers, humiliating its people," and using its lands to stage attacks on Muslim neighbors, namely Iraq. The statement implicates the United States in the destabilization of the region: "if the Americans' aims … are religious and economic, the aim is also to serve the Jews' petty state and divert attention from its occupation of Jerusalem and the murder of Muslims there." The signatories argue, "All these crimes and sins are a clear declaration of war on Allah," which, according to their radical interpretation of the Koran, means the "individual duty for every Muslim" is to kill Americans.

The statement draws its rhetorical power from the frequent and authoritative use of Koranic scripture to justify its ends and means. Because bin Laden was not a religious leader, he knew that in order to elicit support from the Islamic community his statement would have to be founded in scripture. Therefore, he invokes "the words of the Almighty Allah," citing passages that call on Muslims to "fight the pagans all together as they fight you all together" and to "fight [pagans] until there is no more tumult or oppression, and there prevail justice and faith in Allah." He equates pagans with "Satan's U.S. troops and the devil's supporters allying with them," arguing that each Muslim's duty is "to kill the Americans and plunder their money wherever and whenever."

A tone of militancy dominates the statement, beginning with an invocation of Koranic scripture ordering Muslims to "fight and slay the pagans wherever ye find them." Next, bin Laden describes the plight of the Arabian Peninsula, asserting that it has "never—since Allah made it flat, created its desert, and encircled it with seas—been stormed by any forces like the crusader armies spreading in it like locusts." The crusaders, as bin Laden calls Americans, are portrayed as colluding with Israel to continue "occupying" Jerusalem. He calls the relationship between the two nations the "crusader-Zionist alliance" against Allah and thus beckons "Muslim ulema, leaders, youths and soldiers to launch the raid on [the

An undated photo of Osama bin Laden. AP PHOTO

Americans] … and to displace those who are behind them so that they may learn a lesson."

CRITICAL DISCUSSION

Western scholars and journalists had little response to the "World Islamic Front Statement" immediately after its release; most media outlets simply reprinted a translation of the statement. However, after the East African embassy bombings six months later, most Westerners responded with fear and hatred, demurring to examine the document with any depth. One notable exception is Bernard Lewis's 1998 article in *Foreign Affairs,* in which he recognizes the statement as a "magnificent piece of eloquent, at times even poetic Arabic prose." He simultaneously acknowledges the "West must defend itself" against the very real threat the statement presents and submits in defense of his objective analysis that "in devising strategies to fight the terrorists, it would surely be useful to understand the forces that drive them."

Following the October 2000 bombing of the USS *Cole* and the attacks of September 11, 2001, scholars and journalists have revisited the "World Islamic Front Statement," considering it to be the founding document of the World Islamic Front and a symbol of bin Laden's leadership of the international jihadist movement. Although the statement helped to publicly position bin Laden as a major terrorist mastermind and financier, al-Qaeda-sponsored attacks, and the subsequent international military response, tended to overshadow the ideology expressed in the document. Instead of reducing the American presence on the Arabian Peninsula, bin Laden's jihadist attacks

PRIMARY SOURCE

"WORLD ISLAMIC FRONT STATEMENT URGING JIHAD AGAINST JEWS AND CRUSADERS"

Praise be to Allah, who revealed the Book, controls the clouds, defeats factionalism, and says in His Book: "But when the forbidden months are past, then fight and slay the pagans wherever ye find them, seize them, beleaguer them, and lie in wait for them in every stratagem [of war]"; and peace be upon our Prophet, Muhammad Bin-'Abdallah, who said: I have been sent with the sword between my hands to ensure that no one but Allah is worshiped, Allah who put my livelihood under the shadow of my spear and who inflicts humiliation and scorn on those who disobey my orders.

The Arabian Peninsula has never—since Allah made it flat, created its desert, and encircled it with seas—been stormed by any forces like the crusader armies spreading in it like locusts, eating its riches and wiping out its plantations. All this is happening at a time in which nations are attacking Muslims like people fighting over a plate of food. In the light of the grave situation and the lack of support, we and you are obliged to discuss current events, and we should all agree on how to settle the matter.

No one argues today about three facts that are known to everyone; we will list them, in order to remind everyone:

First, for over seven years the United States has been occupying the lands of Islam in the holiest of places, the Arabian Peninsula, plundering its riches, dictating to its rulers, humiliating its people, terrorizing its neighbors, and turning its bases in the Peninsula into a spearhead through which to fight the neighboring Muslim peoples.

If some people have in the past argued about the fact of the occupation, all the people of the Peninsula have now acknowledged it. The best proof of this is the Americans' continuing aggression against the Iraqi people using the Peninsula as a staging post, even though all its rulers are against their territories being used to that end, but they are helpless.

Second, despite the great devastation inflicted on the Iraqi people by the crusader–Zionist alliance, and despite the huge number of those killed, which has exceeded 1 million—despite all this, the Americans are once again trying to repeat the horrific massacres, as though they are not content with the protracted blockade imposed after the ferocious war or the fragmentation and devastation. So here they come to annihilate what is left of this people and to humiliate their Muslim neighbors.

Third, if the Americans' aims behind these wars are religious and economic, the aim is also to serve the Jews' petty state and divert attention from its occupation of Jerusalem and murder of Muslims there. The best proof of this is their eagerness to destroy Iraq, the strongest neighboring Arab state, and their endeavor to fragment all the states of the region such as Iraq, Saudi Arabia, Egypt and Sudan into paper statelets and through their disunion and weakness to guarantee Israel's survival and the continuation of the brutal crusade occupation of the Peninsula.

All these crimes and sins committed by the Americans are a clear declaration of war on Allah, his messenger, and Muslims. And ulema have throughout Islamic history unanimously agreed that the jihad is an individual duty if the enemy destroys the Muslim countries. This was revealed by Imam Bin–Qadamah in "Al–Mughni," Imam al–Kisa'i in "Al–Bada'i," al–Qurtubi in his interpretation, and the shaykh of al–Islam in his books, where he said: "As for the fighting to repulse [an enemy], it is aimed at defending sanctity and religion, and it is a duty as agreed [by the ulema]. Nothing is more sacred than belief except repulsing an enemy who is attacking religion and life."

On that basis, and in compliance with Allah's order, we issue the following fatwa to all Muslims:

The ruling to kill the Americans and their allies—civilians and military—is an individual duty for every Muslim who can do it in any country in which it is possible to do it, in order to liberate the al–Aqsa Mosque and the holy mosque [Mecca] from their grip, and in order for their armies to move out of all the lands of Islam, defeated and unable to threaten any Muslim. This is in accordance with the words of Almighty Allah, "and fight the pagans all together as they fight you all together," and "fight them until there is no more tumult or oppression, and there prevail justice and faith in Allah."

SOURCE: "PBS Newshour," translated by Foreign Broadcast Information Services, February 23, 1998. http://www.pbs.org/newshour/updates/military/jan–june98/fatwa_1998.html

actually increased Western intervention in Middle Eastern politics.

Since 2001 most scholarship on the "World Islamic Front Statement" and on bin Laden has attempted to situate the terrorist leader and his World Islamic Front in the context of international politics and as part of an ongoing war between civilizations. Rosalind Gwynne in a 2006 article in *Religion* states that most scholars have dismissed the question of whether bin Laden's "conduct may be called 'Islamic' … by asserting that bin Ladin is 'using Islam' to cover 'real motives' originating in anything but religion." Therefore, Gwynne examines the theological traditions informing his various interviews, statements, and declarations, reasoning that "if too many of his adversaries dismiss him as 'a devil quoting scripture' … they will not only remain ignorant of the intellectual and emotional basis of his support but also fail to grasp the single most important factor that, sooner or later, will deprive him of that support: credible, authoritative, text-based opposition from Muslims themselves."

BIBLIOGRAPHY

Sources

Gwynne, Rosalind W. "Usama bin Laden, the Qur'an, and Jihad." *Religion* 36.2 (2006): 61-90. *Academic OneFile.* Web. 7 Aug. 2012.

Lewis, Bernard. "License to Kill." *Foreign Affairs* Nov. 1998: 14. *Academic OneFile.* Web. 7 Aug. 2012.

Perry, Marvin, and Howard E. Negrin. *The Theory and Practice of Islamic Terrorism: An Anthology.* New York: Palgrave Macmillan, 2008. Print.

Snyder, Robert S. "Hating America: Bin Laden as a Civilizational Revolutionary." *Review of Politics* 65.4 (2003): 325-49. Print.

Wright, Lawrence. *The Looming Tower: Al-Qaeda and the Road to 9/11.* New York: Random House, 2006. Print.

Further Reading

Albright, Madeleine K., and William Woodward. *The Mighty and the Almighty: Reflections on America, God, and World Affairs.* New York: HarperCollins, 2006. Print.

Calvert, John. *Islamism: A Documentary and Reference Guide.* Westport: Greenwood, 2008. Print.

Kepel, Gilles, Jean-Pierre Milelli, and Pascale Ghazaleh. *Al Qaeda in Its Own Words.* Cambridge: Belknap, 2008. Print.

Lewis, Bernard. *The Crisis of Islam: Holy War and Unholy Terror.* New York: Modern Library, 2003. Print.

Rapoport, David C. *Terrorism: Critical Concepts in Political Science.* Abingdon: Routledge, 2006. Print.

Ruthven, Malise. "The Rise of Muslim Terrorists." *New York Review of Books* 29 May 2008: 33. Print.

Clint Garner

ZAPATISTA MANIFESTO

Zapatista National Liberation Army

✢ **Key Facts**

Time Period:
Late 20th Century

Movement/Issue:
Imperialism; Native
American rights

Place of Publication:
Mexico

**Language of
Publication:**
Spanish

OVERVIEW

Composed by representatives of the Zapatista National Liberation Army (Ejército Zapatista de Liberación Nacional; EZLN), the 1993 "Zapatista Manifesto" was essentially a declaration of war on the Mexican government. The EZLN, a revolutionary group, had formed in support of the Mayan peoples of the state of Chiapas. Its members, known as Zapatistas, objected to the Mexican government's increasing privatization of indigenous land, as well as to its economic policies—including its support of the North American Free Trade Agreement (NAFTA). Addressed explicitly to the "People of Mexico," the manifesto was published in the EZLN newspaper *El Despertador Mexicano* on December 31, 1993. It called for land reform and an end to more than six decades of rule by the Institutional Revolutionary Party (PRI). The day after the manifesto was issued—the same day that NAFTA went into effect—the EZLN staged an armed rebellion.

The "Zapatista Manifesto" and rebellion immediately provoked the Mexican government to militarize Chiapas. Although the uprising ended days later in a cease-fire, the conflict between the EZLN and Mexican authorities continued, sometimes violently, into the twenty-first century. Meanwhile, as the manifesto spread around the world via the Internet, the EZLN gained international support. Expanding its influence, the group soon initiated political programs that, among other goals, aimed to establish ties with resistance groups across Mexico. In 2006, for example, EZLN spokesperson Subcomandante Marcos led the Zapatistas on a national tour known as *La Otra Campaña* (The Other Campaign). Today the "Zapatista Manifesto" is recognized as the political document that brought the EZLN into the public eye. It stands as one of the most powerful demands for indigenous rights in Latin American history.

HISTORICAL AND LITERARY CONTEXT

The primary concern of the "Zapatista Manifesto," also known as the "First Declaration from the Lacandón Jungle," was the Mexican government's infringement of indigenous land rights. The EZLN was based in the Lacandón rainforest, an area of Chiapas that had been settled by Mayan migrants earlier in the twentieth century. Many migrants established villages and adopted a traditional system of governing communal lands, called *ejidos*. In the 1970s, however, the Mexican government declared a large part of the forest a protected area. It designated a small number of indigenous families as tenants and threatened to evict Mayan settlers. The actions of the government, long controlled by the PRI, reflected the historic marginalization and economic exploitation of the indigenous community.

In the early 1990s, in preparation for the implementation of NAFTA, the Mexican government began allowing the privatization of communal ejido lands. Many Maya in Chiapas saw this decision as a direct threat to their security, as it designated their communities as "informal settlements" and rendered them illegal squatters. By that time, the EZLN was active in its support of the Mayan communities of Chiapas. Its leader, who identified himself as Subcomandante Marcos, claimed to have lived in the Lacandón rainforest with the Mayan people since 1983.

The "Zapatista Manifesto" draws from several ideologies, including traditional Mayan culture, liberation theology, and Marxism. The ideals presented in the manifesto were largely influenced by the demands set forth by Mexico's First Indigenous Congress in 1974. Among the influential writings that resulted from that congress were the "Letter from Indigenous Communities," the "Letter from Pátzcuaro," and the founding document of the National Council of Indigenous Peoples. The "Zapatista Manifesto" echoed those works in their call for the egalitarian treatment of indigenous peoples under the law. Both the Indigenous Congress and the Zapatistas were inspired by liberation theology, whose followers apply the teachings of Jesus Christ to freeing the poor from unjust political or socioeconomic conditions. The seminal text of that movement was *A Theology of Liberation* (1971) by Gustavo Gutiérrez. The Zapatista ideology also was clearly influenced by Karl Marx and Friedrich Engels's *Communist Manifesto* (1848). Just as Marx and Engels roused the working class to unite against capitalism, the Zapatistas called on indigenous peoples to unite against the Mexican government.

Since its publication, the "Zapatista Manifesto" has sparked a wealth of commentary, both in support of and in opposition to the Zapatistas' cause. It also has inspired action by indigenous groups in other parts of Latin America. For instance, in 1995 representatives of the Maya in Guatemala and the Guatemalan government signed the Agreement on Identity and Rights of Indigenous Peoples. The agreement addressed such issues as education, language, and spirituality. By 2005 the EZLN had followed its initial manifesto with five more "Declarations from the Lacandón Jungle," which reflect the group's evolving ideology and demands. Books also were published under Marcos's name—for example, *The Other Campaign* (2008) and *¡Ya Basta! Ten Years of the Zapatista Uprising* (2004). Today, the Zapatista movement continues to command significant attention from scholars and activists worldwide.

THEMES AND STYLE

The central theme of the "Zapatista Manifesto" is the EZLN's denunciation of the Mexican government's historic neglect and oppression of the indigenous community. In the opening paragraph, the manifesto declares, "We have been denied the most elemental preparation so that they can use us as cannon fodder and pillage the wealth of our country.... Nor are we able to freely and democratically elect our political representatives ... nor is there peace nor justice for ourselves and our children." After addressing the history of the Maya, the text directly quotes the Mexican Constitution, which grants the people the right to "alter or modify" the national government. Rather than full independence, however, the Zapatistas demand autonomy from the Mexican state, along with control over the extraction of natural resources from their land. The manifesto concludes with explicit orders for the armed forces of the EZLN to wage war against the Mexican Federal Army—while protecting civilians and respecting the lives of prisoners and the wounded.

The manifesto achieves its forceful effect by combining an emotional appeal to the Zapatistas' "Mexican brothers and sisters" with legal justifications for their rebellion against the state. The manifesto proclaims, "[A]s our last hope, after having tried to utilize all legal means based on our Constitution, we go to our Constitution, to apply Article 39, which says: 'National Sovereignty essentially and originally resides in the people.'" By drawing on constitutional law, the Zapatistas legitimate their cause. They further justify a military uprising by addressing international organizations and mentioning international standards of war based on the Geneva Conventions. Rather than presenting a detailed list of demands, the manifesto focuses on clarifying the circumstances that necessitated armed rebellion. (The EZLN issued a list of demands soon afterward, in February 1994.)

The "Zapatista Manifesto" relies on an incensed, condemnatory tone that evokes emotion in its audience and conveys the urgency of the message. One of the first phrases of the manifesto is "ENOUGH IS

SUBCOMANDANTE MARCOS: EZLN SPOKESPERSON AND REVOLUTIONARY

Subcomandante Marcos, the de facto spokesperson for the Zapatista National Liberation Army (EZLN), is a writer and an outspoken opponent of capitalism, globalization, and the economic policy of neoliberalism. His title, which means "subcommander," refers to the fact that he is not indigenous Maya and thus receives directives from an inner circle of Mayan commanders. In the political realm and as leader of "The Other Campaign," Marcos is known as Delegate Zero. In public, he keeps his true identity a secret by wearing a black mask. In 1995 Mexican president Ernesto Zedillo Ponce de León declared Marcos to be Rafael Sebastián Guillén Vicente, a professor of philosophy. Neither Marcos nor the EZLN has confirmed or denied that identification.

On January 1, 1994, Marcos led an army of Mayan peasants in an uprising to protest the North American Free Trade Agreement (NAFTA) as well as the Mexican government's mistreatment of the indigenous community. Since then, he has gained international fame as the most outspoken representative of the EZLN. Marcos has been described as the new Che Guevara—the South American guerrilla who became a leftist icon in the 1960s—and his mask-wearing, pipe-smoking image has been appropriated by popular culture.

ENOUGH!"—an angry refrain meant to rouse its readers to action. It continues its recruiting effort by presenting war as the only remedy for the crimes of the Mexican government: "[W]e thereby call upon our brothers and sisters to join this struggle as the only path ... [against] a clique of traitors ... the same ones who massacred the railroad workers in 1958 and the students in 1968." Despite its heated style, the manifesto's repeated references to constitutional law and historical events reaffirm the logic and justice of the Zapatistas' cause.

CRITICAL DISCUSSION

The "Zapatista Manifesto" received a surprisingly positive international reaction and quickly acquired numerous supporters worldwide. It was republished in the Mexican newspaper *La Jornada* in early January 1994, and domestic and international journalists quoted the text extensively. Journalists from as far away as Italy heralded the Zapatistas: according to Judith A. Hellman's article in the *Socialist Register*, reporters for the Italian newspaper *Il Manifesto* noted that the mobilization of the indigenous people of Chiapas meant "something important for the left." Human rights organizations were quick to defend the Zapatistas by emphasizing the historic powerlessness of the Mexican indigenous population. However, government supporters and investors put financial interests ahead of concerns for the rights of the Maya in

EZLN (Ejército Zapatista de Liberación Nacional) supporters in Morelia, Mexico, in 2007. Also known as the Zapatistas, the EZLN has protested the Mexican government and has produced the "Zapatista Manifesto" (1993). AP PHOTO/ MOYSES ZUNIGA

Chiapas. That attitude was reflected in a 1995 statement by Riordan Roett, a consultant to Chase Manhattan Bank, who was quoted in Juanita Darling's *Latin America, Media, and Revolution* (2008): "While Chiapas, in our opinion, does not pose a fundamental threat to Mexican political stability, it is perceived to be so by many in the investment community. The government will need to eliminate the Zapatistas to demonstrate their effective control of the national territory and of security policy."

The Zapatistas continue to inspire countless scholarly debates and analyses, many of which refer to the EZLN's declaration of war in the 1993 manifesto. Renewing their interest in collective social movements, North American scholars produced numerous theses and book-length studies of the Zapatista movement; many taught entire courses on the issue. Outside academia, the EZLN gained an international following of lower- and middle-class individuals as a result of its publicity on the Internet. As Darling notes, "Communications on the Web sites indicate that Internet users were not merely passive consumers of the information they read about Chiapas. They identified with the Zapatistas' concerns.... They imagined themselves as participants in the same struggle, in a sense, different neighborhoods of the same community of resistance." The "Zapatista Manifesto" still commands the attention of scholars, journalists, and social activists.

Much scholarship on the "Zapatista Manifesto" has focused on its rapid distribution in early 1994, as well as on the central role played by the Internet, social networks, and other media in the ongoing Zapatista movement. In his 1998 article "Rebellion in Chiapas: Insurrection by Internet and Public Relations," Jerry W. Knudson states, "The Internet was perhaps instrumental in spilling more ink than blood in the recent two-year uprising in Chiapas, Mexico.... Marcos fought this shadow war via the Internet, lacing humor with his communiqués demanding justice for the Maya Indians of Chiapas." Other scholars have examined the commonalities between the manifesto and contemporary and historical indigenous narratives. In an article published in 2011, Eric Cheyfitz compares it to a work by contemporary Native American author Leslie Marmon Silko: "Like the 'Zapatista Manifesto', *Almanac of the Dead* works in the space where Marxism and Indigenous philosophy bear a certain relationship to each other, however vexed."

BIBLIOGRAPHY

Sources

Cheyfitz, Eric. "What Is a Just Society? Native American Philosophies and the Limits of Capitalism's Imagination: A Brief Manifesto." *South Atlantic Quarterly.* 110.2 (2011): 291-307. Print.

Darling, Juanita. *Latin America, Media, and Revolution: Communication in Modern Mesoamerica.* New York: Palgrave Macmillan, 2008. Print.

"El Despertador Mexicano: Declaration of War." *Journal of American History.* Web. 31 July 2012.

Hellman, Judith A. "Real and Virtual Chiapas: Magical Realism and the Left." *Socialist Register* 36 (2000): 161-86. Print.

Knudson, Jerry W. "Rebellion in Chiapas: Insurrection by Internet and Public Relations." *Media, Culture & Society* 20.3 (1998): 507-18. Print.

Further Reading

Burke, Patrick. "Indigenous Rights in Latin America, and Methods of Resistance: The Zapatista Liberation Army and the Coordinating Body of the Indigenous Peoples of the Amazon Basin—A Comparison." *University of Toronto.* Web. 2012 July 30.

Collier, George A., and Elizabeth Lowery Quarantiello. *Basta! Land and the Zapatista Rebellion in Chiapas.* Oakland: Food First, 1994. Print.

Ronfeldt, David F. *The Zapatista "Social Netwar" in Mexico.* Santa Monica: Rand, 1998. Print.

Villas Delgado, Claudia. "Producing a 'Space of Dignity.' Knitting Together Space and Dignity in the EZLN Rebellion in Mexico." Diss. New Jersey State U, 2008. Web. 30 July 2012.

Womack, John, Jr. *Rebellion in Chiapas: An Historical Reader.* New York: The New Press, 1999. Print.

Katrina White

PHILOSOPHIES

AN ATHEIST MANIFESTO

Joseph Lewis

OVERVIEW

An Atheist Manifesto, written by Joseph Lewis in 1954, argues that by rejecting organized religion, American society would improve toward a utopian state because of advances afforded by intellectual freedom and an appreciation for life based on independence rather than the restrictive teachings of the Bible. The piece presents God as a fabrication designed to limit the progress of education and demands that society recognize the restrictive nature of organized religion. Lewis believed that, with the adoption of an atheist theology, technological and medical knowledge could advance to improve the lives of people so that they could enjoy living instead of accepting pain and suffering in order to please a religious deity. Written during the Cold War, at a time when atheism was associated with the Soviet Union, *An Atheist Manifesto* recasts atheist beliefs as emblematic of independence and American dreams.

The manifesto immediately caught the attention of Lewis's followers and furthered his fame as a public atheist and activist. His position that atheism represents freedom in the American sense stirred some controversy, although it failed to change public opinion or cause any significant change within the Church. Critics who often deride Lewis for his lack of historical accuracy and improper research methods generally note the strong emotional tenor of the piece, which was unusual for atheist philosophical writing, and call *An Atheist Manifesto* Lewis's most "courageous" and "polemical" piece of writing. As such, any lasting significance the manifesto has is in relation to Lewis's career rather than any major historical event.

HISTORICAL AND LITERARY CONTEXT

In the United States at the time *An Atheist Manifesto* was published, atheism was associated with the communist politics of the Soviet Union, and thus it was generally deemed to be "un-American." In an attempt to change public opinion about the potential of an American utopia, Lewis discusses the Declaration of Independence as an atheist document, suggesting that the very foundation of American independence is based on atheist principles of freedom and the separation of church and state. Thus, Lewis's manifesto presents atheism as the ultimate form of freedom and independence, and he argues that adopting atheism

on a national level would advance America toward the realization of a perfect society.

First appearing during the height of the Cold War in 1954, the manifesto was a daring effort, given popular beliefs about atheism at the time and the general unrest caused by the threat of nuclear war. Known for his individualism, Lewis was a prominent activist who spent his career presenting his beliefs about science, religion, and politics to the general public through his writing and his public campaigns. The publication of *An Atheist Manifesto* during such a politically tense period is seen by modern historian as a bold move, a testament to Lewis's conviction and his firm belief in his atheist philosophy.

Surrounded by likeminded freethinkers from such groups as Freethinkers of America and the American Association for the Advancement of Science, Lewis drew on the support of a network of colleagues in developing the ideas presented in

❖ *Key Facts*

Time Period:
Mid-20th Century

Movement/Issue:
Cold War; Utopianism

Place of Publication:
United States

Language of Publication:
English

JOSEPH LEWIS: AMERICAN, ACTIVIST, ATHEIST

Born in Alabama to a Jewish family, Joseph Lewis (1889-1968) became one of the most prominent American atheists in the early twentieth century, although he never received international recognition for his accomplishments. Forced to leave school for work at age nine because of his family's poverty, Lewis was self-educated, an avid reader who was heavily influenced by the writings of Robert Green Ingersoll and Thomas Paine.

In 1920, Lewis moved to New York, where he joined the atheist group Freethinkers of America. In 1925 he became the group's president, a position he would hold for the rest of his life. Lewis published heavily in the group's publication, *Bulletin of the Freethinkers of America,* later renamed *Freethinker* and the *Age of Reason,* despite accusations that he was using the group to promote his own political and atheist ideas. He also established two publishing firms, Freethought Press Association in 1921 and Eugenics Publishing Company in 1930, which he used to publish his own work. The two companies were his main sources of income throughout his career. Some of Lewis's most influential books include *The Tyranny of God* (1921), *The Bible Unmasked* (1946), and *The Ten Commandments* (1946).

PRIMARY SOURCE

AN ATHEIST MANIFESTO

Many ask what difference does it make whether man believes in a God or not.

It makes a big difference.

It makes all the difference in the world.

It is the difference between being right and being wrong; it is the difference between truth and surmises—facts or delusion.

It is the difference between the earth being flat, and the earth being round.

It is the difference between the earth being the center of the universe, or a tiny speck in this vast and uncharted sea of multitudinous suns and galaxies.

It is the difference in the proper concept of life, or conclusions based upon illusion.

It is the difference between verified knowledge and the faith of religion.

It is a question of Progress or the Dark Ages.

The history of man proves that religion perverts man's concept of life and the universe, and has made him a cringing coward before the blind forces of nature.

If you believe that there is a God; that man was "created"; that he was forbidden to eat of the fruit of the "tree of knowledge"; that he disobeyed; that he is a "fallen angel"; that he is paying the penalty for his "sins," then you devote your time praying to appease an angry and jealous God.

If, on the other hand, you believe that the universe is a great mystery; that man is the product of evolution; that he is born without knowledge; that intelligence comes from experience, then you devote your time and energies to improving his condition with the hope of securing a little happiness here for yourself and your fellow man.

That is the difference.

* * *

We are not "fallen" angels, nor were we "created" perfect.

On the contrary, we are the product of millions of years of an unpurposed evolution.

We are the descendants and inheritors of all the defects of our primitive ancestry—the evolution of the myriad forms of life from the infinitesimal to the mammoth—from the worm to the dinosaur.

The most important step in the development of man is the recognition of the fact that we are born without knowledge, and that the acquisition of knowledge is a slow and painful process.

* * *

As long as there is one person suffering an injustice; as long as one person is forced to bear an unnecessary sorrow; as long as one person is subject to an undeserved pain, the worship of a God is a demoralizing humiliation.

As long as there is one mistake in the universe; as long as one wrong is permitted to exist; as long as there is hatred and antagonism among mankind, the existence of a God is a moral impossibility.

Ingersoll said: "Injustice upon earth renders the justice of heaven impossible."

Man's inhumanity to man will continue as long as man loves God more than he loves his fellow man.

The love of God means wasted love.

* * *

An Atheist Manifesto. Like all of his writings, however, the manifesto also draws heavily on the works of prominent American freethinkers Robert Green Ingersoll and Thomas Paine, particularly Paine's *Age of Reason* (1794-95), which Lewis identified as the text that most influenced his atheist beliefs. Lewis also incorporated ideas developed in his previous publications, including *The Tyranny of God* (1921) and *The Bible Unmasked* (1946), in his discussion of the repressive nature of religion and the liberty represented by atheist principles and scientific education.

The manifesto was moderately successful in the United States, and although it is outshone by Lewis's full-length books on religion, politics, and the promotion of atheist beliefs, it is still regarded as his most courageous work because of its content and the timing of its release. Discussions of the manifesto influenced academic and political debates about the place of religion within American politics and the development of purely secular public schools. Today, however, the manifesto is largely overlooked because discussions about atheism have taken on international and historical perspectives, although the work's relevance to the history of atheism in the United States is still recognized by some modern scholars.

THEMES AND STYLE

The main theme of *An Atheist Manifesto* is that organized religion and the belief in God prevents intellectual progress and therefore hinders societal

Remember this: You are not a depraved human being.

You have no sins to atone for.

There is no need for fear.

There are no ghosts—holy or otherwise.

Stop making yourself miserable for "the love of God."

Drive this monster of tyrannic fear from your mind, and enjoy the inestimable freedom of an emancipated human being.

The only duty you owe is to yourself and to your family.

The duty you owe to yourself is to do the best you can, and the duty you owe to your family is to endeavor to make them happy.

Emancipate yourself from these stultifying creeds, and protect your children from the contamination of religion.

Get off your knees, stand erect, and look the whole world in the face.

Get all the joy and happiness you can out of life.

Enjoy the fruits of your labor and waste it not upon the myth of heaven; support not the parasites of God.

Do not knowingly harm another human being; do not knowingly injure your fellow man.

All forms of life have feeling, do not make them suffer.

AS SHAKESPEARE SAYS:

"The poor beetle, that we tread upon,
In corporal sufferance finds a pang as great
As when a giant dies."

Kindness is a magic solvent.

While we know that sometimes "ingratitude is more strong than traitor's arms," we also know that "mercy is twice blest; it blesses him that gives and him that takes," and, it should be remembered that while Loyalty is the most important of the virtues, Patience is the most valuable.

Become a courageous human being and do the best you can under any and all circumstances in this imperfect and troublesome world.

Be brave enough to live and be brave enough to die, knowing that when the Grim Reaper comes, you did the best you could and that the world is better for your having lived.

A God could do no more.

I will stand between you and the hosts of heaven.

I am not afraid.

I will act as your attorney before the Bar of Judgment.

I will assume all responsibility.

My services are free.

Put the blame on me.

Break the chains of mental slavery to religious superstition.

Arise and become a free and independent human being.

Dignify yourself as a Man, and justify your living by being a Brother to All Mankind and a Citizen of the Universe.

progress and freedom because it encourages people to believe that they will be punished for their sins if they actively pursue happiness. In order to prove this point, Lewis directly relates the Declaration of Independence—used in this piece as a signifier for the separation of church and state—with numerous intellectual advancements made after its composition that improved the day-to-day lives of average people, including electricity, research into the composition of blood, and anesthesia. Lewis states, "No believer in God would have spent his energies to discover anaesthesia. He would have been in mortal fear of the wrath of God for interfering with His 'divine plan' of making man suffer for having eaten of the fruit of the 'Tree of Knowledge.'" Treating religion as education's

opposite, Lewis contends that belief in God is the major downfall of society because it encourages resistance to intellectual progress.

The manifesto achieves its rhetorical effect by making direct binary comparisons that are presented as the obvious results of basic logic. The main binary that Lewis creates and works within is the opposition of religion with independence: he suggests that belief in God is designed to enslave the population through ignorance, while education is designed to enlighten the population through knowledge and freedom. Lewis states, "It is now established by verifiable evidence that religion stultifies the brain and is the great obstacle in the path of intellectual progress." The "verifiable evidence" to which Lewis refers includes

Atheist Joseph Lewis was greatly influenced by and discusses the theories of Robert Ingersoll, pictured here. Ingersoll was known as "The Great Agnostic." © LEBRECHT MUSIC AND ARTS PHOTO LIBRARY/ ALAMY

numerous medical advancements made in recent history, after the composition of the Declaration of Independence, and supposedly by people who upheld atheist beliefs.

Lewis's manifesto uses derogatory language when discussing anything associated with religion, which makes science and education stand out as apparently clear and enlightened societal advancements. He describes the "idiotic text of the Bible" and the "ravings of the religious lunatics" as means of enslaving people and preventing them from freely and independently pursuing education. Lewis's language presents religion as slavery and contrasts it with the freedom and independence he associates with education, thereby creating the binary which he then uses to promote atheist beliefs as an integral part of societal development. The language of the manifesto also destroys any sense of academic objectivity, however, and the emotional tone generated by the use of derogatory terms contradicts Lewis's association of atheist beliefs with intellectual education.

CRITICAL DISCUSSION

The initial reaction to the release of *An Atheist Manifesto* was varied, with some groups responding sympathetically to Lewis's views and others criticizing the work as heretical and misguided in its portrayal of atheist beliefs. The 1958 newsletter published by the Society for Science and the Public hails the work as "a brilliant call for courage in an age of caution" and calls it "a profound argument for intellectual integrity in a time of moral cowardice." Other atheist scholars were disgusted by Lewis's discussion of atheism as an ideology that could lead toward utopia. This viewpoint is evident in George H. Smith's *Atheism: The Case Against God* (1979), in which Smith comments that Lewis's atheist philosophy is "false and misleading" because "[f]rom the mere fact that a person is an atheist, one cannot infer that this person subscribes to any particular positive belief." Atheism, argues Smith, does not produce emotion, and therefore Lewis is mistaken in suggesting it is the key to a happier life and the realization of utopian ideals.

While *An Atheist Manifesto* is admired for presenting atheist beliefs as a symbol of American independence during the politically charged time of the Cold War, its significance in the history of atheism faded after it was categorized as "bourgeois literature" in such scholarly works as William Peter van den Bercken's *Ideology and Atheism in the Soviet Union* (1988). While certain texts stand out today as particularly significant with regard to the atheist movement in America and the beliefs and problems associated with it, *An Atheist Manifesto* is generally not considered to be one of these influential texts. Works by Ingersoll and Paine, Lewis's primary influences, tend to outshine Lewis's manifesto in terms of their political and social importance and the changes they generated in the thinking of certain American citizens.

Current scholarship on atheism in history tends to focus on global perspectives, with emphasis on existentialism in relation to various religious standpoints or on the philosophical breakdown of religious faith in general. Consequently, the manifesto is often overlooked because of its high emotional tone and singular focus on American Christianity. Despite the fact that the reputations of Lewis and his manifesto have declined, some scholars believe that their current obscurity is unwarranted. Robert Morrell, for example, writes in his brief biography of Joseph Lewis that the activist "never achieved the recognition in the international freethought movement that he deserved."

BIBLIOGRAPHY

Sources

Bercken, William Peter van den. *Ideology and Atheism in the Soviet Union.* Trans. H. Wake. Berlin: Mouton de Gruyter, 1989. Print.

"Front Matter." *Science News-Letter* 73.18 (1958): 237-78. *JSTOR.* Web. 27 Aug. 2012.

Morrell, Robert W. "Lewis, Joseph." *The New Encyclopaedia of Unbelief.* Ed. Tom Flynn. Buffalo: Prometheus, 2007. 489-91. Print.

Smith, George H. *Atheism: The Case Against God.* Buffalo: Prometheus, 1979. Print.

Further Reading

Howland, Arthur H. *Joseph Lewis—Enemy of God.* Boston: Stratford, 1932. Print.

Ingersoll, Robert G. "About the Holy Bible (1894)." *The Agnostic Reader.* Ed. S.T. Joshi. Buffalo: Prometheus, 2007. 134-42. Print.

Kirby, Dianne. *Religion and the Cold War.* New York: Palgrave Macmillan, 2003. Print.

Paine, Thomas. *The Age of Reason.* Secaucus: Citadel, 1974. Print.

Stein, Gordon. "Lewis, Joseph." *Biographical Dictionary of American Cult and Sect Leaders.* Ed. J. Gordon Melton. New York: Garland, 1986. 158-59. Print.

Katherine Barker

THE COMPANION SPECIES MANIFESTO

Dogs, People, and Significant Otherness

Donna Haraway

✤ *Key Facts*

Time Period:
Early 21st Century

Movement/Issue:
Animal rights; War on
Terror

Place of Publication:
United States

**Language of
Publication:**
English

OVERVIEW

Written by Donna Haraway in 2003, "The Companion Species Manifesto: Dogs, People, and Significant Otherness" argues that by viewing dog-human relationships in the proper manner, it is possible to better recognize, embrace, and bridge the boundaries that exist between humans along gender, racial, and ideological lines. Published in a slim, pamphlet-like book, the essay begins with a section that is densely packed with terminology and concepts that can easily bewilder first-time readers and can intimidate those who are not well versed in academic and theoretical discourse. As the essay unfolds, Haraway sheds the terminology-heavy language in favor of a historical analysis of dogs' and humans' shared evolution, using detailed anecdotes to describe the real lives of animals.

By the time of the essay's publication, Haraway had earned a reputation as an influential voice in feminist studies and its intersection with popular culture. "The Companion Species Manifesto" was seen as a new direction in her studies, yet it is wholly consistent with her earlier work in that it promotes an understanding of, rather than a direct conflict with, existing power structures and relationships. This idea is, in Haraway's view, best exemplified by the relationship between humans and their companion animals, particularly canines, because of their unique coevolutionary history. Humans, she argues, must rethink their notions of superiority over nonhuman species. In this light, she expresses suspicion toward the anthropocentrism of applying the human notion of "rights" to animals and instead advocates for respecting dogs as dogs, not as quasi-humans. Since the publication of "The Companion Species Manifesto," this view has gained wide acceptance among those concerned with animal welfare.

HISTORICAL AND LITERARY CONTEXT

While "The Companion Species Manifesto" can be seen as a response to emerging concerns over animal welfare and animal rights, Haraway's concerns are not limited to this narrow reading. For Haraway the advances brought forth through earlier feminist thought and writing had yet to truly alter the power dynamics of human interactions. Through reevaluating human-animal relationships, using the term "companion species," Haraway proposes to shed a new light on the interconnectedness of all living things, which she believed were irretrievably tangled in systems of power. Using the shared history of humans and canines as her model, she discusses how the two species are reflections of each other. She also notes that animals are not powerless in this relationship. To view animals as helpless creatures with the capacity for "unconditional love" is a disservice to humans and animals.

The author makes little mention of the historical moment when this essay was written, only noting that the idea for it came to her when she adopted an Australian shepherd dog named Cayenne. However, "The Companion Species Manifesto" was written during the lead-up to the U.S. invasion of Iraq. Haraway seems to allude to this historical context when she calls her essay a "political act of hope in a world on the edge of global war." It is possible to see this text as a guideline for understanding a newly fractured world, intended for an audience still struggling to map the geopolitical landscape in the wake of the terrorist attacks of September 11, 2001.

"The Companion Species Manifesto" is a continuation of Haraway's earlier thinking and advocacy. In her previous writings she is concerned with concepts that are typically thought of as contradictory, intersections of opposing ideas and philosophies. In perhaps her most influential work, "The Cyborg Manifesto," she discusses the ways in which cyborgs can be seen to represent a complex interpenetration of human and machine. Written during the mid-1980s, this earlier work reflected the common anxiety at the time over the emergence and profusion of technology in the everyday sphere. Haraway's prescription was to embrace emerging technology and celebrate the fusion of others it represented. In "The Companion Species Manifesto," the otherness to be embraced is across the species line and can best be exemplified in the relationship between humans and working dogs.

In "The Companion Species Manifesto," Haraway wants "dog writing to be a branch of feminist theory, or the other way around," and this assertion has opened a line of critical inquiry and scholarship into the nature of human-animal relationships and what they signify about the human condition. Since its publication Haraway's essay has been a touchstone for admirers and detractors from the animal studies field and among feminist scholars.

THEMES AND STYLE

The central concern of "The Companion Species Manifesto" is remembering the long coevolutionary history of humans and canines and acknowledging the important impact dogs have had on human communities for tens of thousands of years. Mindful of this, Haraway argues that, in a contemporary capitalistic system, an animal must have a function that increases its value, thus making it less subject to the whims of affection. It is through this breaking down of hierarchies that an animal can achieve the status of "companion species." Through companion species relationships, a kind of mutual communication and cooperation can exist that reduces hierarchical and patriarchal categorization. Conversely, she argues that treating "a dog as a furry child, even metaphorically, demeans the dogs and children—and sets up children to be bitten and dogs to be killed." Haraway sees these human-animal relationships as a model, something that can inform other relationships: "Implicitly, this manifesto is about more than the relation of dogs and people. Dogs and people figure a universe."

The essay starts by providing definitions for some of the more difficult terms and by setting up a theoretical framework for Haraway's larger discussion. During this early portion the writing frequently takes on a postmodern, meta-writing quality, as when she informs the reader that the text "works fractally, re-inscribing similar shapes of attention, listening, and respect." The core of the piece, however, revolves around Haraway's stories of dogs, particularly her own dog, with which she participates in agility competitions. Additionally, she provides a lengthy history of two particular breeds of working dogs, the Great Pyrenees and the Australian shepherd, in order to illustrate the mutually beneficial relationships that are possible between companion species. When she veers off the subject of dogs, she warns herself, "I am violating a major rule of ... my doggish scribblings" and that there should "be no deviation from the animal stories themselves." Clearly, for Haraway, the stories of the dogs and, more importantly, their deeply intertwined historical connections to humans are vital to understanding the nature of companion species relationships.

"The Companion Species Manifesto" is marked by deeply contrasting styles. The earlier sections tend to rely heavily on theory-rich language that can be challenging to decode. Yet Haraway peppers even the densest language thickets with humorous puns such as "dog-eaten props" and "half-trained arguments." The author is also unafraid to be blunt in discussing her subject, such as when she asks, "how might stories about

DONNA HARAWAY: FINGER ON THE PULSE

Throughout her career, Donna Haraway, now a professor emerita in the History of Consciousness Department at the University of California, Santa Cruz, has demonstrated an ability to capture the prevailing concerns and anxieties of the age and develop new models for understanding them—a skill that has enabled her ideas to reach beyond traditional academic circles. Her essay "The Cyborg Manifesto," published in 1985, came on the heels of the film *The Terminator* and William Gibson's novel *Neuromancer.* As Jeffrey Williams notes in his 2009 piece in *Chronicle of Higher Education,* "the 1980s were the Age of the Cyborg." Haraway's essay was widely read and deeply influential in science fiction, film, and performance art.

Similarly, "The Companion Species Manifesto," published in 2003, emerged at a time when the American public was just beginning to rethink the morality and sustainability of its relationship to the natural world. In recent years numerous states have enacted laws limiting puppy mills, dogfighting, and animal cruelty. Additionally, new emphasis has been placed on the conditions in which animals are raised for consumption. For an academic scholar whose primary focus is poststructuralist theory, Haraway has shown an aptitude for capturing the prevailing cultural zeitgeist, thus giving her work a surprisingly broad cultural impact.

dog-human worlds finally convince brain-damaged US Americans ... that history matters in nature cultures?" In the latter sections of the essay, when the author focuses primarily on her understanding of, and relationship with, working dogs, the tone takes on a pastoral sereneness. Not coincidentally these concrete examples tend to be the most readily accessible.

A Great Pyrenees dog with human companion, c. 1992. © YANN ARTHUS-BERTRAND/ CORBIS

CRITICAL DISCUSSION

Throughout her career Haraway has embraced complexity in her writing, and "The Companion Species Manifesto" is no exception. While the breaking down of traditional binaries is a large part of her project, this insistence on making relationships rather than identities has been viewed by some critics as a refusal to take a stand. In her 2009 piece in *Women's Review of Books*, Kathy Rudy notes, "it's not at all clear what we should do after reading Haraway's book." The essay, written as an amalgamation of science, theory, and anecdote, defies criticism from academic specialists because it does not seem to fit comfortably within any one discipline. Additionally, because the overall goal of the piece is to eschew traditional binary definitions, the essay can leave readers wanting a stronger prescription.

As a piece of feminist theory, "The Companion Species Manifesto" has been largely embraced by scholars. As Katy Williams observes in her review in *Women's Studies in Communication,* the essay "has the potential to revolutionize the way we think about ourselves and our relationship to the rest of the world" as it "expands the very definition of feminism and its concerns." However, Haraway's work has had a less welcome reception from those who view it as a piece of activism on behalf of animal rights. This, despite the fact that Haraway herself acknowledges that the "question turns out not to be what are animal rights … but how may a human enter into a rights relationship with an animal?" Critics such as Dax Boria take issue with Haraway's assertion that the athletic routines dogs are trained to perform are a demonstration of mutual companionship; rather, he states, they are simply a symbolic way for humans to assert mastery over animals.

Over time "The Companion Species Manifesto" has helped to initiate a school of thought that attempts to unify the concerns of animal studies and feminist scholarship. Scholar Don Handelman has argued that Haraway has "opened the door" to further study of how relationships with companion animals can inform feminist studies. This opened door has allowed for agreement with and critique of her philosophy. Animal rights activists, in particular, decry Haraway's admission that she continues to eat meat or her assertion that animal testing is acceptable in certain circumstances. Still, Rudy notes that Haraway's manifesto and the writings it has inspired "untangle us from the straightjacket of abstract rights theorization and endorse women's emotional responses as the foundation of care." Thus "The Companion Species Manifesto" has enabled a new paradigm for a broader viewing of the ways in which oppression can be overcome.

BIBLIOGRAPHY

Sources

Caddick, Alison. "I'd Rather Be a Cyborg than a Goddess: Avoiding Difficult Questions." *Arena Magazine* June-July 1998: 10+. *Academic OneFile.* Web. 9 Aug. 2012.

Rudy, Kathy. "Woman's Best Friend." *Women's Review of Books* Jan.-Feb. 2009: 31+. *Academic OneFile.* Web. 9 Aug. 2012.

Vanderwees, Chris. "*Companion Species* under Fire: A Defense of Donna Haraway's *The Companion Species Manifesto.*" *Nebula* 6.2 (2009): 73+. *Academic OneFile.* Web. 12 Aug. 2012.

Williams, Jeffrey. "Donna Haraway's Critters." *Chronicle of Higher Education* 56.9 (2009). *Academic Search Premier.* Web. 9 Aug. 2012.

Williams, Katy. Rev. of *The Companion Species Manifesto: Dog, People, and Significant Otherness,* by Donna Haraway. *Women's Studies in Communication* 30.1 (2007): 145-48. *Academic Search Premier.* Web. 9 Aug. 2012.

Further Reading

Cassidy, Rebecca. "I Want to Know about the Dogs." *Theory Culture Society* 23 (2006): 324-28. Print.

Dekoven, Marianne. "Jouissance, Cyborgs, and Companion Species: Feminist Experiment." *PMLA* 5 (2006): 1690-96. Print.

Haraway, Donna. *When Species Meet.* Minneapolis: U of Minnesota P, 2008. Print.

Haraway, Donna, and Thyrza Goodeve. *How Like a Leaf: An Interview with Donna Haraway.* New York: Routledge, 2000. Print.

Richter, David H., ed. *The Critical Tradition: Classic Texts and Contemporary Trends.* New York: Bedford, 2007. Print.

Schneider, Joseph. *Donna Haraway: Live Theory.* New York: Continuum, 2005. Print.

Giano Cromley

FIRST AS TRAGEDY, THEN AS FARCE

Slavoj Zizek

OVERVIEW

Composed by Slavoj Zizek, *First as Tragedy, Then as Farce* (2009) proclaims that a global rebirth of communist ideals is the only possible means to redress the numerous social ills suffered under the logic of capitalism. Covering the period between the attacks of September 11, 2001, and the global financial crisis of 2008, *First as Tragedy* employs a rich Hegelian-Marxist philosophy coupled with a Lacanian-based analysis of the framework and methods employed by global capitalism. Zizek diagnoses a litany of problems that are exemplified by the two events in order to point out the failure of the political Left in solving these problems. For Zizek, the Left falls victim to glorifying perceived electoral victories (such as the election of Barack Obama in November 2008) when, in fact, it has only addressed a series of crises that the logic of capitalism necessitates for its own growth. Additionally, the author chastises the Left for unwittingly capitulating to the logic of capitalism when it targets particular instances of abuse (such as corrupt bankers or politicians) rather than revealing the dysfunction of the system as a whole.

Like much of Zizek's writings, *First as Tragedy* was met with criticism by scholars on both the Left and the Right. Conservatives derided his Marxist-oriented critique as one that promoted class warfare and drummed up the old lies of socialism, while scholars who were sympathetic to Zizek's views argued that his economic analysis was too reductive because it focused on a simplistic market-based analysis. In spite of the criticism, *First as Tragedy, Then as Farce* offered a rallying point for those on the left by arguing for a standpoint of critique based upon communistic ideals in order to reveal capitalism's perpetual cycle of power and exploitation. The book attempted to galvanize the Left by pushing for an ideological counterattack to the prevailing capitalist system. Using a variety of cultural and political examples, Zizek moves through a descriptive analysis that can only be corrected through the adoption of communist principles.

HISTORICAL AND LITERARY CONTEXT

Written in response to the global market crash of 2008, *First as Tragedy, Then as Farce* runs through a detailed account of the global crisis. Zizek focuses on the ideological justifications for capitalism while juxtaposing them against the ruptures exposed through the state-sponsored bailouts of large corporations. He uses many pop culture references to perform a thorough, and at times tangential, rhetorical analysis of capitalist ideology. He rejects the assertion that capitalism is based on apolitical market strategies, pointing to the widespread state interventions that took place to alleviate the crisis. Zizek then turns to the impotence of liberal projects that attempt to redress capitalism's perceived ills by illustrating how such projects adhere to the same logic that they wish to contest. For Zizek, the only valid solution is a rejuvenated communism that rejects both state and market-based strategies.

Zizek frames the book during the period between the terrorist attacks of September 11, 2001, and the financial meltdown of 2008. By calling attention to the rhetoric used by President George W. Bush, Zizek attacks the principles that lie behind neoliberalism's beliefs in free-market capitalism. He labels the response to the terrorist attacks as the "tragedy" in which fundamental tenets were jettisoned in exchange for preemptive declarations of war and support for torture. The "tragedy" is followed by the "farce" of the 2008 crash, when the economic principles and associated calculus were unable to account for the colossal failure of the market system. Responding to the celebrated principles of liberal democracy coupled with free-market capitalism, *First as Tragedy, Then as Farce* attempts to reveal the utopian beliefs upon which capitalism is predicated as well as how such beliefs permeated and prescribed our reactions to the terrorist attacks and the financial meltdown. Zizek hopes that by dismantling the fallacies of liberal democracy he can flesh out a communist response and reinstate a moment of political praxis.

First as Tragedy, Then as Farce incorporates a wide range of Marxist political and economic philosophy in addition to situating the cultural critique within a nuanced historical analysis. Through the lens of Marx, Zizek situates the discussion within a complex neo-Platonism that is bolstered by Zizek's own psychoanalytic framework. Drawing on the work of thinkers such as Soren Kierkegaard and Immanuel Kant, Zizek illustrates how capitalist ideology betrayed itself in the wake of the two crises by employing socialist rhetoric and policies that inverted the terms of class warfare

⁘ *Key Facts*

Time Period:
Early 21st Century

Movement/Issue:
Communism; Global recession of 2008; Failure of liberal democracy

Place of Publication:
United States

Language of Publication:
English

SLAVOJ ZIZEK: CULT OF THE PHILOSOPHER

Slavoj Zizek (1949-) is a Slovenian philosopher and cultural critic who specializes in Hegelian-Marxist and Lacanian theories. His work covers a wide range of issues, including film theory, political theory, human rights, multiculturalism, postmodernism, and religion. His first book in English, *The Sublime Object of Ideology* (1989), placed him on the international stage. Since its publication, Zizek has been a prolific writer, composing more than fifty books and hundreds of articles in a variety of languages. Throughout his career, Zizek has intrigued and infuriated scholars and critics, becoming one of the most polarizing and though-provoking thinkers of the twentieth and twenty-first centuries.

The volume of Zizek's writing in combination with his flamboyant personality and controversial positions have led many critics to label him as an academic celebrity rather than a philosopher. Scholars and critics have noted that Zizek does not have a system of thought; rather, they argue that he attempts to be all-encompassing to the point that he combines incompatible modes of thought (such as Hegelianism and psychoanalysis) and remains too vague and obscure to amount to a philosopher of praxis. What is lacking in such a criticism, however, is that Zizek does more than merely theorize about potential change; he actively participates in political movements. In the fall of 2011 he spoke at the inaugural Occupy Wall Street site, cautioning the participants not to fall in love with themselves for resisting but to continue to fight for and craft real change.

to argue for the benefit of the wealthy rather than the benefit of the poor. Akin to Zizek's post-September 11 book, *Welcome to the Desert of the Real* (2002), *First as Tragedy* demonstrates how through a variety of false conflicts, the ideological rhetoric of capitalist practices is bolstered by the false rhetoric of "Wall Street versus Main Street" to such an extent that people are facilitating the growth of the system through their very unease and resistance to the system.

In the years that followed its publication, *First as Tragedy, Then as Farce* inspired a renewed debate on the merits of communist ideals. Not surprisingly, neoliberal and conservative critics lambasted Zizek for fostering an anti-American sentiment and promoting redistribution of wealth and labeled his communist agenda as part of a new wave of neosocialism that did not drift too far from fascism. Scholars who were sympathetic with his cause and supportive of his analysis suggested that although Zizek offered a compelling critique, he ventured too far from materialist and historicist concerns by highlighting such groundbreaking events as if they somehow occurred outside of history. Because of criticisms such as these, Zizek's thoughts produced a rich debate on the possibility of communist ideals to spark a radical shift in ideology and policy.

THEMES AND STYLE

Zizek's main claim in *First as Tragedy, Then as Farce* is that return to communism is the only possible route for enacting substantive change to the unbalanced system in which poor people continue to suffer while large banks and corporations are afforded multiple opportunities to succeed. Following Marx's critique of Hegel's historical repetition, Zizek claims that "the formula of a regime which 'only imagines that it believes in itself' nicely captures the cancellation of the performative power ('symbolic efficiency') of the ruling ideology: it no longer effectively functions as the fundamental structure of the social bond." Following this line of reasoning, Zizek maneuvers through a dialectical assault on capitalism's utopian promise. The book illustrates the variety of symbolic operators that function to conflate consumerism with ethical values to such an extent that the variety of images cut off legitimate threat to the capitalist framework.

In addition to the mash-up of philosophical theories, Zizek demonstrates the breadth of the ideological farce by incorporating a variety of anecdotes and witticisms that cover an array of pop culture references, including movies, advertisements, and news coverage. Zizek maintains that it is not out of stupidity or ignorance that people are seduced by capitalism's rhetoric; rather, he argues that the current state of affairs is so rooted in an illusion that it is difficult for any solution within the system to locate a standpoint of critique. Zizek points out that "the self-propelling circulation of Capital thus remains more than ever the ultimate Real of our lives, a beast that by definition cannot be controlled, since it itself controls our activity, blinding us to even the most obvious dangers we are courting." He develops a line of reasoning in which only a return to communism will provide people with a vantage point to assess the current system. For Zizek, only communism can reveal the false choices that capitalism offers. In order to pull back the veil, the author highlights a variety of forms of exploitation and oppression that serve to categorize people as groups with competing interests.

Like most of Zizek's writings, *First as Tragedy, Then as Farce* relies upon a flamboyant tempo mixed with brash humor and dense prose. He abandons the typical model of a philosophical treatise; however, he utilizes his wit and intellect to first diagnose the current systemic problems and then constructs a compelling counternarrative that seeks to give momentum to a sustained moment of communist praxis. Remarking on the sociopolitical status of Haiti, Zizek claims that "what makes capital exceptional is its unique combination of the values of freedom and equality and the facts of exploitation and domination: the gist of Marx's analysis is that the legal-ideological matrix of freedom-equality is not a mere 'mask' concealing exploitation-domination but the very form in which the latter is exercised." Haiti serves as a placeholder for the liberal and progressive policies and rhetoric that seek to offer a "compassionate capitalism." Zizek holds that such policies and rhetoric only serve to strengthen capitalism's oppressive hold on the global economy. Capitalism's economic model has evolved to one that sought to mitigate excess into one that seeks to colonize areas of excess through free-market principles that promise the participants a bigger slice of the economic pie.

CRITICAL DISCUSSION

Since its initial publication in 2009, Zizek's rallying cry for a return to communism has been met with skepticism from all positions along the political spectrum. Scholars are quick to point out that Zizek's analysis is not rooted in economics and relies too much upon theoretical analysis. Feminist and gender critic Judith Butler has engaged in an ongoing critical dialogue with Zizek, arguing that he privileges a masculinist-oedipal paradigm that negates a substantive open-ended subject. In "Competing Universalities," Butler argues that Zizek's psychoanalysis fails to adequately articulate the position of the subject. In response to Zizek, she claims that "the question is not simply what an individual can figure out about his or her psyche and its investments (that would make clinical psychoanalysis into the endpoint of politics), but to investigate what kinds of identifications are made possible, are fostered and compelled, within a given political field, and how certain forms of instability are opened up within that political field by virtue of the process of identification itself." Other critics take issue with Zizek's conflation of economic apparatuses and state apparatuses, arguing that *First as Tragedy, Then as Farce* fails to adequately account for the political processes that guide state activity.

In spite of the criticisms leveled at Zizek's analysis and solution, the socioeconomic and sociopolitical environments of late capitalism provide a rich landscape in which to debate the morality of the system. By highlighting two of the prominent crises of the early twenty-first century, Fiona Allon comments in *Journal of Communication Inquiry* that "the very term 'crisis' is in many respects a misnomer; volatility is actually the normal mode of operation for capitalism." Zizek's ability to illustrate volatility as a necessary condition for capitalism raises serious doubt as to whether so-called "compassionate capitalism" could adequately address the lingering social problems. Critic Neil Turnball, writing for *Space and Culture,* argues that Zizek's solution relies upon a nonexistent subjectivity, and in order for a return to communism to be viable, Zizek "needs to find an alternative metaphysics very quickly if his thought is to find critical traction in the new post-Hegelian era of capitalism

Author Slavoj Zizek in 2011. © ERIC FOUGERE/VIP IMAGES/CORBIS

that will emerge after the sound and fury of this crisis has passed into history."

Much of the scholarship on *First as Tragedy, Then as Farce* attempts to navigate Zizek's opaque style and meandering anecdotes in order to flesh out premises that allow him not only to offer up a sound diagnosis but also to identify communism as the legitimate solution to the current set of problems. Given how prevalent commodity fetishism is within late capitalism, Arsalan Khan and Jason Hickel, in their essay in *Anthropological Quarterly,* argue that Zizek provides a compelling description of a trend in which the Left "make[s] capitalism seem palatable and benevolent. Instead of imagining real alternatives to global capitalism, many progressives today content themselves with promoting" virtuous commodities. Following the semiotic analysis of many postmodern thinkers, Zizek's analysis illustrates the extent to which late capitalism has commodified resistance, leaving an external alternative like communism as the only viable means by which ills such as poverty and oppression can be rectified.

BIBLIOGRAPHY

Sources

Allon, Fiona. "Speculating on Everyday Life: The Cultural Economy of the Quotidian." *Journal of*

Communication Inquiry 34.4 (2010): 366-81. *Project Muse*. Web. 1 Aug. 2012.

Butler, Judith, Ernesto Laclau, and Slavoj Zizek. *Contingency, Hegemony, Universality: Contemporary Dialogues on the Left*. London: Verso, 2000. 136-81. Print.

Boucher, Geoff, and Matthew Sharpe. "Financial Crisis, Social Pathologies and 'Generalised Perversion': Questioning Zizek's Diagnosis of the Times." *New Formations* 72.5 (2011): 64-79. *Project Muse*. Web. 1 Aug. 2012.

Hickel, Jason, and Arsalan Khan. "The Culture of Capitalism and the Crisis of Critique." *Anthropological Quarterly* 85.1 (2012): 203-27. *Project Muse*. Web. 1 Aug. 2012.

Turnball, Neil. Rev. of *First as Tragedy, Then as Farce,* by Slavoj Zizek. *Space and Culture* 14.1 (2011): 131-33. *Project Muse*. Web. 1 Aug. 2012.

Zizek, Slavoj. *First as Tragedy, Then as Farce*. New York: Verso, 2009. Print.

Further Reading

Boucher, Geoff, and Matthew Sharpe, eds. *Zizek and Politics: A Critical Introduction*. Edinburgh: Edinburgh UP, 2010. Print.

Boucher, Geoff, Jason Glynos, and Matthew Sharpe, eds. *Traversing the Fantasy: Critical Responses to Slavoj Zizek*. Burlington: Ashgate, 2005. Print.

Dean, Jodi. *Zizek's Politics*. New York: Routledge, 2006. Print.

Johnston, Adrian. *Zizek's Ontology: A Transcendental Materialist Theory of Subjectivity*. Evanston: Northwestern UP, 2008. Print.

Stavrakakis, Yannis. "The Radical Act: Towards a Spatial Critique." *Planning Theory* 10.4 (2011): 301-24. *Project Muse*. Web. 1 Aug. 2012.

Taylor, Paul. *Zizek and the Media*. Cambridge: Polity, 2010. Print.

Josh Harteis

MANIFESTO FOR PHILOSOPHY

Alain Badiou

OVERVIEW

First published in 1989, Alain Badiou's *Manifesto for Philosophy* presents his own thinking as a sustained case for the continuing necessity of philosophy. Consisting of an introduction and eleven chapters that introduce different concepts from Badiou's larger philosophical project, the work offers a vision of philosophy as radically separate from the production of truth. The text is intended as intervention in the largely professional debates surrounding modernity and postmodernity within academic philosophy. Badiou claims that philosophy, facing the catastrophe of World War II, has decided to "plead guilty." He writes, "Neither scientists … nor the military, nor even politicians have considered that the massacres of the century affected them as a body. Sociologists, historians, psychologists, all prosper in innocence. Only philosophers have … encountered the historical and political crimes of this century … as the tribunal of a collective and historic intellectual forfeiture." It is against this forfeiting that Badiou writes.

Manifesto for Philosophy represents an abbreviated, polemical presentation of Badiou's longer text *Being and Event*. As such, its reception cannot really be separated from the larger trajectory of its author. As of 2012 this history is still being written. Unlike other French intellectual celebrities, Badiou has yet to see his work spawn the legions of English-speaking admirers enjoyed by Jacques Derrida, Michel Foucault, Roland Barthes, and, earlier, Jean-Paul Sartre. This could be due to the delay in the translation of his writing or the complexity of the work itself, which draws heavily on mathematics as surely as it does on the history of philosophy. As a pamphlet-sized version of *Being and Event, Manifesto for Philosophy* certainly helped to cement the reputation of its author as one of the most significant thinkers of the late twentieth and early twenty-first centuries.

HISTORICAL AND LITERARY CONTEXT

Among the first of the author's texts to appear in English, *Manifesto for Philosophy* is a shortened presentation of ideas contained in his longer magnum opus, *Being and Event,* first published in 1988. When he produced the "sequel" to this text, *Logics of Worlds,* Badiou also produced a *Second Manifesto for Philosophy.* In both cases Badiou sees himself as rescuing philosophy from denigration at the hands of its official representatives. By separating philosophy from the production of truth, Badiou hopes to set it moving forward once again. Although the intellectual movement or milieu of which Badiou is a representative has yet to be specifically labeled, there is much to say about the intellectual history surrounding his emergence.

In the late 1980s, the historical conjunction that had come to dominate the philosophical conversation was an argument between structuralism, which held that much of human thought and action was determined by larger sociohistorical conditions sedimented over time, and poststructuralism, which went a step further by saying that these structures were themselves unstable and, hence, unknowable—at least to the extent that one might hope to operate outside of them. Badiou sees this constellation of ideas as unable to account satisfactorily for *identity* and for *agency.* He suggests that if history is merely the play of structures of which humans have little knowledge and less control, how can they make sense of the impact of new ideas? Badiou's solution is to draw on set theory in mathematics to link the two together. It is not that the subject is an epiphenomenon of repressive structures, such as language or the unconscious, but rather that the subject only exists to the extent that it reacts against these structures. The impetus for this reaction is the *event,* which disrupts the everyday thinking of what is possible in a given historical context. He writes that "as long as nothing happens, aside from that which conforms to the rules of a state of things, there can admittedly be cognition, correct statements, accumulated knowledge; there cannot be truth."

According to Badiou biographer Peter Hallward, the wager of *Manifesto for Philosophy,* and what situates it firmly in the history of the genre, is to argue that it is in fidelity to these truth events that the subject constitutes itself and, in so doing, reorganizes what is understood to be possible. His archetypal example of such a process is the relationship between St. Paul and Jesus Christ. The appearance of the latter is the event whose truth Paul constructs via his fidelity toward it, precisely as he produces his own subjectivity at the same time. Thus the Christian idea of

Key Facts

Time Period:
Late 20th Century

Movement/Issue:
Structuralism;
Post-structuralism

Place of Publication:
France

Language of Publication:
French

ALAIN BADIOU AND THE THEATER

Though Alain Badiou has much to say about all the arts, the theater holds a particularly central place for the thinker. A playwright himself, Badiou sees in the theater a perfect metaphor for the functioning of his philosophy. His plays have yet to gain a wide audience in the English-speaking world, but there is a growing interest. Moreover, in his recently translated *Rhapsody for the Theater,* Badiou draws a number of remarkable parallels between aspects of his own thought and different parts of the theater. He writes, "Theatre is the proof, for any real and present state, of the link between being and truth. This proof is valid even when theatre shows signs of faintness on this or that point, which is the case of our current situation."

Badiou uses the arts to support his claims in ways different from other philosophers. A certain, performative style is at work in his writing that is distinct from the poetic style he accuses other philosophers of relying upon too heavily. It appears that every word was written with a large, public audience in mind, as opposed to the solitary reader.

universalism is, for Badiou, the truth constructed by the subject, Paul, out of the event of Christ.

By delimiting four conditions of truth—politics, science, art, and love—that precisely do not include philosophy, Badiou clears the space for later,

French philosopher Alain Badiou, author of *Manifesto for Philosophy.*
© ERIC FOUGERE/VIP IMAGES/CORBIS

philosophical investigations of the same. By charging philosophy with the job of considering the radical coexistence of all of these different engines of truth, none of which it produces itself, Badiou destroys philosophy as a discipline capable of producing truth in order to save it as one capable of speaking of its production elsewhere. Whether this has had the intended effect—of restarting the discipline of philosophy—remains to be seen.

THEMES AND STYLE

The central theme of *Manifesto for Philosophy* is how that discipline has been "sutured" with others, causing it to lose its grasp on what makes it distinct from other discourses. Badiou writes, "[A] suspension of philosophy can result from the restriction or blockage of the free play required to define a regime of passage, or of intellectual circulation between the truth procedures conditions philosophy." Thus the "positivist" or "scientistic" suture "expected science to configurate on its own the completed system of truths of the time." Marxism, by contrast, proposed a suture between philosophy and politics. In this way Badiou reads Karl Marx's famous injunction in the "Theses on Feuerbach"—namely that, hitherto, "philosophers have only interpreted the world, [but] the point is change it"—as a case where "the political is philosophically designated as alone apt to practically configurate the general system of sense."

If the nineteenth century was dominated by the scientific and political suturing of philosophy, the twentieth century was defined by the suture with art, a move Badiou associates with Martin Heidegger, who exemplifies the trend, wherein "all philosophers claim to be poets, they all envy poets." It is against this latest confusion that Badiou seeks to "de-suture" philosophy and "proclaim its renaissance." Badiou pursues this by deploying the category of the event and the four conditions of truth, whose coexistence can only be approached by philosophy.

One of the most obvious differences between Badiou and many other late twentieth-century continental philosophers is his polemical style. He does not rely on wordplay, puns, or other meta-linguistic tropes to convey his message. In sharp contrast to the allusive, elliptical, dense, enigmatic prose associated with thinkers such as Philippe Lacoue-Labarthe, Jean-Luc Nancy, Jacques Lacan, and Derrida, Badiou is focused, clear, and definitive, if not always simple or obvious: "Let me make myself clear, it would be tantamount to making the Jews die a second time if their death brought about the end of the fields to which they decisively contributed revolutionary politics on the one hand, rationalist philosophy on the other." Sentiments such as these explain why not only manifestos but also theses, declarations, and other traditional hallmarks of radical writing make up a great deal of Badiou's work.

CRITICAL DISCUSSION

As with the question of *Manifesto for Philosophy*'s immediate reception, the critical response to it cannot be separated from that directed toward Badiou's larger project. Early responses were chiefly concerned with the question of ethics, which has been compounded, for some commentators, by Badiou's own persistent Maoism. Many commentators note that if the event radically reconfigures what is possible in a given situation, is there then no guarantee that the truth of the event will not turn out to be an authoritarian one? In other words, what keeps a person from seeing regressive, genocidal, or otherwise malignant regimes as resulting from acts of political fidelity? Whereas many thinkers chose to locate the irreducible other at the heart of any account of subjective agency, Badiou specifically substitutes this kind of fidelity (toward the other) with fidelity toward the event. Peter Hallward's landmark book on Badiou, *A Subject to Truth,* contrasts clearly with the various forms of other-directed subjectivity that were dominant at the time of *Manifesto for Philosophy*'s writing. Hallward asks: "Where exactly are we to draw the line between the sort of strictly subjective deliberation that is internal to the elaboration of a truth, and a merely external or ideological opposition? Both of Badiou's examples, Leninist and Jacobin, testify to the uncertainty of such a line as much as they illustrate an inventive approach to the resolution of differences."

Badiou has responded by arguing that it is the corruption of a truth that produces evil. A corrupted truth is one in which the process of naming has been taken too far, becoming an attempt at a total specification of the lifeworld by the terms of one specific truth. This is radically anti-philosophical for Badiou because it is precisely the coexistence of multiple truths that requires philosophy.

Regardless of how one feels about Badiou's engagement with ethical questions, there can be little doubt that he has taken his place as one of the most significant thinkers in recent decades. As the rate of translation of his works has increased, his impact on more and more disciplines has grown. He has not shied away from pronouncing on contemporary politics, art, mathematics, poetry, or history. Philosopher and cultural critic Slavoj Zizek has pronounced him a "giant" on the level of Georg Wilhelm Friedrich Hegel, and much of the critical response to Badiou has fallen in line with similarly epic appraisals, either for or against.

BIBLIOGRAPHY

Sources

Badiou, Alain. *Manifesto for Philosophy.* Trans. Norman Madarasz. Albany: SUNY P, 1999. Print.

———. *Ethics: An Essay on the Understanding of Evil.* Trans. Peter Hallward. New York: Verso, 2000. Print.

———. *Infinite Thought: Truth and the Return to Philosophy.* Trans. and ed. Oliver Feltham and Justin Clemens. London: Continuum, 2003. Print.

———. *Saint Paul: The Foundation of Universalism.* Trans. Ray Brassier. Stanford: Stanford UP, 2003. Print.

———. *Being and Event.* Trans. Oliver Feltham. New York: Continuum, 2005. Print.

———. *Logics of Worlds.* Trans. Alberto Toscano. New York: Continuum, 2009. Print.

———. *Second Manifesto for Philosophy.* Trans. Louise Burchill. New York: Polity, 2011. Print.

Hallward, Peter. *Badiou: A Subject to Truth.* New York: Continuum, 2000. Print.

Further Reading

Badiou, Alain. *Theory of the Subject.* Trans. Bruno Boostels. New York: Continuum, 2010. Print.

Critchley, Simon. "Demanding Approval: On the Ethics of Alain Badiou." *Radical Philosophy* 100 (2000): 16-27. Print.

Hallward, Peter. "Ethics without Others: A Reply to Critchley on Badiou's Ethics." *Radical Philosophy* 102 (2000): 27-30. Print.

Ling, Alex. *Badiou and Cinema.* Edinburgh: Edinburgh UP, 2010. Print.

Pluth, Ed. *Badiou: A Philosophy of the New New York.* Polity, 2010. Print.

Stephen Squibb

REALITY HUNGER

A Manifesto

David Shields

✢ **Key Facts**

Time Period:
Early 21st Century

Movement/Issue:
Aesthetics; Formal
experimentalism

Place of Publication:
United States

**Language of
Publication:**
English

OVERVIEW

In *Reality Hunger: A Manifesto* (2010), David Shields argues that literary realism, specifically the linear narrative as it is rendered in contemporary novels and short fiction, is an outmoded form that does not adequately represent the concerns and preoccupations of a twenty-first-century audience. Although the book focuses mainly on contemporary fiction and nonfiction, Shields repeatedly notes transformations in other forms of art, most notably popular music and film, and claims that if literature is to remain relevant, writers must adapt the form and content of their work just as musicians and filmmakers have. While Shields, a creative writing professor, remains conscious of what he understands to be the preferences of the general readership, he appears to address his concerns primarily to fellow writers, critics, and scholars, frequently citing authors such as John D'Agata, Deborah Tall, David Markson, and Thomas Bernhard, all of whom have adapted their prose to a twenty-first-century audience and are known to a relatively small circle of informed readers. Shields presents his case in a series of 618 aphorisms arranged in twenty-six chapters. Though most of the maxims are the words of other thinkers, Shields presents all of the remarks as his own without attribution.

Reality Hunger stimulated an already heated debate in literary circles about the relative merits of fiction and nonfiction. For many, the most striking feature of the work, aside from what appears to be a series of unattributed quotations, is Shields's impassioned defense of James Frey, who, it was discovered, had fabricated the most sensational aspects of his past in his best-selling memoir *A Million Little Pieces*. Another widely commented upon aspect of the book is Shields's account of events in his life, some dating back to his youth, that caused him to lose faith in traditional fiction. *Reality Hunger* is respected in literary circles as a provocative, intelligent work, even if, as many of its readers claim, Shields is mistaken in his assessment of the shortcomings of the modern novel.

HISTORICAL AND LITERARY CONTEXT

Reality Hunger springs from Shields's conviction that methodically plotted, best-selling novels have "never seemed less central to the culture's sense of itself." While other forms of artistic expression, such as music and film, have evolved, he believes much of contemporary fiction remains stuck in the nineteenth century. In music, Shields observes, the disc jockey who samples or mixes parts of various songs into a coherent piece of music has become as central a figure as the songwriter. Likewise, in contemporary film, the mash-up—a film combining disparate cuts from numerous sources—often attracts more viewers on YouTube than the traditional major studio release lures to the cinema. Shields acknowledges that numerous writers have attempted to chart a new course for fiction and lauds the innovations of V.S. Naipaul and W.G. Sebald, among others, who celebrate the "essentially creole form" of the novel by experimenting with form and content. Nevertheless, Shields despairs that the most recognizable contemporary works, such as Ian McEwan's *Atonement* and Jonathan Franzen's *The Corrections,* "sacrifice too much on the altar of plot."

By the time *Reality Hunger* was published in 2010, the production and consumption of nearly all forms of artistic expression had been affected to a significant degree by the Internet and a host of electronic devices, most notably smartphones and, in the case of literature, e-readers that offered consumers unprecedented access to goods and information and, consequently, sent the market into overdrive. He argues that in such a fast-paced society, readers have come to expect the most important ideas in a piece of writing to be quickly and immediately distilled. They are less willing than ever to wade through hundreds of pages of plot, dialogue, and description to arrive at an insight that could have been communicated in much less space without such encumbrances. Furthermore, Shields believes that consumers are much savvier and have come to regard the mass of cultural production—accounts of the lives of actors, politicians, and athletes and news in general—as meticulously choreographed fiction. Therefore, what readers in contemporary society crave is reality, not more fiction. According to Shields, this accounts for the rise in popularity of confessional memoirs and tell-all biographies, as well as reality shows and amateur documentary films. He believes these same consumers also understand that the brand of reality served in confessional memoirs and on reality television might at times alter the facts.

Prior to *Reality Hunger,* Jonathan Lethem explored many of the ideas that Shields examines throughout his book in "The Ecstasy of Influence," which first appeared in *Harper's Magazine* in 2007. For example, Lethem argues that yesterday's art must be ruthlessly appropriated to make new art. Like *Reality Hunger,* most of Lethem's essay is plagiarized. A work that was possibly influenced by Shields is John D'Agata's *The Lifespan of a Fact* (2012), which views nonfiction as an art that grants its author license to alter the facts for the sake of some larger aim.

THEMES AND STYLE

The central theme of *Reality Hunger* is that traditional fiction has failed to keep pace with the technological innovations of contemporary society and the aesthetic advancements of other aspects of contemporary art and popular culture. Shields's purpose, he claims in the book's opening paragraph, "is to write the *ars poetica* for a burgeoning group of interrelated but unconnected artists in a multitude of forms and media—lyric essay, prose poem, collage novel, visual art, film, television, radio, performance art, rap, stand-up comedy, graffiti—who are breaking larger and larger chunks of 'reality' into their work."

Rather than the well-told tale, Shields promotes collage, the literary equivalent of sampling or the mash-up, a technique wherein content arises not out of plot and character but appears randomly and spontaneously, drawing from an array of sources, intermixing the banal with the spectacular and sensational, and blurring the line between fact and fiction. Collage, by its very nature, involves appropriating the work of others and making it one's own. Shields does exactly this, copying and pasting the words of artists such as James Joyce, Vladimir Nabokov, Kurt Cobain, Sonny Rollins, and Werner Herzog. He does not attribute any quotations to their authors until the appendix of the book, and he does so only because the lawyers at Random House demanded it. In fact, in a brief note preceding the appendix, he urges readers to cut it out of the book.

The language of *Reality Hunger* is relentlessly provocative, often, it seems, merely for the sake of being provocative. Shields uses the example of Frey, whom he calls a "bad writer," to make the case that most forms of nonfiction are more like art than journalism. As such, memoirs should not be fact-checked but rather enjoyed for the sensations they evoke and the ideas they explore. Alluding to *A Million Little Pieces,* Shields writes, "I'm drawn to the confessional mode because I like the way the temperature in the room goes up when I say, 'I did this' (even if I really didn't)."

IAN McEWAN'S *ATONEMENT*

British novelist Ian McEwan may not write the type of books David Shields prefers, but he has appropriated others' work in the manner that Shields endorses. In 2006 McEwan was taken to task for language in his 2001 best seller *Atonement* that is nearly identical to Lucilla Andrews's description of her treatment of English soldiers wounded at Dunkirk in World War II. While many took a charitable view toward McEwan, Jack Shafer, writing for *Slate,* condemned the Booker Prize-winning author, putting the prose of McEwan and Andrews side by side to make his case. Shafer notes that in *No Time for Romance,* her memoir from 1977, Andrews writes, "Our 'nursing' seldom involved more than dabbing gentian violet on ringworm, aquaflavine emulsion on cuts and scratches, lead lotion on bruises and sprains." Meanwhile, in *Atonement* McEwan writes of Briony Tallis, the novel's heroine and a wartime nurse, "In the way of medical treatments, she had already dabbed gentian violet on ringworm, aquaflavine emulsion on a cut, and painted lead lotion on a bruise."

McEwan mentions Andrews in the "Author's Note" at the end of the novel and acknowledges her memoir as a valuable resource at numerous readings and speaking engagements when promoting his book. When the story broke in 2006, several established writers argued on McEwan's behalf, including Martin Amis, Zadie Smith, and, most notably, Thomas Pynchon, who wrote a letter to McEwan's publisher thanking the author for lifting the text and sharing Andrews's irresistible phrasing with a larger audience.

CRITICAL DISCUSSION

Although *Reality Hunger* received mixed reviews and provoked outrage among defenders of contemporary realist fiction, most critics agree Shields has written a timely and passionate argument on behalf of increasing popular forms of literature, namely the lyric essay and the memoir. Fellow writers regard his book as an important contribution to a heated debate in literary circles about the current and future state of literary prose. For example, writing in the *Guardian,* novelist Blake Morrison, who disagrees with nearly all of Shields's claims about contemporary fiction, calls *Reality Hunger* a "spirited polemic on behalf of nonfiction" and concedes, "The fiction vs non-fiction debate has become intense in recent years, and Shields cranks it up a notch." Similarly, in her review for *Bookforum,* novelist Jami Attenburg writes, "Despite my quarrels with the book's premise, I find Shields's book absorbing, even inspiring.... I am grateful for Shields's sometimes brutal interrogation of what I believe. His critiques led me to reconsider my own creative process." Luc Sante, writing for the *New York Times,* observes that *Reality Hunger* "positively throbs with personality" and calls Shields a "broad-minded revolutionary, urging a hundred flowers to bloom, toppling only the outmoded and corrupt institutions."

However, even as they laud Shields for marshaling a compelling set of observations, most critics agree that his denunciation of the traditionally plotted novel is unlikely to have any impact on the form. Attenburg, for example, claims that "the novel is neither dead nor dormant, and it's not going anywhere anytime soon. People are still going to read novels and short stories, since storytelling fulfills a basic human need. Works of fiction continue to comfort, to challenge, and to entertain." Likewise, Tim Parks, writing for the *New York Review of Books,* notes, "So while sharing [Shields'] ennui with a wide range of fiction and thoroughly enjoying his capacity to seduce and perplex, it's hardly a criticism to say I'm not convinced that the novel can't play some exciting cards."

More pointedly, some critics have found that rather than gaining momentum and intellectual credibility, Shields's argument unravels. In the end, these critics claim, by renouncing plot, he ultimately misunderstands how fiction works. According to Morrison, "The real problem [with the book], though, is the central thesis. It's smart, stimulating, and aphoristic, even when the aphorisms are stolen. But the more you think about it, the dodgier it seems." In the final analysis, Morrison contends, "Shields sells fiction short.... Novels with a clear plot and definite resolution can still be full of ambiguity, darkness, and doubt." Likewise, Attenburg suggests that "as the book builds its principal case—as a manifesto against many forms of fiction—it becomes less useful and ultimately less convincing." For Attenburg, fiction is as authentic as the alternatives Shields champions because "authors of fiction always seek an emotional truth—and that's as true a gesture as possible."

BIBLIOGRAPHY

Sources

Attenburg, Jamie. "The Shock of the Real." Rev. of *Reality Hunger: A Manifesto,* by David Shields. *Bookforum.* Bookforum, Feb.-Mar. 2010. Web. 8 Nov. 2012.

Morrison, Blake. Rev. of *Reality Hunger: A Manifesto,* by David Shields. *Guardian.* Guardian News and Media, 19 Feb. 2010. Web. 8 Nov. 2012.

Parks, Tim. "America First?" Rev. of *Reality Hunger: A Manifesto,* by David Shields. *New York Review of Books.* NYREV, 15 July 2010. Web. 8 Nov. 2012.

Sante, Luc. "The Fiction of Memory." Rev. of *Reality Hunger: A Manifesto,* by David Shields. *New York Times.* The New York Times Company, 12 Mar. 2010. Web. 9 Nov. 2012.

Shafer, Jack. "What Did Ian McEwan Do?" *Slate.* The Slate Group, 8 Dec. 2006. Web. 9 Nov. 2012.

Shields, David. *Reality Hunger: A Manifesto.* New York: Vintage, 2010. Print.

Further Reading

D'Agata. John. *The Lifespan of a Fact.* New York: W. W. Norton, 2012. Print.

Frey, James. *A Million Little Pieces.* Norwell: Anchor, 2005. Print.

Gunkel, David. J. "Rethinking the Digital Remix: Mash-ups and the Metaphysics of Sound Recording." *Popular Music and Society* 31.4 (2008): 489-510. Print.

Lethem, Jonathan. *The Ecstasy of Influence: Nonfictions, Etc.* New York: Vintage, 2012. Print.

Markson, David. *This Is Not a Novel.* Berkeley: Counterpoint, 2001. Print.

Shields, David. *Enough about You: Notes toward the New Autobiography.* Berkeley: Soft Skull, 2009. Print.

Tall, Deborah. *A Family of Strangers.* Louisville: Sarabande, 2006.

Widdicombe, Lizzie. "The Plagiarist's Tale." *New Yorker.* Condé Nast, 13 Feb. 2012. Web. 8 Nov. 2012.

Joseph Campana

THE ROMANTIC MANIFESTO
A Philosophy of Literature
Ayn Rand

✣ **Key Facts**

Time Period:
Mid-20th Century

Movement/Issue:
Objectivism; Aesthetics

Place of Publication:
United States

Language of Publication:
English

OVERVIEW

Written by Ayn Rand, *The Romantic Manifesto: A Philosophy of Literature,* a book of aesthetic and literary theory published in 1969 with a revised edition appearing in 1975, elaborates a detailed series of arguments about the nature and function of art in general and literature in particular. Consisting primarily of a series of essays originally published in Rand's newsletter the *Objectivist,* the book proceeds from a set of tenets largely derived from Rand's philosophy of objectivism, which emphasizes individuality and the primacy of human reason as a means of apprehending objective reality. The book asserts that art serves as a way for humans to transform metaphysical concepts into concrete form, allowing them to be contemplated in a conscious way. The nature of this transformation, which is largely determined by the individual artist's values and "sense of life," informs Rand's championing of romanticism over naturalism. The former, in her view, affirms free will through its selective representation of reality, while the latter, also selective but purposefully focusing on banality or bleakness, affirms determinism.

Largely dismissed or ignored upon its initial publication, *The Romantic Manifesto* remains a fairly obscure work, both within the field of aesthetic theory and within Rand's own bibliography. Although objectivism in general—particularly in its political and economic ramifications—has proven to be one of the most influential philosophical movements of the twentieth century and remains a significant ideological force today, this particular manifestation of it made relatively little impact. Since the turn of the twenty-first century, however, the book has attracted renewed critical attention—albeit mostly from scholars specializing in Rand's writing—as an unjustly neglected work, unique in its promulgation of a coherent theory, based on the philosophical principles of objectivism, about the role of art in human life.

HISTORICAL AND LITERARY CONTEXT

Much of *The Romantic Manifesto* is a response to what Rand sees as the debased quality of most modern art and literature, itself the product of contemporary philosophical impoverishment. The literary school of naturalism, which emphasizes everyday realities and the influence of social and biological forces on the shaping of individual lives, had, since its emergence in the late nineteenth century, substantially impacted the state of contemporary literature. Rand rejects this in favor of romanticism, which she somewhat idiosyncratically defines as "a category of art based on the recognition of the principle that man possesses the faculty of volition," although she repudiates the tendency among nineteenth-century romanticists to elevate emotion and irrationality over reason, citing this quality as a primary cause of romanticism's historical defeat by naturalism.

By the time *The Romantic Manifesto* appeared in 1969, the type of romantic literature Rand advocates, characterized by idealized depictions of plot and character that demonstrate the positive potential of humanity, was rare. Some romantic literature appeared in a degraded form in popular genres, such a detective fiction or thrillers, but the prevailing literary climate was largely the product of naturalism, itself "an outgrowth of the altruist morality" and therefore "a long, wailing plea for pity, for tolerance, for the forgiveness of anything," according to Rand. Contemporary literature was marked by a fondness for flawed characters and plots demonstrating the foibles of human nature, a tendency that Rand considered to have progressed beyond naturalism's "journalistic" emphasis on realism, turning instead into a grotesque opposite of romanticism's idealism.

The Romantic Manifesto may be seen as part of a long tradition of writings about the nature and purpose of art and literature. Its most obvious antecedent—and the only one Rand herself cites as an influence—is the work of Aristotle, whose detailed explication of the various aspects of poetry and drama in *Poetics* prefigures Rand's own anatomization of art and literature in much of her text. Likewise, Aristotle's supposed assertion that, as quoted by Rand in her book, "history represents things as they are, while fiction represents them as they might be and ought to be" forms the backbone of many of Rand's arguments in favor of romanticism. These arguments also bear the influence of the aesthetic theories promulgated during the nineteenth century that brought both romanticism and naturalism to prominence.

Although *The Romantic Manifesto*'s influence on subsequent literature is not generally regarded as immense, it may nevertheless be seen as having impacted (directly or indirectly) the countless authors whose work was inspired by Rand or objectivism. Today its most obvious literary relevance lies in its elaboration of the aesthetic principles that ostensibly guided Rand's composition of novels, such as *The Fountainhead* (1943) and *Atlas Shrugged* (1957), both of which have had an influence on contemporary literature. Meanwhile, contemporary authors such as Quent Cordair and Helen Knode are among those who have avowedly applied Rand's aesthetic theory, as expressed in *The Romantic Manifesto*, to their own writing.

THEMES AND STYLE

The principal theme of *The Romantic Manifesto* is that the existence of art serves an important cognitive function, one that romantic art is best suited to perform in a way consistent with objectivist beliefs. Rand defines art as "a selective re-creation of reality according to an artist's metaphysical value-judgments." It provides a way for people to turn abstract concepts into tangible manifestations, "just as language converts abstractions into the psycho-epistemological equivalent of concretes … so art converts man's metaphysical abstractions into the equivalent of concretes, into specific entities open to man's direct perception." These entities vary widely depending on the philosophical outlook of the artist in question, but ideally they should give a person "the experience of living in a world where things are *as they ought to be*. This experience is of crucial importance to him: it is his psychological life line." The sordid "realism" of naturalism is inimical to this project, and Rand counters naturalism's claim to truthfulness by describing herself as a romantic realist.

Since most of *The Romantic Manifesto* originally appeared in Rand's newsletter, it is unsurprisingly characterized by frequent appeals to the ideological tenets of objectivism, particularly its opposition to altruism and its belief in the primacy of human reason. The distaste for heroic protagonists among contemporary intellectuals is thus described as the product of "the stagnant illusion of their altruist-collectivist upbringing: the vision of a cloddish, humble, inarticulate people whose 'voice' (and masters) they were to be." Likewise, the words *rational* and *irrational* are constantly deployed as, respectively, a profound validation and a damning epithet. The book's arguments are generally oriented toward supplementing an already held system of philosophical beliefs with a compatible aesthetic theory.

Stylistically, *The Romantic Manifesto* is generally marked by straightforward, professorial language in

AYN RAND IN THE 1960S

The essays collected in *The Romantic Manifesto* were for the most part originally written and published throughout the 1960s, a decade when Rand's literary output permanently switched from fiction to nonfiction, and her public identity largely shifted from that of a novelist to that of a cultural commentator and philosophical guru. She ceased writing novels following the release of her magnum opus *Atlas Shrugged* in 1957, and she spent much of the following decade giving lectures on college campuses and at other public forums, as well as writing and publishing a total of four books on objectivist philosophy.

Meanwhile, the Nathaniel Branden Institute, founded in 1958 by Rand's friend and former romantic partner Nathaniel Branden, promoted the objectivist cause throughout much of the decade through a series of lecture courses and other material. The institute's operations were abruptly suspended in 1968, following a rancorous falling-out between Rand and Branden, who was thereafter excluded from the objectivist movement along with his separated wife, Barbara, later the author of the first book-length biography of Rand, *The Passion of Ayn Rand* (1986). Rand continued to write steadily, although the tone of her post-1968 writing is often regarded as considerably more bitter.

its lectures on aesthetic philosophy, although more heated and occasionally extravagant language appears in its polemical sections applying that philosophy to specific issues. The book's first half tends toward more theoretical passages; in these even emphatic statements of artistic judgment are made in a relatively restrained manner, as when, during a discussion of literary principles, Rand criticizes Theodore Dreiser's *An American Tragedy* for failing to integrate its plot and theme. She writes, "Here, the author attempts to give significance to a trite story by tacking on to it a theme which is not related to or demonstrated by its events." In contrast, the book's less abstract second half contains intemperate language such as that used to assert that "it is the Romantic or value-oriented vision of life that the Naturalists regard as 'superficial'—and it is the vision which extends as far as the bottom of a garbage can that they regard as 'profound.'"

CRITICAL DISCUSSION

Outside of objectivist circles, *The Romantic Manifesto* attracted relatively little comment, particularly in comparison to some of Rand's other writings. The reviews that it did receive from mainstream publications were generally either dismissive or actively hostile and often seemed to be colored by the reviewer's opinions on Rand's political views. Peter Michelson's scathing assessment in the *New Republic* exemplifies the harsher appraisals, asserting that the book

Stamp commemorating Ayn Rand, whose works include a number of novels and *The Romantic Manifesto: A Philosophy of Literature* (1969). AP PHOTO/U.S. POSTAL SERVICE

and Louis Torres observe that "in contrast with Rand's thought on ethics, politics, and epistemology … her philosophy of art has received little critical or scholarly attention, even among her admirers." It nonetheless serves as a significant theoretical foundation for the disdain often expressed by contemporary objectivists and others for the supposed willful ugliness of much modern and postmodern art.

In the twenty-first century *The Romantic Manifesto* has been the subject of renewed scholarly analysis. Such studies have been predominantly (though not exclusively) by objectivist critics and often take the form of an expansion or elaboration of Rand's theories. A noteworthy example of this trend is Torres and Kamhi's *What Art Is: The Esthetic Philosophy of Ayn Rand* (2000), which elucidates and contextualizes Rand's ideas at great length, then brings them to bear on a largely negative evaluation of the work of specific artists, such as Samuel Beckett and John Cage. Another, more speculative example is Stephen Cox's 2004 article "Completing Rand's Literary Theory," in *Journal of Ayn Rand Studies,* which attempts to extrapolate further principles from what Rand has written. Discussions of *The Romantic Manifesto* outside the confines of explicitly objectivist scholarship is less common, but one example is Tom Anderson's 1988 article "A Structure for Pedagogical Art Criticism," in the journal *Studies in Art Education,* which incorporates Rand's text into its examination of the ways in which art is analyzed.

BIBLIOGRAPHY

Sources

Anderson, Tom. "A Structure for Pedagogical Art Criticism." *Studies in Art Education* 30.1 (1988): 28-38. *JSTOR.* Web. 12 Sept. 2012.

Cox, Stephen. "Completing Rand's Literary Theory." *Journal of Ayn Rand Studies* 6.1 (2004): 67-89. Print.

Kamhi, Michelle Marder, and Louis Torres. "Critical Neglect of Ayn Rand's Theory of Art." *Journal of Ayn Rand Studies* 2.1 (2000): 1-46. Print.

Michelson, Peter. "Fictive Babble." Rev. of *The Romantic Manifesto: A Philosophy of Literature,* by Ayn Rand. *New Republic* 162.8 (1970): 21-24. *New Republic Archive.* Web. 12 Sept. 2012.

Rand, Ayn. *The Romantic Manifesto: A Philosophy of Literature.* Rev. ed. New York: Signet, 1975. Print.

Torres, Louis, and Michelle Marder Kamhi. *What Art Is: The Esthetic Philosophy of Ayn Rand.* Chicago: Open Court, 2000. Print.

Further Reading

Baker, James T. *Ayn Rand.* Boston: Twayne, 1987. Print.

Bissell, Roger E. "Langer and Camus: Unexpected Post-Kantian Affinities with Rand's Aesthetics." *Journal of Ayn Rand Studies* 7.1 (2005): 57-77. Print.

Heller, Anne C. *Ayn Rand and the World She Made.* New York: Talese-Doubleday, 2009. Print.

"augments ignorance with incoherence," mocking Rand's designation of James Bond and Mike Hammer as the closest modern literary approximations of romantic heroes and excoriating what Michelson (along with other reviewers) saw as Rand's woefully misinformed beliefs about the nature of romantic and naturalist art. He writes, "To contend that Romanticism affirms human value while Naturalism denies it is just wrong."

As the book that established the aesthetic principles of objectivism, *The Romantic Manifesto* is a seminal work in the codification of that movement, although its legacy is perhaps less pronounced than that of other objectivist texts. In their 2000 article "Critical Neglect of Ayn Rand's Theory of Art," in *Journal of Ayn Rand Studies,* Michelle Marder Kamhi

Lipp, Ronald F. "*Atlas* and Art." *Ayn Rand's* Atlas Shrugged: *A Philosophical and Literary Companion.* Ed. Edward W. Younkins. Aldershot: Ashgate, 2007. 143-55. Print.

Peikoff, Leonard. *Objectivism: The Philosophy of Ayn Rand.* New York: Dutton, 1991. Print.

Rand, Ayn. *The Art of Fiction: A Guide for Writers and Readers.* Ed. Tore Boeckmann. New York: Plume, 2000. Print.

Riggenbach, Jeff. "Ayn Rand's Influence on American Popular Fiction." *Journal of Ayn Rand Studies* 6.1 (2004): 91-144. Print.

Thomas, William, ed. *The Literary Art of Ayn Rand.* N.p.: Objectivist Center, 2005. Print.

Vacker, Barry. "Skyscrapers, Supermodels, and Strange Attractors: Ayn Rand, Naomi Wolf, and the Third Wave Aesthos." *Feminist Interpretations of Ayn Rand.* Ed. Mimi Reisel Gladstein and Chris Matthew Sciabarra. University Park: Pennsylvania State UP, 1999. 115-56. Print.

James Overholtzer

POETRY AND PERFORMANCE

L.S.D. MANIFESTO

Elizabeth LeCompte

OVERVIEW

Composed by playwright Elizabeth LeCompte and the experimental theater company the Wooster Group, the *L.S.D. Manifesto* (1984) decries the staid state of contemporary American theater and calls for a radically new form of stage performances to reflect the jumbled brutality of modern life. The manifesto was published in conjunction with the production of LeCompte's *L.S.D. (... Just the High Points ...)*, a play she wrote for the Wooster Group. The piece displays a mélange of disparate elements, including interviews, writings, music, dance, video, excerpts from other plays (including Arthur Miller's *The Crucible*), and recreated debates between conservative FBI and White House operative G. Gordon Liddy and psychedelic-drug advocate Timothy Leary. The manifesto describes the aim and form of an original, radically inclusive L.S.D. theater that would offer a skewed—and sometimes drug-altered—take on modern dramatic convention.

While *L.S.D. (... Just the High Points ...)* sparked controversy, in large part for its unapproved use of scenes from *The Crucible*, the *L.S.D. Manifesto* was barely noticed when it was issued. It did, however, help to articulate the avant-garde project of the Wooster Group. Founded in 1975 by LeCompte and playwright Spalding Gray, the company is notable for its creation of a cohesive body of subversive work during its more than thirty-five years in existence. The *L.S.D. Manifesto* explicates the project that has undergirded the group's various productions: to reject the conventions of realism in order to engage more viscerally with the true complexity of reality. Today, the manifesto is seen as an important document in the history of one of America's most important innovative theater groups.

HISTORICAL AND LITERARY CONTEXT

Originating in the mid-1900s, American avant-garde theater exploded in size and relevance in the 1960s, when companies such as New York City's Living Theatre, according to Arnold Aronson's *American Avant-Garde Theatre* (2000), "began to search for new forms of theater that would better express the ideas of a new world." At the time, the civil rights movement, protests against the Vietnam War, and the explosion of the hippie counterculture were transforming how

people saw the world. Aimed at delivering a radical alternative to the conventionality of Broadway shows, these ensembles became known collectively as Off Broadway. In 1967 Richard Schechner formed the pioneering Performance Group, which explored collective creation and methods of involving the audience in dramatic events. Aronson quotes Schechner as describing their productions as "environmental theatre," designed "to demand changes in the social order." LeCompte joined the company in 1970, as did the performer and playwright Spalding Gray. In 1975, ultimately disillusioned with their experience, the two founded the Wooster Group, devoting themselves to exploring (Aronson quotes Gray as saying) "a dialectic between ... life and theatre rather than between role and text." At the time, New York's alternative theater scene involved minimalist solo performances in bars, clubs, and other unconventional spaces. Rather than representing characters acting out a cogent dramatic plot, performers based their work on autobiographical material, informed by self-awareness and the process of communicating with an audience. The Wooster Group's subversive agenda differed in that it experimented with collaborative theatrical performance, staging, and text.

By the time the *L.S.D. Manifesto* was issued in 1984, avant-garde theater had been culturally and artistically marginalized. The 1980s witnessed the growth of alternative but less cutting-edge performance activity, particularly in New York City's East Village. Aronson describes the scene there as a "mixture of performance art and more or less conventional plays, many with gay and lesbian themes and often performed with a strong camp sensibility." By contrast, the Wooster Group was located in the more affluent and traditional Soho neighborhood. Its manifesto acknowledged, engaged with, and undermined classical theater, avant-garde tradition, and the contemporary alternative theater scene in New York.

While drawing on a long tradition of avant-garde manifestos—including the *Futurist Manifesto* (1909), André Breton's *Surrealist Manifesto* (1924), and the Situationist International revolutionary movement's *Report on the Construction of Situations* (1957)—the *L.S.D. Manifesto* explicitly responds to the 1920 *Dada Manifesto*; it opens with "*DADAIST MANIFESTO (1920)*" (Aronson reproduced the manifesto in a 1985

+ *Key Facts*

Time Period:
Late 20th Century

Movement/Issue:
Theatrical avant-gardism

Place of Publication:
United States

Language of Publication:
English

ELIZABETH LeCOMPTE: RADICAL REWORKER

In 1975 Elizabeth LeCompte and Spalding Gray formed the Wooster Group, an acting workshop that emphasizes a more personal approach to the theater than that of the Performance Group, where they had met in 1970. The result was *Sakonnet Pointi* (1975), a play they "composed and directed" cooperatively. The story of Gray's mother's suicide, it was the first play in what would become the autobiographical series *Three Places in Rhode Island,* which also includes *Rumstick Road* (1978), *Nyatt School* (1978), and *Point Judith (an epilog)* (1979). By 1980 the Performance Group had folded and the Wooster Group had taken its place in the Performing Garage on Wooster Street in Manhattan's Soho neighborhood.

With a core group of actors that included Willem Dafoe for twenty-five years, LeCompte led the Wooster Group to the fore of American avant-garde theater. Often appropriating and altering established works, as in *L.S.D. (... Just the High Points ...),* she was known for her irreverent and often controversial take on theatrical convention. In 1982 she lost funding from the New York State Council on the Arts because of her use of blackface in *Route 1 & 9* (1981), which includes sections from Thornton Wilder's 1938 play *Our Town.* In 1991 she received an OBIE award from the *Village Voice* for her work with the Wooster Group. Four years later she was awarded a prestigious MacArthur Fellowship. In 2007 she adapted *Hamlet* as the Wooster Group's first performance of William Shakespeare and described the play on the theater's website as "a hypothetical theater piece from the fragmentary evidence of the edited film." LeCompte and the Wooster Group remain committed to the *L.S.D. Manifesto's* call for "a New *Art* (Theatre)."

(1991), *To You, the Birdie!* (2002), and *Vieux Carré* (2011; a restaging of the 1977 Tennessee Williams play), the group has continued to create new forms of multimedia theater (incorporating film and video, for instance) and to challenge audience expectations, reframing passé performative conventions such as blackface in their ongoing pursuit of "the Realization of New Ideals."

THEMES AND STYLE

The central theme of the *L.S.D. Manifesto* is that theater must engage more directly and deeply with the incomprehensibility and cruelty of contemporary life. The dominant strain of American drama, the manifesto laments, is concerned only with "Respectable civic distinctions" and offers audiences merely the delusion of a "comfortable Life free from *Content* (Ambivalence) or *Strife* (Contradiction)." L.S.D., the designation the manifesto uses for its countercultural approach to theater, offers an antidote to the mainstream's sanitized art. The document proposes acting on the premise that "Life appears as a simultaneous Muddle of Noises, Colors and Spiritual Rhythms, which is taken unmodified into *Dadaist Art* (the Theatre), with all the sensational Screams and Fevers of its Reckless everyday Psyche and with all its brutal Reality."

The manifesto achieves its rhetorical effect through appeals, often using superlatives, to the lofty expectations and demands of American theatergoers. The authors refer to the "highest *Art* (Theater)" and the "best and most extraordinary Artists." Employing the inclusive first-person plural pronoun, the manifesto asks, "Have the Expressionists (Has Today's Theatre) fulfilled our Expectations of an Art that burns the Essence of Life into our Flesh?" Their answer is "NO! NO! NO!" in bold type and centered on the page. The enthusiasm of the manifesto's diction amplifies the stakes of its argument: it calls not for an innovative style of stage play but for a vital response to the world as it is, engaging the reader in this important struggle to reject the "Aesthetic Attitude toward Life" and instead respond viscerally. The manifesto has two parts, the first detailing its artistic aims and the second, *L.S.D. Manifesto (2),* presenting Leary's response to a question about being harassed for his "unorthodox beliefs." Leary replied, "The more energy that is directed against me, the more energy that is available for me." The apparent purpose of this section is to assert that the Wooster Group, like Leary, feeds off those who question its aims.

Stylistically, the *L.S.D. Manifesto* is distinguished by its use of crossed-out words, which imbue the text with a sense of immediacy and extend the scope of its claims by implication rather than argument. The heading that includes the title and year of the *Dadaist Manifesto* lends historical authority to the argument and, in that it is marked as deleted, demonstrates a

essay in *Drama Review*). Written by the poet and painter Francis Picabia, the *Dada Manifesto* declares the antiwar, radical leftist, reason- and logic-resistant, nonsensical, irrational, and intuition-based agenda of a new counter-art movement; it also defends Dada against perceived attacks by the cubists, a rival, earlier-established movement (led by Pablo Picasso and Georges Braque) whose basis Picabia deemed was a "total famine of ideas." By modeling their manifesto on Picabia's, the Wooster Group linked their call for a revolutionary revitalization of American theater to Dada's earlier call for artistic reinvention, a reinvention that included important origins of performance art and avant-garde theater.

In the nearly two decades since its publication, the *L.S.D. Manifesto* has provided a template for the ongoing artistic mission of the Wooster Group. Staged in conjunction with the manifesto's issuance, *L.S.D. (... Just the High Points ...)* is described as "a four-part examination of hysteria and hallucinations" on the group's website. In such plays as *Brace Up!*

desire to break with the past. The first word of the document, "Art," is also crossed out and is replaced with "Theatre" in parentheses. The replacement suggests that the authors could make their case more broadly and that they emphatically refuse to do so. Through the inclusion of deleted words, the text displays the process of its own composition and reflects the manifesto's argument: it includes the chaos, "Noise," and open-endedness that more refined forms of writing would omit. This is further demonstrated in the second part of the manifesto, which consists only of an interview question and answer and which concludes with the phrase "(TO BE CONTINUED)."

CRITICAL RECEPTION

When the *L.S.D. Manifesto* first appeared in 1984, it received little notice except as an addendum to *L.S.D. (… Just the High Points …),* while LeCompte's play generated interest, criticism, and controversy. In a *New York Times* review, Mel Gussow writes that the performance "still seems a work in process" and criticized its lack of subtlety and cohesiveness. In his *Drama Review* article, Aronson summarizes contemporary reviews as "tend[ing] to dismiss the work as mere self-indulgence." The most pointed response to the production came from Miller, whose denunciation of the Wooster Group's use of his *Crucible* text forced the show to close in November 1984, just months after its premiere. The section was then rewritten to address Miller's complaint, and *L.S.D. (… Just the High Points …)* reopened in January 1985.

The *L.S.D. Manifesto* nevertheless remained an important statement of the group's avant-garde aims. According to Aronson's history text, "The group's seemingly steadfast refusal to adopt a point of view—the apparent apoliticism in the context of politically volatile material—served, ironically, to provoke political responses and to create inflammatory reactions where none was necessarily sought." Over the course of the group's existence, the manifesto has served as a statement of this refusal and of a commitment to "(exploding) all the slogans of *Ethics* (Morality), *Culture* (Politics), and *Inwardness* (Psychology)." Since its composition, it has attracted limited scholarly attention for its significance within the history of the Wooster Group and the American avant-garde theater scene at large.

Some theater scholars have studied the manifesto's importance as a link between different eras of international avant-gardism. In *Poetry of the Revolution: Marx, Manifestos, and the Avant-Gardes* (2005), Martin Puchner situates the *L.S.D. Manifesto* within the context of Dadaism and of the writings included in the *Drama Review,* an academic journal founded in 1955 that examines theater within social, economic, and political frameworks. The journal reprinted the manifesto in 1985. Puchner argues that the statement's inclusion of struck-out allusions to Dadaism "corresponds precisely" to the *Drama Review*'s "strategy of turning to the historical avant-garde to revive the avant-garde of the present: if previous manifestos are supposed to stimulate new ones, then these manifestos will be torn between the present and the past, creating the new in the form of a pastiche of the past."

BIBLIOGRAPHY

Sources

Aronson, Arnold. *American Avant-Garde Theatre: A History.* New York: Routledge, 2000. Print.

———. "The Wooster Group's *L.S.D. (… Just the High Points …).*" *Drama Review* 20.2 (1985): 65-77. Print.

Gussow, Mel. "Stage: Wooster Group." Rev. of *L.S.D. (… Just the High Points…).* Dir. Elizabeth LeCompte. *New York Times* 31 Oct. 1984: C28. *ProQuest Historical Newspapers.* Web. 23 July 2012.

Picabia, Francis. *I Am a Beautiful Monster: Poetry, Prose, and Provocation.* Boston: MIT, 2007. Print.

Puchner, Martin. *Poetry of the Revolution: Marx, Manifestos, and the Avant-Gardes.* Princeton: Princeton UP, 2005. Print.

The Wooster Group. The Wooster Group. Web. 16 Aug. 2012.

Further Reading

Auslander, Philip. *Presence and Resistance: Postmodernism and Cultural Politics in Contemporary American Performance.* Ann Arbor: U Michigan P, 1997. Print.

———. "Task and Vision: Willem Defoe in *L.S.D.*" *Drama Review* 20.2 (1985): 94-98. Print.

Callens, J., ed. *The Wooster Group and Its Traditions.* Brussels: Lang, 2004. Print.

Champagne, Lenora. "Always Starting New: Elizabeth LeCompte." *Drama Review* 25.3 (1981): 19-28. Print.

Goldberg, RoseLee. *Performance: Live Art Since 1960.* New York: Abrams, 1998. Print.

Marranca, B. "The Wooster Group: A Dictionary of Ideas." *Performing Arts Journal* 25:2 (2003): 1-18. Print.

Quick, Andrew. *The Wooster Group Workbook.* New York: Routledge, 2007. Print.

Savran, David. "Arthur Miller and *The Crucible.*" *Drama Review* 20.2 (1985): 99-109. Print.

———. *Breaking the Rules: The Wooster Group.* New York: Theatre Communications, 1988. Print.

Schechner, R. *The End of Humanism: Writings on Performance.* New York: Performing Arts Journal, 1982. Print.

Theodore McDermott

A Manifesto for the New Sincerity

Jesse Thorn

OVERVIEW

Posted to the website *Maximum Fun* on March 26, 2006, the brief essay titled "A Manifesto for the New Sincerity" announced the death of irony and tentatively offered an alternative way of appreciating cultural objects in a postmodern world. The manifesto marks Jesse Thorn's foray into an already-crowded critical discussion that intensified after September 11, 2001, when film and literary critics began proffering competing characterizations of the sentiment and style that might replace irony in a new, darker age of American culture. Drawing on an assortment of film, television, and consumer product texts, radio host and author Jesse Thorn articulates a "radical new ethos" to replace irony and sincerity with earnest appreciation. Addressed to readers at large, Thorn's manifesto does not make demands but rather defines "New Sincerity" as a cultural shift already well underway.

Commentators on Thorn's manifesto—including visitors to his website and guests on his radio shows—initially expressed suspicion about the methods and claims of Thorn's new sincerity ethos. Some described it as ultimately indistinguishable from the irony it aimed to replace. Such critics saw Thorn's vision of "irony and sincerity combined like Voltron," a 1980s cartoon robot, as a sarcastic or even cynical rebranding of warmed-over pop cultural artifacts. Nevertheless, Thorn continued to apply the perspective to an ever-widening range of cultural objects via his radio show, *The Sound of Young America* (later continued as *Bullseye*). Although some maintain that new sincerity is one in a poorly differentiated series of cultural impulses with similar names, critics willing to take Thorn at his word have related the phenomenon to highly regarded antecedents in Russian literary history.

HISTORICAL AND LITERARY CONTEXT

"A Manifesto for the New Sincerity" responds to a perceived opportunity to replace irony, a prevailing element of American cultural discourse, with a worthier ethos. Thorn explains that the 9/11 attacks signaled for many the death of irony in mass media. Cultural critic Lynn Spigel notes in a 2004 essay for *American Quarterly* that in late 2001 virtually every major television humorist "met the late-night audience with dead seriousness." In the essay Spigel labels

this backlash a "new sincerity," though she does not construe the term as describing a deliberate or organized movement.

Thorn argues that by 2006, when he published his manifesto, irony had indeed died, though it had not been annihilated in the 9/11 attacks as critics had declared. According to the manifesto, irony passed away "slowly, quietly, of old age." Whereas Spigel expounds on the chilling effect of 9/11 on American media, Thorn emphasizes the resilience of such "great exemplars" of irony as satirical newspaper *The Onion* and television comic Jon Stewart. He envisions a teleological state in which the "old guard" of commentators has permanently given way to sincere appreciation of art and culture, rather than the temporary, commercially motivated candor Spigel observes.

Although Thorn posits new sincerity as a movement largely independent of a particular medium or genre, the idea has clear antecedents in poetry, fiction, music, and visual art criticism. The novelist David Foster Wallace articulates ideals similar to those of new sincerity in a 1993 essay on the commercialization of literature through television, published in the journal *Review of Contemporary Fiction*. Literary theorist Mikhail Epstein in *Russian Postmodernism: New Perspectives on Post-Soviet Culture* (1999) detects a pattern, which he terms "a new sincerity," in the Russian poetry of the late Soviet era. Genre films of the 1990s and early 2000s (most notably horror and sci-fi) tacitly engaged in the critical dialogue over sincerity and irony by becoming increasingly self-referential in their humor.

Despite the continued debate over the role of irony in mass culture, the literary impact of "A Manifesto for the New Sincerity" has been slight. The text, by its own admission, serves more as a description of an emerging trend than as a call to action. Canonical formulations of cultural sincerity, such as those by Epstein or Wallace, have had a much more profound impact on literature and the arts. Nevertheless, Thorn's essay is significant as an art manifesto for its emphasis on the power of readers and viewers, rather than of artists, to vest a work with irony or sincerity.

THEMES AND STYLE

Throughout the manifesto, Thorn posits an essential difference between irony and sincerity that readers must transcend in order to arrive at a more

★ *Key Facts*

Time Period:
Early 21st Century

Movement/Issue:
New Sincerity

Place of Publication:
United States

Language of Publication:
English

THE OLD NEW SINCERITY

Jesse Thorn's invocation of new sincerity may be viewed as a late entrant in an ongoing contest to define the term in a critically useful fashion. A notable predecessor in this effort is Russian American literary theorist Mikhail Epstein, who partitioned the work of poets during the last decade of Soviet rule into several different schools. One of these was termed the new sincerity (also known as postconceptualism), which Epstein describes as "an experiment in resuscitating 'fallen,' dead languages with a renewed pathos of love, sentimentality, and enthusiasm, as if to overcome alienation."

Epstein's and Thorn's ideas share important historical parallels. As with the irony-laden popular culture Thorn describes and implicitly criticizes, Epstein's new sincerity springs from a background of disillusioned poetic movements, such as nihilistic conceptualism and the Great Defeat, both of which explicitly de-emphasize the author. Moreover, like Thorn, who insists that even the most absurd elements of American popular culture are worthy of appreciation, Epstein's postconceptualists see beauty in "anti-lyrical material, comprised of the wastes from the ideological kitchen." Although written against a cultural backdrop quite different from the stars and stripes that adorn Knievel's jumpsuit, the poetry of the Russian new sincerity movement seems to align with the ethos of Thorn's later movement.

satisfying outlook on mass culture. He suggests that the movement is difficult to describe, though it may be approximated as either "irony and sincerity combined" or "the absence of irony and sincerity, where less is (obviously) more." The central figure of the manifesto is daredevil Evel Knievel, whose cultural persona defies (according to Thorn) "literal" esteem but transcends mere ironic appreciation. The stunt artist's dual embodiment of absurd theatrics and legitimate success poses a dilemma to which the ideology of new sincerity is a possible answer.

The manifesto achieves its rhetorical effect by invoking late twentieth- and early twenty-first-century cultural icons to elucidate the differences between irony and sincerity. Thorn's use of such symbols establishes his fluency with the media and narrows his audience to readers who share his cultural knowledge. He packages his high concept of an ideology that transcends its parts, into the figure of Voltron, a gigantic robot formed from smaller vehicles. The metaphor draws on readers' knowledge of the eponymous television series, which was adapted from two earlier Japanese series and thus carries connotations of remixing, editing, and translation. He closes his essay with a fusillade of similarly suggestive allusions that require no explanation to like-minded twenty- and thirty somethings, billing the new sincerity movement as "more Hedwig than Rocky Horror … more Bruce Lee than Chuck Norris."

Thorn writes in a casual, conversational style that assumes the reader's shared enthusiasm for an earnest approach to popular culture. Early in the manifesto, he demonstrates his facility with irony, "that particularly distasteful form of discourse," by invoking sentiments that drip with sarcasm: "Somewhere, an eagle shed a single tear." In his appraisal of Knievel, Thorn is more restrained, stating that the stunt man simply "boggles the mind" and "is, in a word, awesome." In other paragraphs, he inflates his prose with archaic literary conventions only to deflate them with mass cultural inflections: "So now, dear reader, you're in on the Next Big Thing." In a nod to the great ironist Mark Twain, he announces that the "reports of irony's death were greatly exaggerated" only to aver that "the pundits and prognosticators who declared irony dead … were absolutely right." By fluidly oscillating between irony and sincerity, Thorn stylistically models the language of the new sincerity.

CRITICAL DISCUSSION

Initial reactions to Thorn's manifesto were polarized. Some readers openly embraced the author's advocacy of a postironic stance, while others termed the manifesto an ironic ploy in itself. Design and technology blogger Roo Reynolds related the manifesto to Thorn's ongoing work as a radio host, observing that Thorn is engaged in the broader cultural task of imagining a philosophical position to succeed postmodernism. Reynolds claims that Thorn presents a more participatory alternative to the future envisioned by English philosopher Alan Kirby, who abstracts the "death of irony" to the level of a fundamental worldview. In a 2006 essay for the journal *Philosophy Now,* Kirby concludes that "pseudo-modernism," the next phase of contemporary thought, will involve "a new weightless nowhere of silent autism." Unlike Kirby's dark prediction of a future in which a life online "takes the world away," Thorn posits a digital universe in which users can revel in a wealth of cultural artifacts and mine them for social truths.

Although "A Manifesto for the New Sincerity" is often cited as sparking discussions about the decline of irony, detailed treatments of the issue tend to refer instead to earlier texts specific to the disciplines of literature, film, or philosophy. These key texts often develop the basic point that Thorn makes in greater depth but diverge greatly as to the nature of the sincerity achieved by a given medium. For instance, film theorists associate the term "new sincerity" with the work of Jim Collins, who applied the term in 1993 to such films as *Dances with Wolves* (1990) and *Field of Dreams* (1989). For Collins, sincerity means rejecting postmodernism in an examination of American mythology. Art critics often construe new sincerity as a form of earnestness and authenticity, for example in their analysis of early twenty-first-century sculpture, which centers on a return to the spiritual impulse presumed to lie at the root of the plastic arts.

Academic discussion of Thorn's work is almost nonexistent, leaving it to his readers and listeners to apply his new cultural paradigm to a vast array of literary and cultural texts. Unabashed by the diffidence of critics, the author has continued to promote his philosophy through his radio productions and podcasts, applying the ethos to such diverse domains as London tweed merchants, the cinematic oeuvre of Mel Brooks, and artisanal pencil sharpening. Although some readers and listeners have been endeared to Thorn's decidedly uncynical outlook, others dismiss it as a sublimated version of 1990s pop cultural irony.

Daredevil motorcyclist Evel Knievel jumps over seven Mack trucks in 1974. In "Manifesto for a New Sincerity" Jesse Thorn says appreciation of Knievel exemplifies the New Sincerity. AP PHOTO/FILE

BIBLIOGRAPHY

Sources

Epstein, Mikhail, Alexander Genis, and Slobodanka Vladiv-Glover. *Russian Postmodernism: New Perspectives on Post-Soviet Culture*. Trans. and ed. Slobodanka Vladiv-Glover. New York: Berghahn Books, 1999. Print.

Kirby, Alan. "The Death of Postmodernism and Beyond." *Philosophy Now* Nov. 2006: 34-37. Web. 5 July 2012.

Reynolds, Roo. "Welcome to the New Sincerity." *Roo Reynolds—What's Next?* 28 May 2008. Web. 25 June 2012.

Spigel, Lynn. "Entertainment Wars: Television Culture after 9/11." *American Quarterly* 56.2 (2004): 235-70. Web. 25 June 2012.

Wallace, David Foster. "E Unibus Pluram: Television and U.S. Fiction." *Review of Contemporary Fiction* 13.2 (1993): 151-94. Web. 25 June 2012.

Further Reading

Altieri, Charles. "The Fate of the Imaginary in Twentieth-Century American Poetry." *American Literary History* 17.1 (2005): 70-94. Web. 25 June 2012.

Collins, Jim. "Genericity in the Nineties: Eclectic Irony and the New Sincerity." *Film Theory Goes to the Movies*. Ed. Jim Collins et al. New York: Routledge, 1993. Print.

Kelly, Adam. "David Foster Wallace and the New Sincerity in American Fiction." *Consider David Foster Wallace: Critical Essays*. Ed. David Hering. Los Angeles: Sideshow Media Group P, 2010. Print.

Roelstraete, Dieter. "Great Transformations: On the Spiritual in Art, Again." *Afterall: A Journal of Art, Context, and Enquiry* Spring 2009: 5-15. Web. 25 June 2012.

Trilling, Lionel. *Sincerity and Authenticity*. Cambridge: Harvard UP, 1972. Print.

Wee, Valerie. "The *Scream* Trilogy, 'Hyperpostmodernism,' and the Late-Nineties Teen Slasher Film." *Journal of Film and Video* 57.3 (2005): 44-61. Web. 25 June 2012.

Michael Hartwell

NEO-HOODOO MANIFESTO

Ishmael Reed

OVERVIEW

The prose poem "Neo-HooDoo Manifesto" by American author Ishmael Reed, first published in his 1972 collection *Conjure,* advocates an aesthetic, political, and spiritual worldview modeled on principles of the folk magic known as hoodoo. Reed presents contemporary U.S. culture as the latest stage of a historical struggle between two opposing cultural attitudes, typified by their religious representatives. Hoodoo, for Reed, stands for that which is inclusive, improvisatory, and sensual, while Western monotheism embodies the homogenizing and repressive forces of history. The author maintains that he is only the most recent in a long series of reinterpreters of the hoodoo tradition, invoking (among others) a host of famous jazz musicians, the nineteenth-century medium Marie Laveau, and the priests of ancient Egypt. Furthermore, Reed calls out as dishonest the predominantly white "countercultures" that seek to deny their connection to the African and African American traditions from which, the author suggests, they draw their vitality.

"Neo-HooDoo Manifesto" attracted notice in several early appraisals of *Conjure,* though critics were often reluctant to prognosticate as to its broader impact on African American literary culture, let alone American literature in general. Reed himself embraced the neo-hoodoo aesthetic most famously in his "postmodern detective novel" *Mumbo Jumbo* (1972), though it also has proved to be an important concept in academic studies of his subsequent works. Subject to intense critical interest (and a flurry of competing attempts at definition) in the 1980s, "neo-hoodoo" has since become a term of art for describing similarly syncretistic impulses in the work of other, predominantly African American, poets and novelists.

HISTORICAL AND LITERARY CONTEXT

"Neo-HooDoo Manifesto" addresses a primarily U.S. cultural scene in which African influence is increasingly pervasive but, simultaneously, more and more repressed. This basic problem is announced early in the poem: "The reason that HooDoo isn't given the credit it deserves in influencing American culture is because the students of that culture … are uptight closet Jeho-vah revisionists." Reed cites scholar Theodore Roszak's *The Making of a Counter Culture* (1969) as an example of the official illusion of

cultural authority, which—because an illusion—has to be forcefully defended by academic, religious, and government institutions. As Reed notes, this phenomenon is by no means exclusive to the United States: in his prose poem he quotes at length from a timely *New York Times* article about the Vatican forbidding jazz masses in Italy.

In his 1970 chapbook *Catechism of D Neoamerican Hoodoo Church,* Reed had suggested a means of reasserting the culture that Western churches and universities threatened to erase. As in "Neo-HooDoo Manifesto," he used as his central image the American body of folk-magic practices known as hoodoo (sometimes referred to as "conjure"); he argued that hoodoo, not Christianity, was the legitimate religious heritage of the American people and thereby set the terms of a battle between what he dubbed the "Cop Religion" and his own "Neoamerican HooDoo Church."

"Neo-HooDoo Manifesto" arrived at a transitional moment in African American literary history. The controversial Black Arts movement, begun in the late 1960s, had reached its peak, but spokespersons of the New Black Aesthetic (famously described by writer and professor Trey Ellis) had not yet propounded their less combative alternative. Though a claim of direct stylistic influence seems dubious, Reed's prose poem addresses issues also raised in "The Revolutionary Theatre" (1965) by writer LeRoi Jones (now known as Amiri Baraka); for example, Jones rejects much of white Western art as produced "in complete sympathy with the most repressive social forces in the world today." "Neo-HooDoo Manifesto" also acknowledges the link between Western artistic traditions and political oppression, but it mocks those institutions rather than calling overtly for their destruction.

Reed's prose poem was a moderate critical success; its emphasis on personal aesthetics and improvisation spurred discussions of the balance between individual freedom and political imperatives in African American literature. As a term, "neo-hoodoo" has been extended to describe the incorporation of hoodoo motifs in the work of other prominent writers. For example, Keith Cartwright in his 2005 article "Weave a Circle Round Him Thrice" describes the poetry of Pulitzer Prize winner Yusef Komunyakaa as engaged in a "neo-hoodoo balancing act" insofar as it sees the value both in "colonizing bookish traditions" and in "vernacular traditions of ritualizing embodied practice." Neo-hoodoo remains best known, however, as a broad descriptor of the syncretistic tendencies in Reed's own writing.

THEMES AND STYLE

"Neo-HooDoo Manifesto" argues for a neo-hoodoo poetics that shares with hoodoo both its name and its governing values: hoodoo polytheism, for example, implies neo-hoodoo plurality and eclecticism, while the root doctor's resourcefulness becomes the artist's improvisation. Reed sets about constructing a list— part pantheon, part congregation—of the dozens of neo-hoodoos whose lives and works reflect these qualities: among them are jazz musician Sun Ra; Vertamae Grosvenor, author of *Vibration Cooking* (1970); and writer and folklorist Zora Neale Hurston, whom Reed claims as "our theoretician." This poetics of inclusiveness also extends to entire cultures: "Neo-HooDoo," Reed declares, "borrows from Ancient Egyptians ... borrows from Haiti Africa and South America. Neo-HooDoo comes in all styles and moods." Moreover, while Reed's work is generally discussed in the context of African American literature, the poem describes neo-hoodoo as a multiracial phenomenon whose practitioners are "Black Red ... and occasionally White."

The major opponents of neo-hoodoo are, therefore, those forces that do not leave room for spontaneity; diversity; or, for that matter, sensuality. In literature this means such institutions as the Western canon and the Eurocentric literary criticism taught in universities. However, the real villain of the "Neo-HooDoo Manifesto" is monotheism, which Reed personifies in the figure of "Jeho-vah." He specifically arrays a wide variety of irreverent arguments against Christianity, which he views as the clearest modern embodiment of anti-hoodoo repression and conformism. This conflict also runs back to the Old Testament: "Moses," Reed maintains, "had a near heart attack when he saw his sons ... dancing to a 'heathen sound' ... (probably a mixture of Sun Ra and Jimmy Reed played in the nightclub district ...)." The author argues that in a fair fight, neo-hoodoo would easily overtake Jeho-vah (though the terms of such a battle are not exactly clear). Accordingly, "Neo-HooDoo now demands a rematch, the referees were bribed and the adversary had resin on his gloves."

Stylistically, "Neo-HooDoo Manifesto" might be described as a verbal collage. The speaker lampoons traditional symbols of authority, adopting the perspectives of a TV police officer ("We have issued warrants for a god arrest") and an academic historian ("HooDoo challenged the stability of civil authority in New Orleans ..."). In a somewhat subtler jest, Reed obfuscates an allusion to Billy Bird's "Mill Man Blues" (1928) as the text of "an early American HooDoo

Priestess Yaffa, voodoo queen also known as "Rose," prepares to perform a ceremony in New Orleans, Louisiana, circa 1991. © PHILIP GOULD/CORBIS

Song." Elsewhere, he applies these techniques to suggest that the concept of authority itself is of little use to the neo-hoodoo cause. Such emblems of Western civilization as the *New York Times* and the Roman Curia are set up for ridicule, while Milo Rigaud's *Secrets of Voodoo* (1971) is brought in to affirm neo-hoodoo's antihierarchical lineage. More generally, the prose poem achieves an effect that verges on the incantatory through its use of anaphora and litany: the roll call of "Neo-HooDoos" becomes at times an alliterative, unpunctuated list, and many paragraphs open with a newly refocused definition of what "Neo-HooDoo is."

CRITICAL DISCUSSION

Early critics of Reed's "Neo-HooDoo Manifesto" (and of *Conjure*) were generally appreciative but varied in their assessment of the poem's importance.

PRIMARY SOURCE

"NEO-HOODOO MANIFESTO"

Neo-HooDoo is a "Lost American Church" updated. Neo-HooDoo is the music of James Brown without the lyrics and ads for Black Capitalism. Neo-HooDoo is the 8 basic dances of 19-century New Orleans' *Place Congo*— the Calinda the Bamboula the Chacta the Babouille the Conjaille the Juba the Congo and the VooDoo—modernized into the Philly Dog, the Hully Gully, the Funky Chicken, the Popcorn, the Boogaloo and the dance of great American choreographer Buddy Bradley.

Neo-HooDoos would rather "shake that thing" than be stiff and erect. (There were more people performing a Neo-HooDoo sacred dance, the Boogaloo, at Woodstock than chanting Hare Krishna … Hare Hare!) All so-called "Store Front Churches" and "Rock Festivals" receive their matrix in the HooDoo rites of Marie Laveau conducted at New Orleans' Lake Pontchartrain, and Bayou St. John in the 1880's. The power of HooDoo challenged the stability of civil authority in New Orleans and was driven underground where to this day it flourishes in the Black ghettos throughout the country. Thats why in Ralph Ellison's modern novel *Invisible Man* New Orleans is described as "The Home of Mystery." "Everybody from New Orleans got that thing," Louis Armstrong said once.

…

Neo-HooDoo is sexual, sensual and digs the old "heathen" good good loving. An early American HooDoo song says:

Now lady I ain't no mill man
Just the mill man's son
But I can do your grinding
till the mill man comes

Which doesn't mean that women are treated as "sexual toys" in Neo-HooDoo or as one slick Jehovah Revisionist recently said, "victims of a raging hormone imbalance." Neo-HooDoo claims many women philosophers and theoreticians which is more than ugh religions Christianity and its offspring Islam can claim. When our theoretician Zora Neale Hurston asked a *Mambo* (a female priestess in the Haitian VooDoo) a definition of VooDoo the Mambo lifted her skirts and exhibited her Erzulie Seal, her Isis seal. Neo-HooDoo identifies with Julia Jackson who stripped HooDoo of its oppressive Catholic layer— Julia Jackson said when asked the origin of the amulets and talismans in her studio, "I make all my own stuff. It saves money and it's as good. People who has to buy their stuff ain't using their heads."

Neo-HooDoo is not a church for egotripping— it takes its "organization" from Haitian VooDoo of which Milo Rigaud wrote:

Unlike other established religions, there is no heirarchy of bishops, archbishops, cardinals, or a pope in VooDoo. Each oum'phor is a law unto itself, following the traditions of VooDoo but modifying and changing the ceremonies and rituals in various ways. Secrets of VooDoo.

William Heyen, writing for *Poetry* magazine in 1973, praised *Conjure* for its "outpouring of spirit" and expressed cautious admiration for "the way Reed has gone out to what tells him what he is." As to the "Neo-HooDoo Manifesto" itself, however, Heyen noted only that it "defines [Reed's] non-western-civ. head and where it came from." Other critics, such as Chester Fontenot, writing in a 1978 article published in *Black American Literature Forum*, regarded "Neo-HooDoo Manifesto" as a document of great potential significance: "Neo-Hoodoo can endow the Black artist with a mystic sense which will allow him to alter his form according to his experiences and aspirations."

The principles enshrined in the poem also have proved central to analyses of Reed's own work. As early as 1974, scholar Neil Schmitz devoted an essay to examining neo-hoodoo themes and motifs in Reed's published fiction to date. As a set of aesthetic and political criteria, however, the poem has been applied with greatest consistency to two novels: *Mumbo Jumbo* (1972) and *The Last Days of Louisiana Red* (1975). The former, Reed's first long work to deliberately incorporate neo-hoodoo motifs, received widely positive reviews. *Louisiana Red,* however, was considered by major literary critics such as Houston Baker to gainsay the politics of inclusiveness expounded in the poem. In an acrimonious 1975 review of the novel, Baker took Reed to task for "putting down those who stand in his way of love, harmony, common sense, and the neo-hoodoo way." Not altogether surprisingly, this led to a swift reply from Reed titled "Hoodoo Manifesto #2 on Criticism: The Baker-Gayle Fallacy." According to Reginald Martin in a 1987 article for *MELUS*, in "Hoodoo Manifesto #2" Reed reiterated claims familiar from the original

Neo-HooDoo believes that every man is an artist and every artist a priest. You can bring your own creative ideas to Neo-HooDoo. Charlie "Yardbird (Thoth)" Parker is an example of the Neo-HooDoo artist as an innovator and improvisor.

In Neo-HooDoo, Christ the landlord deity ("render unto Caesar") is on probation. This includes "The Black Christ" and "The Hippie Christ." Neo-HooDoo tells Christ to get lost. (Judas Iscariot holds an honorary degree from Neo-HooDoo.)

...

Neo-HooDoo ain't Negritude. Neo-HooDoo never been to France. Neo-HooDoo is "your Mama" as Larry Neal said. Neo-HooDoos Little Richard and Chuck Berry nearly succeeded in converting the Beatles. When the Beatles said they were more popular than Christ they seemed astonished at the resulting outcry. This is because although they could feebly through amplification and technological sham 'mimic' (as if Little Richard and Chuck Berry were Loa [Spirits] practicing ventriloquism on their "Horses") the Beatles failed to realize that they were conjuring the music and ritual (although imitation) of a Forgotten Faith, a traditional enemy of Christianity which Christianity the Cop Religion has had to drive underground each time they meet. Neo-HooDoo now demands a rematch, the referees were bribed and the adversary had resin on his gloves.

Neo-HooDoo is a litany seeking its text

Neo-HooDoo is a Dance and Music closing in on its words

Neo-HooDoo is a Church finding its lyrics

Cecil Brown Al Young Calvin Hernton David Henderson Steve Cannon Quincy Troupe Ted Joans Victor Cruz N.H. Pritchard Ishmael Reed Lennox Raphael Sarah Fabio Ron Welburn are Neo-HooDoo's "Manhattan Project" of writing

...

A Neo-HooDoo celebration will involve the dance music and poetry of Neo-HooDoo and whatever ideas the participating artists might add. A Neo-HooDoo seal is the Face of an Old American Train.

Neo-HooDoo signs are everywhere!

Neo-HooDoo is the Now Locomotive swinging up the Tracks of the American Soul.

Almost 100 years ago HooDoo was forced to say Goodbye to America. Now HooDoo is back as Neo-HooDoo
You can't keep a good church down!

prose poem, charging Baker and his fellow "new black aestheticians" with imposing Western, Eurocentric limits upon their definition of good art. A similar exchange with literary critic Addison Gayle would follow the publication of Reed's 1976 novel *Flight to Canada.*

As neo-hoodoo values have found expression in subsequent works by Reed and others, a variety of critical definitions of neo-hoodoo have emerged. Ashraf H.A. Rushdy, in "Ishmael Reed's Neo-HooDoo Slave Narrative" (1994), notes no fewer than four distinct approaches, each emphasizing different facets of the phenomenon: for some it is "almost strictly an aesthetic principle," or a means of lending coherence to Reed's authorial idiosyncrasies; for others it is "an artistic and a religious sensibility"; for still others it is a means of resisting "Western cultural imperialists." Rushdy suggests, however, that given the emphasis on plurality and diversity evident in the original prose poem, "the fact that Neo-HooDoo has not been strictly defined as a monolith probably doesn't bother Reed all that much."

BIBLIOGRAPHY

Sources

Baker, Houston. "*The Last Days of Louisiana Red*—A Review." *Umnum Newsletter* 4.3-4 (1975): 6. Print.

Cartwright, Keith. "Weave a Circle Round Him Thrice: Komunyakaa's Hoodoo Balancing Act." *Callaloo* 28.3 (2005): 851-63. *JSTOR.* Web. 3 Oct. 2012.

Fontenot, Chester J. "Ishmael Reed and the Politics of Aesthetics, or Shake Hands and Come Out Conjuring." *Black American Literature Forum* 12.1 (1978): 20-23. *JSTOR.* Web. 3 Oct. 2012.

Heyen, William. "Four Realities." *Poetry* 122.4 (1973): 237-40. *JSTOR.* Web. 3 Oct. 2012.

Jones, LeRoi (Amiri Baraka). "The Revolutionary Theatre." *Liberator* July 1965: 4-6. *University of Illinois Department of English*. Web. 3 Oct. 2012.

Martin, Reginald. "The FreeLance PallBearer Confronts the Terrible Threes: Ishmael Reed and the New Black Aesthetic Critics." *MELUS* 14.2 (1987): 35-49. *JSTOR*. Web. 3 Oct. 2012.

Rushdy, Ashraf H.A. "Ishmael Reed's Neo-HooDoo Slave Narrative." *Narrative* 2.2 (1994): 112-39. *JSTOR*. Web. 3 Oct. 2012.

Schmitz, Neil. "Neo-HooDoo: The Experimental Fiction of Ishmael Reed." *Twentieth-Century Literature* 20.2 (1974): 126-40. *JSTOR*. Web. 3 Oct. 2012.

Further Reading

Fox, Robert Elliot. "Blacking the Zero: Toward a Semiotics of Neo-Hoodoo." *Black American Literature Forum* 18 (1984): 95-99. Print.

Gates, Henry Louis, Jr. "The 'Blackness of Blackness': A Critique of the Sign and the Signifying Monkey." *Critical Inquiry* 9.4 (1983): 685-723. *JSTOR*. Web. 3 Oct. 2012.

Lock, Helen. "'A Man's Story Is His Gris-Gris': Ishmael Reed's Neo-HooDoo Aesthetic and the African-American Tradition." *South Central Review* 10.1 (1993): 67-77. *JSTOR*. Web. 3 Oct. 2012.

McGee, Patrick. *Ishmael Reed and the Ends of Race*. New York: St. Martin's, 1997. Print.

Nazareth, Peter. "An Interview with Ishmael Reed." *Iowa Review* 13.2 (1982): 117-31. *JSTOR*. Web. 3 Oct. 2012.

Zapf, Harald. "Ishmael Reed's Rooted Cosmopolitanism: American 'Patriotism' and Global Writing." *Amerikastudien / American Studies* 47.2 (2002): 285-99. *JSTOR*. Web. 3 Oct. 2012.

Michael Hartwell

ONTOLOGICAL-HYSTERIC MANIFESTO I

Richard Foreman

OVERVIEW

Written by Richard Foreman and first published in 1972 in *Performance* magazine, "Ontological-Hysteric Manifesto I" is an essay that describes a new form of theater that rejects traditional dramatic elements, such as character and narrative, in order to frustrate the audience's viewing experience, thereby drawing attention to the process and habits of that act of perception. The appearance of the essay coincided with the production of Foreman's ontological-hysteric plays, such as *Angelface,* his first, which contains characters in ordinary domestic situations that converse in dialogue that makes no conventional sense. "Ontological-Hysteric Manifesto I" provides a theoretical foundation for these plays.

While the ontological-hysteric plays attracted a small amount of interest and criticism within the world of avant-garde theater, Foreman's essay received little attention at first. The text, however, helps articulate the aesthetic of Foreman's theatrical works, an aesthetic that he revised and refined in two subsequent ontological-hysteric essays in 1974 and 1975. The Ontological-Hysteric Theater, founded by Foreman in New York in 1968, is notable for the theoretical cohesiveness of its body of work, which has spanned more than four decades. "Ontological-Hysteric Manifesto I" explicates the intellectual foundation that guides Foreman's theatrical productions: to break with traditional dramatic tactics that reinforce socially prescriptive modes of perception.

HISTORICAL AND LITERARY CONTEXT

"Ontological-Hysteric Manifesto I" addresses the state of American theater in the 1960s, when avant-garde theater ensembles inspired by the work of Antonin Artaud began to challenge traditional notions of drama and performance. The Open Theatre, established by Joseph Chaikin in the early 1960s, became a prominent force in the avant-garde theater with plays such as *The Serpent,* which combines passages and imagery from the book of Genesis and President John F. Kennedy's assassination. In 1968 the Performance Group, an experimental theater troupe founded by Richard Schechner, performed *Dionysus in 69,* a groundbreaking play that seeks to break down the wall between spectator and actor by encouraging audience participation. Foreman argues that these

experimental groups failed to break with the traditions of dramaturgy in so much as they attempted to create emotional identification with the audience.

By the time *Performance* magazine published "Ontological-Hysteric Manifesto I" in 1972, a more formalized and highly intellectualized avant-garde was in ascendance. Along with the productions of the Ontological-Hysteric Theater, which began with *Angelface* in 1969, the emergence of the New American Cinema and directors such as Jack Smith had a profound impact on Foreman's theater. These films, according to author Arnold Aronson in his book *American Avant-Garde Theatre: A History,* "shifted the locus of the work of art from the content not simply to the form, but to the raw elements of the creative process." The work of Foreman's contemporary Robert Wilson shows striking technical similarities, such as painstakingly slow pacing and movement, which, according to Aronson, placed "a burden on the spectator to develop a new means of watching." When the "Ontological-Hysteric Manifesto I" appeared, it provided a theoretical foundation for Foreman's theater and articulated many of the dominant trends of the avant-garde of the 1970s.

"Ontological-Hysteric Manifesto I" incorporates much of Gertrude Stein's 1936 book, *The Geographical History of America or the Relations of Human Nature to the Human Mind,* a mélange of Stein's prose pieces, dialogues, philosophical meditations, and short plays. In his article "A Short History of Richard Foreman's Ontological-Hysteric Theatre," Markus Wessendorf argues that Foreman's theoretical underpinnings draw on two of Stein's ideas about writing: "the notion of writing in a state of continuous presence and the concept of continually 'beginning again' in the writing."

"Ontological-Hysteric Manifesto I" provides a theoretical foundation for the ongoing production of the Ontological-Hysteric Theater. Along with the publication of his two subsequent ontological-hysteric essays, which refine his theatrical aesthetics, as of late 2012 Foreman continues to produce plays on an almost annual basis. On Foreman's continued artistic production, Aronson writes, "If it is no longer avant-garde in the sense that it is relatively familiar, even comforting to long-time supporters, it still has the power to challenge, surprise, even to shock." In the early twenty-first century, the Ontological-Hysteric

❖ Key Facts

Time Period:
Mid-20th Century

Movement/Issue:
Dramatic aesthetics;
Avant-gardism

Place of Publication:
United States

Language of Publication:
English

Avant-garde playwright Richard Foreman, founder of the Ontological-Hysteric Theater, photographed in 1987. © ISABELLE WEINGARTEN/SYGMA/ CORBIS

Theater still commands significant scholarly interest as one of the most important contributors to avant-garde theater in the United States.

THEMES AND STYLE

The central theme of "Ontological-Hysteric Manifesto I" is that contemporary theater does not challenge the expectations and understanding of audiences. The form of theater that the essay proposes eschews traditional dramaturgy in favor of a variety of techniques, such as prerecorded dialogue, trance-like pacing, and abrasive sounds that are intended to alter the audience's habitual modes of perception, thereby opening the possibility of new understandings of being that have hitherto remained hidden. Foreman articulates the distinctions between these two forms of theater in his essay: "Old notions of drama (up thru Grotowski-Brook-Chaikin) = the danger of circumstance turning in such a way that we are 'trapped' in an emotional commitment." He argues that the new ontological mode "forces the unseeable to cast shadows."

"Ontological-Hysteric Manifesto I" achieves its rhetorical effect by laying down a challenge to contemporary avant-garde theatergoers. Foreman often frames the act of viewing his ontological theater as difficult, as if it is a test that only certain viewers will undertake. He writes, "The artistic experience must be an ordeal to be undergone." He explains that his primary theatrical concern is to create a performance in which the audience experiences the "danger of art" as a "possible decision he (spectator) may make upon the occasion of confronting the work of art. The work of art as a contest between object (or process) and viewer." By acknowledging the difficulty and importance of his work, the essay appeals to people who consider themselves capable of understanding and enduring the challenges of art.

Stylistically, "Ontological-Hysteric Manifesto I" is distinguished by its inclusion of drawings and lines that often interrupt and comment on the text itself. These lines, arrows, and stars serve to draw connections between, and give greater emphasis to, certain written aspects of the essay. For example, the opening statement, "Theatre in the past has used language to build: what follows what?" is illustrated by a drawing that consists of the underlined word "old" followed by a series of arrows that suggest the linear nature of traditional dramatic narrative. The use of handwritten question marks contributes to the sense that the work is a continuing exploration of the author's thought, not a fully worked-out theoretical system. The drawings often cause the essay to feel jumbled or disjointed, but in so doing, they become a stylistic embodiment of one of the Ontological-Hysteric Theater's driving theoretical goals: to foreground the cluttered and often discontinuous nature of perception and consciousness.

CRITICAL DISCUSSION

When "Ontological-Hysteric Manifesto I" appeared in *Performance,* it received little notice other than as an addendum to the plays of the Ontological-Hysteric Theater, which generated interest and criticism in the theater world. Stanley Kauffmann, in a review in *New Republic,* criticizes Foreman's play *Pandering to the Masses: A Misrepresentation* and the "essay" included in its program, writing that "presumably Foreman needs to believe he is accomplishing this thematic end [of a writer casting off 'the habit of thinking we think in logical, linear, monophonic ways'] in order to create his pictures," but Kauffmann sees the play only as "a series of effects, visual and aural, many of which were ingenious and amusing, none of which was moving or mindblowing." Other criticism was more favorable. According to Gerald Rabkin, editor of the book *Art + Performance: Richard Foreman,* critic Arthur Sainer's review of *Total Recall* in *Village Voice* describes the play as a "cunning, forceful, and brilliant work."

In the decades following the appearance of "Ontological-Hysteric Manifesto I," the text remains an important articulation of Foreman's aesthetic aims. In her 1976 introduction to *Plays and Manifestos,* an anthology of Foreman's work, Kate Davy describes Foreman as "one of the most important avant-garde artists working in the theatre today." In 1995 the playwright received one of the most prestigious awards in the United States, the MacArthur Fellowship, which is awarded on the basis of exceptional creativity and the possibility of future work.

According to Davy, "Foreman takes the fundamental conflict (hysteric) basis of most traditional theatre and renders it phenomenologically—retarding and breaking up the hysterical situation or state, and focusing on the moment-to-moment reality of things-in-and-of-themselves." In an article in *Theatre Journal,* Martin Puchner uses Foreman's essay, which Puchner notes seeks "to make visible and manifest through its own structure the fact that theatre and manifesto are firmly entangled in each other," as a starting point for the analysis of theatricality and performativity in the manifesto genre. Puchner traces these elements in reverse, through the history of the avant-garde to *The Communist Manifesto* by Karl Marx and Friedrich Engels.

BIBLIOGRAPHY

Sources

Aronson, Arnold. *American Avant-Garde Theatre: A History.* London: Routledge, 2000. Print.

Davy, Kate. Introduction. *Plays and Manifestos,* by Richard Foreman. Ed. Kate Davy. New York: New York UP, 1976. Print.

Foreman, Richard. "Ontological-Hysteric Manifesto." 1972. *Plays and Manifestos,* ed. Kate Davy. New York: New York UP, 1976. 67-80. Print.

Kauffmann, Stanley. Rev. of *Pandering to the Masses: A Misrepresentation,* by Richard Foreman. *New Republic* 175.6 (1975): 22. Print.

Puchner, Martin. "Manifesto = Theatre" *Theatre Journal* 54.3 (2002): 449-65. *JSTOR.* Web. 4 Oct. 2012.

Rabkin, Gerald. "Richard Foreman: An Introduction." *Art + Performance: Richard Foreman.* Ed. Gerald Rabkin. Baltimore: Johns Hopkins UP, 1999. 1-22. Print.

Further Reading

Cumbie, Janet. *Richard Foreman's Ontological-Hysteric Theatre: A Philosophical Inquiry.* Greensboro: U of North Carolina at Greensboro, 1982. Print.

Davy, Kate. *Richard Foreman and the Ontological-Hysteric Theatre.* Ann Arbor: UMI Research, 1981. Print.

Ebrahimian, Babak. *The Cinematic Theatre.* Oxford: Scarecrow, 2004. Print.

Foreman, Richard. *Reverberation Machines.* Barrytown: Station Hill, 1985. Print.

Shank, Theodore. *Beyond the Boundaries: American Alternative Theatre.* Ann Arbor: U of Michigan P, 2002. Print.

Wessendorf, Markus. "A Short History of Richard Foreman's Ontological-Hysteric Theatre [1999]." *University of Hawai'i at Manoa.* Web. 27 Oct. 2012.

Woods, Tim. *Beginning Postmodernism.* Manchester: Manchester UP, 1999. Print.

Gregory Luther

PERSONISM

A Manifesto

Frank O'Hara

✢ *Key Facts*

Time Period:
Mid-20th Century

Movement/Issue:
New York School; Beat
Movement; Black
Mountain School

Place of Publication:
United States

**Language of
Publication:**
English

OVERVIEW

"Personism: A Manifesto" (1959) is an essay by Frank O'Hara that mocks the self-importance of literary manifestos and poetic formulas by inventing a nonexistent literary movement that he calls "Personism" and explaining its poetic principles. Originally written for Donald Allen's anthology *The New American Poetry* (1960) but ultimately not included, "Personism" first appeared in the Beat literary magazine *Yugen* in 1961. Despite the manifesto's flippant tone, it encapsulates many of O'Hara's ideas about what a poem should be, poetry's place within American culture, and the relationship between poetry and painting. As such, "Personism" offers a valuable entry point into the poetry of O'Hara and the New York school.

Although Allen rejected the essay because he felt it did not adequately account for O'Hara's odes (and perhaps out of some concern that its elements of parody would prove distracting), "Personism" was recognized by the time of O'Hara's death in 1966 as one of his definitive statements on poetry. In "Personism," O'Hara reveals his poetic principles primarily by what he rejects. Dismissing the traditional justifications of poetry in terms of morality or philosophy, O'Hara refuses to proscribe formal rules for the composition of a poem or to delimit a poem's subject matter. His manifesto demonstrates through its own insouciant style that the poet must be witty and spontaneous, creating poems that fuse abstraction and intense emotion, blend the everyday and the erudite, and speak to the reader with the effortless immediacy of a telephone call. Because he published only two brief essays about his own writing in his lifetime ("Personism" and "Statement for *The New American Poetry*"), the manifesto assumes an outsized importance for anyone evaluating O'Hara's theories of poetry.

HISTORICAL AND LITERARY CONTEXT

When O'Hara wrote "Personism: A Manifesto," postwar American poetry was divided into two camps: poets writing in traditional (or "closed") poetic forms and practitioners using an "open" form. As a member of the New York school, O'Hara, along with the Black Mountain poets and Beats, was clearly affiliated with the latter camp. The anthology that nearly included his manifesto, Allen's *The New American Poetry,* championed open-form poetry and included a number of statements by Black Mountain, Beat, and New York poets on the meaning and function of the open-form poem. In essence, O'Hara's manifesto sidesteps this larger debate over closed and open poetic forms by mocking the many manifestos that attempted to systematize the elements of poetry and proscribe rules for the line, syllable, and sound.

Written in New York City during the height of the abstract expressionist movement, "Personism" draws on O'Hara's familiarity with the work of painters such as William de Kooning, Jackson Pollock, and Jasper Johns. These abstract expressionists defined art in terms of a spontaneous process of creation and therefore developed techniques of "action painting," such as Pollock's method of dripping or flinging paint at the canvas. Rather than seeking to represent a recognizable reality, abstract expressionists emphasized art as the expression of feeling (specifically, the painter's feelings toward the emerging painting). Although focused on the process of creation, the abstract expressionists also placed great importance on the formal elements of the finished painting, such as its composition in terms of color and texture. As a curator at the Museum of Modern Art, O'Hara became friends with many of the abstract expressionists, championed their work, and collaborated with contemporary painters to produce art that blended poetry, painting, and pop culture. In his manifesto, O'Hara refers to the abstract expressionists to suggest that poetry like painting should be considered a process—not a finished product—that incorporates but also abstracts personal feeling.

Although "Personism: A Manifesto" responds most directly to Allen Ginsberg's article "Abstraction in Poetry" (1959) about O'Hara's long poem *Second Avenue,* its more formative influence is Charles Olson's manifesto "Projective Verse" (1950). In this manifesto, Olson makes the case that open-form poetry is a natural mode of poetic creation and integral to the tradition of English and American literature. His manifesto proved enormously influential in inspiring many poets to turn from formal poetry to experimental verse. Despite sharing Olson's belief in the importance of open-form poetry and admiration for William Carlos Williams, O'Hara distances himself in his own manifesto from Olson's categorical statements and oracular style.

In the decades following its publication, "Personism" influenced many American poets and schools of poetry. Within a few years of its publication, O'Hara's manifesto was generally acknowledged to represent the aesthetic theories of the New York poets. In the 1970s and 1980s, O'Hara's theories of poetic abstraction were shared by some of the early language poets. Since then, his emphasis on spontaneity and colloquial speech has become axiomatic for many contemporary American poets. Today, "Personism" continues to generate considerable scholarly interest, and its aesthetic continues to influence a generation of poets, especially those working in traditions closely connected to language poetry, the history of New York, and queer politics.

THEMES AND STYLE

The overriding theme of "Personism" is that poetic manifestos and other critical commentary detract from the qualities of spontaneity, personal feeling, and audacity that convey the energy of a poem from the poet to the reader. Pointing out that such commentary can be superfluous to the poem, O'Hara asserts quite simply, "everything is in the poems" and (as a poet) "you just go on your nerve." Comparing poetry to a life-or-death situation, he jokes, "If someone's chasing you down the street with a knife you just run, you don't turn around and shout, 'Give it up! I was a track star for Mineola Prep.'" Throughout the manifesto, O'Hara attempts to puncture momentous claims about the value or function of poetry. Arguing that poetry should not be confused with morality or self-improvement, he compares contemporary poets to "a middle-aged mother trying to get her kids to eat too much cooked meat." Although no less facetious, O'Hara's explanation of personism (the nonexistent literary movement that he claims to have founded) is significant because it reveals his poetic influences and convictions. Comparing poetry to painting, he discusses two methods of creating abstraction in poetry: (1) removing the poet's personality from the poem and (2) providing the illusion of the personal by redirecting the poet's feelings for a person into the poem. Through the latter method's abstract rendering of personal feelings, the poem "evok[es] overtones of love without destroying love's life-giving vulgarity, and sustain[s] the poet's feelings towards the poem while preventing love from distracting him into feelings about the person." Concluding that this element of connection and feeling "between the poet and the person" matters most, O'Hara light-heartedly undermines his own manifesto by proclaiming the telephone an acceptable substitute for the poem.

Rhetorically, "Personism" achieves its irreverent insight by balancing its elements of parody

FRANK O'HARA: NEW YORK POET

After moving to New York at age twenty-four in 1950, Frank O'Hara quickly emerged as a noteworthy figure in the city's communities of poets and painters. He became friends with John Ashbery, James Schuyler, and Kenneth Koch, the principal members of the New York school of poets. Through his job as a curator at the Museum of Modern Art, O'Hara met and collaborated with many contemporary painters, including Larry Rivers and Jasper Johns.

As a poet, O'Hara had many influences. In addition to the poets and painters of the New York school, he was influenced by the experimental poetry of William Carlos Williams and French surrealists such as Apollinaire and Rimbaud. O'Hara's own poems are marked by a strange blend of randomness and intimacy. His "I-do-this-I-do-that" poems move from one subject to another without logical connections, in a manner reminiscent of free association or a walk down a city street. "The Day Lady Died," written for Billie Holiday, is a famous example. Given the context of the 1950s, O'Hara's poetry is often surprisingly direct about his homosexuality.

O'Hara died at the age of forty after being struck by a Jeep on Fire Island. On his gravestone is carved a line from his poem "In Memory of My Feelings": "Grace to be born and live as variously as possible."

The poet Frank O'Hara in his apartment in New York, 1964. FRED W. MCDARRAH/GETTY IMAGES

against an intricate series of allusions. The manifesto's moments of parody frequently depend on implicit (and incongruous) metaphors that compare poetry to "believ[ing] in god," falling in love, and wearing a tight pair of pants. Yet O'Hara also incorporates serious discussion of aesthetics through his allusions to poets such as John Keats, Stéphane Mallarmé, Wallace Stephens, and Pierre-Jean de Béranger and painters such as Giorgio di Chirico and Jean Dubuffet. Because of the manifesto's blend of parody and allusion, it is often difficult for the reader to decide which statements to take seriously.

Stylistically, "Personism" is marked by its cheerful tongue-in-cheek tone and casual confessionalism. Whether referring to the adverse effects of writing or love, O'Hara maintains his sense of jaunty indifference. For example, when he declares that personism "may be the death of literature as we know it," he only admits to "certain regrets" about that. Similarly, when making his case to the reader that poetic criticism is as useless as arguing with a lover, he declares, "you just let all the different bodies fall where they may, and they always do may after a few months." Here O'Hara presents himself as pleasantly inured to the inevitable failure of relationships. This studied casualness is again on display as O'Hara alerts the reader to his homosexuality with the statement that he founded personism on a day he had lunch with LeRoi Jones (*Yugen*'s editor, who later changed his name to Amiri Baraka) and he was in love with a male "someone." Although O'Hara mentions homosexuality nonchalantly, as he does again when characterizing the poem as a homosexual threesome with the phrase "Lucky Pierre style," it is clear that gay relationships serve not only as an occasion for O'Hara's cheerfully self-revelatory style but also as a frame of reference for his conception of the poem and its audience.

CRITICAL DISCUSSION

Because "Personism" was published in the small journal *Yugen* rather than the groundbreaking anthology *The New American Poetry,* it received little notice from writers, scholars, or the general public until a reappraisal of O'Hara's status as a minor poet after his death in 1966. However, one important early response to the manifesto was Donald Allen's judgment that it served as an incomplete explanation of O'Hara's poetic project because it accounted for his love poems but not his odes. O'Hara's early death caused a reevaluation of his reputation as a minor poet, with his *Collected Poems* appearing in 1971 and Marjorie Perloff's full-length study, *Frank O'Hara: Poet among Painters* appearing in 1977. Following Perloff's lead, many scholars see "Personism" as O'Hara's definitive statement on his poetry.

In the half-century since its publication, as poetic norms have shifted toward O'Hara's more colloquial and fragmented style, the connection between "Personism" and O'Hara's poetry has received sustained critical attention from scholars and poets. Marjorie Perloff argued that the manifesto is significant in defining O'Hara's poetic "aesthetic of attention" (the poems' attempts to render the ordinary unfamiliar by focusing on surfaces or generating unexpected juxtapositions). She declares, "The notion that *recognition* is central to art is the cornerstone of O'Hara's 'Personism.'" Many scholars have linked the manifesto's joke about the telephone to the elements of gossip, fragmented conversation, and casual address that appear in the poems. In contrast, some scholars such as Lytle Shaw contend that the focus on "Personism" has led readers to ignore the social and political concerns of O'Hara's poetry. Today, "Personism" remains the subject of scholarly focus, especially in studies of race and sexuality.

Much scholarship has focused on the literary history of "Personism" and what it signifies about O'Hara's relationship to literary movements such as the New York school, the Beats, and confessional poets. For example, in "Confessional Counterpublics," Anne Hartman argues that O'Hara should be considered a confessional poet. In the last two decades, a great deal of commentary has focused on the sexual politics of O'Hara's writing, especially its affiliations with what was termed "gayspeak" and "queertalk" by earlier critics. Additional new historical scholarship has focused on the contexts of the Cold War, O'Hara's work at the Museum of Modern Art, racial politics, and the influence of films of the 1950s on O'Hara's poetics.

BIBLIOGRAPHY

Sources

Diggory, Terence. "Abstract Expressionism." *Encyclopedia of the New York School Poets. Facts On File Library of American Literature: Literary Movements.* New York: Facts On File, 2009: 2-3. *Gale Virtual Reference Library.* Web. 22 July 2012.

Feldman, Alan. *Frank O'Hara.* Boston: Twayne, 1979. Print.

Gooch, Brad. *City Poet: The Life and Times of Frank O'Hara.* New York: Knopf, 1993. Print.

Mattix, Micah. *Frank O'Hara and the Poetics of Saying "I."* Madison, NJ: Fairleigh Dickinson UP and Rowman & Littlefield, 2011. Print.

Perloff, Marjorie. *Frank O'Hara: Poet among Painters.* Chicago: U of Chicago P, 1998. Print.

Ramazani, Jahan, Richard Ellmann, and Robert O'Clair. "Introduction." *The Norton Anthology of Modern and Contemporary Poetry: Volume 2.* New York: Norton, 2003. xiii-lxvii. Print.

Further Reading

Cappucci, Paul R. *William Carlos Williams, Frank O'Hara, and the New York Art Scene.* Madison, NJ: Fairleigh Dickinson UP, 2010. Print.

Epstein, Andrew. *Beautiful Enemies: Friendship and Postwar American Poetry.* New York: Oxford UP, 2006. Print.

Frank O'Hara Now: New Essays on the New York Poet. Ed. Robert Hampson and Will Montgomery. Cambridge: Liverpool UP, 2010. Print.

Hartman, Anne. "Confessional Counterpublics." *Journal of Modern Literature* 28.4 (2005): 40-56. Web. 22 July 2012.

Herring, Terrell Scott. "Frank O'Hara's Open Closet." *PMLA* 117:3 (2002): 414-27. Web. 22 July 2012.

Lehman, David. *The Last Avant-Garde: The Making of the New York School of Poets.* New York: Doubleday, 1998. Print.

Magee, Michael. "Tribes of New York: Frank O'Hara, Amiri Baraka, and the Poetics of the Five Spot." *Contemporary Literature* 44.4 (2001): 694-726. Web. 22 July 2012.

Shaw, Lytle. *Frank O'Hara: The Poetics of Coterie.* Iowa City: U of Iowa P, 2006. Print.

Smith, Hazel. *Hyperscapes in the Poetry of Frank O'Hara: Difference/Homosexuality/Topography.* Cambridge: Liverpool UP, 2000. Print.

Sweet, David L. "Parodic Nostalgia for the Aesthetic Manifesto." *Journal of Modern Literature* 23.3-4 (2000): 375-91. Web. 22 July 2012.

Kevin Cooney

PILOT PLAN FOR CONCRETE POETRY

Augusto de Campos, Haroldo de Campos, Décio Pignatari

❖ **Key Facts**

Time Period:
Mid-20th Century

Movement/Issue:
Poesia concreta
movement; Avant-
gardism; Aesthetics

Place of Publication:
Brazil

**Language of
Publication:**
Portuguese

OVERVIEW

Published in 1958 by Brazilians Augusto de Campos, Haroldo de Campos, and Décio Pignatari, "Pilot Plan for Concrete Poetry" calls for a new, formalist style of poetry that is "aware of graphic space as a structural agent" and that utilizes the physicality of words on a page to elaborate meaning. European artists Max Bill and Öyving Fahlström first coined the term *concrete poetry* in the early 1950s to describe poetry that embraces rationality while rejecting expressionism and lyrical abstraction. In the mid-1950s the de Campos brothers and Pignatari, along with the Swiss-Bolivian poet Eugen Gomringer, founded an organized movement that espoused the virtues of a minimalist, anti-expressionist poetic practice in which the typographical arrangement of words is as critical to the piece as the words themselves. The "Pilot Plan" offers a formal declaration of the movement's aims and techniques. The first works of the movement, known as *poesia concreta,* were unveiled in 1956 at the National Exhibition of Concrete Art at the Museum of Modern Art of São Paulo. Two years later, the rules and philosophy behind concrete poetry were further expounded upon in the "Pilot Plan," which was intended to expose the unaware to this new movement in Brazil's literary scene.

The "Pilot Plan" was the first piece of writing to describe the concrete poetry movement, and it immediately caught the attention of other abstract and experimental poets, who embraced the manifesto's ability to bring context to such an avant-garde style. Spurred on by the manifesto, the concrete poetry movement reached the height of its popularity in the 1960s, as many conventional poets began to adopt the genre in its basic poetic form, rather than as a combination of literature and visual art. In response to the movement's popularity, artists used the term *poesia visiva* to describe more experimental attempts to blend words and images. *Poesia visiva* has now grown to include the use of photography, film, and soundscapes, among other artistic mediums.

HISTORICAL AND LITERARY CONTEXT

Although the "Pilot Plan" seemed like it was conveying new literary advances in the 1950s—with its shared focus on the typographical arrangement of words and conventional poetic elements—the roots of concrete poetry can be traced as far back as the third century BCE, when Greek Alexandrians used words as decorative elements in religious art. A more immediate model for the *poesia concreta* movement can be found in lettrism, an avant-garde movement that emerged in Paris after World War II. The lettrists sought to dismantle the conventional conception of words as signifiers by initiating a purely formal, rather than expressive or semantic, poetics. Founded by the poet Isidore Isou under the influence of Dadaism and futurism, lettrism was prominent in the 1940s and helped to inform the emergence of concrete poetry in the early 1950s.

By the time the "Pilot Plan" was published in 1958, *poesia concreta* was already a cohesive movement. The de Campos brothers and Pignatari first came together in the early 1950s to translate *The Cantos of Ezra Pound.* Inspired by Pound's explorations and innovations of the formal and stylistic conventions of poetry, the de Campos brothers and Pignatari founded *Noigrandes,* a São Paulo journal devoted to experimental poetry, in 1952. Soon, the three became known as the Noigrandes group and founded the larger concrete poetry movement. In 1953 de Campos published his first work of concrete poetry, titled *poetamenos.* By 1955 the de Campos brothers, along with Pignatari, had established the basic principles of concrete poetry through their various works in Brazilian newspapers. Augusto de Campos defined the poem as "the tension of word-things in space-time." Pignatari declared that concrete poetry reached its "polemic phase" with the 1956 National Exhibition of Concrete Art in São Paulo.

In composing the "Pilot Plan," the authors drew from an array of literary influences. Their most substantial influence may have been the *Manifesto of Lettrist Poetry.* Composed by Isidore Isou in 1942, the manifesto offers an aphoristic, fragmented call for a formally innovative poetics. The various futurist and Dadaist manifestos from earlier in the twentieth century also provided a precedent for the "Pilot Plan." In addition, the de Campos brothers and Pignatari were inspired by extraliterary developments, such as architect Lúcio Costa's pilot plan for the country's new modern capital, Brasília, which was under construction at that time.

Since the publication of the "Pilot Plan," many poets have continued to interpret the underlying aesthetic assumptions and innovations of the concrete poetry movement. For example, poet Jennifer Kathleen Phillips created the interactive puzzle poetry form, with poems within poems or visual messages displayed by the sound or shape of the poem's words and letters. Although the "Pilot Plan" may not be as widely read today as it was in the late 1950s and early 1960s, it is still considered an important document that has helped introduce a broad audience to the innovations of concrete poetry.

THEMES AND STYLE

The "Pilot Plan" served to introduce a larger audience to the movement's origins and aims. Here was a new medium that the de Campos brothers and Pignatari had been working with extensively—and yet it had not been written about in prose. The three men corrected this deficiency with their essay, framing it as an introduction of sorts to this new poetic movement. The "Pilot Plan" begins with a definition "Concrete poetry: product of a critical evolution of forms"—and proceeds to explain that definition in more detail. The manifesto's authors then name various writers who influenced the movement, including E.E. Cummings and Guillaume Apollinaire, and point to such avant-garde precedents as Dadaism and futurism. They go on to explain their theory of how formal structure informs poetic meaning. The "Pilot Plan" relies on fractured, staccato syntax to convey the underlying theory, aims, and techniques of the concrete poetry movement, thus demonstrating the movement's distrust of the expressive potential of language.

To persuade their readers that concrete poetry offers a vital and valid style of poetry, the de Campos brothers and Pignatari employ a prose style that embodies the characteristics of their poetic ideals. They write, "Concrete poetry: total responsibility before language. Total realism. Against a subjective and hedonistic poetry of expression. To create precise problems and to solve them in terms of sensible language. A general art of the word. The poem-product: useful object." In this way, the authors offer a clipped and urgent statement of concrete poetry's place in the world. Though seemingly radical and experimental, concrete poetry is faithful to language ("total responsibility before language"), and this allows for unparalleled fidelity to reality ("Total realism"). The result is not merely art but a "useful object," a tangible and utilitarian thing.

Through its use of abstract language and its rebellion against proper grammatical convention,

AUGUSTO DE CAMPOS: ONE-THIRD OF THE PILOT PLAN

Although not alone in his authorship of "Pilot Plan for Concrete Poetry," Augusto de Campos was one of the key figures in the movement. A lifelong writer, de Campos was born on February 14, 1931, in São Paulo, Brazil. After founding the *Noigandres* literary magazine with his brother, Haroldo, in 1952, de Campos and his peers went on to declare concrete poetry as an emerging movement.

Between the 1950s and 1970s, de Campos experimented mostly with concrete poetry. Later, in the 1980s, he added different mediums to his oeuvre, experimenting with electric billboards, videotext, hologram and laser effects, computer graphics, and different multimedia events. After forming a friendship with Brazilian musician Caetano Veloso, de Campos partnered with Veloso in a video show entitled *Pulsar* in 1984. Several years later, he also collaborated with his son, Cid, on a multimedia performance titled *Poesia é risco* (Poetry is risk), which utilized a combination of poetry, music, and images. The show has since been presented in Brazil and several other countries around the world.

"Pilot Plan" is written in a prose style that suggests the poetic innovations that its authors are advocating. The essay's most notable break with the conventions of prose is its lack of complete sentences. By omitting verbs, the authors insist on the fragmented nature of language and resist the conventional purpose of prose, which is to convey meaning. Rather, with their pared down and fractured style, the authors seek to purify the prose of conventional syntax and thus emphasize the notion of words as discrete (and concrete) units of meaning.

CRITICAL DISCUSSION

When the manifesto was originally published, it received praise from other writers who were curious about this new movement and now had answers to their questions. However, there were several dissenting opinions about the text. A group of writers from Brazil, referred to as the Rio group, argued that they favored intuitive composition to a priori composition—unlike the de Campos brothers and Pignatari. The Rio group decided to write their own manifesto in response to the "Pilot Plan" and published *Neoconcrete Manifesto* in 1959, describing poetry as a quasi-corpus rather than as a "machine" or "object," as the "Pilot Plan" authors did.

From an aesthetic standpoint, the "Pilot Plan" had a lasting impact on the world of conceptual and experimental poetry. It gave meaning and symbolism to an emerging genre. Although concrete poetry

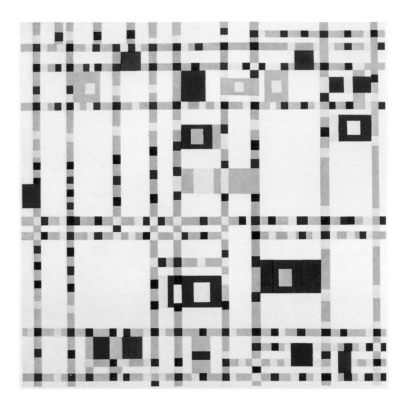

Piet Mondrian's painting *Broadway Boogie-Woogie* (1942-1943). In "Pilot Plan for Concrete Poetry," the authors point to the paintings of Mondrian, specifically the "Boogie-Woogie" series, as a visual-arts example of concrete poetry. © DENNIS HALLINAN/ALAMY

reached its popularity in the 1960s, it continues to be utilized today. If the de Campos brothers and Pignatari had never written their manifesto and had merely continued writing short pieces in Brazilian newspapers instead, it is possible that concrete poetry would have died out early on without a manifest to guide it along. Not much has been written about the actual manifesto since its publication, but the concrete poetry movement itself is still highly revered as an important mode of abstract poetry writing.

Most of the scholarly writing that addresses the "Pilot Plan" focuses on the authors' dedication to the subject. Although they published their manifesto in 1958, all three men still continue to experiment with various literature and visual forms. Since 1980 Augusto de Campos has shifted his creative efforts to new media representations, showcasing his poems on billboards, and utilizing computer graphics and hologram and laser effects. His brother, Haroldo, turned to the critical side of art, working as a theorist and a translator. Meanwhile, Pignatari spent time teaching at the Superior School of Industrial Design in Rio. Despite their different paths, all three continue to demonstrate the creativity that drove them to introduce concrete poetry to a large-scale audience.

BIBLIOGRAPHY

Sources

"A Brief Guide to Concrete Poetry." *Poets.org.* Poets.org, n.d. Web. 1 Sept. 2012.

De Campos, Augusto, Décio Pignatari, and Haroldo de Campos. "Pilot Plan for Concrete Poetry." *Noigandres* 4 (1958): n. pag. Print.

Franchetti, Paulo. "Poetry and Technique: Concrete Poetry in Brazil." *Portuguese Studies* 24.1 (2008): 56. *Literature Resource Center.* Web. 30 Aug. 2012.

Jackson, K.D., and Irene Small. "POEM/ART Brazilian Concrete Poetry." *Ciberletras* 17 (2007): n. pag. Web. 1 Sept. 2012.

Further Reading

Campos, Augusto de. *Poetamenos.* São Paulo: Edições Invenção, 1973. Print.

Herbert, George, and F.E. Hutchinson. *The Works of George Herbert.* Oxford: Clarendon, 1941. Print.

Higgins, Dick. *Pattern Poetry: Guide to an Unknown Literature.* Albany: State U of New York, 1987. Print.

Perrone, Charles A. *Seven Faces: Brazilian Poetry since Modernism.* Durham: Duke UP, 1996. Print.

Rothenberg, Jerome, Pierre Joris, and Jeffrey Cane Robinson. *Poems for the Millennium: The University of California Book of Modern & Postmodern Poetry.* Berkeley: U of California P, 1995. Print.

Anna Deem

PLACE IN FICTION

Eudora Welty

OVERVIEW

First delivered as a paper at the 1954 Fulbright Conference on American Studies at Oxford University and later published as an essay, Eudora Welty's "Place in Fiction" advances the idea that the most effective, lasting fiction expresses its origins with a strong sense of place. Welty's fiction is primarily set in the American South and is steeped in southern geography, community, social customs, and history. As a result, her work was open to the charge of regionalism, and critics often classed her, along with William Faulkner and Katherine Anne Porter, as a "southern writer." Opposing such characterizations, Welty asserts in "Place in Fiction" that "'regional' is an outsider's term; it has no meaning for the insider who is doing the writing, because as far as he knows he is simply writing about life." More generally, the essay is propelled by Welty's conviction that fiction rooted in the daily life of a particular place can "focus the gigantic, voracious eye of genius and bring its gaze to point," illuminating universal human experiences and building a world that strongly engages the reader.

"Place in Fiction" was a highlight of the 1954 Fulbright Conference. When it was published two years later as an essay in *South Atlantic Quarterly,* it was again well received. The piece was not widely read, however, until it was published in *Eye of the Story: Selected Essays and Reviews* (1979), a collection of Welty's work. Although significant scholarship devoted exclusively to the essay has not appeared, "Place in Fiction" remains influential in the literary criticism of Welty's fiction.

HISTORICAL AND LITERARY CONTEXT

"Place in Fiction" is Welty's response to use of the term "regionalist," which was often applied to Welty and other southern writers, particularly to imply provincialism, antebellum sentimentality, or a refusal to engage with racial issues. Her early work was generally well reviewed, but critics such as Diana Trilling commented on her refusal to acknowledge racial injustice. Welty was further troubled by critics' stereotypes of southern writers and of their command of logic and craft, as discussed by Dan Flower in the *Hudson Review.* Flower recounts Welty's exchange with critic Edmund Wilson following his *New Yorker* review of William Faulkner's *Intruder in the Dust.* Although the review was not entirely negative, Wilson did suggest that writers who resided in an "antiquated community" could not fully command the art of modern fiction, which in his view was properly a by-product of industrial cities. Welty wrote a spirited defense of Faulkner, articulating ideas that she would develop further in "Place in Fiction."

An American cultural movement known as the Southern Literary Renaissance was coming to a close when "Place in Fiction" appeared. During this period, which spanned about thirty years from the early to mid-twentieth century, the South became the locus of significant American literary activity. Unlike their predecessors—who tended to invoke a plantation idyll or the bravery of the Confederate army—writers such as Faulkner wrote about slaves, descendants of slaves, and poor whites and made serious, if not entirely successful, attempts to grapple with the South's troubled history of race relations. Southern writers, protesting the encroachment of northern industry on the South's rural, farm-based culture, also dealt with themes of city versus country. Welty biographers have noted that although she was influenced by a variety of Southern Renaissance writers, she did not align herself with any particular school, and her fiction was more concerned with individual and family relationships than explicitly political issues.

"Place in Fiction" is part of a literary tradition of southern writers engaging with southern concerns, especially the changes in the physical and social landscape brought on by industrialization in the twentieth century. Upholding the value of the South's agrarian way of life in contrast to an urban one centered on industrialization, a group of twelve American novelists, poets, and essayists known as the Southern Agrarians produced a manifesto called *I'll Take My Stand: The South and the Agrarian Tradition* (1930). It sought to define "proper living" by using the Old South as a sort of mythic model, with a demonstrable terrain, history, and inherited way of life. Welty disavowed any close association between her fiction and the political concerns of this group, but some scholars have referred to her as a sort of literary Agrarian, pointing, for example, to her descriptive essay "Some Notes on River Country," which evokes lost towns on the Mississippi River between Jackson and Natchez. Exploring the appeal of these lost places, she writes,

✤ *Key Facts*

Time Period:
Mid-20th Century

Movement/Issue:
Aesthetics; Southern literature

Place of Publication:
United States

Language of Publication:
English

EUDORA WELTY: PHOTOGRAPHER

During the 1930s, Eudora Welty took photographs while traveling as a publicity agent for the Works Project Administration. Later in her life she said that she had photographed people because they were a part of real life and that she was recording reality. Welty's photographs primarily depicted the rural poor, both whites and blacks, and are a record of a little-documented time and place in American history. In her memoir, *One Writer's Beginnings,* Welty discusses the importance of photography in developing technique as a fiction writer. She writes, "Photography taught me that to be able to capture transience … was the greatest need I had." She further stated that "these were things a story writer needed to know. And I felt the need to hold transient life in words—there's so much more of life that only words can convey."

During her lifetime, Welty published two books of photographs, *One Time, One Place: Mississippi in the Depression: A Snapshot Album* (1971) and *Photographs* (1989). A body of scholarship has developed that relates Welty's photography to her fiction. Some critics have sought to connect specific pictures to her stories, as, for example, a picture of a woman from Hinds County in 1935 with the character Phoenix Jackson from Welty's 1941 short story "A Worn Path."

"A place that once is lived in is like a fire that never goes out."

In the decades following the publication of "Place in Fiction," critics have used the essay as a touchstone for interpreting not only the treatment of place by Welty but also in southern fiction more generally. Controversy continues, however, about the extent to which Welty can be tied to the Agrarian movement. Welty herself responded to some of the criticisms about her treatment of race relations in the South in her 1965 essay "Must the Novelist Crusade?" In the essay she poses the question, "Is writing a novel *something we can do about it*?" Her ultimate answer is "no." For Welty, fiction has aims distinct from those of journalism or crusading, valuable though such activities may be. She affirms "that morality as shown through human relationships is the whole heart of fiction," but she resists the notion that injustice can be explicitly argued against there, opining instead that arguments introduce a false "neatness" into fiction that ultimately undermines "the shared act of imagination" that makes it true and meaningful. Two of Welty's short stories of particular interest in light of her critical discourse concerning race are "Where Is This Voice Coming From?" (1963) and "The Demonstrators" (1966).

THEMES AND STYLE

In "Place in Fiction" Welty stresses the primacy of place in establishing a believable fictional world, which she believes is key in expressing universal elements of human experience. The author emphasizes that all fiction is "regional" in the sense that it arises from a particular writer at a particular time. The notion of place developed in the essay goes beyond mere physical location to include the social and cultural aspects of place, including the human emotions bound up with it. "Location," she writes, "is the ground conductor of all the currents of emotion and belief and moral conviction" and needs "the warm hard earth underfoot, the light and lift of air, the stir and play of mood, the softening of bath of atmosphere that give the likeness-to-life that life needs." Welty also identifies place as the origin of a given writer's point of view: "Place … bestows on us our original awareness; and our critical powers spring up from the study of it and the growth of experience inside it."

Welty's manifesto achieves its rhetorical effect by positing a "we" who have had certain shared emotional experiences as people and as readers and by appealing to examples from canonical fiction to question what "regional" can mean. Developing the theme that the external world presented in a novel is a vehicle to illuminate essential truths about life, Welty describes how "some of us grew up with the china night-light, the little lamp whose lighting showed its secret and with that spread its enchantment." She calls upon the reader's experience with works such as *Wuthering Heights* to illustrate that it is the nature of all fiction to be "bound up in the local." "I say, 'The Yorkshire Moors,'" she explains, "and you will say, 'Wuthering Heights.'" She goes on to invite readers to imagine moving Marcel Proust's *Swann's Way* to London or Thomas Mann's *Magic Mountain* to Spain. Finally she asks explicitly, "Jane Austen, Emily Brontë … the authors of the books of the Old Testament, all confined themselves to regions, great or small—but are they regional?"

Stylistically, "Place in Fiction" is distinguished by its conversational tone, which underlines Welty's notion that good writing communicates and is about "you and me, here." Throughout the work, she addresses readers directly, developing her themes through a dialogue of questions and replies. Although conversational, Welty's language is also imaginative and lyrical. She refers to place, for instance, as "one of the lesser angels that watch over the racing hand of fiction."

CRITICAL DISCUSSION

"Place in Fiction" was well received when delivered at Cambridge in 1954 and also after it was published in *South Atlantic Quarterly.* Over the next few years, Welty gave readings of the essay, including a presentation at the Women's College at Duke University in 1955. The essay did not gain a wide audience, however, until it was included in *Eye of the Story.* Biographers have noted that Welty always felt a bit uncomfortable as an essayist and had to be urged by a longtime friend, the novelist Kenneth Millar, to reissue the piece. In correspondence urging that "Place in Fiction" as well as several other essays be republished, he writes, "They are not written in the language of the schools, into which even most artists tend to shift when they write criticism. And partly for that reason they manage to get and stay closer to the workings of fiction than almost anything I can remember."

In the years following the publication of "Place in Fiction," critics less commonly treated literature from the South, including Welty's, as a distinct category of American literature. This shift in perception has been attributed, at least in part, to feminist arguments that "regional" is a diminutive term far more commonly applied to women's writing than to that of their male peers. For example, in 1991 Candace Waid noted in *Modern American Women Writers* that decades after "Place in Fiction" was published, Welty's *Collected Stories* still came with a disclaimer in the introduction that they were not to be dismissed as regional. "Such backhanded compliments," she writes, "usually go on to praise the work of writers such as Welty as being 'universal.' Masking anxiety about the representation of cultural difference and reflecting a particularly 'American' concern with aesthetic and literary nationalism, this use of 'universal' may strike Southern writers as provincial as well as condescending." Most contemporary readings of Welty are in line with this analysis and have focused on other issues.

Since its publication in 1956, "Place in Fiction" has been used as a primer in reading Welty's fiction but has yet to generate a substantive body of critical scholarship as a stand-alone literary manifesto. Jan Gretlund's 1994 *Eudora Welty's Aesthetics of Place,* one of the only book-length discussions of Welty's conception of place, broadly argues that "Welty's work represents a cultural continuity of basic Agrarian ideas from their origin in the rural South to their presence in the urbanized South." More recent Welty scholarship has focused on topics not closely related to place, although some feminist treatments of elements of the grotesque in Welty's work offer a counterpoint to more traditional readings of the South in her fiction.

Author Eudora Welty at her home in Jackson, Mississippi, in 1992. © PHILIP GOULD/CORBIS

BIBLIOGRAPHY

Sources

Flower, Dan. "Eudora Welty and Racism." *Hudson Review.* Hudson Review, Summer 2007. Web. 2 June 2012.

Gretlund, Jan Nordby. *Eudora Welty's Aesthetics of Place.* Odense UP and the U of Delaware P, 1994. *Google Book Search.* Web. 3 June 2012.

Marrs, Suzanne. *Eudora Welty: A Biography.* Orlando: Harcourt, 2005. Print.

———. "Place and Displaced in Eudora Welty's 'The Bride of Innisfallen.'" *Mississippi Quarterly* 22 Sept. 1997: 647-68. *Literature Sources from Gale.* Web. 3 June 2012.

Prenshaw, Peggy Whitman. "Eudora Welty." *The History of Southern Literature.* Ed. Louis D. Rubin Jr. et al. Baton Rouge: Louisiana State UP, 1985. 470-75. Print.

Waid, Candace. "Eudora Welty." *Modern American Women Writers.* Ed. Elaine Showalter, Lea Baechler, and A. Walton Litz. New York: Scribner's, 1991. *Literature Sources from Gale.* Web. 3 June 2012.

Welty, Eudora. "Must the Novelist Crusade?" *The Eye of the Story: Selected Essays and Reviews.* New York: Random House, 1977. Print.

Further Reading

Eudora Welty and Politics: Did the Novelist Crusade? Ed. Harriet Pollack and Suzanne Marrs. Baton Rouge: Louisiana State UP, 2001. Print.

Gleason-White, Sarah. "A Particularly Southern Form of Ugliness: Eudora Welty, Carson McCullers, and Flannery O'Connor." *Southern Literary Journal* 36.1 (2003): 46-57. Print.

Kreyling, Michael. *Inventing Southern Literature.* Jackson: UP of Mississippi, 1998. Print.

Prenshaw, Peggy Whitman. *Eudora Welty: Critical Essays.* Jackson: UP of Mississippi, 1979. Print.

Waldron, Ann. *Eudora: A Writer's Life.* New York: Anchor Books, 1998. Print.

Welty, Eudora. *One Writer's Beginnings.* New York: Warner Books, 1983. Print.

———. *Photographs.* Jackson: UP of Mississippi, 1983. Print.

Daisy Gard

POETIC MANIFESTO

Dylan Thomas

❖ *Key Facts*

Time Period:
Mid-20th Century

Movement/Issue:
Aesthetics; Modernism;
Freudianism

Place of Publication:
United States

**Language of
Publication:**
English

OVERVIEW

In "Poetic Manifesto," written in 1951 in response to a letter from a doctoral student, Dylan Thomas explains his theories of poetry, early influences, and poetic techniques. The letter was not presented as a manifesto, however, until it was published by Richard Jones as "Dylan Thomas's Poetic Manifesto" in the winter 1961 issue of *Texas Quarterly,* eight years after Thomas's death. Thomas used portions of the letter to introduce his poetry to audiences, including a notable reading at the Massachusetts Institute of Technology on March 7, 1952. In "Poetic Manifesto," Thomas insists on the verbal craft of his poetry, its religious frame of reference, and the value of poetry residing in the reader's emotional response to words.

Since its publication, the "Poetic Manifesto" has been regarded as a generally reliable statement of Thomas's beliefs about poetry, and it has played an influential role in rehabilitating Thomas's reputation as a poet. When the manifesto was first published in 1961, Thomas's literary reputation had already declined significantly since his death in 1953. Rumors of his drinking and womanizing, confirmed in biographies such as John Malcolm Brinnin's *Dylan Thomas in America* (1955), led many readers to interpret the poetry in light of the biography, either by focusing on Thomas himself as a defiant romantic or by ascribing Thomas's faults to his poetry. In addition, English poetry and literary criticism of the 1950s and 1960s was dominated by the Movement, a group of writers including Kingsley Amis, Philip Larkin, and Donald Davie who rejected the stylistic exuberance and mythic elements of Thomas's poetry. Reprinted in Constantine FitzGibbon's more sympathetic biography, *Dylan Thomas: A Life* (1965), the "Poetic Manifesto" has since prompted more nuanced evaluations of Thomas's theories and his place among twentieth-century poets.

HISTORICAL AND LITERARY CONTEXT

Although it does not, like most manifestos, make broad claims about how literature in its era should be written, Dylan Thomas's "Poetic Manifesto" indicates how his poetry might be read productively in connection with an earlier generation of modernist writers. Asked about the influence of James Joyce, Sigmund Freud, the surrealists, and the Bible on his poetry,

Thomas stresses his differences from the modernists by declaring that, of these four, only the Bible could be counted as a formative influence. It is possible, however, that Thomas is being slightly disingenuous in denying the influence of Joyce, Freud, and the surrealists. For instance, when asked a similar question about Freud in "Answers to an Enquiry" (1934), Thomas described poetry as an extension of Freud's work: "Whatever is hidden should be made naked.... [P]oetry must drag further into the clean nakedness of light more even of the hidden causes than Freud could realize." Like Freud's theories of sexual energy, Joyce's verbal techniques are regarded as an important influence on Thomas's poems. Considering the dominance of Joyce's brand of high modernism and Freud's psychological theories within the academy at the time, Thomas's decision to downplay their influence might reflect his conception of himself as a literary amateur or outsider.

Like Thomas's poetry, his "Poetic Manifesto" does not lend itself to easy historical categorization. It does not mention the London Blitz, his status as a Welsh poet living in England, his work reading poetry on BBC radio broadcasts, or his celebrated reading tours of America, even though all of these were important influences on his poetry. Perhaps paradoxically, the most historical element of Thomas's manifesto may be his emphasis on the beauty of words as distinct from their referents or meanings. This emphasis on the sound and texture of words was certainly characteristic of surrealist writers and prompted many contemporaries to link Thomas's obscurity with surrealism. At the same time, Thomas's insistence on the primacy of words, in connection with the techniques of "puns, portmanteau-words, paradox, allusion, paronomasia, paragram, catachresis, [and] slang" resembles New Criticism's theories of the poem as an aesthetic object that must be analyzed according to its own internal logic rather than in terms of mimesis.

The "Poetic Manifesto" represents Thomas's mature statement of his poetic theories, and it expands on, and occasionally reverses, his earlier responses to a reader's questions in "Answers to an Enquiry." Significantly, in both cases Thomas's statements on poetry emerge in response to general questions from a reader rather than as a more polemical manifesto addressed to other writers. In both statements on poetry,

Thomas envisions his poems as written for the common reader.

Because of Thomas's early and unexpected death at the age of thirty-nine, the "Poetic Manifesto" stands as a retrospective summary of his poetic aims and achievements. In the decades following its publication, the "Poetic Manifesto" has influenced scholarly studies of Thomas and his place in twentieth-century poetry. Thomas's popularity declined significantly in the late twentieth century, and studies of his poetry appear somewhat infrequently.

THEMES AND STYLE

The main theme of Dylan Thomas's "Poetic Manifesto" is the poet's development from a young child "in love with words" to a mature poet conscious of his influences and his own poetic aims. Throughout the manifesto, Thomas traces his love of words from the nursery rhymes, verses, and ballads that appealed to him in infancy to the writers that he learned to imitate. Among his first influences, he lists "nursery rhymes and folk tales, the Scottish Ballads, a few lines of hymns, the most famous Bible stories and the rhythms of the Bible, Blake's Songs of Innocence, and the quite incomprehensible magical majesty and nonsense of Shakespeare." Thomas stresses that, at a young age, understanding the meaning of the words was less important than the feelings conjured up by the words themselves: from the sound of words "came love and terror and pity and pain and wonder and all the other vague abstractions that make our ephemeral lives dangerous, great, and bearable." As he grew older, he learned to write poetry by focusing primarily on the craft of wordplay: "What I like to do is to treat words as a craftsman does his wood or stone or what-have-you, to hew, carve, mould, coil, polish and plane them into patterns, sequences, sculptures, fugues of sound expressing some lyrical impulse, some spiritual doubt or conviction, some dimly-realised truth I must try to reach and realise." Yet, despite his emphasis on craft, Thomas concludes by stressing the reader's experience of pleasure and the poem as more than the sum of its parts—"so that something that is not in the poem can creep, crawl, flash, or thunder in."

The major rhetorical technique of "Poetic Manifesto" is its use of similes and metaphors to describe words as physical things. For example, Thomas writes, "[T]hese words were, to me, as the notes of bells, the sounds of musical instruments, the noises of wind, sea, and rain, the rattle of milk-carts, the clopping of hooves on cobbles, the fingering of branches on the window pane, might be to someone, deaf from birth, who has miraculously found his hearing." Through this catalogue of images and associations, he stresses the physicality of words and associates them with the natural world.

The dominant tone of the manifesto is that of enthusiasm. Describing his youthful experiences with writing, Thomas dramatizes the power and mystery

DYLAN THOMAS: NEO-ROMANTIC POET

Born in Swansea, Wales, in 1914, Dylan Thomas began writing poetry at a young age. Formally schooled at Swansea Grammar School from 1925 to 1931, Thomas spent three years writing poetry in Wales before leaving for London in 1934. Thomas wrote "The Force That through the Green Fuse Drives the Flower" and "And Death Shall Have No Dominion" during this early period of productivity. These poems work to fuse contrasting themes of birth and death, and sex and Christianity.

In London, Thomas adopted a bohemian lifestyle, befriending a group of poets known as the Apocalyptics, and married Caitlin Macnamara, a dancer and writer with whom he had three children. He wrote scripts and later read poetry for the BBC in London during World War II. In 1950, he made his first trip to the United States on a reading tour. His American tours, marked by drinking and philandering, impaired his health, and he died on November 9, 1953, at the age of thirty-nine. Although known for such famous poems as "Fern Hill," "Do Not Go Gentle into That Good Night," and "A Refusal to Mourn the Death, by Fire, of a Child in London," Thomas was also an accomplished writer of short fiction and screenplays.

The Welsh poet Dylan Thomas, author of "Poetic Manifesto," in 1948. © MIRRORPIX/LEBRECHT AUTHORS/THE IMAGE WORKS

of words through his descriptions and comparisons. For example, he describes his youthful perception that his first poems were "wonderfully original things, like eggs laid by tigers." Like the sensation of wonder he is describing, Thomas's simile is an original way of highlighting the elements of mystery in the natural (and written) world. In his conclusion to the manifesto, Thomas returns to the theme of enthusiasm: "The joy and function of poetry is, and was, the celebration of man, which is also the celebration of God."

CRITICAL DISCUSSION

When first published in the *Texas Quarterly*, the "Poetic Manifesto" revived debates over Dylan Thomas's character as well as his poetic theories. Constantine FitzGibbon, comparing Thomas's responses in the "Poetic Manifesto" to his responses in "Answers to an Enquiry," declares, "[W]hile there was no change of purpose, almost no change of view, in the seventeen years that had elapsed, there was a widening and a deepening both of perception and of humility. He was, in fact, the same poet only more so." Other scholars have noted that, while the manifesto provides some sense of Thomas as a man, it remains vague about his poetic ideas and methods. R.B. Kershner, Jr. writes, "[T]he most Thomas is willing to do, in speaking about the genesis and execution of his work, is to hint at attitudes and areas of concern; one receives the impression that he not so much would not as could not describe his working method in easily accessible terms."

As the scholarly debate shifted from Thomas's personality to his legacy as a poet, the "Poetic Manifesto" continued to inform evaluations of Thomas's poetry. The scholarly consensus is that Thomas's poetry, while shaped in many ways by modernist poets like T.S. Eliot and Ezra Pound, also constituted a reaction against the unsentimental, intellectual style of modernist poems. However, unlike the 1930s poetry of W.H. Auden and C. Day Lewis, which was also written in reaction against modernism, Thomas's poetry is not marked by broad social themes or an ironic mode. What distinguishes Thomas from these poets has been variously attributed to neo-romanticism or the bardic tradition and traced to Thomas's emphasis on personality (Karl Shapiro) or stress on feeling rather than ideas (Stephen Spender). In the half century since the "Poetic Manifesto" was first published, it continues to motivate a diminishing number of studies of Thomas's Welsh origins, social conscience, and poetic technique.

Early studies of the "Poetic Manifesto" focused on Thomas's poetic principles and how well they correspond with his poems. From the 1950s to the 1970s, many studies of Thomas's prosody appeared, addressing such questions as the relation between image and structure, narration and rhyme scheme, and spoken versus written rhythms within the poems. From the 1980s to the present, fewer studies of Thomas's poetics have appeared as the scholarly focus has shifted from religious and aesthetic themes to historical and political contexts.

BIBLIOGRAPHY

Sources

Brinnin, John Malcolm, ed. *A Casebook on Dylan Thomas*. New York: Crowell, 1960. Print.

Davies, Walford, ed. *Dylan Thomas: New Critical Essays*. London: Dent, 1972. Print.

"Dylan Thomas (1914-1953)." *Poetry Criticism*. Volume 52. Ed. David Galens. Detroit: Thomson Gale, 2004: 207-338. *Dictionary of Literary Biography*. Web. 9 Aug. 2012.

"Dylan Thomas 1914-1953." *Poetry Foundation*. Poetry Foundation, n.d. Web. 9 Aug. 2012.

FitzGibbon, Constantine. *The Life of Dylan Thomas*. Boston: Little, Brown, 1965. Print.

Kershner, R.B., Jr. *Dylan Thomas: The Poet and His Critics*. Chicago: American Lib. Assn., 1976. Print.

Lewis, Wyndham, et al. "Answers to an Enquiry." *New Verse* 11 (1934): 7-8. Print.

Thomas, Dylan. *Early Prose Writings*. Ed. Walford Davies. London: Dent, 1971. Print.

Further Reading

Crehan, Stewart. "The Lips of Time." *Dylan Thomas*. Eds. John Goodby and Chris Wigginton. New York: Palgrave, 2001. 46-64. Print.

Ferris, Paul. *Dylan Thomas, The Biography: New Edition*. Washington, DC: Counterpoint, 2000. Print.

Gordon, John. "Dylan Thomas: The Great War and Recovered Memory." *ANQ* 18.4 (2005): 39-42. Print.

Heaney, Seamus. "Dylan the Durable? On Dylan Thomas." *Salmagundi* 100 (1993): 66-85. Print.

McNees, Eleanor Jane. *Eucharistic Poetry: The Search for Presence in the Writings of John Donne, Gerald Manley Hopkins, Dylan Thomas, and Geoffrey Hill*. Lewisburg: Bucknell UP, 1992. Print.

Moynihan, William T. *The Craft and Art of Dylan Thomas*. Ithaca: Cornell UP, 1966. Print.

Kevin Cooney

POETRY AND THE PRIMITIVE
Notes on Poetry as an Ecological Survival Technique
Gary Snyder

OVERVIEW

Written by American poet Gary Snyder, "Poetry and the Primitive: Notes on Poetry as an Ecological Survival Technique" calls for a radical re-evaluation of Western ecological ethics using principles gleaned from poetics, anthropology, and indigenous traditions. Snyder first delivered the manifesto as a lecture at the 1965 Berkeley Poetry Conference alongside Beat poets Allen Ginsberg and Robert Creeley, later publishing the work in the prose collection *Earth House Hold* (1969). Heavily influenced by the American Indian culture he experienced while growing up in the Pacific Northwest and by the Zen Buddhism he encountered on a six-year sojourn to Asia, Snyder incorporates indigenous and Eastern worldviews into a philosophy of maintaining ecological balance and preventing further environmental destruction. Presented to an American audience in the midst of a cultural revolution, Snyder's message fit seamlessly with the nascent ecological interests of the hippie movement.

In a climate predisposed to Snyder's politics, "Poetry and the Primitive" met with a generally positive response, although critics from indigenous communities opposed his appropriation of American Indian tenets without acknowledging their origins. The manifesto's themes of historical continuity, appreciation of animals, and interconnectedness align closely with the philosophies of 1960s countercultural movements and refer to an era when ecological concerns first entered American cultural consciousness. "Poetry and the Primitive" established a need to diverge from traditional Western values in environmental matters, which impelled the later deep-ecology and eco-critical movements. The manifesto also demonstrated an important intersection of poetry and political discourse, which Snyder continues to explore in his prose and poetry.

HISTORICAL AND LITERARY CONTEXT

"Poetry and the Primitive: Notes on Poetry as an Ecological Survival Technique" responds to the disconnected and disrespectful Western view of the natural environment, which Snyder saw as highly destructive. Though Western history is replete with examples of humans exploiting the natural world, it was not until the Industrial Revolution that concerns over the deterioration of resources and habitats began to challenge assumptions that humans were meant to dominate nature. The late 19th century European "Back-to-Nature" movement as well as conservationist activities in early 20th century America emphasized the preservation of wilderness over exploitation as man's moral obligation. While many efforts were successful, consumption and destruction of natural resources continued unabated through the post-WWII era. By the mid-20th century, environmental thinking had shifted to a more reciprocal understanding of the relationship between humans and nature as a way to better address impending environmental crises.

By the time "Poetry and the Primitive" was published, countercultural groups had begun exploring Eastern and Native American philosophies as alternatives to what they perceived as a restrictive and hegemonic Western perspective. Such worldviews emphasized interconnectedness and respect for ecological systems with regard to the natural world. As part of the Beat Generation, Gary Snyder shared that group's values of experimentation, rejection of consumerism, and freedom of expression, however Snyder's upbringing in the rural Northwest and affinity for the wilderness set him apart from his urban-dwelling peers such as Ginsburg and novelist Jack Kerouac. Even before delivering his environmental manifesto in 1965, Snyder was often compared with transcendentalist writer Henry David Thoreau. "Poetry and the Primitive" unified and underscored these various influences in order to propose a paradigm shift in environmental thinking.

"Poetry and the Primitive" draws on a long lineage of American nature writing that is often traced back to Thoreau's *Walden* (1854). Chronicling two years spent in a cabin by Walden Pond, Massachusetts, Thoreau proffers closeness with nature as a remedy for social ills. Building from this precedent, Aldo Leopold's book *A Sand County Almanac* (1949) promotes a "land ethic" of stewardship and conservation based on the principle that all living beings deserve respect, and that humans are part of an ecological community. Echoes of this ethic are observable in

✣ *Key Facts*

Time Period:
Mid-20th Century

Movement/Issue:
Aesthetics; Primitivism;
Environmentalism

Place of Publication:
United States

**Language of
Publication:**
English

GARY SNYDER: ZEN POET

From a young age, Gary Snyder showed a keen interest in the cultures and religions of the Far East, because, he has said, he recognized in those traditions a mirror of his own sentiments about the Northwestern landscape in which he was raised. This interest grew into a life passion. Amid a trendy interest in Asian culture in 1950s San Francisco, Snyder pursued graduate work in East Asian studies. In 1956—before completing his degree—Snyder left the United States on a scholarship from the First Zen Institute of America for Kyoto, Japan where he would spend the next ten years in formal training to become a Zen Buddhist monk. By 1958 Snyder had been immortalized as the fictional character Japhey Ryder, a Buddhist spiritualist, in Jack Kerouac's novel *The Dharma Bums*. Ryder introduces the main character to Zen and mountaineering, which mirrored the real-life friendship between Snyder and Kerouac and spurred a renewed craze for Zen.

In addition to extensive work with Chinese and Japanese translations, Snyder's poetry demonstrates the influence of Zen practice in both form and content. James Campbell writes, "Even when it goes unmentioned in the verse itself, the meditative tendency sits behind his work and nature poems. He writes about repairing a car with the same attentiveness he gives to Zen ritual." While Snyder attested in 2005 that "Being a Buddhist doesn't necessarily mean you have to be a good Buddhist," the writer's poetry, politics, and daily life are guided by the Buddhist principles of non-harming, honoring the non-human world, and fully inhabiting one's environment.

Snyder's manifesto. By the 1960s environmental writing found traction in American culture, notably with Rachel Carson's seminal work *Silent Spring* (1962) whose condemnation of industrial chemicals incited a grassroots political movement. While all of these texts suggest different methodologies for environmental preservation, in considering the role of humans in their natural environment each manifesto encourages attentiveness to the impact of human activity on the non-human environment.

"Poetry and the Primitive" stands out as a harbinger of ecological literature and theories. While counterculture movements of the 1950s and 1960s gave rise to the modern environmental movement, these impulses intensified and diversified in the 1970s. Snyder's manifesto most closely aligns with the Deep Ecology movement, which espouses an ethic of respect for nature and the inherent value of all living beings. Eco-poets and environmental writers have proliferated in the latter 20th century; writers such as Barry Lopez, Terry Tempest Williams, and Wendell Berry all follow in Snyder's model, incorporating non-Western worldviews and fusing poetics and politics. As environmental concerns have moved to the forefront of life in the early 21st century, literature dealing with the intersection of human and non-human worlds continues to be compelling for contemporary readers.

THEMES AND STYLE

The central theme of "Poetry and the Primitive" is that interdependence between humans and the natural world is necessary to mitigate environmental destruction. Snyder sets up a binary opposition between civilization and primitivism throughout the manifesto to illustrate the superior ability of "primitive" cultures to connect with their natural environment. "One of the most remarkable intuitions in Western thought was Rousseau's Noble Savage: the idea that perhaps civilization has something to learn from the primitive." Using examples from Eastern and Native American traditions, as well as from Western anthropology, Snyder argues that a worldview of interconnection promotes deeper respect and honor for nature. Ultimately, the goal of that interconnection and of the manifesto is to encourage a new ecological ethic: "The primitive world view, far-out scientific knowledge and the poetic imagination are related forces which may help if not save the world or humanity, at least to same the Redwoods."

The manifesto achieves its rhetorical effect through appeals to a transcendent unity that bespeaks the 1960s countercultural rejection of Western mores, harmony, and appreciation for diversity. This sense of unity is primarily demonstrated through anecdotal evidence of various primitive cultures and from anthropological observations. Ostensibly, the manifesto addresses Snyder's peers of like-minded writers, who share his affinity for non-Western philosophy, but do not have the same depth of knowledge in such areas. While the manifesto is not didactic, Snyder takes on the role of educator, and is at times chiding: "We all know what primitive cultures don't have. What they *do* have is this knowledge and connection and responsibility which amounts to a spiritual ascesis for the whole community." His own deep conviction in the strength of this alternative worldview is further abetted by examples from texts by Claude Levi-Strauss and anthropologist Stanley Diamond.

"Poetry and the Primitive" is organized as a logical argument. The manifesto is divided into four sections: Bilateral Symmetry, Making Love with Animals, The Voice as a Girl, and Hopscotch and Cats Cradles, each of which treats one pillar of the overarching theme of interconnection. Logical organization and a cogent discussion of each point appeals to Western reader's appreciation for the rational, while the examples vacillate between the spiritual and the empirical. In doing so, Snyder negotiates his Western audience's likely interest in the subject matter, but mediates the message with an academic style that is familiar and understandable to them. Moreover, as ecology and environmentalism were in their nascent stages when the manifesto first appeared, Snyder's choice for a meditative tenor and logical organization betrays not a sense of urgency, but rather one of contemplation of strategy at the outset of a new era.

CRITICAL DISCUSSION

Initial discussion of "Poetry and the Primitive" failed to recognize the essay as an environmentalist manifesto, instead considering it a guidebook for Snyder's poetry. Reviews of the essay often lumped it with the other prose essays in 1969's *Earth House Hold,* which was frequently discussed in concert with a poetry collection published the same year, *Regarding Wave.* As one critic, Paul Sherman, noted, "*Earth House Hold* [...] provides an excellent introduction to a poet whose poetry, because of its autobiographical nature and allusions to Oriental and American Indian lore, is not always readily available..." (76). About the manifesto, Thomas Parkinson said, "The several segments of the books connect and culminate in the crystallizing form of the essay "Poetry and the Primitive" in confirming Snyder's ethos (448). Without a specific discussion of the ecological ramifications of the manifesto, both Parkinson and Sherman asserted that, as a collection, *Earth House Hold* established the writer's deepening awareness of the environment and its effect on him.

Don McLeod stated that "Snyder's main impact on the Beat Generation, and on American literature since, has been as a spokesman for the natural world and the values associated with primitive cultures..." (NP). As the countercultural movements of the 1960s faded, environmentalism gained momentum through the remainder of the 20th century. "Poetry and the Primitive" served as a model for this movement. The manifesto's themes of interconnection, reciprocity, and living in concert with one's environment became tenets of the environmental movement as well as of several of its offshoots. The environmental ethic of the manifesto also persisted in Snyder's subsequent prose and poetry, becoming more concretized in later texts such as the 1990 prose collection, *The Practice of the Wild.*

"Poetry and the Primitive" has received significant attention for its de-emphasis of an American anthropocentric perspective. In one vein of study, scholars have identified the manifesto's promotion of a non-Western worldview as its legacy. Mary Ann Caws considers the essay a manifesto of "neoprimitivism," while Trevor Carolan's interest lies in the potential to understand post-nationalism through the sense of connection depicted in the essay. In another vein, ecocritics have taken up "Poetry and the Primitive" as a model of the "vital spirit of ecology," one that underscores compassion for the non-human world. In his 2006 article "Nature Writing in American Literature," Petr Kopecky traces the roots of the Deep Ecology movement—which regards all living beings as

Poet Gary Snyder in Berkeley, California, in 2008. His "Poetry and the Primitive" asserts the fundamental importance of man's relationship with the environment. © PAUL CHINN/SAN FRANCISCO CHRONICLE/CORBIS

equals—to several California writers, hailing Snyder's "ecophilosophical platform" as integral to the movement's mission (80).

BIBLIOGRAPHY

Sources

Carolan, Trevor. "Ecosystems, Mandalas and Watersheds: The Dharma Citizenship of Gary Snyder." *The University of Fraser Valley Research Review* 3.1 (2010): 144-60. Print.

Caws, Mary Ann ed. "Primitivism and Neoprimitivism." *Manifesto: A Century of Isms.* Lincoln: U of Nebraska P, 2001: 98-102. Print.

Disch, Robert ed. *The Ecological Conscience: Values for Survival.* Englewood Cliffs, N.J.: Prentice-Hall, 1970. Print.

Kopecky, Petr. "Nature Writing in American Literature: Inspirations, Interrelations, and Impacts of California Authors on the Deep Ecology Movement." *The Trumpeter* 22.2 (2006): 77-89. Print.

Murphy, Patrick D. "The Waves of Household and Marriage: *Earth House Hold* and *Regarding Wave.*" *Understanding Gary Snyder.* Columbia: U of South Carolina P, 1992. 92-108. Print.

Sherman, Paul. "From 'Lookout to Ashram: The Way of Gary Snyder': Part One." *The Iowa Review.* 1.3 (1970): 76-89. Print.

———. "From 'Lookout to Ashram: The Way of Gary Snyder: Part Two (Conclusion)." *The Iowa Review* 1. 4 (1970): 70-85. Print.

McLeod, Dan. "Gary Snyder." *Dictionary of Literary Biography, Volume 16: The Beats: Literary Bohemians in Postwar America.* Detroit: Gale Research Co., 1983. 486-500. Print.

Parkinson, Thomas. "The Theory and Practice of Gary Snyder." *Journal of Modern Literature* 2.3 (1971/1972): 448-452. Print.

Steuding, Bob. *Gary Snyder.* New York: Twayne, 1976. Print.

Further Reading

"Biography: Gary Snyder." *The Poetry Foundation.* The Poetry Foundation, 2009. Web. 21 May 2012.

Campbell, James. "Saturday Review Profile: Gary Snyder: High Peak Haikus." *The Guardian.* 16 July 2005. Print.

Davidson, Michael. *The San Francisco Renaissance: Poetics and Community at Mid-Century.* Cambridge, UK: Cambridge UP, 1989. Print.

Goodyear, Dana. "Zen Master: Gary Snyder and the Art of Life." *The New Yorker.* 20 Oct 2008. 66-75. Print.

Gottleib, Robert. *Forcing the Spring: The Transformation of the American Environmental Movement.* Washington, D.C.: Island Press, 2005. Print.

Gray, Timothy. *Gary Snyder and the Pacific Rim: Creating Countercultural Community.* Iowa City: U of Iowa P, 2006. Print.

Halper, Jon, ed. *Gary Snyder Dimensions of a Life.* New York: Random House, 1991. Print.

Jung, HwaYol, and Petee Jung. "Gary Snyder's Ecopiety." *Environmental History Review* 14.3 (1990): 74-87. Print.

Molesworth, Charles. *Gary Snyder's Vision: Poetry and the Real Work.* Columbia: U of Missouri P, 1983. Print.

Quetchenbach, Bernard W. "Gary Snyder." *Back from the Far Field: American Nature Poetry in the Late Twentieth Century.* Charlottesville: U of Virginia P, 2000. 85-122. Print.

Snyder, Gary. *Earth House Hold: Technical Notes and Queries to Fellow Dharma Revolutionaries.* New York: New Directions Publishing, 1969. Print.

———. *The Gary Snyder Reader: Prose, Poetry, and Translations 1952-1998.* Washington, DC: Counterpoint, 1999. Print.

———. *The Practice of the Wild.* San Francisco: North Point Press, 1990. Print.

Elizabeth Boeheim

PROJECTIVE VERSE

Charles Olson

OVERVIEW

Charles Olson's influential "Projective Verse" (1950) defines poetry not in terms of the formal unities and self-contained meaning emphasized by New Criticism but in terms of its energy and openness. Written when the New Critics' model was widely accepted (and only two years after T.S. Eliot won the Nobel Prize for Literature), Olson's essay uncovers new possibilities for poetry by drawing on alternative traditions, such as the modernism of Ezra Pound and William Carlos Williams, the anthropology of Leo Frobenius, and the expansive social vision and polyphonic vernacular of Herman Melville. Specifically, he argues that the meter and rhyme of "closed" poems could be discarded in favor of "open" projective verse that would appear, on the page, like a musical scoring of the poet's breath. Olson claims that this conception of the poem leads poets to perceive their relationship to the world differently; without the sense of superiority inherent in the lyrical ego, the poet can unite his voice with the natural world.

"Projective Verse" received a great deal of immediate favorable attention. Notably, Williams quoted a large portion of the essay approvingly in his *Autobiography* (1951). Poets Robert Creeley and Edward Dorn (both from Black Mountain College) wrote positive reviews. "Projective Verse" had an enormous influence not only on the emerging Black Mountain School but also on the Beats and the New York poets. The essay has become the foremost statement for the poetry produced by these three movements. While it also received many early negative reviews, "Projective Verse" has inspired a broad range of poets and movements connected with the experimental postmodernism of the 1970s, 1980s, and 1990s, including poets as diverse as Amiri Baraka (LeRoi Jones) of the Black Arts Movement, Language poet Susan Howe, and feminist poet Adrienne Rich.

HISTORICAL AND LITERARY CONTEXT

"Projective Verse" takes issue with the formalism that dominated colleges, universities, and academic journals in the post–World War II period. This formalist methodology, known as New Criticism, originated in the 1920s and 1930s in the literary criticism of Eliot as well as in the writings of American and British poet-critics Allen Tate, John Crowe Ransom, Robert Penn

Warren, Yvor Winters, I. A. Richards, and William Empson. Ascribing the poem's meaning to its rhetorical techniques and formal structure (as opposed to the poet's intention or the social/historical context), these writers prized the techniques of paradox, ambiguity, and irony for promoting nuance and complexity. The influence of these critics was felt throughout the postwar period, especially as studies like Cleanth Brooks's *The Well-Wrought Urn* (1947) and W. K. Wimsatt and Monroe Beardsley's *The Verbal Icon* (1954) developed new formulations for the teaching and study of poetry.

By the time "Projective Verse" was published in *Poetry New York* in 1950, many writers were beginning to question the conservatism and orthodoxy of New Criticism's precepts. Figures later associated with the Beats, the San Francisco Renaissance, the New York poets, and the Black Mountain School were already experimenting with open forms and non-Western traditions. As "Projective Verse" was reprinted and discussed throughout the 1950s, it influenced the direction of these and other poetic movements. Certainly, the manifesto was instrumental in bringing together the Black Mountain School, a loosely affiliated group of teachers, students, and poets. By the time "Projective Verse" was published in the anthology *New American Poetry* (1960), these movements were better known and had produced a considerable body of work.

Olson's essay draws heavily on the writings of Pound and Williams. Many of Olson's statements about the poem echo Pound's statements on music in *Antheil and the Treatise on Harmony* (1924), on sculpture in *Gaudier-Brzeska* (1916), and on poetry and interpretation in *ABC of Reading* (1934). Similarly, Olson builds on Williams's statements on the poem as a field from his essay "The Poem as a Field of Action" (1948). "Projective Verse" was also influenced by the editing suggestions and theoretical contributions Creeley made to early drafts.

"Projective Verse" has inspired a body of commentary, other manifestos, and a great deal of open-form poetry. In the 1950s and 1960s, many writers responded to Olson's essay, and it became a lightning rod for criticism of open-form poetry. The work also inspired imitations and parodies. Most famously, Frank O'Hara's "Personism: A Manifesto" (1959)

✣ **Key Facts**

Time Period:
Mid-20th Century

Movement/Issue:
Aesthetics; Black Mountain School; The Beats; New York poets

Place of Publication:
United States

Language of Publication:
English

CHARLES OLSON: BLACK MOUNTAIN POET

A major figure in twentieth-century American poetry, Charles Olson laid the groundwork for postmodern poetics through his assimilation of modernist principles. Born in Massachusetts in 1910, Olson spent his summers vacationing with his family in Gloucester, a small fishing village that later formed the backdrop for his major work, *The Maximus Poems* (published in three volumes, 1960, 1968, 1970). Educated at Wesleyan University and Harvard, Olson accepted a Guggenheim fellowship and later published *Call Me Ishmael* (1947), his study of Herman Melville's *Moby Dick*.

During World War II, Olson worked in the Office of War Information and seemed poised for a career in politics with the Democratic Party; however, he abandoned politics for poetry. In 1948 he began teaching at Black Mountain College, a liberal arts school located near Asheville, North Carolina. From 1951 to 1956 he served as a lecturer and rector there, meeting Robert Creeley, Robert Duncan, and other poets who would become known as the Black Mountain School. After the college closed in 1956, Olson moved to Gloucester, where he continued to work on *The Maximus Poems* until his death in 1970. He is best known for "Projective Verse," his epic *The Maximus Poems,* and his poem "The Kingfishers."

Poet Charles Olson reading at an art museum in 1957. NAT FARBMAN//TIME LIFE PICTURES/GETTY IMAGES

mocks elements of Olson's style while largely supporting his claims about the need for open-form poetry and his metaphor of the poem as a field. Since its publication, "Projective Verse" has motivated many poets to write outside of traditional forms. It continues to command scholarly interest and to influence postmodern poets, Language poets, and individual poets in many other genres.

THEMES AND STYLE

"Projective Verse" explores the idea that poetry must rediscover its natural force in the rhythms of breath and the open field of the page and develop a form that is both more natural and more crafted. Olson stresses the open, natural elements of projective verse. He traces the basic elements of the poem to the physicality of the poet: "The two halves [of the poem] are: / the HEAD, by the way of the EAR, to the SYLLABLE / the HEART, by way of the BREATH, to the LINE." Olson compares the poem to an open field and the poet to an explorer: "From the moment he ventures into FIELD COMPOSITION—puts himself in the open—he can go by no track other than the one the poem under hand declares." Olson defines the poem, like a law of physics, in terms of its kinetic energy: "A poem is energy transferred from where the poet got it … to … the reader." Although he compares the poem to a natural landscape and emphasizes the poet's unity of head and heart, his vision is not primarily romantic. Olson endorses technology as well as nature, noting that the typewriter provides the poet with "the stave and bar a musician has had." He claims that the goal of projective verse is a new worldview, namely "objectism," which consists of "getting rid of the lyrical interference of the individual as ego, of the 'subject' and his soul." He hopes to replace Wordsworth's "egotistical sublime" with a truer account based on the recognition that man is one creature ("object") among many.

"Projective Verse" sets its provisional observations about poetry within a rigorously logical structure. Although he declares that his essay is intended "merely to get things started," Olson puts forth theories about the definition, origins, and purpose of projective verse and objectism that are far from tentative. His systematic approach uses groupings—including the poem's kinetics, projective principles, and the poet's writing process—to unify a manifesto that ranges throughout world literature, from Homer and Euripides to Eliot and "from the late Elizabethans to Ezra Pound."

"Projective Verse" strikes a tone of informal erudition through stylistic devices—capitalization, direct addresses to the reader, and allusions. Olson uses capitals to highlight key principles, such as Creeley's insight, "FORM IS NEVER MORE THAN AN EXTENSION OF CONTENT." This marks the essay as informal and nonacademic; nevertheless,

Olson's scholarly expertise is evident. His exclamation to the poet to move quickly from one perception to another—"MOVE, INSTANTER, ON ANOTHER"—combines the informality of direct address with Latin and anachronistic phrasing. His direct addresses to the reader frequently follow quotations from Pound or Williams: Olson describes projective verse as "much more … than simply such a one as Pound put … to get us started: 'the musical phrase,' go by it, boys, rather than by, the metronome." Olson's informal direct address makes his allusion more immediate to the reader.

CRITICAL DISCUSSION

Early responses to "Projective Verse" were starkly divided. When it was first published in *Poetry New York,* the essay received enthusiastic admiration from Williams, Creeley, Dorn, and others, but when it was reprinted in *New American Poetry* it met with a barrage of overwhelmingly negative reviews from academic poets, including James Wright, James Dickey, Marianne Moore, and Robert Bly. In a characteristic example of this criticism, Moore dismissed Olson's theories by describing projective verse as "weedy and colorless like suckers from an un-sunned tuber." As Tom Clark notes in *Charles Olson: The Allegory of a Poet's Life* (1991), "The sheer unanimity of the ensuing critical rejection of his art and ideas by the ascendant academic establishment of the time appears in retrospect not so much a considered aesthetic or intellectual judgment as the defensive campaign of a threatened orthodoxy."

In addition to its enormous influence on the Beats, the New York poets, and the Black Mountain poets, "Projective Verse" provided a rationale for a fundamental shift in American poetry in the late 1950s and early 1960s. While not all American open-form poetry after 1950 can be attributed to the influence of Olson's essay, it was the first to articulate both the aesthetic rationale for open form and the historical forces that propelled it; it persuaded many poets to experiment with open-form poetry. In addition, Olson's theory of objectism renewed many poets' interest in writing about the natural world during the 1960s and 1970s. "Projective Verse" significantly influenced the development of later movements, such as postmodern and Language poetry. It continues to be the subject of critical commentary regarding its links to modernism and postmodernism, its influence on postwar American poetry, and its connection to Olson's own poems.

A good deal of scholarship has focused on Olson's citations from Pound and Williams in order to determine whether "Projective Verse" announces a break with modernism or a restatement of modernist principles. This question has led scholars to focus on the relationship between Olson's manifesto and his poetry, especially *The Maximus Poems* (published as three volumes). As Anne Day Dewey summarizes, "Critics have either placed Olson's work in the tradition of the Modernist epic 'poem including history' or emphasized his break with Modernism in the tendency of his poetics to ground an ideal cultural order in nature." More recent studies have focused on Olson's relationships with the Black Mountain poets and his political ideals.

BIBLIOGRAPHY

Sources

Castle, Gregory. "New Criticism." *The Blackwell Guide to Literary Theory.* Malden: Blackwell, 2007. 122-28. *Gale Literature Resource Center.* Web. 28 Aug. 2012.

"Charles Olson (1910-1970)." *Poetry Criticism: Volume 19.* Ed. Carol T. Gaffke. Detroit: Gale, 1997. 265-323. *Dictionary of Literary Biography.* Web. 28 Aug. 2012.

Clark, Tom. *Charles Olson: The Allegory of a Poet's Life.* New York: Norton, 1991. Print.

Dewey, Anne Day. *Beyond Maximus: The Construction of Public Voice in Black Mountain Poetry.* Stanford: Stanford UP, 2007. Print.

Rifkin, Libbie. *Career Moves: Olson, Creeley, Zukofsky, Berrigan, and the American Avant-Garde.* Madison: U of Wisconsin P, 2000.

Von Hallberg, Robert. *Charles Olson: The Scholar's Art.* Cambridge: Harvard UP, 1978. Print.

Further Reading

Berry, Eleanor. "The Emergence of Charles Olson's Prosody of the Page Space." *Journal of English Linguistics* 30.1 (2002): 51-72. Web. 28 Aug. 2012.

Fredman, Stephen. *The Grounding of American Poetry: Charles Olson and the Emersonian Tradition.* New York: Cambridge UP, 1993. Print.

Jaussen, Paul. "Charles Olson Keeps House: Rewriting John Smith for Contemporary America." *Journal of Modern Literature* 34.1 (2010): 107-24. Web. 28 Aug. 2012.

Mackey, Nathaniel. *Discrepant Engagement.* Cambridge: Cambridge UP, 1993. Print.

Maud, Ralph. *Charles Olson's Reading: A Biography.* Carbondale: Southern Illinois UP, 1996. Print.

———. *What Does Not Change: The Significance of Charles Olson's "The Kingfishers."* Madison: Fairleigh Dickinson UP, 1988. Print.

Mossin, Andrew. "'In Thicket': Charles Olson, Frances Boldereff, Robert Creeley and the Crisis of Masculinity at Mid-Century." *Journal of Modern Literature* 28.4 (2005): 13-39. Web. 28 Aug. 2012.

Paul, Sherman. *Olson's Push: Origin, Black Mountain, and Recent American Poetry.* Baton Rouge: Louisiana State UP, 1978. Print.

Kevin Cooney

THE REJECTION OF CLOSURE

Lyn Hejinian

✣ *Key Facts*

Time Period:
Late 20th Century

Movement/Issue:
Aesthetics; Third-wave
feminism

Place of Publication:
United States

**Language of
Publication:**
English

OVERVIEW

Initially delivered as a talk in April 1983, Lyn Hejinian's essay "The Rejection of Closure" sought to break with long-standing images of "the poet as guardian to Truth" and to celebrate in his place the experimental, exploratory poetics that characterized the late-twentieth-century language writing movement. "Closed" texts, Hejinian argued, offer a "stable, calm and calming (and fundamentally unepiphanic) vision of the world," which might be acceptable in a work of detective fiction but could easily become "coercive" in the medium of lyric poetry; "open" texts "acknowledge[d] the vastness of the world" without attempting to contain or complete it. Hejinian's talk was reprinted in the 1985 volume *Writing/Talks,* edited by Bob Perelman; its publication led to a wider discussion of the nature of closure in writing.

In essay form, "The Rejection of Closure" quickly became a classic of postmodern poetics, praised, debated, qualified, and extended by a variety of critics and authors. Scholars seeking to understand the language poets and their legacy of formal experimentation often invoked "The Rejection of Closure" as a starting point; the essay also proved useful in considering the merits of Hejinian's own work as a poet. As this discussion took shape, Hejinian would continue to elaborate her position on closure, notably in the later clarification "Continuing against Closure" (2001) and in the formal example of *My Life,* an ongoing poetic autobiography. "The Rejection of Closure" continues to be seen as an emblematic moment in the history of experimental poetics and as a lens for reappraising the products of the language movement.

HISTORICAL AND LITERARY CONTEXT

"The Rejection of Closure" is primarily a declaration of an aesthetic rather than an overtly political stance, but Hejinian construed her critique of closure as related to a larger "ethics of meaning," especially when applied to women's writing. She notes in the preface to her 1985 essay that "within the writing community, discussions of gender were frequent, and they were addressed both to perceptible practical problems (instances of injustice) ... and to longer-term questions of power." "The Rejection of Closure" is aimed primarily at the latter, as an attempt to elucidate the varieties of poetry that might counter a tradition of linear, authoritative, and sometimes oppressive discourse.

Indeed, when Hejinian delivered her initial talk in 1983, the "third wave" of the feminist movement was well under way, though it would not be labeled as such for several years. "The Rejection of Closure" made specific reference to the newly prominent politics of cultural inclusiveness in feminist discourse, suggesting a connection between literary forms and the diverse world they represent. Hejinian drew on noted theorist Luce Irigaray to show how the emphasis on "generative rather than directive" writing might be "posit[ed] ... within a feminine sphere of discourse." Likewise, Hejinian invoked poet Carla Harryman's "radiant critique (one might even say trashing) of conventional (patriarchal) power structures" as an example of the efficacy of the "power of invention" and the "power of performance."

More generally, "The Rejection of Closure" presented an opportunity to take stock of the variety of formal approaches that best typified language poetry for its readers and critics. Hejinian cites the "field work" of American poets Robert Grenier and Bruce Andrews, both of whom worked in a poster-style medium in which words are as much visual artifacts as bearers of literal meaning. It is worth noting that many so-called language authors were ambivalent at best about the term, which they initially saw as an external label largely applied by critics. In an instance of poetic irony, Hejinian's essay lent further closure to critical conceptions of the language movement even as it championed openness of form.

It is difficult to point out specific poems influenced by "The Rejection of Closure" rather than by the overall milieu of language poetics or by other specific poetic works. The principles explicated in the essay, however, have been seen to apply to a wide range of poetry by language and other writers; indeed, Hejinian names several poets (including Bernadette Mayer and Jackson Mac Low) who share her approach to form. Hejinian's own work, too, provides a further exemplification of her stance on closure: notable in this regard is her ongoing poetic "autography" *My Life,* to which, with each new edition, the poet has added new layers of material that complicate, contradict, and enrich what has come before.

THEMES AND STYLE

The central issue for "The Rejection of Closure" is a perceived dichotomy between "closed" literary works, which shepherd the reader toward a single possible interpretation, and "open" works, which leave room for multiple possibilities. Hejinian quickly qualifies this distinction by noting that there are few examples of strictly "closed" writing (the above-mentioned detective fiction and some unnamed works of lyric poetry). The majority of the essay therefore develops this distinction from a simple binary to a spectrum of possible approaches, relating it especially to the formal structure of a work. Hejinian observes that far from being a "container" for meaning, a poem's form is a dynamic participant in the ways its meaning can be constructed: "form is not a fixture but an activity."

Hejinian also goes to considerable length to establish the historicity of the openness/closure distinction by examining the presence of similar attitudes in the work of poets across centuries and languages. Notably, she detects in German author Johann Wolfgang von Goethe's long poem *Faust* a clear acknowledgement of the way in which "language induces a yearning for comprehension, for perfect and complete expression, [but] also guards against it." A similar self-conscious desire is read into English poet William Wordsworth's *Cambridge and the Alps*; not surprisingly, these concerns also find expression in the work of Hejinian's contemporaries, including American poet Bob Perelman and French author Hélène Cixous, the latter of whom also reinforces Hejinian's connection between closure and the "feminine textual body." Portions of the essay also cite Hejinian's own poetry for its attempts ("I don't mean to suggest that I succeeded," the poet cautions) to achieve openness through juxtaposition of disparate subjects and syntaxes.

While "The Rejection of Closure" bears the overall structure of a literary or academic essay, much of its language can itself be seen as a demonstration of Hejinian's views on closure. To begin, the sentences of the essay frequently (and with evident relish) undercut, qualify, and parallel themselves through a heavy use of parentheses—to say nothing of Hejinian's use of dashes to achieve similar ends. A small but typical instance of this self-echoing tendency comes in Hejinian's description of "the gap between what one wants to say (or what one perceives there is to say) and what one can say (what is sayable)." Moreover, rather than develop a single, linear route of argumentation, Hejinian seems primarily to transpose the initial theme of closure/openness into a variety of topical keys, ranging from the literary history of the Romantics to psychoanalysis to linguistically ambiguous "jokes, puns, riddles … chants and rhymes."

CRITICAL DISCUSSION

From the perspective of literary critics, "The Rejection of Closure" initially served as one of a set of essays characterizing the language movement overall

THE LANGUAGE (OR L=A=N=G=U=A=G=E) POETS

As scholar Kornelia Freitag, among others, notes, "Hejinian's work has gained recognition in the context of the loosely structured movement that is known as 'Language Writing.'" This movement drew its name, along with its common and unusually styled variant, from the magazine L=A=N=G=U=A=G=E, edited by Charles Bernstein and Bruce Andrews and printed from 1978 to 1982. Poems in this publication, and those associated with language writing in general, displayed a high degree of formal inventiveness, with some taking the shape of fields of text scattered across the page and others appearing as unfinished typescripts composed entirely of nonsense words. The heavily stylized book reviews in a given issue often proved superficially indistinguishable from the verse.

Hejinian was closely involved with L=A=N=G=U=A=G=E, with her poetry and prose appearing in several numbers of the publication. Moreover, her links to language writing at large were reinforced by quotations, in "The Rejection of Closure," from several L=A=N=G=U=A=G=E alumni. Serious critical discussion of language writing as a phenomenon began with poetry scholar Marjorie Perloff, whose initial essays on the subject were published in the same few years that "The Rejection of Closure" was taking shape; both contributed to the recognition of language writing as a major movement in American literary history.

(and thereby authorizing discussions of poetry and politics under that name). As such, it has often been read alongside other prose works by poets such as Charles Bernstein and Ron Silliman. One comparative study was undertaken by Michael Greer in his

Lyn Hejinian in 1985. In "Rejection of Closure," Hejinian, a founding figure of the Language writing movement, explores the concept of the "open text." © CHRISTOPHER FELVER/CORBIS

1989 article on the ideology of language poetry published in *boundary 2*. Greer reads Hejinian's essay as a "turn 'inward,' toward a consideration of the subject," in contrast to Silliman's Marxist analysis of the "outward" role of poetry in an explicitly political sphere. Christopher Beach in "Poetic Positionings" (1997) cites "The Rejection of Closure" as an extended example of the ways in which Hejinian and other language poets stood "diametrically opposed" to a "poetic mainstream," represented by such figures as Stephen Dobyns.

Scholars soon realized the value of "The Rejection of Closure" as a lens for critiquing contemporary poetry and for identifying historical antecedents to the language movement. To a considerable extent, these critics have also applied the essay's principles as a context for examining Hejinian's own work. In a 1997 *Modern Language Studies* essay arguing for the literary canonization of Hejinian's *My Life,* Lisa Samuels cites "The Rejection of Closure" as an exposition of the gender politics at work in the volume. Kornelia Freitag, in "'A Pause, a Rose, Something on Paper': Autobiography as Language Writing in Lyn Hejinian's 'My Life'" (1998), explores the connections among "Rejection," *My Life,* and earlier works by modernist poet Gertrude Stein. Benjamin Friedlander, in a 2001 essay published in *Qui Parle* that is itself an unusual formal experiment, further establishes Hejinian's work on closure as a central element of language poetry criticism.

Not all critics, however, are in agreement as to the success, or even the possibility, of the "openness" Hejinian declares. Jacob Edmond, writing in *Contemporary Literature* in 2009, declares that, on the contrary, some degree of closure is inescapable in language, as the poet's own work is shown to attest, and cautions against allowing a "rhetoric of openness" to itself foreclose further conversation on the issue. Hejinian, meanwhile, has continued to develop and extend her definitions of "openness" and "closure" in a series of essays. Her brief 2001 article "Continuing against Closure" is among the more direct resumptions of this discussion; *The Language of Inquiry* (2000) provides a fuller treatment, though largely en route to a broader point about the interrelationship of poetry and poetics.

BIBLIOGRAPHY

Sources

Beach, Christopher. "Poetic Positionings: Stephen Dobyns and Lyn Hejinian in Cultural Context." *Contemporary Literature* 38.1 (1997): 44-77. Print.

Edmond, Jacob. "The Closures of the Open Text: Lyn Hejinian's 'Paradise Found.'" *Contemporary Literature* 50.2 (2009): 240-72. Web. 16 July 2012.

Freitag, Kornelia. "'A Pause, a Rose, Something on Paper': Autobiography as Language Writing in Lyn Hejinian's 'My Life.'" *Amerikastudien/American Studies* 43.2 (1998): 313-27. Print.

Friedlander, Benjamin. "A Short History of Language Poetry/According to 'Hecuba Whimsy.'" *Qui Parle* 12.2 (2001): 107-42. Print.

Greer, Michael. "Ideology and Theory in Recent Experimental Writing, or, The Naming of 'Language Poetry.'" *boundary 2* 16.2-3 (1989): 335-55. Print.

Samuels, Lisa. "Eight Justifications for Canonizing Lyn Hejinian's *My Life.*" *Modern Language Studies* 27.2 (1997): 103-19. Print.

Further Reading

Hejinian, Lyn. "Continuing against Closure." *Jacket* 14 (2001): n.p. Web. 16 July 2012.

———. *My Life.* 2nd ed. Los Angeles: Sun & Moon, 1987. Print.

———. *The Language of Inquiry.* Berkeley: U of California P, 2000. Print.

Jarraway, David R. "*My Life* through the Eighties: The Exemplary L=A=N=G=U=A=G=E of Lyn Hejinian." *Contemporary Literature* 33.2 (1992): 319-36. Print.

Marsh, Nicky. "'Infidelity to an Impossible Task': Postmodernism, Feminism and Lyn Hejinian's *My Life.*" *Feminist Review* 74 (2003): 70-80. Print.

Perelman, Bob. "An Introduction to Language Writing." *Revue française d'études américaines* 67 (1996): 70-89. Print.

Reddy, Srikanth. "Changing the *Sjuzet*: Lyn Hejinian's Digressive Narratologies." *Contemporary Literature* 50.1 (2009): 54-93. Web. 16 July 2012.

Michael Hartwell

SPEECH AND IMAGE
An African Tradition of the Surreal
Léopold Sédar Senghor

OVERVIEW

The 1965 essay "Speech and Image: An African Tradition of the Surreal" by Senegalese poet and political leader Léopold Sédar Senghor attempts to define an African tradition of surrealism by contrasting it with European surrealism. (Surrealism, broadly, was a movement in art and literature that advocated the expression of unconscious as well as conscious experience.) The essay carries on the African surrealist movement that black intellectuals from France and its colonies had initiated decades earlier in Paris, and it is deeply intertwined with the *négritude* movement, which Senghor cofounded. "Speech and Image" was published years after Senghor had left France, during the initial years of his presidency in Senegal, and reflected his pride in African culture and aesthetics as unique and autonomous from European colonial influences. The essay is addressed to an international audience, specifically European intellectuals who were generally unfamiliar with African culture. Differing from earlier conceptions of surrealism, including that of Aimé Césaire, "Speech and Image" argues that words are ideograms, or symbols for ideas—a notion that Senghor claims is derived from an inherently African metaphysical worldview, one that is in direct contrast to the European empirical worldview.

The first known version of "Speech and Image" appeared in *Prose and Poetry*, a collection of Senghor's essays and poetry published in English in 1965. The essay, and the book in general, did not garner much attention at the time, as it emerged after the heyday of surrealism had passed. "Speech and Image" is significant within Senghor's body of work, however, in its reflection of the aesthetic values on which all of his writing, especially his poetry, was based. It can therefore be read as a manifesto proclaiming his personal version of African surrealism. The impact of "Speech and Image" and other works by Senghor on the surrealist and négritude movements is widely recognized today.

HISTORICAL AND LITERARY CONTEXT

"Speech and Image" reflects Senghor's continued effort to champion a distinctly African intellectual and artistic culture—a project begun years earlier as part of his participation in the négritude movement.

Senghor's rich exchanges over several decades with black intellectuals, such as Martinican author and politician Césaire and French Guianan author Léon Damas, inspired him to refine his notions of African surrealism as well as his theories regarding the common heritage of those who were part of the African diaspora. Senghor shared the disdain of his black contemporaries for French colonial racism. His promotion of an African solidarity based on shared traditions and values is reflected in his conception of surrealism in "Speech and Image."

"Speech and Image" emerged in 1965, in the aftermath of Senegal's independence from France and Senghor's election as president in 1960. It is likely that the essay was written earlier, perhaps in the 1950s, but not published immediately because of Senghor's intense political activities. His anticolonial politics, a central theme in his poetry and prose, came to fruition with France's exit from West Africa. In 1959 Senegal joined other French West African colonies in the Mali Federation. The following year Senegal seceded to become an independent republic, with Senghor as its head. Senghor's cultural and intellectual activities continued throughout his presidency. His writing promoted national pride in Senegal's unique heritage, an exceptionalism made evident in the notion of African surrealism presented in "Speech and Image."

Senghor's essay was inspired by the work of other négritude writers and of black intellectuals involved in similar movements (e.g., *negrismo*, a literary movement in the Hispanic Caribbean that championed the hybrid identity of Afro-Caribbean people, and the Harlem Renaissance in the United States), as well as that of the surrealist André Breton. A publication that undoubtedly influenced Senghor's composition of "Speech and Image" is the 1932 radical journal *Légitime Défense* ("Legitimate Defense"), which combined the promotion of a shared black identity with the creation of a literary style based on surrealism. Other influential works include Césaire's book-length poem *Cahier d'un retour au pays natal* (1939; "Return to My Native Land") and much of the writing in the négritude journal *L'Etudiant Noir* ("The Black Student"), which Senghor cofounded with Césaire and Damas. The writings of Breton, a cofounder of the surrealist movement, had perhaps the strongest

❖ *Key Facts*

Time Period:
Mid-20th Century

Movement/Issue:
African surrealism;
Négritude

Place of Publication:
Senegal

**Language of
Publication:**
English

LÉOPOLD SÉDAR SENGHOR: SENEGALESE POET AND POLITICIAN

Léopold Sédar Senghor was a poet, cultural theorist, and politician from Senegal. Born near Dakar in 1906, he attended L'École Nationale de la France d'Outre-Mer in Paris, where he met Aimé Césaire and other black intellectuals who would later contribute to the négritude and surrealist movements. Senghor taught in France for several years before he was drafted into the French army during World War II. He served in an all-African unit until he was captured by the Nazis in 1940; he then spent eighteen months in a German prison camp. After the war Senghor served several terms as the Senegalese representative in the French National Assembly before returning to Senegal in the mid-1950s. He played a pivotal role in Senegal's independence movement and became the country's first democratically elected president in 1960. Reelected three times, he retired from the presidency in 1980.

Senghor is as well known for his writing as he is for his role in colonial French and African politics. During his residence in France, he wrote many of his better-known poems, which were read as statements of resistance and as evocations of black identity and experience. He published several collections of poetry throughout his lifetime, including *Chants d'ombre* (1945; *Songs of Shadow*) and *Nocturnes* (1961). Senghor is perhaps most recognized for his role as cofounder, with Césaire, of the négritude movement, which promoted unique African cultural traditions and aesthetics that opposed European colonial influence and exploitation. He was also a founder of the literary journal *Présence Africaine* and, from 1984, the first black member of the French Academy. Senghor died in France in 2001, at the age of ninety-five. He is considered one of the most important African intellectuals of the twentieth century.

impact on Senghor. "Speech and Image" recalls such works as *Manifesto of Surrealism* (1924) and directly quotes *Signe ascendant* (1947; "Ascendant Sign"), in which Breton proclaims the inextricable relationship between the ethics and aesthetics of surrealism.

Senegalese writers and cultural theorists have carried on the work embodied in "Speech and Image." Its legacy is particularly evident in the Pan-African journal *Présence Africaine* ("African Presence"), cofounded by Senghor and Alioune Diop. Still in circulation today, the journal is recognized as one of the most prominent examples of postcolonial African literature. The scholarship of Senegalese author and literary theorist Hamidou Dia furthers Senghor's promotion of black literature and aesthetics independent from European cultural influence, as evidenced in *Introduction à la littérature négro-africaine* (1983; "Introduction to Black African Literature"). The work of Beninese historian and linguist Dieudonné Gnammankou in recovering Africa's cultural legacy also reflects Senghor's influence. While "Speech and Image" has received little scholarly attention in its own right, Senghor's body of

work continues to be regarded for its vital contribution to African and Pan-African literature.

THEMES AND STYLE

One of the main themes of "Speech and Image" is that European surrealism and African surrealism are inherently dissimilar. Senghor writes, "But as you would suppose, African surrealism is different from European surrealism. European surrealism is empirical. African surrealism is mystical and metaphysical." The essay's central objective is to reveal these differences. To legitimate his claim, Senghor directly quotes Breton, who notes, "The poetic [European] analogy … proceeds in a completely empirical way." He goes on to argue that African languages (and thus African modes of thinking) are better suited to surrealist expression than European ones. To Senghor, the African use of words as ideograms—symbols standing for ideas—echoes African oral tradition, which relies on abstract speech, rather than concrete writing, to express experience. This symbolic form of expression represents a more metaphysical, otherworldly understanding of life that he characterizes as African surrealism.

Senghor's essay achieves its impact through formal rhetoric that appeals to an educated European audience. His arguments assume knowledge of the discourses surrounding surrealism and aesthetics: "Two and two do not make four, but five, as Aimé Césaire has told us. The object does not mean what it represents but what it suggests, what it creates." Senghor also draws on the renown of prominent cultural theorists such as Breton to speak directly to a European intelligentsia familiar with their works. Nevertheless, Senghor does not address his audience uncritically. Rather, he incorporates a veiled condemnation of Europe's oppressive role in the African colonies: "the astonishment of the first Europeans when they found that the 'natives' did not understand their pictures or even the logic of their arguments!"

Senghor employs a celebratory and at times ironic tone in his explanation of the differences between European and African understandings of words and imagery. The author clearly privileges what he calls the mystical nature of African surrealism over Europe's empirical perspective. Senghor writes, "The African image is not then an image by equation but an image by *analogy,* a surrealist image…. The image, I repeat, is not an equation but a *symbol,* an ideogramme. Not only the figuration of the image but also its material … stone, earth, copper, gold, fibre." The author praises what he sees as the Africans' more complex notion of imagery. He also uses italics to highlight what he perceives as the distinct, superior qualities of African surrealism.

CRITICAL DISCUSSION

"Speech and Image" did not receive much direct scholarly attention upon its publication in 1965. Later critics of Senghor's notion of surrealism remarked on his influence on both African and European aesthetics. In *Symposium of the Whole: A Range of Discourse Toward an Ethnopoetics* (1983), Jerome and Diane Rothenberg note, "[Senghor's] poetics drew from a base in African oral tradition, illuminated by and in turn illuminating the explorations of European Surrealism." Certain scholars, including Marc A. Christophe in "Léopold Sédar Senghor as Racial Theorist" (1987), accused Senghor of promoting a racist understanding of the African worldview, thereby perpetuating a European ethnocentric view of Africans as uncivilized savages.

Senghor's "Speech and Image" added to his extensive body of work on surrealism and the promotion of an autonomous African literature. It enriched the anticolonial discourse of his contemporaries involved in surrealism and négritude. Yet the somewhat controversial approach of these writers gained them many opponents as well as supporters. As Dale Tomich explains in "The Dialectic of Colonialism and Culture," "For Césaire, Senghor, Damas, and their compatriots, the implications of the question of Black identity were so broad that they challenged the foundations of Western culture and Western civilization"; these writers aimed to "destroy the myth of 'savage Africa' and to carve themselves an identity other than that of 'Frenchmen with Black skins.'" In the decades since the publication of "Speech and Image," Senghor's notion of surrealism has been the subject of extensive scholarly criticism.

Much scholarship on "Speech and Image" has focused on the binary opposition it establishes between Africa and Europe. In *Race, Culture, and Identity* (2006), Shireen Lewis notes the potentially problematic nature of Senghor's theory in "the appearance that his thinking on black identity privileges one side of the binary (the colonizer or white European) while withholding value from the other side (the colonized or black African). It is this appearance that has contributed to accusations that his construction of black identity is racist and reinforces racist stereotypes of black people." Other scholars explore the ideological differences between Senghor's theory and those of his contemporaries. As Ranjana Khanna observes in *Dark Continents* (2003), "Contrasting his surrealism with that of Breton … Senghor nonetheless assumed a collective mystical unconscious, which he suggested has concrete basis in a variety of African languages…. While Césaire at times assumed a precolonial pan-Africanism, it did not follow this form of mysticism."

BIBLIOGRAPHY

Sources

Christophe, Marc A. "Léopold Sédar Senghor as Racial Theorist: A Comparison of His Thoughts with Those of Frobenius and Gobineau." *Obsidian II: Black Literature in Review* 2.3 (1987): 46-53. Print.

Khanna, Ranjana. *Dark Continents: Psychoanalysis and Colonialism.* Durham: Duke UP, 2003. Print.

Senegelese president Léopold Sédar Senghor wears the uniform of the French Academy of Moral and Political Sciences in a 1969 photograph. Senghor was also a prominent writer and philosopher who penned works such as "Speech and Image: An African Tradition of the Surreal" AP PHOTO

Lewis, Shireen. *Race, Culture, and Identity: Francophone West African and Caribbean Literature and Theory from Négritude to Créolité.* Lanham: Lexington, 2006.

Rothenberg, Diane, and Jerome Rothenberg, eds. *Symposium of the Whole: A Range of Discourse toward an Ethnopoetics.* Berkeley: U of California P, 1983. Print.

Senghor, Léopold. "Speech and Image: An African Tradition of the Surreal." *Surrealist Painters and Poets: An Anthology.* Ed. Mary Ann Caws. Cambridge: MIT P, 2001. 391-92. Print.

Tomich, Dale. "The Dialectic of Colonialism and Culture: The Origins of the Négritude of Aimé Césaire." *Review (Fernand Braudel Center)* 2.3 (1979), 351-85. Print.

Further Reading

Balakian, Anna. "The Progress of Surrealism." *Journal of General Education* 27.1 (1975), 69-82. Print.

Caws, Mary Ann, ed. *Manifesto: A Century of Isms.* Lincoln: U of Nebraska P, 2001. Print.

———. *Surrealist Painters and Poets: An Anthology.* Cambridge: MIT P, 2001. Print.

Senghor, Léopold Sédar. *Prose and Poetry.* Ed. J. Reed and C. Wake. London: Oxford UP, 1965. Print.

Songolo, Aliko. "Surrealism and Black Literatures in French." *French Review* 55.6 (1982), 724-32. Print.

Katrina White

QUEER POLITICS

GAY LIBERATION FRONT MANIFESTO

Anonymous

OVERVIEW

The *Gay Liberation Front Manifesto*, written in 1971 by a UK chapter of the Gay Liberation Front (GLF) and published anonymously, details the oppression experienced by gay people and the actions they can take against the oppression. At the end of their manifesto, the authors explain their intent in publishing it: "We recognise that it leaves many questions unanswered and open-ended but hope it will lead to the furtherance of a scientific analysis of sexism and our oppression as gay people." Although the work was written for "our gay sisters and brothers," the GLF clearly intended for the document to be used as educational material for those whom the gay community views as oppressors.

Most of the early reactions to the GLF's manifesto centered not on the document itself but on the high-profile, direct actions that the group carried out after its publication, including a disruption of the 1971 launch of a church-based morality campaign called the Festival of Light. In the first "kiss-in," GLF members dressed in drag and invaded the Methodist Central Hall, where they kissed one other and sounded horns, making a large commotion. Their actions were meant to provoke festival organizers Mary Whitehouse, Cliff Richard, and Malcolm Muggeridge, who all openly opposed gay rights. Whitehouse identified specific "evils" that she wanted to eliminate, including extramarital sex, pornography in films, sex on TV, abortion rights, and openly gay lifestyles. Ultimately the manifesto can be viewed as a guide to the direct actions upon which the GLF would later embark.

HISTORICAL AND LITERARY CONTEXT

The *Gay Liberation Front Manifesto* was a reaction to the 1969 Stonewall riots and the subsequent formation of the first GLF groups in New York City. The text was written to remedy the injustices toward the gay community after the riots brought these grievances to the public's attention. The riots resulted from a police raid of the Stonewall Inn—a bar that openly welcomed gays and lesbians as well as others on the fringes of society in New York City's Greenwich Village. At the time, police raids on gay bars were very frequent, but the raid on Stonewall went awry because of the refusal of bar patrons to cooperate with police and the fact that the patrons outnumbered police. The confrontation erupted into a spontaneous riot, forcing the rest of the country—and other nations, such as the United Kingdom—to sit up and take notice of the injustices that were occurring against the gay community.

The UK GLF group held its first meeting on October 13, 1970, in the basement of the London School of Economics. According to founders Bob Mellors and Aubrey Walter, the group's purpose was to create "a parallel movement based on revolutionary politics and alternative lifestyles." A year later, as the group became recognized as a political movement in the press and as their weekly meeting attendance increased to as many as 500 people, the UK GLF published its manifesto, explaining exactly how the gay community was still being oppressed and what group members planned to do to combat the oppression.

The *Gay Liberation Front Manifesto* was inspired by the original New York GLF, despite the fact that the New York GLF never formally wrote a manifesto. Instead, the UK group used the New York group's original ideas as inspiration to document the ideals of the entire GLF movement, with the goal of giving the GLF a worldwide presence and showing solidarity with the New York movement. Mellors took much of his inspiration for the formation of the UK GLF and its manifesto from his visit to New York in 1970, alongside Walter, and their meeting with the Black Panthers.

Since its publication, the *Gay Liberation Front Manifesto* has been read widely, both within and outside the gay community. The U.S. GLF disbanded in 1972, and the UK group broke up in 1974. Both groups—and the UK GLF's manifesto—were responsible for starting the conversation about gay rights but were not necessarily the direct reason behind the social and political changes that followed. Their disbandment did not diminish the popularity of the manifesto, as it continued to be widely read and inspire other gay activists who started their own groups, such as OutRage!, the Organisation for Lesbian and Gay Action (OLGA), Stonewall, and the Lesbian Avengers.

✥ *Key Facts*

Time Period:
Mid-20th Century

Movement/Issue:
Gay rights

Place of Publication:
England

Language of Publication:
English

BOB MELLORS: THE MAN BEHIND THE UK GAY LIBERATION FRONT

Although the writers of the *Gay Liberation Front Manifesto* are referred to as "anonymous," the UK GLF cofounders Bob Mellors and Aubrey Walter played a large role in assembling the beliefs and philosophy that formed the group's manifesto. Mellors specifically was a key figure in the early formation of the gay community in the United Kingdom. Born in 1950, he envisioned a GLF chapter in England, a dream that became a reality after he visited New York and became friends with Walter. Mellors and Walter met with the Black Panthers, who helped form the young men's early ideas on gay liberation and push them to create their own chapter.

Because of his job at the London School of Economics, Mellors was able to book a room at the institution to hold the first GLF meeting in 1970. In 1974, when the GLF split apart, Mellors helped more specialized gay and lesbian groups grow out of the disbanded GLF. In 1994 Mellors moved to Warsaw, Poland, and continued working in the gay community, as well as teaching English to native Polish speakers. On March 24, 1996, Mellors was stabbed to death in his home in Warsaw, a victim of a robbery. He is buried in Nottinghamshire, England.

The Gay Liberation Front staged protests in London in the early 1970s. Here, a member of the organization holds a poster promoting one such event in 1971. EVENING STANDARD/GETTY IMAGES

THEMES AND STYLE

The *Gay Liberation Front Manifesto* is organized around two distinct themes: how and why the gay community is being oppressed and what can be done about the problem. The "how" aspect is explained through several key header topics, including family, school, the media, employment, the law, physical violence, and psychiatry, while the "why"

aspect discusses conventional gender roles and the "threat" that the gay community presents to those roles. To do something about the "how" and the "why," the manifesto urges readers to engage in a liberated lifestyle and not to succumb to "particularly oppressive aspects of gay society," such as "the youth cult, butch and femme role-playing, and compulsive monogamy." The text concludes by asking its audience to "free their heads" and campaign and defend their interests as gay people, specifically noting that "we do not intend to ask for anything. *We intend to stand firm and assert our basic rights.* If this involves violence, it will not be we who initiate this, but those who attempt to stand in our way to freedom."

To persuade the gay community and to inform its oppressors, the authors use several rhetorical strategies in the manifesto, such as providing copious real-life examples and detailing direct actions that their audience can put into practice. These examples, such as the following excerpt from the media section, are what make the piece particularly compelling:

> Anti-homosexual morality and ideology, at every level of society, manifest themselves in a special vocabulary for denigrating gay people. There is abuse like 'pansy', 'fairy', 'lesbo' to hurl at men and women who can't or won't fit stereotyped preconceptions. There are words like 'sick', 'bent' and 'neurotic' for destroying the credence of gay people. But there are no positive words.

This type of example is persuasive because it presents the much-discussed topic of gay slurs from a new angle, noting that there are many negative words but no positive words to use in reference to gay people. Backing up the examples are multiple actions that the GLF urges readers to take, such as developing consciousness-raising groups and gay communes and forming an alliance with the women's liberation movement.

The persuasive argument of the manifesto is strengthened by its encouraging and optimistic tone. Although its subject matter is rather gloomy—especially in its discussion of the injustices that the gay community faces—the language is still hopeful and encourages readers to feel that they can make a difference. The work declares that "by freeing our heads we get the confidence to come out publicly and proudly as gay people, and to win over our gay brothers and sisters to the ideas of gay liberation," reassuring readers that "victory will come. If we're convinced of the importance of the new life-style, we can be strong and we can win." Such strong proclamations cut through the dark descriptions of oppression with their encouraging appeal.

CRITICAL DISCUSSION

After the GLF published its manifesto, the initial reaction was felt mainly throughout the gay community. The text was not widely distributed and was given mainly to members and people who were considering joining the group. Despite the relatively small distribution of the manifesto, by January 1971 up to 500 people were attending the weekly general meeting, suggesting that the document's message was passed on fairly quickly via word of mouth in the UK gay community.

Since its initial appearance, the *Gay Liberation Front Manifesto* has served as a template to future activist groups as to how to organize and formulate their beliefs in a meaningful way and connect to a large community of people. Later manifestos, such as the *Dyke Manifesto* from the Lesbian Avengers (a 1990s radical direct-action group), were strongly influenced by the UK GLF's text. Like its predecessor, the *Dyke Manifesto* is also divided into sections with different headers (such as "Who are the Lesbian Avengers?" and "What is direct action?") and uses persuasive language and declarative statements to cultivate a heightened sense of urgency in readers.

Although the *Gay Liberation Front Manifesto* inspired future activist groups and has appeared in some radical readers and anthologies, it has not garnered much attention from critics since its publication. Despite the fact that the document followed on the heels of the Stonewall riots and was responsible for forming one of the first organized gay movements in the United Kingdom, most critical writings about the GLF movement delve only into the formation of the group's UK chapter and the fact that it published a manifesto, without ever openly critiquing its message. In 2010, the fortieth anniversary of the UK group was celebrated back where it started, on the campus of the London School of Economics (LSE). Sue Donnelly, one of the school's archivists, comments on the school's stance toward the GLF: "LSE is proud that it was, and it remains, a platform for the discussion of sexuality, rights and equality in a neutral, open and safe environment." The *Gay Liberation Front Manifesto* may not have drawn substantial reaction from critics, but the legacy of the GLF's UK chapter is still being celebrated.

BIBLIOGRAPHY

Sources

"A Brief History of the Gay Liberation Front, 1970-73." *Libcom.org.* Libcom, 21 Nov. 2007. Web. 24 Aug. 2012.

Donnelly, Sue. "Celebrating the 40th Anniversary of the Gay Liberation Front." *Out of the Box: News and Comment from LSE Archives.* London School of Economics, 7 Oct. 2010. Web. 11 Sept. 2012.

Dyke Manifesto: Calling All Lesbians!: Wake Up! New York: Lesbian Avengers, 1993. Print.

PRIMARY SOURCE

GAY LIBERATION FRONT MANIFESTO

The starting point of our liberation must be to rid ourselves of the oppression which lies in the head of every one of us. This means freeing our heads from self oppression and male chauvinism, and no longer organising our lives according to the patterns with which we are indoctrinated by straight society. It means that we must *root out* the idea that homosexuality is bad, sick or immoral, and develop a gay *pride*. In order to survive, most of us have either knuckled under to pretended that no oppression exists, and the result of this has been further to distort our heads. Within gay liberation, a number of consciousness-raising groups have already developed, in which we try to understand our oppression and learn new ways of thinking and behaving. The aim is to step outside the experience permitted by straight society, and to learn to love and trust one another. This is the precondition for acting and struggling together.

By freeing our heads we get the confidence to come out publicly and proudly as gay people, and to win over our gay brothers and sisters to the ideas of gay liberation.

CAMPAIGN Before we can create the new society of the future, we have to defend our interests as gay people here and now against all forms of oppression and victimisation. We have therefore drawn up the following list of immediate demands.

- that all discrimination against gay people, male and female, by the law, by employers, and by society at large, should end.

- that all people who feel attracted to a member of their own sex be taught that such feeling are perfectly valid.

- that sex education in schools stop being exclusively heterosexual.

- that psychiatrists stop treating homosexuality as though it were a sickness, thereby giving gay people senseless guilt complexes.

- that gay people be as legally free to contact other gay people, though newspaper ads, on the streets and by any other means they may want as are heterosexuals, and that police harassment should cease right now.

- that employers should no longer be allowed to discriminate against anyone on account of their sexual preferences.

- that the age of consent for gay males be reduced to the same as for straight.

- that gay people be free to hold hands and kiss in public, as are heterosexuals.

Gay Liberation Front: Manifesto. 1971. *Internet History Sourcebooks Project.* Fordham U, n.d. Web. 24 Aug. 2012.

Further Reading

Carter, David. *Stonewall: The Riots That Sparked the Gay Revolution.* New York: St. Martin's, 2004. Print.

Kissack, Terence. "Freaking Fag Revolutionaries: New York's Gay Liberation Front, 1969-1971." *Radical History Review* 62 (1995): 105-34. Print.

Lucas, Ian. *OutRage!: An Oral History.* London: Cassell, 1998. Print.

Power, Lisa. *No Bath but Plenty of Bubbles: An Oral History of the Gay Liberation Front, 1970-1973.* London: Cassell, 1995. Print.

Shumsky, Ellen. "Radicalesbians. *Gay & Lesbian Review Worldwide* 16.4 (2009): 17+. *Literature Resource Center.* Web. 24 Aug. 2012.

Walter, Aubrey. *Come Together: The Years of Gay Liberation, 1970-73.* London: Gay Men's, 1980. Print.

Anna Deem

A GAY MANIFESTO

Carl Wittman, Tom Hayden

OVERVIEW

A Gay Manifesto, written by Carl Wittman in 1970, serves as the author's personal manifesto about coming out of the closet later in life and what it was like to be part of the gay community in the late 1960s. After marrying Mimi Feingold in 1966, Wittman moved to San Francisco in the summer of 1967. There, feelings that Wittman had tried to ignore came to the surface, prompting him to seek sexual liberation and freedom from his marriage. He divorced Feingold the following year and began circulating among his friends drafts of an essay that ultimately became *A Gay Manifesto.* Wittman wrote his manifesto as a primer for the gay community about homosexuality and lesbianism, as well as the actions that gay men in San Francisco were taking.

Wittman's manifesto was embraced by the gay community, especially in San Francisco, where many saw it as one of the first pieces of literature to accurately and openly discuss the gay lifestyle as a viable option. The rise of gay activism in San Francisco was influenced in part by events such as the 1969 Stonewall riots in New York City. D.E. Mungello, who became friends with Wittman in San Francisco, writes in "A Spirit of the 60's": "Carl and I lived gay liberation. There was a shock element in Gay Lib as a political movement, and we were energized by doing things that were scandalous to most of the people we knew." Today, *A Gay Manifesto* is seen as an important early guide to homosexual activism and life that provided the gay community with a powerful piece of foundational literature.

HISTORICAL AND LITERARY CONTEXT

Wittman finished the final pre-published draft of *A Gay Manifesto* in 1969, one month before the Stonewall riots occurred on June 28. The manifesto sought to allay tensions between the gay community and mainstream society. Such tensions were brought to light during the Stonewall riots, when the Stonewall Inn—a bar in New York City's Greenwich Village that openly catered to gays and others on society's fringes—was raided by police. Though this was merely another in a long line of raids, the police lost control of the massive crowd and riots erupted. After the protests, which were marked by numerous violent encounters between the police and protesters, died

down, the gay community took steps to ensure that it had a voice, forming activist groups and establishing places for gays to feel welcome.

The riots in New York affected Wittman, who felt that gays in San Francisco suffered from similar injustices. Indeed, the San Francisco police were also raiding gay bars and persecuting gay men. Oral sex was considered a felony, and anyone caught engaging in homosexual sex in a rented apartment faced eviction. Many gay men began having sex in public parks as a result, and in 1971, 2,800 gay men were arrested for public sex. Different activist groups, such as the Society for Individual Rights and the Daughters of Bilitis, spoke out against police actions. So, too, did Wittman, whose essay spoke particularly to gay men.

Wittman's manifesto is just one of several pieces of literature that emerged in the late 1960s and early 1970s about gay life. Many members of the Gay Liberation Front (GLF)—a group formed in New York in 1969 in response to the Stonewall riots—felt that gays needed to mobilize. In 1971, the United Kingdom chapter of the GLF published a manifesto, the

❖ *Key Facts*

Time Period:
Mid-20th Century

Movement/Issue:
Gay liberation

Place of Publication:
America

Language of Publication:
English

THE CHARISMATIC CARL WITTMAN

Born on February 23, 1943, Carl Wittman lived most of his life speaking out for causes in which he believed. His interest in activism started early on when he was a member of the national council for the Students for a Democratic Society. Although Wittman was actively gay from the age of fourteen, he did not openly acknowledge his sexuality until the late 1960s, when the article "Waves of Resistance," published in November 1968 in the magazine *Liberation,* inspired him to openly embrace his sexual identity.

After Wittman came out and became more involved in the gay community, he began writing about his experiences. He cowrote "An Interracial Movement of the Poor" in 1963 with Tom Hayden and followed it up with *A Gay Manifesto,* which was reprinted as a pamphlet by the Red Butterfly cell of the Gay Liberation Front. Having grown tired of San Francisco, Wittman moved to Wolf Creek, Oregon, in 1971. On January 22, 1986, Wittman died of an AIDS-related illness.

THEMES AND STYLE

Wittman's manifesto focuses primarily on embracing the gay lifestyle and enlightening others by "freeing the homosexual in everyone." Wittman, who had spent most of his life repressing his true feelings, calls for self-acceptance in the gay community, using his own experiences to show fellow gays why they need to step out of the closet and not be ashamed of who they are. In the conclusion of his manifesto, Wittman notes: "We've been playing an act for a long time, so we're consummate actors. Now we can begin to be, and it'll be a good show!" Wittman was much happier after he revealed his true self, and he wanted to pass this message on to other gay men in the hope that they would embrace their own feelings and fight back against their oppressors.

Wittman's persuasive push for enlightenment is structured around several key strategies, including establishing his personal connection with his audience and devising an informative primer on the main elements of homosexuality. Wittman immediately draws the audience into his world, establishing an intimate connection. He uses his vast firsthand knowledge of the homosexual lifestyle to clear up misconceptions and explain in full what it actually means to be a gay man or woman in the United States of the late 1960s. "Homosexuality is not a lot of things," he writes. "It is not a makeshift in the absence of the opposite sex; it is not hatred or rejection of the opposite sex; it is not genetic; it is not the result of broken homes except inasmuch as we could see the sham of American marriage. Homosexuality is the capacity to love someone of the same sex." His understanding of homosexuality, delivered matter-of-factly, forces readers to think about what their lives would be like if they were in his shoes.

Because the subject is of such a personal nature, Wittman's writing has a candid quality that both enlightens and taps into the emotions of the reader. Early in the manifesto, he writes:

> Where once there was frustration, alienation, and cynicism, there are new characteristics among us. We are full of love for each other and are showing it; we are full of anger at what has been done to us. And as we recall all the self-censorship and repression for so many years, a reservoir of tears pours out of our eyes. And we are euphoric, high, with the initial flourish of a movement.

Wittman's language in this passage is both moving and heartfelt, focusing on the positivity of his message instead of dwelling on the discrimination the gay community has endured.

CRITICAL DISCUSSION

A Gay Manifesto was well received by Wittman's intended audience, which was made up primarily of gay men. Due to the formation of the Gay Liberation

Gay Liberation Front Manifesto, for that very purpose. Speaking for all GLF chapters, the manifesto details the oppression experienced by gays and the actions that could be taken to oppose it.

Since its publication, *A Gay Manifesto* has continued to exert a great influence the gay community. Although laws such as the banning of oral sex have been officially taken off the books, the gay community still faces various types of oppression. For example, nonreproductive sex is considered immoral by many conservatives, and the legalization of gay marriage in the United States is a divisive topic. Early activist literature, including *A Gay Manifesto,* helped pave the way for the legalization of gay marriage in an increasing number of states. This push has garnered support from influential figures such as U.S. president Barack Obama, who stated in 2012 that he would support gay marriage legislation.

Front in 1969 and the Stonewall riots that same year, his manifesto was topical and generated discussion among his peers, many of whom viewed it as a valuable resource for those still struggling with their sexuality and for fellow activists who were searching for positive reinforcement in a socially and politically confusing era. In "A Spirit of the 60's," Mungello describes Wittman's dedication to the gay cause:

> Carl stayed true to the values he expressed in the *Gay Manifesto.* He wrote that the first thing needed was "to free ourselves; that means clearing our heads of the garbage that's been poured into them." He thought that ghettos, whether black, white, straight, or gay, were a bad thing. So in 1971 he left San Francisco for good, because it was becoming a gay ghetto, and moved to Wolf Creek, Oregon, where he tried to build a gay commune.

A Gay Manifesto continues to exert a political and social influence. Literature such as Wittman's essay prompted American society to begin grappling with the issue of equal rights for gays. Writing for the the *Lambda Book Report,* Michael Bronski describes the legacy of the manifesto and similar works from the early years of the gay movement:

> From Carl Wittman's vastly influential "Gay Manifesto" to Jill Johnston's weekly column in the Village Voice the movement was continually driven, pushed, chided and nourished. There were no lack of ideas, theories, propositions, demands and analysis— everyone had an opinion. This led to enormous agreements, disagreements and at times confusion but the intellectual stimulation of the times were breathtaking: thinking, really thinking was a political act we realized could change our lives.

Despite the influence of *A Gay Manifesto,* scholarship on the work has been limited. The most salient pieces of writing on the manifesto's significance have come from San Francisco writers who witnessed the rise of the gay community. Mungello, for example,

comments further on his experiences with Wittman: "Fortunately, history is constantly being rewritten, forgotten people are being rediscovered, and excluded people are being added. I will always remember that sunny spring day of our first meeting and sex and kissing Carl good-bye on a busy Berkeley street in 1969. He is someone we should all remember." Indeed, many within the gay community do remember Wittman. His manifesto has been reprinted numerous times in publications such as the *Harvard Crimson,* the *San Francisco Free Press,* and *Guerilla Magazine* and in Neil Miller's book *Out of the Past: Gay and Lesbian History from 1869 to the Present* (1994).

BIBLIOGRAPHY

Sources

Amico, Michael. "Gay Youths as 'Whorified Virgins.'" *Gay & Lesbian Review Worldwide* 12.4 (2005): 34+. *Literature Resource Center.* Web. 30 Aug. 2012.

Bronski, Michael. "Public Sex: The Culture of Radical Sex." *Lambda Book Report* Jan.-Feb. 1995: 16+. *Literature Resource Center.* Web. 30 Aug. 2012.

Mungello, D.E. "A Spirit of the 60's." *Gay & Lesbian Review Worldwide* 15.3 (2008): 20+. *Literature Resource Center.* Web. 28 Aug. 2012.

Wittman, Carl. *A Gay Manifesto.* Boston: New England Free, 1970. Print.

Further Reading

"A Brief History of the Gay Liberation Front, 1970-73." *Libcom.org.* Libcom, 21 Nov. 2007. Web. 24 Aug. 2012.

Carter, David. *Stonewall: The Riots That Sparked the Gay Revolution.* New York: St. Martin's, 2004. Print.

"Gay Liberation Front: Manifesto." *Internet History Sourcebooks Project.* Fordham University, n.d. Web. 24 Aug. 2012.

Lucas, Ian. *OutRage!: An Oral History.* London: Cassell, 1998. Print.

Miller, Neil. *Out of the Past: Gay and Lesbian History from 1869 to the Present.* New York: Vintage, 1994. Print.

Power, Lisa. *No Bath but Plenty of Bubbles: An Oral History of the Gay Liberation Front, 1970-1973.* London: Cassell, 1995. Print.

Anna Deem

OUT AGAINST THE RIGHT

The Dyke Manifesto

Lesbian Avengers' Civil Rights Organizing Project

✥ Key Facts

Time Period:
Late 20th Century

Movement/Issue:
Gay Rights

Place of Publication:
United States

Language of Publication:
English

OVERVIEW

Composed by the Lesbian Avengers' Civil Rights Organizing Project (LACROP), *Out against the Right: The Dyke Manifesto* (1994) is a polemic against the antigay initiatives championed by the Christian Right. The manifesto also criticized the gay rights movement for not taking strong stands against the racism, sexism, and elitism evident within its own ranks, and the document decried the heterosexism that continued to pervade the feminist movement. Moreover, it sought to counter the invisibility experienced by lesbians, transsexuals, and trans-gender individuals within the gay rights and feminist movements. Printed on a two-sided broadsheet boldly designed by Carrie Moyer, the *Dyke Manifesto* was distributed en masse at the New York City LGBT Pride Parade on June 26, 1994. In compiling the manifesto, LACROP contacted activists working in states plagued by antigay legislation, sharing their grassroots organizing models and suggesting innovative ways to fight back. Their testimonials are printed on the reverse of the manifesto and encourage other lesbians to mobilize against bigotry. The manifesto, which is addressed to "you pervert, freak, bulldagger, unfit, sicko, lesbian, bitch," incites lesbians to political action by reminding them of the derogatory language used by members of the Christian Right and other homophobes.

Although the manifesto did not engender a specific movement, it was a unique intervention aimed at giving the political concerns of lesbians a priority they had not had in earlier rights movements, and it was a significant contribution to literary works produced by the gay movements of the 1980s and 1990s. LACROP touted the manifesto's ideas in the besieged communities it helped and successfully employed many of the strategies suggested on the reverse of the broadsheet. The group was notably successful in northern Idaho, where its presence and out-and-proud campaign efforts helped defeat Proposition One, a multipronged initiative to limit legal protections for gay and lesbian citizens and to prevent schools and libraries from making available information that affirms gay and lesbian identity. Eventually, the manifesto and its accompanying testimonials were expanded upon and became the *Out Against the Right:*

An Organizing Handbook (1995), which documents LACROP's experiences with grassroots campaign efforts and offers further strategies for mobilization against the Christian Right.

HISTORICAL AND LITERARY CONTEXT

Out Against the Right: The Dyke Manifesto responds to the political crises facing the American gay and lesbian population in the mid-1990s, when antigay ballot initiatives were cropping up all over the United States. By 1992, the Christian Right had become America's most powerful special interest group and was openly pitting itself against the gay and lesbian community, claiming that gays and lesbians threatened the American family and way of life. Extreme right-wing organizations such as the Christian Coalition, Concerned Women for America, and Focus on the Family were intensifying their attacks on both lesbians and gay men. In November 1992, Christian Right organizations backed state constitutional amendments, including Colorado's Amendment 2 and Oregon's Measure 9, that sought to repeal existing antidiscrimination ordinances and prohibit local or state governments from ever again passing such ordinances. Although Oregon's Measure 9 was defeated, Colorado's Amendment 2 passed; it was declared unconstitutional in 1996 by the U.S. Supreme Court.

By the time *Out Against the Right: The Dyke Manifesto* was written in 1994, eight states were facing antigay ballot initiatives. Among the most radical advocates for change was New York Lesbian Avengers, a direct action group formed in 1992. In the fall of that year, New York Lesbian Avengers sent activists to Lewiston, Maine, to combat the Christian Right's initiative to repeal the town's antidiscrimination ordinance. The Lewiston initiative passed despite the group's efforts, but the Avengers' experience with local independent activists inspired the formation of LACROP, a grassroots mobilization effort created in January 1994 to assist lesbian and gay activists in communities besieged by the Christian Right. *The Dyke Manifesto* provided a platform around which gay and lesbian activists in both rural and urban areas could coalesce.

Out Against the Right: The Dyke Manifesto draws on a history of declarations of the rights of women and gay men. In *Manifestoes: Provocations of the Modern* (1999), Janet Lyon draws parallels between *The Dyke Manifesto* and the 1871 women's manifesto of the Paris Commune. In an effort to rouse women into action, the Commune tract declares, "The final hour has struck … The place of the workers is back at their barricades … Action! Energy! The tree of liberty is best nourished by the blood of its enemies!" The same militant passion is seen in LACROP's manifesto: "Now's the time to fight back and fight forward … Join the struggle, take the streets … 1000's OF ANGRY DYKES CAN'T BE WRONG—AND WON'T GIVE IN. EVER." Both manifestos angrily reject half-measures, demand action, and sound the cry for women to take to the streets. In composing the 1994 manifesto, LACROP imitated the urgent tone, strident wording, and powerful graphics of the original 1993 *Lesbian Avengers' Dyke Manifesto.*

In the year following its distribution, *Out Against the Right: The Dyke Manifesto* was reworked into a grassroots political activists' manual called *Out Against the Right: An Organizing Handbook.* In her 1995 article, "Gay Politics in the Heartland: With the Lesbian Avengers in Idaho," Sara Pursley details LACROP's triumphant 1994 experience in Idaho, which was central to the discussion and strategies outlined in the 1995 handbook. Despite having been written almost two decades ago, the handbook is still touted as an "invaluable resource to grassroots organizing" on the Lesbian Avengers' official website. Although the Lesbian Avengers' social impact and their 1993 manifesto are discussed in a number of queer and feminist works, *Out Against the Right: The Dyke Manifesto* is mentioned infrequently.

THEMES AND STYLE

The central theme of *Out Against the Right: The Dyke Manifesto* is that the civil rights of gay and lesbian Americans are being threatened by extreme Christian right-wing political groups. The manifesto warns the lesbian public about right-wing movements: "The Christian Right is on our homosexual heels and it's time we started kicking … THEY'RE REACHING DEEP INTO OUR SAFEST CLOSETS with legislation that will get us at our jobs, in the streets—*even* in our homes." The latter half of the manifesto claims that mainstream campaigns formed to combat the Christian Right's initiatives are impotent and further repress lesbians and gays in the name of campaign strategy. Angered that traditional activist campaigns require less "respectable" gay individuals to stay in the closet, the manifesto declares, "Butch, femme and androgynous dykes, leather queers, drag kings and queens, transsexuals and trans-genders will not be thrown to the wolves so that straight-acting 'gay people' can beg for acceptance at our expense." To this

THE LESBIAN AVENGERS: MOBILIZING QUEER AMERICA

Founded in New York in 1992 by Anne-Christine d'Adesky, Marie Honan, Anne Maguire, Sarah Schulman, Ana Simo, and Maxine Wolfe, the Lesbian Avengers describe themselves as "a direct action group focused on issues vital to lesbian visibility and survival." The founders were longtime queer activists who had been involved in LGBT groups such as ACT-UP and Queer Nation, but they had grown tired of women's issues being ignored by these groups. The Lesbian Avengers' first exploit occurred on September 9, 1992, at an elementary school in Queens where local right-wing activists were attempting to suppress a multicultural curriculum that included information about lesbian and gay lives. The Avengers descended upon the school with a marching band and passed out lavender balloons instructing children to "Ask about lesbian lives." The Avengers became known for such controversial "zaps," in which small groups would often trail politicians to draw attention to their antigay initiatives.

According to the Lesbian Avengers' *Dyke Manifesto,* the Avengers engage in "creative activism: loud, bold, sexy, silly, fierce, tasty, and dramatic." Their visual creativity was seen in Carrie Moyer's eye-catching flyers and at their fire-eating demonstrations, where they would chant the slogan "The fire will not consume us. We take it and make it our own." In addition to communiqué-style newsletters, the Avengers penned two manifestos and two handbooks dedicated to educating lesbians to force political and cultural change by conducting out-and-proud actions. Although the New York Lesbian Avengers performed their last action in 1995, chapters across the nation remain active. The annual Dyke March, held in dozens of cities around the world, is the most visible of the Avengers' legacies.

end, the reverse side of the manifesto outlines non-traditional strategies for organizing and fighting the Christian Right without compromising gay and lesbian identity.

The manifesto achieves its incendiary rhetorical effect by continually reminding lesbians of the Christian Right's hate-filled language and actions. These reminders are achieved through strident language and irony. Addressing the lesbian audience as, "pervert, freak, bulldagger, unfit, sicko, lesbian, bitch," *The Dyke Manifesto* uses right-wing hate words to provoke angry lesbians into action. The tract then juxtaposes these hateful epithets with an ironic statement about the Christian Right: "UPSTANDING, FAMILY-VALUED, GOD-FEARING AMERICA WANTS YOU GONE." The irony is compounded by the inclusion of a picture depicting a family with three young children in which the father holds a sign stating, "It's not diversity. It's perversity." The juxtaposition draws attention to the ugly hypocrisy of

family-valued, God-fearing America's intolerance and the hate that is being taught to their children.

Stylistically, *Out Against the Right: The Dyke Manifesto* is distinguished by its fiercely energetic tone. The color of the increasingly bold typeface alternates between black and orange, suggesting fiery anger. This rage is further highlighted by a picture of fist-pumping dykes at a demonstration in Lewiston, Maine. The strategically placed bull's-eye behind the words "freak, bulldagger, unfit" is yet another reminder that lesbians are constantly targeted by the hostile Christian Right. The large typeface, color choices, and eye-catching graphics command attention while simultaneously feeding the fire of lesbian anger. The in-your-face strategies suggested on the reverse of the manifesto are echoed in LACROP's decision to print it on thousands of broadsheets, to design it as a flyer, and to distribute it at New York City's LGBT Pride Parade. By implementing the very tactics proposed in the manifesto, LACROP demonstrates the power of passion and exhorts others to unleash their fierce energy in order to fight back: "GIVE US YOUR VISION, YOUR PASSION. JOIN THE STRUGGLE. TAKE THE STREETS...."

CRITICAL DISCUSSION

When *Out Against the Right: The Dyke Manifesto* was first distributed in 1994, it was largely ignored by mainstream media. However, though the manifesto did not garner much contemporary attention, LACROP successfully used it as a springboard to combat both the Christian Right and traditional reformist campaigns in the communities it served. LACROP's tract gave hope to gays and lesbians by vehemently rejecting the homogeneous view of gay and lesbian identity proffered by both the Christian Right and mainstream antidiscrimination campaigns. As Lyon

suggests, the tract rejects stereotypes by redefining the terms "lesbian" and "dyke": "*The Dyke Manifesto* lays open the ostensibly static category of 'lesbian' and reveals within it an extraordinary motion of bodies, partial identities, public struggles, class-based oppressions, and political passions." Lyon asserts that in the manifesto, a "dyke" is not just a lesbian, but "a lesbian subject pushed to action and shaped by an array of alliances ... 'dyke' is a political identity brought to life by the kiss of righteous rage." By offering this new multifaceted identity, the manifesto inspires hope and political drive in queer communities around the nation.

The impact of *Out Against the Right: The Dyke Manifesto* is evident in LACROP's successful defeat of Idaho's Proposition One in 1994. Although LACROP left northern Idaho on November 23, 1994, Pursley observes that "the legacy of its work remains in the form of two Lesbian Avengers chapters ... the Lewiston Lesbian and Gay Society, a Lesbian and Gay Rural Organizing Project, a pro-lesbian and pro-gay youth group at Sandpoint High School, and the seeds of an antiviolence project." The manifesto's legacy is apparent in the Supreme Court's 1996 decision to overturn Colorado's Amendment Two, a piece of legislation that the Lesbian Avengers vocally opposed. In the nearly two decades since the manifesto was first written, it has been the occasional subject of criticism that has considered its importance in polemic, feminist, and social terms.

Much scholarship discusses the social impact of the Lesbian Avengers' deeds, though *Out Against the Right: The Dyke Manifesto* is only sporadically mentioned. *The Dyke Manifesto* is most extensively treated in Lyon's *Manifestoes: Provocations of the Modern.* Lyon discusses the tract's value as a manifesto, stating, "As with other manifestoes, the Dyke Manifesto operated by lighting up a polemical field scorched by the failed promises of an incomplete or incompetent political order, and by challenging the status of the 'universal subject' on which that order is implicitly based." In chapter 2 of *Community Activism and Feminist Politics,* Leila J. Rupp and Verta Taylor consider the feminist importance of lesbian communities such as the Avengers: "we see lesbian feminist communities as sustaining the radical feminist tradition and bequeathing a legacy, however imperfect, to feminists of the future." Commentators have also drawn attention to the Avengers' inclusion in the lesbian chic phenomenon of the 1990s, even though *The Dyke Manifesto* angrily states, "FUCK LESBIAN CHIC." For example, in *Risking Resistance: Rhetorical Agency in Queer Theory and Queer Activism,* Erin J. Rand claims the activist practices of the Lesbian Avengers are, "hip, stylish, fashionable, fun, and sexually available to men; consequently, they are able to make sense as lesbian chic."

BIBLIOGRAPHY

Sources

Barron, Alexandra. "Lesbian Avengers." *LGBTQ America Today: An Encyclopedia.* Ed. John C. Hawley. Vol. 2. Westport: Greenwood, 2009. 664-666. *Gale Virtual Reference Library.* Web. 21 June 2012.

Bull, Chris, and John Gallagher. *Perfect Enemies: The Religious Right, the Gay Movement, and the Politics of the 1990s.* New York: Crown, 1996. Print.

LACROP. *Out Against the Right: The Dyke Manifesto.* LGBT/Queer Studies and Services Institute. Illinois State University, 1994. Web. 21 June 2012.

———. *Out Against the Right: An Organizing Handbook.* Octobertech, 1995. Web. 21 Jun 2012.

Lesbian Avengers, The. "Lesbian Avengers Civil Rights Organizing Project." *The Lesbian Avengers International Communiqué.* May 1994: 1-2. Print.

Lyon, Janet. *Manifestoes: Provocations of the Modern.* Ithaca: Cornell UP, 1999. Print.

Pursley, Sara. "Gay Politics in the Heartland: With the Lesbian Avengers in Idaho." *Nation* 23 Jan. 1995: 90-94. Print.

Rand, Erin J. *Risking Resistance: Rhetorical Agency in Queer Theory and Queer Activism.* Ann Arbor: ProQuest, 2006. Print.

Rupp, Leila J., and Verta Taylor. "Women's Culture and Lesbian Feminist Activism." *Community Activism and Feminist Politics: Organizing Across Race, Class, and Gender.* Ed. Nancy A. Naples. New York: Routledge, 1998. Print.

Further Reading

Boucher, Cindy. "Lesbian Avengers." *Qualia Folk … dedicated to LGBT scholarship.* Qualia Folk, 8 Dec 2011. Web. 24 Jun 2012.

Brandt, Pamela Robin, and Lindsy Van Gelder. *The Girls Next Door: Into the Heart of Lesbian America.* New York: Simon, 1996. Print.

Cvetkovich, Ann. "Fierce Pussies and Lesbian Avengers: Dyke Activism Meets Celebrity Culture." *Feminist Consequences: Theory for the New Century.* Ed. Elisabeth Bronfen and Misha Kavka. New York: Columbia UP, 2000. 283-318. Print.

Love, Heather. *Feeling Backward: Loss and the Politics of Queer History.* Boston: Harvard UP, 2007. Print.

Schulman, Sarah. *My American History: Lesbian and Gay Life during the Reagan/Bush Years.* New York: Routledge, 1994. Print.

Maggie Magno

QUEERS READ THIS

Anonymous

+⁘ *Key Facts*

Time Period:
Late 20th Century

Movement/Issue:
Gay rights; AIDS crisis

Place of Publication:
United States

**Language of
Publication:**
English

OVERVIEW

Although written anonymously for distribution at the Pride March in New York City, 1990, the manifesto *Queers Read This* is associated with the activist group Queer Nation and was written in response to the marginalization and violence directed towards the gay community, which escalated during the AIDS crisis of the previous decade. The manifesto is addressed to the "queer" brothers and sisters of America, and it centers upon the idea that queers are at war with straight (heterosexual) people because abuses of gay people's rights—including violent gay bashings, verbal attacks, and political inequality—had become the norm. Written at a time of great change for the queer community, the manifesto was part of a new activism that focused on public displays of queer existence. The text is an attempt to rally gay troops for war against straights, as this seemed to be the only reasonable response, in the view of the writers, to the explosion of homophobic violence that threatened the lives of queers at the time.

Although initially received with mixed feelings about the assertive public behavior encouraged by the manifesto and by its reconstitution of the word queer, the manifesto was largely embraced by the gay community for its message of unity. Although many did not heed the call for retaliatory violence, the manifesto did inspire a mass outing of queers to their families, friends, and colleagues, which ultimately contributed to a reduction in the blatant homophobia and violence that had escalated in the late 1980s. While the militant style of activism that produced this manifesto had run its course by the early 1990s, the use of the word queer to describe anybody who was not heterosexual became more prevalent, although some are still reluctant to use the term today.

HISTORICAL AND LITERARY CONTEXT

Queers Read This was written largely in response to the violent homophobia that emerged in the 1980s because of the association of AIDS with the lifestyles of gay men. While gay rights movements had made considerable progress during the 1970s—along with other civil rights movements of the time—the AIDS epidemic negatively influenced public opinion about sexual minorities. Most of the earliest cases of AIDS in the United States seemed to involve men who engaged in anal sex with men, and for a time in the early 1980s the disease was called gay-related immune deficiency, or GRID, a name that drew protests from gay rights groups. Doctors and medical researchers soon realized, however, that the disease was affecting other populations as well; the name acquired immunodeficiency disorder was proposed in 1982 as a more accurate characterization of the disease. Nevertheless, the link between gay men and the poorly understood disorder fueled homophobic fears, and it was not until the cause of the disease was identified in 1984 and the reportage of several high-profile cases involving AIDS patients who were not gay—including tennis star Arthur Ashe and a young hemophiliac named Ryan White, both infected by blood treatments—that such fears began slowly to dissipate. Despite growing public understanding of AIDS, many nonetheless continued to look on the disease as a symbol of the perceived sinfulness or abnormality of homosexuality, and gays remained at risk for violent attacks.

The deep-rooted prejudice that the AIDS crisis brought to light caused outrage within the gay community and led to the formation of activist groups such as ACT UP (AIDS Coalition to Unleash Power), GLAAD (Gay & Lesbian Alliance Against Defamation), and Queer Nation. These groups promoted unity within the queer community through a style of militant activism, which included strong messages that grew out of anger over injustices suffered by the community.

Released at the height of this militant activism, *Queers Read This* was written to combat attempts to equate homosexuality with AIDS and thus encourage—in some cases, violent—homophobia. The manifesto adopted the tone of the bold new activism, which was characterized by orchestrated displays of gay affection, marches, and chants—such as "We're here. We're queer. Get used to it"—to challenge the image of AIDS as a disease of gay men who were infecting the heterosexual population by way of public washrooms and pay phones. The writers of the manifesto were inspired by the need to stop the homophobic panic created by misunderstanding of the AIDS crisis and to discourage the passive acceptance of violence by members of the queer community who would not publicly announce their sexuality but instead attempted to blend in with the heterosexual population.

The manifesto and its legacy among activits helped change the popular and political images of homosexuals. It also generated a great deal of criticism related to the use of the word queer as a unifying term for the members of sexual minorities. Theories about identity, performance, and acceptability in mainstream culture emerged in relation to this unifying concept of queerness, and writers were inspired by these emerging theories and the blunt, unapologetic language of the movement to compose gritty literature about the struggles of specific sexual minorities. Universities created departments to study this emerging genre of theory and literature. Queer studies is still developing as a field of study in modern academia.

THEMES AND STYLE

The central theme of *Queers Read This* is that queers are at war with straights and must unite through their common rage to fight for basic freedoms and rights. The manifesto revolves around incidents of discrimination, such as teenagers shouting "Faggot's gonna die" on the street, and political injustices: the writers assert that President Ronald Reagan "mass-murdered" queers with AIDS "for eight years" by ignoring the disease until it began affecting straights. Such incidents reflect varying degrees and forms of violence toward members of the queer community, and the references to them are intended to inspire hatred: the hatred that the authors believe queers should feel toward straights in response to the hatred that straights exhibit toward queers in acts of bigotry and intolerance. The manifesto argues that it is only by unifying as queers who share a common hatred of straight people can gays, lesbians, and other sexual minorities recognize attacks on gays as acts of war and fight back accordingly for social and political equality.

The rhetorical effect of this pamphlet is achieved through the use of multiple narrators who share a common sense of outrage but express it in different ways. The manifesto begins with declarations about the dangers of being queer and the need to unite as an army against straights: "It is easier to fight when you know who your enemy is. Straight people are your enemy." The pamphlet then describes the hatred that straight people exhibit towards queers and argues that queers should reciprocate. Although the pamphlet gives voice to the angry perspectives of lesbians, artists, people with AIDS, clubbers, and others who fit under the banner of queer, the main thrust of its argument is the need for all queers to stand united as an army against discrimination.

The pamphlet uses strong language designed to offend the reader and to reinforce the claim that unification through anger is the only way to win the war for equality against the straights. In addition to using such provocative terms as "hate," "fuck," "faggot," and "dyke," the manifesto demands that gays and lesbians unite under the label queer because,

THE AIDS CRISIS: FROM A "GAY DISEASE" TO A STRAIGHT PROBLEM

Officially identified in America in 1981, AIDS (acquired immunodeficiency syndrome), transferred in the form of HIV (human immunodeficiency virus) through bodily fluids, is a disease that disables the immune system, leaving an infected person vulnerable to life-threatening diseases. By 1987, AIDS had become an epidemic with more than 40,000 recorded cases, a number that subsequently rose rapidly. For a number of years, the infection was popularly associated with homosexual men and intravenous drug users, groups already regarded with widespread disapprobation. Even as medical researchers made new discoveries about the cause, transmission, and incidence of the disease, many Americans continued to fear that they could become infected through casual contact.

Public opinion began to change, however, with the case of Ryan White, a young, straight teenager who acquired AIDS through a blood transfusion. Because of the taboos surrounding AIDS as a sexually transmitted "gay disease," White was refused admittance to school once his illness became known. The resulting controversy led to efforts to better inform the public about the disease and prompted the government to increase funding for HIV/AIDS research. Many members of the queer community felt outraged, however, that so many of their friends and lovers died unnoticed and that it took the infection of a straight man to finally bring about full recognition of the terrible impact of the disease.

although it "can be a rough word" because of its association with strangeness and otherness, "it is also a sly and ironic weapon we can steal from the homophobe's hands and use against him." In embracing the word queer and other words straights have used to degrade people who do not fit the heterosexual norm, the pamphlet makes the point that gays and lesbians must not only recognize verbal assault as an act of war but that they also must admit to their own hatred and desire to fight for their rights and freedoms. Thus, the strong language inspires, and is inspired by, the anger that queers feel both as individuals who suffer personally the effects of discrimination and as a united community defending against violence.

CRITICAL DISCUSSION

The initial reaction to the distribution of *Queers Read This* was an excitement that resulted in the formation of numerous Queer Nation chapters in major cities across the United States. Contemporary response to the bold nature of the manifesto and Queer Nation at large was mixed: some were offended by the bluntness of the language while others felt empowered by the militant activism. Allan Bérubé and Jeffrey Escoffier, in their 1991 discussion of the Queer Nation, praises

People marching in the street to commemorate Gay Pride Day in New York City. EDUCATION IMAGES/ UIG/GETTY IMAGES

the manifesto for its uniqueness. "A new generation of activists is here," he writes. "They may be the first wave of activists to embrace the retrofuture/classic contemporary styles of postmodernism." Other scholars, such as poet Jason Schneiderman, argue that "the word 'queer' is a problem" because it suggests a "big tent approach to sexual minorities" that, despite its unifying effect, largely oversimplifies the differences among sexual minorities and their associated issues of discrimination.

The reconstitution of the word queer to describe the unification of non-heterosexual minorities is the legacy of the Queer Nation manifesto. Members of various sexual minorities have expressed ambivalence about the word queer because of its offensive origins and the overgeneralization it represents. Susan Stryker writes in *glbtq: An Encyclopedia of Gay, Lesbian, Bisexual, Transgender, and Queer Culture* (2004) that "use of the term 'queer' was never universally embraced by all segments of the constituencies that the concept of 'queerness' could potentially represent." Theorists such as Michael Trask agree. The word queer, he notes, "routes itself through a polymorphous body politic in which it might be possible for anyone to assume the name 'queer'" although "it is impossible for anyone to 'own' it." Even in current scholarship, the bold nature of the word queer and the unification of sexual minorities as outlined in *Queers Read This* remains cause for debate.

Opinions in the debate over the use of the word queer continue to range between open acceptance and blatant distaste. Nevertheless, the manifesto succeeded in generating discussion about the rights and freedoms of various sexual minority groups under its umbrella. Donald E. Hall in his "Introduction: Queer Works" (1997) describes the use of the word queer as "something like that of a loose cannon" in its effectiveness, but he notes that it "worked to stimulate a public discussion among individuals who otherwise might never have confronted issues surrounding sexual and social non-conformity."

BIBLIOGRAPHY

Sources

Bérubé, Allan, and Jeffrey Escoffier. "Queer/Nation." *OUT/Look: National Lesbian and Gay Quarterly* 11 (Winter 1991): 13-14. Rpt. *American Homo Community and Perversity*. Ed. Jeffrey Escoffier. California: U of C Press, 1998. 202-204.

Chauncey, George. *Why Marriage? The History Shaping Today's Debate over Gay Equality*. New York: Basic, 2004. *Ebrary*. Web. 20 July 2012.

Hall, Donald E. "Introduction: Queer Works." *College Literature* 24.1 (1997): 2-10. *JSTOR*. Web. 20 July 2012.

Schneiderman, Jason. "In Defense of Queer Theory." *The Gay & Lesbian Review Worldwide* 17.1 (2010): 11-15. *Literature Resource Center*. Web. 19 July 2012.

Stryker, Susan. "Queer Nation." *glbtq: An Encyclopedia of Gay, Lesbian, Bisexual, Transgender, and Queer Culture*. Ed. Claude J. Summers. glbtq, 2004. Web. 19 July 2012.

Trask, Michael. "Merging with the Masses: The Queer Identity Politics of Leftist Modernism." *Differences* 8.1

(1996): 94+. *Literature Resource Center.* Web. 20 July 2012.

Further Reading

Abelove, Henry, Michèle Aina Barale, and David M. Halperin, eds. *The Lesbian and Gay Studies Reader.* New York: Routledge, 1993. Print.

Battis, Jes. *Homofiles: Theory, Sexuality, and Graduate Studies.* Lanham: Lexington, 2011. Print.

Berlant, Lauren, and Michael Warner. "What Does Queer Theory Teach Us About X?" *PMLA* 110.3 (1995): 343-49. Print.

Castiglia, Christopher. *If Memory Serves: Gay Men, AIDS, and the Promise of the Queer Past.* Minneapolis: U of Minneapolis P, 2012. Print.

Huffer, Lynne. *Mad for Foucault: Rethinking the Foundations of Queer Theory.* New York: Columbia UP, 2010. Print.

James Kinsella, *Covering the Plague: AIDS and the American Media.* New Brunswick: Rutgers UP, 1989. Print.

Katherine Barker

RACIAL POLITICS

BLACK ART

Amiri Baraka

OVERVIEW

The poem "Black Art" by Amiri Baraka, first published in January 1966, demands that black writers create a new form of poetry inspired by and written for the black community. From the poem's first line— "Poems are bullshit unless they are teeth or trees or lemons piled on a step"—"Black Art" decrees that poetry must be about action toward racial equality and a new black aesthetic. Written in the wake of the assassination of the human rights activist Malcolm X, "Black Art" is considered the manifesto of the Black Arts movement founded by Baraka in 1965 in Harlem. "Black Art" marks Baraka's departure from integrated bohemian artist and Beat poet to black nationalist leader and revolutionary.

"Black Art" received mixed reviews from critics, largely because of the poem's inflammatory tone and overt racism. The poem became a manifesto for a large number of black artists, including Maya Angelou, Nikki Giovanni, Ron Karenga, Larry Neal, and Sonia Sanchez, who joined Baraka's Black Arts movement in direct response to his words. In many ways this organization served as the artistic branch of the Black Power movement, encouraging a new generation of black voices to write and to create publishing houses in New York and other U.S. cities. Many mainstream critics deemed "Black Art" antiwhite, specifically toward members of the Jewish faith. For this reason, Baraka would later face harsh scrutiny and attempted censure from a number of his contemporaries who felt that the delivery of his message was too abrasive. Baraka's "Black Art" served its intended purpose in creating a new form of poetry, one that calls people to action and that facilitates change for African Americans.

HISTORICAL AND LITERARY CONTEXT

"Black Art" challenges black artists to disband their preconceived notions of poetry and art to create a new form that champions the black cause. The assassination of Malcolm X motivated Baraka to give up efforts at integration and to pursue a more revolutionary path as a black activist. He explains this concept in his autobiography: "The solution is revolution.... We thought it meant killing white folks. But it is a system that's got to be killed." Baraka urges writers to use their art for social change.

Malcolm X was assassinated on February 21, 1965, and this event directly inspired the composition of "Black Art." In a 2012 article in *Our Weekly LA*, Baraka explains that "after Malcolm X was assassinated, we came to believe there really was a war against Black people and not just the work of some disconnected racist White folk." Malcolm X's assassination, he says, "drove us from Greenwich Village to Harlem." Baraka and Neal's Black Arts Repertory Theatre, established in Harlem in 1964, served as a focal point for the Black Arts movement. In his 1968 essay "The Black Arts Movement," Neal defines Black Art as "the aesthetic and spiritual sister of the Black Power concept." Baraka's poem, Neal asserts, "comes to stand for the collective conscious and unconscious of Black America—the real impulse in the back of the Black Power movement, which is the will toward self-determination and nationhood, a radical reordering of the nature and function of both art and the artist."

"Black Art" was not the first manifesto written by an African American author on the subject of race and art, although its form and tone are unique. The essays "Negro Artist and the Racial Mountain" by Langston Hughes and "Criteria of Negro Art" by W. E. B. Du Bois both address the purpose of art for the black community. Baraka was also influenced by the speeches of Malcolm X, with his "by any means necessary" approach to the civil rights movement and the struggle for African American rights. Although Baraka was an integrated poet prior to Malcolm X's assassination, his earlier essays "The Revolutionary Theatre" (1964) and "State Meant" (1965) develop themes similar to those in "Black Art." In his 1968 essay "Black Cultural Nationalism," Karenga concisely explains the Black Arts movement's concept of art: "Black Art, like everything else in the black community, must respond positively to the reality of revolution."

Upon its publication, "Black Art" inspired a wave of black writers, publishers, and dramatists to create art for the social advancement of blacks in cities across the United States. Baraka's militant stance on art brought him notoriety among his peers, but it also had negative effects on his career, resulting in censure, loss of tenure, and even imprisonment. After Baraka was arrested on gun charges during the Newark riots in 1968, the judge read segments of his poetry to justify imprisonment, a conviction that was later overturned.

❖ *Key Facts*

Time Period:
Mid-20th Century

Movement/Issue:
Aesthetics; Black Arts movement; Black Power movement

Place of Publication:
United States

Language of Publication:
English

BROADSIDE PRESS

As the Black Arts movement grew during the 1960s, a number of African American-owned publishing houses emerged in various U.S. cities. One of the most important of these was inaugurated in Detroit in 1965, when a local librarian and poet printed a broadside edition of one of his works. He had written the poem two years earlier in response to the bombing of the 16th Street Baptist Church in Birmingham, Alabama. The poem was "The Ballad of Birmingham," the poet was Dudley Randall, and the new publishing house was Broadside Press. Over the next year Broadside exclusively printed verse in the single-sheet format that gave the press its name. The first six were reprints of works by various prominent black writers, including Gwendolyn Brooks and Robert Hayden. These were known collectively as "Poems of the Negro Revolt."

In 1966 Broadside published poet Margaret Danner and Randall's collaboration *Poem Counterpoem,* its first book-length work. In answer to race riots that rocked Detroit in 1967, Randall's first solo collection, *Cities Burning,* appeared in 1968. That year the press began to focus on emerging rather than established black poets. During the next decade it issued broadsides on an almost monthly basis, producing works by Amiri Baraka and many other important black writers. Although Randall sold the press in 1985, it remains in operation and continues to publish the socially engaged writing of familiar and new black voices.

Although Baraka renounced his ties with the Black Arts movement in 1974 to adopt a socialist ideology, his legacy as the movement's founder remains. The Black Arts movement was a driving force in establishing African American studies programs at universities across the United States, thus legitimizing black literature as viable for future generations to study.

THEMES AND STYLE

The main theme of "Black Art" is that blacks should create art that separates them from white society, promotes their own causes, and strives for social change. "Black Art" is written as a mantra, criticizing the genre and deeming poems to be "bullshit." Baraka's commentary on artists who emulate whites is evident when he advocates smearing black poems "on girdle-mamma mulatto bitches / whose brains are red jelly stuck / between 'lizbeth taylor's toes." He urges his audience to create art in their own image:

> We want a black poem. And a
>
> Black World.
>
> Let the world be a Black Poem
>
> And Let All Black People Speak This Poem
>
> Silently
>
> or LOUD

By pointing out the different types of black stereotypes, Baraka raises his poem to a political level. He criticizes jocks, mulattoes, and different types of black leaders in an effort to promote social change: "There's a negroleader pinned to / a bar stool in Sardi's ... / ... Another negroleader on the steps of the white house." Baraka uses language, sound, and stereotype to convey his theme of a separate Black Arts movement.

"Black Art" relies on abrasive language and violent images to provoke the reader into action. Written in the first-person plural point of view, the poem conveys a sense of unity, as if a whole generation is crying out against the confines of structure, espousing revolution. Baraka proclaims, "We want live / words of the hip live flesh and / coursing blood." The images become increasingly violent as the poem progresses:

"We want 'poems that kill.' Assassin poems, Poems that shoot guns. Poems that wrestle cops into alleys and take their weapons leaving them dead...."

Baraka's use of inflammatory language to agitate the reader is evident in both words and sounds. In the middle of the poem, he breaks into the sounds "rrrrrrrrrrrrrr" and "tuhtuhtuhtuhtuhtuhtuhtuhtuh" to simulate an airplane flying and firing. These sounds also resemble the sound of jazz drumbeats and vocal scatting. Baraka originally read his poem on drummer Sonny Murray's album *Sonny's Time Now* (1965).

In "Black Art," Baraka relies heavily on confrontational language and racially charged phrases to shock the reader into action. He presents images of dead Irish policemen, promotes the killing of Mafia drug dealers, and recommends "Setting fire ... to / whities ass." While all of these images are graphic, Baraka's depiction of Jewish people in the poem is the most apparent. He makes multiple violent references to Jews, calling for "dagger poems in the slimy bellies / of the owner-jews" and "Another bad poem cracking / steel knuckles in a jewlady's mouth." When Baraka abandoned his bohemian lifestyle as a Beat poet for the role of Black Arts movement activist, he also divorced his Jewish wife. In many ways these references are viewed as a direct renunciation of their relationship.

CRITICAL DISCUSSION

The initial reaction to "Black Art" was polarized: Black Power leaders and artists saw the poem as a rallying cry for their cause, deeming Baraka the founder of the Black Arts movement. Many white readers viewed the poem as a direct affront to their way of life and well-being, and some felt that it was anti-Semitic, sexist, racist, and homophobic, although Baraka's critique of blacks as well as other races serves as a backward testament to equality among his subjects. In his essay "Amiri Baraka and the Black Arts of Black Art," David L. Smith explains, "Baraka is attempting to take the ethnic animosities common to black urban

Author and poet Amiri Baraka in Newark, New Jersey, July, 1967. Also known as LeRoi Jones, Baraka was injured during the Newark riots. AP PHOTO

communities, to give them sharp political focus, and to transfer this politically informed emotion to his readers."

Smith also criticizes "Black Art," writing that when it is "viewed as a symbolic statement of defiance, the poem is mildly interesting and effective; but viewed as an exhortation, it is exceedingly dangerous." The close relation of the literary Black Arts movement and the political Black Power movement made many readers feel that Baraka's poem was an actual call to arms, endorsing violence against a white-dominated society and power structure. Although Baraka renounced his allegiance to the Black Arts movement in 1974, he still faced harsh scrutiny throughout his career for "Black Art" and other controversial poems.

Viewed as a metaphor for black revolution rather than a physical threat of revolution, "Black Art" is a strong example of black nationalist manifesto in direct response to the racial injustices of the civil rights and Black Power era. In her essay "On the Sound of Water," Sherry Brennan calls "Black Art" a "difficult poem … written during Baraka's black nationalist period, and reflects his political and ideological beliefs at the time." Brennan asserts that the poem's difficulties lie "in its race and gender violence, in its violence against peoples," noting that it is nevertheless "a remarkably tender poem, as well. It calls, at its end, for virtue and love, and for a black poem."

Although the poem is often criticized for its racism and violence, "Black Art" is Baraka's lasting legacy in the founding of the Black Arts movement.

BIBLIOGRAPHY

Sources

"Amiri Baraka Talks Black Arts." *Our Weekly LA*, 21 June 2012. Web. 31 Aug. 2012.

Baraka, Amiri. *The Autobiography of LeRoi Jones/Amiri Baraka.* New York: Freundlich Books, 1984. Print.

———. "Black Art." *The Norton Anthology of African American Literature.* Ed. Henry Louis Gates Jr. and Nellie Y. McKay. New York: Norton, 1997. 1883-84. Print.

Brennan, Sherry. "On the Sound of Water: Amiri Baraka's 'Black Art.'" *African American Review* 37.2/3 (2003): 299-311. Web. 31 Aug. 2012.

Karenga, Ron. "Black Cultural Nationalism." *Negro Digest* 17.3 (1968): 5-9. *GoogleBooks.* Web. 31 Aug. 2012.

Neal, Larry. "The Black Arts Movement." *Tulane Drama Review* 12.4 (1968): 29-39. Print.

Smith, David L. "Amiri Baraka and the Black Arts of Black Art." *boundary 2* 15.1-2 (1986-87): 235-54. *MLA International Bibliography.* Web. 31 Aug. 2012.

Further Reading

Baraka, Amiri. *The Politics and Art of a Black Intellectual.* New York: New York UP, 2001. Print.

Baraka, Amiri, and Charlie Reilly. *Conversations with Amiri Baraka.* Jackson: UP of Mississippi, 1994. Print.

Brown, Lloyd W. *Amiri Baraka.* Boston: Twayne, 1980. Print.

Hudson, Theodore. *From LeRoi Jones to Amiri Baraka: The Literary Works.* Durham, NC: Duke UP, 1973. Print.

Lee, Maurice A. *The Aesthetics of LeRoi Jones/Amiri Baraka: The Rebel Poet.* Valencia: Universidad de Valencia, 2004. Print.

Ron Horton

BLACK PANTHER PARTY PLATFORM

Huey P. Newton, Bobby Seale

OVERVIEW

The Black Panther Party Platform, drafted by Huey P. Newton and Bobby Seale in 1966, is the founding document of the Black Panther Party (BPP), then called the Black Panther Party for Self-Defense. Influenced by the writings of Nation of Islam leader Malcolm X, Chinese communist leader Mao Zedong, and West Indian social philosopher Frantz Fanon, Newton and Seale articulate the BPP's critique of American racism and capitalism and announce the party as a militant and revolutionary organization committed to armed self-defense. According to Newton, the platform was intended to be accessible to "black people and especially brothers on the block" and to raise political consciousness among them. Also known as the Ten-Point Program, the platform consists of ten demands juxtaposed with ten beliefs, each beginning with "we want" and "we believe," respectively. The tenth point summarizes these demands as "land, bread, housing, education, clothing, justice and peace." Other demands include an exemption from military service and a general amnesty for all black men.

The Black Panther Party Platform did not receive widespread attention during the first year of its publication. Newton and Seale initially printed 1,000 copies of the platform and distributed them to members of the black community in Oakland, California. Later, the text regularly appeared in issues of the organization's newspaper, the *Black Panther,* which began publication in 1967. As the BPP gained fame and notoriety, the pamphlet was considered the central theoretical text of the party and a notable counterpoint to the more mainstream nonviolent ideologies of the civil rights era.

HISTORICAL AND LITERARY CONTEXT

The Black Panther Party Platform can be read as a response to racial tensions of the 1960s, a time when racist discrimination and police brutality were widespread, especially in black communities such as Oakland. Often these tensions led to large-scale outbreaks of violence, where many black men and women were killed at the hands of police. According to the *Encyclopedia of American Race Riots* (2007), of the roughly seventy race-related riots in the United States since 1850, about twenty occurred during the 1960s, more than any other decade in the 19th and 20th centuries.

Furthermore, political science scholar Judson Jeffries has stated that from 1960 to 1968, 51 percent of those killed by police were black—a disproportionately large number, considering that black people made up roughly 10 percent of the U.S. population at the time. The encyclopedia also notes that in 1965 riots in the Watts neighborhood of Los Angeles left thirty-four dead and more than one thousand injured. Newton blames this outcome on the police underresponse and cites the incident as one of the motivating factors behind the founding of the BPP. In light of this violence, Newton viewed the nonviolent tactics of Martin Luther King Jr. and others as futile. "We do not believe in passive and nonviolent tactics," he explained to a *New York Times* interviewer in 1967. "They haven't worked for us black people. They are bankrupt."

The drafting of the platform, which took place in Oakland in 1966, places it well within the anti-Vietnam War movement. To some degree, the document may also be read as an antiwar manifesto. A 1967 article in *Ebony* magazine by Robert J. Ellison points out that black servicemen, whether volunteers or draftees, made up 23 percent of those fighting in the Vietnam War, a fact partially attributed to unemployment in the black community. Newton's call for exemption from military service, therefore, and the party's later alignment with the National Liberation Front—the Vietnamese political organization seeking to overthrow the South Vietnamese government— might be read, in part, as reactions to the Vietnam War draft and its effects on black communities.

The Black Panther Party Platform owes much of its black nationalist stance to forerunners such as Marcus Garvey and the Nation of Islam, but it also stands apart from most civil-rights-era rhetoric in its socialist and anticolonialist influences. Newton claims as his influences Fanon's *The Wretched of the Earth* (1961), Mao's *Selected Works* (5 volumes in English, 1954-62), and Argentine revolutionary Che Guevara's *Guerrilla Warfare* (English translation, 1961). An unacknowledged influence may be the work of civil rights activist Stokely Carmichael, who popularized the term "black power" and who facilitated the Alabama-based Lowndes County Freedom Organization, a political party predating the BPP, whose emblem was the black panther. In his paper titled "The Basis of Black

Time Period:
Mid-20th Century

Movement/Issue:
Black nationalism

Place of Publication:
United States

Language of Publication:
English

HUEY P. NEWTON

Huey P. Newton, a cofounder of the Black Panther Party and its minister of defense, is one of the more intriguing figures of the black power movement of the 1960s. He was among the party's major theorists, as well as one of its combatants. Illiterate upon his graduation from high school, he taught himself to read using Plato's *Republic*. In September 1968 Newton was convicted for the voluntary manslaughter of police officer John Frey, but the charges were dropped by 1970. In the interim, "Free Huey" became the mantra of the Black Panther Party. The newspaper the *Black Panther* featured full-page ads proclaiming the slogan, and members waved flags that displayed the same sentiment.

In the mid-1970s, Newton published a book of poems with City Lights Press in which San Francisco's Zen Center abbot Richard Baker calls him "one of the great men of our or any time." During this period Newton was accused of killing Oakland prostitute Kathleen Smith and fled to Havana, Cuba, until 1977. After returning to the United States (he was never convicted for the Smith murder), he earned a Ph.D. in social philosophy from the University of California at Santa Cruz, where he wrote a dissertation titled *War against the Panthers: A Study of Repression in America*. He was murdered in 1989 by a drug dealer in Oakland.

Power," Carmichael declares (like Newton in the first of his ten-point plan) that "we must determine our own destiny." Similarly, Carmichael's 1966 book on black power was titled, like the first ten points of the Black Panther Party Platform, *What We Want*.

Various forms of the Black Panther Party Platform appeared in most of the issues of the *Black Panther*. According to Seale, the platform was the primary political education for party members. Beginning with the publication of "Rules of the Black Panther Party" in 1969, each member was required to "know and understand" the ten points of the platform. Its tenets were repeated frequently during speeches, especially those that Seale delivered. According to some historians, the platform influenced the work of later party members and black power activists, including Angela Davis, Assata Shakur, Mumia Abu-Jamal, and H. Rap Brown.

THEMES AND STYLE

The Black Panther Party Platform is centrally concerned with meeting the immediate needs—education, employment, safety, and housing—of a disenfranchised community. Newton believes the government has deprived African Americans of these rights and cites, in particular, General William Tecumseh Sherman's Civil War promise of 40 acres and a mule (here rendered as "two mules") for each former slave—restitutions that were later revoked by

President Andrew Johnson. The platform demands that this promise be finally fulfilled: "We will accept the payment in currency which will be distributed to our many communities."

The platform's poignancy might be said to be derived from its colloquial language, brevity, and repetition of the key phrases "we want" and "we believe." In early versions of the platform, the ten short, numbered points beginning "we want" are followed by ten longer, unnumbered points that start with "we believe." In later versions, these two categories are fused, assigning one "we believe" paragraph to each line beginning "we want." This structure recalls Mao's ten-point "Specific Programme" of the Chinese Communist Party and his "Ten Demands to the Kuomintang." G. Louis Heath in *Off the Pigs!* (1976) has done much to point out the similarities between Black Panther and Maoist doctrines, noting that one version of the BPP "Rules," which appeared in early 1969, included, "without attribution," Mao's "8 points of attention" and "3 main rules of discipline." The party's debt to Mao, however, is more than simply ideological: in 1967 the Black Panthers bought their first shotguns with money they earned from the sales of the "Little Red Book" of Mao's quotations recently shipped from China.

The language of the Black Panther Party Platform also borrows heavily from German philosopher Karl Marx and U.S. president Thomas Jefferson. On the subject of employment, it suggests that "the means of production should be taken from the businessmen and placed in the community." The platform ends with an unattributed passage pulled from the Declaration of Independence, thereby reframing the struggle of the Black Panthers as an analogue of that of the American Revolutionists of 1776: "whenever any form of government becomes destructive of these ends, it is the right of the people to alter or to abolish it." The stylistic echoes of these revolutionaries situate the Black Panther Party in a long tradition of militant anti-imperialists.

CRITICAL DISCUSSION

Much of the early media attention paid to the Black Panther Party reacted strongly to its actions but mostly ignored the group's writings. From the point of view of the mainstream news media at least, the early pre-1969 incarnation of the party seemed to have acted much more aggressively than its manifesto would predict. In May 1967 a group of armed Panthers entered a meeting of the California legislature to protest a bill that would restrict the right to openly carry weapons, and early news reports on the Panthers emphasized the paramilitary nature of the party. One such article from the *New York Times* on May 21, 1967, ran with the headline "A Gun Is Power, Black Panther Says." It quotes Newton on the use of force but ignores his thoughts on education and land reform. Sol Stern has a more sympathetic

A Black Panther Party poster (1969) designed by Emory Douglas, the party's minister of culture. SNARK/ART RESOURCE, NY

article in an August 1967 issue of the *New York Times Magazine*, which juxtaposes the Panthers' violent rhetoric with the real violence of "police malpractice in the ghetto." "To write off the Panthers as a fringe group is to miss the point," Stern argues. "What matters is that there are a thousand black people in the ghetto thinking privately what any Panther says out loud."

As the organization grew, the Black Panthers and their rhetoric polarized commentators. Some, including leaders of the Students for a Democratic Society, called them the vanguard of the coming revolution. Others were less flattering. In a 1993 book review, for example, U.S. writer Alice Walker claims that the Black Panthers abused their women and were confused by their homoeroticism. Cedric Johnson, in his book *Revolutionaries to Race Leaders* (2007), states that Roy Wilkins, then head of the National Association for the Advancement of Colored People, called militant organizations such as the BPP "a reverse Ku Klux Klan."

Seale responded to allegations of racism by reasserting the party's foundation as one of self-defense: "We believe our fight is a class struggle and not a race struggle." In seeming contradiction, the Black Panther Party Platform's phrase "robbery by the capitalist" became "robbery by the white man" by 1967. Although no consensus may ever be reached, critical attention continues to be paid to the Black Panther Party Platform and the BPP's place in the civil rights movement.

The Panthers and their rhetoric have enjoyed a fair amount of scholarly discussion into the 21st century. In the 1970s, Jimmy Mori's "The Ideological Development of the Black Panther Party" charts with the rigor of a linguist the party's ideological shift from guns to free breakfasts, from "Off the Pigs" to "Serve the People." A recent anthology, *The Black Panther Party (Reconsidered)* (1998), collects primary sources and contemporary commentary. A 2010 article in the *Journal of American Studies* conducts a retrospective of

Black Panther historiography and shows the tremendous breadth of criticism that has appeared on the subject in the last forty years.

BIBLIOGRAPHY

Sources

Carmichael, Stokely. *The Basis of Black Power.* 1966. Student Nonviolent Coordinating Committee Position Paper: The Basis of Black Power. University of Virginia. The Sixties Project, 1993. Web. 30 Jan. 2013.

Ellison, Robert J. "Viet Nam: Every Youth Must Face the Fact of Involvement." *Ebony* Aug. 1967: 23-28. Print.

Heath, G. Louis. *Off the Pigs! The History and Literature of the Black Panther Party.* Metuchen, NJ: Scarecrow, 1976. Print.

Hillard, David. *Huey: Spirit of the Panther.* New York: Thunder's Mouth, 2006. Print.

Jeffries, Judson L. *Huey P. Newton: The Radical Theorist.* Jackson: UP of Mississippi, 2002. Print.

Jeffries, Judson L., et al., eds. *The Black Panther Party (Reconsidered).* Baltimore: Black Classic, 1998. Print.

Johnson, Cedric. *Revolutionaries to Race Leaders.* Minneapolis: U of Minnesota P, 2007. Print.

Mao, Tse-Tung. *Selected Works of Mao Tse-Tung.* Vol. 3. London: Lawrence & Wishart, 1954. Print.

———. *Selected Works of Mao Tse-Tung.* Vol. 3. Peking: Foreign Languages, 1967. Print.

Mori, Jimmy. "The Ideological Development of the Black Panther Party." *Cornell Journal of Social Relations* 12.2 (1977): 137-55. Print.

Newton, Huey P. *To Die for the People: The Writings of Huey P. Newton.* Ed. Toni Morrison. New York: Random, 1972. Print.

———. *The Huey P. Newton Reader.* New York: Seven Stories, 2002. Print.

Rucker, Walter, and James Nathaniel Upton, eds. *Encyclopedia of American Race Riots.* 2 vols. Westport, CT: Greenwood, 2007. Print.

Seale, Bobby. *Seize the Time: The Story of the Black Panther Party and Huey P. Newton.* New York: Random, 1970. Print.

Stern, Sol. "The Call of the Black Panthers." *New York Times Magazine* 6 Aug. 1967: 10-11.

Street, Joe. "The Historiography of the Black Panther Party." *Journal of American Studies* 44.2 (2010): 351-75. Web.

Walker, Alice. Rev. of *A Taste of Power,* by Elaine Brown. *New York Times* 5 May 1993. Print.

Further Reading

Churchill, Ward, and Jim Vander Wall. *Agents of Repression: The FBI's Secret Wars against the Black Panther Party and the American Indian Movement.* Boston: South End, 1988. Print.

Newton, Huey P. *War against the Panthers: A Study of Repression in America.* New York: Harlem River, 2000. Print.

Newton, Huey P., and Erika Huggins. *Insights and Poems.* San Francisco: City Lights, 1975. Print.

Jonathan Reeve

BORDERLANDS/LA FRONTERA

The New Mestiza

Gloria Anzaldúa

OVERVIEW

Borderlands/La Frontera: The New Mestiza (1987), a semiautobiographical book by Chicana scholar Gloria Anzaldúa, has been extremely influential in the fields of Chicano studies, gay and lesbian studies, border theory, cultural studies, and feminist theory. Emerging at a time when female authors of Mexican descent were still marginalized from the male-dominated sphere of U.S. Chicano literature, Anzaldúa's text not only challenges the patriarchal nature of Chicano culture but also asserts her identity as a lesbian Chicana author. *Borderlands/La Frontera* was published during a transitional period between second- and third-wave feminism, when women of color such as Anzaldúa began to question the movement's essentialism and its marginalization of minority females. The text speaks to a female, primarily Chicana audience that is able to identify with Anzaldúa's experiences, yet it also addresses issues concerning masculinity. Thematically, *Borderlands/La Frontera* is a celebration of the Chicana woman's hybrid identity, which Anzaldúa refers to as the "new mestiza."

Borderlands/La Frontera generally received a positive response from scholars, many of whom connected with Anzaldúa's innovative, personal approach to exploring Chicana feminism and identity as well as life along the border. Although some conservative male Chicano authors either derided or ignored what they saw as a radical text, *Borderlands/La Frontera* has had a lasting impact in the literary arena and is now one of the most prominent books in Chicana/o literature. Numerous other scholars have expanded upon the work that Anzaldúa began with *Borderlands/La Frontera*. In part because of the way it creates new categories and interconnections and establishes alliances and dialogues among diverse peoples, *Borderlands/La Frontera* has remained relevant.

HISTORICAL AND LITERARY CONTEXT

When *Borderlands/La Frontera* was published in 1987, the third-wave feminist movement was still taking shape, spurred on primarily by women of color. In the wake of the second-wave feminism movement, which was dominated primarily by white middle-class women, both female and queer scholars of color began to speak out against the polarizing effects of a liberation movement that only represented a privileged sector of the U.S. population. In addition, scholars such as Anzaldúa, bell hooks, and Chela Sandoval responded to the male-dominated civil rights and Chicano movements that preceded the 1980s by creating a new space that, independent of men, was representative of the experiences of women from minority ethnic communities.

The many legal and institutional rights obtained by women of the second-wave feminist movement served as a foundation for the third wave. The second wave's notable accomplishments included public recognition of the abuse and rape of women, establishment of domestic abuse shelters for women and children, and access to contraception and other reproductive services. Anzaldúa and her peers took on additional issues that were becoming increasingly relevant. For example, in the Southwest, especially along the United States-Mexico border, Chicanas and Chicanos (female and male Americans of Mexican descent, respectively) faced heightened discrimination and were often blamed for economic issues such as rising unemployment rates. Chicanas in particular faced derogatory treatment, both within and outside the Chicano community.

Anzaldúa expanded on the writings of feminists such as Marta Cotera ("Among the Feminists: Racist Classist Issues—1976") and Anna Nieto Gomez ("La Femenista," 1974), whose works introduced a transnational feminist consciousness that, according to Sonia Saldívar-Hull in her introduction to the second edition of *Borderlands/La Frontera*, "built new coalitions with other U.S. Latinas and U.S. women of color." In 1981 Anzaldúa published the anthology *This Bridge Called My Back* with Cherríe Moraga, which engages with this consciousness and calls for race-related subjectivities to play a more central role within the feminist movement. *Borderlands/La Frontera* continues this progressive approach to feminism, strengthening cross-cultural alliances not only among women but also with queer-identified men and introducing a socio-politically specific context for this dialogue by forging coalitions between women across the United States-Mexico border.

❖ *Key Facts*

Time Period:
Late 20th Century

Movement/Issue:
Third-wave feminism; Chicana identity

Place of Publication:
United States

Language of Publication:
English and Spanish

GLORIA ANZALDÚA: CHICANA TRAILBLAZER

Gloria Anzaldúa (1942-2004) was a renowned Chicana scholar who worked in feminist studies, queer theory, creative writing, and cultural theory. Best known for her groundbreaking text on the Chicana mestiza identity, *Borderlands/La Frontera: The New Mestiza* (1987), Anzaldúa was among the first Chicana scholars to publicly declare and embrace her lesbian identity. Her work also laid the foundation for border theory, specifically that related to the United States-Mexico border and the identity of those individuals living in what she coined the "borderlands." Anzaldúa advocated embracing the hybrid nature of Chicana identity and its multiple cultural and religious influences.

Anzaldúa grew up in Rio Grande Valley, Texas, where her family had resided for six generations. She received a Bachelor of Arts degree from Pan American University and a Master of Arts degree in English and education from the University of Texas at Austin. In addition to publishing theoretical essays and adult and children's fiction, Anzaldúa was coeditor of *This Bridge Called My Back: Writings by Radical Women of Color* (1981) and editor of *Making Face, Making Soul: Haciendo Caras* (1990). She received numerous honors during her lifetime, including the National Endowment for the Arts Fiction Award in 1991.

In the years following its publication, *Borderlands/La Frontera* influenced a large body of scholarship that explores and elaborates on the ideas of a new mestiza consciousness, a feminist Chicana identity, and the notion of the borderlands as a fluid space. These texts include *Talking Back: Thinking Feminist, Thinking Black* (1989) by bell hooks and *Decolonizing Methodologies: Research and Indigenous Peoples* (1999) by Linda Tuhiwai Smith. Over the past two decades, self-identifying lesbian Chicana scholars such as Cherríe Moraga, Carla Mari Trujillo, and Alicia Gaspar de Alba have also taken the path followed by Anzaldúa, forging new categories and cross-disciplinary dialogue and expanding the fields of queer theory, women's studies, and gay and lesbian studies.

THEMES AND STYLE

The central theme of *Borderlands/La Frontera* is the historical oppression and marginalization experienced by Chicanas living along the United States-Mexico border. One of the best-known sections begins with a long epigraph in Spanish, which functions as a proclamation of independence for new mestizas from the historical patriarchy of Mexican and Chicano culture. In one of the book's many intensely personal anecdotes, Anzaldúa describes how she had to leave home in order to discover her true identity: "If going home is denied me then I will have to stand and claim my space, making a new culture—*una cultura mestiza*—with my own lumber, my own bricks and mortar and my own feminist architecture." Here, Anzaldúa sets up the foundation for the feminist treatise that she develops later in the book, literally *claiming* a new, unique space for the Chicana.

Anzaldúa's work relies on an intimate rhetoric that establishes a connection with the reader through first-person narration and specific personal anecdotes. The author's inclusion of numerous Spanish phrases and passages gestures to the hybrid Chicana/o identity that she is portraying and speaks to the bilingual audience for whom she is writing. In many sections, the author employs a fictional narrative strategy, telling stories to draw in the reader. Anzaldúa opens her section on the Virgin of Guadalupe with a Spanish-language anecdote about her childhood as a Roman Catholic, an experience with which the majority of her Chicana readership can relate. Yet the book's Spanish passages alienated some English monolingual readers who were unable to decipher the text.

Borderlands/La Frontera is notable for its inclusion of numerous literary genres, including essays, poems, stories, and folklore. This mixture reflects her goal of establishing dialogues and connections across the traditionally fixed boundaries of sexual orientation, gender, culture, and geopolitics. It also gives the book an informal tone, like that of a personal diary rather than a work of cultural theory. Anzaldúa transitions smoothly from prose to poetry to reflect her internal dialogue. For example, she writes, "Why do I cast no shadow? / Are there lights from all sides shining on me? / Ahead, ahead … I knew at that instant: something must change / or I'd die." Despite the lack of a structural break between this poem and the essay that follows, the text reads in a natural, flow-of-consciousness manner. Anzaldúa's mixed-genre approach made the book accessible to a wider, non-academic Chicana audience that recognized many of the cultural and folkloric anecdotes.

CRITICAL DISCUSSION

Upon its publication, *Borderlands/La Frontera* received mainly favorable reviews from both Chicana/o and Caucasian scholars. Many female reviewers identified with the text, reading it as an exploration of female identity as much as a discussion of Chicana/o history and the borderlands. Referring to several poems from the book, Margaret Randall writes, "I have gone back … and each time find new doors challenging me to open them and walk through. I will walk through again and again, discovering with each passage further demands upon my own cultural myopia, racism, conformity." Critics such as Randall appreciated the book's complex, layered structure and found that their engagement with its ideas and worldview became further enriched over time.

As the fields of gay and lesbian studies and queer theory have grown and transformed over the past few decades, scholars have continued to cite *Borderlands/La Frontera* as an important source. Similarly, despite the evolution of third-wave feminism and its incorporation of new issues in recent years, Anzaldúa's now-canonical work remains part of the discourse. "Anzaldúa's exploration of the 'borderland' consciousness powerfully asserts itself as feminist ... [it] reveal[s] different modes of multiple positioning and practices around issues of feminists and feminism," writes Inderpal Grewal in "Autobiographic Subjects, Diasporic Locations." As Grewal recognizes, the text's attention to the multiple positionalities of women of color and their hybrid identities is a central element of today's evolving feminist movement.

Many Chicana and feminist scholars have engaged specifically with Anzaldúa's direct denunciation of the exclusionary, heteronormative nature of the traditional academy. "Borderland-mestizaje 'feminism,' then, is an evolution, extension, or perhaps a mutation *que nace* [that is born] from the bodies of Chicana feminists ... who recognized the androcentric, nationalistic, and homophobic tendency of Chican'o' border theory and cultural studies," writes C.M. Saavedra and E.D. Nymark in "Borderland-Mestizaje Feminism: The New Tribalism." Anzaldúa's new mestiza consciousness has been adopted and expanded upon by scholars such as Saavedra and Nymark, who believe its centering of the experience of women from minority communities is significant and relevant to the U.S. public at large. In her introduction to *Chicana Feminisms: A Critical Reader*, Gabriela F. Arredondo praises the text for stressing how the "praxis of feminists of color is often not recognized or sanctioned in the academy." New scholarship has carried on this practice of inserting the voices of feminists of color into feminist discourse, including *Displacing Whiteness: Essays in Social and Cultural Criticism* (1997), edited by Ruth Frankenberg; *Women Reading Women Writing: Self-Invention in Paula Gunn Allen, Gloria Anzaldúa, and Audre Lorde* (1996) by AnaLouise Keating; and *Colonize This!: Young Women of Color on Today's Feminism* (2002), edited by Daisy Hernández and Bushra Rehman.

Photo of the U.S.-Mexico border at Tijuana. Author Gloria Anzaldúa's *Borderlands/La Frontera* is based on her experience growing up as a Mexican-American near the border. © MARK KARRASS/CORBIS

BIBLIOGRAPHY

Sources

Arredondo, Gabriela F. et al., eds. Introduction. *Chicana Feminisms: A Critical Reader*. Duke UP, 2003. Print.

Grewal, Inderpal. "Autobiographic Subjects, Diasporic Locations." *Scattered Hegemonies: Postmodernity and Trasnational Feminist Practices*. I. Grewal and C. Kaplan, eds. Minneapolis: U. of Minnesota P, 1994. Print.

Randall, Margaret. "Una Conciencia de Mujer." Rev. of *Borderlands/La Frontera: The New Mestiza*, by Gloria Anzaldúa. *The Women's Review of Books* 5.3 (Dec. 1987): 8-9. Print.

Saavedra, C.M., and E.D. Nymark. "Borderland-Mestizaje Feminism: The New Tribalism." *Handbook of Critical and Indigenous Methodologies*. N. K. Denzin, Y. S. Lincoln, and L. Tuhiwai-Smith, eds. Thousand Oaks: Sage, 2008. Print.

Saldívar-Hull, Sonia. "Introduction to the Second Edition." *Borderlands/La Frontera: The New Mestiza:* 2nd ed. San Francisco: Aunt Lute Books, 1999. Print.

Further Reading

Anzaldúa, Gloria, ed. *Making Face, Making Soul: Haciendo Caras: Creative and Critical Perspectives by Women of Color*. San Francisco: Aunt Lute Foundation Books, 1990. Print.

Anzaldúa, Gloria, and AnaLouise Keating. *The Gloria Anzaldúa Reader*. Durham: Duke UP, 2009. Print.

Anzaldúa, Gloria, and Cherríe Moraga, eds. *This Bridge Called My Back: Writings by Radical Women of Color*. Watertown: Persephone Press, 1981. Print.

Barnard, Ian. Queer Race: Cultural Interventions in the Racial Politics of Queer Theory. New York: Peter Lang, 2004. Print.

Frankenberg, Ruth, ed. *Displacing Whiteness: Essays in Social and Cultural Criticism.* Durham: Duke UP, 1997. Print.

Hernández, Daisy, and Bushra Rehman, eds. *Colonize This!: Young Women of Color on Today's Feminism.* Emeryville, CA: Seal, 2002. Print.

Keating, AnaLouise. *Women Reading Women Writing: Self-Invention in Paula Gunn Allen, Gloria Anzaldúa, and Audre Lorde.* Philadelphia: Temple UP, 1996. Print.

Moraga, Cherríe. *A Xicana Codex of Changing Consciousness: Writings, 2000-2010.* Durham: Duke UP, 2011. Print.

Saldívar-Hull, Sonia. *Feminism on the Border: Chicana Gender Politics and Literature.* Berkeley: U of California P, 2000. Print.

Yarbro-Bejarano, Yvonne. "Gloria Anzaldúa's *Borderlands/La Frontera*: Cultural Studies, 'Difference,' and the Non-Unitary Subject." *Cultural Critique* 28 (Autumn 1994): 5-28. Print.

Katrina White

Chicano Manifesto

Armando B. Rendón

OVERVIEW

Written by Armando B. Rendón, *Chicano Manifesto* (1971) is the first book by an American of Mexican descent to explain the spirit, history, and purpose of the Chicano movement. By drawing wider attention to a series of uprisings that took place in the Southwest in the 1960s, Rendón extended the call for Chicanos throughout the United States to organize and take political action in response to their continued political, cultural, social, and economic oppression within the United States. The manifesto encompasses a unique record of events in the history of Chicanos—a political term of self-identification used by many U.S.-born individuals of Mexican-American descent—that led to the rise of the Chicano movement in the mid-1960s and the creation of La Raza Unida, a U.S. political party, to represent Chicanos. Rendón's book was published at a turning point for the Chicano population, a period of politicization and social organizing that began in the Southwest. Addressed primarily to American readers of Mexican descent, the *Chicano Manifesto* reflects the reality facing Chicano people at the time of its publication.

Despite Rendón's aspiration that his manifesto be warmly embraced by the Chicano community as a whole, the work was given a mixed reception. Chicano reviewers criticized Rendón's lack of differentiation between the terms Chicano and Mexican American and maintained that he had failed to adequately document certain historical facts. Nevertheless, Chicano scholars saw value in Rendón's examination of contemporary issues, including the United Farm Workers' strike and third-party politics. Although the manifesto did not attract wide attention from non-Chicano audiences, many Caucasian readers saw an overt message of animosity in the manifesto's antagonistic portrayal of Anglos, or whites, as historical oppressors of the Chicano community. In recent decades, the ambitious three-hundred-page work has received little scholarly attention, and, although it did serve as an impetus for the political mobilization of the larger Chicano community, major scholars have not widely recognized it as a foundational Chicano text.

HISTORICAL AND LITERARY CONTEXT

The *Chicano Manifesto* addresses the growing unrest in the Chicano community that resulted from increasing discrimination, police brutality, and exploitation of Chicano labor during the mid-twentieth century. The continued presence of Mexican laborers, who were first brought to the United States in 1942 by the Bracero Program in response to growing demand for manual labor during World War II, drew resentment from Americans who felt their livelihood was being threatened. After the program expired and the United States began the massive deportation of Mexican migrants through such programs as Operation Wetback in 1954, open hostility toward legal and illegal Mexican immigrants grew. In addition, Chicano soldiers who enlisted in the U.S. military often faced discriminatory treatment, including denial of veterans' benefits.

When the *Chicano Manifesto* was published in 1971, Chicanos continued to face limited access to minimum wage jobs, social and political oppression, poverty, and crime. Law enforcement unfairly targeted Chicano youths, labeling them as criminals and subjecting them to police brutality, especially in communities with a high concentration of Chicano residents, such as East Los Angeles. Armando B. Rendón was one of many young Chicano college students who had protested against these oppressive conditions in the early 1960s. Such resistance had its roots in such earlier protests as the Zoot Suit Riots in Los Angeles during the 1940s, when police and U.S. sailors and Marines targeted and attacked Mexican American youths dressed as "zoot suiters" or "pachucos." The zoot suit consisted of high-waisted, wide-legged trousers and a long coat and was associated with the showy—often interpreted as defiant—public appearance of groups of Mexican American youths on the streets of Los Angeles. The riots are often associated with the murder of José Díaz in Los Angeles in August 1942. The murder and subsequent trial, in which twenty-one young Latino men were charged, led to a public outcry against the perceived threat of the zoot suiters and spurred violence against Mexican American youths during the following year. Such violence, condoned and perpetrated by police and other representatives of government, contributed to the unrest and disillusionment of the Mexican American community.

Rendón's work draws on the Mexican and Mexican American political traditions of the manifesto and the *testimonio,* a politically charged first-person

✤ *Key Facts*

Time Period:
Late 20th Century

Movement/Issue:
Chicano identity and civil rights

Place of Publication:
United States

Language of Publication:
English

DEFINING AN ERA: THE CHICANO MOVEMENT

The Chicano movement of the 1960s and 1970s emerged (in conjunction with the anti-Vietnam War movement) as a response to blatant discrimination against Chicanos in the United States and the violation of their civil rights. The movement was concentrated in the Southwest, primarily in Arizona, California, New Mexico, and Texas. Its leaders included Reies López Tijerina, Rodolfo "Corky" Gonzales, Dr. Hector P. García, and Cesar Chávez. Also known as El Movimiento, it addressed a broad range of issues, including farm workers' rights, disproportionate military recruitment, equal access to higher education, restoration of land grants, and voting and other political rights. Leaders of the movement rejected the label Mexican American, preferring Chicano (alternatively spelled Xicano) as a symbol of ethnic pride and self-determination that reflected their indigenous Mexican roots.

In addition to political and social issues, Chicanos organized around a burgeoning cultural renaissance that included visual art, theater, and literature and reflected the community's growing awareness of a collective history. Many significant works emerged during this period, including Rodolfo Gonzales's poem "I Am Joaquin," numerous plays produced by El Teatro Campesino, Oscar Zeta Acosta's *The Autobiography of a Brown Buffalo* (1972), and works by writers Tomás Rivera and Abelardo Gonzales. However, male cultural and political leadership heavily dominated the Chicano movement and failed to acknowledge the interests and rights of Chicanas. The mainstream Chicano movement did not begin to directly address Chicanas' rights until the late 1980s and early 1990s.

account that relates an experience of injustice or oppression. One particularly influential *testimonio* is Miguel Barnet's *Biografía de un Cimarrón* (1966), which denounces the institution of slavery through the first-person account of former slave Esteban Montejo. The *Chicano Manifesto* shares the personal nature of Barnet's text and its emphasis on specific injustices. *Plan Espiritual de Aztlán* (1969), published by the First National Chicano Liberation Youth Conference, was inspired by the burgeoning Chicano movement and the push toward empowerment and political self-realization within the Chicano community, goals that Rendón also incorporated in his manifesto.

In the years following the publication of the *Chicano Manifesto*, numerous similar texts were published, largely overshadowing Rendón's reflection on the Chicano cause. Works such as Richard Santillan's *Chicano Politics: La Raza Unida* (1973) and collections of Chicano-authored reflective essays such as *The Chicanos: As We See Ourselves* (1979), present a more complex and better-developed understanding of Chicano identity and politicization during this

period. Although some later Chicano publications, such as Rolando Hinojosa's essay on Mexican-American literature, published in *Books Abroad* (1975), reference the *Chicano Manifesto* as an early source on Chicanos and the Chicano movement, Rendón's work often has been omitted from the study of Chicano literature at the university level.

THEMES AND STYLE

The central theme of the *Chicano Manifesto* is that a united Chicano community must respond to oppression by the Anglo system and fight for recognition and equal social and political status. Rendón emphasizes the denigration inherent in negative Chicano caricatures—such as the Frito Bandito—disseminated in mass media and popular culture. He confronts the stereotype of the lazy Mexican using elements of Chicano history largely forgotten by Americans: "Who built the railroad in most of the Southwest and helped put down the rails in the Midwest? ... The Chicano." He expounds on Chicano oppression by drawing on specific examples of injustice and by sharing personal anecdotes to illustrate his points. Having exposed the complicity of the American public in the oppression of Chicanos, he arrives at the necessity of political action in the form of La Raza Unida, a tool for challenging Anglo control and instituting change at a national level.

The manifesto makes rhetorical appeals to Chicanos' collective identity and shared indigenous roots in order to foster solidarity and support for the Chicano movement. Rendón repeatedly references Aztlán, the Aztec homeland, as Chicanos' collective birthplace, emphasizing Mexican Americans' common cultural origins. The manifesto, which is divided into sixteen chapters, begins with a discussion of identity and an exploration of the ancestral homeland. Rendón uses the idea of Chicanos' shared cultural heritage as the "people of Aztlán" to support his argument in the second half of the book that Chicanos' current political reality demands revolution. He reinforces notions of Chicano collectivity and commonality in these later chapters by arguing that "the power and motivation of the Chicano revolt generate essentially from the Mexican American people."

Contrary to the formal nature of many political manifestos, the *Chicano Manifesto* is informal in tone and language. In order to appeal to working-class readers, Rendón writes in the first person and uses colloquial language in some parts of the text in order to personalize his discussion of the Chicano cause. In the final chapter of the manifesto, he recalls a moment from his childhood: "at an evening gathering of almost the whole family—uncles, aunts, nephews, nieces, my abuelita—we sat outdoors through the dusk ... someone brought out a Mexican card game, the Lotería El Diablito." By personalizing the history of Chicano movement with Spanish-language terms and cultural references, Rendón extends a warm invitation to fellow first- and second-generation Mexican Americans to join the Chicano collective.

CRITICAL DISCUSSION

The *Chicano Manifesto* received little media or scholarly attention when it was published in 1971. Some scholars have explained the lack of media coverage by pointing to the numerous similar works by Chicanos published at the same time. Although Chicano reviewers such as Richard Emilio López have found the manifesto's revolutionary fervor potentially inspiring, they have criticized Rendón's failure to clearly define the term *Chicano* and explain his characterization of Chicanos as a superior race. Additionally, many scholars have found the manifesto's exaggerated rhetoric and essentialist nature problematic. In a 1974 review of the book in *International Migration Review,* Ruth Horowitz concludes that Rendón's book "fails to catch the ethos of the Chicano as the *Autobiography of Malcolm X* or *Soul on Ice* does for Blacks."

Since the dissolution of the Chicano movement in the early 1980s, the *Chicano Manifesto* has received little attention. The most extensive analysis of Rendón's work is in Sheila Marie Contreras's *Blood Lines: Myth, Indigenism, and Chicana/o Literature* (2008), which examines Rendón's representation of the spiritual aspect of Chicano identity. However, Contreras and Angie Chabram-Dernersesian criticize the *Chicano Manifesto* for its negative portrayal of Chicanas and exaltation of machismo as a central element of Chicano identity. Because of such criticism, Rendón's manifesto is rarely mentioned in most Chicano, Latino, and ethnic studies programs despite growing scholarly interest in the Chicano movement.

Rendón's manifesto remains a valuable historical resource, and many scholars continue to cite it as such. In *Law & Society Review* (2005), however, Mary Romero argues that other works from the same period are much more powerful and informative. Several scholars have discussed Rendón's conceptualization of the term *machismo* and have condemned his manifesto for its glorification of an oppressive patriarchal tradition. In *Next of Kin: The Family in Chicano/a Cultural Politics* (2009), Richard T. Rodríguez disagrees with such criticism, arguing "Rendón's comprehension of machismo recasts the term from a male-specific trait to one that acts as a mobilizing force for nation formation." Despite the controversy over Rendón's portrayal of masculinity in Chicano culture and the exclusion of his manifesto from academic surveys of the Chicano movement, the *Chicano Manifesto* remains notable as part of the Chicano literary tradition and as an early source on the fight for Chicano equality. As Richard Emilio López recognizes, the manifesto "focus[es] on important issues

Armando Rendón, author of the *Chicano Manifesto,* at a press conference in 1970. He holds a chart arguing that Chicano soldiers in the Vietnam War were dying at a disproportionately high rate. © BETTMANN/CORBIS

affecting Chicanos, for example, unequal educational opportunities and the 1970 Census problem ... [and] presents a host of facts" from the formative years of the Chicano movement.

BIBLIOGRAPHY

Sources

Contreras, Sheila Marie. *Blood Lines: Myth, Indigenism, and Chicana/o Literature.* Austin: U of Texas P, 2008. Print.

Horowitz, Ruth. Rev. of *Chicano Manifesto,* by Armando Rendón. *International Migration Review* 8.1 (1974): 86-87. Web. 4 June 2012.

López, Richard Emilio. "Manifesto for Chicanos." Rev. of *Chicano Manifesto,* by Armando Rendón. *Review of Politics* 35.4 (1973): 581-83. Web. 4 June 2012.

McCluskey, Cynthia, and Francisco Villarruel. "Policing the Latino Community: Key Issues and Directions for Future Research." *Latinos in a Changing Society.* Ed. Martha Montero-Sieburth and Edwin Melendez. Westport: Praeger, 2007. 183-99. Print.

Rodríguez, Richard T. *Next of Kin: The Family in Chicano/a Cultural Politics.* Durham: Duke UP, 2009. Print.

Romero, Mary. "Brown Is Beautiful." *Law & Society Review* 39.1 (2005): 211-34. Web. 5 June 2012.

Further Reading

Chabram-Dernersesian, Angie. "I Throw Punches for My Race, but I Don't Want to Be a Man." *The Chicana/o Cultural Studies Reader.* Ed. A. Chabram-Dernersesian. New York: Routledge, 2006. Print. 165-82.

Chávez, Ernesto. *My People First! "Mi Raza Primero!" Nationalism, Identity and Insurgency in the Chicano Movement in Los Angeles, 1966-1978.* Berkeley: U of California P, 2002. Print.

García, Chris F., ed. *La Causa Politica: A Chicano Political Reader.* Notre Dame: U of Notre Dame P, 1974. Print.

Hinojosa, Rolando. "Mexican-American Literature: Toward an Identification." *Books Abroad* 49.3 (1975): 422-30. Print.

Macklin, June, and Stanley A. West, eds. *The Chicano Experience.* Boulder: Westview, 1979. Print.

Mariscal, George. *Brown-Eyed Children of the Sun: Lessons from the Chicano Movement, 1965-1975.* Albuquerque: U of New Mexico, 2005. Print.

Muños, Carlos. *Youth, Identity, Power: The Chicano Movement.* New York: Verso, 1989. Print.

Santillan, Richard. *Chicano Politics: La Raza Unida.* Los Angeles: Tlaquilo, 1973. Print.

Trejo, Arnulfo D., ed. *The Chicanos: As We See Ourselves.* Tucson: U of Arizona P, 1979. Print.

Katrina White

CUSTER DIED FOR YOUR SINS

An Indian Manifesto

Vine Deloria, Jr.

OVERVIEW

Custer Died for Your Sins: An Indian Manifesto (1969), by Standing Rock Sioux writer and lawyer Vine Deloria, Jr., denounces discriminatory treatment of Native Americans in the United States and advocates for political and cultural sovereignty. Chief among Deloria's concerns is the integration of American Indians into mainstream American society without the renunciation of tribal identity. Intended for an audience of Native and non-Native Americans, Deloria's text chronicles numerous injustices suffered by American Indians throughout U.S. history and in modern society. The manifesto emerged in an era of activism and served to galvanize the Red Power movement through its cogent reasoning and clarity. In plain language, with acerbic humor, and from a decidedly Indian point of view, *Custer Died for Your Sins* engages the most important and problematic aspects of mainstream society's relationship with Native Americans.

An instant best seller, *Custer Died for Your Sins* electrified Native American communities and forced non-Native Americans to reconsider their own perspective on and treatment of indigenous Americans. In drawing attention to the plight of Native Americans, Deloria helped alter the way they were viewed. Indian activists praised *Custer* for its lucid explanation of their demands: political self-determination, economic independence, increased educational opportunities, and cultural preservation. Deloria's critique of institutions such as the Bureau of Indian Affairs and the anthropology departments of American universities prompted practical changes in the ways in which they interacted with American Indian communities. Today, *Custer Died for Your Sins* is considered among the most significant nonfiction Native American texts and is recognized as a catalyst in the advancement of indigenous rights and the development of indigenous studies around the world.

HISTORICAL AND LITERARY CONTEXT

Custer Died for Your Sins responds to demeaning attitudes and paternalistic institutional policies toward American Indians, which had become increasingly intolerable for educated and integrated Native Americans coming of age in the 1960s. Although extreme anti-Indian practices had disappeared by the mid-twentieth century, many government-sanctioned policies continued to regulate Native American life. Moreover, stereotypes and misconceptions about American Indians dominated mainstream U.S. culture. Many Native Americans felt politically and culturally invisible, as decisions were being made on their behalf without their input. *Custer* asserts Native Americans' right to self-determination and self-representation.

Appearing in a time of general societal protest in the United States, *Custer Died for Your Sins* aligned itself with the burgeoning minority rights movements. In the year *Custer* was published, Native American activism was in its early stages. One source of discontent was the official federal policy of "relocation and termination." Promoting the abandonment of reservations and the end of treaty agreements, the policy sought ultimately to sever U.S. government ties to Indian communities, with the aim of discontinuing federal medical, financial, and educational support. This plan, as well as the policy of assimilation, signaled the potential demise of Native American ways of life. In a time of fear and frustration, *Custer* provided an opening for Native Americans to participate in the discourse surrounding their future.

The publication of *Custer Died for Your Sins* coincided with a renaissance of Native American literature. The manifesto draws on the work of Deloria's peers in the humanities and social sciences. Until the mid-twentieth century, literature written by Native Americans was scarce, but interest in Indian texts exploded in the 1960s. In the same year *Custer* appeared, Kiowa author N. Scott Momaday won the Pulitzer Prize for his novel *House Made of Dawn*. Anthologies and reprints of older Native American fiction and poetry helped satisfy the new demand, and more Indian-authored works appeared. Importantly, these texts focused on subjects of concern to Indians. Deloria applied this model to his manifesto.

In the years following its publication, *Custer Died for Your Sins* significantly elevated the profile of Native Americans in the United States. The text stimulated the growth of such groups as the American Indian Movement and the National Council of

✦ *Key Facts*

Time Period:
Mid-20th Century

Movement/Issue:
Native American rights

Place of Publication:
United States

Language of Publication:
English

ALCATRAZ OCCUPATION

Most Americans think of Alcatraz Island as the location of a penitentiary that once housed notorious criminals such as Al Capone and George "Machine Gun" Kelly. However, prior to colonial settlement, the island was an important Native American site for gathering food and escaping early European explorers. When the prison closed in 1964, indigenous groups saw an opportunity to reclaim the island. Citing an 1868 treaty entitling Native Americans to surplus federal lands, seventy-nine American Indians successfully sailed to Alcatraz on November 20, 1969, where they then remained for nineteen months.

Demanding recognition for Indian rights, the occupiers found considerable support in mainstream society. Several celebrities spoke out in favor of the protest and traveled to Alcatraz in a show of solidarity, making Indian rights a national issue and pressuring the government to honor the occupiers' demands. As the occupation wore on, though, violence and controversy mounted, and on June 11, 1971, government forces expelled the seventeen remaining occupiers. The success of the Alcatraz occupation in attracting attention to the plight of Native Americans set the tone for activists in the next decade and proved that American Indians would no longer be silenced and that their demands could no longer be ignored.

American Indians. In addition, many of the policy and attitude changes Deloria called for came to pass. As Deloria's first text, *Custer* served as a springboard for the lawyer-activist, who went on to write more than twenty additional books and numerous articles focusing on the position of Native Americans in modern society. Deloria set the precedent for other treatises on Indian experience, such as Dee Brown's *Bury My Heart at Wounded Knee* (1970) and Edgar Cahn and David Hearne's *Our Brother's Keeper: The Indian in White America* (1972). The forcefulness of *Custer,* combined with increased activism and education within the Indian community, gave impetus to a proliferation of Native American texts, as well as expansions of the academic study of Native American culture and literature.

THEMES AND STYLE

Two themes persist throughout *Custer Died for Your Sins*: acknowledgement of the persecution of American Indians in the United States and affirmation of Native Americans' right to sovereignty. Over twelve chapters, Deloria censures those who have hindered American Indians' ability to govern and speak for themselves. Using historical and anecdotal evidence, the author depicts the federal government, anthropologists, missionaries, and others claiming to offer help as malicious at worst and hapless at best. In doing so, he demonstrates that putting Indian matters into the hands of non-Indians has consistently hampered Native

American advancement. Deloria observes, "Everywhere an Indian turns he is deluged with offers of assistance, with good, bad, and irrelevant advice, and with proposals designed to cure everything from poverty to dandruff. Rarely does anyone ask an Indian what he thinks about the modern world." In *Custer,* Deloria seeks to redress this exclusion of Native American views.

The manifesto achieves its rhetorical effect through the representation of a Native American worldview that challenges commonly held beliefs. To present an Indian perspective, Deloria repeatedly describes what "Indians think," how "Indians feel," and what "Indians believe." Deloria presumes, rightly or wrongly, to speak for modern American Indians in order to describe their unique and often maligned position in society. Addressing an audience of both Native and mainstream Americans, Deloria endeavors to inform readers of an alternate narrative not presented in textbooks or popular media. "Most books about Indians cover some abstract and esoteric topic of the last century," he writes. "Contemporary books are predominantly by whites trying to solve the 'Indian problem.' Between the two extremes lives a dynamic people in a social structure of their own, asking only to be freed from cultural oppression." Notably absent from the manifesto is any lengthy discussion of the differences in opinion or experience among Native Americans, the presence of which would potentially undermine Deloria's argument.

The manifesto is marked by the use of exaggeration and sardonic humor in concert with clear, direct language. Deloria's text avoids exhaustive research but candidly lays out complex issues in a manner that is both captivating and comprehensible to a general audience: "Wherein, you may ask, does all of the controversy—particularly the charge of paternalism—originate, if everything is operating so smoothly in the bureau?" At times, the language is hyperbolic, yet his vehemence underscores the exigency of his message. Humor is employed throughout the text, even when Deloria is launching an attack. For example, he writes, "An old Indian once told me that when the missionaries arrived they fell on their knees and prayed. Then they got up, fell on the Indians, and preyed." The author's jokes exemplify Indian humor, a previously under-researched aspect of Native American culture to which Deloria devotes an entire chapter.

CRITICAL DISCUSSION

Although initial responses to *Custer Died for Your Sins* were mixed, they were all impassioned, nonetheless. The manifesto was read in academic circles and popular culture, by Indians and non-Indians alike. Reviews such as Edward Abbey's in the *New York Times* praised Deloria for candidly pointing out oversights in the dominant discussions about American Indians. Harsher critics derided the book's lack of methodical research, as well as the author's overgeneralizations and exaggerations.

John Trudell, a member of the Sioux, stands next to a teepee on Alcatraz Island after Native Americans occupied it in 1969. In that year, Vine Deloria, Jr. discussed the relationship between Native Americans and the American government in *Custer Died for Your Sins.* AP PHOTO

Those most incensed by the manifesto were among Deloria's targets: anthropologists; however, one anthropologist, Mark E. Randall, endorsed Deloria's critique of his discipline. Randall's essay in turn provoked an immediate rebuttal decrying anthropologists' role in Indian oppression. This debate was emblematic of the broader discussion the manifesto engendered. When *Time* magazine entered the fray with a feature article titled "The Angry American Indian: Starting Down the Protest Trail" (1970), it was clear that *Custer* had struck a nerve throughout the United States.

Custer Died for Your Sins proved to be pivotal in the development of efforts to promote and validate Native American perspectives in political and theoretical discourse. Activist groups such as the Red Power movement immediately took up Deloria's cause, making enormous strides for Indian rights. Awareness of Indian rights has continued to grow in the decades since the manifesto's publication; indigenous groups have won more political battles, and Native American scholars have followed Deloria's example. *Custer* helped change Native American views with respect to sovereignty and identity, leading to a fundamental shift in Indians' relationship to the federal government, mainstream society, and themselves.

Deloria's manifesto has continued to generate interest within a variety of academic and professional fields. Anthropologists continue to ponder Deloria's indictment of their discipline: for example, the book *Indians and Anthropologists: Vine Deloria, Jr. and the*

Critique of Anthropology (1997), edited by Thomas Biolsi and Larry Zimmerman, examines the period of Indian and non-Indian relations inaugurated by *Custer* and its consequences. The chapter in *Custer* titled "Indian Humor" has engendered its own body of scholarship as well, from Ruth Dean's 2003 article on the use of Native American humor in transcultural nursing care to Eva Gruber's book *Humor in Contemporary Native North American Literature* (2008). Perhaps the issue most frequently taken up by scholars has been the role Deloria and his manifesto have played in indelibly shifting the way Native Americans think about themselves. As Charles Wilkinson writes in *Blood Struggle: The Rise of Modern Indian Nations* (2005), "For Indians, *Custer* inspired empowerment and pride. It offered hope in a time when hope seemed the province of all in America save Natives." The depth of Deloria's manifesto has ensured that it will fuel scholarly research and critical discussion well into the twenty-first century.

BIBLIOGRAPHY

Sources

"The Angry American Indian: Starting Down the Protest Trail." *Time* 9 Feb. 1970: 16-26. Print.

Deloria, Vine, Jr. *Custer Died For Your Sins: An Indian Manifesto.* London: Macmillan, 1969. Print.

Heidenreich, C. Adrian. "The Sins of Custer Are Not Anthropological Sins: A Reply to Mark E. Randall." *American Anthropologist* 74.4 (1972): 1032-34. Print.

Johnson, Kirk. "Vine Deloria, Jr., Champion of Indian Rights, Dies at 72." *New York Times*. New York Times, 15 Nov. 2005. Web. 18 July 2012.

Newcomb, Steve. "A Scholar's Influence in Indian Country." *Indian Country Today*. Indian Country Today Media Network, 12 Jan. 2005. Web. 9 Aug. 2012.

Ortiz, Alfonso. "*Custer Died for Your Sins*." *American Anthropologist* 73.4 (1971): 953-55. Print.

Randall, Mark E. "Custer Died for Our Sins." *American Anthropologist* 73.4 (1971): 985. Print.

Schweninger, Lee. "Vine Deloria, Jr." *American Indian Biographies*. Ed. Harvey Markowitz and Carole A. Barrett. Pasadena: Salem, 2005. 145-46. Print.

Further Reading

Biolsi, Thomas, and Larry J. Zimmerman, eds. *Indians and Anthropologists: Vine Deloria, Jr. and the Critique of Anthropology*. Tucson: U of Arizona P, 1997. Print.

Deloria, Barbara, Kristen Foehner, and Sam Scinta, eds. *Spirit & Reason: The Vine Deloria, Jr. Reader*. Golden: Fulcrum, 1999. Print.

Pavlik, Steve, and Daniel R. Wildcat. *Destroying Dogma: Vine Deloria, Jr. and His Influence on American Society*. Golden: Fulcrum, 2006. Print.

Smith, Sherry L. *Hippies, Indians, and the Fight for Red Power*. New York: Oxford UP, 2012. Print.

Warrior, Robert Allen. *Tribal Secrets: Recovering American Indian Intellectual Traditions*. Minneapolis: U of Minnesota P, 1995. Print.

Wilkinson, Charles F. *Blood Struggle: The Rise of Modern Indian Nations*. New York: Norton, 2005. Print.

Elizabeth Boeheim

IN PRAISE OF CREOLENESS

Jean Bernabé, Patrick Chamoiseau, Raphaël Confiant

OVERVIEW

Coauthored by three Martinican writers—Jean Bernabé, Patrick Chamoiseau, and Raphaël Confiant—*Éloge de la Créolité,* or *In Praise of Creoleness* (1989), proposes "Creoleness" as a means of self-representation. In doing so, the work defines the term to reflect the shared history, culture, and language of the French Caribbean rather than in terms of nation, race, or geography. *In Praise of Creoleness* is foremost a literary manifesto that calls on Francophone Caribbean writers to be candid in depictions of their background by incorporating, for example, the influences of the native Creole language into their predominantly French-language literary works.

First delivered as a speech by its three authors, *In Praise of Creoleness* was initially received as an invigorating force in Caribbean studies, albeit a controversial one, for its rejection of prior notions of Martinican identity and representation. The manifesto disputes the dominance of French language and culture in the Antilles, but also rejects exclusive identification with the African diaspora as promoted by the Négritude movement, which also had its foundations in Martinique. Instead, the manifesto advocated for a more authentic representation of French Caribbean reality, which the authors felt was a *blend* of indigenous, European, African, and Asian influences. The manifesto engendered a literary movement, *Créolité,* which in turn created a wider readership of French Caribbean texts, an expanded network of writers concerned with an accurate portrayal of French Caribbean life, and a more formalized study of Creole language. Today, *In Praise of Creoleness* is considered a seminal work in Caribbean studies and integral to sustaining the mixed heritage and language of the French Caribbean.

HISTORICAL AND LITERARY CONTEXT

Historically, *In Praise of Creoleness* responds to centuries of colonial domination that enslaved, displaced, and dehumanized non-Europeans. Martinique remained a colony until 1946, when it became a French overseas department. The resulting bureaucratic shift increased legal rights and political representation for inhabitants of Martinique and led to a policy of assimilation, codifying French as the official language and the franc

(and later the Euro) as the official currency. Such changes, however, heightened nonwhite Martinicans' sense of alienation. French Caribbean thinkers began to define a new cultural identity out of the desire to achieve true cultural identity and the fear that continued European influence would extinguish Creole languages.

By the late twentieth century, the process of decolonization left many inhabitants of the former colonies questioning what would come next. Activism and politicization then present throughout the Caribbean endeavored to establish regional cultures to break from the past violence and oppression of their colonizers. When *In Praise of Creoleness* was published in 1989, the authors of the manifesto felt that some cultural agendas were mistakenly continuing to seek validation outside of instead of within their native culture. Feeling deprived of self-determination and fearful of losing their hybridized Creole language, Bernabé, Chamoiseau, and Confiant put to paper a declaration of Creoleness, which galvanized the *Créolité* literary movement.

In Praise of Creoleness marked the culmination of nearly a century of literary movements that sought to redefine Caribbean culture, race, and history. In particular, the manifesto draws on the precedent set by several Martinican writers. Poet and politician Aimé Césaire founded the Négritude movement in his epic, *Cahier d'un retour au pays natal / Return to My Native Land* (1939), which stressed ideological identification with Africa, valorizing this aspect of French Caribbean identity. Writer Édouard Glissant later incorporated indigenous Caribbean and Asian immigrant influences to this identity in the 1981 essay collection, *Le discours antillais / Caribbean Discourse,* naming his approach *Antillanité.* Further refining these treatises, *In Praise of Creoleness* defined Creoleness in terms of its diversity and its language, arriving at the concept of *Créolité.*

The French-language publication of *In Praise of Creoleness* stirred Francophone Caribbean studies by endorsing the use of Creole language into French Caribbean texts. The linguistic hybridization described in the manifesto appealed to both French Caribbean readers and the wider Francophone world, which made the budding trend a much more viable option for French Caribbean

✣ *Key Facts*

Time Period:
Late 20th Century

Movement/Issue:
Creole Identity;
Postcolonialism

Place of Publication:
Martinique

**Language of
Publication:**
French

writers. Among others, Confiant and Chamoiseau have been lauded for incorporating Creole into their fiction. In 1990 an abridged English-language version of the manifesto appeared in the journal of African Diaspora art and culture, *Callaloo*, greatly increasing circulation of the *Créolité* idea. Confiant and Chamoiseau further developed the concept in *Lettres créoles* (1991), which delineated in greater detail the anthropological and modern history informing the evolution of contemporary Francophone Caribbean literature. Postcolonial theoretical texts such as Edward Said's *Orientalism* and Gyatri Spivak's *Can the Subaltern Speak?* pursued similar issues to those raised by *In Praise of Creoleness*, such as pluralism and self-determination. Today, *In Praise of Creoleness* is seen as a seminal text in French Caribbean literary studies.

THEMES AND STYLE

The central theme of *In Praise of Creoleness* is that French Caribbean identity should be conceived within its blended culture and should represent that hybrid rather than merely replicate its European and African heritages. Of the utmost concern for Bernabé Chamoiseau, and Confiant is the development of a previously suppressed worldview: "We have seen the world through the filter of western values, and our foundation was 'exoticized' by the French vision we had to adopt. It is a terrible condition to perceive one's interior architecture, one's world, the instants of one's days, one's own values, with the eyes of the other." The manifesto builds upon Négritude's rejection of Eurocentric values, but unlike its predecessors, *In Praise of Creoleness* also denies African lineage as the predominant marker of French Caribbean identity. "Neither Europeans, nor Africans, nor Asians, we proclaim ourselves Creoles." The manifesto offers instead a definition of Creoleness that embraces the markers of lived experience.

The primary goals of *In Praise of Creoleness* are to establish French Caribbean Creole identity from within its cultural and linguistic history and to demand its recognition by outsiders. Writers and artists make up the manifesto's targeted audience, since such individuals are capable of preserving and disseminating Creoleness through their works. The manifesto's persuasive force arises from its appeal to French Caribbean solidarity in defiance of colonialism and its emphasis on self-representation. This sense of solidarity is achieved by a first-person plural point of view: "We cannot reach Caribbeanness without interior vision. And interior vision is nothing without the unconditional acceptance of our Creoleness. We declare ourselves Creoles." The use of "we" refers to multiple authorship; more importantly, this point of view unifies the unrepresented Caribbean Creoles on whose behalf Bernabé, Chamoiseau, and Confiant write.

Written as a declaration of a new school of thought, the manifesto uses the language of critical theory and draws on a postcolonial framework, which addresses the legacy of colonialism in culture, identity, and ideology. The main body of the document is broken into three sections: Toward Interior Vision and Self-Acceptance (which outlines the history and philosophical evolution leading to *Creolité*), Creoleness (which delineates four common attributes of the designation), and Constant Dynamics (which declares the authors' hopes for the movement). The tenor of the piece is generally didactic but veers toward fervor at the close of the text: "Creole literature will have nothing to do with the Universal, or this disguised adherence to Western values." Although dedicated to sustaining Creole language and culture, *In Praise of Creoleness* was originally written in French. This choice, in concert with its academic diction and postcolonial rhetoric, conveys the sense that the manifesto is in part tailored to an international audience even though it is speaking on behalf of the inhabitants of the French Caribbean.

CRITICAL DISCUSSION

The provocative and defiant stance of *In Praise of Creoleness* polarized contemporary readers. Given as a speech before its publication, the manifesto was initially poorly received. Bernabé, Chamoiseau, and Confiant were understood to be renouncing Négritude, and their perceived arrogance shocked and angered audience members. Nervertheless, the manifesto's release caused excitement among Caribbean scholars: David Scott asserted "It was something of an intellectual *event*." Francophone Caribbean studies were stimulated by the manifesto's revolutionary tone, but critics were incensed by its simplification of French Caribbean ties to Africa, and they rebuked the authors' romanticization of the past. Among the authors' peers, several commentators took issue with the manifesto's theoretical approach. Rather than the inclusive diversity claimed in the manifesto, Guadeloupean writer Maryse Condé saw in the text a new system of exclusions on the basis of authenticity, prompting her to ask, "What is a Caribbean person, and consequently what is a Caribbean writer? Are they always Creole? Where are they born, and where do they live?" and to call for a redefinition of the term.

In Praise of Creoleness stimulated an entire literary movement, encompassing literary analysis, political and cultural theory, and a linguistic aesthetic. Emerging at a critical moment in the development of postcolonial theory, *In Praise of Creoleness* has become a foundational text for the continued growth of the discipline, validating Creoleness as an articulation of postcolonial experience, but it is not without controversy. Sally and Richard Price lauded the text as "an embracing of all the strands that have contributed to the making of the Antillean" before censuring the manifesto's predominantly Francophone "intellectual antecedents." Nevertheless, the manifesto achieved its

Opposite page:
Poster advertising the Antillean line of a French transatlantic shipping company. *In Praise of Creoleness* investigates assumptions of Creole identity and critiques the European legacy in the Caribbean. THE BRIDGEMAN ART LIBRARY

authors' intent: Creole-language literary works and readership grew, and the language itself was recognized as a legitimate field of study, ensuring its survival.

In the decades following its publication, much of the scholarship of *In Praise of Creoleness* has refined the definition and application of *Créolité*. Caribbean scholars frequently invoke the manifesto as a gauge to evaluate a text's Creoleness. A 1993 conference at the University of Maryland, entitled "Expanding the Definition of *Créolité*," demonstrated both the breadth of the term and its oversights. In the conference's keynote address, as recounted in H. Adlai Murdoch's *Creole Identity in the French Caribbean Novel*, critic A. James Arnold admonished the manifesto's omission of women, and he disputed the weight accorded to the maroon figure in Caribbean history, stating that "these are imaginary, rather than historical, heroes." Papers from the conference were later compiled in the 1995 tome *Penser la créolité,* edited by vocal critic Maryse Condé, as well as Madeleine Cottenet-Hage. Condé, along with several other scholars, has addressed one of the most persevering trends in *Créolité* studies: theorizing French Caribbean women's identity, which was not discussed in the manifesto. Where Bernabé, Chamoiseau, and Confiant fall short, an entire corpus of intellectual works endeavors to compensate.

BIBLIOGRAPHY

Sources

Condé, Maryse. "*Créolité* without the Creole Language?" *Caribbean Creolization: Reflections on the Cultural Dynamics of Language, Literature, and Identity.* Eds. Kathleen M. Balutansky and Marie-Agnès Sourieau. Gainesville: UP of Florida, 1998: 101-109. *Google Book Search.* Web. 16 Aug. 2012.

Murdoch, H. Adlai. *Creole Identity in the French Caribbean Novel.* Gainesville: UP of Florida, 2001. Print.

Ormerod, Beverley. "The Martinican Concept of 'Creoleness': A Multiracial Redefinition of Culture." *Mots Pluriels.* University of Western Australia, July 1998. Web. 14 Aug. 2012.

Price, Richard and Sally Price. "Shadowboxing in the Mangrove." *Cultural Anthropology* 12.1 (1997): 3-36. Print.

Scott, David. "Preface: Islands of *Creolité?*" *Small Axe* 13.30 (2009): vii-x. Print.

Further Reading

Bensmaïa, Réda, and Alyson Waters. "Francophonie." *Yale French Studies* 103 (2003): 17-23. Print.

Cohen, Robin. *The Creolization Reader: Studies in Mixed Identities and Cultures.* New York: Routledge, 2009. Print.

Condé, Maryse, and Madeleine Cottenet-Hage, eds. *Penser la créolité.* Paris: Karthala, 1995. Print.

Glissant, Édouard. *Le discours Antillais.* Paris: du Seuil. 1981. Print.

Knepper, Wendy. *Patrick Camoiseau: A Critical Introduction.* Jackson: UP of Mississippi, 2012. Print.

Mehta, Brinda. *Notions of Identity: Diaspora, and Gender in Caribbean Women's Writing.* New York: Palgrave Macmillan, 2009. Print.

Oakley, Seanna. "'A Way to Cross Over': Caribbean Literary Criticism." *Literature Compass* 1.1 (2004): 1-15. Print.

Poddar, Prem, and David Johnson. *A Historical Companion to Postcolonial Thought in English.* New York: Columbia UP, 2005. Print.

Taylor, Lucien. "Créolité Bites: A Conversation with Patrick Chamoiseau, Raphaël Confiant, and Jean Bernabé." *Transition* 74 (1997): 124-161. Print.

Tcheuyap, Alexie, and R.H. Mitsch. "Creolist Mystification: Oral Writing in the Works of Patrick Chamoiseau and Simone Schwartz-Bart." *Research in African Literatures* 32.4 (2001): 44-60. Print.

Elizabeth Boeheim

PAN-AFRICAN CULTURAL MANIFESTO

Organization of African Unity

OVERVIEW

Created and published in 1969 by the Organization of African Unity (OAU), *Pan-African Cultural Manifesto* is the result of several group discussions conducted during the first Pan-African Cultural Festival, which was held in Algiers, Algeria, in 1969 and attended by artists, intellectuals, and writers from thirty-one different African nations. By compiling the notes of three major commissions, the Realities of African Culture, the Role of African Culture in the Liberation Struggle and African Unity, and the Role of Culture in the Economic and Social Development of Africa, the OAU sought to inspire Africans to put aside their individual national differences and focus on Africanity in an effort to embrace their shared culture and history while striving to compete scientifically and economically in the modern world. The manifesto suggests that by endorsing their culture, Africans can maintain independence from colonial rule while also learning how to contribute to and succeed in a modern, global economy.

Pan-African Cultural Manifesto received mixed reviews from critics. Anticolonialists and supporters of the many revolutionary groups present at the festival rallied behind OAU's notion of Africanity through cultural and political independence. Many members of the African elite who had gained their power through assimilation with the colonial government did not agree with the manifesto's cry for a unified African cultural heritage. The influence of the *Pan-African Cultural Manifesto* extended beyond Africa to the Black Panther Party, which used it to explore members' African roots in the group's revolt against its perceived oppressor, the United States government. The creation of the manifesto was historically significant because it marked one of the first occasions in which leaders of African nations came together to explore their collective culture in a unified effort to end colonial rule.

HISTORICAL AND LITERARY CONTEXT

Pan-African Cultural Manifesto is, at its very core, an anticolonial document. The OAU believed that the main decentralizing factor in African progress lay in colonialism and its long-lasting effects. Under colonial rule, Africans were not allowed to celebrate their culture or speak their original languages. In this sense,

the voice of Africans had been stolen by colonization, and the manifesto sought to give the back to the masses the common language of Africanity by turning writers, artists, and intellectuals into revolutionaries.

Pan-African Cultural Manifesto was created during a time when Algeria was struggling with decolonizing after 132 years of foreign occupation and an eight-year civil war. However, given that Algeria had gained its independence in 1963, Algiers, the capital, served as the perfect stage for African leaders to meet and discuss the fate of their countries. In his essay, "Anti-Negritude in Algiers," published in a 1970 issue of *Africa Today,* Bernth Lindfors explains, "The very structure of the Festival's Symposium on African Culture ... seemed deliberately designed to minimize friction and maximize opportunities for agreement ... The Manifesto was endorsed unanimously, and Chairman Mohamed Benyahia of Algeria concluded the Symposium by urging that 'after this conference we must not allow anyone to say there are substantial differences between us.'"

The first Pan-African Cultural Festival and the *Pan-African Cultural Manifesto* were both inspired by earlier Pan-African congresses. The manifesto drew inspiration from Pan-African authors, such as American W.E.B. Du Bois and Algerian Frantz Fanon, who urged their audiences to reject nationalism and colonialism and fight for a unified African culture. The manifesto was also directly influenced by Algerian president Houari Boumedienne's July 21, 1969, inaugural speech for the festival. The president stated,

> This first Pan-African Cultural Festival is concerned, not only with our values and sensitivies, but also with our very existence as Africans and our common future. This festival ... should ... make a direct connection to our vast effort of construction. It constitutes an intrinsic part of the struggle we are all pursuing in Africa— whether that of development, of the struggle against racialism, or of national liberation.

Pan-African Cultural Manifesto inspired a number of artistic works and writings, such as *Cultural Charter for Africa* published by the OAU in 1976. The charter's theme is similar to that of the *Pan-African Cultural Manifesto* in its call for artistic inspiration for future African art and writing to promote Africanity.

✤ *Key Facts*

Time Period
Mid-20th Century

Movement/Issue:
Pan-Africanism;
Anticolonialism;
Decolonization

Place of Publication:
Algeria

Language of Publication:
English

PAN-AFRICANISM AND THE ORGANIZATION OF AFRICAN UNITY

Pan-Africanism dates to the early slave writings and abolitionist movements of the late eighteenth and early nineteenth centuries. The movement became more organized by Henry Sylvester-Williams, who founded the African Association (later renamed Pan-African Association) which held the first Pan-African Conference in London in 1900. Pan-Africanism called for a return to traditional African values of culture, society, and unity. Pan-African leaders sought to overthrow colonial rule and gain control of their own governments and natural resources. Some popular leaders in the Pan-African movement were Ghana's president Kwame Nkrumah, NAACP founder and writer W.E.B. Du Bois, "back to Africa" movement founder Marcus Garvey, and civil rights leader Malcolm X.

The Organization of African Unity (OAU) was founded on May 25, 1963, by thirty-two independent African states, and it addressed issues of united Africanity, promoted political independence and economic success, and fought oppressive colonial rule. When it disbanded in 2002, fifty-three of the fifty-four African states were members. Criticized as being ineffective for not having an armed force and failing to interfere in member states' affairs, the OAU was often referred to as a "dictator's club." The organization was lauded more for its successful negotiations, such as the end of apartheid in South Africa, than it was for taking action against individual African leaders. On July 9, 2002, the African Union replaced the OAU as the main Pan-African organization.

THEMES AND STYLE

The main theme of *Pan-African Cultural Manifesto* is Africanity, which is described in the work as a "gigantic effort to recover Africa's cultural heritage and adapt it to the needs of technological civilization." Artists with scientists and other thinkers can together help make "known the common inspiration and common heritage which go to make up Africanity." The OAU drafted the manifesto from small group discussions based on the following three topics: the realities of African culture, the role of African culture in the liberation struggle and African unity, and the role of culture in the economic and social development of Africa. The overall theme of the manifesto suggests that only through embracing its culture and heritage can Africa begin to educate the masses into continued revolt against colonialism in an effort to promote social and economic growth across the continent. It states, "Our artists, authors and intellectuals must, if they are to be of service to Africa, find their inspiration in Africa."

The manifesto develops its theme by introducing each of the three main topics individually and then building an argument upon them. It leads the reader through the same steps necessary for Africa to assert independence. The first section champions a celebration of African culture and a return to traditions abandoned during the colonial period. Once African intellectuals, writers, and artists embrace their unique culture, they can use their craft to promote revolution and independence. The final step to building an economically and technologically advanced Africa is through educating the masses to be stewards of African culture and defenders of African tradition. The manifesto states, "It has become now both urgent and necessary to promote the permanent education of the masses in every field to develop in them a scientific, technological, and critical spirit and attitude and to render popular culture fully effective."

Pan-African Cultural Manifesto, the result of a unified effort derived through group consensus, is structured in an orderly fashion and written in a calm tone. It does not include much of the deliberation or the argumentative tenor of the debates that occurred within the group discussions at the event. The OAU decided this approach was necessary in order to promote the harmony that would be needed among African nations to reach the manifesto's goals. The document states, "Africanity obeys the law of a dialectic of the particular, the general and the future, of specificity and universality, in other words of variety at the origin and starting point and unity at the destination." The OAU wanted *Pan-African Cultural Manifesto* to serve as an example of the collaboration necessary to promote Africanity.

CRITICAL DISCUSSION

In his essay "From Harlem to Algiers," Samir Meghelli describes the initial reaction to the manifesto:

> In the immediate aftermath of the festival, one could not find a great deal of evidence of meaningful reflection, just as evidence of its significance cannot be easily found in the secondary historical literature now. And yet it is clear that the First All African Cultural Festival ... represents a watershed moment in the history of linkages between the African American and African freedom movements. The festival gave voice to these important ideas and provided the context for a broad range of African and African diasporic intellectuals, artists, activists, and students come into conversation with one another, in some cases literally, and in others, symbolically.

After winning a war for independence against colonial forces, Algeria became a Mecca for liberation movements. Black Panther leader Eldridge Cleaver was present at the 1969 festival, and he and his wife later sought asylum in Algiers after fleeing the United States during an FBI investigation. In his article "Our Other Man in Algiers," published in a 1970 issue of *New York Times Magazine,* author Sanche De Gramont explains, "In Algiers, the Panthers are

In Buchanan, Liberia, a chief leads his people in singing and dancing. CHRISTOPHER HERWIG/ LONELY PLANET IMAGES/ GETTY IMAGES

respected as one of approximately a dozen liberation movements accredited by the Algerian Government and provided with assistance and support in their task of overthrowing the governments in power in their respective countries." *Pan-African Cultural Manifesto* inspired many African American artists, intellectuals, and writers to join the Pan-African movement, seeking inspiration for their respective arts in African culture and tradition.

Pan-African Cultural Manifesto not only inspired writers and musicians to embrace their African roots but also prompted universities to create Pan-African or African studies programs. It served as a political call to arms against colonialism as well as a cultural renaissance for all Africans and the African diaspora. In his 1971 book, *Journey to Africa,* author Hoyt Fuller explains that "Pan Africanism is an idea whose time has come" and the festival in "Algiers was the Black World coming of Age." In 2009 the 2nd Pan-African Cultural Festival was also held in Algiers to inspire a new generation of artists, intellectuals, musicians, and writers to seek inspiration in African culture and tradition, thus continuing to promote Africanity in the modern world.

BIBLIOGRAPHY

Sources

Boumedienne, Houari. "The Algerian Festival: Inaugural Address 1969." *New African Literature and the Arts,* Vol. 3. Ed. Joseph Okpaku. New York: Third, 1973. *Google Book Search.* Web. 21 Aug. 2012.

Fuller, Hoyt. *Journey to Africa.* Chicago: Third World, 1971. Print.

Gramont, Sanche De. "Our Other Man in Algiers." *New York Times Magazine* 1 Nov. 1970. *ProQuest.* Web. 21 Aug. 2012.

Lindfors, Bernth. "Anti-Negritude in Algiers." *Africa Today* Jan./Feb. 1970. *JSTOR.* Web. 21 Aug. 2012.

Meghelli, Samir. "From Harlem to Algiers: Transnational Solidarities between the African American Freedom Movement and Algeria, 1962-1978." *Black Routes to Islam.* Eds. Manning Marable and Hishaam D. Aidi. New York: Palgrave-Macmillan, 2009.

Organization of African Unity. *Pan-African Cultural Manifesto. Africa Today* Jan./Feb. 1970. *JSTOR.* Web. 21 Aug. 2012.

Further Reading

Andemicael, Berhanykun. *The OAU and the UN: Relations between the Organization of African Unity and the United Nations.* New York: Africana, 1976. Print.

Cervenka, Zdenek. *The Organization of African Unity.* New York: Praeger, 1968. Print.

———. *The Unfinished Quest for Unity: Africa and the OAU.* New York: Africana, 1977. Print.

Fanon, Frantz. *The Wretched of the Earth.* Preface by Jean-Paul Sartre. Trans. Constance Farrington. New York: Grove Press, 1963.

Geiss, Imanuel. *The Pan-African Movement: A History of Pan-Africanism in America, Europe, and Africa.* New York: Africana, 1974. Print.

Ron Horton

THE WRETCHED OF THE EARTH

Frantz Fanon

❖ *Key Facts*

Time Period:
Mid-20th Century

Movement/Issue:
Colonialism; Racisim

Place of Publication:
France

**Language of
Publication:**
French

OVERVIEW

Written by Frantz Fanon and published in 1961, *The Wretched of the Earth* describes Europe's prolonged colonization and exploitation of the third world and calls for a new "history of Man" driven by those nations that were formerly colonized. Although Fanon adopts a language of universalism, his experiences in Africa serve as a model for his broader understanding of decolonization. Born in the French colony of Martinique in 1925, Fanon became actively involved in the Algerian War of Independence (1954-1962) when he worked at the psychiatric hospital in Blida, Algeria. Addressed to the colonized peoples of the third world, *The Wretched of the Earth* demands the invention of new institutions, intellectual approaches, and techniques of government that will avoid the same atrocities and crimes that stained European humanism. The language and tone of the manifesto is Marxian, although Fanon's focus on the peasantry, or the lumpenproletariat, rather than the proletariat, or working class, throughout the text distinguishes *The Wretched of the Earth* from other works in the same tradition.

The Wretched of the Earth received mixed reviews within France but was embraced by oppressed groups of the third world as well as the African American community in the United States. The book has been called the "Bible of decolonization," and it influenced anticolonial revolutions, postindependence struggles for equality, and black consciousness movements around the world. In the early twenty-first century, *The Wretched of the Earth* is recognized as a foundational text on the psychology of colonialism and anticolonial struggle, and it continues to find new applications within critical and political theory.

HISTORICAL AND LITERARY CONTEXT

The Wretched of the Earth responds to the period of widespread decolonization of European colonies that began after World War II (1939-1945), highlighting the perceived decline of Europe and its displacement by the third world. Europe was only able to achieve its tremendous wealth, intellectual and technological development, and ideological supremacy through the exploitation of its colonies and the oppression of the colonized peoples. The French *mission civilisatrice*, or civilizing mission, that helped justify colonialism and shape colonial policy sought to make the colonized

people citizens of the republic but simultaneously withheld true equality in order to maintain the difference that elevated the colonizer to a position of economic and political privilege over the colonized. The blatantly racial basis of economic oppression in the colonial context, which displaced the more subtle inequality of class that was the subject of traditional Marxian manifestos, demanded a redistribution of wealth. Fanon writes in *The Wretched of the Earth* that "the economic infrastructure is also a superstructure. The cause is effect: you are rich because you are white, you are white because you are rich."

When Fanon wrote *The Wretched of the Earth*, the majority of France's former colonies had already attained their independence, and most of Africa was independent. Algeria, however, was still engaged in its war of independence. This struggle was particularly protracted and violent because Algeria was home to a large settler community and was viewed as an integral part of France rather than as a colony. After working at the psychiatric hospital in Blida, where he treated both the victims and the perpetrators of torture, Fanon shifted from a political dedication to the independence movement to near self-identification as an Algerian.

Also, while Fanon wrote *The Wretched of the Earth*, vocal opposition to the ongoing occupation of Algeria was growing. In 1960 a group of French intellectuals signed the *Declaration of the Right to Insubordination in the Algerian War*, which supported the Algerian independence movement and declared the right of French citizens to refuse to participate in acts of aggression against the Algerian people, even if this meant deserting from the military. Prior to writing *The Wretched of the Earth*, Fanon wrote two other full-length texts dealing with colonialism: *Black Skin, White Masks* (1952), which addresses the psychological impact of racism and draws on Fanon's own experiences as a black man from Martinique studying medicine and psychiatry in France, and *A Dying Colonialism* (1959), which deals directly with the Algerian war.

Despite early criticism that the historical particularity of the text would limit its applicability, *The Wretched of the Earth* has been widely influential. When Fanon died on December 6, 1961, just months after *The Wretched of the Earth* was published, the French police confiscated copies of the text from Paris bookshops. Bobby Seale and Huey Newton, who founded the African American Black Panther Party in 1966, adapted Fanon's idea of the revolutionary role of the peasantry to their own philosophy. Steve Biko, who founded the Black Consciousness movement in South Africa in the late 1960s, and Ali Shariati, one of the intellectual luminaries of the 1979 Iranian Revolution, were similarly influenced by Fanon. *The Wretched of the Earth* remains an important historical record of the period of decolonization as well as a reminder of the economic oppression of developing countries that continues in the twenty-first century.

THEMES AND STYLE

The central theme of *The Wretched of the Earth* is that the period of European colonialism and supremacy is at an end and that the third world, through its successful revolution and decolonization, must lead the way to a new humanism. Europe, although it aspired to this humanism, was never able to advance intellectually, technologically, or economically without committing concurrent acts of exploitation. Fanon writes, "[T]oday we know with what sufferings humanity has paid for every one of [Europe's] triumphs of the mind." Throughout his work, Fanon is adamant about the necessity of rejecting a Cold War mentality that leaves the formerly colonized in a "Manichaean world" that restrains economic and ideological development. He writes, "Let us decide not to imitate Europe; let us combine our muscles and our brains in a new direction. Let us try to create the whole man, whom Europe has been incapable of bringing to triumphant birth."

Fanon's work achieves its rhetorical effect through its universalist discourse, although its call for unity is addressed only to the third world and demands that it "not forget Europe's crimes, of which the most horrible was committed in the heart of man, and consisted of … the crumbling away of his unity." Originally written and published in French, the language of the colonizer, the text repeatedly references the atrocities and crimes committed by Europe, and Fanon does not acknowledge his European readers or grant them a formative role in the coming age. Instead, he explains that the third world is responsible for bringing Europe into this period of new humanism as well: "[I]f we wish to reply to the expectations of the people of Europe, it is no good sending them back a reflection, even an ideal reflection, of their society and their thought with which from time to time they feel immeasurably sickened."

Stylistically, *The Wretched of the Earth* possesses a fiery tone and draws on Marxist rhetoric to communicate its message. Fanon writes, "Come, then, comrades; it would be as well to decide at once to change our ways. We must shake off the heavy darkness in which we were plunged, and leave it behind. The new day which is already at hand must find us firm, prudent and resolute." Europe's crimes are broadly outlined in vivid language that communicates the urgency of the manifesto's message and perpetuates the violent tone

set by Fanon in his opening chapter. Europe "killed and devoured" men, while the United States, serving as a cautionary tale for former European colonies that might want to imitate Europe, "became a monster, in which the taints, the sickness and the inhumanity of Europe have grown to appalling dimensions."

CRITICAL DISCUSSION

When *The Wretched of the Earth* was first published in 1961, French reactions to the text were mixed, while it received an enthusiastic response in Africa and within the African American community. Critics condemned Fanon's idealism as well as his failure to lay out a concrete economic plan for the redistribution of wealth. Marxists disapproved of his focus on the peasantry or rural masses rather than the proletariat as the driving force of revolution and also questioned his attention to the psychology of colonial oppression.

EL MOUDJAHID

ORGANE CENTRAL DU FRONT DE LIBERATION NATIONALE
N° 77 – 29 Janvier 1961
PRIX 40 FRANCS

LA REVOLUTION PAR LE PEUPLE ET POUR LE PEUPLE

LA QUESTION DE LA MINORITE EUROPEENNE

A l'ombre du para, la rencontre impossible

The front page of a 1961 issue of *El Moudjahid* discussing colonialism in Africa. Frantz Fanon wrote pro-Algerian pieces for this publication and others. He also supports African independence in his 1961 book *The Wretched of the Earth*. © PHOTOS 12/ ALAMY

PRIMARY SOURCE

THE WRETCHED OF THE EARTH

Come, then, comrades; it would be as well to decide at once to change our ways. We must shake off the heavy darkness in which we were plunged, and leave it behind. The new day which is already at hand must find us firm, prudent and resolute.

We must leave our dreams and abandon our old beliefs and friendships of the time before life began. Let us waste no time in sterile litanies and nauseating mimicry. Leave this Europe where they are never done talking of Man, yet murder men everywhere they find them, at the corner of every one of their own streets, in all the corners of the globe. For centuries they have stifled almost the whole of humanity in the name of a so-called spiritual experience. Look at them today swaying between atomic and spiritual disintegration....

So, my brothers, how is it that we do not understand that we have better things to do than to follow that same Europe?

That same Europe where they were never done talking of Man, and where they never stopped proclaiming that they were only anxious for the welfare of Man: today we know with what sufferings humanity has paid for every one of their triumphs of the mind....

...The pretext of catching up must not be used to push man around, to tear him away from himself or from his privacy, to break and kill him.

No, we do not want to catch up with anyone. What we want to do is to go forward all the time, night and day, in the company of Man, in the company of all men. The caravan should not be stretched out, for in that case each line will hardly see those who precede it; and men who no longer recognise each other meet less and less together, and talk to each other less and less.

It is a question of the Third World starting a new history of Man, a history which will have regard to the sometimes prodigious theses which Europe has put forward, but which will also not forget Europe's crimes, of which the most horrible was committed in the heart of man, and consisted of the pathological tearing apart of his functions and the crumbling away of his unity. And in the framework of the collectivity there were the differentiations, the stratification and the bloodthirsty tensions fed by classes; and finally, on the immense scale of humanity, there were racial hatreds, slavery, exploitation and above all the bloodless genocide which consisted in the setting aside of fifteen thousand millions of men.

So, comrades, let us not pay tribute to Europe by creating states, institutions and societies which draw their inspiration from her.

Humanity is waiting for something other from us than such an imitation, which would be almost an obscene caricature.

If we want to turn Africa into a new Europe, and America into a new Europe, then let us leave the destiny of our countries to Europeans. They will know how to do it better than the most gifted among us.

But if we want humanity to advance a step further, if we want to bring it up to a different level than that which Europe has shown it, then we must invent and we must make discoveries.

If we wish to live up to our peoples' expectations, we must seek the response elsewhere than in Europe.

Moreover, if we wish to reply to the expectations of the people of Europe, it is no good sending them back a reflection, even an ideal reflection, of their society and their thought with which from time to time they feel immeasurably sickened.

For Europe, for ourselves and for humanity, comrades, we must turn over a new leaf, we must work out new concepts, and try to set afoot a new man....

SOURCE: Grove, 1963. Pp. 311-312, 314-316.

Others reproached Fanon's criticism of Europe and his attempt to extrapolate a theory on decolonization based largely on his experiences in Africa, and chiefly Algeria, arguing that the extreme violence described in the text reflects the particularities of a settler colony. However, it is Fanon's attitude toward violence that received the most critical attention. In his 1961 preface to *The Wretched of the Earth*, Jean-Paul Sartre, a French novelist, playwright, and philosopher, addresses a European audience, stressing the necessity of violence to the anticolonial struggle and its role in the emergence of a new humanism and arguing that as the "offspring of violence," the colonized "draws every moment of his humanity from it: we were men at his expense, he becomes a man at ours. Another man: a man of higher quality." In contrast, Gilbert Comte, writing in the French weekly *La Nation française* in 1962, called *The Wretched of the Earth* a "*Mein Kampf* of decolonization," invoking the political ideology of German dictator Adolf Hitler.

In the decades that followed, scholars continued to debate Fanon's views on violence. American political scientist Hannah Arendt condemned the text, and especially Sartre's preface, in her 1970 book, *On Violence*, writing, "No body politic I know of was ever founded on equality before death and its actualization in violence." Arendt questions the argument that collective violence can predictably result in the emergence of a "new man." Since its publication, *The Wretched of the Earth* has been the subject of an extensive body of criticism that considers it from historical, political, postcolonial, and literary perspectives.

Much scholarship focuses on the application of *The Wretched of the Earth* to contemporary political realities. In his foreword to Richard Philcox's 2004 translation of *The Wretched of the Earth,* Homi K. Bhabha draws a comparison between Fanon's historical context and the economic challenges of globalization, highlighting "the poignant proximity of the incomplete project of decolonization to the dispossessed subjects of globalization." Bhabha argues that the poverty and inequality of formerly colonized nations continue in part because of the implementation of International Monetary Fund (IMF) and World Bank policies that have "the feel of the colonial ruler," in the words of Joseph Stiglitz, former chief economist of the World Bank.

BIBLIOGRAPHY

Sources

Arendt, Hannah. *On Violence.* New York: Harcourt, 1970. Print.

Bhabha, Homi K. Foreword. *The Wretched of the Earth.* By Frantz Fanon. New York: Grove, 2004. vii-xli. Print.

Comte, Gilbert. "Un *Mein Kampf* de la décolonisation." *La Nation francaise.* 21 Mar. 1962. Print.

Horne, Alistair. *A Savage War of Peace: Algeria, 1954-1962.* London: Papermac, 1987. Print.

Sartre, Jean-Paul. Preface. *The Wretched of the Earth.* By Frantz Fanon. New York: Grove, 2004. xliii-lxii. Print.

Young, Robert J. C. *Postcolonialism: An Historical Introduction.* Oxford: Blackwells, 2001. 274-92. Print.

Further Reading

Bulhan, Hussein Abdilahi. *Frantz Fanon and the Psychology of Oppression.* New York: Plenum, 1985. Print.

Cherki, Alice. *Frantz Fanon: A Portrait.* Ithaca: Cornell UP, 2006. Print.

Fanon, Frantz. *Black Skin, White Masks.* Trans. Richard Philcox. New York: Grove, 2008. Print.

———. *A Dying Colonialism.* Trans. Haakon Chevalier. New York: Grove, 1965. Print.

Gates, Henry Louis, Jr. "Critical Fanonism." *Critical Inquiry* 17.3 (1991): 457-70. Print.

Macey, David. *Frantz Fanon: A Life.* London: Granta, 2000. Print.

Memmi, Albert. *The Colonizer and the Colonized.* Trans. Howard Greenfield. Boston: Beacon, 1991. Print.

Allison Blecker

STUDENTS, ACTIVISTS, AND SITUATIONS

BEYOND VIETNAM: A TIME TO BREAK SILENCE

Martin Luther King, Jr.

OVERVIEW

On April 4, 1967, Martin Luther King, Jr. delivered a sermon from the pulpit of Manhattan's Riverside Church titled "Beyond Vietnam: A Time to Break Silence." Drafted for King by African American historian and religious scholar Vincent Harding, the powerful speech denounces the involvement of the United States in the Vietnam War. It urges young men of all races who perceived the war as immoral or unjust to apply for conscientious objector status. King charges the United States with being "the greatest purveyor of violence in the world today." The address lists his reasons for opposing the war and proposes steps toward peace. Intended to foster in the peace movement the same level of fervor driving the civil rights movement and to link the two, King's speech was reprinted in the political/literary journal *Ramparts* in May and subsequently in several other media outlets.

Only a handful of antiwar activists and a select few print publications sympathetic to the antiwar cause supported the declaration. Overall, however, it was met with resistance. King was forced to defend himself in the face of accusations—not only from opponents but also from supporters and colleagues (including those at the NAACP)—that he was either diverting attention away from the civil rights movement to the antiwar movement or proposing an unacceptable merger of the two. He insisted that he had no such purpose but was advocating an equal sense of urgency in the individual pursuit of each cause. The speech represented a revision in King's civil rights agenda; his previous focus on legal and political aims shifted during the final years of his life to a pursuit of more solid economic and social changes for African Americans. Later, in the wake of the speech and the declining popularity of the war, the movement did indeed follow this path.

HISTORICAL AND LITERARY CONTEXT

The mid-to late 1960s were marked by an increasing overlap of the civil rights and antiwar movements. Student Nonviolent Coordinating Committee (SNCC) leader Bob Moses noted that the bodies of three civil rights workers—two white and one black—lynched in Nashoba County, Mississippi, in June 1964 were discovered just as the United States dropped its first bombs on North Vietnam. While nearly all civil rights leaders were opposed to the war, many felt that devoting too much attention to antiwar campaigns would slow the momentum that the civil rights movement had gained during the past decade of activism. Others, King chief among them, were disillusioned with the movement's failure to improve the day-to-day lives of African Americans. They saw the war as symptomatic of the same societal problems faced by American blacks and aspired to fight on both fronts at once.

King's opposition to the war went far beyond that of many pacifists. By 1967 reports had surfaced that during one documented period, 31 percent of white men and 67 percent of black men eligible for the draft had been called up. King saw in these statistics the same "cruel manipulation of the poor" that was at the heart of enfranchised racism in U.S. domestic policy. Despite having gained political rights, African Americans continued to be denied access to social status and economic opportunities and were prey to governmental abuse in myriad forms. In "Beyond Vietnam," King decries the U.S. government's devotion of resources to (allegedly) securing liberties for another country's citizens rather than for its own. He implicates the oppressive tendencies of capitalism in providing the foundation of both racism and violent imperialism.

In crafting the speech, King drew most heavily from the praxis of his own oratory legacy. His 1963 "I have a dream" speech, a call for racial equality delivered from the steps of the Lincoln Memorial, had already reached iconic status. The power of his delivery and the deftness of his rhetoric had galvanized his fellow activists, and the extra pressure exerted on the Kennedy administration thereafter expedited the advancement of several pieces of civil rights legislation. King's work on civil rights earned him the 1964 Nobel Peace Prize. In his Vietnam speech, King called the Nobel Committee's earlier decision to award him the prize "a commission to work harder than I had ever worked before for 'the brotherhood of man.'"

"Beyond Vietnam" marked a turning point in King's approach and his public career. Although he maintained in the speech the sermonic tone and delivery for which he was known, he took a less poised approach to the subject matter than in his earlier addresses. Until that point he had advocated impassivity and professionalism in activist conduct; he was growing weary, however, of both the slow pace

Key Facts

Time Period:
Mid-20th Century

Movement/Issue:
Vietnam War

Place of Publication:
United States

Language of Publication:
English

THE GENESIS OF KING'S SPEECH

King's friend and fellow activist Vincent Harding drafted the speech King delivered at Riverside in 1967. In an interview with *Sojourners* magazine's associate editor Rose Marie Berger in 2007, Harding recalled that "by and large Martin seemed fairly satisfied with what I provided and most of the speech was based on that draft," with King adding the closing lines. A noticeable shift in voice between Harding's original text and King's amendments elicited critical responses. Harding recalled that he and King "often laughed about the fact that [...historian] Henry Steele Commager [...] was going around after the speech telling everybody that he knew exactly what was going on there, that King had written the major part and somebody else put on an ending."

According to Harding, King had already publicly stated his opposition to the war on several occasions. Most were passing remarks that received little attention, however. "What [King] began to look for," Harding remembered, "were occasions and settings he could feel were the right places and times for him to speak out"—that is, a venue conducive to moral rather than just political opposition to the war. Although Harding did not recall "how or under what circumstances" the civil rights leader was invited to speak at Riverside Church, he did recall King recognizing it as exactly the venue he had been looking for.

of progress and his colleagues' insistence that he not involve himself in antiwar campaigns. In his opening remarks to the speech, he articulated a desire to "break the betrayals of [his] own silences" in order to finally speak his disapproval of the war. Unfortunately for King, the press and public were prepared neither for the message nor for the frustration he expressed to the congregation that evening, and he endured persistent criticism during his final years.

THEMES AND STYLE

The dominant theme of "Beyond Vietnam" is the denunciation of American involvement in Vietnam as an extension of the racism that still plagued domestic policy. Citing moments of "real promise of hope for the poor" and marginalized members of society that he had witnessed during the Poverty Program in 1964, King laments that in the escalating war effort he has seen "the program broken and eviscerated as if it were some idle political plaything of a society gone mad on war." He notes, too, the hypocrisy inherent in U.S. offensive strategies in Vietnam that mandate slaughtering citizens while pretending to liberate them. He asks, "What do the peasants think as we ally ourselves with the landlords and [...] charge them with violence while we pour new weapons of death into their land?" King's purpose is also to exhort Americans to work for peace, which would necessitate an ecumenical, human-oriented, "positive revolution of values."

Powering King's rhetoric are the candor and vexation he had been denying himself as the war progressed. He describes a government that "continued to draw men and skills and money like some demonic, destructive suction tube," making "incandescently clear" his perception of the war "as an enemy of the poor" and his intention "to attack it as such." He chastises the government for sending poor black and white men "eight thousand miles away to guarantee liberties in Southeast Asia which they [themselves] had not found in Southwest Georgia and East Harlem." King could no longer keep silent in the face of a war he saw as "but a symptom of a far deeper malady within the American spirit."

In addition to employing a more critical tone, King conveyed in the speech a hopelessness his followers found uncharacteristic and unsavory; it belied the success that they believed the movement had achieved, which King now felt was negligible. Many of his remarks betray a sense of defeat and exhaustion, as when he declares that if the United States continues to pursue the war, "There will be no doubt in my mind and in the mind of the world that we have no honorable intentions in Vietnam." Recognizing in the government's attitudes toward the war the same "malady" that persisted in sanctioning and institutionalizing racism, King confesses to believing that in entreating peace, the world demanded a "maturity of America that we may not be able to achieve."

CRITICAL DISCUSSION

Immediately following King's delivery of "Beyond Vietnam," both the black press and white press lambasted him for calling for an end to the war in Vietnam, with 168 newspapers and periodicals denouncing his position as treasonous. *Time* and *Newsweek* agreed with the *U.S. News and World Report,* which held that "King should have kept silent and inferred that black leaders had no business speaking about such matters." The *Washington Post* dismissed "Beyond Vietnam" as "sheer inventions of unsupported fantasy" and declared that many who had respected King in the past would "never again accord him the same confidence." *Life* contended that King went "beyond his personal right to dissent" when he advocated a plan that amounted to "abject surrender in Vietnam." He was even portrayed by *Time,* who had named him Man of the Year in 1963, as "an opportunist trying desperately to maintain his leadership of the civil rights movement," in the words of Richard Lentz.

Most of King's critics later changed their positions. In fact, by August 1967 public support for the war had dropped from 72 percent to 61 percent, and the number who believed in the fight for a negotiated peace dropped from 57 percent to 37 percent. Then, in March 1968 the Gallup Poll revealed that 49 percent of the population believed that U.S. military involvement in Vietnam was wrong. Although the war continued until 1975, some scholars feel that

King's speech anticipated the shift in public opinion that eventually ended the war.

Contemporary scholarship on "Beyond Vietnam" emphasizes the change in opinions about the speech over the decades. In their 1986 article "King on Vietnam and Beyond," Henry E. Darby and Margaret N. Rowley argue that the "criticisms" King offered at Riverside Church that evening were "prophetic." Benjamin Harrison's "Impact of the Vietnam War on the Civil Rights Movement in the Midsixties" (1996) assesses King's grasp of the issues surrounding the war as sound and well informed, writing that "hindsight indicates his views were more accurate" than those of the politicians conducting the war. Hindsight has afforded these critics a certain sobriety, however, as even Harrison concludes that King's critics were proven right in their belief that antiwar activism "marked the beginning of the end for the one social movement that truly had the potential for improving twentieth century race relations in America." With the expulsion of whites from the SNCC and the rise of the militant Black Panthers in the late 1960s, the civil rights movement began to splinter.

American soldiers in South Vietnam during the Vietnam War. AP-PHOTO

BIBLIOGRAPHY

Sources

Berger, Rose Marie. "Web Exclusive: Extended Interview with Vincent G. Harding." *Sojourners* magazine. Sojourners, 4 Apr. 2007. Web. 13 Aug. 2012.

Darby, Henry E., and Margaret N. Rowley. "King on Vietnam and Beyond." *Phylon* 47.1 (1986): 43-50. *JSTOR*. Web. 20 July 2012.

Harrison, Benjamin T. "Impact of the Vietnam War on the Civil Rights Movement in the Midsixties." *Studies in Conflict and Terrorism* 19.3 (1996): 261+. *Academic OneFile*. Web. 20 July 2012.

King, Martin Luther, Jr. "Beyond Vietnam: A Time to Break Silence." *A Call to Conscience: The Landmark Speeches of Dr. Martin Luther King, Jr.* Ed. Clayborne Carson and Kris Shepard. New York: IPM/Warner, 2001. Print.

Lentz, Richard. *A Symbols, the New Magazines, and Martin Luther King.* Baton Rouge: Louisiana State UP, 1990.

"A Tragedy." *Washington Post and Times-Herald* 6 Apr. 1967: A20. *ProQuest Historical Newspapers.* Web. 20 July 2012.

"Dr. King's Disservice to the Cause," *Life* 21 Apr. 1967: 4. Print.

"Dr. King's Error." *New York Times* 7 Apr. 1967: 36. *ProQuest Historical Newspapers.* Web. 20 July 2012.

"Gallup Poll Reports 49% Believe Involvement in Vietnam an Error." *New York Times* 10 Mar. 1968: 36. *ProQuest Historical Newspapers.* Web. 20 July 2012.

"Is Vietnam to Become a Civil Rights Issue?" *U.S. News and World Report* 19 July 1965: 12. Print.

Further Reading

Bernstein, Irving. *Guns or Butter: The Presidency of Lyndon Johnson.* New York: Oxford UP, 1996. Print.

Branch, Taylor. *At Canaan's Edge: America in the King Years, 1965-68.* New York: Simon & Schuster, 2006. Print.

Dionisopoulos, George N., et al. "Martin Luther King, the American Dream and Vietnam: A Collision of Rhetorical Trajectories." *Western Journal of Communication* 56.2 (1992): 91+. *Academic OneFile.* Web. 20 July 2012.

Dyson, Michael Eric. *I May Not Get There with You: The True Martin Luther King, Jr.* New York: The Free Press, 2000. Print.

Gerstle, Gary. *American Crucible: Race and Nation in the Twentieth Century.* Princeton: Princeton UP, 2001. Print.

King, Martin Luther, Jr. Ed. Clayborne Carson. *The Autobiography of Martin Luther King, Jr.* New York: IPM/Warner, 1998. Print.

Clint Garner

THE COMING INSURRECTION

Invisible Committee

✣ Key Facts

Time Period:
Early 21st Century

Movement/Issue:
Great recession;
Anticapitalism

Place of Publication:
France

**Language of
Publication:**
French

OVERVIEW

Composed by the Invisible Committee, an anonymous French collective, *The Coming Insurrection* (2007; reissued 2009) describes the causes of contemporary social unrest and anticipates the collapse of capitalist society. The book was issued in the midst of worldwide revolutions. In 2005, two years before its initial publication, riots broke out in France in protest of perceived social, racial, and economic inequality. In 2009, a deep economic recession sparked demonstrations across Europe and around the world. According to the book's authors, these crises are the latest developments in the inevitable process of the capitalist system's collapse. Influenced by the revolutionary group Situationist International, which helped spark the French May 1968 uprisings, *The Coming Insurrection* argues that capitalism has profoundly alienated humans from themselves and proposes a kind of anarchic communism as the solution.

When *The Coming Insurrection* was published in France, it greatly disturbed the French political establishment and the government of President Nicolas Sarkozy. In 2008 nine of the text's supposed authors were arrested in France for allegedly sabotaging French railways and for "criminal association for the purposes of terrorist activity." Although charges were dropped against eight of the accused, and the ninth, Julien Coupat, was acquitted at trial (none of them were definitively proved have authored the manifesto), their arrest and Coupat's trial only brought greater attention to the book and its message. In 2009 *The Coming Insurrection* was reissued with a new introductory section and was published in English, drawing a strong response not only from international anarchists and revolutionary sympathizers but from conservative activists and commentators. Today, *The Coming Insurrection* is considered one of the most important revolutionary statements to emerge from the worldwide social unrest that continues to foment in the wake of the 2008 financial crisis and economic downturn.

HISTORICAL AND LITERARY CONTEXT

The Coming Insurrection analyzes the social unrest in France and elsewhere in the West at the dawn of the twenty-first century, when social and economic injustice led to demonstrations—in many cases, violent protests—against systems of economic and political power. The wave of unrest started with protests against the World Trade Organization in Seattle in late 1999. This outburst against globalization and corporatization led to a resurgence in anarchist, communist, and other radical left-wing movements. In France, growing disaffection among youth, immigrants, and the poor erupted in violence on October 27, 2005, after two teenagers were killed while allegedly hiding from police. Over the next month, riots—motivated by perceptions of racial discrimination and pervasive economic injustice—broke out all over the country.

When *The Coming Insurrection* was published in March 2007, the protest movement in France was gathering strength and momentum. The passage of a 2006 law deregulating labor inspired a wave of protest led by young people and students. Protesters occupied universities, rallied by the hundreds of thousands, went on strike, burned cars, and clashed with police. Eventually, the demonstrations were successful and the law was scrapped. Meanwhile, in a remote corner of France, near the village of Tarnac, Coupat and other alleged members of the Invisible Committee "created their very own ecocommunity and velvet underground, rehabbed an ancient cottage, reenergized a worn out bar, reorganized as a cooperative an adjacent *épicerie,* helped out with the running of a mobile library and *ciné-club,* and participated in the daily affairs of the traditionally communist commune," according to scholar Andy Merrifield in his 2010 piece in *Environment and Planning D.*

The Coming Insurrection draws on a history of radical writing and, in particular, on Guy Debord's *The Society of the Spectacle* (1967), which offers a harsh critique of modern consumerist, capitalist society: "All that once was directly lived has become mere representation." The authors of *The Coming Insurrection* echo Debord's critique of the artificiality and superficiality of contemporary life. The Invisible Committee's book also shows the influence of Giorgio Agamben's *The Coming Community* (1993). According to Merrifield, Agamben's book foresees and advocates the creation of human communities based on "'inessential commonality,' a belief that one's existence now hinges on one's possibility or potentiality, on what one can become in the future." Other important influences on *The Coming Insurrection* include theorists Martin Heidegger, Michel Foucault, Gilles Deleuze, and Félix Guattari.

The Coming Insurrection helped to inspire a range of polemical writings that accompanied protest movements in Europe and the United States. In 2011, for example, members of Occupy Wall Street issued their *Declaration of the Occupation of New York City,* a document that echoed disaffection expressed in *The Coming Insurrection.* It, too, was authored collectively and anonymously and advocated for an inclusive, communitarian response to the injustices of capitalism. As the Occupy movement spread around the world and anti-austerity riots broke out in Europe between 2008 and 2012, echoes of *The Coming Insurrection* could be detected in other writings that emerged.

THEMES AND STYLE

The central theme of *The Coming Insurrection* is that contemporary capitalist society is on the verge of total collapse. The manifesto's original version opens, "From whatever angle you approach it, the present offers no way out." The 2009 version begins with the same idea, expressed somewhat more emphatically: "Everyone agrees. It's about to explode." In both versions, *The Coming Insurrection* assuredly declares that the end of contemporary culture is nigh and proceeds to illustrate the causes of the coming collapse and to outline a procedure for creating a new communitarian system of social organization. The faults of capitalist society are described as seven hellish circles. These circles, which are given evocative subtitles such as "The environment is an industrial challenge," describe problematic aspects of the dominant culture, such as ecology and economics. The book then offers a series of steps for a violent insurrection that will leave power in "majestic ruins" and replace it with an egalitarian, inclusive, and communitarian society.

In terms of rhetorical style, *The Coming Insurrection* appeals to a sense of disenchantment and alienation so deep and pervasive that it has left people with nothing to lose. Written in a plural first-person voice that emphasizes its communal origins and aims, *The Coming Insurrection* harnesses despair, particularly that of youth, to the possibility of total revolutionary change. "Children of the metropolis," the authors write, "we offer this wager: that it's in the most profound deprivation of existence, perpetually stifled, perpetually conjured away, that the possibility of communism resides." The authors describe contemporary life in the bleakest of terms and offer their audience the possibility for effective defiance. "*GET GOING!*" the text implores. "*Get organized in order to no longer have to work.*" *The Coming Insurrection* depicts revolution as a means of overturning the bland despair of capitalist alienation.

Stylistically, *The Coming Insurrection* is relatively sober and conventional, in contrast with the bold radicalism of its argument. Rather than a rash call for action, the book makes a deliberate and often self-effacing case for its cause. "We can no longer even see

how an insurrection might begin," the authors concede, despite advocating for one. "We're setting out from a point of extreme isolation, of extreme weakness," they write. "Nothing appears less likely than an insurrection, but nothing is more necessary." By admitting their doubt and reluctance, the authors appeal to the perceived alienation of their youthful and disenfranchised audience. They also present the kind of sober analysis that legitimates the book's critique as something more substantial and rigorous than mere anger or disenchantment.

CRITICAL DISCUSSION

The Coming Insurrection immediately disturbed the French establishment and inspired the radical left wing. Of the response in France, the French newspaper *Le Monde* notes, "one hasn't seen power become so fearful of a book for a very long time." When the work was translated into English in 2009, it drew a strong response, particularly from the American right. Conservative commentator Glenn Beck, for example, featured *The Coming Insurrection* on his television show, calling it "a dangerous book" and warning viewers that it would help foment unrest in the United States. Less alarmist responses to the book were included in the *New York Times* and *Adbusters.* Among anarchist and other radical leftist groups, the book has been viewed alternately as inspirational and misguidedly simplistic.

As unrest has continued to spread in France, *The Coming Insurrection* has become increasingly prominent. Late in 2007, months after the book's publication, a new wave of riots started in France. Like the demonstrations of 2005 and 2006, the unrest was led by youths and was motivated by racial and economic injustice. On November 11, 2008, one year after the release of *The Coming Insurrection,* French police raided the rural commune run by the book's nine alleged authors. They were charged with "criminal association for the purpose of terrorist activity,"

The Coming Insurrection was written in the wake of riots in France in November 2005. Here, firefighters in Toulouse, France, try to put out car fires set by rioters. The riots started in suburbs, where many youth had no prospects. AP PHOTO/REMY GABALDA

PRIMARY SOURCE

THE COMING INSURRECTION

"I AM WHAT I AM." My body belongs to me.
I am me, you are you, and *something's wrong*. Mass personalization. Individualization of all conditions—life, work and misery. Diffuse schizophrenia. Rampant depression. Atomization into fine paranoiac particles. Hysterization of contact. The more I want to be me, the more I feel an emptiness. The more I express myself, the more I am drained. The more I run after myself, the more tired I get. We cling to our self like a coveted job title. We've become our own representatives in a strange commerce, guarantors of a personalization that feels, in the end, a lot more like an amputation. We insure ourselves to the point of bankruptcy, with a more or less disguised clumsiness....

The injunction, everywhere, to "be someone" maintains the pathological state that makes this society necessary. The injunction to be strong produces the very weakness by which it maintains itself, so that *everything seems to take on a therapeutic character,* even working, even love. All those "how's it goings?" that we exchange give the impression of a society composed of patients taking each other's temperatures. Sociability is now made up of a thousand little niches, a thousand little refuges where you can take shelter. Where it's always better than the bitter cold outside. Where everything's false, since it's all just a pretext for getting warmed up. Where nothing can happen since we're all too busy shivering silently together. Soon this society will only be held together by the mere tension of all the social atoms straining towards an illusory cure. It's a power plant that runs its turbines on a gigantic reservoir of unwept tears, always on the verge of spilling over.

...

France wouldn't be the land of anxiety pills that it's become, the paradise of anti-depressants, the Mecca of neurosis, if it weren't also the European champion of hourly productivity. Sickness, fatigue, depression, can be seen as the *individual* symptoms of what needs to be cured. They contribute to the maintenance of the existing order, to my docile adjustment to idiotic norms, and to the modernization of my crutches. They specify the selection of my opportune, compliant, and productive tendencies, as well as those that

must be gently discarded. "It's never too late to change, you know." But taken as *facts,* my failings can also lead to the dismantling of the hypothesis of the self. They then become acts of resistance in the current war. They become a rebellion and a force against everything that conspires to normalize us, to amputate us. The self is not something within us that is in a state of crisis; it is the form they mean to stamp upon us. They want to make our self something sharply defined, separate, assessable in terms of qualities, controllable, when in fact we are creatures among creatures, singularities among similars, living flesh weaving the flesh of the world. Contrary to what has been repeated to us since childhood, intelligence doesn't mean knowing how to adapt—or if that is a kind of intelligence, it's the intelligence of slaves. *Our inadaptability,* our fatigue, are only *problems* from the standpoint of what aims to subjugate us. They indicate rather a departure point, a meeting point, for new complicities. They reveal a landscape more damaged, but infinitely more sharable than all the fantasy lands this society maintains for its purposes.

...

In reality, the decomposition of all social forms is a blessing. It is for us the ideal condition for a wild, massive experimentation with new arrangements, new fidelities. The famous "parental resignation" has imposed on us a confrontation with the world that demands a precocious lucidity, and foreshadows lovely revolts to come. In the death of the couple, we see the birth of troubling forms of collective affectivity, now that sex is all used up and masculinity and femininity parade around in such moth-eaten clothes, now that three decades of non-stop pornographic innovation have exhausted all the allure of transgression and liberation. We count on making that which is unconditional in relationships the armor of a political solidarity as impenetrable to state interference as a gypsy camp. There is no reason that the interminable subsidies that numerous relatives are compelled to offload onto their proletarianized progeny can't become a form of patronage in favor of social subversion. "Becoming autonomous," could just as easily mean learning to fight in the street, to occupy empty houses, to cease working, to love each other madly, and to shoplift.

SOURCE: Semiotext(e), 2009, pp. 29–31.

but lack of evidence—including proof that they did, in fact, coauthor the text—forced the police to drop charges against eight of the nine. Coupat was held for six months and was put on trial, but he was eventually acquitted. The group became known in France as "the Tarnac Nine," and their seemingly unjust persecution—along with the fact that they seemingly "beat the system"—helped bring greater attention to *The Coming Insurrection* and its message of radical change.

Critics debate the importance of *The Coming Insurrection*'s message. In the *New Statesman,* Daniel Miller declares, "*The Coming Insurrection* is without a doubt the most thought-provoking radical text to be published in the past ten years. It deserves to be read and discussed." Not all scholars have been as impressed with the work. Writing in *Anarchist Studies,* Iain McKay argues that "the work is lacking in real analysis and strategy" and that it offers "a remarkably reformist and quietist vision of dropping-out and tending your allotment." Other commentators have placed the manifesto's message within a historical context of radical left-wing writing. In a 2012 review for *Critical Quarterly,* Timothy Ivison writes of the apparent influence of the Situationists and argues that *The Coming Insurrection* "clearly attempts to transcend the stultification of radical history with a new programme of intervention."

BIBLIOGRAPHY

Sources

Debord, Guy. *The Society of the Spectacle.* New York: Zone Books, 1994. Print.

Invisible Committee. *The Coming Insurrection.* Cambridge: MIT P, 2009. Print.

Ivison, Timothy. Rev. of *The Situationists and the City,* ed. Tom McDonough; *The Coming Insurrection,* by the Invisible Committee; and *50 Years of Recuperation of the Situationist International. Critical Quarterly* 54.2 (2012): 92-97. Print.

McKay, Iain. "The Coming Insurrection." *Anarchist Studies* 19.1 (2011): 124+. *Academic OneFile.* Web. 23 Aug. 2012.

Merrifield, Andy. "The Coming of *The Coming Insurrection*: Notes on a Politics of Neocommunism." *Environment and Planning D: Society and Space* 28.2 (2010): 202-16. Web. 23 Aug. 2012.

Miller, Daniel. "Back to Meinhof." *New Statesman* [1996] 19 Oct. 2009: 52+. *Academic OneFile.* Web. 23 Aug. 2012.

Further Reading

Agamben, Giorgio. *The Coming Community.* Minneapolis: U of Minnesota P, 1993. Print.

Amster, Randall. *Anarchism Today.* Santa Barbara: Praeger, 2012. Print.

Barney, Darin. "'Excuse Us if We Don't Give a Fuck': The (Anti-) Political Career of Participation." *Jeunesse: Young People, Texts, Cultures* 2.2 (2010): 138+. *Academic OneFile.* Web. 23 Aug. 2012.

Hoffman, Robert, ed. *Anarchism.* New York: Atherton, 1970. Print.

May, Todd. *The Political Philosophy of Poststructuralist Anarchism.* University Park: Pennsylvania State UP, 1994. Print.

Perlin, Terry M. *Contemporary Anarchism.* New Brunswick: Transaction Books, 1979. Print.

Theodore McDermott

LE MANIFESTE DE MONTRÉAL

AIDS ACTION NOW!, AIDS Coalition to Unleash Power

❖ *Key Facts*

Time Period:
Late 20th Century

Movement/Issue:
AIDS treatment

Place of Publication:
United States

**Language of
Publication:**
French; English; Spanish

OVERVIEW

Jointly issued by Toronto-based AIDS ACTION NOW! (AAN!) and the New York chapter of AIDS Coalition to Unleash Power (ACT UP), *Le Manifeste de Montréal* (1989) is an international bill of rights for people living with AIDS that outlines the responsibilities of governments, international organizations, corporations, health care agencies, and private citizens who work with or care for people living with the disease. The manifesto, which builds upon the demands made during the founding of AAN! in February 1988, was presented at the Palais de congrès in Montreal before the opening of the Fifth International AIDS Conference. A response to public misconceptions about HIV/AIDS and a critique of the drug testing and approval process, the manifesto was intended to raise international awareness of the plight of people living with the disease and to lobby for proper health care and ethical treatment. Although the manifesto sought to increase public awareness of the needs of all people infected with HIV/AIDS, it also urged recognition of the diverse populations affected by the disease—including prisoners, intravenous drug users, and women—and thus drew attention to the broad political and economic ramifications of HIV/AIDS and its treatment. Addressing the problem of HIV/AIDS, as the manifesto makes clear, was going to require political and social action, not just scientific research. Addressed to the international community at large, the document lists ten major demands that seek to reform the global community's understanding of HIV/AIDS and outline how those living with the disease should be treated.

Emboldened by the manifesto's international release, activists picketed pharmaceutical company Bristol Myers, insisting it make didanosine, an antiretroviral drug that helps control HIV, available for public use. The company soon acceded to activists' demands, and Canadian health minister Perrin Beatty announced funding for a national treatment registry. In the United States, members of ACT UP staged a series of public demonstrations calling for affordable HIV/AIDS medication, prompting pharmaceutical manufacturer Burroughs Wellcome to lower the price of its antiretroviral AZT. *Le Manifeste de Montréal* is known as the first proclamation to address the concerns of people living with HIV/AIDS and has influenced the missions of many world organizations, such as the United Nations Programme on HIV/AIDS.

HISTORICAL AND LITERARY CONTEXT

Le Manifeste de Montréal responds to medical neglect and cultural marginalization experienced by people living with HIV/AIDS during the 1980s. The Centers for Disease Control and Prevention (CDC) first recognized HIV/AIDS in 1981. One year later, the Public Health Agency of Canada (PHAC) recorded that country's first case of HIV/AIDS. In reaction to the worldwide epidemic, the International AIDS Society (IAS) organized the International AIDS Conference in 1985 to discuss health and developmental issues related to the retrovirus. Motivated by the problems faced by people living with the disease and the perceived inaction of IAS, CDC, and PHAC, Michael Lynch organized AAN! and Herb Spiers formed ACT UP two years after the first conference.

In the period between the formation of AAN! and ACT UP in 1987 and the 1989 International AIDS Conference, government support of people living with HIV/AIDS was minimal, and scientific research aimed at finding a cure progressed sluggishly. AAN! and ACT UP sought to bring the matter to public attention through a series of pickets, protests, and boycotts. Under the guidance of Lynch and Spiers, activists formed a coalition in early 1989 and cooperatively composed the original drafts of *Le Manifeste de Montréal* in New York and Toronto. On May 22, 1989, Spiers sent a revised draft to AAN! member Chuck Grochmal for final proofing; two weeks later ACT UP member Conyers Thompson read it at the opening ceremonies of the fifth annual International AIDS Conference.

Le Manifeste de Montréal builds upon "The Gay Rights Freud," an article Lynch and Spiers wrote collaboratively. Published in the journal *Body Politic* in 1977, the article outlines the manner in which Freud opposed social policies that were detrimental to men and women who identified as homosexual. The article references Freud's "Letter to a Mother of a Homosexual," in which the famed psychoanalyst claims that homosexuality "is nothing to be ashamed of, no vice, no degradation, it cannot be classified as an illness." In a plea for empathy, Lynch and Spiers cite Freud's *Three Essays on the Theory of Sexuality,* which expresses the belief that all humans express both homosexual and heterosexual libidinous attachments. The influence of Lynch and Spiers's earlier document can be seen in *Le Manifeste de Montréal*'s call for basic human rights for people living with HIV/AIDS regardless of sexual orientation.

In the years that followed, *Le Manifeste de Montréal* influenced the language of many international HIV/AIDS organizations' mission statements. One goal of the United Nations Programme on HIV/AIDS, for example, is to unite the efforts of "civil society, national governments, the private sector, global institutions and people living with and most affected by HIV." This goal echoes the collaborative nature of and global concerns addressed in *Le Manifeste de Montréal*. In *Manifestoes* (1999), Janet Lyon argues that AAN! and ACT UP's jointly composed document "demonstrates the force that can be delivered by a manifesto's *provisional* collectivity" by creating a contingent and diverse "we." The force of the manifesto stems in part from the fact that its authors drafted the document in three languages and from its call for direct action through public agitation.

THEMES AND STYLE

Thematically, *Le Manifeste de Montréal* provides a united voice for people living with HIV/AIDS around the world in an effort to attain the same ethical medical treatment and basic human rights afforded to those who have not contracted the disease. The manifesto's preamble states that HIV/AIDS "is a world wide epidemic affecting every country. People are infected, sick and struggling to stay alive. Their voices must be heard and their special needs met." The document's architects intended the voices of those living with the disease to reach "all peoples, governments international bodies, multinational corporations, and health care providers" in order to confront HIV/AIDS "positively," declaring that the global community has a "social and moral obligation" to listen to and carry out the manifesto's demands. To this end, the document continually addresses and references the "international" community, not only in its preamble but within each subsequent demand.

In order to achieve its rhetorical effect, the manifesto emphasizes the disease's ubiquity, calling it "a world wide epidemic affecting every country" that should be a concern for all citizens worldwide. Likewise, the document attempts to dispel the notion that people living with HIV/AIDS are a threat to society, stating that the disease "is not highly infectious." Moreover, *Le Manifeste de Montréal* argues that people infected with the disease are no different, fundamentally, from those who have not been infected; as such, the manifesto states that the global community should "acknowledge and preserve the humanity of people with HIV." The manifesto's third demand elaborates upon these basic human rights by outlining fourteen sub-points, focusing on "anti-discrimination legislation," "active involvement" by people living with the disease in policy-making that relates to HIV/AIDS, "guaranteed access" to medical treatments and facilities, as well as "full legal recognition of lesbian and gay relationships."

TIMOTHY RAY BROWN: THE BERLIN PATIENT

One of the central issues addressed by *Le Manifeste de Montréal* is access to experimental treatments that may lead to a cure or help those living with HIV/AIDS manage side effects more easily. Since the document's release, the scientific community and pharmaceutical companies have been more understanding of this demand. In 2007 and 2008, Timothy Ray Brown, a German man infected with HIV, received two bone marrow transplants from a donor whose genes contained a mutation that made him immune to HIV/AIDS because he lacked the necessary receptors, CD4 and CCR5, for the virus to gain entry to his cells.

After the transplants, the HIV in Brown's body disappeared completely, even though he stopped taking anti-HIV medicines. Doctors and researchers declared him cured. While new tests in 2012 showed minute traces of partial HIV cells in some of his tissue, those remnants were incapable of producing a new infection. In a February 2009 article in the *New England Journal of Medicine* titled "Long-Term Control of HIV by *CCR5* Delta32/Delta32 Stem-Cell Transplantation," researchers address Brown's case and claim that the key to controlling and curing HIV/AIDS resides in further experimentation with these receptors. The article's authors encourage "further investigation of the development of CCR5-targeted treatment options."

The authors of *Le Manifeste de Montréal* composed the document as a series of terse, direct statements that clearly articulate their demands. Because of this the document evinces a sense of authority, confidence, and urgency. Most importantly, the manifesto's authors created three versions of the document: one in English, one in French, and one in Spanish. The simultaneous release of a single text composed in three of the world's most prominent languages further emphasizes the international agenda AAN! and ACT UP wanted to promote.

CRITICAL DISCUSSION

The initial response by the groups associated with *Le Manifeste de Montréal* and those sympathetic to its cause were not critical or literary; instead, reactions took the form of a radical activism, including pickets and protests that targeted major pharmaceutical companies, such as Burroughs Wellcome, and the U.S. Food and Drug Administration. Protesters demanded easier access to antiretroviral drugs and other medical treatments that curbed the effects of HIV/AIDS and made living with the disease less difficult. In the United States, members of ACT UP chained themselves to the VIP balcony on the floor of the New York Stock Exchange, bringing trading to a halt, and called for affordable HIV/AIDS medications. Four days later Burroughs Wellcome lowered the price of its antiretroviral drug AZT by 20 percent. Being one of the first public declarations of the rights of people living with HIV/AIDS, *Le Manifeste*

An AIDS activist holds a sign during an ACT UP demonstration in San Francisco, California, on June 25, 1990. © CHUCK NACKE/ALAMY

manifesto's influence in raising awareness of the ethical issues surrounding the treatment and care of those living with the disease. *The Ontario Accord,* a 2012 joint statement released by Greater Involvement of People with HIV/AIDS and Meaningful Involvement of People with HIV/AIDS, acknowledged the role that *Le Manifeste de Montréal* played in "the foundational work that continues to inspire us," which the groups also recognized in following "the precedent of naming our work after its geographic birthplace." Similarly, in a February 2012 issue of *The Connection,* a Canada-based newsletter addressing issues related to HIV/AIDS, the creation of *Le Manifeste de Montréal* is identified as "a defining moment" in the history of HIV/AIDS activism that demonstrated the power of "individual and collective voices" and their ability to "profoundly influence subsequent approaches to HIV research."

BIBLIOGRAPHY

Sources

Brier, Jennifer. *Infectious Ideas: U.S. Political Responses to the AIDS Crisis.* Chapel Hill: U of North Carolina P, 2009. Print.

Freud, Sigmund. "Letter to a Mother of a Homosexual." *American Journal of Psychiatry* 107 (1951): 787. Print.

Greater Involvement of People with HIV/AIDS and Meaningful Involvement of People with HIV/AIDS. *The Ontario Accord.* 2012. Ontario AIDS Network, 2013. Web. 31 Jan. 2013.

Joint United Nations Programme on HIV/AIDS. *International Guidelines on HIV/AIDS and Human Rights: 2006 Consolidated Version.* Geneva: Office of the High Commission on Human Rights, 2006. Web. 5 June 2012.

Katz, Jonathan Ned. "Herbert Spiers: November 8, 1945-March 2, 2011." *OutHistory.org.* Out History, 8 Oct. 2011. Web. 1 June 2012.

Lester, Brian. "The Ontario Accord: Commitment to GIPA/MIPA." *The Connection.* Regional HIV/AIDS Connection, Feb. 2012. Web. 5 June 2012.

Lyon, Janet. *Manifestoes: Provocations of the Modern.* Ithaca: Cornell UP, 1999. Print.

Further Reading

Epstein, Steve. *Impure Science: AIDS, Activism, and the Politics of Knowledge (Medicine and Society).* Berkeley: U of California P, 2006. Print.

Freud, Sigmund. *Three Essays on the Theory of Sexuality.* New York: Basic, 2000. Print.

Herman, Didi, and Carl Stychin. *Legal Inversions: Lesbians, Gay Men, and the Politics of Law.* Philadelphia: Temple UP, 1995. Print.

Pepin, Jacques. *The Origin of AIDS.* New York: Cambridge UP, 2011. Print.

Silversides, Ann. *AIDS Activist: Michael Lynch and the Politics of Community.* Toronto: Between the Lines, 2003. Print.

Smith, Raymond and Patricia Siplon. *Drugs into Bodies: Global AIDS Treatment Activism.* Santa Barbara: Praeger, 2006. Print.

de Montréal influenced subsequent documents as well. For example, in 1992 the AIDS Consortium, a South African human rights organization, wrote its Charter of Rights for people living with HIV. Drafted by Edwin Cameron, Edward Swanson, and Mahendra Chetty, the document drew heavily from AAN! and ACT UP's manifesto. In 2006 the United Nations released its *International Guidelines on HIV/AIDS and Human Rights,* wherein it recognizes *Le Manifeste de Montréal* as a document of importance in advocating for the rights of those infected. In her book *Infectious Ideas: U.S. Political Responses to the AIDS Crisis* (2009), Jennifer Brier argues that *Le Manifeste de Montréal* exemplifies the way in which AIDS activism "became a central site for opposition to modern conservatism."

While scholars have conducted little research on *Le Manifeste de Montréal* outside of the brief analysis provided by Lyon in *Manifestoes,* many groups advocating for HIV/AIDS research have acknowledged the

Joshua Ware

Manifesto of the 121

Maurice Blanchot, Dionys Mascolo, Jean Schuster

OVERVIEW

Written primarily by Maurice Blanchot with Dionys Mascolo and Jean Schuster, *Declaration of the Right to Insubordination in the Algerian War* (1960), commonly known as the *Manifesto of the 121,* condemns the ongoing Algerian War as a racist and imperialist effort by the French to oppress the Algerian people. The war began in 1954 when Algerian Muslims revolted against the French government, which reacted violently in order to maintain control of the North African nation, the largest and only remaining French colony. Under French rule, Muslims had been segregated from Europeans and treated as an inferior class, and French colonists, seeking to preserve their wealth and property, had worked to prevent pro-Muslim reforms. Primarily addressed to the French people, the manifesto affirms the right of French citizens to aid Algerians in their struggle for independence and declares that French citizens have the right to refuse to participate in acts of aggression.

Many French intellectuals and public figures embraced the *Manifesto of the 121,* although the document also met with widespread criticism. Some supporters of Algerian independence criticized the manifesto's endorsement of violence. The French government accused the signatories of treason for openly opposing the army and sanctioning desertion, acts of insubordination, and assistance for the Algerian nationalist movement. The declaration even inspired a countermanifesto affirming the French presence in Algeria and denouncing the signatories of the *Manifesto of the 121.* Blanchot, preferring the solidarity of authorship by an anonymous collective, denied his principal role in the composition of the declaration, which went through multiple revisions at the hands of various authors. Today the manifesto is considered a key document in fomenting French resistance to the Algerian War.

HISTORICAL AND LITERARY CONTEXT

The *Manifesto of the 121* responds to the French colonial presence in Algeria and the French army's use of violence and torture during the Algerian War. After the French invasion of Algeria in 1830, European settlers, known as *pieds-noirs,* formed a large, vocal, and deeply entrenched community. By the outbreak of the Algerian War in 1954, French public opinion on Algeria was widely governed by the idea, expressed by French minister François Mitterrand, that "Algeria is France." However, the ongoing occupation primarily served the interests of the army and the *pied-noir* community, particularly as the conflict became increasingly protracted and brutal. French citizens who criticized the army's use of torture, and the colonial project more broadly, were condemned for their opposition, and French soldiers who committed acts of insubordination or deserted were denounced and imprisoned.

When the manifesto was written, French political discourse focused on expressing unity with French Algeria and left little space for support of Algerian independence. Moreover, any division in public opinion was largely suppressed by the press and other official institutions. The manifesto was released in July 1960, shortly before the September start of the Jeanson trial, in which nineteen French citizens and six Algerians were accused of assisting the Algerian National Liberation Front (FLN), a revolutionary group dedicated to obtaining independence from France. The signatories' support of these "suitcase carriers," so named for the papers and funds the rebels transported for the Algerian resistance movement, generated much of the controversy surrounding the manifesto.

The *Manifesto of the 121* distinguishes itself from earlier protest manifestos that represent a call to action in that it does not seek to effect immediate political change. Rather, it presents a judgment about the right to refuse and emphasizes the personal responsibility of each individual to determine his or her own position. The declaration's central concern with the right to refuse echoes Blanchot's "*Le Refus*" ("Refusal"), published in *Le 14 juillet* in 1958, disputing the legitimacy of French president Charles de Gaulle's return to power in May 1958. In the statement Blanchot advocates refusal and the power of saying no as an exercise of political power.

Although there was massive debate over the declaration, the text was not widely published within France. Dissidents mostly circulated the manifesto in secret because Blanchot and other signatories had been accused of treason and charged with—in

❖ *Key Facts*

Time Period:
Mid-20th Century

Movement/Issue:
Algerian War; Algerian independence; Colonialism

Place of Publication:
France

Language of Publication:
French

MAURICE BLANCHOT: POLITICAL WRITINGS

Maurice Blanchot was the author of eleven novels, including *Thomas the Obscure* (1941), and of numerous essays, articles, and fragments. While his early work reveals Far-Right leanings, his later work demonstrates a shift to the Far Left. All of his writings reflect his commitment to dissidence and refusal. His signature on numerous manifestos throughout his life—from *Manifesto of the 121* in 1960 to the *Not in Our Name* petition against the Iraq War in 2002, which he signed shortly before his death the following year—indicate a lifelong commitment to political writing.

However, Blanchot perceived his body of work as decidedly nonpolitical. In published fragments, he states that he signed the *Manifesto of the 121* "as a nonpolitical writer led to comment seriously and firmly on essential problems." Unlike other political writers of his day, he was concerned less with applying a specific political ideology than with creating a paradigm by which citizens could meaningfully refuse or affirm political events. Zakir Paul in *Maurice Blanchot: Political Writings, 1953-1993* (2010) explains, "For Blanchot, 'political writing' has little to do with lending one's signature to a cause as a writer; rather, it is an attempt to find the impossible language that would allow one to refuse and contest certain political events while watchfully preserving the possibility of others."

Blanchot's words—"inciting insubordination and desertion" and "provoking soldiers to disobedience." Although the charges were later dropped, the 121 original signatories were forbidden from appearing on national radio and television, and the major French daily newspaper *Le Figaro* could not publish their writings. In October 1960 a countermanifesto titled "Manifesto of French Intellectuals" was published supporting French Algeria and condemning the signatories "professors of treason." Today the *Manifesto of the 121* is often read in relationship to its well-known signatories, such as André Breton, Marguerite Duras, and Jean-Paul Sartre, as a public declaration of values in the face of government repression.

THEMES AND STYLE

The central theme of the *Manifesto of the 121* is that the absolute right to refuse transcends political context and derives its legitimacy not from a greater power or authority, such as the law, but from the notion of individual responsibility. The declaration does not directly address the men and women faced with the moral dilemma posed by the Algerian War, who must either signal their consent through their participation in acts of torture and unjust aggression or indicate their refusal through insubordination. Rather, the manifesto targets institutions, such as

judiciary bodies and the press, that play a role in the formation of public opinion and that condemn citizens who choose refusal. According to the manifesto, the signatories "have the duty to intervene, not to give advice to men who have to decide personally when faced with such grave problems, but to ask those who judge them not to be taken in by the equivocal aspect of words and values."

The manifesto achieves its rhetorical effect by outlining the injustices that the French have committed in order to maintain control over Algeria. Although the ongoing conflict in Algeria is a war of independence for the Algerians, the declaration categorizes the war from the French perspective as "neither a war of conquest nor a war of 'national defense.'" The *Manifesto of the 121* argues that the military presence continues to serve solely the limited interests of the army and the *pied-noir* community: "Today, it is mainly the will of the army that maintains this criminal and absurd combat, and this army, by the political role that many of its high ranking representatives make it play, sometimes acts openly and violently outside of any legality." Because of the army's adoption of a political role, which Blanchot elsewhere likens to a political party, each Frenchman has the right to refuse to participate in and to openly oppose the military.

Stylistically, the manifesto is distinguished by its direct language and probing tone. The declaration needles the reader with rhetorical questions to highlight the moral dilemma presented by the Algerian War: "when, through the will of those who use it as an instrument of racist or ideological domination, the army places itself in a state of open or latent revolt against democratic institutions, doesn't revolt against the army take on a new meaning?" Invoking the trauma of World War II, the declaration asks, "Is it necessary to recall that fifteen years after the destruction of the Hitlerian order, French militarism, as a result of the exigencies of this war, has managed to reinstate torture and to make it an institution in Europe once again?" By probing the logic of French involvement in Algeria, the authors model the kind of independent inquiry and judgment they urge French citizens to exercise.

CRITICAL DISCUSSION

When the *Manifesto of the 121* was first published in 1960, reactions to the declaration were mixed. By October the number of signatories had grown to more than four hundred and included such luminaries as Simone de Beauvoir, Henri Lefebvre, and Sartre. However, other intellectuals, such as philosopher Maurice Merleau-Ponty, refused to add their names to the declaration because of the signatories' support for the collaborators charged in the Jeanson trial and for the FLN, which used torture and terror tactics. Michel Cournot, a French writer and journalist, denounced the *Manifesto of the 121* as bourgeois, arguing that its elevated language and abstract message made it inaccessible to the proletariat and therefore ineffectual.

After Algeria gained its independence from France in 1962, the declaration remained an important historical and legal document. Through its justification of refusal and dissidence, it effectively contested the idea that only a homogeneous French identity could provide a strong foundation for Algeria. In a 2004 essay for *Journal of Law and Society,* Patrick Hanafin observes, "this document [unsettled] the stabilised political order" and represented "in counter-opposition to the writing or inscribing of a community through the written constitution … an exscribing, an unwriting, an undoing." Through its focus on dissidence as the foundation for community, the declaration challenged the government's obsession with unity and undermined the strength of political authority by locating the right to insubordination outside of the law, as well as outside any formal system or moral code. Thus, by shifting the discourse from civic duty to civic rights, and by emphasizing personal responsibility, the manifesto became—according to Leslie Hill in *Blanchot: Extreme Contemporary* (1997)—"one of the first texts, in France, to contest and rethink the figure of the intellectual as universal conscious."

Recent scholarship has focused on the significance of the *Manifesto of the 121* to human rights discourse. As Hanafin explains, the declaration expresses "an absolute right based on an impossible responsibility to the other to whom we may have no duty to defend." Such a formulation transcends the traditional concept of universal human rights, which depends on a greater moral or political power for its legitimization; thus, human rights are limited by political and moral power. In an essay for the *Routledge International Handbook of Cosmopolitan Studies* (2012), Hanafin writes, "What Blanchot was enacting here was a right dislodged from the repressive state apparatus, an example of [the] 'right to have rights.'"

BIBLIOGRAPHY

Sources

Hanafin, Patrick. "A Right to Politics? Towards an Agonistic Cosmopolitics of Human Rights." *Routledge International Handbook of Cosmopolitan Studies.* Ed. Gerard Delanty. New York: Routledge, 2012. 326-39. Print.

———. "The Writer's Refusal and Law's Malady." *Journal of Law and Society* 31.1 (2004): 3-14. Print.

Hart, Kevin. "Foreword: The Friendship of the No." *Maurice Blanchot: Political Writings, 1953-1993.* Trans. Zakir Paul. New York: Fordham UP, 2010. xi-xxx. Print.

Hill, Leslie. *Blanchot: Extreme Contemporary.* New York: Routledge, 1997. Print.

Naylor, Phillip C. *France and Algeria: A History of Decolonization and Transformation.* Gainesville: U of Florida P, 2000. Print.

Paul, Zakir. "Introduction: 'Affirming the Rupture.'" *Maurice Blanchot: Political Writings, 1953-1993.* Trans. Zakir Paul. New York: Fordham UP, 2010. xxxi-lvi. Print.

Further Reading

Blanchot, Maurice. *Maurice Blanchot: Political Writings, 1953-1993.* Trans. Zakir Paul. New York: Fordham UP, 2010. Print.

De Baecque, Antoine, and Serge Toubiana. "The Manifesto of the 121." *Truffaut: A Biography.* Berkeley: U of California P, 2000. 165-67. Print.

Horne, Alistair. *A Savage War of Peace: Algeria 1954-1962.* London: Macmillan, 1977. Print.

Schalk, David L. *War and the Ivory Tower: Algeria and Vietnam.* New York: Oxford UP, 1991. Print.

Ungar, Steven. *Scandal and Aftereffect: Blanchot and France since 1930.* Minneapolis: U of Minnesota P, 1995. Print.

While the *Manifesto of the 121* supported the Algerians and anticolonialism during the Algerian War, other organizations, including OAR (Organisation de l'armée secrète, or Organization of the Secret Army), were dedicated to preventing Algeria from seceding as a French colony. This OAR propaganda poster depicts an Algerian man on the left and a French man on the right, calling them brothers. KHARBINE-TAPABOR/THE ART ARCHIVE AT ART RESOURCE, NY

Allison Blecker

Nanterre Manifesto

Anonymous

✧ *Key Facts*

Time Period:
Mid-20th Century

Movement/Issue:
Student movement;
Socialist cultural
revolution; May of '68

Place of Publication:
France

**Language of
Publication:**
French

OVERVIEW

Written on June 11, 1968, by an anonymous group of French students at Nanterre University near Paris, the *Nanterre Manifesto* describes the impetus for the student and worker strikes of May 1968 and calls for continued cooperation between workers and students in a revolution to end political and cultural repression. The Interdisciplinary Committee of the Faculty of Letters and Social Science of Nanterre, a group of students and teachers that occupied the university following the strikes of May, composed the document as a committee report to help restructure the university. Although the text primarily focuses on the structure of the university, its recognition of the importance of the working-class struggle attests to its broad cultural purview. Central to the report are six points that outline a critique of the hierarchical relations in modern society and aim to build solidarity between workers and students in their shared goal of cultural revolution.

The *Nanterre Manifesto* was one of many committee reports written in the occupied French universities following the strikes of May 1968. As such, it provoked little response outside of the stakeholders directly involved with the political restructuring of Nanterre University. Earlier, however, in the winter and spring of 1968, students at the university had played a critical role in the development of the revolutionary student movement by organizing massive strikes and occupations and leveling demands for reform at the administration. Today the *Nanterre Manifesto* is recognized as among the many important political documents of the cultural revolution of the late 1960s.

HISTORICAL AND LITERARY CONTEXT

The *Nanterre Manifesto* responds to the economic and educational problems facing France following World War II. Just prior to the war, student enrollment at French universities was estimated at sixty thousand. By 1967 enrollment had grown more than tenfold to 750,000, a situation that led to one of the worst instructor-to-student ratios in Western Europe, as well as to authoritarian decrees to alter egalitarian admissions procedures and the creation of suburban universities such as Nanterre, a place noted for its industrial design and absence of windows. Moreover, in 1953, fifteen years prior to the

publication of the report, millions of striking workers successfully defended their retirement and promotion benefits, a victory that encouraged unionism and mass protest.

By the time the *Nanterre Manifesto* was written, the events of May 1968 had already erupted. Only a few months prior, on March 22, Daniel Cohn-Bendit and twenty other students at Nanterre had invaded and occupied the administration building. By April 2 the general assembly of the student movement at Nanterre had attracted 1,500 students, and by early May the student strikes had spread to other universities, attracting more than 25,000 students. Tens of thousands of wage earners marched in unity with the students against state repression and for better wages and working conditions. On May 13 all of the major unions called for a general strike, effectively shutting down the country—though the rumor of military intervention and the Communist Party's agreement with French president Charles de Gaulle's call for new elections caused the majority of the strikes and protests to end within a few months.

The *Nanterre Manifesto* draws on a long history of revolutionary manifestos that can be traced back to Karl Marx and Friedrich Engels's *The Communist Manifesto* (1848). The report's most immediate literary precedent is another manifesto composed at Nanterre following the occupation of the administration building on March 22. One hundred forty-two participants in the occupation, including Cohn-Bendit, approved the *Manifesto of the 142* (1968), which attacks the state's use of a repressive police force against political protestors and vows to retaliate against these acts of repression with increasing force. Thus, by criticizing the French state for its repressive policies, the *Manifesto of the 142* articulates many of the concerns of the *Nanterre Manifesto*.

In the decades following its issuance, the *Nanterre Manifesto* has served as a point of populist pride among participants in the student movements of the late 1960s. Although it is infrequently referenced, the movement in which it played a part has been the subject of many popular books and films that focus not only on the political events and actors but also on the radical milieu of 1968. With the passage of the Law of Orientation, which restructured higher education in France, the revolution helped secure university reforms such as decentralized governance and the encouragement of multidisciplinary studies. Today the *Nanterre Manifesto* commands interest as a significant document in the history of 1968.

THEMES AND STYLE

The central theme of the *Nanterre Manifesto* is that the organization of contemporary French society has created political oppression, socioeconomic exploitation, and cultural alienation. With the force of the May revolution behind it, the report argues that political and social institutions have not been alone in reinforcing this subjugation. The text states, "Repression is not only a question of police clubs or electoral trickery, nor even exclusively a question of pressures on salaries and work outputs"; rather "it permeates the content and forms of culture." The document goes on to critique the ruling class's use of media to establish and consolidate power, implying that the revolution, if it hopes to succeed, must comprise physical struggle, illegality, strike, and occupation, as well as a revolution of the word.

The *Nanterre Manifesto* achieves its rhetorical effect by appealing to a union of students and workers. During the May crisis, the French Communist Party denounced student activists in an attempt to maintain its claim as the primary leftist revolutionary force (however, the party would later undermine its credibility by agreeing to participate in President de Gaulle's June 23 election). The *Nanterre Manifesto* courts the involvement of the proletariat by cataloging their accomplishments: "The workers contribute their experience and their denunciation of exploitation." The report also attempts to establish the necessity of the student movement, which aids the working class in establishing a theoretical dimension, a "denunciation of culture and values," that prevents the revolution from becoming "confined" to mere professional demands. It seeks an "embryonic union" that "is not a subordination, either of workers to students, or student to workers"; rather through collaboration it aims to achieve its revolutionary objectives.

Stylistically, the *Nanterre Manifesto* is distinguished by its formality. Written as a report, it demands credibility as an official document. The text seeks to use its validity as a platform to launch the criticism that will "subvert the whole academic institution from the functions assigned to it by the ruling class." By drafting the report as part of a parity committee including students and teachers, its authors achieve one of their revolutionary objectives: to subvert the "hierarchical relationship between master and disciple."

CRITICAL DISCUSSION

When the *Nanterre Manifesto* was first published, it received little attention except as an addendum to the events of the revolution of May 1968, which provoked interest and criticism around the world.

DANIEL COHN-BENDIT: RADICAL STUDENT

Born in 1945 to German Jewish parents in a newly liberated France, Daniel Cohn-Bendit was raised in a family whose members prided themselves for their leftist politics. According to Mark Kurlansky in *1968: The Year That Rocked the World* (2005), Cohn-Bendit's father had been an attorney in Germany known for defending left-wing dissidents. However, the family was forced to leave when Hitler took power in 1933. They survived the war and eventually settled in Paris.

In 1959 Cohn-Bendit returned to Germany, and by 1960 he had become a German citizen in order to avoid French military service. Four years later he received a scholarship to study sociology in France at Nanterre University. At Nanterre he became instrumental in the foundation of radical anarchist groups. He helped lead the charge in the occupation of the administration building in March of 1968 and played a role in the composition of the *Manifesto of the 142*. His sense of humor and charm made him something of a celebrity in the media, and by the time the strikes broke out in May of that year, Cohn-Bendit was one of the most important and recognizable student radicals in France. In the 1990s, decades after his political involvement, he became a television talk show host.

Michael Seidman in *The Imaginary Revolution: Parisian Students and Workers in 1968* (2004) recalls how in the 1968 *L'Explosion de mai,* journalists Lucien Roux and René Backmann speak, perhaps prematurely, of the profound impact of the crisis: "In several weeks everything—the old ways, habits, customs, and ideas—collapsed…. From now on, French history after World War II will be divided into pre- and post- 1968." Alain Touraine, a sociologist at Nanterre, echoes those sentiments, arguing that students and workers had reinvented the class struggle by battling the contemporary French technocracy. Others, such as the French sociologist Raymond Aron, see the revolution's goals as ridiculous and impossible.

After the events of May 1968, the *Nanterre Manifesto* remained an important source of political inspiration among students. While many of the demands and hopes of the May crisis led to little change, the university saw significant reform under the leadership of Edgar Faure, the newly named minister of education. His Law of Orientation established many of the objectives set forth in the *Nanterre Manifesto,* such as student participation in university decision making, albeit in more moderate forms. In the decades since the report was first published, it has been the subject of a small body of criticism that has considered its legacy in historical and political terms.

Most scholarship has focused on the development of the student movement leading up to the crisis of May 1968 but not specifically on the *Nanterre*

At a 1968 student protest in Paris, participants carry a banner exalting the rights of Nanterre University. MARIO DE BIASI;SERGIO DEL GRANDE/MONDADORI PORTFOLIO VIA GETTY IMAGES

Manifesto. Seidman uses official university and police archives to establish a narrative of social unrest among students in the early 1960s that culminates with the participation of working-class strikers during the revolution of 1968: "The radical students who started the chain of events that led to the greatest strike wave in French history lashed out against capitalism, the state, and the property." Julian Bourg's *From Revolution to Ethics* (2007) traces a shift and growth in ethical discourse in contemporary theory following the events of May 1968, while Kristin Ross takes a historiographical stance in her book *May'68 and Its Afterlives* (2010), in which she argues that "'the events of May'68'

cannot now be considered separately from the social memory and forgetting that surround them."

BIBLIOGRAPHY

Sources

Bourg, Julian. *From Revolution to Ethics: May 1968 and Contemporary French Thought.* Montreal: McGill-Queen's UP, 2007. Print.

Kapote, Christopher, and Paul Zolbrod. *The Rhetoric of Revolution.* Toronto: MacMillan, 1970. Print.

Kurlansky, Mark. *1968: The Year That Rocked the World.* New York: Random House, 2005. Print.

Ross, Kristin. *May '68 and Its Afterlives.* Chicago: U of Chicago P, 2010. *E-brary.* Web. 22 Oct. 2012.

Seidman, Michael. *The Imaginary Revolution: Parisian Students and Workers in 1968.* New York: Berghahn, 2004. Print.

Further Reading

Caldwell, Wilber. *1968: Dreams of Revolution.* New York: Algora, 2009. Print.

Fraser, Ronald. *1968: A Student Generation in Revolt.* London: Chatto & Windus, 1988. Print.

Horn, Gard-Ranier. *The Spirit of '68: Rebellion in Western Europe and North America, 1956-1976.* Oxford: Oxford UP, 2007. *E-brary.* Web. 22 Oct. 2012.

Katsiaficas, George. *The Imagination of the New Left: A Global Analysis of 1968.* Boston: South End, 1987. Print.

Quattrocchi, Angelo, and Tom Nairn. *The Beginning of the End.* London: Verso, 1998. Print.

Gregory Luther

ON THE POVERTY OF STUDENT LIFE

Association Fédérative Générale des Étudiants de Strasbourg

OVERVIEW

On the Poverty of Student Life (*De la misère en milieu étudiant*) is a situationist political pamphlet first published by the Association Fédérative Générale des Étudiants de Strasbourg (AFGES) in 1966. While the title page attributes the work to "members of the Situationist International and students of Strasbourg University," the text was written by Tunisian situationist Mustapha Khayati. Composed during a period of mounting social unrest in France, *On the Poverty of Student Life* levels a searing attack on the nation's university system, asserting that modern education has become a method for transforming students into "low-level functionaries" capable of maintaining the "totalitarian spectacle" of modern capitalism. At the same time, the pamphlet exhorts students to develop an awareness of their oppressed political situation, with the aim of dismantling the capitalist economy and rebuilding society based on egalitarian principles. The pamphlet's full title, *On the Poverty of Student Life: Considered in Its Economic, Political, Psychological, Sexual and Especially Intellectual Aspects, with a Modest Proposal for Doing Away with It*, offers a glimpse into the scope and ambition of the situationist project.

On the Poverty of Student Life sparked controversy throughout France following its initial publication. Traditional media outlets derided the work for contributing to what cultural critic Greil Marcus in *Lipstick Traces* (1988) called the "collapse of decency, morality, order, the university, and Western civilization itself," and several weeks after its release, a judge ordered the students responsible for the publication to be ousted from the AFGES. The work's scathing critique of the modern leftist movement also alienated a number of radical political groups, notably the French Communist Party. In spite of this widespread condemnation, the pamphlet proved galvanizing to a small following of radicals who had become disenchanted with mainstream efforts at political reform, and it was instrumental in helping the situationist movement gain nationwide recognition. Translations of *On the Poverty of Student Life* soon appeared in countries throughout Europe, and the tract eventually became a foundational text for activists during the massive student and worker protests that paralyzed France in May 1968.

HISTORICAL AND LITERARY CONTEXT

On one level, *On the Poverty of Student Life* offers a Marxist critique of modern capitalism, albeit one that has been updated to reflect the new economic and political problems confronting Europe in the post–World War II era. For the situationists, the oppression of the proletariat was driven by the capitalist "spectacle," a form of ideological control exerted by mass media and other forms of political and cultural manipulation, with the aim of compelling individuals to devote their lives to upholding the free-market system. At the same time, *On the Poverty of Student Life* reflects the disillusionment among many leftists with the ultimate failure of the Soviet revolution, particularly during Joseph Stalin's reign (1922-53). In the work, Khayati argues that modern communist political systems, with their massive bureaucracies and authoritarian forms of control, are ultimately no different from the capitalist ideology they claim to oppose. In the face of these developments, the situationists argued, the idea of world revolution had devolved into an illusion.

According to Khayati, the university student of the 1960s was particularly susceptible to this illusion. In the face of considerable postwar economic expansion, students found themselves subjected to a curriculum that had become a mere tool of the capitalist economy, one designed to train obedient managers rather than free thinkers. Shaped by this highly specialized instruction, students lacked the "revolutionary consciousness" necessary to overcome capitalist forms of social control. As part of a generation that had grown up in the age of mass advertising, the average student was little more than a "conspicuous consumer," the "perfect spectator" in a commodity-driven culture. In Khayati's view, one of the most insidious cultural products of the postwar capitalist economy was the "Idea of Youth," a type of "publicity myth" designed to channel the imaginative and political energies of the students into the perpetuation of consumer society.

On the Poverty of Student Life belongs to a revolutionary tradition that originated during World War I and was shaped to a large degree by the ideas of agitator Rosa Luxemburg and other members of the German Spartacist movement. Like the Spartacists, the situationists opposed the Marxist-Leninist

Key Facts

Time Period:
Mid-20th Century

Movement/Issue:
Situationism; Student protest movement; Marxism

Place of Publication:
France

Language of Publication:
French

THE RETURN OF THE DURUTTI COLUMN

The origins of *On the Poverty of Student Life* can be traced to May 1966, when a small group of students at France's University of Strasbourg, inspired by the situationists, decided to seek election to the Student Union, with the express aim of dismantling it. After winning the election, the students immediately began preparing two publications for distribution in the fall. The first of these was a four-page comic by student André Bertrand called *The Return of the Durutti Column* (*Le Retour de la Colonne Durutti*). The title derives from a misspelling of Buenaventura Durruti, the leader of an anarchist group during the Spanish Civil War of the 1930s. Inspired in part by the collage techniques of the Dada artists of the World War I era, Bertrand's comic featured various images from films, advertisements, and cartoons, accompanied by subversive commentary. In one panel, two toothbrushes take turns disparaging various political factions; another features two cowboys on horseback discussing Marx's theory of reification. Bertrand's technique provides a representative example of the situationist practice of *détournement,* a process through which images derived from the capitalist system are reformulated to produce a critique of that system. On its final page, *The Return of the Durutti Column* announces the upcoming publication of "the most scandalous brochure of the century," *On the Poverty of Student Life,* before proceeding to describe the pamphlet as a "cardiogram of everyday reality that will allow you to choose for yourself, whether you are for or against the current misery, for or against the powers that by taking your own history away from you prevent you from living."

notion of a "vanguard party," which argued that the proletariat could only achieve authentic revolutionary consciousness through the guidance of communist leaders. By contrast, the situationists espoused Luxemburg's belief that absolute individual freedom, or what Khayati terms "generalized self-management," was the only legitimate form of political power. *On the Poverty of Student Life* also owes a debt to French sociologist and philosopher Henri Lefebvre's landmark *Critique of Everyday Life* (originally published as *Critique de la vie quotidienne* in 1947), a Marxist study of the individual in a capitalist society. Drawing from German socialist Karl Marx's theories of alienation, Lefebvre argued that the modern worker had become corrupted by the capitalist division of labor and leisure time, to the point where the individual had lost the power to determine the course of his or her own life.

Lefebvre's concept of alienation was later explored in various situationist writings from the 1950s and 1960s, before becoming one of the central theses of Khayati's 1966 pamphlet. *On the Poverty of Student Life* is especially noteworthy for locating modern alienation within the context of the spectacle, an idea that would

receive more in-depth analysis in French Marxist Guy Debord's groundbreaking 1967 work *The Society of the Spectacle* (*La Société du spectacle*). That same year, another situationist writer, Raoul Vaneigem, published *The Revolution of Everyday Life* (1967; *Traité de savoir-vivre à l'usage des jeunes générations*), an examination of the ways in which modern capitalist society perverts and undermines authentic human experience. All three works exerted a profound influence on the development of radical political activity in French universities during 1967 and 1968. In subsequent decades, *On the Poverty of Student Life* became widely recognized as a central text of the situationist movement, not only influencing such political tracts as *The Coming Insurrection* (2009; *L'insurrection qui vient,* 2007) but also becoming essential reading for members of the various Occupy movements of 2011 and 2012.

THEMES AND STYLE

On the Poverty of Student Life represents an attempt to reinvigorate radical politics through a "revolutionary critique of the world of the commodity." The foundation of this critique lies in the systematic negation of all facets of the capitalist system, from the forced alienation of the individual to the cult of consumerism propagated by the media. In order to participate in this revolution, Khayati argues, modern university students must become liberated from the "complacency" and "illusory glamour" imposed on them by mass culture. For the situationists, this liberation involves breaking free not only from the commodity-driven economic structure but also from the "passionless polemics" of the leading "celebrities of Unintelligence"—a group that includes leftist theorists such as Roland Barthes, Louis Althusser, and Lefebvre. Only through "a contestation of the entire society," the pamphlet asserts, can the individual hope to achieve the level of consciousness necessary to supersede entrenched forms of political domination.

On the Poverty of Student Life is divided into three parts. The opening section, "To make shame more shameful still by making it public," presents a thorough analysis of the economic, cultural, and intellectual "poverty" of the modern student within the framework of a detailed critique of the modern university system. In the second section, titled "It is not enough for theory to seek its realization in practice; practice must seek its theory," Khayati provides assessments of various leftist political activities in the decades following World War II, evaluating protest movements in the United States, Western and Eastern Europe, and Japan. The pamphlet's third section, "To create at last a situation that goes beyond the point of no return," exposes several of the common fallacies crippling modern radical thought, ultimately arguing that only by engaging with the capitalist system "in terms of the *totality*" and inhabiting a "living critique of that system" can the struggle to overcome alienation succeed.

The publication of *On the Poverty of Student Life* helped set the stage for violent student rioting and a general uprising throughout France for two weeks in 1968, which left the city looking like a war zone. AP PHOTO

Khayati delivers this message in a polemical style, attacking both university students and the predominant leftist groups of the era with a combination of methodical logic and unqualified scorn. The pamphlet's general tone becomes apparent in the opening line, as Khayati describes the modern student as the "most universally despised creature in France, apart from the policeman and the priest." Throughout *On the Poverty of Student Life,* Khayati characterizes his principal subject in ruthless terms: the student is a "stoical slave" with an "unhealthy propensity to wallow in his own alienation." Professors, meanwhile, "have lost their former role as guard-dogs serving the future masters" of society, only to adopt "the considerably less noble function of sheep-dogs in charge of herding white-collar flocks to their respective factories and offices." In spite of its generally vitriolic tone, *On the Poverty of Student Life* ultimately concludes on a positive note, projecting a future society freed from the demands of the commodity and based instead on principles of "free creativity" and "poetry made by all," a world in which all individuals are free to "live without dead time and to enjoy without restraints."

CRITICAL DISCUSSION

On the Poverty of Student Life caused immediate scandal in the fall of 1966, when members of the AFGES at the University of Strasbourg distributed 10,000 copies of the pamphlet to administration, faculty, and students at the opening assembly of the academic year. The event attracted nationwide attention, with most media coverage expressing a mix of outrage and bewilderment at the work's radical political philosophy. Although the reaction among mainstream sectors of society was largely negative, the pamphlet quickly gained an avid following in the growing student protest movement. A second edition of the work appeared in March 1967 and was soon circulating among students at the University of Paris at Nanterre, where the impetus behind the May 1968 student riots would originate. In the months following its initial appearance in France, pirated translations of the work began appearing at universities throughout Europe. Scholars have estimated that by 1969, between 250,000 and 500,000 copies of *On the Poverty of Student Life* had been disseminated worldwide.

As the student movement began to subside at the end of the 1960s, *On the Poverty of Student Life* ceased to function as a guide for aspiring revolutionaries. After publisher Éditions Gérard Lebovici issued a new edition of the work in 1976, Khayati famously disavowed it, asserting that the pamphlet was intended to be free and that any attempt to generate revenue from its distribution stood in direct opposition to the work's theoretical aims. The work began to receive renewed attention in the 1980s as critics began to identify a link between the radical social revolution proposed by the situationists and various underground cultural movements of the 1970s and 1980s, notably punk rock. By the early twenty-first century, however, the pamphlet once again gained political relevance as a new generation of protestors began to reexamine the text's theories of alienation and contestation. In a 2006 article published in the journal *Social Justice,* Simeon Hunter described the work as a "manual for political intervention."

Over the years, scholars have analyzed *On the Poverty of Student Life* both for its style and its political impact. In the article "French Leftism" (1972), Richard Gombin asserted that the work's "cultural and subjective view of the revolutionary act" distinguished it from the predominantly economic philosophy of Marx and Friedrich Engels, while suggesting that the text belonged more to the romantic and symbolic literary traditions. Ironically, Lefebvre, who had come under attack by both Khayati and his own students, later acknowledged that the pamphlet was a major success for the student movement. Reflecting on its original publication, Lefebvre remarked in a 1983 interview that it was a "very good brochure, without a doubt." Marcus declared that *On the Poverty of Student Life* was unlike any other manifesto of its time, suggesting that public reaction to the work "could not have been more extreme if the student union had spent its money on guns." Michael Seidman offered an in-depth analysis of the pamphlet's central ideas and its impact on subsequent revolutionary events in his 2004 study *The Imaginary Revolution: Parisian Students and Workers in 1968.*

BIBLIOGRAPHY

Sources

Gombin, Richard. "French Leftism." *Journal of Contemporary History* 7.1/2 (1972): 27-50. Print.

Hunter, Simeon. "Situating Situationism/Supporting Its Legacy: Reply to Mikkel Bolt Rasmussen." *Social Justice* 33.2 (2006): 16-28. Print.

Kaufman, Vincent. *Guy Debord: Revolution in the Service of Poetry.* Trans. Robert Bononno. Minneapolis: U of Minnesota P, 2006. Print.

Marcus, Greil. *Lipstick Traces: A Secret History of the Twentieth Century.* Cambridge: Harvard UP, 1988. Print.

Ross, Kristin, and Henri Lefebvre. "Lefebvre on the Situationists: An Interview." *October* 79 (1997): 69-83. Print.

Seidman, Michael. *The Imaginary Revolution: Parisian Students and Workers in 1968.* New York: Berghahn, 2004. Print.

Further Reading

Cohn-Bendit, Daniel, and Gabriel Cohn-Bendit. *Obsolete Communism: The Left-Wing Alternative.* Trans. Arnold Pomerans. London: Deutsch, 1968. Print.

Comité Invisible. *The Coming Insurrection.* Los Angeles: Semiotext(e), 2009. Print.

Dark Star. *Beneath the Paving Stones: Situationists and the Beach, May 1968.* Edinburgh: AK, 2001. Print.

Debord, Guy. *The Society of the Spectacle.* Trans. Donald Nicholson-Smith. New York: Zone, 1990. Print.

Gardiner, Michael. *Critiques of Everyday Life.* London: Routledge, 2000. Print.

Horn, Gerd-Rainer. *The Spirit of '68: Rebellion in Western Europe and North America, 1956-1976.* Oxford: Oxford UP, 2007. Print.

Lecourt, Dominique. *The Mediocracy: French Philosophy since the Mid-1970s.* Trans. Gregory Elliott. London: Verso, 2001. Print.

Lefebvre, Henri. *Critique of Everyday Life.* Trans. John Moore. London: Verso, 1991.

Wilby, Peter. "Humanity's Last Rage." *New Statesman* 12 May 2008: 26-29. Print

Stephen Meyer

PORT HURON STATEMENT

Tom Hayden

OVERVIEW

Largely written by Tom Hayden and adopted in June 1962 by Students for a Democratic Society (SDS), the Port Huron Statement galvanized the period's student protest movement. The manifesto focuses on the idea of participatory democracy, in which all citizens work to facilitate change, and also addresses the need for racial equality and nuclear disarmament. Its opening sentence captures the unrest of the time: "We are people of this generation, bred in at least modest comfort, housed now in universities, looking uncomfortably to the world we inherit." The manifesto goes on to lay out the concerns of the New Left, a political movement during the 1960s that consisted mainly of students and other youths and focused on racial equality, women's liberation, and protesting the Vietnam War.

Hayden began writing the Port Huron Statement in 1961 when he was just twenty-two years old, and the finished document provided his peers with a sense of political purpose. Inspired by the Freedom Rides and the student sit-ins in the South protesting segregation, the manifesto articulates the concept of participatory democracy. It was adopted during the first SDS convention, near Port Huron, Michigan. Intended as the founding document of the group, the manifesto was supposed to be five to ten pages long but grew to fifty pages. It has continued to influence pro-democracy movements around the world, including the Occupy Wall Street movement in the 2010s.

HISTORICAL AND LITERARY CONTEXT

The Port Huron Statement was written in response to what Hayden and SDS perceived as the injustices of the Cold War, racial inequality, and the apathy of the Old Left. Made up primarily of people who had come of age during the Great Depression, the Old Left was influenced by Communist politics. Its members had organized the student movements of the 1930s and were considered even more radical than the supporters of Franklin Roosevelt's New Deal. The strain of World War II and the desire for a return to normal life, however, left many in the Old Left unwilling to confront the political and social problems that plagued the United States at mid-century, including the persistent and institutionalized prejudices that limited the social, political,

and educational opportunities available to African Americans and other ethnic minorities. At the same time, international stability and progress were threatened by the Cold War militarism of both the Soviet bloc and the United States. After World War II ended in 1945, U.S. president Harry Truman and Soviet premier Joseph Stalin, who had been allies during the war, disagreed on how Germany's government and economy should be structured. Growing mutual distrust between the United States and the communist Soviet Union led to the Cold War, in which the Soviets tried to expand their sphere of influence and the Americans sought to contain the spread of communism. In 1947, Truman signed the National Securities Act to keep the communist threat at bay. That same year, he created the Central Intelligence Agency, which initiated "Red hunts" to identify communists in the United States government. Tension between the Soviet Union and the United States increased, sparking the Korean War (1950-53), which ended in a cease-fire after newly elected president Dwight D. Eisenhower threatened to use nuclear weapons. In the ensuing years, the United States continued to amass nuclear weapons and bolster its military forces, activities that Hayden and SDS found unjust and immoral.

When the Port Huron Statement appeared in 1962, John F. Kennedy was president and the civil rights movement was fomenting. On December 1, 1955, Rosa Parks had been arrested in Montgomery, Alabama, for refusing to give up her seat on a bus to a white man, spurring the Montgomery Bus Boycott and then sit-ins at lunch counters and Freedom Rides. The atmosphere of racial intolerance, coupled with the events of the Cold War, left many students and other youths feeling disenfranchised and searching for change. The Port Huron Statement articulates this discontentment and provides strategies to fight social injustice and stop the nuclear arms race. In his 2005 essay "The Way We Were and the Future of the Port Huron Statement," Hayden writes, "Rarely, if ever, had students thought of themselves as a force in history or, as we phrased it, an 'agency of social change.' We were rebelling against the experience of apathy, not against a single specific oppression."

Pinpointing apathy within American society as the underlying cause of the social and political injustices, the Port Huron Statement offers participatory

❖ *Key Facts*

Time Period:
Mid-20th Century

Movement/Issue:
New Left; Vietnam War; Civil Rights Movement; Women's liberation

Place of Publication:
United States

Language of Publication:
English

THE LIFE OF TOM HAYDEN

Social and political activist Thomas Emmet Hayden was born December 11, 1939, in Royal Oak, Michigan. During the early 1960s, Hayden became involved with the Student Nonviolent Coordinating Committee (SNCC) while studying at the University of Michigan in Ann Arbor. He became a writer for the university's newspaper, the *Michigan Daily,* and traveled to the South to report on the civil rights movement. In 1961, he was arrested in Albany, Georgia, after completing a freedom ride to protest the segregation of public transportation. While in jail, he began writing the Port Huron Statement for Students for a Democratic Society (SDS).

Hayden served as SDS president in 1962 and 1963 then moved on to other social justice projects. In 1965 Hayden traveled to North Vietnam with Yale professor Staughton Lynd and historian Herbert Aptheker to meet with officials from that communist state. Lynd and Hayden coauthored *The Other Side,* which questioned the United States' involvement in the Vietnam War. Three years later, Hayden helped organize antiwar demonstrations outside the Democratic National Convention in Chicago. He and six other protestors, later known as the Chicago Seven, were jailed and sentenced on contempt-of-court charges. The convictions were later overturned. He has since written several books about political activism, and served as a California state legislator from 1982 to 2000.

democracy as a solution. Arnold Kaufman (1927–1971), a political philosopher and professor at the University of Michigan, coined the term and helped Hayden develop the Port Huron Statement. They were inspired by Thomas Paine's *Rights of Man* and, more importantly, by Henry David Thoreau's *Civil Disobedience,* which states, "Cast your whole vote, not a strip merely, but your whole influence." SDS also attributed the concept of participatory democracy to John Dewey, the leader of the League for Industrial Democracy (LID), which sponsored SDS.

The influence of the Port Huron Statement can best be viewed in political terms. In the early 1960s, young people started joining demonstrations for nuclear disarmament and against the House Un-American Activities Committee. Motivated by the fight against Jim Crow segregation and the United States' increased involvement in Vietnam, Alan Haber founded SDS in 1960. A year later, Haber asked Hayden to draft a document articulating SDS's vision. Hayden submitted his draft to the attendees of the first SDS convention, which included students from around the country and delegates from organizations such as Student Nonviolent Coordinating Committee (SNCC) and LID. During the five-day convention, members debated the manifesto before submitting it to Hayden for the final draft, which continues to reverberate in certain political circles. The legacy of

SDS and the Port Huron Statement can be seen in the Arab Spring uprisings against repressive governments in the Middle East, for example, as well as the protests against economic inequality organized by the Occupy Wall Street movement, which drafted its own statement in 2011.

THEMES AND STYLE

The central theme of the Port Huron Statement focuses on individual political ownership in the form of participatory democracy. Unlike representative democracy, in which elected officials represent constituents, participatory democracy emphasizes the involvement of all citizens in government. The manifesto does not, however, define participatory democracy merely in governmental terms. Rather, it describes participatory democracy as a way of life. Following the ideas of Dewey, Thoreau, and sociologist C. Wright Mills, the manifesto defines democracy as a system that starts at the bottom rungs of society and moves up, unlike the trickle-down theory that has been utilized at times in American politics. Hayden writes that "ordinary people should have a voice in the decisions that affect their lives' because it was necessary for their dignity, not simply a blueprint for greater accountability."

To help achieve its effect, the manifesto draws attention to paradoxes in American life. For example, it argues that racial inequality, especially segregation in the South, contradicts the nation's cornerstone notion that "all men are created equal." In addition, the text highlights the inherent conflict in a society where the upper third controls most of the wealth while the rest of the population suffers from hunger and malnutrition. The Port Huron Statement contends that these problems can be countered by educating people who previously thought they had no right to participate in government. Through education, the disenfranchised can challenge the elite and the government, thus creating a participatory democracy in which continuous social movements address problems and eradicate apathy.

The Port Huron Statement begins with the collective *we* to include the reader as part of the disenfranchised population. It later employs the third person, referring to indifferent students and universities as *they.* This distinction distances the reader from groups that the document holds are apathetic. In an interview with the *Nation,* Hayden said that he and SDS were influenced by the communication style of Ella Baker, an elder advisor for SNCC:

> Listening and speaking in clear vernacular English was crucial. Books were treasured, but where you stood, with whom and against what risks was even more important, because if the people you were organizing couldn't understand your theories, you had to adjust. This led to a language and a form of thinking cleansed

of ideological infection, with an emphasis on trying to say what people were already thinking but hadn't put into words.

Nevertheless, in a *Los Angeles Times* article, Hayden admitted to problems within the text, saying, "It was hardly a perfect document. It contained sexist language."

CRITICAL DISCUSSION

When the Port Huron Statement was unveiled at the SDS convention, it by no means garnered unanimous support. For example, LID delegate Donald Slaiman criticized the statement's lack of anticommunist rhetoric and its criticism of the American Federation of Labor and Congress of Industrial Organizations (AFL-CIO), saying, "The American labor movement has won more for its members than any labor movement in the world! You people have some nerve attacking the labor movement." This strained the relationship between SDS and LID, and the two organizations formally severed ties in 1965.

The Port Huron Statement has influenced protest movements all over the world, from those against the Vietnam War in the 1960s to the Arab Spring uprisings in the 2010s. The idea of participatory democracy inspired contemporary students to lobby for the Dream Act and protest rising tuition costs. In addition, the first principle of Occupy Wall Street's "Principles of Solidarity" stresses engagement in "direct and transparent participatory democracy." The latter document harks back to the work of Hayden, who, in an article for the *Boston Review*, attributes the ongoing impact of his manifesto to the notion that its "core message is timeless but not dogmatic": we all need participatory democracy.

Most contemporary scholarship on the Port Huron Statement takes a historical or political approach. Georgetown professor Michael Kazin calls the final draft "the most ambitious, the most specific and the most eloquent manifesto in the history of the American left." However, as quoted in the *New York Times*, author Diane Ravitch sees the document as dated, especially in its "sort of naïve belief that human nature itself might be transformed through appeal to idealism, and that somehow our institutions will be malleable in the face of idealism mobilized." Another scholar, Heather Murray, analyzes the text from a literary perspective, comparing its discussion of labor in relation to the women's and lesbian rights movement: "The Port Huron Statement called for work that was 'educative, not stultifying; creative, not mechanical; self directed, not manipulated.' At the heart of these observations was a meditation about how workers thought of time, and this challenge was felt particularly by women who often saw their potentially creative leisure eroded by another form of meaningless work: housework."

Tom Hayden, author of the Port Huron Statement, speaking at a political rally in Washington, DC, in 2002. PHOTO BY VISIONS OF AMERICA/UIG VIA GETTY IMAGES

BIBLIOGRAPHY

Sources

Hayden, Tom. "A Framework for Democratic Change." *Boston Review.* Boston Review, 10 Apr. 2012. Web. 20 June 2012.

———. "Participatory Democracy: From the Port Huron Statement to Occupy Wall Street." *Nation.* Nation, 27 Mar. 2012. Web. 2 Aug. 2012.

———. "The Port Huron Statement: A Manifesto Reconsidered." *Los Angeles Times.* Tribune Newspapers, 6 May 2012. Web. 2 Aug. 2012.

Hayden, Tom. *The Port Huron Statement: The Visionary Call of the 1960s Revolution.* New York: Thunder's Mouth, 2005. Print.

Murray, Heather. "Free for All Lesbians: Lesbian Cultural Production and Consumption in the United States during the 1970s." *Journal of the History of Sexuality* 16.2 (2007): 251-75. Print.

"Principles of Solidarity." *Occupied Wall Street Journal.* Occupied Wall Street Journal, 14 Oct. 2011. Web. 16 Aug. 2012.

Roberts, Sam. "The Port Huron Statement at 50." *New York Times.* New York Times, 4 Mar. 2012. Web. 20 June 2012.

Thoreau, Henry David. *Civil Disobedience.* Boston: Godine, 1969. Print.

Further Reading

Lytle, Mark. "Making Sense of the Sixties." *Irish Journal of American Studies* 10 (2001): 1-17. Print.

McMillian, John, and Paul Buhle. "The New Left Revisited (Critical Perspectives on the Past)." Philadelphia: Temple UP, 2002. Print.

Miller, James. *Democracy is in the Streets: From Port Huron to the Siege of Chicago.* Cambridge: Harvard UP, 1994. Print.

Roussopoulos, Dimitrios. *The New Left: Legacy and Continuity.* Montréal: Black Rose, 2007. Print.

Strout, Cushing. "Sixties Protest Culture and What Happened at Cornell." *New England Review* 19.2 (1998): 110-36. Print.

Hannah Soukup

Report on the Construction of Situations and on the Terms of Organization and Action of the International Situationist Tendency

Guy Debord

OVERVIEW

Guy Debord's "Rapport sur la construction des situations et sur les conditions de l'organisation et de l'action de la tendance situationniste internationale" ("Report on the Construction of Situations and on the Terms of Organization and Action of the International Situationist Tendency") (1957) is the founding document for an avant-garde collective called the Situationist International (1957-72). It lays the groundwork for a new experiment in urban living based on the construction of situations ("ensembles of impressions determining the quality of a moment"), emphasizing ephemeral events over permanent structures and reimagining the city as a configurable environment rather than an assemblage of static architectural forms. The situationists saw themselves as the most recent in a line of twentieth-century avant-garde art movements, each of which had tried but failed to improve the quality of life. Through the construction of situations, the situationists hoped to improve the quality and quantity of laborers' leisure time, which had been largely co-opted and degraded by capitalist culture. Calling "revolutionary artists and intellectuals" to join the Situationist International in experimenting with new practices of urban living, the report lists a specific but loosely defined set of tools for the creation of situations (*dérive*, permanent play, psychogeography, and *détournement*) marshaled under two main categories of experimental behavior and unitary urbanism.

The report served as an influential touchstone for the Situationist International and its various splinter factions over the decade that followed, as the group sought to work out the pragmatic relationship between art, politics, and everyday life. Debord prepared the document to present at the Situationist International's first conference in Cosio d'Arroscia, Italy. Today competing interpretations and experimental implementations of Debord's report are still discussed among media theorists and art historians, and the document continues to inspire experimental artists, urban theorists, and political utopianists.

HISTORICAL AND LITERARY CONTEXT

In the report, Debord laments the failure of prior avant-garde art movements—futurism, Dada, and surrealism—to pragmatically alter everyday urban life. By 1957 art had become a segregated commodity emptied of its radical potential to improve life. The situationists felt there were enough goods being produced with the aid of machines to allow for a decrease in labor and an increase in play; however what inhibited this shift from labor to leisure was a capitalist system of propaganda that duped laborers into consuming more. Situationist International believed the solution was to construct a form of experimental living that achieved a total, unified revolution in the realm of everyday life.

The Situationist International was formed by several former members of earlier art movements, notably Debord, Constant Nieuwenhuys, Asger Jorn, and Giuseppe Pinot-Gallizio. Debord's report represents an attempt to synthesize concepts and opinions from each of these artists on architecture and urbanism, experimental forms of painting, and novel interpretations of topology and time. The situationists were indebted to Henri Lefebvre's emphasis on everyday life and admired Bertolt Brecht's confrontational form of epic theater. They also were united in their criticism of the modern, utilitarian architecture of Le Corbusier. (They were interested in architecture only insofar as it created ambient environments that fostered evocative situations.) They felt that other contemporary Western European and American art movements, such as abstract expressionism, cynically celebrated nothingness and that the Eastern European art of socialist realism was a reactionary retreat to an irrelevant past. Thus, they saw themselves as the true heirs of the failed surrealist movement and the most viable hope for a relevant contemporary avant-garde.

Debord's report sets forth the goals and tenets of the nascent Situationist International movement. From futurism to Dada to surrealism to the movements that directly led to the Situationist

✣ *Key Facts*

Time Period:
Mid-20th Century

Movement/Issue:
Situationism;
Avant-gardism

Place of Publication:
France

Language of Publication:
French

THE MEMOIRS OF GUY DEBORD AND ASGER JORN

Situationists Guy Debord and Asger Jorn collaborated on two *détourned* books, the second of which is titled *Mémoires* (1959). Loosely about Debord's time in the Lettrist International, *Mémoires* consists of city maps of Paris and London cut up and reassembled in various positions—a form of situationist psychogeography, or the study of the relationship between the city environment and the human feelings it evokes. The book also contains cut-up texts from various sources reassembled at odd angles, war illustrations and diagrams, photographs of people, and cartoons from newspapers. All of these collaged sources are then partially covered by colored paint drippings.

Debord felt that all of history was a resource for playful appropriation. *Détournement* is the practice of appropriating historical resources (such as a television advertisement or an architectural structure) and putting them to new uses. In fact, the cover for the first edition of *Mémoires* was made out of sandpaper so that repeatedly removing the book from and replacing it back onto a bookshelf would cause it to gradually eat away at the covers of the neighboring books. Debord is listed as the author, and Jorn is credited for providing "load-bearing structures"—presumably the dripped paint forms. *Mémoires* represents one of several situationist experiments at the intersection of art, politics, and everyday life.

International (namely Lettrist International, CoBrA, and the International Movement for an Imaginist Bauhaus), manifestos had been used throughout the early twentieth-century to distinguish priorities and to critique contemporary culture. Debord's report purposefully continues in this tradition of art manifestos due to the situationists' belief that they were the legitimate heirs of these prior movements. Thus, instead of inventing entirely new concepts, the report synthesizes existing ideas brought to the group by its members (especially Jorn, Gallizio, Constant, and Debord)— hence the use of the term *report,* which indicates an assessment of an experiment already in progress.

The report set an important precedent for future situationist writing and is a useful point of comparison for subsequent texts by Debord, who would not publish a longer piece of writing until his most famous work, *Society of the Spectacle,* in 1967. By then he had developed the idea of "decomposition" into the fully articulated theory of a "spectacular society." Whereas in 1957 he was still optimistically seeking an escape via experimental art and living from the decomposition of contemporary culture, by 1967 his diagnosis of the state of contemporary capitalist society had grown increasingly dire. In both documents he maintains his faith in the inevitability of a proletariat uprising, and he calls for a holistic urban revolution rather than a series of gradual improvements. Unlike *Society,* the report is not a concrete media theory but rather a provocation for a kind of lived, experimental practice. In its advocacy of experimentation, it is much less proscriptive than Debord's later writing and continues to appeal to contemporary critical artists.

THEMES AND STYLE

"Report on the Construction of Situations" proposes a new art movement that would holistically alter the quality of everyday life via the construction of situations, defined as "the concrete construction of temporary settings of life and their transformation into a higher, passionate nature." Essentially situations are "collective environments, ensembles of impressions determining the quality of a moment." According to scholar McKenzie Wark, Jorn saw situations as an active knot: a uniquely enfolding, complex, nonuniform, time/space event capable of activating human desire and constructed via "unitary urbanism" (a holistic reimagining of the city) and "experimental behavior." One such behavior is *dérive* (literally "drift"). Situationists would move through the city according to their attractions and repulsions, reforming the time and space of the city to their desires (personally and subjectively, if not yet architecturally). Another form of experimental behavior is *détournement,* which involves the reappropriation and repurposing of the city and all its media, including advertisements, architecture, and food and drink. The report advocates pragmatic change rather than mere cultural analysis and promotes artistic experimentation carried out with purposeful rigor: "We must collectively define our program and carry it out in a disciplined manner, through all means—even artistic ones."

Structurally, the manifesto proceeds in a logical manner, almost as a proof. First, it details the weaknesses of preceding art movements. Next, it critiques current problems with Western and Eastern European art. Then it proposes some provisional experimental plans, lists some long-term goals, and concludes with a few immediate pragmatic concerns. The report advocates a holistic, unified approach to art and politics, and theory and practice. It stays true to this balanced emphasis by beginning with an analysis of past problems and proceeding to a pragmatic (if sometimes oblique) call to action. In order to ennoble and persuade his readers, Debord inclusively describes them as involved participants in art rather than removed observers of art: "The situation is thus made to be lived by its constructors. The role of the 'public,' if not passive at least a walk-on, must ever diminish, while the share of those who cannot be called actors but, in a new meaning of the term, 'livers,' will increase."

Debord's tone throughout the piece is confident and critical but not categorically damning or exclusionary. His style is meant to demonstrate

La prison ou la mort pour les jeunes (1950) by French artist Ivan Chtcheglov is shown in the 2007 exhibit "The Situationist International (1957-1972), in girum imus nocte et consumimur igni" at the Museum Tinguely, Switzerland. KEYSTONE/ GEORGIOS KEFALAS

Situationist International's legitimacy as a contemporary heir to the bold critical art movements of the past. His conciliatory and hopeful tone is meant to persuade "revolutionary artists and intellectuals" to join the Situationist International (or at least to forestall their criticism). Stylistically, he uses a dialectical prose influenced by the early works of Karl Marx and Georg Wilhelm Friedrich Hegel, a literary technique he continued to develop and refine into his signature style as presented in *Society.* He uses poetically paradoxical phrases such as "essentially ephemeral," a terse description of "our entire program." His characterization of the situationist project is intentionally suggestive and open because the Situationist International had not fully experimented with these techniques, and he wanted to avoid unnecessarily overdetermining their potential outcomes. Thus, the language of the report is provocative and suggestive without being terribly specific.

CRITICAL DISCUSSION

The report describes the founding principles of the Situationist International and provides the theoretical underpinnings for Constant's continued *New Babylon* experiments in situationist architecture, Jorn and Debord's *détourned* book experiments, Jorn's *détourned* paintings, Gallizio's industrial paintings and installations, and the publication and distribution of the Situationst International journal, *Internationale Situationniste.* Subsequent interpretation of the report within the movement became a kind of litmus test for its infamous splits, expulsions, purges, and recriminations. For example, the text states, "The only valid experimental approach is one based on the uncompromising critique of existing conditions and their conscious supersession." The interpretation of this criterion became increasingly stringent as Debord's position became increasingly uncompromising. Between 1961 and 1962, the Situationist International was radically restructured, with Jorn, Constant, and Gallizio all departing on various terms. One common interpretation among art historians is that the group focused on art prior to 1961 and on politics after 1962. However, in *50 Years of Recuperation of the Situationist International* (2008), Wark challenges this assumption, arguing that the continuing thread throughout the organization's life was a persistent interest in strategies beyond art and politics for revolutionizing everyday existence.

"Report on the Construction of Situations" has had a profound influence on tactical media artists, such as the Radical Software Group and Critical Art Ensemble, and on artists who consider the city their medium, such as Glowlab. The concept of situations has also indirectly influenced the Occupy movement in the United States, and the practice of *détournement* has been applied by disruptive political artists such as the Yes Men and the culture-jamming magazine *Adbusters*. Numerous architectural books, essays, and exhibitions have been devoted to unitary urbanism and Constant's *New Babylon* project. However, despite the efforts of the Situationist International and others, a unitary, holistic, utopian, situationist city has yet to emerge. Against the charge that the situationist project was a failure, Peter Wollen concedes in *Raiding the Icebox: Reflections on Twentieth-Century Culture* (1993), "The Situationist International left a legacy of great value. The wasteful luxury of utopian projects, however doomed, is no bad thing." In provocatively Debordian fashion, Wark argues that the situationist project was never meant to be subdivided and recuperated in parts; for those who would continue successfully in its spirit, "recuperation must be all or nothing."

Debord's manifesto has been approached by scholars from a number of different perspectives based on their respective disciplines. Art historians find in the report several novel approaches to art making that continue to influence artists in a variety of experimental genres. Media theorists note Debord's nascent suspicion of the spectacular society, while social theorists such as Michel de Certeau find in the document an emphasis on experimental everyday living as a radical form of political resistance. However, the art collective Spurse has criticized Debord for his presumption that there is an immediate, authentic human experience to be found beneath the decomposition of capitalist culture. In a 2008 interview with *Drain Magazine,* they state, "The desire for unmediated and direct connections to the real or each other is to misunderstand the status of things, representations and events. Rather than seeing these things as what get in the way of contact with the real, they are what make the real."

BIBLIOGRAPHY

Sources

Hinderliter, Beth. "An Interview with Spurse." *Drain Magazine* 5.2 (2008). Web. 21 Sept. 2012.

McDonough, Tom. *Guy Debord and the Situationist International: Texts and Documents.* Cambridge: MIT, 2002. Print.

Wark, McKenzie. *50 Years of Recuperation of the Situationist International.* New York: Temple Hoyne Buell Center for the Study of American Architecture, 2008. Print.

Wollen, Peter. *Raiding the Icebox: Reflections on Twentieth-Century Culture.* Bloomington: Indiana UP, 1993. Print.

Further Reading

Knabb, Ken. *Situationist International Anthology.* Berkeley: Bureau of Public Secrets, 1981. Print.

Lefebvre, Henri. *Critique of Everyday Life.* Vol 1. London: Verso, 2008. Print.

Marcus, Greil. *Lipstick Traces: A Secret History of the Twentieth Century.* Cambridge: Harvard UP, 1989. Print.

Plant, Sadie. *The Most Radical Gesture: The Situationist International in a Postmodern Age.* London: Routledge, 1992. Print.

Wark, McKenzie. *The Beach beneath the Street: The Everyday Life and Glorious Times of the Situationist International.* London: Verso, 2011. Print.

Curt Cloninger

SITUATIONIST THESES ON TRAFFIC

Guy Debord

OVERVIEW

First published in the November 1959 issue of the French journal *Situationist International* (*Internationale Situationniste*), Guy Debord's "Situationist Theses on Traffic" (*Positions situationnistes sur la circulation*) offers a piercing analysis of the role of the automobile in promoting and perpetuating the capitalist system. Debord's work outlines the situationist opposition to the automobile in political terms. He identifies the car as "the most notable material symbol of the notion of happiness that developed capitalism tends to spread throughout the society," while drawing a link between the automobile and the Marxist theory of surplus labor. By designing cities that require workers to commute to their jobs, Debord argues, urban planners have transformed the concept of travel into a mere "adjunct of work," one that necessarily reduces the degree to which individuals are able to assert control over their time. In its incisive critique of the modern city's increasing reliance on automobile transportation, "Situationist Theses on Traffic" represents one of the situationist movement's most pointed statements on the problem of urban existence in the postwar era.

Although "Situationist Theses on Traffic" attracted relatively little notice when it first appeared, it formed an integral part of the broader situationist critique of the alienating effects of the capitalist economy on the individual. Throughout the 1950s, the situationists elucidated a concept known as unitary urbanism, an experimental approach to social organization based on exploration and imaginative play rather than the pursuit of status and material gain. In "Situationist Theses on Traffic," Debord suggests that car culture has undermined what he calls the "dialectic of the human milieu," eroding traditional forms of interaction by replacing entire neighborhoods and other public spaces with freeways. Describing the automobile's centrality to modern architecture as "the most unrealistic misapprehension" of the "real problems" confronting urban society, Debord urges "revolutionary urbanists" to shun the imperatives of economic efficiency in order to build city environments that enable the individual to lead an "authentic life." Although "Situationist Theses on Traffic" offers no detailed remedies for the problems traffic presents, several of Debord's key concepts, notably his proposal to ban automobiles from central or historic districts of cities, helped shape urban planning theories into the twenty-first century.

HISTORICAL AND LITERARY CONTEXT

Debord's "Situationist Theses on Traffic" developed in response to the radical process of urbanization underway in Paris during the 1950s, as well as to the growing influence of American consumerism in the years following World War II. For the situationists the automobile had become part of a general program of capitalist propaganda, which presented car ownership "as supreme good of an alienated life and as an essential product of the capitalist market." Although Debord and the situationists did not object to the automobile as a means of travel, they viewed its increasingly "massive and parasitical" presence in society as exerting an almost tyrannical control over urban design. According to Debord, modern architecture must reckon with "the whole development of society," rather than one particular aspect of it.

At the same time, the "Situationist Theses on Traffic" represents a repudiation of the approach to urban planning developed by the International Congresses of Modern Architecture (Congres internationaux d'architecture moderne, or CIAM), a group led by modernist French architect Le Corbusier. In their concept of a functional city, Le Corbusier and his colleagues envisioned an urban landscape divided into three distinct zones (work, residential, and leisure), according to the basic needs and desires of society. In Le Corbusier's ideal city, traffic would exist solely as a means of linking these three zones in the most efficient manner possible. From the time of their formation, the situationists were openly hostile to Le Corbusier's vision of the ideal urban landscape. In his seminal 1953 treatise "Formulary for a New Urbanism" (*Formulaire pour un urbanisme nouveau*), Debord ally Ivan Chtcheglov expresses his disdain for the architect in no uncertain terms. "A Le Corbusier model is the only image that arouses in me the idea of immediate suicide," Chtcheglov writes. "He is destroying the last remnants of joy. And of love, passion, freedom."

In contrast to the idea of a functional city, "Situationist Theses on Traffic" posits the development of the modern urban setting based on the principles of unitary urbanism. Unlike the complex social

✛ *Key Facts*

Time Period:
Mid-20th Century

Movement/Issue:
Situationism;
Urbanization; Marxism

Place of Publication:
France

Language of Publication:
French

PRIMARY SOURCE

"SITUATIONIST THESES ON TRAFFIC"

1

A MISTAKE MADE by all the city planners is to consider the private automobile (and its by-products, such as the motorcycle) as essentially a means of transportation. In reality, it is the most notable material symbol of the notion of happiness that developed capitalism tends to spread throughout the society. The automobile is at the center of this general propaganda, both as supreme good of an alienated life and as essential product of the capitalist market: It is generally being said this year that American economic prosperity is soon going to depend on the success of the slogan "Two cars per family."

2

COMMUTING TIME, as Le Corbusier rightly noted, is a surplus labor which correspondingly reduces the amount of "free" time.

3

WE MUST REPLACE travel as an adjunct to work with travel as a pleasure.

4

TO WANT TO REDESIGN architecture to accord with the needs of the present massive and parasitical existence of private automobiles reflects the most unrealistic misapprehension of where the real problems lie. Instead, architecture must be transformed to accord with the whole development of the society, criticizing all the transitory values linked to obsolete forms of social relationships (in the first rank of which is the family).

5

EVEN IF, during a transitional period, we temporarily accept a rigid division between work zones and residence zones, we must at least envisage a third sphere: that of life itself (the sphere of freedom and leisure—the essence of life). Unitary urbanism acknowledges no boundaries; it aims to form an integrated human milieu in which separations such as work/leisure or public/private will finally be dissolved. But before this is possible, the minimum action of unitary urbanism is to extend the terrain of play to all desirable constructions. This terrain will be at the level of complexity of an old city.

organization proposed by Le Corbusier and other functionalist thinkers, the situationist vision of the modern city was deliberately unplanned and rooted in the continuous and often unpredictable flow of social activity. While "Situationist Theses on Traffic" acknowledges Le Corbusier's fundamental criticism of the surplus labor embedded into the worker's daily commute, it remains adamantly opposed to the architect's notion of a "rigid division" between different spheres of everyday existence. According to Debord, unitary urbanism "acknowledges no boundaries," ultimately seeking to establish "an integrated human milieu in which separations such as work/leisure or public/private will finally be dissolved."

"Situationist Theses on Traffic" represents the most concise expression of Debord's concept of the experimental city, an idea he elucidates in several of his earlier writings for *Situationist International*, notably his 1957 "Report on the Construction of Situations" (*Rapport sur la construction des situations*). Debord's perception of the automobile as a potential agent of social ill also finds an echo in his 1967 *The Society of the Spectacle* (*La Société du spectacle*). In Thesis 174 of this work, Debord blames the "dictatorship of the automobile" for scarring the landscape with a "dominance of freeways, which tear up the old urban centers and promote an ever-wider dispersal." In the ensuing decades, social critics elaborated further on the automobile's role in perpetuating the capitalist "spectacle," among them David Inglis in his essay, "Auto Couture: Thinking the Car in Post-War France," published in a 2004 issue of the journal *Theory, Culture & Society*.

THEMES AND STYLE

At its core, "Situationist Theses on Traffic" concerns the struggle of the individual to retain freedom and authenticity in the face of a consumer-driven capitalist society. For Debord, the primary battleground for this struggle is the modern city. As planners and architects continue to shape urban development according to purely economic criteria, Debord calls upon "revolutionary urbanists" to resist this false "notion of happiness" through direct, imaginative engagement with the urban landscape. Through the practice of unitary urbanism, individuals have the power to "extend the terrain of play to all desirable constructions," in the process reinventing an urban setting that achieves "the level of complexity of an old city." "Situationist Theses on Traffic" derives this concept of urban exploration from three central tenets of situationist thought: dérive, an experimental practice in which the individual drifts through diverse urban landscapes;

6

IT IS NOT a matter of opposing the automobile as an evil in itself. It is its extreme concentration in the cities that has led to the negation of its function. Urbanism should certainly not ignore the automobile, but even less should it accept it as its central theme. It should reckon on gradually phasing it out. In any case, we can envision the banning of auto traffic from the central areas of certain new complexes, as well as from a few old cities.

7

THOSE WHO BELIEVE that the automobile is eternal are not thinking, even from a strictly technological standpoint, of other future forms of transportation. For example, certain models of one-man helicopters currently being tested by the US Army will probably have spread to the general public within twenty years.

8

THE BREAKING UP of the dialectic of the human milieu in favor of automobiles (the projected freeways in Paris will entail the demolition of thousands of houses and apartments although the housing crisis is continually worsening) masks its irrationality under pseudopractical justifications. But it is practically necessary only in the context of a specific social set-up. Those who believe that the particulars of the problem are permanent want in fact to believe in the permanence of the present society.

9

REVOLUTIONARY UBRANISTS will not limit their concern to the circulation of things, or to the circulation of human beings trapped in a world of things. They will try to break these topological chains, paving the way with their experiments for a human journey through authentic life.

SOURCE: *Situationist International* #3, Paris, December 1959. Translation by Ken Knabb, *Situationist International Anthology* (revised and expanded edition, 2006). No copyright.

---

détournement, the act of juxtaposing various artistic or textual elements toward creating a new and surprising social milieu; and psychogeography, the general study of an environment on an individual's emotional state. In this respect, "Situationist Theses on Traffic" posits a type of social process rather than a concrete vision of an ideal city.

"Situationist Theses on Traffic" comprises nine theses of varying lengths. The central theme of the work unfolds indirectly, as Debord interweaves statements on the goals of unitary urbanism with criticisms of the automobile, modern architectural planning, and the capitalist spectacle in general. While "Situationist Theses on Traffic" invites readers to participate in a form of revolutionary action with the aim of liberating individuals from the thrall of consumerism, it never actually outlines a concrete or coherent program. The manifesto's indeterminate quality reflects the situationists' broader preoccupation with the temporal aspects of imaginative activity, as opposed to the potential products of this activity. In other words, Debord's experimental journey is inherently dynamic, defined by its movement through time and space rather than by a fixed destination or landmark.

Stylistically, Debord uses a range of rhetorical devices in "Situationist Theses on Traffic." For the most part, he crafts his argument in polemical language, establishing a clear demarcation between the

"pseudopractical" demands of progress and the "desirable" and "authentic" underpinnings of the situationist project. Debord attacks the capitalist spectacle in sweeping fashion, repeatedly describing the problem confronting modern society in absolute terms. In Debord's view, capitalism operates within a realm of "general propaganda," where the automobile is marketed as a "supreme good" and an "essential product." At the same time, Debord inserts unexpected propositions into various points of his analysis, as when

Traffic on the Boulevard Périphérique, a highway in Paris. Guy Debord's "Situationist Theses on Traffic" spoke out against the way in which Paris was being changed in order to accommodate increasing numbers of automobiles.
© COROT2/ALAMY

he suggests that the automobile might soon be supplanted by one-man helicopters as the principal mode of urban transport. While this notion seems improbable on the surface, its originality stands in stark contrast to the imaginative constraints of urban planners, whose faith in the "permanence of the present society" has rendered them unable to recognize the real problems confronting the modern city.

CRITICAL DISCUSSION

"Situationist Theses on Traffic" emerged at a time when the theory of unitary urbanism was the basis of the situationist critique of modern capitalist society. During the 1950s and 1960s, the notion of contesting urban spaces had begun to gain widespread attention, both in Europe and the United States. In their 1961 essay "Banning Automobiles from Manhattan," Paul Goodman and Percival Goodman express similar concern with the increasing dominance of car culture in modern cities, while offering a detailed proposal for a radical reconfiguration of road usage in New York City. In contrast to Debord's declamatory and general critique, Goodman and Goodman offer a detailed and systematic approach, offering a range of specific suggestions on such subjects as parking, public transport, and civic codes.

In the ensuing decades, Debord's "Situationist Theses on Traffic" exerted a wide influence over a range of scholarly disciplines, notably sociology, urban planning, and cultural studies. In her book, *City Images: Perspectives from Literature, Philosophy, and Film,* author Mary Ann Caws interprets Debord's opposition to capitalist urban development as a form of resistance against the increasing presence of postmodern architecture. In his essay "Auto Couture," Inglis offers a Marxist reading of the manifesto, focusing on Debord's critique of the surplus labor involved with car ownership. Other critics comment on Debord's rhetorical strategy in "Situationist Theses on Traffic." In his book, *The Situationist City,* Simon Sadler draws a link between Debord's critique of the automobile and the "Athens Charter" (*Charte d'Athenes*), Le Corbusier's landmark 1943 manifesto on the subject of modern urban planning. Whereas Le Corbusier views the automobile in terms of its function in practical transportation, Sadler argues, Debord subverts this notion entirely, asserting that the principal value of travel is as a form of pleasure.

Over the years, scholars attempted to locate "Situationist Theses on Traffic" within specific historic or cultural contexts. In his book, *Guy Debord: Revolution in the Service of Poetry,* author Vincent Kaufmann, speaking generally about the situationist theory of unitary urbanism, describes Debord's critique of modern city planning as an "attempt to reappropriate the urban space," an act that "assumes a contested relation to a space considered to have been occupied by the enemy." In his book, *Visions of the City: Utopianism, Power and Politics in Twentieth-Century Urbanism,* David Pinder locates Debord's critique of car culture within the broader framework of the widespread demolition of working-class districts of Paris and its surroundings during the 1950s. Paul F. Downton, author of *Ecopolis: Architecture and Cities for a Changing Climate,* cites Debord's theories in drawing attention to the "misapprehension" that continues to plague urban planning in the twenty-first century.

BIBLIOGRAPHY

Sources

Chtcheglov, Ivan. "Formulary for a New Urbanism." Trans. Ken Knabb. *Bureau of Public Secrets.* Ken Knabb, 2006. Web. 14 Aug. 2012.

Debord, Guy. *The Society of the Spectacle.* Trans. Donald Nicholson-Smith. New York: Zone, 1990. Print.

Downton, Paul F. *Ecopolis: Architecture and Cities for a Changing Climate.* Berlin: Springer Netherland, 2008. Print.

Inglis, David. "Auto Couture: Thinking the Car in Post-War France." *Theory, Culture & Society* 21.4/5 (2004): 197-219. Print.

Kaufmann, Vincent. *Guy Debord: Revolution in the Service of Poetry.* Trans. Robert Bononno. Minneapolis: U of Minnesota P. 2006. Print.

Sadler, Simon. *The Situationist City.* Cambridge: MIT, 1998. Print.

Further Reading

Beckman, Karen Redrobe. *Crash: Cinema and the Politics of Speed and Stasis.* Durham: Duke UP, 2010. Print.

Caws, Mary Ann. *City Images: Perspectives from Literature, Philosophy, and Film.* New York: Gordon and Breach, 1991. Print.

Clavier, Berndt. *John Barth and Postmodernism: Spatiality, Travel, Montage.* New York: Lang, 2007. Print.

Davis, Mike. *City of Quartz: Excavating the Future in Los Angeles.* London: Verso, 1990. Print.

Goodman, Paul, and Percival Goodman. "Banning Cars from Manhattan." *Bureau of Public Secrets.* Ken Knabb, 1961. Web. 14 Aug. 2012.

Harold, Christine. *OurSpace: Resisting the Corporate Control of Culture.* Minneapolis: U of Minnesota P, 2007. Print.

Pinder, David. *Visions of the City: Utopianism, Power and Politics in Twentieth-Century Urbanism.* New York: Routledge, 2005. Print.

Plant, Sadie. *The Most Radical Gesture: The Situationist International in a Postmodern Age.* New York: Routledge, 1992. Print.

Ross, Kristin. *Fast Cars, Clean Bodies: Decolonization and the Reordering of French Culture.* Cambridge: MIT, 1995. Print.

Stephen Meyer

THE SOCIETY OF THE SPECTACLE

Guy Debord

OVERVIEW

The Society of the Spectacle (1967), French Marxist Guy Debord's most succinct and influential piece of theoretical and political writing, describes Western capitalist culture as a parade of images that mediate relations between people and distract consumers from living "real" experiences. The book is a product of the situationist movement founded in 1957 by Debord and other Western intellectuals to respond to the unbridled growth of consumerism. Situationism holds as its central tenets the rejection of passive consumption and the awakening of class consciousness through the practical application of theory. Addressed to a general audience, *The Society of the Spectacle* defines spectacle and its effects on society in nine chapters, addressing topics from "The Commodity as Spectacle" to "Negation and Consumption within Culture."

Debord's book, which was embraced most notably by a radical contingent of Parisian students, was circulated on the eve of the May 1968 student and worker uprising in France. The text at least indirectly contributed to the May 1968 zeitgeist by calling for a wholesale rejection of contemporary society and for the replacement of government with a collection of democratic workers' councils. As students engaged in sometimes violent protests and workers began to occupy numerous factories throughout France, the situationists were elected to various committees within the movement—although they never sought to hierarchically control it (such control would have undermined the self-autonomy for which they advocated). Today *The Society of the Spectacle* is known as a landmark work of utopian revolutionary action in the late twentieth century and as a seminal text of neo-Marxist media theory in a range of disciplines, from film theory to the social sciences.

HISTORICAL AND LITERARY CONTEXT

Debord's book addresses the concern that capitalism underwent a transformation after the late 1920s that resulted in the spectacular accumulation of surplus commodities. His ideas build on several decades of thought around the work of philosopher Karl Marx, who in the mid-nineteenth century theorized that mass production had moved society beyond a state of "being" to merely "having." In the early twentieth century, philosopher György Lukács developed Marx's

theories, in particular the idea of commodity fetishization as the central problem of capitalist societies. As a result, Lukács fashioned a unique brand of Western Marxism focused on analysis of consumption instead of analysis of production. French Marxist Henri Lefebvre, who was particularly influential for Debord, also developed Marx's theories about consumption, exploring in the influential three-volume *Critique of Everyday Life* the pervasiveness of consumer culture and the impoverished thinking that emerged as a result.

By 1967, when *The Society of the Spectacle* was published, Debord was the most prominent member of the situationist movement. In 1957 he had helped found Situationist International, an organization comprised mainly of artists, to challenge the suppression of art in a consumer-driven society. His criticism not only of Western capitalism but also of communist bureaucracy in Eastern Europe and China made him popular among students, leftists, and other radicals. To them, socialist labor unions that purported to represent the desire of the workers had become as ideological and spectacular as the system of Western capitalism they meant to oppose. Therefore, Debord and the situationists believed that the solution lay in local workers' councils, wherein any councilperson could be removed from office by majority vote at any time.

Situationist International followed in a long line of manifesto-producing twentieth-century art movements, beginning with futurism and continuing through Dada, surrealism, CoBrA, the International Movement for an Imaginist Bauhaus, and the Lettrist International. In 1957 Debord wrote the situationist movement's founding manifesto, *Report on the Construction of Situations,* and over the following decade he found himself increasingly interested in pragmatic politics. Accordingly, he was influenced by such Marxist works as Marx and Friedrich Engels's *The Communist Manifesto* (1848) and Lukács's *History and Class Consciousness* (1923).

The dialectic style and suspicious tenor of *The Society of the Spectacle* influenced a subsequent body of critical writing on media and their relationship to culture. After disbanding Situationist International in 1972, Debord himself encouraged ongoing dialogue about the book through two subsequent films—*The Society of the Spectacle* (1973) and *Refutation of All Judgments* (1975)—as well as another manifesto

✤ *Key Facts*

Time Period:
Mid-20th Century

Movement/Issue:
Situationism; Neo-Marxism; Collectivism

Place of Publication:
France

Language of Publication:
French

THE SOCIETY OF THE SPECTACLE: A 1973 FILM

Guy Debord's 1973 film *The Society of the Spectacle* is composed of found news footage of various historical events, television advertisements, stills of magazine advertisements, industrial instructional films, and scenes from Soviet and Hollywood movies. In addition, typography is occasionally superimposed over the images. Debord performs the voiceovers for the film by reading excerpts from his text of the same name. Many of the excerpts are either direct plagiarisms or altered (*détourned*) versions of texts by Karl Marx, Georg Wilhelm Friedrich Hegel, and others.

Processing the rapidly edited imagery, spoken words, and written language is a cognitively jarring experience for many viewers. The effect is much more unsettling—and to some more enlivening—than Debord's textual manifesto, which must rely on the printed word alone to achieve the author's goal of awakening class consciousness. The film therefore serves as a mediated enaction of the dialectic style that Debord achieves in his book. It also provides an excellent example of what Situationist International prized as the application of written theory to the praxis of art.

("Comments on the Society of the Spectacle" [1988]). Debord's penchant for terse, paradoxical, dialectic aphorisms is also taken up in Hakim Bey's *The Temporary Autonomous Zone* (1991), McKenzie Wark's *Hacker Manifesto* (2004), and the later philosophical writings of Jean Baudrillard (particularly *Simulacra and Simulation* [1981]). In the tradition of art manifestos, Debord's literary style also has influenced the theoretical writing of tactical media artists such as the Critical Art Ensemble.

THEMES AND STYLE

The Society of the Spectacle makes the broad claim that consumers have come to live a spectacular, mediated existence separate from any experience of the real. In the first chapter, Debord defines spectacle in a variety of evocative terms: "a social relationship between people that is mediated by images"; "the very heart of society's real unreality"; "an enormous positivity, out of reach and beyond dispute"; and "the bad dream of modern society in chains, expressing nothing more than its wish for sleep." The spectacle is not limited to advertising and mass marketing; it also pervades news journalism, politics, higher education, the art market, leisure, and every other sector of life. A major function of the spectacle, according to Debord, is to imprison workers in an ahistorical present tense without consciousness of past or future noncapitalist systems. Debord's solution (following Lukács) is to awaken workers to an awareness of their own class, agency, and destiny to change the world.

Debord employs several rhetorical strategies to decalcify and revivify the ideas of Marx and the surrealists, which he states have been co-opted and neutered by the spectacle. His main rhetorical strategy for bringing about a mass awakening is the use of dialectic prose. Following Hegelian and early Marxist theory, he uses a pattern of thesis and antithesis, or negation, to frame his argument. Thus, *The Society of the Spectacle* is filled with paradoxical, contradictory phrases. At one point, he even uses the dialectic to explain his use of the dialectic: "Critical theory … is not a negation of style, but the style of negation." He also employs the situationist tactic of *détournement* (derailment) by rephrasing and recontextualizing key source texts. Finally, he repeats source texts verbatim without quotation marks or citation, explaining, "Plagiarism is necessary. Progress demands it." (Aptly, this explanation itself is directly plagiarized from the poet Comte de Lautréamont.)

Stylistically, in the tradition of early twentieth-century art manifestos, *The Society of the Spectacle* is intended to be polemical, hyperbolic, and polarizing. In order to establish the overall cosmology of spectacular society, the first three chapters are even more hyperbolic than the latter chapters. Debord was critical of any theory that did not arise from and inject itself back into praxis—the exercise of everyday living. According to Debord, received and calcified ideology is the enemy of praxis, but theory is its ally. Therefore, his book is not meant to be logical "proof" of his theory of a spectacular society. Rather, it is meant to be a provocation and a wake-up call for those duped by the numbing effects of the spectacle. Thus, throughout the text, the use of dialectic is at work in the hopes of awakening class consciousness.

CRITICAL DISCUSSION

In light of its association with the May 1968 uprising in France, *The Society of the Spectacle* was received as a piece of incendiary revolutionary writing. Many of the French academics who experienced the uprising in Paris went on to recuperate, adapt, and theoretically expand upon the text. The book also gained a sympathetic following among nonacademic Marxist and anarchist activists (dubbed "pro-situs") of various stripes and nationalities. Nonacademics, including Debord, began to accuse scholars of spectacularizing the manifesto by overly associating it with theory devoid of praxis. Only in 1992 could philosopher Sadie Plant in *The Most Radical Gesture: The Situationist International in a Postmodern Age* declare, "There is no longer any damage to be done to its ideas by introducing them into the profoundly non-revolutionary milieu of contemporary intellectual debate."

Decades after its publication, *The Society of the Spectacle* continues to be discussed in political and philosophical circles, and its influence has extended further into the fields of media theory and art. It has inspired a number of artists and designers, including

Martha Rosler, the Yes Men, and *Adbusters* magazine, to continue to undermine and *détour* spectacular media imagery. However, the book is not without its critics. For many, Debord's suspicion of imagery is itself suspicious. In *The Emancipated Spectator* (2009), philosopher Jacques Rancière argues that, as consumers, people are not merely passive receivers of imagery but active participants in constructing the images they apperceive.

Scholarship regarding *The Society of the Spectacle* reveals several conflicting trends. Those who view it as a proto-post-structuralist text often see Debord's spectacle as a precursor of Jean Baudrillard's simulacrum, a term for a facsimile that itself becomes truth. However, whereas Debord thought the spectacle masked an underlying reality that must be uncovered, Baudrillard postulated that the spectacle replaces reality altogether. In *Simulacra and Simulation* (1981) Baudrillard asserts, "The territory no longer precedes the map, nor does it survive it. It is nevertheless the map that precedes the territory." In contrast, philosopher Anselm Jappe convincingly places the book as the last in a line of radical Western Marxist positions—a descendant of Lukács rather than a progenitor of Baudrillard. In his biography of Debord, Jappe contends, "It would be a serious error to try to associate Debord with more or less 'postmodern' theories concerned with communication, images, and simulation. When adepts of such theories hail Debord for his alleged 'prophetic' gifts, they are clearly laboring under a misapprehension."

BIBLIOGRAPHY

Sources

Baudrillard, Jean. *Simulacra and Simulation.* Ann Arbor: U of Michigan P, 1994. Print.

Debord, Guy. *Comments on the Society of the Spectacle.* New York: Verso, 1998. Print.

———. "Report on the Construction of Situations and on the International Situationist Tendency's Conditions of Organization and Action." *Situationist International Anthology.* Ed. Ken Knabb. Berkeley: Bureau of Public Secrets, 1981. 25-43. Print.

———. *The Society of the Spectacle.* New York: Zone, 1994. Print.

Jappe, Anselm. *Guy Debord.* Berkeley: U of California P, 1999. 134. Print.

Plant, Sadie. *The Most Radical Gesture: The Situationist International in a Postmodern Age.* London: Routledge, 1992. Print.

Rancière, Jacques, and Gregory Elliott. *The Emancipated Spectator.* London: Verso, 2009. Print.

Situationist International. "The Beginning of an Era." *Situationist International Anthology.* Ed. Ken Knabb. Berkeley: Bureau of Public Secrets, 1981. 308. Print.

Further Reading

Cubitt, Sean. *Simulation and Social Theory.* London: Sage, 2001. Print.

Gray, Christopher. *Leaving the 20th Century: Incomplete Work of the Situationist International.* London: Rebel, 1998. Print.

Lukács, György. *History and Class Consciousness: Studies in Marxist Dialectics.* Cambridge: MIT, 1971. Print.

Marcus, Greil. *Lipstick Traces: A Secret History of the Twentieth Century.* Cambridge: Harvard UP, 1989. Print.

Reid, Jamie, and Jon Savage. *Up They Rise: The Incomplete Works of Jamie Reid.* London: Faber & Faber, 1987. Print.

Viénet, René. *Enragés and Situationists in the Occupation Movement, France, May 1968.* New York: Autonomedia, 1992. Print.

Curt Cloninger

A poster from the May 1968 student revolt in France announces "the beginning of a long struggle." Guy Debord's book *The Society of the Spectacle* is thought by many to have been a catalyst for the revolt. ERICH LESSING/ART RESOURCE, NY

TWENTY POINTS

Henry L. Adams

✣ **Key Facts**

Time Period:
Mid-20th Century

Movement/Issue:
American Indian
Movement (AIM); Civil
Rights Movement

Place of Publication:
United States

**Language of
Publication:**
English

OVERVIEW

The Twenty Points position paper, composed primarily by Native American protest leader Henry L. Adams, delineates the demands of the Trail of Broken Treaties Caravan protest, a 1972 cross-country demonstration for Indian rights. As several hundred American Indians from across the United States prepared to march on Washington DC, Adams and other leaders of the protest convened in Minneapolis, Minnesota, to formalize the objective of their protest by presenting the Twenty Points to the administration of President Richard Nixon. The points called for legislative and judicial action reestablishing treaty rights and protecting Indian sovereignty. Directly addressing Congress and the executive branch, Twenty Points proposed to redefine U.S.-Indian relations.

It is difficult to separate reception of the Twenty Points manifesto from the Trail of Broken Treaties protest and the ensuing occupation of the Bureau of Indian Affairs (BIA) building. In subsequent news coverage and negotiations, the occupation of BIA offices overshadowed the manifesto's call to action, which was outlined in twenty specific demands for governmental changes to the management of and transactions with American Indian tribes. To appease protesters, government officials agreed to consider the Twenty Points over a six-month period but ultimately rejected all the propositions, many of which sought far-reaching revisions to current policies. Despite this dismissal, the Twenty Points paper stands out for its eloquent and direct demands for a reconsideration of U.S.-Indian negotiations. Unfortunately, today many remember the violence and destruction associated with the Trail of Broken Treaties protest more than they recall the pleas for self-determination and sovereignty expressed in the Twenty Points position paper.

HISTORICAL AND LITERARY CONTEXT

The "Twenty Points" manifesto responds to decades of dissatisfaction in Native American communities stemming from discrimination, lack of sovereignty, and disregarded treaty rights. The position paper's chief demand is for the restoration of treaty-making authority, which would officially acknowledge Native Americans' unique cultural and political standing among U.S. citizens. In the mid-twentieth century, many Native American communities faced extreme poverty and the impending loss of traditional culture. For the manifesto's writers, renewal of treaty negotiations offered a resolution to these challenges. By demanding treaty-making authority, American Indian tribes could assert themselves as sovereign nations as well as improve the lot of Native Americans throughout the United States.

When the Twenty Points position paper was written in 1972, a Native American political resistance movement was well under way. Founded in the late 1960s, the American Indian Movement (AIM) directed collective Native American attention on reversing "ruinous" colonialist policies of the United States. Amid an atmosphere of political protest and rising identity politics in the United States, AIM organized Native Americans from around the country, including smaller groups also working for Indian rights. The original purpose of the Trail of Broken Treaties caravan, which included an estimated 1,000 participants and was planned primarily by AIM, was to present the Twenty Points paper to the federal government. Eventually, the protest followed the pattern of more violent Native American demonstrations as it culminated in the occupation of BIA offices.

Written near the end of the Red Power movement, an indigenous-rights protest movement of the 1960s modeled after the Black Power movement of the same era, the Trail of Broken Treaties Twenty Points position paper bears the marks of other literary works from the Indian Rights movement. In form, the manifesto is a list of demands and reveals echoes of documentation from similar protests, such as the Alcatraz Proclamation from that island's 1969 occupation. The content of the manifesto, particularly its assertion of sovereignty, draws on the precedence of prior Indian manifestos such as Vine Deloria, Jr.'s *Custer Died for Your Sins: An Indian Manifesto* (1969), which argued for Indian self-representation and self-determination. However, the legal context and formal presentation as a position paper separates Twenty Points from its predecessors.

In the months following the presentation of the Twenty Points position paper, government officials and media outlets seemed to all but forget about the manifesto. The position paper was also roundly rejected by the Nixon administration. However, despite its political impotence, the paper demonstrated that Native Americans could unite against white America. Preeminent Native American lawyer and scholar Vine Deloria, Jr. took up the Trail of Broken Treaties cause, penning the book-length discussion of the event and its implications in *Behind the Trail of Broken Treaties* (1974). Soon after the Trail of Broken Treaties caravan, protesters descended on Wounded Knee in South Dakota, again imploring the government for self-determination. Today, the Twenty Points paper is generally thought of as a political failure for its inability to incite legislative change, however, it represents a watershed moment in Native American protest: American Indians recognized the untapped power in collective action, which inaugurated a new era in U.S.-Indian relations.

THEMES AND STYLE

The central theme of the Twenty Points position paper is the restructuring of the relationship between the U.S. government and Native American communities so that decision-making power is more evenly distributed, ensuring tribal sovereignty. Three objectives put forth in the manifesto's preamble infuse each of the Twenty Points in an attempt to achieve this balance of power: the renewal of government contracts, the restoration of Native American communities, and the safeguard of American Indians' future in the United States. More than half of the Twenty Points deal principally with treaty reform in various ways. The first and second points address future treaty negotiations, calling for the "restoration of constitutional treaty-making authority" and the "establishment of treaty commission to make new treaties," respectively. Points four and five address mismanagement of past treaties, calling for a "commission to review treaty commitments and violations" and "resubmission of unratified treaties to the Senate". Predominant among the other points is a strategy to reconstruct U.S.-Indian relations, including the creation of a congressional joint committee, plans for land reform, and the dissolution of the BIA.

The manifesto achieves its rhetorical effect by appealing for transparent and fair dealings between Native Americans and the U.S. government. Targeting the presidential administration, the manifesto takes a diplomatic and formal approach, using legalese characteristic of political discourse. For example, point sixteen declares that the paper is a "remedy [for] the break-down in constitutionally-prescribed relationships between the United States and Indian Nations and people and to alleviate the destructive impact that distortion in those relationships has rendered upon the lives of Indian People." To separate Twenty Points from previous Indian appeals, the manifesto asserts that it is not "another recitation of past complaints [or] … redundant dialogue of discontent" and instead offers practical tactics to move forward

THE ACTUAL PROTEST: BIA TAKEOVER

The Trail of Broken Treaties caravaners never intended to occupy the Bureau of Indian Affairs facilities. Their initial intent was to raise awareness of Indian rights through peaceful demonstrations and to present the Twenty Points paper to the Nixon administration on the eve of the 1972 presidential election. However, when the several hundred caravaners arrived in Washington DC, they discovered that accommodations were either unavailable or no longer offered. The group sought assistance from the BIA but were disappointed by the organization's failure to help. Believing the lack of housing was an intentional obstruction, the protesters seized BIA offices and took out much of their pent-up aggression on the building.

During the occupation, which lasted from November 2 to 9, 1972, protesters vandalized and damaged the building and its contents. The occupation finally ended when newly reelected President Nixon, concerned chiefly with ending the protest, agreed to review the Twenty Point position paper if the protesters abandoned the BIA building. Protesters were given $36,66,000 for their travel home, but some faced potential criminal charges for stealing artifacts and classified documents and for an estimated $36,700,000 in damages caused to the building. In the end, rather than enlightening non-Indians about the plight facing many Native Americans throughout the United States, the violence that erupted at BIA not only obscured important issues but also may have turned supporters away from the cause of Indian rights.

productively. To do so, point twenty asks for "the most creative, if demanding and disciplined forms of community development and purposeful initiatives" for health, education, and economic development in conjunction with cost estimates for these provisions. The manifesto takes a proactive stance—guided by an underlying philosophy of self-determination—in tackling what its authors perceive as problematic aspects of U.S.-Indian relations,

Stylistically the Twenty Points manifesto adheres to characteristics of a position paper, its self-proclaimed genre. Typically found in legal and political contexts, position papers present an opinion about an issue, most often when a thorough understanding of an opponent's view is necessary. The manifesto's bulleted format and its detailed, coherent explanation of demands conform to this genre and make explicit the controversial and weighty issues at stake. The authoritative tone of the manifesto emphasizes its strategic approach to political renegotiations. Forceful statements, such as the declaration that "Congress should by law provide for a new system of federal court jurisdiction and procedure, when Indian treaty or governmental rights are at issue," reinforce the authors' passion for their cause, though it is at times

American Indian Movement (AIM) leader Dennis Banks, participating in a march in 1976. AIM was one of many Native American groups involved in the Trail of Broken Treaties protest.
© BETTMANN/CORBIS

tempered by the manifesto's objective stance. Such passion comes through in discussion of Indian youths' suffering from governmental neglect. The manifesto asserts that "death remains a standard cure for environmentally induced diseases afflicting many Indian children without adequate housing facilities, heating systems, and pure water sources." The manifesto derives its rhetorical force from its coherent practical approach, as well as from its authors' subtle, yet fervent, conviction.

CRITICAL DISCUSSION

The Twenty Points position paper was declared a failure by many observers. When the manifesto was first presented to the government as the terms of negotiation in the Trail of Broken Treaties protest, the Nixon administration and news outlets ignored it. Eclipsed by the violent conflict erupting in the occupation of BIA offices, the manifesto itself received little attention. Caravaners were depicted as "communist-inspired radicals" intent on demolition, and the government "deftly avoided" discussion of the Twenty Points. Eventually the manifesto reached its intended audience, as federal officials agreed to review the Twenty Points on the condition that protesters peacefully abandon the BIA building. Following six months of consideration, officials announced that treaty reform was impossible and other concerns raised in the Twenty Points would continue to be studied. Ultimately, none of the proposed reforms was enacted.

Although the manifesto's demands were not met, Twenty Points demonstrated the organizational power and resilience of Native Americans to Indians and non-Indians alike. According to John Sanchez, The Trail of Broken Treaties "signaled American Indian determination to persist in the face of public indifference and government hostility" and the Twenty Points paper functions as a symbol of this

persistence. Sanchez observes that the Twenty Points was also significant because it attempted to alter "both the Indians' self-perception and government policy," appealing to younger, urban Indians' desire for action as well as older, reservation-based Native Americans' need for autonomy. Three years after the Trail of Broken Treaties caravan, the Indian Self-Determination and Education Assistance Act of 1975 got at some of the concerns raised by the protest. Although the act did not address treaty making, it did establish self-determination as an official federal policy and ensured the provision of resources and protections for Native Americans. The Twenty Points manifesto may not be directly responsible for these changes, but the position paper is a notable piece of a broader sea change in U.S.-Indian interactions.

The bulk of scholarship on Twenty Points has been focused on the rhetoric of Native American protest and its impact on Indian-white relations. Scholars have considered the rhetoric used in Twenty Points to understand Native American protest discourse on its own. Some scholars have also looked to rhetoric to understand the failure of Twenty Points to convince non-Indians to invest in Native American issues. In "Enacting Red Power: The Consummatory Function in Native American Protest Rhetoric," Randall A. Lake defends the supposed ineffectiveness of protest rhetoric, asserting that Indians address other Indians rather than attempt to convince outsiders, so that protest documents have been evaluated with the wrong audience in mind. Tim Baylor's research of media framing of Native American protest demonstrates again the misunderstanding between Indians and non-Indians, showing that only a minority of news reports about the Trail of Broken Treaties included discussion of treaty rights, the protesters' central issue. Most scholars and participants agree that even though immediate policy goals were not accomplished, the long-term impact of the Trail of Broken Treaties has been to inspire three generations of American Indians.

BIBLIOGRAPHY

Sources

Heppler, Jason. *Framing Red Power: Newspapers, the Trail of Broken Treaties, and the Politics of Media.* U of Nebraska-Lincoln: Center for Digital Research in the Humanities. n.d. Web. 2 Aug 2012.

Margolis, Richard J. "Indians: A Long List of Grievances." *New York Times* 12 Nov 1972. Print.

Salomon, Larry. "Movement History: A Trail of Broken Treaties." *Third Force* 3.1 (1995): 35. Print.

Shown, Susan. "Trail of Broken Treaties: A 30th Anniversary Memory." *Indian Country Today* 6 Nov 2006: A5. Print.

"Trail of Broken Treaties Caravan." *Redhawk's Lodge.* William Redhawk. 21 May 2004. Web. 2 Aug 2012.

"Trail of Broken Treaties 20-Point Position Paper." *American Indian Movement.* American Indian Movement Grand Governing Council. Web. 2 Aug 2012.

Further Reading

Baird-Olson, Karen. "Reflections of an AIM Activist: Has It All Been Worth It?" *American Indian Culture and Research Journal* 18.4 (1994): 233-52. Print.

Baylor, Tim. "Media Framing of Movement Protest: The Case of American Indian Protest." *The Social Science Journal* 33.3 (1996): 241-55. Print.

Deloria, Vine, Jr. *Behind the Trail of Broken Treaties: An Indian Declaration of Independence.* New York: Delacorte, 1974. Print.

Johnson, Troy, Joane Nagel, and Duane Champagne, eds. *American Indian Activism: Alcatraz to the Longest Walk.* Champaign: U of Illinois, 1997. Print.

Lake, Randall L. "Enacting Red Power: The Consummatory Function of Native American Protest Rhetoric." *Quarterly Journal of Speech* 69 (1983): 127-42. Print.

Nagel, Joane. *American Indian Ethic Renewal: Red Power and the Resurgence of Identity and Culture.* New York: Oxford UP, 1996. Print.

Sanchez, John, and Mary E. Stuckey. "The Rhetoric of American Indian Activism in the 1960s and 1970s." *Communication Quarterly* 48.2 (2000): 120-36. Print.

Elizabeth Boeheim

YIPPIE MANIFESTO

Jerry Rubin

OVERVIEW

The *Yippie Manifesto,* written in 1969 by social activist Jerry Rubin and published in the counterculture journal *Evergreen Review,* is a tongue-in-cheek essay that reads as a radically themed political protest against perceived police and governmental injustice. The document heralded the views of the Youth International Party, founded in the United States in late 1967 by Rubin and antiwar activist Abbie Hoffman. The Yippies, as they called themselves, were not a formal political party so much as a loose collection of hippies, anti-Vietnam War activists, and mischief makers who saw themselves as cultural rebels challenging entrenched middle-class American values. They broadcast their demands for political and social change through elaborately choreographed street theater. Rubin's essay demanded, among other things, an immediate end to the war in Vietnam, an overhaul of the U.S. prison system, an end to all censorship, and the abolishment of money. His exhortation for his audience to "RISE UP AND ABANDON THE CREEPING MEATBALL!" embodies the *Yippie Manifesto*'s provocative, irreverent opposition to the existing political and cultural paradigms.

Although it was an important testament to the originality and approach of the Youth International Party, the *Yippie Manifesto* did not significantly affect the movement. In keeping with the pranks the Yippies used to attract media attention, the essay relied on outrageous claims and absurdist symbolism. Other left-leaning activists and many of those involved in the antiwar movement viewed Yippie tactics as street theater devoid of substance. Mainstream Americans in the late 1960s did not embrace the Yippies' demands or approaches, and the essay likely did more to reinforce biases against the fringe factions of the movement than gain adherents. The document catalogs several of the most notable Yippie events, including their much-publicized protest at the 1968 Democratic National Convention in Chicago, where Rubin and seven others were arrested and tried on charges of conspiracy and inciting to riot.

HISTORICAL AND LITERARY CONTEXT

By the time Rubin wrote the *Yippie Manifesto,* more than 13,000 Americans had died in the Vietnam War and public support for it was waning. Resistance to the draft was intensifying, which also catalyzed public activism around other social and political issues. Protests against the war, such as the October 1967 march on the Pentagon, gave participants a forum to express their outrage not only at the war but also at the traditional structures of power. In the early and mid-1960s, a number of anti-disciplinary and counterculture groups were organized to oppose conventional civil, social, or political institutions. Groups such as the Diggers, the Merry Pranksters, and Up Against the Wall Motherfucker briefly flourished and contributed to a broadening expression of dissent over the war, consumerism, traditional values, sexual mores, and popular culture.

In 1967 the Yippies staged a theatrical demonstration against capitalistic greed at the New York Stock Exchange, where they flung dollar bills from the observation gallery and laughed as traders scrambled to pocket them. The same year, during a 100,000-person protest against the Vietnam War, Hoffman led the Yippies in a so-called exorcism of the Pentagon. The Yippies also played a prominent role among the thousands of antiwar protesters who gathered in the streets of Chicago during the 1968 Democratic National Convention. Hoffman, Rubin, and six others were arrested after they presented Pigasus the Pig as the Yippie Party's own candidate for president. The *Yippie Manifesto* sought to stir youth energy and rebellion by dramatizing scenarios in which oppression—whether societal, police, or political—occurs.

The *Yippie Manifesto* draws from a wide array of the polemical writing that emerged from the antiwar movement and from the *Port Huron Statement,* in particular. Composed in 1962, the *Port Huron Statement* called for the end of U.S. involvement in the war in Vietnam and its Cold War foreign policy of engagement in general. It also demanded an end to domestic economic and racial inequality. Written primarily by Tom Hayden, founder of Students for a Democratic Society, the *Port Huron Statement* was an important call to action and established the student and youth voice in the antiwar and antiestablishment movement. The *Yippie Manifesto* built on the *Port Huron Statement*'s brand of grassroots activism, while also making an irreverent, glib, and absurdist rant that draws from a rich tradition of avant-garde prose writing. Inspired by the manifestos of such early twentieth century art movements as Dadaism, the *Yippie Manifesto* rejects linear logic just as it rejects the dominant culture's reliance on rationality to establish its authority.

Long after the countercultural foment of the 1960s subsided, the *Yippie Manifesto*'s rejection of the capitalist status quo remained a source of inspiration for left-wing activists. This lingering influence can be felt, for example, in the *Declaration of the Occupation of New York City*. Composed and issued by members of the Occupy Wall Street movement in 2011, the declaration indicts the "corporate forces of the world" for perpetuating social, economic, and political injustice around the world. Like Rubin, the Occupy Wall Street leaders make a case not for a specific, limited political cause but rather for an upending of the status quo and the creation of "solutions accessible to everyone." Today, the *Yippie Manifesto* is considered an important contribution to left-wing activism in the United States.

THEMES AND STYLE

The central theme of the *Yippie Manifesto* is that the Yippie movement offers an antidote to the "great spiritual crisis" of contemporary capitalism and democracy in America. It advocates for a world that is communal and borderless and for a society in which the individual is self-governing. In keeping with counterculture messaging, it rejects systems and policies that lead to inequality. It engages youth and calls them to activism, irrationality, and joyous self-expression, as well as to wage war on the establishment. As Rubin writes, "We offer: sex, drugs, rebellion, heroism, brotherhood. They offer: responsibility, fear, Puritanism, repression." The document also declares a spiritual aspect of the Yippie movement, stating that "political demonstrations should make people dream and fantasize. A religious-political movement is concerned with people's souls, with the creation of a magic world which we make real." This vein was reinforced by the antiauthoritarian, antimaterialist anarchist belief that "rules are made to be broken" and "there are no such things as borders."

The essay achieves its rhetorical effect through provocative, spontaneous appeals that simultaneously flaunt, cajole, argue, question, rage, sneer, and despair. Devoid of organizing structures, such as paragraphs or extensively developed ideas, the document's message comes across as a spontaneously formed, improvisational, and mostly personal expression. The appeal for a freedom of being and expression is embodied in the freeform style of the writing and its open-ended format. The sense of impermanence is achieved through its rapidly shifting, abstract, seeming incongruous statements, such as:

> We are a new generation, species, race. We are bred on affluence, turned on by drugs, at home in our bodies, and excited by the future and its possibilities.

JERRY RUBIN: PARADOX OF THE SIXTIES

Remembered for his passion in forming the Yippie movement and his vocal complaints about American capitalism and materialism, Jerry Rubin ultimately became an entrepreneur and businessman in his own right, which damaged his reputation among many of his early followers. Born in 1938, Rubin started protesting left-wing causes in Berkeley, California, after he dropped out of the university. In 1965 he helped form the Vietnam Day Committee, a group that organized protests against the Vietnam War. As the visionary behind the Yippies' protests against the New York Stock Exchange and the Pentagon, both in 1967, and the Democratic National Convention in Chicago in 1968, Rubin, along with Abbie Hoffman, was perceived as the visionary behind the Yippie brand of theatrical protest. He was arrested numerous times and, following the 1968 convention in Chicago, was indicted on federal charges of conspiracy and incitement to riot. The "Chicago Seven Trial," in which he and six others were tried, was one of the most significant political events of the late 1960s.

In the 1970s and 1980s Rubin went into business, becoming a marketing analyst and venture capitalist, and shifted his message, voicing the opinion that he believed the creation of wealth and distribution of wealth into impoverished communities was the way to make change in U.S. society. He accumulated great wealth and was criticized for becoming a Yuppie (the 1980's moniker for a Young Urban Professional). He died in 1994 after being hit by a car while he was jaywalking across Wilshire Boulevard in Santa Monica, California.

> Everything for us is an experience, done for love or not done at all.

> We live off the fat of society. Our fathers worked all-year round for a two-week vacation. Our entire life is a vacation.

Unique, even anomalistic among other manifestos, Rubin's work defies categorization in recognized literary terms; in mocking so many institutional frameworks, it also mocks traditional forms of questioning them.

Stylistically, the *Yippie Manifesto* is distinguished by its colorful and informal tone of outrage, defiance, and nihilism. Written as personal testimony that draws on a mixture of seemingly random accounts, established events, and brief segments of dialogue with anonymous Americans, the essay makes its appeal not as an official document but as a voice of the unofficial, the unlicensed, and the unsanctioned:

> The economy is closed. It does not need us. Everything is built.

> So the purpose of the universities is: to get us off the streets. Schools are baby-sitting agencies.

Abbie Hoffman during the 1968 Democratic National Convention. Hoffman was a cofounder and the most famous member of the revolutionary countercultural group the Yippies. JULIAN WASSER/ TIME & LIFE PICTURES/ GETTY IMAGES

The purpose of the Vietnam War is: to get rid of blacks. They are a nuisance. America got the work she needed out of blacks, but now she has no use for them.

Rubin demonstrates his alignment with the radical counterculture by exemplifying rejection of established protest language. By using colloquial speech and a tone of ranting outrage, the *Yippie Manifesto* makes the case ironically (as in the above statement regarding African Americans) for upending of the status quo.

CRITICAL DISCUSSION

The Yippies were the among the most high-profile political activists of the 1960s, thanks to their media-courting activities, and their essay was condemned outside the counterculture and debated within it. In his 1970 essay "The New Left and the Counter-Culture," critic David Crownfield typified the response to Rubin's writing. "Rubin," Crownfield writes, "is not only obscene, theatrical, funny, surrealistic; he is disorganized, tedious, and unoriginal. But the incongruities he creates and exposes are essential…. [It is] the creation of an imagination which can recognize absurdity, which can entertain alternatives, which ceases to take for granted the whole straight established system of values." Crownfield's critique of Rubin's argument and praise of his overarching project was typical of the left-wing reaction to the text. While many activists sought the same kind of fundamental change called for in Rubin's essay, they mostly viewed it and the Yippie movement as a distraction to serious and effective protest. Among political conservatives, the *Yippie Manifesto* and its message were met with derision and even fear, despite Rubin's declared commitment to nonviolence.

More recently, many critics have reassessed the Yippies' contribution to grassroots protest, political theater, and street theater. In *Anti-Disciplinary Protest: Sixties Radicalism and Post-Modernism,* Julie Stephens argues that "in the Yippie notion of guerilla theatre, the streets were … a canvas, a backdrop full of engrossing and useful props and actors. [It was] the most appropriate site for a political satire which drew simultaneously from fantasy and burlesque as well as from the melodrama of a violent clash with the police." Commentators have also argued that more recent grassroots street protests, such as at the World Trade Organization protests in Seattle in 1999 and the Occupy Wall Street protest in 2012, take their tone of outrage and theatrical color from the Yippies.

Scholars have placed Rubin's writing within the context of polemical countercultural writing in the United States during the 1960s. Stephens argues that the strategy of incorporating "popular ingredients" and an informal rhetorical tone was part of a deliberate effort "to counter the piety of more conventional Left strategies, to taint the purity of movements supposedly based on selfless ideals and noble ancestry, and to playfully incorporate seductive items from the everyday into an arena often noted for its autonomy and specialization." Other commentators have noted the Yippies' efforts to "commandeer the media" in various ways, as scholar Todd Gitlin writes in *The Sixties: Years of Hope, Days of Rage,* including through the distribution of the *Yippie Manifesto.* Gitlin observes that the Yippie attitude toward the media reflected their "belief that the turned-on baby-boom generation was already 'the revolution in embryo'; that what the media were calling its 'lifestyle' prefigured a kind of small-c communism remaining only to be taken up by the rest of sluggish America."

BIBLIOGRAPHY

Sources

Crownfield, David. "The New Left and the Counter-Culture." Rev. of *Do IT!* by Jerry Rubin. *North American Review* 255.3 (1970): 70-76. Print.

"Declaration of the Occupation of New York City." *New York City General Assembly.* 29 Sept. 2011. Web. 2 Aug. 2012.

Farber, David. *Chicago, '68.* Chicago: U of Chicago P, 1988. Print.

Gitlin, Todd. *The Sixties: Years of Hope, Days of Rage.* New York: Bantam Books, 1987. Print.

Leen, Jeff. "The Vietnam Protests: When Worlds Collided." *Washington Post* 27 Sept. 1999, A1. *Academic OneFile.* Web. 24 Sept. 2012.

Rubin, Jerry. "Yippie Manifesto." *Evergreen Review* 13.66 (1969). Print.

Santoski, Teresa. "Daily TWiP—Abbie Hoffman and Fellow Yippies Fling Dollar Bills at Stock Traders Today in 1967." *Nashua Telegraph.* Telegraph Publishing, 24 Aug. 2010. Web. 6 Nov. 2012.

Stephens, Julie. *Anti-Disciplinary Protest: Sixties Radicalism and Post-Modernism.* New York: Cambridge UP, 1998. Print.

Further Reading

Albert, Judith Clavir, and Stewart Edward Albert. *The Sixties Papers: Documents of a Rebellious Decade.* Westport: Praeger, 1984. Print.

De Groot, Gerard J. *The Sixties Unplugged: A Kaleidoscopic History of Disorderly Decade.* Cambridge: Harvard UP, 2008. Print.

O'Neill, William L. *The New Left: A History.* Wheeling: Harlan Davidson, 2001. Print.

Sossi, Ron, Tom Hayden, and Frank Condon. *Voices of the Chicago Eight: A Generation on Trial.* San Francisco: City Lights, 2008. Print.

Rubin, Jerry. *Growing (Up) at Thirty-Seven.* New York: M. Evans, 1976. Print.

Stein, David Lewis. *Living the Revolution: The Yippies in Chicago.* Indianapolis: Bobbs-Merrill, 1969. Print.

Martha Sutro

TECHNOLOGIES

CRYPTO ANARCHIST MANIFESTO

Timothy C. May

OVERVIEW

The *Crypto Anarchist Manifesto,* written by Timothy C. May in 1988 for the Crypto'88 conference and widely published on the Internet in 1992, discusses the potential for an anarchist revolution through the development of new encryption technologies that would allow people to access information, to freely (and sometimes illegally) trade without government regulation or taxes, and to interact anonymously so that no corporations could control their interactions. The purpose of the manifesto is to alert the public to the rapid advancements in encryption technology and the societal anarchy that would result from everyday use of technology. May suggests that once this technology is in the hands of the general public, a new form of anarchy—complete freedom of information and anonymity online—will drastically alter the control of corporations that govern intellectual information. Released when Internet technology was still relatively new and expanding exponentially, the manifesto predicts that it would be only a matter of time until online interaction became completely untraceable and anonymous.

The manifesto was initially embraced by the organization from which May developed his free encryption software ideas, a group that called itself the cypherpunks. The point of the group was to devise ways to access information on encryption technology and anonymously publish that information on the Internet. They predicted both positive and negative repercussions from the public use of online encryption: people would be able to securely trade goods and post controversial opinions without prosecution, but crime and black market activity would increase because of the anonymity created through strong encryption software. The manifesto succeeded in making readers aware of the work being done to publicize encryption technology and the pros and cons associated with that publication.

HISTORICAL AND LITERARY CONTEXT

The manifesto was released at a time when the Internet, developed by the U.S. military, was becoming accessible to private users. The development of new technology enabled devices such as home computers to make this resource a usable tool in the day-to-day lives of the average person. The cypherpunks

demanded that encryption technology, developed by the military to protect its assets, be made public, believing that true anonymity should be obtainable within the online community to facilitate total freedom of speech. May believed the development of this technology would change how social and economic interactions affect people in much the same way that the development of printing technology changed medieval society by reducing the power of the guilds. In addition to facilitating anonymous transactions, encryption technology could enable methods of identification, such as online signatures and privacy measures, which would enhance security surrounding online purchases and credit transactions.

As a retired Intel physicist, May was aware of the rapidly developing capabilities of the Internet and the amount of information being withheld from the public. He brought his knowledge about Intel's inner workings to the cypherpunk group, where it was used by mathematicians, programmers, libertarians, and free-market advocates to freely publicize encryption technologies to the public. Today May is still known for his ideas about usable and accessible encryption technology that would allow total freedom of information.

The *Crypto Anarchist Manifesto* was influenced by the ideas being debated in the activist writings of the cypherpunks and by May's own writing about accessible encryption technology as a means of social change. May admits to writing the manifesto rather quickly and states that although there are sections he would change if given the chance, he keeps it in its original form for historical reasons. In the manifesto, he uses elements of style and tone that he remembered from Karl Marx's *The Communist Manifesto* to add a sense of irony to the text.

After its online publication, May's manifesto influenced subsequent writing about restricted access to cybertechnology and freedom in the rapidly expanding online community. May continued to write about government restrictions on encryption and published a number of essays including "The Cyphernomicon" and "True Nyms and Crypto Anarchy." Other activists began to discuss aspects of government laws concerning the control of Internet use, and manifestos appeared about the freedoms—especially freedom of speech—that some of these laws

✧ *Key Facts*

Time Period:
Late 20th Century

Movement/Issue:
Anarchism; Internet freedom; Information access

Place of Publication:
United States (Online)

Language of Publication:
English

CYPHERPUNKS: ONLINE SOCIAL ANARCHISTS

Existing as an informal activist group since the late 1980s, the cypherpunks are determined to promote social and political change through the open publication of encryption technology. Begun as an e-mail list with scattered meetings, the cypherpunk group discussed issues of privacy in the newly developing medium of the Internet and the cryptography in place to govern privacy and anonymity. Digital codes to enable anonymous transactions and verifiable signatures were discussed and developed via e-mail, and opinions were debated about the ethical and political implications of developing such codes in the name of crypto anarchy. Among the group's prominent members are Arthur Abraham, Eric Hughes, and Timothy C. May.

Some members of the group worked anonymously to "liberate" scholarly work on cypher technology by purchasing academic journals and duplicating the material on the Internet for free. Republishing these copyrighted articles without leaving traces to the original source was difficult if not impossible; a feat which members of the group felt was unjust. The Supreme Court upheld that every American had the right to distribute pamphlets anonymously, and the cypherpunks involved in liberating scholarly work felt they were unable to exercise that right without sophisticated, accessible encryption technology.

A button displaying the common symbol for anarchy. Timothy May, in his *Crypto Anarchist Manifesto*, argues that computer technology and related cryptologic methods will lead to a revolution. As the title suggests, this revolution will bring a type of anarchy. © ALEX SEGRE/ALAMY

violated. In 1996, for example, the Telecommunications Reform Act was the first to include Internet communications. Writer John Perry Barlow immediately published his rapidly successful and somewhat controversial "Declaration of the Independence of Cyberspace" as a response to the act. This work uses many of the ideas about freedom of speech and the right of anonymity outlined in the *Crypto Anarchist Manifesto*.

THEMES AND STYLE

The main theme of the *Crypto Anarchist Manifesto* is that the development of computer capabilities and encrypted Internet access will allow free and anonymous access to information, which will ultimately change the nature of trade, social interactions, and government control. May states that this will be "both a social and economic revolution," which previously existed in theory but did not have the technology to come to fruition. The new society resulting from this revolution would be one of anarchy—or crypto anarchy, due to its reliance on encrypted information—because trade would become unregulated and untaxed, national secrets would be revealed, and people would communicate anonymously.

The manifesto achieves its rhetorical effect through the presentation of information from an objective standpoint. The majority of the manifesto reads as a news report or an information bulletin. At the end, the author directly encourages readers: "Arise, you have nothing to lose but your barbed wire fences!" The comparison between cutting down barbed wire fences and using encrypted access to change the concept of ownership aligns the digital revolution with the Industrial Revolution, when ideas about land ownership butted against the communal farming that had existed for centuries. This comparison contextualizes the social changes that the manifesto predicts will accompany the development of encryption technology—namely the dissolution of government and corporate control over online transactions and communication. According to May, the medium of the debate has changed because of new encryption technologies and the advancement of computer technology, but the ideas of anarchy—and of the ungoverned freedom over the exchange and use of intellectual property—provide the foundation of the manifesto.

The language used in the manifesto attempts to describe the quickly changing technology of the early 1990s without sounding too technical for the average reader. Terms such as *True Name* and *CryptoNet* make the manifesto sound technologically advanced, on the one hand, but they also have a strong resemblance to themes and ideas discussed in science fiction literature. These terms appeal to the manifesto's intended audience, who would be versed in such literature and ideas, but the language also emphasizes the newness and strangeness of the medium in which the anarchist revolution will take place. Although these terms reflect the newness of technology as a medium for social change, they are modestly placed within the manifesto to emphasize that the technology in question is still being developed. May predicts that the anarchist revolution associated with the development of this technology will change society, the economy, and governing structures so that information will be freely and anonymously available to the public without the interference of government control.

CRITICAL DISCUSSION

The publication of the manifesto initially created discussion about government control and basic rights and freedoms within the developing online community.

PRIMARY SOURCE

CRYPTO ANARCHIST MANIFESTO

A specter is haunting the modern world, the specter of crypto anarchy.

Computer technology is on the verge of providing the ability for individuals and groups to communicate and interact with each other in a totally anonymous manner. Two persons may exchange messages, conduct business, and negotiate electronic contracts without ever knowing the True Name, or legal identity, of the other. Interactions over networks will be untraceable, via extensive rerouting of encrypted packets and tamper-proof boxes which implement cryptographic protocols with nearly perfect assurance against any tampering. Reputations will be of central importance, far more important in dealings than even the credit ratings of today. These developments will alter completely the nature of government regulation, the ability to tax and control economic interactions, the ability to keep information secret, and will even alter the nature of trust and reputation.

The technology for this revolution—and it surely will be both a social and economic revolution—has existed in theory for the past decade. The methods are based upon public-key encryption, zero-knowledge interactive proof systems, and various software protocols for interaction, authentication, and verification. The focus has until now been on academic conferences in Europe and the U.S., conferences monitored closely by the National Security Agency. But only recently have computer networks and personal computers attained sufficient speed to make the ideas practically realizable. And the next ten years will bring enough additional speed to make the ideas economically feasible and essentially unstoppable. High-speed networks, ISDN, tamper-proof boxes,

smart cards, satellites, Ku-band transmitters, multi-MIPS personal computers, and encryption chips now under development will be some of the enabling technologies.

The State will of course try to slow or halt the spread of this technology, citing national security concerns, use of the technology by drug dealers and tax evaders, and fears of societal disintegration. Many of these concerns will be valid; crypto anarchy will allow national secrets to be trade freely and will allow illicit and stolen materials to be traded. An anonymous computerized market will even make possible abhorrent markets for assassinations and extortion. Various criminal and foreign elements will be active users of CryptoNet. But this will not halt the spread of crypto anarchy.

Just as the technology of printing altered and reduced the power of medieval guilds and the social power structure, so too will cryptologic methods fundamentally alter the nature of corporations and of government interference in economic transactions. Combined with emerging information markets, crypto anarchy will create a liquid market for any and all material which can be put into words and pictures. And just as a seemingly minor invention like barbed wire made possible the fencing-off of vast ranches and farms, thus altering forever the concepts of land and property rights in the frontier West, so too will the seemingly minor discovery out of an arcane branch of mathematics come to be the wire clippers which dismantle the barbed wire around intellectual property.

Arise, you have nothing to lose but your barbed wire fences!

While not all scholars agree that the development and practical application of encryption technology will create crypto anarchy, government control of the export of this information may be seen as hindrance to the development of this technology and the funding required. Peter Neumann, in a 1994 article for *Issues in Science and Technology,* writes, "Easing export controls on sensible encryption technology to create a larger market would create a powerful incentive for U.S. firms to invest more in the development of encryption." Other scholars view May's crypto anarchy beliefs as frightening because, according to Kevin Kelly in *Out of Control* (1995), "pervasive encryption removes economic activity—one driving force of our society—from any hope of central control. Encryption breeds out-of-controllness."

The mixed opinions about freedom of speech and the cypherpunks' goals continue to generate

discussion about privacy and government control online and the potential outcomes of openly publicizing encryption technology. Some scholars point out the flaws in May's anarchist ideas, such as Dorothy Denning in an essay in *Crypto Anarchy, Cyberstates, and Pirate Utopias* (1996). She argues that while a free market with its associated benefits is an outcome most people would desire, anarchy—the complete lack of governance—is not desirable, even on the Internet: "Thus, the crypto anarchists' claims come close to asserting that technology will take us to an outcome that most of us would not choose." Other activists defend May's beliefs that crypto anarchy is both inevitable and a highly desirable goal. Duncan Frissell responds to Denning's criticism, also in *Crypto Anarchy,* by calling the American government a cult that will always exist because "the deregulation of human interaction will make it easier for more oppressive cults to exist than is possible today."

Current trends in scholarship surrounding encryption technology and the Internet tend to focus on issues of privacy and security rather than on societal philosophies such as anarchy. For example, account information was stolen from the electronic resources of the Bank of America in 2007, which led to questions about why the information was not encrypted for security reasons. In 2005 bank analysts told *All Things Considered* that encryption was not used because it is "a pain to manage" and "particularly unwieldy for information that's constantly in use." The use of encryption and its practical applications are still being researched by corporations but have apparently limited potential for the general population because of encryption's cumbersome intricacies.

BIBLIOGRAPHY

Sources

"Analysis: Reluctance of American Businesses to Use Encryption Technology." *All Things Considered* 22 June 2005: n. pag. *Literature Resource Center*. Web. 4 Sept. 2012.

Denning, Dorothy E. "The Future of Cryptography." *Crypto Anarchy, Cyberstates, and Pirate Utopias*. Ed. Peter Ludlow. Cambridge: MIT, 2001. 85-101. *Scribd*. Web. 4 Sept. 2012.

Frissell, Duncan. "Re: Denning's Crypto Anarchy." *Crypto Anarchy, Cyberstates, and Pirate Utopias*. Ed. Peter Ludlow. Cambridge: MIT, 2001. 105-14. *Scribd*. Web. 4 Sept. 2012.

Kelly, Kevin. *Out of Control: The New Biology of Machines, Social Systems, and the Economic World*. New York: Perseus, 1995. Web. 4 Sept. 2012.

Neumann, Peter G. "Computer Insecurity." *Issues in Science and Technology* 11.1 (1994): 50-54. *Gale Opposing Viewpoints in Context*. Web. 4 Sept. 2012.

Further Reading

Beeson, Ann. "Should the Internet Be Regulated? Openness Should Be Preserved." *World & I* 13.2 (1998): 68-69. Web. 4 Sept. 2012.

Branscomb, Anne W. *Who Owns Information? From Privacy to Public Access*. New York: Basic, 1994. Print.

Cavoukian, Ann. *Who Knows? Safeguarding Your Privacy in a Networked World*. Toronto: Random, 1995. Print.

Kahin, Brian, and Charles Nesson, eds. *Borders in Cyberspace: Information Policy and the Global Information Infrastructure*. Cambridge: MIT, 1997. Print.

May, Timothy C. "Crypto Anarchy and Virtual Communities." *Crypto Anarchy, Cyberstates, and Pirate Utopias*. Ed. Peter Ludlow. Cambridge: MIT, 2001. 65-79. *Scribd*. Web. 4 Sept. 2012.

Katherine Barker

A Declaration of the Independence of Cyberspace

John Perry Barlow

OVERVIEW

John Perry Barlow's "A Declaration of the Independence of Cyberspace," originally distributed via e-mail in February 1996, declares the information exchange taking place on the computer networks of the world (a phenomenon he spatializes as "cyberspace") to be legally and ideologically independent from the physical world. Barlow asserts the sovereignty of the Internet based on its incompatibility with preexisting legal and organizational paradigms. The declaration came during the rapid initial growth of the Internet and the associated legal debates over jurisdiction. Addressed to "Governments of the Industrial World," it declares the laws that attempt to regulate cyberspace to be inapplicable to its reality and ultimately ineffectual. Furthermore, it claims that many of the legal concepts of the physical world, such as property and identity, are not categories that can cleanly apply in the domain of information.

Immediately after its email circulation, the declaration generated prolific discussions from both supporters and detractors. It was reprinted in newspapers throughout the United States, discussed in computer science journals, and widely reposted on the Internet. In May 1996 there were more than five thousand sites reposting Barlow's message. By November of that year the number was estimated at forty thousand. In a June article in *Wired,* Barlow claimed that he received around three hundred e-mails a day concerning the declaration. Although it was considered by some to be brash or idealistic, the declaration was prescient in forecasting many of the transformations in the Internet and its associated laws.

HISTORICAL AND LITERARY CONTEXT

"A Declaration of the Independence of Cyberspace" was a direct response to the Telecommunications Act of 1996, which deregulated broadcasting and imposed restrictions on electronic communications. Title V of the bill, called the Communications Decency Act (CDA), attempted to restrict obscene language and images on the Internet. As Barlow put it, the act made it "unlawful, and punishable by $250,000, to say 'shit' online." Shortly after the bill passed, a large-scale protest campaign began on the Internet. Barlow's

Electronic Frontier Foundation (EFF) initiated a Blue Ribbon Campaign for Online Freedom of Speech, Press, and Association. Its website was to become, according to the EFF, "one of the 4 most-linked-to sites on the Web." In the 1997 Supreme Court case *Reno v. ACLU,* the CDA was declared unconstitutional and struck from the Telecommunications Act.

By the time Barlow sent his e-mail in 1996, the Internet was growing at an exponential rate. At the inception of the World Wide Web in 1990, the Internet consisted of roughly two million users—mostly computer programmers, government employees, and college students. By 1996, however, there were 73 million Internet users, a number that would grow to 400 million by the year 2000. Widespread file sharing was beginning to challenge existing copyright law, and the issue was greatly intensified with the release of Napster in 1999. The introduction of the encryption program Pretty Good Privacy (PGP) in the 1990s gave Internet users military-grade cryptographic tools that provided a degree of privacy for files and e-mails.

Structurally, Barlow's declaration builds from the *Declaration of Independence,* written by Thomas Jefferson, whom Barlow references. Barlow contends that the Telecommunications Act "insults the dreams of Jefferson" and others, and his e-mail signature contains a quote from Jefferson: "It is error alone which needs the support of government. Truth can stand by itself." In a 2004 article in *Reason,* Brian Doherty calls Barlow "the Thomas Jefferson of cyberspace." Barlow adopted the word "cyberspace" from science fiction author William Gibson, and by applying it to Internet communications effectively extended the spatial metaphor implicit in the terms "website" or "chat room" to the level of a community or nation.

The declaration continued to be influential into the twenty-first century. In March 2012 the hacker activist group Anonymous released its own "Declaration of the Independence of Cyberspace." The Anonymous version replaces the now somewhat antiquated word "cyberspace" with "Internet" and adds passages that are critical of the proposed copyright laws known as the Stop Online Piracy Act (SOPA) and Protect IP Act (PIPA). Although Barlow's declaration is no longer discussed to the same degree it was

❖ *Key Facts*

Time Period:
Late 20th Century

Movement/Issue:
Internet freedom

Place of Publication:
United States

Language of Publication:
English

JOHN PERRY BARLOW: NEW MEDIA THEORETICIAN

John Perry Barlow has had a diverse set of occupations throughout his career. From 1971 to 1988 he worked as a cattle rancher, running the Bar Cross Land and Livestock Company. At the same time he was writing lyrics for the Grateful Dead and continued to do so until the band dissolved in 1995. In 1990, with Mitchell Kapor, he cofounded the Electronic Frontier Foundation (EFF), a nonprofit civil liberties advocacy group involved with legally defending users of technology. The EFF has been instrumental in many of the major technology court cases of the past several years, especially those involving file sharing, digital rights management, and bloggers' rights.

At various points, Barlow has been a Republican Party county chairman, a Democratic Party member, and an anarchist. He has written several notable works, particularly "The Economy of Ideas," an influential theoretical work in copyright law, and "Pretty Bad Problem," the preface to the *Pretty Good Privacy (PGP) User's Guide.* His essays have appeared widely in such publications as *Wired* and the *New York Times.* Barlow was known as the Professor of Cyberspace at the European Graduate School, where he taught a summer workshop, and he is currently a fellow at Harvard Law School's Berkman Center for Internet and Society.

in the mid-1990s, it remains a relevant document and frequent topic of debate among theoreticians of new media. The 2012 "Declaration of Internet Freedom," for instance, which Barlow supported, shares many principles with Barlow's declaration.

THEMES AND STYLE

"A Declaration of the Independence of Cyberspace" centers on the idea that cyberspace, which it refers to as the "new home of Mind," exists outside of the world of "flesh and steel"—what Barlow elsewhere calls "meatspace"—and therefore does not fall under its jurisdiction. "Our identities have no bodies," he argues, "so, unlike you [governments], we cannot obtain order by physical coercion." Furthermore, Barlow argues, as an anarchic entity with "no elected government," cyberspace allows for the creation of "a world that all may enter without privilege or prejudice accorded by race, economic power, military force, or station of birth." In contrast to regimes like the U.S. government, which, he argues, create laws "that claim to own speech itself," Barlow envisions a world where the only law would be the Golden Rule.

The rhetorical arc of "A Declaration of the Independence of Cyberspace" begins with separatism and ends by proposing a virtual nation. The opening paragraphs stress the differences between the old governments: "You of the past," and the new: "We

of the future." Barlow clearly differentiates between these two categories, insisting, "You are not welcome among us…. We did not invite you." He sets forth the principles of the new cyberspace nation, repeating the phrase "We are creating a world…" along with descriptions of this utopia. The final paragraph begins, "We will create a civilization of the Mind in Cyberspace." The structure emulates Jefferson's *Declaration of Independence,* where grievances begin with the word "He" (King George) and are answered with resolutions beginning with "We."

The language of the declaration is bold, concise, and abstract. Barlow achieves a pointed directness through his repeated use of pronouns and second-person address. He invokes a sense of further immediacy through the use of short, staccato sentences: "Do not think that you can build it [cyberspace], as though it were a public construction project. You cannot." Here, "you cannot" is an anapest that rhythmically emphasizes the division Barlow attempts to draw between traditional governments and the inhabitants of cyberspace. The paragraph structure mirrors this rhythm—some paragraphs in the middle section of the declaration, like those in Jefferson's, consist of only one sentence. Barlow also uses archaic words and structures that evoke a somewhat Jeffersonian tone—his use of the word "commonweal," for instance, and his Germanic capitalization of nouns such as "Mind" recall the language of eighteenth-century revolutionaries.

CRITICAL DISCUSSION

When the declaration first became available to the public shortly after its initial e-mail distribution in February 1996, most public reactions were critical or skeptical. In an August 1996 article in *Salon,* Scott Rosenberg calls Barlow's concept of a sovereign cyberspace "alluring, but hardly practical." Although he admits that the work is "a stirring, admittedly grandiose call to virtual arms" and "worth reading in full," he asks Barlow, in an extension of the American revolutionary metaphor, "when the first digital redcoats arrive to reassert the rule of some nation's law over the net, what e-mail minutemen will ride to defend the cause of freedom?" Similarly, in 1997 Virginia Postrel points out the naïveté of Barlow's dismissal of the physical. Whereas Barlow declares that "the global conveyance of thought no longer requires your factories," Postrel replies, "This is silly. Netizens do not communicate via telepathy—machines of metal, plastic, silicon, and glass are very much involved…. The worldwide network of computers depends on factories."

Later assessments of Barlow's work remained critical, although his declaration would be seriously discussed in legal and theoretical circles. At the annual meeting of the American Society of International Law in 1999, for instance, a discussion panel heard the voices of "decentralists" who "think territorially based governmental regulation will inevitably fail in cyberspace," quoting from Barlow's declaration to support their argument. Javier Beltran, writing in the *Boston College Intellectual Property and Technology Forum,* concedes that the declaration "is typical of the time that it was made" yet quotes liberally from it as a work that exemplifies "legal uncertainty in cyberspace."

Contemporary scholarship tends to highlight the dated, optimistic language of the declaration, while maintaining respect for its landmark historical status. In an article titled "An Impossible Future," Aimée Hope Morrison contends, "Attention to the rhetorical strategies of the piece—its slippery pronouns and complex structure of allusions and metaphors—reveals a wealth of contradictions and misdirection: newness is rooted in history; revolution is effected by commercial transaction; and liberal democracy becomes libertarianism." In his 2001 *Crypto Anarchy, Cyberstates, and Pirate Utopias,* however, Peter Ludlow claims that "whatever the merits of political independence for cyberspace, it would be a mistake to conclude that it is unfeasible on technological grounds." As evidence, Ludlow cites the tenets of crypto-anarchism, a philosophy that envisions a stateless virtual society facilitated by strong encryption of communications that enables privacy and erodes governmental control. Similarly, Lawrence Lessig's 1999 *Code and Other Laws of Cyberspace,* which argues for a regulated Internet, cites Barlow as an early utopian theoretician.

BIBLIOGRAPHY

Sources

Anonymous [activist group]. "A Declaration of the Independence of CyberSpace." *Tumblr.* Web. 21 July 2012.

Barlow, John Perry. "Subject: A Cyberspace Independence Declaration." 9 Feb. 1996. E-mail.

———. "Declaring Independence." *Wired* June 1996. Web. 21 July 2012.

Beltran, Javier. "What a Local Internet Company Can Do about Legal Uncertainty in Cyberspace." *Boston College Intellectual Property and Technology Forum.* Web. 21 July 2012.

"Blue Ribbon Campaign." *Electronic Frontier Foundation.* Web. 21 July 2012.

Doherty, Brian. "John Perry Barlow 2.0." *Reason.* Aug./Sept. 2004. Web. 21 July 2012.

Ludlow, Peter, ed. *Crypto Anarchy, Cyberstates, and Pirate Utopias.* Cambridge: MIT P, 2001. Print.

Morrison, Aimée Hope. "An Impossible Future: John Perry Barlow's 'Declaration of the Independence of Cyberspace.'" *New Media & Society* 11.1 (2009): 53-72. *SAGE.* Web. 21 July 2012.

Postrel, Virginia. "Their Own Worst Enemies." *Forbes* 7 Apr. 1997: 96. *ProQuest.* Web. 21 July 2012.

Rosenberg, Scott. "Independence Daze." *Salon* 1 Aug. 1996. Web. 21 July 2012.

Further Reading

Barlow, John Perry. "Barlow Home(stead) Page." *Electronic Frontier Foundation.* Web. 21 July 2012.

———. "The Economy of Ideas." *Wired* Mar. 1994. Web. 18 July 2012.

Berman, Paul Schiff. "The Culture of Cyberspace." *American Society of International Law. Proceedings of the Annual Meeting* 1999: 354-56. *ProQuest.* Web. 20 July 2012.

Johnson, David R., and David Post. "Law and Borders: The Rise of Law in Cyberspace." *Stanford Law Review* 48.5 (1996): 1367-1402. *JSTOR.* Web. 21 July 2012.

Jones, Reilly. "A Critique of Barlow's 'A Declaration of the Independence of Cyberspace.'" *Extropy* 8.2 (1996). Web. 21 July 2012.

Lessig, Lawrence. *Code and Other Laws of Cyberspace.* New York: Basic Books, 1999. Print.

Pangburn, D.J. "'Anonymous' Declaration of Independence and the Question of Internet Sovereignty." *Death and Taxes.* Web. 21 July 2012.

Thill, Scott. "March 17, 1948: William Gibson, Father of Cyberspace." *Wired* 17 Mar. 2009. Web. 21 July 2012.

Van Der Leun, Gerard, and Thomas Mandel. *Rules of the Net: On-Line Operating Instructions for Human Beings.* New York: Hyperion, 1996. Print.

Jonathan Reeve

President Bill Clinton signs the Telecommunications Reform Act in 1996 as Vice President Al Gore watches. In "A Declaration of the Independence of Cyberspace," John Perry Barlow criticizes the act, which covers the Internet as well as more traditional types of telecommunication. AP PHOTO/DOUG MILLS

DIGITAL HUMANITIES MANIFESTO 2.0

Todd Presner, et al.

❖ *Key Facts*

Time Period:
Early 21st Century

Movement/Issue:
Digital scholarship

Place of Publication:
United States

Language of Publication:
English

OVERVIEW

Written by Todd Presner, Jeffrey Schnapp, Peter Lunenfeld, and others in 2009, the "Digital Humanities Manifesto 2.0" is an online document meant to spark intellectual debate regarding how the humanities should contribute to the digital culture of the twenty-first century. Authored primarily by Presner and Schnapp, the manifesto is a product of a collaboration that was born over the course of nine seminars held at UCLA in 2009. Presner and his group first composed the manifesto as an attempt to introduce the humanities to the digital age; then the project was reimagined in its 2.0 format as an open debate encouraging a redefinition of the humanities in an era when the main format of information is digital. Addressed to "digital humanists," the manifesto is written in a way that encourages its readers to shape the discussion through annotations and blog comments. Central to the manifesto's argument is the idea that the definition of digital humanities is ever changing and should be redefined frequently as digital media changes.

First published as a blog post, version 2.0 of the manifesto received immediate, positive public reaction. A specialized platform allowed readers to add comments in the blog's margins, offering critiques and praise to help revise the document. The final form of the manifesto is a PDF file that describes what the digital humanities should be. Written by professionals in the humanities, students in related fields, and online readers of its early versions, the "Digital Humanities Manifesto 2.0" is recognized today as a significant achievement that demonstrates how digital media can be used to shape intellectual thought in the humanities.

HISTORICAL AND LITERARY CONTEXT

As the world entered the twenty-first century, the development of communications technology was advancing at a rapid rate. Study of the humanities in the twentieth century, as Patricia Cohen writes in a 2010 article for *The New York Times,* was concerned primarily with "'isms'—formalism, Freudism, structuralism, postcolonialism—grand intellectual cathedrals from which assorted interpretations of literature, politics, and culture spread." However, as communications technology proliferated, scholars of the humanities found themselves struggling to keep up. Access to data was limited because digitized information was not available. In addition, the concept of digital humanities did not exist. As a result, groups of humanists began to research ways to merge the study of the humanities with the technological advances of the new century.

As version 2.0 of the manifesto indicates, the first wave of the digital humanities "was quantitative." Rather than facilitating discussion of these issues, it "looked backward" and "replicated the world of scholarly communications that print gradually codified over the course of five centuries." The initial vision of the project was to develop digital research techniques, making ideas that are prevalent in the humanities available in digital format to a wider audience. Schnapp of Stanford and Presner of UCLA, along with a group of other professionals, pushed for the humanities to actively engage in the digital world, using the virtual landscape of the Internet and online information databases to form new ideas about what constitutes the humanities. They envisioned a movement that would engender digital discussion and revision of ideas that formerly only existed on paper or within the walls of academic institutions.

The "Digital Humanities Manifesto 2.0" comes from a long tradition of published papers examining the state of knowledge and academics—in particular one study called *The Postmodern Condition.* Written in 1979 by Jean-François Lyotard, this "report on knowledge" examines how knowledge has changed with the introduction of computers and other technologies in the postmodern world. Presner and the other writers of the "Digital Humanities Manifesto 2.0" adopt numerous ideas from Lyotard, including the challenges related to the idea of control and ownership of information as it passes through technologies.

Written first as a blog entry, the "Digital Humanities Manifesto 2.0" encouraged comments that would result in "redrafting," with the end result being an open discussion of the definition of the digital humanities. The primary writers of the manifesto continue to redefine the digital humanities and facilitate discussion about the field's future. In keeping with the idea of free exchange of information, Schnapp and Presner both maintain websites to further the discussion of the ideas put forth in their manifesto. Readers of the 2.0 version also have been invited to join the dialogue through a number of scholarly articles published on the subject.

THEMES AND STYLE

At the core of the "Digital Humanities Manifesto 2.0" is the idea of free exchange of ideas. The manifesto opens with instructions to the reader to "comment, engage, retort, spread the word," and "throw an idea." From the beginning, the manifesto emphasizes the idea that commentary from readers will shape future versions of the manifesto. The manifesto answers the question, "Will there be a 3.0 release?" by including a picture of a hand giving a thumbs-up, suggesting that the manifesto is a work in progress. Although a new version has not yet appeared, other academics, such as those at the Day of DH project at the University of Alberta, have continued the discussion. Information and knowledge belongs to everyone, the writers suggest, and the digital humanities are a result of "co-creation" and "teamwork."

Rhetorically, the manifesto encourages open exchange by presenting the work as something unfinished. The personal pronoun *you* is used not only to create familiarity with the reader, which in turn creates the sense of dialogue between the authors and the readers, but also to reinforce the idea that the manifesto belongs to readers. Rather than relying on traditional paragraphs, the manifesto is structured in bulleted lists and follows a stream of consciousness-style logic, highlighting the idea that the manifesto is a work in progress. The writers use a strike-through font for certain words in the text to suggest that revision is necessary: "Process is the new god; ~~not product.~~"

Stylistically, the manifesto strives for informality and attempts to redefine what language can be, using not only words but also picture icons to express ideas. When discussing the idea that there is "ample room under the Digital Humanities" umbrella, the writers omit the word *umbrella* in favor of an icon of an umbrella. Using pictures instead of words to enhance ideas not only adds to the informal style of the document but also helps to emphasize the manifesto's overall theme: that the digital humanities are ever-changing and are composed of more than just the traditional arts and literature of the past. The umbrella icon appears once again on the penultimate page of the manifesto, tying the document together as it seeks "to reshape and reinvigorate contemporary arts and humanities practices, and expand their boundaries." The icons effectively expand the boundaries of what the written language can be in the digital age.

CRITICAL DISCUSSION

The "Digital Humanities Manifesto 2.0" was eagerly received by scholars of the digital humanities, who reposted the manifesto, in whole and in part, on blogs across the Internet. While most considered the manifesto a good idea, others were skeptical. One such post appeared in 2009 at *Generation Bubble*, where blogger

THE DIGITAL HUMANITIES: AN EMERGING FIELD

The word *humanities* is the general term for the academic disciplines that study what makes people human. Specifically, the humanities are traditionally composed of languages, literature, religion, art, philosophy, and history. The field of digital humanities, then, examines how technology, specifically computers and the online world, affect the study of humanities. Although the field has roots much earlier in the twentieth century, the digital humanities began to garner attention in the 1990s when scholars began to archive literature in digital databases.

Nearly a decade later Susan Schreibman, Ray Siemens, and John Unsworth published *A Companion to Digital Humanities,* an essay collection that attempted to look at the digital humanities not just as a way to document the study of the humanities but also as way to create the humanities. This marked a new approach for humanists to examine technology and how it is used to create culture, thereby creating the humanities. Some believe that digital technology is becoming so integral to the study of the humanities that the digital humanities are simply the humanities as they will be studied in the future.

Anton Steinpilz criticizes the document for being "by turns oracular, confrontational and unclear" and "like all manifestos … more about effect than exegesis." This criticism sums up the view of the majority of the manifesto's opponents, who judge it to be more about creating debate and less about generating useful information.

The "Digital Humanities Manifesto 2.0" accomplished its goal by opening a forum for people to discuss the future of the humanities in the digital age. The debate was unwelcome to some scholars who feared older ways of cataloguing information would be lost in the face of new technology. Curt Hopkins writes in 2012 for *Ars Technica* that the argument surrounding the digital humanities "comes from two extremes: those who believe the digital half of digital humanities will save the humanities and those who believe it will destroy it." David M. Berry in *Understanding Digital Humanities* (2012) sees the manifesto as an example of "second wave digital humanities" that is "crucial to understanding" the field, particularly as new technology is introduced. The manifesto has garnered reactions from a range of readers, from a casual Internet audience to accomplished scholars, and has been assigned as a text in core courses of the growing digital humanities field.

While the manifesto itself is not a central subject of much criticism, the digital humanities as an emerging academic field has attracted some scholarly attention. Appropriate to the nature of the manifesto, much of the criticism has come in the form of blogs

This image of an ancient Greek mosaic floor with the head of Dionysus is used as an illustration in the *Digital Humanities Manifesto 2.0.* © PETER EASTLAND/ALAMY

and online articles. Patrik Svensson, writing in 2012 for *Digital Humanities Quarterly*, notes, "the terrain of digital humanities is not stable nor fixed." Svensson calls the manifesto's "radical projections" on the future of information technology visionary and at the forefront of an emerging field. Some critics, most in the humanities field, such as N. Katherine Hayles in *Understanding Digital Humanities* (2012), see the digital humanities as "computational techniques" that are useful for "modes of enquiry, research, publication, and dissemination." As digital technology advances, so will the field of digital humanities.

BIBLIOGRAPHY

Sources

Berry, David M. "Introduction: Understanding the Digital Humanities." *Understanding Digital Humanities.* Ed. David M. Berry. New York: Palgrave Macmillan, 2012. 1-20. Print.

Cohen, Patricia. "Digital Keys for Unlocking the Humanities' Riches." *New York Times.* New York Times, 16 Nov. 2010. Web. 15 Sept. 2012.

Hayles, N. Katherine. "How We Think: Transforming Power and Digital Humanities." *Understanding Digital Humanities.* Ed. David M. Berry. New York: Palgrave Macmillan, 2012. 42-66. Print.

Hopkins, Curt. "Future U: Rise of the Digital Humanities." *Ars Technica.* Condé Nast, 17 June 2012. Web. 17 Sept. 2012.

Lyotard, Jean-François. *The Postmodern Condition: A Report on Knowledge.* Manchester: Manchester UP, 1984. Print.

Presner, Todd, et al. "The Digital Humanities Manifesto 2.0." *Humanities Blast.* WordPress, 10 Oct. 2011. Web. 12 Sept. 2012.

Steinpilz, Anton. "Let's Kill Off the Copyright: The Mellon Seminar's 'Digital Humanities Manifesto' and the Future of Intellectual Property." *Generation Bubble.* Generation Bubble, 17 June 2009. Web. 18 Sept. 2012.

Svensson, Patrik. "Envisioning the Digital Humanities." *Digital Humanities Quarterly* 6.1 (2012): n. pag. Web. 17 Sept. 2012.

Further Reading

Davidson, Cathy N. "Humanities 2.0: Promise, Perils, Predictions." *PMLA* 123.3 (2008): 707-17. Print.

Fish, Stanley. "The Digital Humanities and the Transcending of Mortality." *New York Times.* New York Times, 9 Jan. 2012. Web. 17 Sept. 2012.

Flanders, Julia. "The Productive Unease of 21st-Century Digital Scholarship." *Digital Humanities Quarterly* 3.3 (2009): n. pag. Web. 17 Sept. 2012.

Gold, Matthew K. *Debates in the Digital Humanities.* Minneapolis: U of Minnesota P, 2012. Print.

"How Do You Define DH?" *Day of DH 2012.* University of Alberta, 26 Mar. 2012. Web. 3 Oct. 2012.

Liu, Alan. "Digital Humanities and Academic Change." *ELN* 47.1 (2009): 17-35. Print.

Presner, Todd. "Digital Humanities 2.0: A Report on Knowledge." *Connexions.* Rice University, 8 June 2010. Web. 15 Sept. 2012.

Schreibman, Susan, Ray Siemens, and John Unsworth, eds. *A Companion to Digital Humanities.* Oxford: Blackwell, 2004. Print.

Lisa Kroger

GNU Manifesto

Richard Stallman

OVERVIEW

The *GNU Manifesto,* written by Richard Stallman and first published in *Dr. Dobb's Journal* in 1985, is the inaugural document of the free and open source software movement. The manifesto sets forth the aims and principles of the GNU Project, a collaborative effort to create a UNIX-compatible operating system freely available for anyone to use, modify, and share. GNU, a recursive acronym for "GNU's Not Unix" and pronounced "guh-noo," was born in response to a growing trend among software companies in the mid-1980s to copyright, license, and otherwise restrict the use of software. The manifesto, addressed primarily to computer programmers "for whom building community spirit is as important as making money," sought to garner volunteers who would contribute to the construction of the operating system. Although much of the document concerns the technical goals of GNU software, the manifesto's philosophy of placing value on transparency and on community remains of central importance to many software developers.

Outside the software community, the *GNU Manifesto* was not widely discussed until the early 1990s, when Linus Torvalds's Linux kernel was added to a group of software components that had been developed by the GNU Project. The combination of these components with the kernel, a type of software that manages such resources as the computer's memory for the other software, yielded the GNU/Linux software operating system, which quickly began to be adopted worldwide. Today, GNU/Linux is the most common operating system on webservers and supercomputers, and it is also used by tens of millions of users on their personal computers. As a consequence, the philosophy and methodology behind the creation of GNU/Linux and the terms of its distribution—the GNU General Public License (GPL)—are increasingly important. Even among nonprogrammers, the principle of transparent collaboration expressed in the manifesto has rapidly spread, notably with organizations such as Creative Commons and the Wikimedia Foundation. The *GNU Manifesto* and the ideals of the free and open source movement continue to make a profound impact in the fields of computer software development and copyright law.

HISTORICAL AND LITERARY CONTEXT

Stallman began the GNU Project in 1983 in response to growing frustrations caused by proprietary, closed-source software where he worked at the Artificial Intelligence (AI) Laboratory of the Massachusetts Institute of Technology (MIT). In the early 1980s, the Xerox Company gave the lab a new laser printer without the printer's source code, the human-readable and modifiable software instructions that serve as the basis for the software controlling the printer. Previously, programmers at the lab had had access to such code to customize and troubleshoot the software. Around the same time, AT&T ceased distributing free copies of the UNIX operating system, and instead began charging a prohibitively large licensing fee for its use. On the basis of these and other changes in the software climate, Stallman decided to quit working at the lab and start developing a system that was free and open.

The publication of the *GNU Manifesto* came at a pivotal moment in the history of software development. Up until that point, programmer ethics at MIT and other institutions had been community-oriented, meaning that innovations and solutions to problems were shared freely, especially in academic communities. Many large software companies, however, were beginning to guard their source code with increasingly complex end-user license agreements (EULAs) and they required persons with access to the code to sign nondisclosure contracts. In 1976 Microsoft's Bill Gates wrote an "open letter to hobbyists" that equated software sharing with "theft." In contrast, Stallman insisted that sharing software is an ethical necessity: "I consider that the golden rule requires that if I like a program I must share it with other people who like it," he said in a 1983 announcement of the GNU Project. "I cannot in good conscience sign a nondisclosure agreement or a software license agreement."

The *GNU Manifesto* builds on a system of "hacker ethics," which declares that "all information should be free," an ethos that was already in place at MIT when Stallman joined the AI Lab. (The term "hacker," in its original sense, did not mean "computer criminal," as it often does today but rather referred to creative and capable users of technology.) As Steven Levy notes in *Hackers: Heroes of the Computer Revolution,* this ethic included the following dictum: "Access to computers—and anything that might teach you

❖ *Key Facts*

Time Period:
Late 20th Century

Movement/Issue:
Intellectual freedom

Place of Publication:
United States

Language of Publication:
English

RICHARD STALLMAN: FREE SOFTWARE PIONEER

Richard Stallman, founder of the Free Software Foundation and its primary theorist, has been one of the most vocal activists of the free software movement. In an introduction to a collection of Stallman's essays, *Free Software, Free Society,* Lawrence Lessig beams: "Our generation has a philosopher. He is not an artist, or a professional writer. He is a programmer." However, in the same introduction, he concedes: "I know him [Stallman] well enough to know he is a hard man to like. He is driven, often impatient. His anger can flare at friend as easily as foe." Stallman delivers lectures worldwide in English, French, and Spanish, advocating for copyleft and protesting restrictive practices such as Digital Rights Management (DRM).

As a programmer, he is the primary author of a number of essential programs that are in wide use today, notably GNU coreutils, GNU compilers, and the popular programmer's text editor Emacs. While working at the MIT Artificial Intelligence Laboratory, he studied physics at Harvard, where he graduated *magna cum laude.* His achievements include a Macarthur grant (1990) and numerous honorary doctorate degrees from universities around the world. An atheist with a sense of humor, Stallman is also considered a saint ("Saint iGNUcius") in the parodic Church of Emacs.

something about the way the world works—should be unlimited and total." Initially referring to physical access to computers, the dictum also came to mean access to software source code.

In the decades after it appeared, the *GNU Manifesto* proved to be highly influential. The GNU General Public License, whose principles are based on the manifesto, spawned a number of similar "copyleft" licenses intended to promote the free exchange of information, and these licenses are in widespread use today. In 1999, in an article titled "The Free Universal Encyclopedia and Learning Resource," Stallman called for an encyclopedia to be produced under free software principles; two years later, Jimmy Wales founded the free encyclopedia Wikipedia based on similar principles. Most of the text of Wikipedia is now released under GNU licenses. Also in 2001, Lawrence Lessig founded the organization Creative Commons, inspired by the GPL, to promote free culture and to provide the means for artists to copyleft their works. As of 2010, there were roughly one-half million works released under Creative Commons licenses.

THEMES AND STYLE

A central theme of the *GNU Manifesto* is that of community solidarity. "Software sellers want to divide the users and conquer them," Stallman argues, "making each user agree not to share with others. I refuse to break solidarity with other users in this way."

Stallman's rejection of software ownership shares facets of Marx's abolition of bourgeois private property, but he denies that GNU philosophy is compatible with the authoritarian hierarchy of Bolshevik communism. This decentralized model also recalls Peter Kropotkin's anarchist theory of mutual aid. In a 2010 interview on Reddit.com, Stallman said that "free software clearly does have Anarchist aspects." Unlike abstract political works, however, the GNU manifesto details concrete ways in which the readers can contribute to the project and specifically calls for donations of "machines and money … programs and work."

The rhetoric of the manifesto makes use of a number of semantic distinctions. The word "free" in "free software," for instance, is defined in terms of liberty rather than the lack of price. Although much free software is available gratis, price is not a concern of the manifesto. "Think of 'free speech,'" Stallman explains in a later essay, "not 'free beer'." The second half of the manifesto, titled "Some Easily Rebutted Objections to GNU's Goals," uses a format similar to an FAQ (frequently asked questions) document, anticipating concerns about the manifesto's proposed development methodology. Here, Stallman responds to questions such as, "Won't programmers starve?" with sketches for new business models that do not rely exclusively on the sale and licensing of software. In this way, he correctly predicted the business model of many current open source software companies, whose primary streams of income come from software-related services rather than software sales.

The *GNU Manifesto* employs a colloquial style. The question-and-answer format recalls FAQs of early-1980s usenet newsgroups and, in so doing, lightens the tone by placing the manifesto in the context of those informal discussion threads. In fact, the manifesto borrows from Stallman's 1983 announcements of the GNU Project on net.unix-wizards and other newsgroups. The gravitas of the manifesto's political and legal implications, juxtaposed with its conversational style, mirrors the strategy of the GNU Project, which aimed to make software development more collaborative and, thus, more "conversational." The manifesto also appeals to the unity of computer users by asserting that "all computer users will benefit" from GNU and that "everyone will be able to obtain good system software free."

CRITICAL DISCUSSION

Early responses to GNU ideologies were mixed. A 1983 usenet message by software engineer Brad Templeton expressed fear that GNU "could be the most dangerous thing to the world of software, and could result in tremendous setbacks in the advancement of software quality." In contrast, computer scientist Barry Shein, then a professor at Boston University, wrote that GNU was "both valuable and highly credible." Rick Spanbauer of the State University of New York agreed, adding that "the commonly accepted principal [*sic*] of free flow of scientific knowledge should apply in the case of programs."

In the 1990s, with the success of GNU/Linux as an operating system, the GNU model began to gain wider attention. Eric Raymond's seminal 1997 paper "The Cathedral and the Bazaar" made a strong case for the GNU/Linux development strategy, to the degree that it influenced Netscape to release its web browser under the GNU license. The Netscape browser later became Firefox, one of the world's most popular web browsers and one of the greatest success stories for open source software. In the book *Open Sources: Voices from the Open Source Revolution,* Raymond describes Netscape's success as unexpected: "many saw this as flying in the face of conventional wisdom for the commercial software business." Now, however, this model is well accepted, and, as Raymond states in *Open Sources,* "rare is the software company today that does not emulate our strategy in one way or another."

GNU continues to generate controversy. In a 2001 speech delivered to New York University's business school, Microsoft's Craig Mundie criticized the GPL as "viral" and claimed it "poses a threat to the intellectual property of any organization making use of it." Stallman responded by accusing Microsoft of "taking away users' freedom to cooperate and form an ethical society." That same year, Siva Vaidhyanathan published a book, *Copyrights & Copywrongs: The Rise of Intellectual Property and How It Threatens Creativity,* that discusses Stallman's manifesto and argues for "'thin' copyright protection: just strong enough to encourage and reward aspiring artists … yet porous enough to allow full and rich democratic speech and the free flow of information." Since then, dozens of works have been published about open source software—software that, although not identical to the GNU type, shares important characteristics. Steven Weber's 2004 *Success of Open Source,* for instance, argues that open source software is an economic and political success, in addition to being an effective development methodology.

BIBLIOGRAPHY

Sources

Levy, Steven. *Hackers: Heroes of the Computer Revolution.* Sebastapol: O'Reilly, 2010. Print.

Mundie, Craig. "The Commercial Software Model." The New York University Stern School of Business. 3 May 2001. *Microsoft News Center.* Microsoft. Web. 19 June 2012. Transcript.

Raymond, Eric S. "The Cathedral and the Bazaar." Web. 19 June 2012.

"RMS AMA." Interview with Richard Stallman. Reddit. com. Web. 19 June 2012.

Shein, Barry. "Public Domain EMACS available from GNU Project." Newsgroup net.unix-wizards. 21 March 1985. *Google Groups.* Google. Web. 19 June 2012.

Spanbauer, Rick. "What's GNU With You?" Newsgroup net.unix-wizards. 5 Oct. 1983. *Google Groups.* Google. Web. 19 June 2012.

Stallman, Richard. *Free Software, Free Society: Selected Essays of Richard M. Stallman.* Free Software Foundation, 2010. PDF file.

———. "Free Software: Freedom and Cooperation." New York University. 29 May 2001. *GNU Operating System.* Free Software Foundation. Web. 19 June 2012. Transcript.

Templeton, Brad. "GNU Considered Harmful to Software Quality." Newsgroup net.unix-wizards. 7 Oct. 1983. *Google Groups.* Google. Web. 19 June 2012.

Vaidhyanathan, Siva. *Copyrights & Copywrongs: The Rise of Intellectual Property and How It Threatens Creativity.* New York: New York UP, 2001. Print.

Further Reading

Deek, Fadi P., and James A. McHugh. *Open Source: Technology and Policy.* Cambridge: Cambridge UP, 2007.

Hammerly, Jim, and Tom Paquin. "Freeing the Source: The Story of Mozilla." *Open Sources: Voices from the Open Source Revolution.* Eds. Chris DiBona and Sam Ockman. Sebastapol: O'Reilly, 1999. Print.

Muffatto, Moreno. *Open Source: A Multidisciplinary Approach.* London: Imperial College, 2006. Print.

Open Sources: Voices from the Open Source Revolution. Eds. Chris DiBona and Sam Ockman. Sebastapol: O'Reilly, 1999. Print.

St. Laurent, Andrew M. *Understanding Open Source and Free Software Licensing.* Sebastapol: O'Reilly, 2004. PDF file.

Wardrip-Fruin, Noah, and Nick Montfort. *New Media Reader.* Cambridge, MA: MIT, 2003. Print.

Weber, Steven. *Success of Open Source.* Cambridge: Harvard UP, 2004. Print.

Williams, Sam. *Free as in Freedom (2.0): Richard Stallman and the Free Software Revolution.* Boston: Free Software Foundation, 2010. PDF file.

Jonathan Reeve

People working on computers using Linux software in São Paulo, Brazil, in 2003. That year Brazilian president Luiz Inácio Lula da Silva encouraged government agencies to use open-source programs. AP PHOTO/ALEXANDRE MENEGHINI

A HACKER MANIFESTO

McKenzie Wark

✤ *Key Facts*

Time Period:
Eary 21st Century

Movement/Issue:
Marxism; Intellectual
freedom

Place of Publication:
United States

**Language of
Publication:**
English

OVERVIEW

McKenzie Wark's *A Hacker Manifesto* (2004) is a restatement of Marxist thought in the context of the Internet and of twenty-first century forces of globalization. Wark defines two classes that have formed in the past century: the hacker class and the vectoralist class. The hacker class, a kind of new proletariat, is made up of artists, philosophers, programmers, and others producing new ideas in various mediums. The vectoralist class is "the emergent ruling class of our time," owners of multinational corporations that attempt, through the concept of intellectual property, to own and profit from the work of the hacker class and to control the flow of information through society. *A Hacker Manifesto* was published during a period of intensifying attempts by corporations to strengthen legal protections against piracy and other unauthorized use of proprietary information. The manifesto is an academic analysis but also a call to (virtual) arms for the hacker class to preserve control over its work and to keep information free.

A Hacker Manifesto received mixed reviews on publication. Some theorists praised Wark's work as perceptive and provocative. Others questioned his conception of a hacker class, and yet others objected to the term "hacker," tied as it often is to Internet crime even though the term also simply refers to expert, creative computer coders. On balance, *A Hacker Manifesto* has been viewed as an interesting if sometimes obscure contribution to discussions of intellectual property. Although it has not effected significant change, the work provides a solid base for ongoing debates over problems specific to the information age.

HISTORICAL AND LITERARY CONTEXT

A Hacker Manifesto addresses the increasing regulation of intellectual property, particularly when such regulation benefits corporate interests. Reflecting the rise of the Internet, the Digital Millennium Copyright Law of 1998 expanded the category of copyright-protected works to include software and database-related material. The law also made it illegal to circumvent a copyright-protecting access device—for example, encryption on a DVD—even if copyright was not being infringed upon in the process. With the legislation came numerous lawsuits seeking damages,

and more importantly, a clearer definition and even an expansion of the body of protected intellectual property. Meanwhile, academic debates and broader cultural conversations were keeping step with and commenting on the legal wrangling over copyright.

Wark calls the rebellions and demonstrations held in 1989 by disenfranchised students and protestors in China, Germany, Korea, and the Philippines "the signal events of our times" and sees them as the beginning of the hacker revolution he envisions in his manifesto. Antiglobalization protests took shape throughout the 1990s, with culture jamming—a form of street art pioneered by Ron English that uses altered commercial billboards to advance anticommercialist messages—and other movements gaining currency, especially with young adults. Discussions about the right of corporations to own ideas or discoveries—for instance, the human genome—also grew increasingly heated.

A Hacker Manifesto draws on the work of Guy Debord and Gilles Deleuze, two influential philosophers writing in the twentieth century. Debord, founder of the revolutionary group Situationist International, was an early critic of mass media and the effect of mass-produced images on human thought and relationships. He was particularly concerned with what he saw as the substitution of representations of life for actual living. His theoretical work *The Society of the Spectacle* (1967) is an acknowledged influence on Wark, whose manifesto is similarly constructed of paragraph-length aphorisms grouped in chapters by subject. Deleuze and his collaborator, Félix Guattari, are much cited in Wark's notes, particularly in relation to their work *What Is Philosophy?* (1991). Their general answer to this question, in Wark's view, is that philosophy is "a tool to be used to escape from the commodification of information as communication," and the necessity of achieving this end is a central theme in *A Hacker Manifesto*.

In *A Hacker Manifesto,* Wark joins an ongoing dialog about the meaning of the term "hacker," which had been in contention since it entered the vocabulary of mainstream culture. Although the book has not inspired a particularly large body of academic work, it has been discussed online—an appropriate platform for a theoretician with a confessed interest in "low theory." Wark has gone on to write on gamer theory and the situationist movement, as in his work *The Beach Beneath the Street* (2011). Wark has also been politically active, participating in the Occupy Wall Street movement with a reading from his manifesto at the Washington Square Park Assembly in November 2011.

THEMES AND STYLE

A Hacker Manifesto lays out the conflict between the rising hacker class, which produces "new concepts, new perceptions, new sensations," and the vectoralist class, the twenty-first century's bourgeoisie, which seeks to control not only the content the hacker class creates but the means of producing and disseminating that content. The manifesto calls on hackers as a collective to wrest control of their innovations from the vectoralists. For Wark, the commodification of information creates a false sense of scarcity. It is artificial because information is not finite in the way that physical property might be, and it cannot be used up or lost. Moreover, commodification limits access to information that the hacker class can use as source material to create new information. The manifesto is directed to a largely academic audience, and it achieves its force through arguments from and references to other important philosophical works, namely those by Karl Marx and Debord. The book itself, which is small and bound in red, is an obvious and oft-noted nod to another little red book, *Quotations from Chairman Mao Tse-Tung* (1964), which was distributed across China during the Communist Cultural Revolution. In structure, *A Hacker Manifesto* is often compared to Debord's *The Society of the Spectacle,* with sections treating such topics as abstraction, information, representation, and the world.

A Hacker Manifesto is distinguished by its formal, philosophical language, which echoes Marx's *The Communist Manifesto* (1848) and demands to be treated seriously as a modern-day formulation of Marx and as a legitimate manifesto. The opening "A double spooks the world, a double of abstraction" clearly echoes Marx, whose *Communist Manifesto* begins "A spectre is haunting Europe—the spectre of Communism." Wark further develops this affinity with the words he uses to describe the problems he sees in the present day, referring repeatedly to "class," "production," and "commodities," and echoing Marx in tone and argument in aphorisms such as "out of the abstraction of nature comes its productivity, and the production of a surplus over and above the necessities of survival." This style is in stark contrast to Wark's final section of notes, which is written in a more accessible manner.

CRITICAL DISCUSSION

Upon publication, *A Hacker Manifesto* was received with mixed reviews. Writing in *The Nation,* Terry Eagleton calls it "a perceptive, provocative study packed to the seams with acute analysis." Eagleton is somewhat critical, however, of Wark's use of the term "hacker,"

SITUATIONIST INTERNATIONAL AND *THE SOCIETY OF THE SPECTACLE*

Guy Debord's *The Society of the Spectacle* (1967) is considered the defining text of the Situationist International, a group of radicals formed by Debord, Asger Jorn, and other former members of Isidore Isou's Lettrist Movement, which was itself strongly influenced by the European avant-garde. Established in the summer of 1957, the group was considered part art movement, part political movement, although political theory and activism became the group's focus by the early to middle 1960s. Situationist International members became famous for their dense, theoretical texts, and for their involvement in the May 1968 occupation of the Sorbonne and in the rioting and labor strikes that followed. The general strikes involved millions of French workers over the duration of two weeks and resulted in the near collapse of Charles de Gaulle's government.

The *Society of the Spectacle* takes a neo-Marxist view of twentieth-century mass-media culture, arguing that mass-produced images create a false spectacle that serves to distract the masses from the emptiness of wage slavery and from true engagement with life. Many view the punk-rock culture of the 1970s as a direct ideological descendent of the Situationists, although others have argued that groups such as the Sex Pistols represent a cynical co-opting of Situationist ideas for profit. Wark, who has written two books on the Situationist International, points to organizations such as the Luther Blissett Project and the Radical Software Group as the modern-day heirs of Situationist thought and practice.

calling it "perverse" and "unduly romanticizing" to "hang a connection between intellectual workers and criminalized code-busters on an arbitrary metaphor." Further, Eagleton does not agree that Wark's description of hackers is really a description of a class in the Marxist sense of the word: In Marxist theory, people of a class are singular in their position within the capitalist machine, not simply people who share a vision or opinion of the capitalist machine. Eagleton is leery of Wark's more bombastic statements, such as "Education is slavery," viewing them as indicative of a mind that sometimes misses nuances. In a piece for *Technology Review,* Simson Garfinkel is also critical of Wark's use of "hacker," pointing out that Wark completely ignores the class of hackers who engage in criminal activity, as well as those who hack hardware. Wark's title, Garfinkel concludes, is a bit of a misnomer, and though he reasons that Marx's communists would see themselves in *The Communist Manifesto,* he does not necessarily think that all people who consider themselves hackers—Wark's target audience—will recognize themselves enough to appropriate Wark's agenda. Garfinkel does praise Wark for identifying the vectoralist class as the enemy who generates the oppression of information that all hacking activity seeks to remedy,

Chinese students hold a sit-in during pro-democracy protests in China in 1989. In "A Hacker Manifesto," McKenzie Wark identifies this and other 1989 rebellions and demonstrations as "signal events" marking the beginning of the revolution he envisions in the manifesto. AP PHOTO/ MARK AVERY

was discussed, derided, dismissed, but also reposted, put up on websites, and so on. It led an underground existence, as one of those texts with which people in the net art and theory world may have some glancing acquaintance."

Although some level of analysis is present in the reviews by Eagleton and Garfinkel, *A Hacker Manifesto* has yet to become the subject of in-depth scholarly treatment in books or peer-reviewed journals. In the spirit of Wark's ideas, some intelligent analysis is available and freely accessible on various blogs. Perhaps a bit ironically, the Harvard University Press blog cites French theorist Jean Baudrillard's comment, "This text by Ken is unprecedented … a jubilation. It makes me laugh and it interests me."

BIBLIOGRAPHY

Sources

Davis, Ben. "What Occupy Wall Street Can Learn from the Situationists (A Cautionary Tale)." *ArtInfo.* 17 Oct. 2011. Web. 28 June 2012.

Eagleton, Terry. "Office Politics." *The Nation* 25 Oct. 2004: 40. *General OneFile.* Web. 27 June 2012.

Garfinkel, Simson. "Hack License: Recent Books Struggle to Define Hacking and Its Economic and Social Legitimacy." *Technology Review* Mar. 2005: 75+. *General OneFile.* Web. 27 June 2012.

"Jean Baudrillard on *A Hacker Manifesto*." *Harvard University Press Blog.* 11 Dec. 2006. Web. 28 June 2012.

Wark, McKenzie. *50 Years of Recuperation of the Situationist International.* New York: Princeton Architectural, 2008. Print.

———. *A Hacker Manifesto.* Cambridge: Harvard UP, 2004. Print.

———. "Copyright, Copyleft, Copygift." *Meanjin* 69.1 (2010). Meanland. Web. 28 June 2012.

Further Reading

Debord, Guy. *The Society of the Spectacle.* Detroit: Black and Red, 1983. Print.

Hyde, Lewis. *Common as Air: Revolution, Art and Ownership.* New York: Farrar, Straus and Giroux, 2010. Print.

Lessig, Lawrence. *The Future of Ideas: The Fate of the Commons in a Connected World.* New York: Vintage, 2002. Print.

Levy, Stephen. *Hackers: Heroes of the Computer Revolution.* New York: Penguin, 1994. Print.

Klein, Naomi. *No Logo.* London: Harper Collins, 2000. Print.

Raymond, Eric S. *The Cathedral and the Bazaar: Musings on Linux and Open Source by an Accidental Revolutionary.* Sebastopol, CA: O'Reilly, 1999. Print.

Daisy Gard

an identification he views as Wark's primary contribution to the intellectual-property debate.

Wark has given an account of the influence of his work, which he has offered free online at various times, as "on a tiny scale, the new gift economy in action." For Wark, the new gift economy is an alternative to intellectual property and functions like karma—share something at no charge, and others will share in return, even if only by spending their time analyzing the work, hence adding to the discussion. Wark may not have originated this idea, but it is very much in keeping with the political views he expresses in *A Hacker Manifesto.* Of the work, Wark writes, "It

THE HACKER MANIFESTO

Loyd Blankenship

OVERVIEW

Loyd Blankenship's 1986 essay "The Hacker Manifesto," also known as "The Conscience of a Hacker," protests the systematic persecution of the young and technologically savvy and states that hacking, contrary to popular belief, is about intellectual curiosity and can be considered a constructive, rather than a destructive and criminal, force. Published in the underground e-zine *Phrack,* the essay addresses authority figures but is written with a hacker audience in mind. Slight, coming in at a mere 520 words, the manifesto is punctuated by references to the "damn kids" who constitute its audience, echoing newspapers, parents, and teachers, then responding through the voice of a hacker. Blankenship, also known by his hacker handle, the Mentor, was part of several elite hacking groups during the 1980s. He wrote "The Hacker Manifesto" in response to his 1986 arrest.

At the time of publication, "The Hacker Manifesto" was largely ignored by the mainstream media but was embraced by hackers. It has since been considered a founding document in hacker culture and its philosophy. In the decades since the manifesto was written, *hacktivism,* which is generally understood to refer to the use of information technology to achieve political ends, has become an important cultural force, with the work of such groups as the Chaos Computer Club and WikiLeaks the subject of much debate. The manifesto remains widely available on the Internet and is still considered relevant by new generations of hackers, some of whom have run afoul of the law, much as Blankenship did in his day.

HISTORICAL AND LITERARY CONTEXT

"The Hacker Manifesto" responds to the U.S. government's criminalization and crackdown on computer hacking during the 1980s, as well as public perceptions about the nature of the practice. At the time, hackers were largely suburban high school or college students, mostly male, who had no arrest record or history of trouble with the law. Many treated hacking as an intellectual exercise or a way to satisfy their curiosity about the way computer networks function. Public perception of hacking, however, often characterized hackers as malicious, and acts of hacking were increasingly treated as criminal, particularly when they targeted large institutional databases that contained personal information.

The 1980s saw a rapid increase in personal computing technology and, with it, growing fears about computer crime. During the early part of the decade, a number of computer hacking groups, consisting mostly of adolescent males, broke into computer systems at a number of high-profile institutions, including the Memorial Sloan-Kettering Cancer Center in Manhattan. The Sloan-Kettering break-in was covered by *Newsweek* and other magazines, and the publicity led to a U.S. Congressional investigation. Six bills relating to computer hacking were introduced into Congress in 1983 alone. In 1986 Congress passed the Computer Fraud and Abuse Act, making it a crime to hack into computer networks. Arrests soon followed, including that of Blankenship.

"The Hacker Manifesto" joined a growing tide of writings on technology and culture that accompanied the increasing presence of computers in the national landscape. Douglas Thomas cites "A Manifesto for Cyborgs," Donna Haraway's seminal work of feminist scholarship, as one antecedent. "The Hacker Manifesto" also continues a tradition of writing by and for hackers of various stripes, including Steven Levy's *Hackers: Heroes of the Computer Revolution* (1984) and Hugo Cornwall's *The Hacker's Handbook* (1985). Blankenship has cited Robert Heinlein's *The Moon Is a Harsh Mistress,* which he was reading at the time he was writing his manifesto, as a source of inspiration, dealing as it does with revolution.

In the decades following the appearance of "The Hacker Manifesto," a number of online manifestos have been published, most notably Timothy C. May's "The Crypto Anarchist Manifesto" (1992) and Eric Hughes's "A Cypherpunk's Manifesto" (1993). "The Hacker Manifesto" made the Mentor something of a hero in hacker circles. More than ten years after the manifesto's original publication, the Mentor was asked to give a reading of his essay at H2K2, the 2002 Hackers on Planet Earth convention. He has since retired from hacking and encourages youth to concentrate on legal alternatives.

THEMES AND STYLE

"The Hacker Manifesto" attempts to articulate the motivations of hackers, and to demonstrate the value of their activity, as opposed to societal perceptions that hacking is solely destructive and criminal. With

+ **Key Facts**

Time Period:
Late 20th Century

Movement/Issue:
Computer hacking

Place of Publication:
United States

Language of Publication:
English

"THE HACKER MANIFESTO" AND "A MANIFESTO FOR CYBORGS" IN DOUGLAS THOMAS'S *HACKER CULTURE*: A CLOSER LOOK

In his discussion of hacking as the performance of technology, Douglas Thomas asserts that the hacker is situated relative to technology very much like Donna Haraway's cyborg in "A Manifesto for Cyborgs." Haraway, like many of her contemporaries, argues against essentialism and notions of binary opposition in feminist discourse. Her work posits, in Thomas's reading, the cyborg as a "space of enactment" between the poles of technology and humanity from which "one may both enact discourses of technology, and critique them." Thomas views "The Hacker Manifesto" as grappling with the artificial categories of technology and culture and, through its explication of a hacker's conscience, unpacking how each category blends into the other. From the opening of "The Hacker Manifesto," Thomas traces "a split sense of interpretation," wherein the Mentor's language, such as "they're all alike," both parodies the misrepresentation of hackers by mainstream culture and accurately represents the view that most people have of hackers. For the hacker, technology is both the source of this split and a means of liberation. Outdated discourses of technology view it as an instrument, but the activity of hacking opens up a world and creates a space free of some of the worst aspects of the broader culture, which uses technology (such as nuclear bombs) to destroy. By developing these contradictions, "The Hacker Manifesto" points out what the hacker knows—that technology is part of culture, not a separate category.

the many headlines announcing the arrest of teenage hackers as the background, the manifesto opens by inviting someone, presumably an adult outside of hacker circles, to "take a look behind the eyes of a hacker." The hacker's world, according to Blankenship, starts in school, which is intellectually unchallenging and peopled mainly by educators who are sadistic or apathetic. Further, the hacker lives in a larger world where adults "build atomic bombs … murder, cheat and lie to us and try to make us believe it's for our own good." Computers, by contrast, teach without bias and create a virtual space where people can exist "without skin color, without nationality, without religious bias."

The manifesto achieves its rhetorical effect by contrasting an outsider, authority figure's view of hackers with the hacker's own view. Through the first half of "The Hacker Manifesto," the Mentor repeats the refrain "They're all alike," as the adult response to anything kids, and specifically hackers, do wrong. The "damn kids," another phrase used repeatedly for effect, are underachievers who cheat and spend their time playing games and tying up the phone lines.

In contrast, the hacker's self-description is of someone who is bored in school but curious nevertheless. Computers—unlike teachers, who may pass judgment based on a student's appearance or personality—provide an unbiased opportunity for students to explore and learn. The essay concludes by admitting some of the charges against hackers—"Yes, I am a criminal"—but subverts the meaning of the term by adding, "My crime is that of outsmarting you, something that you will never forgive me for." The manifesto closes by pointing out that society can stop a single hacker but not the hacker project as a whole, because, "after all, we're all alike."

The tone of "The Hacker Manifesto" is mocking and confrontational, further serving to underscore the hacker's youth and place outside mainstream society. The hacker sneers at adults and their "three-piece psychology" and outmoded "1950's technobrain," which is unable to see, for example, the difference between teenage rebellion, for rebellion's sake, and the rebellion of hackers, which has legitimate purpose. After repeating stereotype after stereotype, the manifesto's tone becomes angry, much like a kid exploding after years of harassment. "You bet your ass we're all alike," because "we've been spoon-fed baby food at school" and "we've been dominated by sadists."

CRITICAL DISCUSSION

When the "The Hacker Manifesto" was first published in 1986, it drew little attention outside the close-knit hacker community, within which it was warmly received. Many hackers considered the manifesto a reflection of their own motivations for hacking as well as a justification for it. Cyberculture studies did not gain currency until the 1990s, and even then, few treated the manifesto except as a footnote.

Commentators have noted that "The Hacker Manifesto" is still widely available and still considered important decades after its publication, making it unique among Internet documents, which usually have a short shelf life. It has also become better known with age. References to the document appear in the wider culture, for example, in the 1995 movie *Hackers*. Furthermore, hacking has become a ubiquitous topic in the mainstream press, as computer-based fraud has risen and, with it, concerns about privacy and security. Hacktivism has also been a growing topic of interest. WikiLeaks, one of the most famous examples of a hacktivist group, has been responsible for leaking a large number of classified documents to the public, justifying these leaks with the idea that information should be free and that hacking is acceptable to achieve this end. Peter Ludlow, writing in the *Nation,* traces this attitude back to "The Hacker Manifesto," among other early hacker documents. Quoting the Mentor's assertion that "you can't stop them all," Ludlow agrees that "indeed, you can't," noting that WikiLeaks founder Julian Assange first went online a year after the manifesto was published and, since then, "that basic hacker philosophy has not been abandoned, and indeed has evolved into a broad cultural movement."

Although "The Hacker Manifesto" is still discussed today, little serious scholarship has treated it as a stand-alone text. One notable exception is the discussion by S.M. Furnell et al. exploring the security ramifications of the ideas presented by the Mentor. Furnell asserts that the Mentor ignores many of the wider issues concerning hacking and that, in the Mentor's view of hackers as explorers, he fails to acknowledge that this exploration amounts to trespassing, which, even if done without malicious intent, can cause damage and compromise individual privacy. Moreover, the manifesto can be used by less conscientious hackers to justify malicious activity, because it makes no specific claims about what sort of hacking is ethical and what is not. Although Furnell does not advocate censorship of "The Hacker Manifesto," he does suggest that it should be published alongside material that offers alternate points of view on hacking. Thomas develops a more academic treatment of the manifesto in *Hacker Culture*. Comparing "The Hacker Manifesto" to "A Manifesto for Cyborgs," Thomas reads hackers as "hybrid figures," much like Haraway's cyborgs, who "blur the boundary between the technological and the cultural."

BIBLIOGRAPHY

Sources

Blankenship, Loyd. "The Conscience of a Hacker." *Phrack*. Phrack Inc., 28 July 1987. Web. 29 June 2012.

Furnell, S.M., P.S. Dowland, and P.W. Sanders. "Dissecting the 'Hacker Manifesto.'" *Information Management & Computer Security* 7.2 (1999): 69-75. Print.

Haraway, Donna. "A Manifesto for Cyborgs." *Feminism/Postmodernism*. Ed. Linda Nicholson. New York: Routledge, 1990. Print.

Ludlow, Peter. "WikiLeaks and Hacktivist Culture." *Nation*. The Nation, 15 Sept. 2010. Web. 24 June 2012.

Thomas, Douglas. *Hacker Culture*. Minneapolis: U of Minnesota P, 2002. Print.

Further Reading

Critical Cyber-Culture Studies. Ed. David Silver and Adrienne Massanari. New York: NYU Press, 2006. Print.

Ito, Mizuko. *Hanging Out, Messing Around, and Geeking Out: Kids Living and Learning with New Media*. Cambridge: MIT Press, 2010. Print.

Jordan, Tim, and Paul Taylor. *Hacktivism and Cyberwars: Rebels with a Cause?* London: Routledge, 2004. Print.

Levy, Steven. *Hackers: Heroes of the Computer Revolution*. New York: Penguin, 2001. Print.

Menn, Joseph. "They're Watching. And They Can Bring You Down." *Financial Times*. Financial Times, 23 Sept. 2011. Web. 24 June 2012.

The New Media and Cybercultures Anthology. Ed. Praymod Nayhar. Oxford: Wiley, 2010. Print.

Daisy Gard

A participant uses a laptop as he attends the annual Chaos Communication Congress of the Chaos Computer Club in 2010 in Berlin, Germany. The Chaos Computer Club is Europe's biggest network of computer hackers, and its annual congress draws up to 3,000 participants. SEAN GALLUP/GETTY IMAGES

INDUSTRIAL SOCIETY AND ITS FUTURE

Theodore Kaczynski

✥ *Key Facts*

Time Period:
Late 20th Century

Movement/Issue:
Technology; Revolution

Place of Publication:
United States

**Language of
Publication:**
English

OVERVIEW

Composed by Theodore Kaczynski, *Industrial Society and Its Future* (1995) argues that technological innovation has caused widespread human suffering and the destruction of nature; therefore, industrial society should be eradicated. By the time of the treatise's publication in the *New York Times* and the *Washington Post*, Kaczynski, known in the media only as the Unabomber, had killed three people and wounded twenty-three more during a nearly two-decade-long bombing campaign targeting professors, scientists, and others. The manifesto seeks to diagnose the ills of modern culture as the products of industrialization and to advocate for revolution that would overthrow the "economic and technological basis of the present society." Addressed to the public at large, Kaczynski's treatise, popularly known as the *Unabomber Manifesto*, was published after he claimed he would cease the bombings if either the *Times* or *Post* printed it. Formatted as a series of numbered paragraphs, the manifesto attempts to make a rational case against gradual reform in favor of enacting society's total collapse.

Widely dismissed as the rantings of a dangerous criminal, *Industrial Society and Its Future* nevertheless received measured and admiring appraisals by several mainstream writers and critics. The *New York Times* environmental writer Kirkpatrick Sale describes the manifesto's author as "a rational man" and states, "his principal beliefs are, if hardly mainstream, entirely reasonable." Magazines such as *Time* and the *New Yorker* featured prudent assessments of Kaczynski's critique of technology and society. Although the manifesto garnered the attention its author sought, it also led to his identification and arrest. Today, Kaczynski's manifesto, though popularly dismissed as the deluded ravings of a madman, continues to attract the attention of philosophers, environmentalists, and political radicals.

HISTORICAL AND LITERARY CONTEXT

Industrial Society and Its Future responds to a perceived political, social, environmental, and spiritual crisis at the end of the twentieth century. Kaczynski traces the foundations of the crisis to the Industrial Revolution, which he calls "a disaster for the human race." During the late nineteenth and early twentieth centuries,

many writers and activists criticized the unchecked pollution, pillaging of natural resources, and inhumane working conditions that came with rapid industrialization. In the 1960s counterculturalists extended this criticism to the U.S. military-industrial complex and the Vietnam War, maintaining that humankind had become enslaved to its own machine. During Kaczynski's time at the University of Michigan and the University of California at Berkeley, where he was a graduate student and professor, respectively, he witnessed many antiwar and antiestablishment protests, which undoubtedly influenced his perception of technological progress as the root of society's problems.

By the time he published his manifesto in 1995, radical environmental groups had become prominent antiestablishment forces, advocating sabotage, vandalism, and violence to defend the natural world. The organization Earth First! was notorious for organizing violent actions against the U.S. Forest Service, lumber companies, and university researchers during the 1980s and early 1990s. An even more radical group, the Earth Liberation Front, conducted bombings and arsons designed to advance animal rights and environmentalism. Kaczynski was particularly influenced by the environmental newspaper *Live Wild or Die!*, which in the early 1990s published a list of enemies of nature and placed Gilbert Murray, president of the California Forestry Association, at the top. On April 24, 1995, just months before his manifesto was published, Kaczynski used what would be his last mail bomb to kill Murray.

Industrial Society and Its Future draws from a diverse array of environmental, political, and sociological writings. *The Technological Society* (1954) by French sociologist Jacques Ellul, which was translated into English in 1964, describes technology's domination of society and the present and future implications of this dominance. Ellul's emphasis on technology's tendency to erode morality features prominently in Kaczynski's tract (Kaczynski, after his arrest, acknowledged Ellul as an influence). Another significant work for Kaczynski was *The True Believer: Thoughts on the Nature of Mass Movements* (1951), by Eric Hoffer, which describes the appeal of leftism to the disaffected.

Since its publication, *Industrial Society and Its Future* has had a profound influence on the writings of extremists sympathetic to Kaczynski's critique of progress and violent program for change. In 2011, before killing more than seventy people in the name of anti-Islamic nationalism, a Norwegian named Anders Behring Breivik published a 1,500-page manifesto that liberally quotes from *Industrial Society and Its Future* but substitutes "multiculturalists" or "cultural Marxists" wherever Kaczynski uses the word "leftists." Contemporary scholars have written about Kaczynski's manifesto as part of a small but growing body of scholarship that examines extremist philosophies. Scholars have also begun to view *Industrial Society and Its Future* as an apt analysis of the dehumanizing potential of technological and economic development. Kaczynski's critique became increasingly relevant in the early twenty-first century, when increasing globalization and worldwide recession coincided, spurring poverty rates and economic instability in many countries.

THEMES AND STYLE

The central theme of *Industrial Society and Its Future* is that economic growth and technological innovation are ruinous forces and must be destroyed. The manifesto opens with the declaration, "The Industrial Revolution and its consequences have been a disaster for the human race." It charges that the effects of industrialization "have destabilized society, have made life unfulfilling, have subjected human beings to indignities, have led to widespread psychological suffering … and have inflicted severe damage on the natural world." The manifesto advocates "a revolution against the industrial system" whose object is to "overthrow not governments but the economic and technological basis of the present society." To reinforce the immediacy of the problem, Kaczynski disparages attempts to make moderate reforms or gradual modifications to the entrenched social and economic order, concluding that "revolution is much easier than reform." This appeal for revolution entails a nihilistic argument for the expendability of humanity relative to the greater goal of social change. Kaczynski acknowledges that destroying the current social system may mean "many people will die," but he excuses this outcome, arguing that "revolutionaries, by hastening the onset of the breakdown, will be reducing the extent of the disaster."

The manifesto achieves its rhetorical aim through appeals to logic and reason. Kaczynski takes a measured, rational approach to explaining his argument in order to make his extremist views more palatable to mainstream readers. He numbers each paragraph of the essay to signal the methodical nature of his argument, a technique borrowed from other philosophical works, such as Ludwig Wittgenstein's *Tractatus Logico-Philosophicus* (1921), to lend the manifesto seriousness and authority. Kaczynski uses the first-person plural to imply that he is not alone in his beliefs: "We do not mean to imply that primitive cultures ARE inferior

THEODORE KACZYNSKI: MATHEMATICAL THINKER

Before Theodore Kaczynski moved to a cabin in the Montana woods in 1971 and eventually began mailing bombs around the United States, he was a respected mathematician. A graduate of suburban Chicago public schools, he enrolled at Harvard University at age sixteen and at twenty began graduate school at the University of Michigan. During his five years in Ann Arbor, he established a reputation for brilliance. He solved previously unsolvable problems, published in prestigious journals, and received a prize for the university's best mathematics thesis. Yet, even before he graduated, he fantasized about escaping society and living in solitude in the wilderness.

In 1967 he took a professorial position at the University of California at Berkeley. Although he was on track to have a distinguished career as a mathematician, he abruptly quit in 1969 and returned to his parents' home in Illinois. While looking for land to live on in pursuit of his dream of living in isolation, he sent letters of complaint to various publications about everything from advertising to motorcycles. Finally, in 1971 he found the home he was searching for—a ten-by-twelve-foot cabin outside of Lincoln, Montana, where he remained until his arrest in 1996.

Theodore Kaczynski, also known as the Unabomber, being escorted to court in 1996 for his arraignment on charges that he planted bombs that killed three people and injured twenty-three. © RALF-FINN HESTOFT/CORBIS

to ours. We merely point out the hypersensitivity of leftish anthropologists." To reinforce the notion that there are many who share his extremist views, he signs the manifesto "FC," which stands for Freedom Club, a nonexistent terrorist group.

Stylistically, *Industrial Society and Its Future* assumes a dry, detached tone in order to evoke an objective point of view. Throughout the manifesto, Kaczynski defines and refines his terms as a means of gaining credibility from a skeptical audience. The convoluted wording of many of these definitions gives his argument an esoteric quality: "We use the term 'surrogate activity' to designate an activity that is directed toward an artificial goal that people set up for themselves merely in order to have some goal to work toward, or, let us say, merely for the sake of the 'fulfillment' of that goal." The manifesto's extensive and digressive endnotes reinforce the intellectual and academic authority of the document. However, underlying these stylistic formalities is the presumption that the reader distrusts the writer's authority. The manifesto even engages in self-criticism, saying it has failed to adequately reflect the author's argument: "Throughout this article we've made imprecise statements and statements that ought to have had all sorts of qualifications and reservations attached to them … So we don't claim that this article expresses more than a crude approximation to the truth."

CRITICAL DISCUSSION

When *Industrial Society and Its Future* first appeared in 1995, it was received as a fanatical screed published not for its inherent value but to forestall Kaczynski's threat of further violence. Many scholars and critics questioned the decision to publish it. Although most readers were repulsed by the manifesto, others saw logic and value in the points it raised. Alston Chase (2000) writes in the *Atlantic,* "The Unabomber's manifesto was greeted in 1995 by many thoughtful people as a work of genius, or at least profundity, and as quite sane." Distinguished literary critic Cynthia Ozick writes in a 1997 essay for the *New Yorker* that Kaczynski is a "philosophical criminal of exceptional intelligence and humanitarian purpose, who is driven to commit murder out of an uncompromising idealism."

After Kaczynski's arrest in 1996, the manifesto was seen less as an argument about technology and humanity and more as evidence of the insanity of a serial killer. William Glaberson wrote in a 1998 article for the *New York Times,* "It seems hard to believe now, but it wasn't very long ago that the Unabomber seemed like a serious person. To read about him in many newspaper and magazine accounts was to hear of a mysterious philosopher: dangerous yet compelling, brilliant, intriguing." When court psychiatrists labeled Kaczynski a paranoid schizophrenic, the diagnosis seemed to seal the manifesto's legacy as the work of a madman. Today, *Industrial Society and Its Future* is the subject of balanced criticism of its sociological, technological, and environmental argument.

Much scholarship has focused on the aptness of Kaczynski's critique despite the indefensibility of his actions. In *What Technology Wants* (2010), Kevin Kelly writes, "in meticulous, scholarly precision, Kaczynski makes his primary claim that 'freedom and technological progress are incompatible' and that therefore technological progress must be undone." Nevertheless, Kelly disagrees with Kaczynski's tactics and conclusions: "Kaczynski was misled because he followed logic divorced from ethics, but as befits a mathematician, his logic was insightful." Commentators have explored the manifesto in the larger context of radicalism and polemical writing. Conservative scholar Ralph Reiland (1998) writes in *American Enterprise,* "The ideological links between radical environmentalism and Kaczynski's savagery have been mostly ignored by the media … But the Unabomber was no intellectual loner." In fact, Chase argues that the ideas expressed in the manifesto are so pervasive, the document serves as a kind of pastiche, "an academic—and popular—cliché."

BIBLIOGRAPHY

Sources

Chase, Alston. "Harvard and the Unmaking of the Unabomber." *Atlantic* June 2000: 41-65. Web. 10 Jun. 2012.

Glaberson, William. "The Nation; Rethinking a Myth: 'Who Was That Masked Man?'" *New York Times.* New York Times, 18 Jan. 1998. Web. 11 Jun. 2012.

Kaczynski, Theodore J. *Technological Slavery: The Collected Writings of Theodore J. Kaczynski, a.k.a. "The Unabomber."* 2nd ed. Ed. David J. Skrbina. Port Townsend: Feral House, 2010. Print.

Kelly, Kevin. *What Technology Wants.* New York: Viking, 2010. Print.

McFadden, Robert D. "Prisoner of Rage: From a Child of Promise to the Unabom Suspect." *New York Times.* New York Times, 26 May 1996. Web. 11 June 2012.

Mello, Michael. *The United States of America vs Theodore John Kaczynski: Ethics, Power, and the Invention of the Unabomber.* New York: Context, 1999. Print.

Ozick, Cynthia. "A Critic at Large, Dostoyevsky's Unabomber." *New Yorker* 24 Feb. 1997: 114. Web. 11 June 2012.

Reiland, Ralph. "Inspiring the Unabomber." *American Enterprise* 9.3 (1998): 10. Web. 11 June 2012.

Further Reading

Chase, Alston. *Harvard and the Unabomber: The Education of an American Terrorist.* New York: Norton, 2003. Print.

Douglas, John, and Mark Olshaker. *The Anatomy of Motive.* New York: Scribner, 1999. Print.

Finnegan, William. "Defending the Unabomber." *New Yorker.* Condé Nast, 16 Mar. 1998. Web. 11 Jun. 2012.

Gelernter, David. *Drawing Life: Surviving the Unabomber.* New York: Free Press, 1997. Print.

Graysmith, Robert. *Unabomber: A Desire To Kill.* Washington, DC: Regnery, 1997. Print.

Haberfeld, M.R., and Agostino Von Hassell, eds. *A New Understanding of Terrorism: Case Studies, Trajectories and Lessons Learned.* New York: Springer, 2009. Print.

Lloyd, Marion, and Jeffrey R. Young. "Nanotechnologists Are Targets of Unabomber Copycat, Alarming Universities." *Chronicle of Higher Education* 2 Sept. 2011: A20. *Academic OneFile.* Web. 11 June 2012.

Waits, Chris, and Dave Shors. *Unabomber: The Secret Life of Ted Kaczynski.* Helena: Farcountry, 1999. Print.

Young, Jeffrey R. "The Unabomber's Pen Pal." *Chronicle Review* 25 May 2012: B6-B11. *Academic OneFile.* Web. 11 June 2012.

Theodore McDermott

Intimate Bureaucracies: A Manifesto

dj readies

❖ **Key Facts**

Time Period:
Early 21st Century

Movement/Issue:
Occupy Movement;
Avant-gardism

Place of Publication:
United States

Language of Publication:
English

OVERVIEW

Composed by dj readies (a pseudonym for academic cultural theorist Craig J. Saper), the pamphlet *Intimate Bureaucracies: A Manifesto* (2012) explores the historical relationship between art, community, social media, and political agitation in relation to the Occupy Wall Street (OWS) protest encampment in Manhattan's Zuccotti Park in 2011 and artist George Maciunas's Fluxhouse cooperatives in SoHo in the 1960s. Saper argues that these communities represent "sociopoetic systems," a neologism describing how artists "perform, manipulate, and score social situations using social networks as a canvass." Saper theorizes that such systems can lead to the formation of more humane, "intimate bureaucracies" within the greater bureaucratic structure of society. Punctum Books, an independent open-access and print-on-demand publisher, released *Intimate Bureaucracies* in pamphlet form and also as an e-book in collaboration with AK Press Tactical Media and Minor Compositions; the publishers made the e-book version available for free.

Intimate Bureaucracies was well received in the avant-garde academic and artistic communities of New York and Paris but received little attention from mainstream media. Saper had already established a strong reputation as a cultural theorist within these communities with the publication of a similar work, *Networked Art* (2001), which explored the role of sociopoetic systems within the art world and greater society. Saper originally coined the term "intimate bureaucracies" to describe these systems in *Networked Art* and emphasized the term's salience for the art community in the second half of the twentieth century. *Intimate Bureaucracies* is most significant for updating Saper's theories to address the Occupy Wall Street movement and for reemphasizing the role of interconnected artistic niche communities functioning in opposition to a twenty-first century corporate bureaucracy.

HISTORICAL AND LITERARY CONTEXT

The historical roots of *Intimate Bureaucracies* lic in the history of twentieth century networked art experiments, notably the pre-Internet mail art experiments of the 1960s, 1970s, and 1980s in which artists from around the world collaborated with each other through the postal system to create hybrid works of art and stage shows. (Dick Higgins's and Robert Rehfeldt's artistic collaborations serve as a useful example.) Situationist artistic interventions in 1960s France and Maciunas's Fluxhouse cooperatives also influenced Saper's theories by providing historic examples of artistic concerns that drew together a group of disconnected individuals in the interest of collaborating toward a common sociopolitical goal. Maciunas's Fluxhouse cooperatives, an extension of his Fluxus Project in which artists, architects, composers, and designers lived together and engaged in performance art exhibitions known as happenings under Maciunas's loose direction, are especially crucial to Saper's theories. Other artists whose work can be considered as networked, such as Anna Freud Banana; Guy Blcus; Randall Packer; Geof Huth; and mIEKA-Land and Lyx Ish, creators of the Dreamtime Village online community, also feature prominently in Saper's history of networked art.

The Occupy Wall Street movement of 2011 provided the impetus for Saper's publication of *Intimate Bureaucracies*. The movement initially grew out of generalized dissatisfaction with the perceived social, economic, and political status quo in the United States among college-educated American youth. This dissatisfaction led to the establishment of protest encampments in many U.S. cities, where digitally literate protestors used social media to coordinate movement organization and communicate demands. These protest encampments also drew in members of the working poor, the unemployed, the homeless community, organized labor, and the veteran community and spread to other cities around the world. The protesters generated political protest art and practiced small-scale corporate communication dynamics that Saper suggests are exemplary of sociopoetic systems and the function of an intimate bureaucracy within the greater society it claims to resist. He also identifies the emergence of social entrepreneurial websites such as Kiva and Kickstarter as byproducts of this socially conscious, media-enabled community.

The literary context of *Intimate Bureaucracies* draws on notable works of academic theory in the cultural studies field, including French philosopher and theorist Guy Debord's *The Society of the Spectacle* (1967), an analysis of the use of popular historical images to contextualize contemporary society, and Roland Barthes's *Mythologies* (1957), which examines the role of myth as a frame for viewing contemporary culture. *T.A.Z.: The Temporary Autonomous Zone* (1991) by Hakim Bey (a pseudonym for author Peter Lamborn Wilson), also influenced *Intimate Bureaucracies* through its exploration of the anarchistic artistic possibilities of the early Internet, as did *Bolo'bolo* (1983), a work by pseudonymed author p.m. in the avant-garde journal *Semiotext(e)* that outlines a hypothetical future societal formation of pluralistic groups of mutual interest. Saper's previous works, *Networked Art* and *Artificial Mythologies* (1997), also raised many of the themes present in *Intimate Bureaucracies*.

The recent publication of *Intimate Bureaucracies* has not allowed for the manifesto to achieve significant literary influence. Saper did give a lecture on *Intimate Bureaucracies* in April 2012 at the Digital Legacies of the Avant-Garde Conference in Paris along with Manfred Mohr ("A Programmed Aesthetic") and Christiane Paul ("Feedback: New Media and Histories"). Packer also interviewed Saper concerning *Intimate Bureaucracies* in June 2012 on *The Post Reality Show: TALK MEDIA!* Saper continues to teach in the Language, Literacy, and Culture program at the University of Maryland, Baltimore, and serves as the reviews editor for the online journal *Rhizomes: Cultural Studies in Emerging Knowledge*.

THEMES AND STYLE

The central theme of *Intimate Bureaucracies* is the importance of sociopoetic systems functioning as self-contained intimate bureaucracies within the greater societal system. Saper argues this function requires "participator decentralization" among members of an intimate bureaucracy who seek "to project intimacy onto otherwise impersonal systems" and form a community. For Saper, this more intimate adaptation of corporate bureaucracy can result in a "new productive mythology surrounding the electronic world wide web" and that sociopoetic systems can be new "organizational and communication systems … that represent necessities, models, goals, and demands—an intimate bureaucracy that is a paradoxical mix of artisanal production, mass-distribution techniques, and belief in the democratizing potential of social media." Saper also emphasizes how "electronic networks combine a bureaucracy with its codes, passwords, links … with niche marketing, intimate personal contacts[,] … creating a hybrid situation or performance." He discusses the ways in which Occupy Wall Street and Fluxhouse represent "a model of social organization … that coalesces beyond any particular protest[,] … a working model of an intimate bureaucracy [which] threatens the dominant model of social organization."

Saper's rhetorical strategy in *Intimate Bureaucracies* relies on inductive academic argument and historical example. After initially emphasizing the role of the Occupy Wall Street movement as an intimate

BOB BROWN'S READING MACHINE

In addition to writing *Intimate Bureaucracies: A Manifesto*, *Networked Art*, and *Artificial Mythologies*, Craig Saper has done extensive research on New York-based avant-garde poet Bob Brown (1886-1959), including Brown's manifesto *The Readies* (1930), which included a description of a new form of "reading machine" that would allow readers to dispense with books and use machinery to scan microscopic text line by line. Saper argues that Brown's proposed reading machine eerily predates the technological advances of electronic textual media, claiming that "today, Brown's research on reading seems remarkably prescient in light of text-messaging (with its abbreviated language), electronic text readers, and even online books" and that "Brown's practical plans for his reading machine, and his descriptions of its meaning and implications for reading in general, were at least fifty years ahead of their time." In tribute to Brown, Saper has made several of the texts Brown intended for use in his reading machine available online, as well as a working digital model of the machine itself.

bureaucracy, Saper focuses more on the history of networked art and the Fluxhouse cooperatives as historical examples of sociopoetic systems. He argues that "OWS's most profound politics may have less to do with the injustices of the current tax codes, wealth disparity, or even, economic collapse, and more to do with its systems and practices of organization and communication." He draws limited parallels between Occupy Wall Street and Fluxhouse and relies on loose inductive arguments to relate the two. Saper's use of the academic first-person voice lends credibility to his assertions, but the overall argument of *Intimate Bureaucracies* is largely left to the reader. This allows for broad academic interpretation of his thesis.

The language of *Intimate Bureaucracies* is densely academic and sometimes difficult to interpret without a scholarly knowledge of the cultural studies field. ("By highlighting the existing aesthetic relationships as well as performance settings, distribution systems, measurement machinery, or the social apparatus, my project does not demythologize, but displaces, the frame to focus on the sociopoetic dimension.") The language is more accessible in the sections in which Saper explores historical examples of sociopoetic systems, including substantial histories of the Fluxhouse cooperative and mail art. His dense, heavily theoretic language ultimately serves to broaden the possibilities of his argument to a point of high abstraction.

CRITICAL DISCUSSION

Critical reaction to *Intimate Bureaucracies* has been limited by its recent publication, but the work has been favorably compared to Saper's earlier work, *Networked Art*, and served as one of the inspirations for

an art exhibition, *Intimate Bureaucracies: Art and the Mail,* held at the University of Essex in the United Kingdom in February and March of 2012. In his 2002 review in the journal *symploke,* Jon McKenzie compared *Networked Art* to other notable cultural theory works, such as Manuel Castell's *The Rise of the Network Society* (2002), Fredrich Kittler's *Discourse Networks, 1800/1900* (1992), and Simon S. Haykin's *Neutral Networks* (2009). McKenzie calls *Networked Art* "a start-up manual for the 21st century" and writes how the book "goes back to the future to investigate an untimely nexus of cultural creativity, social organization, and technical infrastructure. He claims that "'Intimate Bureaucracies' functions as the secret title of this important book."

Other critics have emphasized the importance of Saper's concept of intimate bureaucracies as originally put forward in *Networked Art.* Fellow cultural theorist Packer calls Saper's term, "intimate bureaucracy," "not ... an oxymoron, but rather a profound commentary on alternative culture." Packer refers to the idea of intimate bureaucracy as the "mantra" behind his founding of the "U.S. Department of Art and Technology," Parker's own avant-garde artistic organization. Stefaan Van Ryssen's 2003 review of *Networked Art* notes how the book "will certainly appeal to the general reader who is interested in the origins of networked art.... On the other hand, it lacks the rigor and detail to be a real lexicon, and its sinuous argument makes it sometimes difficult to follow."

Other scholars have focused on the role of the political within Saper's conception of intimate bureaucracies and sociopoetic systems. Jeanne Marie Kusina writes in her 2005 article "The Evolution and Revolutions of the Networked Art Aesthetic" that, while "anarchist tendencies are certainly in evidence" in much networked art, "the motivations behind these acts point toward a desire to foster human interaction in areas where it seems to be absent." Kusina emphasizes how members of sociopoetic systems choose to engage in greater society in a politically active way, writing, "Instead of opting out of a societal system they disagree with, network artists choose to *opt-in* with the creation of a new entity in line with their values and codes." Previous scholarly consensus on the importance of the study of networked art suggests that *Intimate Bureaucracies* represents another important step in a burgeoning field of academic consideration.

BIBLIOGRAPHY

Sources

Khatib, Kate. "Intimate Bureaucracies: A New Tactical Media Release!" *Revolution by the Book.* The AK Press, 16 Apr. 2012. Web. 7 Nov. 2012.

Kusina, Jeanne Marie. "The Evolution and Revolutions of the Networked Art Aesthetic." *Contemporary Aesthetics* March 2005. *Mpublishing, U of Michigan Library.* Web. 7 Nov. 2012.

McKenzie, Jon. Rev. of *Networked Art,* by Craig J. Saper. *symploke* 10.1 (2002): 205-06. *Project MUSE.* Web. 7 Nov. 2012.

Packer, Randall. "The Intimate Bureaucracy of the Capital Fringe." *Reportage from the Aesthetic Edge*. Randall Packer, 19 June 2012. Web. 7 Nov. 2012.

readies, dj (pseudonym for Craig J. Saper). *Intimate Bureaucracies: A Manifesto*. Brooklyn: Punctum Books, 2012. Print.

Van Ryssen, Stefan. Rev. of *Networked Art,* by Craig J. Saper. *Leonardo Reviews*. Leonardo On-Line, 2 Jan. 2003. Web. 7 Nov. 2012.

Further Reading

Barthes, Roland. *Mythologies*. Trans. Annette Lavers. New York: Farrar, Straus and Giroux, 1972. Print.

Bey, Hakim (pseudonym for Peter Lamborn Wilson). *T.A.Z.: The Temporary Autonomous Zone, Ontological Anarchy, Poetic Terrorism*. New York: Autonomedia, 1991. *Hermetic Library*. Web. 14 Nov. 2012.

Debord, Guy. *The Society of the Spectacle*. 1967. Trans. Donald Nicholson-Smith. New York: Zone Books, 1995. Print.

Friedman, Ken, ed. *The Fluxus Reader*. London: Academy Editions, 1998. Print.

p.m. (pseudonym). *Bolo'bolo*. Foreign Agents Series. Ed. Jim Fleming and Sylvere Lotringer. Cambridge: Semiotext(e)/MIT P, 1985. Print.

Saper, Craig J. *Artificial Mythologies: A Guide to Cultural Invention*. Minneapolis: U of Minnesota P, 1997. Print.

———. *Networked Art*. Minneapolis: U of Minnesota P, 2001. Print.

Wark, McKenzie. *A Hacker Manifesto*. Cambridge: Harvard UP, 2004. Print.

Taylor Evans

MANIFESTO FOR CYBORGS
Science, Technology, and Socialist Feminism in the 1980s
Donna Haraway

✣ *Key Facts*

Time Period:
Late 20th Century

Movement/Issue:
Technology; Feminism;
Postmodernism

Place of Publication:
United States

**Language of
Publication:**
English

OVERVIEW

"Manifesto for Cyborgs: Science, Technology, and Socialist Feminism in the 1980s" (1985) is a germinal work on technology and gender by Donna Haraway. It is more commonly known by the title given to its slightly revised 1991 incarnation, "A Cyborg Manifesto: Science, Technology, and Socialist-Feminism in the Late Twentieth Century." In this postmodern manifesto, Haraway presents the cyborg as an image of the power that resides in the social other, which she argues is inevitably both natural and socially constructed, both organic and cybernetic (subject to automatic control, usually electrical or electronic). Haraway's manifesto suggests that feminists embrace the chaotic fragmentation of identity categories that, in her view, technology perpetuates; she locates the possibility of transformational change in fracture rather than in wholeness, in critical contrast to many Marxist and psychoanalytic ideological frames.

Upon its initial publication, Haraway's manifesto was almost immediately recognized as a significant document adding to the continuing discussion of gender and technology. The widespread reception of the manifesto would lead to its eventual revision and republication. As both a biologist and a philosopher, Haraway has pursued an ongoing project to examine the boundaries of identity and species categories; "Manifesto for Cyborgs" forms part one of her endeavor. In the manifesto, Haraway expounds on both the consequence and the opportunities created for feminism by the transformation of labor, the body, and communication at the dawn of the digital age. The manifesto had a profound impact on postmodern and feminist scholarship, becoming the foundational text of a still-growing body of "cyborg theory." Haraway embraces technoculture, rejecting second-wave feminist appeals to nature and gender essentialism; as a result, her work has only grown more relevant as virtual and microtechnological innovations have transformed the post-1980s world. Haraway's explication of the cyborg as a metaphor for oppressed persons has also affected pop culture and cyberculture, as virtual personae have become commonplace and science fiction cyborgs have proliferated.

HISTORICAL AND LITERARY CONTEXT

Haraway's "Manifesto for Cyborgs" addresses the intersection between changes in technology and gender roles that were occurring in the late twentieth century, proposing the existence of a unique connection between them. By the mid-1980s technological innovations in robotics, computer science, and communications were beginning to produce a "new industrial revolution," transforming both the economic and personal spheres. Computers became increasingly central to all sorts of businesses and the processing and exchange of information. Microelectronics and silicone chip technology integrated machines with daily life and necessitated the restructuring of labor from factory-style mass-assembly work to information management, data entry, and programming.

By 1985, the year in which the manifesto was first published, an estimated 71 percent of women between the ages of twenty-five and forty-four participated in the workforce, and half of all college graduates in 1985 were women. Advancements in technology transformed the workplace, blurring the lines between commonly accepted gender roles. Traditionally feminine tasks, such as typing and organization, became significant skill sets, and arguments about women's physical inferiority to men ceased to be relevant. This change coincided with gains made in women's rights by the feminist second wave. Haraway's manifesto provided a frame for the continuance of women's empowerment in the cybernetic era.

The manifesto responds to a number of academic trends and fractures: the predominance of psychoanalytic theories that position women as natural or primitive; the fragmentation that was taking place in the feminist community as core terms of gender, sexuality, race, and class came into question; and the mounting pressures of postmodernism on traditional concepts and methodologies in academic research. A growing body of work questioned the basic ways in which academic disciplines regulated knowledge; such black feminists as Audre Lorde and Barbara Smith exposed the ways in which epistemology contributed to structural racism, while such scholars as Evelyn Fox-Keller, Helen Longino, Sandra Harding, and Nancy Tuana discussed the ways in which feminism challenged the scientific method. Haraway's manifesto brings these questions together with the insights produced by feminist authors of science fiction, including Joanna Russ, Samuel Delany, John Varley, James Tiptree Jr., Ursula K. Le Guin, and Vonda McIntyre.

"Manifesto for Cyborgs" articulates concepts, frames, and metaphors that resonated tremendously with its historical moment and has continued to be relevant to the intersection of gender and technology in the twenty-first century. Haraway's *Simians, Cyborgs and Women: The Reinvention of Nature* (1991) furthers the development of her theory of the cyborg. Since 1985 the rise of the Internet has made cyberculture increasingly central to culture as a whole—visible in such literary and pop-cultural trends as cyberpunk, as well as the growing significance of digital media in political movements and the increasing concern with cyberspace rights and legalities—thus ensuring the continued importance of Haraway's manifesto.

THEMES AND STYLE

"Manifesto for Cyborgs" argues that the social apparatus of control and normalization that maintains gender and sexual roles can be understood as a technology, one that is produced by human culture as a way of managing society while at the same time it is producing the individuals who make up society. Haraway asserts that "naturalistic" tendencies in social theory are, by nature, oppressive because they insist on unity by suppressing diversity. She explores the ways in which communication technologies allow women to reshape both themselves and their realities, arguing that feminist "cyborg writing" could have the ability dynamically to transform, destabilize, or destroy gender and class norms.

Haraway self-consciously poses her cyborg as a "myth," keeping her metaphor transparent: "By the late twentieth century, our time, a mythic time, we are all chimeras, theorized and fabricated hybrids of machine and organism; in short, we are cyborgs." By positioning herself as a cyborg, Haraway employs the collectivist rhetoric of the manifesto form, allying herself with other proponents of the cyborg against dominant ideas of hierarchical wholeness. For Haraway, the oppressed in particular inevitably occupy a cyborgian position, part nature and part social construct. However, instead of disavowing this cyborg identity and striving for either a natural or a united womanhood, Haraway suggests that feminism embrace this hybrid, fragmented identity, "insist[ing] on noise and advocat[ing] pollution, rejoicing in the illegitimate fusions of animal and machine." In a deconstructive move, Haraway notes that gender and race oppression work through the construction of binaries, such as male/female, civilized/primitive, and whole/part; her myth of the cyborg, both natural and technological, challenges these dualisms and ultimately reveals

THE GENESIS OF "CYBORG"

The word "cyborg" is a relatively recent coinage, dating to the 1960s. Older terms for living machines include the ancient Greek "android," literally "man-machine," and "robot," which originally referred to a central European system of serfdom but which became the term of choice for animate machines when Karel Čapek used it in his 1920 play *R.U.R.: Rossum's Universal Robots*. "Cyborg" as a term places unique emphasis on the blended or chimeric nature of the figure, combining the 1940s term "cybernetic" (relating to or exhibiting automatic control) and the Old English-derived "organism" (an individual plant, animal, or single-celled life form). The term was coined by Manfred Clynes and Nathan S. Kline, who used it in a 1960 article on the self-regulating human-machine systems that would be necessary for a human being to survive in outer space. Although the word "cyborg" conjures up images from science fiction, some have theorized that assistive devices, such as cochlear implants and contact lenses, may have already transformed people into cyborgs. Emergent technologies, such as the C-Leg system, which replaces an amputated limb with a sensitive prosthesis, or the implanted brain-computer interfaces that have been used experimentally to treat acquired blindness, continue to blur the lines between human and machine.

their construction, as well as the mutually constitutive nature of their terms.

Haraway's style is dense, poetic, referential, and self-conscious. Her manifesto alternates between metaphorical assertions and explications of specific instances. Perhaps taking her own recommendation for a mode of writing responsive to "the struggle for language and the struggle against perfect communication, against the one code that translates all meaning perfectly, the central dogma of phallogocentrism," Haraway delivers prose that is nonlinear, often inconclusive or multiple, and frequently circular. ("Phallogocentrism," a term coined by the French feminist Luce Irigaray, refers to the linkage of language, masculinity, and privilege that authorizes male speech.) Haraway's style, which in its nonlinear complexity deviates from and deconstructs the form and tone of the traditional manifesto, has been critiqued as a weakness of the essay. For example, Roger Smith characterizes Haraway's prose as "formidable and excluding" and admits to a wish for "fewer words"; similar criticisms have frequently been applied to works written in the vein of academic postmodernism to which Haraway belongs, a scholarly trend that seeks to deconstruct the sociocultural power of language. In her book *Manifestoes: Provocations of the Modern*, Janet Lyon cites "A Cyborg Manifesto" as an example of the tension between postmodern style and the "formation of audience and the mobilization of passional activism" that Haraway implicitly seeks to effect through her prose.

to explore postmodernism, posthumanism, gender, and technology in the twenty-first century, often branching out from Haraway's archive to consider new applications of her cyborg figure. Significant works in this critical vein include *A Cyborg Handbook* (1995), edited by Chris Hables Cray, Steven Mentor, and Heidi Figueroa-Sarriera; *Cyborg Babies: From Techno-Sex to Techno-Tots* (1998), edited by R. Davies-Floyd and Joseph Dumit; and *The Gendered Cyborg: A Reader* (1999), edited by Gill Kirkup, Linda Janes, Fiona Hovenden, and Kathryn Woodward. Haraway herself has remained an active participant in cyborg theory debates, continuing to refine her conceptualization of consciousness and her understanding of its historical and contextual situation. "Manifesto for Cyborgs," something of a crossover success, has also enjoyed wide nonacademic readership, particularly among creators and fans of speculative fiction and media. Groups and genres of the 1990s, including cyberpunk culture, hacker collectives, participants in the industrial music scene, and the creators of *The Matrix,* to mention only a few, drew on ideas expressed in Haraway's work, which appeals to nonacademic readers through its imaginative portrayal of social justice issues.

Texts on cyborg theory abounded throughout the 1990s, frequently citing Haraway's work, as scholars strove to grasp the nature and implications of the cyborg. In the twenty-first century critics have examined "Manifesto for Cyborgs" by applying cyborg theory to various literary and cultural texts, as widely divergent as *The Stepford Wives,* Japanese cyberculture, and the poetry of Eavan Boland. Addresses to the manifesto as a primary source have become somewhat rare, as criticism instead tests and explores the conceptual limits of the cyborg through the concrete examples provided by life or literature. However, some scholars, including Melissa Colleen Stevenson, Sarah Kember, and Kirsten Campbell, have also worked to apply Haraway's insights into the unique relationship between gender and technology to the situation of women in scientific and technological fields, examining the nonmetaphorical cyborgs formed by women working with and through machines.

BIBLIOGRAPHY

Sources

Haraway, Donna. "Manifesto for Cyborgs: Science, Technology, and Socialist Feminism in the 1980s." *Socialist Review* 80 (1985): 65-108. Print.

———. "A Cyborg Manifesto: Science, Technology, and Socialist-Feminism in the Late Twentieth Century." *Simians, Cyborgs, and Women: The Reinvention of Nature.* New York: Routledge, 1991. 149-182. Print.

Lyon, Janet. *Manifestoes: Provocations of the Modern.* Ithaca: Cornell UP, 1999. Print.

McNeil, Maureen. Rev. of *Simians, Cyborgs, and Women: The Reinvention of Nature,* by Donna Haraway. *Science, Technology, and Human Values* 19.1 (1994): 110-13. Print.

Actress Daryl Hannah as a "replicant,' or cyborg, in Ridley Scott's 1982 film *Blade Runner,* which is considered a seminal film in the cyberpunk genre. ©WARNER BROS/ COURTESY EVERETT COLLECTION

CRITICAL DISCUSSION

Haraway's manifesto almost instantly became a significant text in ongoing debates about gender, technology, and postmodernism. According to Maureen McNeil, after the 1985 publication of "Manifesto for Cyborgs" in the *Socialist Review,* the essay was "widely circulated, revised, and republished," attesting to the breadth and urgency of its reception. Jeffrey J. Williams notes in the *Chronicle of Higher Education* (2009) that Haraway's manifesto "was an unlikely candidate to capture the zeitgeist. But it struck a chord, characterizing one aspect of postmodernism, of the world changing from nature to simulation, from things to information."

"Manifesto for Cyborgs" is credited with having launched "cyborg theory," which has continued

Smith, Roger. Rev. of *Simians, Cyborgs, and Women: The Reinvention of Nature,* by Donna Haraway. *Isis* 83.2 (1992): 350-51. Print.

Williams, Jeffrey J. "A Theory of Critters." *Chronicle of Higher Education.* Chronicle of Higher Education, 18 Oct. 2009. Web. 27 June 2012.

Further Reading

Balinisteanu, Tudor. "The Cyborg Goddess: Social Myths of Women as Goddesses of Technologized Otherworlds." *Feminist Studies* 33.2 (2007): 394-423. Print.

Balsamo, Anne. *Technologies of the Gendered Body: Reading Cyborg Women.* Durham: Duke UP, 1999. Print.

Burfoot, Annette. "Feminist Technoscience: A Solution to Theoretical Conundrums and the Wane of Feminist Politics?" *Resources for Feminist Research* 33.3-4 (2010): 71. Print.

Chilcoat, Michelle. "Brain Sex, Cyberpunk Cinema, Feminism, and the Dis/Location of Heterosexuality." *NWSA Journal* 16.2 (2004): 156-76. Print.

Haraway, Donna. *The Haraway Reader.* New York: Routledge, 2004. Print.

———. *Modest_Witness@Second_Millennium. FemaleMan_Meets_OncoMouse: Feminism and Technoscience.* New York: Routledge, 1997. Print.

Hayles, N. Katherine. *How We Became Posthuman: Virtual Bodies in Cybernetics, Literature, and Informatics.* Chicago: U of Chicago P, 1999. Print.

Schueller, Malini Johar. "Analogy and (White) Feminist Theory: Thinking Race and the Color of the Cyborg Body." *Signs* 31.1 (2005): 63-92. Print.

Stevenson, Melissa Colleen. "Trying to Plug In: Posthuman Cyborgs and the Search for Connection." *Science Fiction Studies* 34.1 (2007): 87-105. Print.

Carina Saxon

ONE HALF A MANIFESTO

Jaron Lanier

❖ *Key Facts*

Time Period:
Early 21st Century

Movement/Issue:
Technological
advancement

Place of Publication:
United States

**Language of
Publication:**
English

OVERVIEW

In "One Half a Manifesto," published in the online magazine *Edge* on September 25, 2000, computer scientist Jaron Lanier refutes arguments that rapid technological development will continue unabated until cybernetics eventually governs all of human existence—including all human creativity and culture. During the late twentieth century, in light of significant advances in computing, some scientists hypothesized that technological growth, and by extension human culture, was in fact governed by scientific laws and followed an exponential model. However, Lanier describes such beliefs as "cybernetic totalism," or the beliefs that reality can be reduced to a system of cybernetic patterns and that computers will soon permanently change the nature of human existence. Addressed to computer scientists and "cybernetic totalists," the essay argues that "bloated" software and inefficient processes have retarded the development of technology such that the "cyber-armageddon" that many have predicted could never occur.

The essay's criticism of prevailing theories of technological development elicited mixed reactions from computer scientists. A series of comments from members of the Reality Club—a group of intellectual and cultural figures hosted by *Edge*—call Lanier's writing everything from "a beautiful work" to a persuasive argument written "in a social vacuum." The text was one of the first to criticize the foundation for a new generation of online information sharing, later dubbed Web 2.0, helping to launch significant conversations about the future role of technology in society. The piece is also notable because it does not attempt to predict the future of computer culture—ostensibly the other half of the "One Half a Manifesto." Nevertheless, it remains one of several important works by Lanier on the topic of cybernetic dogma, including "Digital Maoism: The Hazards of the New Online Collectivism" (2006), "Beware the Online Collective" (2006), and *You Are Not a Gadget: A Manifesto* (2010).

HISTORICAL AND LITERARY CONTEXT

"One Half a Manifesto" responds to the theories of writers and scientists who believe that computers will one day become as powerful as human brains. In 1965 Intel cofounder Gordon E. Moore delineated a powerful theory, dubbed Moore's Law, which states that the number of transistors on a semiconductor chip will double approximately every two years. Author Ray Kurzweil described a similar theory in 1999, called the Law of Accelerating Returns, which states that technological development, like evolutionary development, follows a model of exponential growth. Such theories of rapid, unchecked technological growth led many to believe that the development of transformative artificial intelligence was little more than decades away.

Lanier's essay was published at the end of the dot-com bubble, when the technology sector was struggling to determine how to exploit the Internet's interactive capabilities. Other technological developments that paved the way for "One Half a Manifesto" included the Windows 2000 operating system, music-sharing sites such as Napster, and global leaps in broadband Internet usage. In 2000 Lanier, already well established in his field, was employed as chief scientist of Advanced Network and Services, which included the nonprofit company Internet2, as lead scientist of the National Tele-immersion Initiative and as a visiting scholar at the Department of Computer Science at Columbia University.

Although "One Half a Manifesto" was the first text to extensively discuss cybernetic totalism, Lanier was not alone in his beliefs. In formulating the essay, he was influenced by several other scientists. For example, while in his early twenties, he met Nobel Prize-winning physicists Richard Feynman and Murray Gell-Mann at the California Institute of Technology. According to Lanier, they helped expose him to "the culture of theoretical physics ... the most refined culture for applying maths to life." The essay was also likely influenced by the time Lanier spent working for Atari, where he struck up a friendship with Thomas Zimmerman, the inventor of the data glove.

After its publication, "One Half a Manifesto" helped launch Lanier's literary career and enhance his reputation as a leading critic of Web 2.0. His later works build on the ideas expressed in the piece, questioning conventional wisdom about the role of technology in society. In "Digital Maoism" he challenges the notion that "the collective is all-wise [and] that it is desirable to have influence concentrated in a bottleneck that can channel the collective with the most verity and force." In *You Are Not a Gadget,* he chronicles the effects of Web 2.0 on the "Facebook Generation": "Something like missionary reductionism has happened to the Internet with the rise of Web 2.0…. The strangeness is being leached away in the mush-making process." Today "One Half a Manifesto" remains relevant to discussions of the future of technology, as scientists have increasingly called into question the relevance of firmly held theories such as Moore's Law.

THEMES AND STYLE

The central theme of "One Half a Manifesto" is the fallacy that computers will someday be as highly functioning as the human brain and will bring about an "eschatological cataclysm in our lifetimes" as "ultra-intelligent masters of physical matter and life." To develop this theme, Lanier organizes his essay into six beliefs of cybernetic totalism. The first three address the convictions that "cybernetic patterns of information provide the ultimate and best way to understand reality"; "people are no more than cybernetic patterns"; and "subjective experience either doesn't exist, or is unimportant." The fourth and fifth sections challenge beliefs that Darwinian theories of evolution and Moore's Law in fact govern human technology, creativity, and culture. The final section addresses a belief in "the coming cybernetic cataclysm" in which "biology and physics will merge with computer science … resulting in life and the physical universe becoming mercurial."

In each of the six sections, Lanier uses wisdom gained through experience to deflate his opponents' fantasies of a world run by computers. Whereas his colleagues see in technological advances the basis for developing artificial intelligence, Lanier sees self-delusion: "We make ourselves stupid in order to make the computer software seem smart." He portrays himself as a silent observer who has worked alongside cybernetic totalists but has resisted the urge to publicly comment on the subject: "My position is unpopular and even resented in my professional and social environment." He states that he was ultimately compelled to write the manifesto because his opponents' ideas "might end up essentially built into the software that runs our society and our lives … caus[ing] suffering for millions of people." Thus, he concludes that pragmatism, skepticism, and humility are the only appropriate antidotes to cybernetic totality.

In "One Half a Manifesto," Lanier uses a humorous, philosophical tone to connect with his audience and to reflect the creativity that he believes underlies all technological innovation. For example, after addressing the application of evolutionary theory to cybernetics, he concludes, "So, while I love Darwin, I won't count on him to write code," alluding to his belief that personal experience, not scientific theory, lies at the root of important technological advances. Similarly, when he states in his conclusion, "I'll

JARON LANIER: VIRTUAL REALITY PIONEER

Writer and computer scientist Jaron Lanier first came to prominence for coining the term "virtual reality" (VR) to describe an interactive, multidimensional computer-generated environment. His work with VR began in the 1980s when he founded VPL Research, a VR equipment purveyor that developed the first multiuser virtual worlds using head-mounted displays. He also helped pioneer the use of avatars, or digital images that represent users and may be manipulated by them, in a VR setting.

Although VR became notable for its entertainment applications in the 1990s, Lanier and VPL Research explored a host of other uses, including prototyping of vehicle interiors and surgical simulation. In the late 1990s VPL Research was sold to Sun Microsystems, and Lanier applied his significant VR experience to his work at the National Tele-immersion Initiative and Advanced Network and Service. In a 1989 interview with *Whole Earth Review,* he explains his vision that virtual reality would enhance, not supplant, human existence: "Virtual Reality is the first medium that's large enough not to limit human nature. It's the first medium that's broad enough to express us as natural beings. It's the first medium within which we can express our nature and the whole of nature to each other."

Jaron Lanier, author of "One Half a Manifesto," plays an ancient Lao flute during an advertising conference at Microsoft headquarters in Redmond, Washington, in 2011. KEVIN P. CASEY/ BLOOMBERG VIA GETTY IMAGES

PRIMARY SOURCE

"ONE HALF A MANIFESTO"

For the last twenty years, I have found myself on the inside of a revolution, but on the outside of its resplendent dogma. Now that the revolution has not only hit the mainstream, but bludgeoned it into submission by taking over the economy, it's probably time for me to cry out my dissent more loudly than I have before. (* see below)

And so I'll here share my thoughts with the respondents of edge.org, many of whom are, as much as anyone, responsible for this revolution, one which champions the assent of cybernetic technology *as* culture.

The dogma I object to is composed of a set of interlocking beliefs and doesn't have a generally accepted overarching name as yet, though I sometimes call it "cybernetic totalism". It has the potential to transform human experience more powerfully than any prior ideology, religion, or political system ever has, partly because it can be so pleasing to the mind, at least initially, but mostly because it gets a free ride on the overwhelmingly powerful technologies that happen to be created by people who are, to a large degree, true believers.

Edge readers might be surprised by my use of the word "cybernetic". I find the word problematic, so I'd like to explain why I chose it. I searched for a term that united the diverse ideas I was exploring, and also connected current thinking and culture with earlier generations of thinkers who touched on similar topics. The original usage of "cybernetic", as by Norbert Weiner, was certainly not restricted to digital computers. It was originally meant to suggest a metaphor between marine navigation and a feedback device that governs a mechanical system, such as a thermostat. Weiner certainly recognized and humanely explored the extraordinary reach of this metaphor, one of the most powerful ever expressed.

I hope no one will think I'm equating Cybernetics and what I'm calling Cybernetic Totalism. The distance between recognizing a great metaphor and treating it as the only metaphor is the same as the distance between humble science and dogmatic religion.

Here is a partial roster of the component beliefs of cybernetic totalism:

1. That cybernetic patterns of information provide the ultimate and best way to understand reality.

2. That people are no more than cybernetic patterns.

3. That subjective experience either doesn't exist, or is unimportant because it is some sort of ambient or peripheral effect.

4. That what Darwin described in biology, or something like it, is in fact also the singular, superior description of all creativity and culture.

5. That qualitative as well as quantitative aspects of information systems will be accelerated by Moore's Law.

And finally, the most dramatic:

6. That biology and physics will merge with computer science (becoming biotechnology and nanotechnology), resulting in life and the physical universe becoming mercurial; achieving the supposed nature of computer software.

Furthermore, all of this will happen very soon! Since computers are improving so quickly, they will overwhelm all the other cybernetic processes, like people, and will fundamentally change the nature of what's going on in the familiar neighborhood of Earth at some moment when a new "criticality" is achieved- maybe in about the year 2020. To be a human after that moment will be either impossible or something very different than we now can know.

SOURCE: Jaron Lanier, "One Half a Manifesto," www.edge.org, November 11, 2000. Copyright © 2012 By Edge Foundation, Inc. All Rights Reserved. http://edge.org/conversation/one-halfa-manifesto

worry about the future of human culture more than I'll worry about the gadgets," he contrasts his own pragmatic view of technology with his opponents' confused and detached notions of "intelligent agents" and "expert systems." For Lanier, cultural context, not technological theory, is key. Without it, he jokes, "I don't think Martians would necessarily be able to distinguish a Macintosh from a space heater."

CRITICAL DISCUSSION

Responses to "One Half a Manifesto" came almost immediately, mostly in the form of online comments. In fact, several remarks from members of the Reality Club were published alongside of the essay, emphasizing its purpose of stimulating dialogue. Several wrote encouraging opinions, commending the author for tackling a frequently ignored topic. Science writer Margaret Wertheim writes, "I heartily agree that what he called 'cybernetic totalism' needs to be exposed." Other early reactions from Lanier's peers expanded on the document, strengthening it with their own arguments. Writer Cliff Barney states, "I wish Lanier had written the other half of his manifesto…. This is more likely to affect Armageddon than Dr. Moore's relentlessly shrinking etchings." However, former MIT professor Rodney A. Brooks took issue with Lanier's argument: "The first problem I have is with his dismissal of Artificial Intelligence as being based on an intellectual mistake. His argument is all smoke and mirrors with no viable logic."

The online dialogue continued in the months and years following the essay's publication. On November 11, 2000, Lanier publicly responded to the comments of his Reality Club colleagues on *Edge,* with remarks ranging from personal statements ("A warm, brotherly bear hug for you!") to clarifications about his intentions ("I hope it's clear that I was being snide and flip when I brought up nanobots.") In addition, he clarifies the intellectual distinctions between Kurzweil's theories and his own, essentially outlining a seventh section to "One Half a Manifesto" that addresses the totalist belief that "fundamental intellectual achievement" is "inexorably speeding up." The new comments prompted Kurzweil in 2001 to respond on his website, *Kurzweil Accelerating Intelligence,* that Lanier "mischaracterizes many of the views he objects to" and that many of the scientist's arguments "aren't really arguments at all, but an amalgamation of mentally filed anecdotes and engineering frustrations."

More than a decade after the publication of "One Half a Manifesto," criticism has died down. Most critics tend to focus on Lanier's more recent works, specifically his 2010 book *You Are Not a Gadget,* which builds on the concepts he established in "One Half a Manifesto." He cites Web 2.0 developments such as Wikipedia and Linux as glorifying the collective at the expense of the individual. In a 2011 *New Yorker* profile of the computer scientist, writer Jennifer Kahn calls him "an unusual figure: he is a technology expert who dislikes what technology has become."

BIBLIOGRAPHY

Sources

Appleyard, Bryan. "Jaron Lanier: The Father of Virtual Reality." *Sunday Times* (London). Times Newspapers Ltd., 17 Jan. 2010. Web. 24 Aug. 2012.

Kahn, Jennifer. "The Visionary." *New Yorker* 11 July 2011: 46. *Literature Resource Center.* Web. 23 Aug. 2012.

Kurzweil, Ray. "One Half of an Argument." *Kurzweil Accelerating Intelligence.* Kurzweil Accelerating Intelligence, 31 July 2001. Web. 24 Aug. 2012.

Lanier, Jaron. "One Half a Manifesto." *Edge.* Edge, 25 Sept. 2000. Web. 24 Aug. 2012.

"The Reality Club: One Half a Manifesto: Part I." *Edge.* Edge, 11 Nov. 2000. Web. 24 Aug. 2012.

"The Reality Club: One Half a Manifesto: Part II." *Edge.* Edge, 11 Nov. 2000. Web. 24 Aug. 2012.

"Virtual Reality: An Interview with Jaron Lanier." *Whole Earth Review* 64 (1989): 108-19. Web. 24 Aug. 2012.

Further Reading

Brock, David C., and Gordon E. Moore. *Understanding Moore's Law: Four Decades of Innovation.* Philadelphia: Chemical Heritage Foundation, 2006. Print.

Kurzweil, Ray. *The Age of Spiritual Machines: When Computers Exceed Human Intelligence.* New York: Viking, 1999. Print.

Lanier, Jaron. "Beware the Online Collective." *Edge.* Edge, 25 Dec. 2006. Web. 24 Aug. 2012.

———. "Digital Maoism: The Hazards of the New Online Collectivism." *Edge.* Edge, 30 May 2006. Web. 24 Aug. 2012.

———. *You Are Not a Gadget: A Manifesto.* New York: Knopf, 2010. Print.

Anna Deem

RUSSELL-EINSTEIN MANIFESTO

Bertrand Russell, Albert Einstein

❖ *Key Facts*

Time Period:
Mid-20th Century

Movement/Issue:
Nuclear disarmament

Place of Publication:
England; United States

**Language of
Publication:**
English

OVERVIEW

Composed by the British philosopher, social critic, and antiwar activist Bertrand Russell in consultation with German-born physicist Albert Einstein, the *Russell-Einstein Manifesto* (1955) outlines the dangers that nuclear weapons pose to humanity and calls for a conference of scientists to assess what the authors deemed a growing crisis. The manifesto, which built on comments Russell had made just days after the bombings of Hiroshima and Nagasaki in August 1945, was delivered at a press conference at Caxton Hall, London, on July 9, 1955. Its intended audience included members of the applied physics and foreign-policy communities; the document was sent to the leaders of all nuclear and potentially nuclear countries. The cultural diversity of the document's eleven signatorics—ten of whom were, or would become, Nobel laureates—helped ensure the political neutrality of their plea for nonproliferation and eventual nuclear disarmament.

Although initially greeted with resistance, the manifesto eventually gained traction among reporters who had attended the press conference. Thereafter, it received a great deal of favorable press, which helped inaugurate the Pugwash Conferences on Science and World Affairs. Taking the *Russell-Einstein Manifesto* as a founding charter, the conferences gather Eastern and Western scientists to work toward morally sound solutions to problems related to armed conflict and global security. The first such meeting was held in Pugwash, Nova Scotia, in 1957 and was financed by Canadian Cyrus Eaton, a Chicago industrialist who had corresponded with Russell since 1938. Both the resultant Pugwash movement and Russell played important roles in urging a peaceful settlement of the 1962 Cuban Missile Crisis and negotiating the ensuing Partial Test Ban Treaty (1963)—the first limitative treaty on nuclear weapons—signed by the Soviet Union, the United Kingdom, and the United States. More than fifty regional organizations operate today under the umbrella of the Pugwash Conferences. The manifesto itself set the tone for worldwide antinuclear movements, including the still-robust Campaign for Nuclear Disarmament, founded in 1957 in England.

HISTORICAL AND LITERARY CONTEXT

The *Russell-Einstein Manifesto* responded to the increasingly tense political climate surrounding the rapid advancement of thermonuclear weapons technology in the early 1950s. On November 1, 1952, the United States tested the world's first hydrogen bomb (a weapon based on nuclear fusion), which had an explosive yield of 10.4 megatons (the equivalent of about 10 million tons of TNT), or 500 times more powerful than the atom bombs that had devastated Hiroshima and Nagasaki. The Soviet Union quickly followed, detonating its first hydrogen bomb in 1953. Becoming engaged in an arms race, the United States on March 1, 1954, exploded on Bikini Atoll in the Pacific Ocean a hydrogen bomb with a 15-megaton yield, about twice as powerful as its designers had anticipated. Sailors aboard a Japanese fishing vessel were contaminated, and one later died—the first recorded victim of a hydrogen bomb. On December 23, 1954, Russell delivered a BBC radio talk titled "Man's Peril," in large part motivated by the events on Bikini Atoll. The manuscript was published in the BBC magazine the *Listener* the following week, setting the stage for Russell and Einstein's collaboration.

Russell had been formulating the manifesto for ten years when, on March 16, 1955, President Dwight D. Eisenhower addressed the possibility that the United States might intervene in Chinese conflicts in the Taiwan Straits, saying publicly of atom bombs, "I see no reason why they shouldn't be used just exactly as you would use a bullet..." Einstein, who had been corresponding with Russell during the previous months, agreed then that the document was necessary and suggested that it would carry more weight if it were signed by a small number of reputable scientists. The two quickly enlisted the help of Joseph Rotblat, the only scientist who had left the Manhattan Project (the program that developed the atom bomb) for moral reasons. Russell drafted the statement on April 5, 1955, and six days later Einstein enthusiastically became the first signatory.

The *Russell-Einstein Manifesto* resembles such major documents as the ubiquitous *Communist Manifesto* (1848) in its performative drama: its ringing final phrase, reiterated from Russell's original BBC discourse, is "Remember your humanity, and forget the rest." Although Russell was not a pacifist at the outset of the 1898 Boer War, he was persuaded to become one in 1900 by the French logician Louis Couturat in a series of letters exchanged over several years. Russell later ambivalently supported World War II, nevertheless believing that war was an evil in itself, destructive of life and liberty.

Along with the *Mainau Declaration*—a statement similar to Russell's issued by German scientists Otto Hahn and Max Born in July 1955—the *Russell-Einstein Manifesto* fostered an open conversation about the dangers of nuclear proliferation. From August 3 to 5, 1955, the World Association of Parliamentarians for World Government (founded in 1951) met in London and approved a resolution based on the manifesto. After Russell led a failed attempt to organize a disarmament meeting in India hosted by nonaligned leaders, the Indian government commissioned a book titled *Nuclear Explosions and Their Effects* (1956). The manifesto also provided an academic foundation for artistic inquiry. The risks outlined in the manifesto have become part of popular culture through both satire—as in Stanley Kubrick's iconic film, *Dr. Strangelove, or How I Learned to Stop Worrying and Love the Bomb* (1964)—and speculative political fiction, including Tom Clancy's novels *Patriot Games* (1987) and *The Sum of All Fears* (1991). Russell himself saw the postapocalyptic film *On the Beach* (1959), starring Gregory Peck and Ava Gardner, which no doubt reinforced his views.

THEMES AND STYLE

The central concern of the *Russell-Einstein Manifesto* is the eventual abolition of war. Recognizing that advances in thermonuclear technology cannot be unmade, the document acknowledges that "an agreed prohibition of nuclear weapons, while it might be useful in lessening tension, would not afford a solution, since such weapons would certainly be manufactured and used in a great war in spite of previous agreements to the contrary." Knowing that progress would be slow, the manifesto calls in the meantime for nuclear disarmament and urges political leaders to adopt "a way of thinking which shall make such avoidance [of war] possible," thereby limiting the risk of nuclear devastation. The manifesto also cites the potential benefits of technological advancement in general and the use of nuclear fusion and fission to produce energy in particular, and it demands that all relevant fields of study, especially applied nuclear physics, employ conscientious, ethical practices and make considered decisions based on morality.

A plea for political and cultural neutrality serves as the manifesto's main rhetorical strategy, with the authors submitting that, although "most of us are not neutral in feeling […] as human beings […] whether Communist or anti-Communist, whether Asian or European or American, whether White or Black," we

JOSEPH ROTBLAT: PHYSICIST AND PACIFIST

Joseph Rotblat (1908-2005) lived a quiet, unassuming life dedicated to peace and the abolition of nuclear weapons. At the age of thirty, he accepted a fellowship working with physicist and Nobel laureate James Chadwick in London, leaving his hometown of Warsaw just days before the Nazi invasion of Poland. The fellowship led to his involvement first with the British atomic bomb project and then with the American Manhattan Project. He left the latter on moral grounds seven months before the first atom bomb was tested and learned of the bomb's successful creation only after its use on Hiroshima and Nagasaki was reported in the news. Stunned by the decision to bomb civilian populations, he committed to working for nuclear disarmament and global peace.

Rotblat served as a consulting expert for Bertrand Russell during the drafting of the *Russell-Einstein Manifesto* (1955) and coordinated the first Pugwash Conference in 1957. He was the secretary-general of Pugwash from 1957 to 1973 and was president of the organization from 1988 to 1997. In 1995 he and Pugwash were jointly awarded the Nobel Peace Prize for "their efforts to diminish the part played by nuclear arms in international politics and, in the longer run, to eliminate such arms."

must not decide political disagreements by means of war. Knowing that a document expressing even a hint of ideological bias would be dismissed immediately, Russell chose instead to appeal to each individual's sense of moral conscience and common humanity. The manifesto is composed of a preamble by Russell in the first person, explaining the intent and history of the manifesto; a central statement written from the perspective of the signatories (designated as "we"); and a resolution. An initial more formal tone gives way to a personal address in which the signatories petition their readers: "Here, then, is the problem which we present to you, stark and dreadful and inescapable: Shall we put an end to the human race; or shall mankind renounce war?"

In these final entreaties the emotional timbre of the manifesto takes shape most clearly. Written as a public address, it relies on its early formality to establish a credible foundation from which to offer its concluding request. It states with certitude that "there lies before us, if we choose, continual progress in happiness, knowledge, and wisdom," implying a certain amount of faith in the audience's optimism and rational capacity. It appeals to the same faculty in invoking each person's humanity. The closing petition, "Remember your humanity, and forget the rest," became a shibboleth, effectively defining the ethos of

Bertrand Russell reading the *Russell-Einstein Manifesto* in London in 1955. © BETTMANN/ CORBIS

the nonproliferation movement, as well as the movement to ban testing of nuclear weapons, which Russell also supported. The phrase still appears as the slogan for Pugwash Conferences.

CRITICAL DISCUSSION

The *Russell-Einstein Manifesto* was greeted at the press conference in London with a flurry of questions, most expressing concern about a perceived disregard of the security risks posed by disarmament. Many of the reporters present (most of whom were English) were mollified by Russell's responses; the most common view expressed in print, however, was that although the manifesto was praiseworthy, it was too idealistic. The *New York Times* reproduced the document in full the next day, buried among ads for dresses on page twenty-five. The event itself was widely reported, in part because it was the last document Einstein signed before his death on April 18, 1955. The academic community was hesitant to comment, perhaps because it was charged with much of the responsibility for the changes advocated in the manifesto.

The issue was already of public concern, however, and the manifesto helped launch the antinuclear lobby. Progress toward disarmament and global pacifism was slow and limited, but the continued efforts of signatory Rotblat and his peers at the Pugwash Conferences helped bring the nonproliferation and test ban movements to public notice. The recognition that accompanied Einstein's association with the manifesto eased the efforts of other activists, such as Irish minister for external affairs Frank Aiken, who initiated work on the international Treaty on the Non-Proliferation of Nuclear Weapons (commonly known as the Non-Proliferation Treaty, or NPT) in 1958. The treaty was enacted in 1970, taking as its basis three "pillars": nonproliferation, disarmament, and the peaceful development of nuclear energy technology. The document has transcended political boundaries, with 45 nations signing and ratifying immediately and 189 others joining by 1992—more than have entered into any other such agreement.

The tenth anniversary of the Pugwash Conferences stimulated a wave of rigorous academic scrutiny of the *Russell-Einstein Manifesto.* By then, most scholars favored the views held by the authors and lamented how little change the document and the conferences had brought about. Some negative assessments persisted. In a 1967 article for *International Affairs,* Leonard Schwartz expressed concern over the authors' claims of neutrality, asserting that in their early eagerness for action, they too readily accepted support from backers and hosts with left-leaning ideological biases—most notably Eaton, host of the first conference. Later critics have leveled the opposite accusation of complicity with political power structures. Eva Senghaas-Knobloch and Birgit Volmerg, in "Towards a Social Psychology of Peace" (1988), maintained that both the document and the conferences too closely aligned themselves with the governments they were petitioning for change. Knobloch and Volmerg felt that, rather than appealing to heads of state, a successful peace movement would instead address "all citizens and in so doing [express] a personal disagreement with the position of governments."

BIBLIOGRAPHY

Sources

Butcher, Sandra I. *The Origins of the Russell-Einstein Manifesto.* Washington, DC: Pugwash Conferences on Science and World Affairs, 2005. Print.

Holdren, John P. "Joseph Rotblat (1908-2005)." *Science* 28 Oct. 2005: 633. *Academic OneFile.* Web. 11 June 2012.

Krieger, David. "After Fifty Years, Do We Remember Our Humanity?" *Humanist* 65.4 (2005): 23-30. *Academic Search Complete.* Web. 11 June 2012.

Schwartz, Leonard E. "Perspective on Pugwash." *International Affairs* 43.3 (1967):498-515. *JSTOR.* Web. 11 June 2012.

Senghaas-Knobloch, Eva, and Birgit Volmerg. "Towards a Social Psychology of Peace." *Journal of Peace Research* 25.3 (1988): 245-56. *JSTOR.* Web. 11 June 2012.

Further Reading

Boutwell, Jeffrey, and Joseph Rotblat. *Addressing the Nuclear Weapons Threat: The Russell-Einstein Manifesto Fifty Years On.* Rome: Pugwash Conferences on Science and World Affairs, 2005. Print.

Bry, Ilse, and Janet Doe. "War and Men of Science." *Science* 11 Nov. 1955: 911-13. *JSTOR.* Web. 11 June 2012.

Kelly, Cynthia C. *The Manhattan Project: The Birth of the Atomic Bomb in the Words of Its Creators, Eyewitnesses, and Historians.* New York: Black Dog & Leventhal, 2007. Print.

Kothari, D.S., and Jawaharlal Nehru. *Nuclear Explosions and Their Effects.* Delhi: Government of India Publications Division, Ministry of Information and Broadcasting, 1956. Print.

Rotblat, Joseph. "The Threat Today." *Bulletin of the Atomic Scientists* 37.1 (1981): 33-36. *Academic Search Complete.* Web. 11 June 2012.

Russell, Bertrand. "The Russell-Einstein Manifesto." *Bertrand Russell: Man's Peril, 1954-55.* Ed. Andrew Bone. London: Routledge, 2003. Print. 304-33.

Collected Papers of Bertrand Russell. Ed. Kenneth Blackwell. Vol. 28. London: Allen, 1983-

Seltzer, Richard. "Arms Control Work Wins Scientists Nobel Prize." *Chemical & Engineering News* 23 Oct. 1995: 9. *Academic OneFile.* Web. 11 June 2012.

Tarnow, David, and Michael Douglas. *Nobel Voices for Disarmament: 1901-2001.* Washington, D.C.: Smithsonian Folkways Recordings, 2007. CD.

Clint Garner

WHY FACEBOOK EXISTS

Mark Zuckerberg

✦ *Key Facts*

Time Period:
Early 21st Century

Movement/Issue:
Online Social
networking;
Democratization;
Internet freedom

Place of Publication:
United States

**Language of
Publication:**
English

OVERVIEW

Composed by Facebook founder and CEO Mark Zuckerberg, *Why Facebook Exists* (2012) describes the social networking company's mission to increase interpersonal connectivity and thereby democratize social, political, and economic institutions. Zuckerberg, who for many years had resisted taking the company public, composed the statement as part of Facebook's filing for an initial public offering (IPO), the second largest ever for a U.S. company. Explaining Facebook's methods and motivations in social rather than financial terms, Zuckerberg places the social networking site in a long tradition of revolutionary communications technologies, such as the printing press and television. Addressed to potential shareholders, *Why Facebook Exists* expresses reluctance even to consider Facebook a company and denies that the social networking site is motivated by profit. Central to the document is a set of five commandments that guide Zuckerberg's leadership of Facebook: focus on impact, move fast, be bold, be open, and build social value.

When the letter was issued three months before the company's IPO, the business and technology communities were skeptical. Many doubted the sincerity of Zuckerberg's altruistic claims, pointing out that he and other Facebook insiders stood to profit greatly from the sale of stock. Others questioned the CEO's professionalism, arguing that he was abdicating his responsibility to potential investors by renouncing profit as a motive. After the much-anticipated debut of Facebook stock, the company's share price quickly declined, disappointing investors. Analysts blamed sluggish trading on Zuckerberg's handling of the IPO, which they said benefited Facebook insiders at the expense of outside traders. Nevertheless, *Why Facebook Exists* is considered an important declaration of values during the early history of social networking and the Internet.

HISTORICAL AND LITERARY CONTEXT

Why Facebook Exists meditates on Facebook's impending transformation from a private to a public company after years of rapid growth during which Zuckerberg had resisted relinquishing control. The website, initially called thefacebook, debuted in 2004, when social networking sites Friendster and MySpace,

both of which launched in 2003, dominated the fledgling industry. Within ten months, thefacebook had a million users and was attracting the interest of wealthy investors in California's Silicon Valley. Zuckerberg initially resisted the investment out of concern that he would be pressured to take the company public. After he became CEO in 2005 and the site was rebranded as Facebook, the company experienced explosive growth. He refused offers—from Yahoo!, Microsoft, and others—to buy out Facebook and purposely delayed the company's IPO, despite a contractual obligation to investors to go public.

By the time *Why Facebook Exists* was issued in 2012, pressure for the company to go public was high. Zuckerberg remained reluctant, although many analysts predicted that an IPO would infuse the company with needed capital and make its founder personally wealthy. Zuckerberg was concerned that a public offering would force him to relinquish creative and financial control of the company and lead to a shift in priorities that would place corporate profit ahead of the goal of facilitating social progress. A talented software developer, he had built Facebook in his Harvard dorm room, dropping out of college after his sophomore year in order to dedicate all of his energy to expanding the website.

Why Facebook Exists draws on a tradition of corporate writing about social commitment, in particular founders' letters, or statements about the founding principles of an organization. A prominent example is the 2004 Google founders' letter, written prior to Google's transformation into a public company. In the letter, a self-described "'Owner's Manual' for Google's Shareholders," Google founders Larry Page and Sergey Brin outline their vision of how they will make "Google a long term success and the world a better place." Like Page and Brin, Zuckerberg in his IPO letter portrays his company's mission in altruistic terms, assuring potential investors that his social mission makes good business sense as well.

Following its issuance, *Why Facebook Exists* inspired satires that mocked Zuckerberg's lofty idealism and perceived sanctimoniousness. Comedian and writer Andy Borowitz posted "A Letter from Mark Zuckerberg" to his *New Yorker* blog on May 17, 2012, undermining Zuckerberg's notion that Facebook can create radical social and political change. Borowitz writes that the site is a tool for "enabling millions to share information of no interest with people they barely know." Several months later, on July 26, 2012, Borowitz posted another satirical letter in response to the company's plummeting share price. Despite the lampooning, Zuckerberg's letter generated considerable interest because of the insights it offered into his views on Facebook and the future of social networking.

THEMES AND STYLE

The central theme of *Why Facebook Exists* is that Facebook is motivated by an idealistic vision of social progress rather than by profit. The manifesto opens, "Facebook was not originally created to be a company. It was built to accomplish a social mission—to make the world more open and connected." Zuckerberg argues throughout the rest of the text that the company's mission is ongoing and will not change because Facebook is owned by shareholders. However, Zuckerberg argues that profit and altruism are interrelated: "By focusing on our mission and building great services, we believe we will create the most value for our shareholders and partners over the long term—and this in turn will enable us to keep attracting the best people and building more great services." Similarly, the manifesto's five core values—focus on impact, move fast, be bold, be open, and build social value— apply equally to maximizing profit and to "making Facebook the best place for great people to have a big impact on the world."

The manifesto achieves its rhetorical effect through appeals to the altruistic nature of potential investors. The concept of selfless ambition is evoked through repeated references to the possibility of creating a more united and engaged humanity: "There is a huge need and a huge opportunity to get everyone in the world connected, to give everyone a voice and to help transform society for the future." However, Zuckerberg's calls for large-scale social transformation are tempered by language that personalizes the manifesto's appeal: "Even if our mission sounds big, it starts small—with the relationship between two people." The use of the first person plural suggests that Zuckerberg's vision is a movement, greater than any one person, while his use of the first person singular maintains the sense that his letter is a personal and direct appeal to investors.

Stylistically, *Why Facebook Exists* is distinguished by its informality. Its casual tone, personal form of address, and lack of technical language belie the text's status as part of a financial filing for a multi-billion-dollar company, as does Zuckerberg's emphasis on the company's "social mission." Although this approach is unconventional, it gives insight into Zuckerberg's style as CEO and demonstrates his ability to work with investors to develop the company. He describe

FACEBOOK AND PRIVACY CONCERNS

One early and enduring criticism of Facebook has been its handling of users' private information. The first major backlash against the site occurred in November 2007 when Facebook debuted the Beacon advertising platform, which automatically posted information about users' purchases to their profiles. Although the project was ultimately dismantled in response to a public outcry, several features of the platform were used for later applications. Moreover, as the website grew, users feared Facebook would claim ownership of user-generated content, such as photos and videos, and use it for commercial purposes. In response the company revised its terms of service and allowed users to have input on certain policies.

Users reacted again in 2009 after system problems made public some users' private information. In addition, it was revealed that the site had been sharing users' information with advertisers without permission, allowing advertisers to personally identify users and to collect their personal information. Facebook again responded to public protest, which included a bill of rights drafted by *PC World,* by making corrections to its code and simplifying its privacy settings. Nevertheless, in 2011 the U.S. Federal Trade Commission announced that Facebook would be subject to independent consumer privacy audits for the next twenty years for its failure to adequately protect users' privacy.

his vision of Facebook's relationship to the business world in plain language with relatively little jargon: "These days I think more and more people want to use services from companies that believe in something beyond simply maximizing profits." His candor serves to reassure investors that his vision is sound, honest, and forward-looking, taking to heart the best interest of the company's customers and its shareholders.

CRITICAL DISCUSSION

When *Why Facebook Exists* was published in February 2012, it had a mixed reception in the business and technology communities. Writer Steven Levy's response in *Wired* typifies the cautious approval with which critics received Zuckerberg's letter. Levy writes, "Even the best founder's letters straddle the line between bombast and brilliance, and that is certainly the case in the Facebook [letter]." In a 2012 article for *Time,* Sam Gustin writes admiringly of Zuckerberg's commitment to social change and places the founder's altruistic ambition within the context of similarly motivated entrepreneurs: "Zuckerberg is clearly an idealist of the first order and he's not alone. Increasingly, young entrepreneurs, particularly in technology, are looking to create businesses that contribute to the public good as well as make money." Others expressed wariness about the letter's casual insistence that profit

Facebook founder Mark Zuckerberg ringing the NASDAQ stock market's opening bell to celebrate Facebook's 2012 initial public offering (IPO). In conjunction with this offering, Zuckerberg wrote the letter "Why Facebook Exists." AP PHOTO/ NASDAQ VIA FACEBOOK, ZEF NIKOLLA

was a secondary motive for the company. In a 2012 article for the *Wall Street Journal,* Joe Walker observes, "For a guy asking investors for $5 billion to grow his company, Mark Zuckerberg sounded awfully nonchalant about the money-making part of taking Facebook public."

Following Facebook's IPO and the disappointing performance of the company's stock, many commentators began to question the sincerity of the altruistic claims made in *Why Facebook Exists*. In a 2012 article for the *New Yorker,* John Cassidy writes, "By the time Facebook's stock started trading on the public market, insiders—the company's founders, employees, and venture-capitalist backers—had bagged most, if not all, of the company's value for themselves." Other critics echoed this sentiment, questioning Zuckerberg's and Facebook's alleged disinterest in profit. Although the manifesto attracted numerous journalistic and popular responses online and in print, *Why Facebook Exists* generated limited scholarly responses in the first months after it was issued.

In a 2012 essay for *New Perspective Quarterly,* Nathan Gardels offers one of the few scholarly responses to Zuckerberg's manifesto. He analyzes the document with respect to the ways in which online social networking sites alter the "balance of power between the utility and the user, the gatekeeper and the gated." According to Gardels, "Connectivity among the newly empowered voices is unraveling the last hanging threads of authority—cultural, social and political—and weaving another pattern of power." He argues that Facebook's

potential for social change is limited by the company's failure to commit to an ideology that "ties people together into a united mindset and defines with authority what is included and what is excluded from the political agenda."

BIBLIOGRAPHY

Sources

Borowitz, Andy. "A Letter from Mark Zuckerberg." *New Yorker.* New Yorker, 17 May 2012. Web. 26 July 2012.

———. "A Letter from Mark Zuckerberg." *New Yorker.* New Yorker, 26 July 2012. Web. 26 July 2012.

Cassidy, John. "Inside Job: Facebook I.P.O. Shows System Is Broken." *New Yorker.* New Yorker, 21 May 2012. Web. 26 July 2012.

Gardels, Nathan. "Who, Whom?" *New Perspectives Quarterly* 29.2 (2012): 2-5. Web. 26 July 2012.

Gustin, Sam. "Why Facebook's IPO Matters." *Time.* Time, 2 Feb. 2012. Web. 10 Aug. 2012.

Levy, Steven. "Mark Zuckerberg, the Hacker Way and the Art of the Founder's Letter." *Wired.* Wired, 3 Feb. 2012. Web. 26 July 2012.

Page, Larry, and Sergey Brin. "2004 Founders' IPO Letter." *Google Investor Relations.* Google, 2004. Web. 26 July 2012.

Further Reading

Andrews, Lori. *I Know Who You Are and I Saw What You Did: Social Networks and the Death of Privacy.* New York: Free, 2011. Print.

Eaglesham, Jean, and Telis Demos. "Lawmakers Push for Overhaul of IPO Process." *Wall Street Journal.* Dow Jones, 22 June 2012. Web. 10 Aug. 2012.

Kirkpatrick, David. *The Facebook Effect: The Inside Story of the Company That Is Connecting the World.* New York: Simon, 2010. Print.

Lacy, Sarah. *Once You're Lucky, Twice You're Good: The Rebirth of Silicon Valley and the Rise of Web 2.0.* New York: Gotham, 2008. Print.

Mezrich, Ben. *Accidental Billionaires: The Founding of Facebook: A Tale of Sex, Money, Genius and Betrayal.* Westminster: Anchor, 2010. Web. 25 July 2012.

Theodore McDermott

WikiLeaks Manifesto

Julian Assange

❖ *Key Facts*

Time Period:
Early 21st Century

Movement/Issue:
Intellectual freedom;
Authoritarianism; War
on Terror

Place of Publication:
Online

**Language of
Publication:**
English

OVERVIEW

Composed by Julian Assange, the *WikiLeaks Manifesto* (2010) describes the conspiratorial relationship between the political and corporate elite and how disruption of communication can reduce the power of this conspiracy. Assange is the founder, editor in chief, and spokesperson of WikiLeaks, a highly controversial media website that publishes the confidential documents of governments and other institutions. His manifesto was a slightly modified version of two prior essays, *State and Terrorist Conspiracies* and *Conspiracy as Governance,* both published in 2006. When the manifesto was issued on August 1, 2010, WikiLeaks had been online for three and a half years, during which time Assange and his collaborators had posted secret documents exposing everything from the corruption of African politicians to the inner workings of the Church of Scientology to the standard operating procedure of guards at the Guantanamo Bay prison. In 2010 the site had begun to draw increasing scrutiny for distributing and publishing confidential documentation from the U.S. wars in Iraq and Afghanistan. The *WikiLeaks Manifesto* makes the case that disrupting the transfer of information is a means of reducing the conspiratorial power of oppressive regimes.

When it first appeared online, the *WikiLeaks Manifesto* was generally met with approval from those sympathetic to Assange. Some online commenters noted, however, that the manifesto was an almost exact copy of his *State and Terrorist Conspiracies* and *Conspiracy as Governance.* As part of a much larger WikiLeaks campaign of advocating institutional transparency, these documents helped to catalyze passionate debate about the legitimacy of governmental secrecy, the value of informational openness, and the evolving role of journalism. Several months after the manifesto was issued, in November 2010, WikiLeaks released more than 200,000 secret, confidential, and unclassified U.S. diplomatic cables. A month after that, Assange was arrested in England for rape and sexual assault in Sweden, and WikiLeaks became decreasingly active. Today the *WikiLeaks Manifesto* is regarded as an important document in the ongoing debate about the function of confidentiality and transparency in the information age.

HISTORICAL AND LITERARY CONTEXT

The *WikiLeaks Manifesto* responds to the international political upheaval and military conflict at the beginning of the twenty-first century, when the United States and its Western allies initiated a wide-ranging War on Terror in the Middle East, in Asia, and elsewhere in the Islamic world. On September 11, 2001, nine years before the *WikiLeaks Manifesto* appeared, a series of coordinated terrorist attacks occurred in New York and Washington, D.C. Soon after the United States and its allies in the North Atlantic Treaty Organization (NATO) invaded Afghanistan, which had harbored Osama bin Laden, the alleged mastermind of the attacks. Then, in 2003, while the war in Afghanistan continued, the United States, despite objections from many of its allies as well as from the United Nations, launched an invasion of Iraq. The United States considered Iraq a new theater in the War on Terror, though the connection was considered by many observers to be tenuous at best.

By the time the *WikiLeaks Manifesto* was issued in 2010, the United States and its allies were still mired in conflict in Afghanistan, and the U.S. occupation of Iraq was winding down after years of struggle and violence. Four years before, in 2006, Assange started WikiLeaks and authored *State and Terrorist Conspiracies* and *Conspiracy as Governance,* two nearly identical versions of the manifesto. At that time the violence and bloodshed in Iraq had reached its peak. Resistance to the U.S. coalition's occupation was strengthening, while sectarian conflict was growing into what many feared would become a civil war. Meanwhile, coalition operations and casualties were on the rise in Afghanistan. As a result, opposition to the War on Terror was growing not only in the United States but throughout the rest of the world. In April 2010, just before the *WikiLeaks Manifesto* was issued, Assange released a 2007 video that showed U.S. soldiers in Iraq killing eighteen people, including two journalists, from a helicopter. In July 2010 WikiLeaks released some 90,000 documents related to the war in Afghanistan. The release of these documents was considered treasonous by many governmental officials and was seen as a powerful act of opposition by many who were critical of the War on Terror.

Assange's earlier essays, *State and Terrorist Conspiracy* and *Conspiracy as Governance,* drew on a tradition of writing about information, technology, and transparency that can be traced to *A Magna Carta for the Knowledge Age*. Written in 1994 by a group of technology theorists that included Esther Dyson, George Gilder, George Keyworth, and Alvin Toffler, *A Magna Carta for the Knowledge Age* describes the revolutionary political, social, and economic implications of a world population that inhabits cyberspace rather than the physical world. This new paradigm, the authors argue, is one that will be controlled by information rather than by things: "The central event of the 20th century is the overthrow of matter.... The powers of mind are everywhere ascendant over the brute force of things." In composing *State and Terrorist Conspiracy* and *Conspiracy as Governance*, Assange drew from this notion that information forms the structure of political and radical systems.

In the years since its publication, the *WikiLeaks Manifesto* has been followed by new writings from Assange on various topics and has also inspired compositions by others in support of the organization's aims. On June 4, 2012, for example, *Friends of WikiLeaks Manifesto* was distributed online. The document enumerates a list of "broad ideals" that guide its authors' commitment "to defend WikiLeaks" as well as its sources and sympathizers. Since 2010 numerous editorials and press releases have been issued on the WikiLeaks website. These documents have included interviews with Assange; announcements of WikiLeaks activities; and even a statement from Assange regarding his new Russian television show, in which he writes that "corporate media and regime propaganda machines alike excel in the mass production of sensationalist smears against individuals and organisations they perceive to be social, political or economic competition. Fortunately WikiLeaks is all three." Today the *WikiLeaks Manifesto* is viewed as a vital document in the ongoing controversy surrounding Assange's group.

THEMES AND STYLE

The central theme of the *WikiLeaks Manifesto* is that obstructing communication can help dismantle the authoritarian power of conspiratorial institutions. The manifesto opens with the following declaration: "To radically shift regime behavior we must think clearly and boldly for if we have learned anything, it is that regimes do not want to be changed." Assange then identifies "conspiratorial interactions ... as the primary planning methodology behind maintaining or strengthening authoritarian power." The manifesto describes these "conspiratorial interactions" as webs of communication that function as the "cognitive devices" of groups. By blocking or destroying connective pathways between members of powerful groups, insurgents can disrupt conspiracy and reduce the "total conspiratorial power" of authoritarian regimes.

The manifesto achieves its rhetorical effect by analogizing the structure of governmental institutions

JULIAN ASSANGE

Julian Assange was born in 1971 in Australia and was raised in an unconventional household. During his childhood he moved thirty-seven times and rarely attended school. Despite his lack of formal education, he studied with his mother and by mail, and he read voraciously. As a teenager, Assange became interested in computer programming and lived on the run with his mother, who was trying to keep her whereabouts unknown from an abusive ex-boyfriend. Then, in 1987, before the Internet even existed, Assange learned to hack into computer networks and joined a group of hackers that later became known as the International Subversives.

As Assange became an adult, he retained his childhood habit of itinerancy and his adolescent interest in hacking. When he was twenty, his illegal online activities attracted the interest of the Australian Federal Police, who arrested him. Though he got off with only a small fine, it would not be his last run-in with authorities. In 2006 he began to build the elaborately secure WikiLeaks website. The site published its first secret document in December of that year: a Somali rebel leader's directive to kill government officials. Over the next four years, as WikiLeaks published more documents, Assange drew increasing criticism and attention. Then, in 2010, Assange was arrested in England on charges of rape and sexual assault in Sweden. Many of his supporters suspect that his arrest was motivated by a conspiracy of his critics, who hoped to silence him. His critics, however, insist that the charges are valid.

to that of terrorist groups. Assange describes how analysts for the U.S. government "look at terrorist conspiracies as connected graphs." He then writes, "We extend this understanding of terrorist organizations and turn it on the likes of its creators where it becomes a knife to dissect the power conspiracies used to maintain authoritarian government." In this way the *WikiLeaks Manifesto* undermines the legitimacy of institutional authority while empowering those in opposition to it. The use of the first-person plural "we" involves the reader in this conspiracy of opposition and resistance. The metaphor of a graph is employed, according to the manifesto itself, "as way [*sic*] to harness the spatial reasoning ability of the brain to think in a new way about political relationships." This use of spatial metaphor also provides the manifesto's audience with a means of visualizing the process of dismantling authoritarian conspiracy.

Stylistically, the *WikiLeaks Manifesto* is distinguished by its formal mode of argumentation. Assange assumes a tone of exaggerated rationality as a means of legitimizing the manifesto's controversial argument about the conspiratorial nature of institutional authority. For example, he writes, "The 'importance' of communication passing through a link difficult to evaluate apriori, since it its [*sic*] true value depends on

Julian Assange arrives at court in London in 2012. The founder of WikiLeaks and the author of the *WikiLeaks Manifesto,* Assange faced significant legal challenges because of his website and challenge of authority. AP PHOTO/ KIRSTY WIGGLESWORTH, FILE

the outcome of the conspiracy." With this careful kind of language, Assange distances his manifesto from the passionate cries typically associated with radical stands against authority and establishes the logical underpinnings of his case. He also employs quotes from sources as diverse as President Theodore Roosevelt, William Shakespeare, and Machiavelli in order to legitimize his argument. The manifesto's careful and logical tone has a second function: it co-opts and satirizes the detached objectivity that is a hallmark of governmental documents. This emphasizes the rhetorical connection between institutional and terroristic conspiracies.

CRITICAL DISCUSSION

When the *WikiLeaks Manifesto* was published in 2010, it received little attention outside the online community of WikiLeaks sympathizers, many of whom pointed out that the manifesto was nearly identical to *State and Terrorist Conspiracy* and *Conspiracy as Governance,* which appeared on Assange's personal website in 2006, soon after he founded WikiLeaks. After the *WikiLeaks Manifesto* was issued, WikiLeaks released hundreds of thousands of U.S. diplomatic cables, and Assange was arrested for rape and sexual assault. This resulted in increased scrutiny of Assange and his ideas about the revolutionary potential of information. Jason Pontin writes in *Technology Review* that "'State and Terrorist Conspiracy' and 'Conspiracy as Governance' are extraordinary documents: supple, original, and, it must be declared, nuts."

After the arrest of Assange in 2010, the *WikiLeaks Manifesto* remained an important statement of WikiLeaks's foundational aims, despite the absence of the group's founder. Raffi Khatchadourian, in a 2012 essay for the *New Yorker,* describes *Conspiracy and Governance* as a "manifesto of sorts" that "argued that, when a regime's lines of internal communication are disrupted, the information flow among conspirators must dwindle, and that, as the flow approaches

zero, the conspiracy dissolves. Leaks were an instrument of information warfare." These ideas, which were repeated in the *WikiLeaks Manifesto,* guided the actions of Assange's organization, even after his arrest and decreased prominence. In the few years since the manifesto was issued, it has not attracted significant scholarly interest, though the organization itself has been the subject of an extensive body of criticism that has considered its role in questioning institutional secrecy, informational transparency, and journalistic practice.

Much of the scholarship has been focused on the aim of WikiLeaks to, as the *WikiLeaks Manifesto* puts it, "radically shift regime behavior" by disrupting the flow of information between the conspirators in powerful institutions. Many commentators have analyzed the unintended complications arising from this seemingly straightforward objective. According to scholar John Steel in *Journalism and Free Speech* (2012), "The WikiLeaks controversy exposes the tension related to trying to balance individual liberty with state security." Clare Birchall, in "Transparency, Interrupted: Secrets of the Left" (2011), argues that WikiLeaks's fight for access to information has turned the organization into a conspiracy that's as elaborately guarded as those it seeks to counter. WikiLeaks, she writes, "demands a level of secrecy equivalent to that practised by the state."

BIBLIOGRAPHY

Sources

Assange, Julian. *Conspiracy and Governance.* IQ.org. 3 Dec. 2006. Web. 1 Aug. 2012.

———. *State and Terrorist Conspiracies.* IQ.org. 10 Nov. 2006. Web. 1 Aug. 2012.

———. *WikiLeaks Manifesto.* The Comment Factory. 1 Aug. 2010. Web. 27 July 2012.

Birchall, Clare. "Transparency, Interrupted: Secrets of the Left." *Theory Culture Society* 28.7-8 (2011): 60-84. Web. 1 Aug. 2012.

Dyson, Esther, et al. "A Magna Carta for the Knowledge Age." Alamut. 22 Aug. 1994. Web. 1 Aug. 2012.

"Friends of WikiLeaks Manifesto." LegionNet. 4 June 2012. Web. 1 Aug. 2012.

Khatchadourian, Raffi. "No Secrets: Julian Assange's Mission for Total Transparency." *New Yorker.* Condé Nast, 7 June 2012. Web. 27 July 2012.

Pontin, Jason. "Transparency and Secrets." *Technology Review* 114.2 (2011): 70-73. *Academic Search Elite.* Web. 1 Aug. 2012.

Steel, John. *Journalism and Free Speech.* New York: Routledge, 2012. Print.

Further Reading

Alford, Roger P., and Simon Chesterman. "Espionage and the First Amendment after Wikileaks." *Proceedings of the Annual Meeting-American Society of International Law Annual.* Washington, D.C.: American Society of International Law, 2011. 147+. *Academic OneFile.* Web. 13 Aug. 2012.

Kovel, Joel. "WikiLeaks Forever." *Capitalism Nature Socialism* 22.1 (2011): 1-3. Print.

Krotoski, Aleks. "Wikileaks and the New, Transparent World Order." *Political Quarterly* 82.4 (2011): 526-30. Print.

Leigh, David, and Luke Harding. *Wikileaks: Inside Julian Assange's War on Secrecy.* New York: Public Affairs, 2011. Print.

MacKinnon, Rebecca. *Consent of the Networked: The World-wide Struggle for Internet Freedom.* New York: Basic, 2012. Print.

Sifry, Micah L. *Wikileaks and the Age of Transparency.* Berkeley: Counterpoint, 2011. Print.

Theodore McDermott

SUBJECT INDEX

Bold *volume and page numbers (e.g.,* **3:269–272***) refer to the main entry on the subject.*
Page numbers in italics refer to photographs and illustrations.

AUTHOR INDEX

The author index includes author names represented in The Manifesto in Literature. *Numbers in* **Bold** *indicate volume, with page numbers following after colons.*

TITLE INDEX

The title index includes works that are represented in The Manifesto in Literature. *Numbers in* **Bold** *indicate volume, with page numbers following after colons.*